Windows CE

From the Ground Up

Jean Louis Gareau

Annabooks
San Diego

Windows CE from the Ground Up

by

Jean Louis Gareau

PUBLISHED BY

Annabooks
11838 Bernardo Plaza Court
San Diego, CA 92128-2414
USA

619-673-0870
http://www.annabooks.com

Printed in the United States of America

ISBN 0-929392-65-5

First Printing May 1999

Information provided in this publication is derived from various sources, standards, and analyses. Any errors or omissions shall not imply any liability for direct or indirect consequences arising from the use of this information. The publisher, authors, and reviewers make no warranty for the correctness or for the use of this information, and assume no liability for direct or indirect damages of any kind arising from technical interpretation or technical explanations in this book, for typographical or printing errors, or for any subsequent changes.

The publisher and authors reserve the right to make changes in this publication without notice and without incurring any liability.

All trademarks mentioned in this book are the property of their respective owners. Annabooks has attempted to properly capitalize and punctuate trademarks, but cannot guarantee that it has done so properly in every case.

Dedication

For my wife, Martha, with love,
and to my parents, with gratitude.

Contents

Foreword

As you probably know, Windows CE is a brand-new operating system, built from the ground up to allow the Windows family to be extended into a wide variety of dedicated applications. Microsoft made a major commitment to Windows CE, and is continuing to invest heavily in further improvements in both the operating system and the development tools. It therefore gratifies us to see hardware and software engineers and their companies worldwide make similar commitments to Windows CE. It is certainly obvious from the contents of this book that Jean Louis Gareau has personally invested considerable time and effort into understanding and teaching the details of Windows CE.

Sometimes publications tend to specialize in one or another aspect of deploying an operating system, by concentrating on only one level, such as writing applications. However, particularly in the case of Windows CE, the lower levels are just as important, where you adapt the OS to your specific hardware. In the world of applied computing, we who develop the operating system cannot begin to foresee the devices and appliances that you will develop in the future. It is therefore our job to make Windows CE modular and customizable for use in a huge variety of presently unknown applications, while keeping it familiar to those of you who are established Windows programmers.

This operating system flexibility places some additional burdens on you, the developer, however. You receive the benefit of scalability, but you need to be able to include and exclude various parts of the OS in order to make use of that benefit. And while we work hard to provide tools to help, you sometimes need advice on how to use those tools.

You will need to interface hardware devices to Windows CE that we (or you!) haven't yet anticipated. So none of us can expect to always find the driver we need sitting and waiting for us to use. But when a teacher like Jean uses his extensive experience to explain the methods, you are much more likely to succeed sooner rather than later. The less trouble you have, and the faster you get your target system up and running, the happier we all are.

So whether you're working at ground level where the OS meets the hardware, or at the top level porting an application to Windows CE, you will save considerable time by following the examples and insider tips Jean provides in this book. *Windows CE from the Ground Up* will become an immediate worldwide reference for all of you using Windows CE.

Harel Kodesh
Vice President
Information Appliance Division
Microsoft Corporation

Preface

I got the opportunity to work on Windows CE when version 2.0 was introduced, in early 1998. Like my co-workers and other interested people I met in conferences, it took me quite a while to understand how to do something useful with it in a reasonable amount of time. And there's a good reason for that: Windows CE is a pioneer at the junction of two technological worlds: embedded systems and Windows applications. The former is focused in producing small and fast systems, with almost no underlying operating system and with a minimum of hardware components (*e.g.*, a few KB of ROM and RAM), and commonly using 8-bit or 16-bit processors. On the other hand, the latter makes liberal use of as many resources as possible (*e.g.*, desktop systems with 25GB hard disks and 256MB of RAM), the fastest CPUs (500MHz), and sophisticated operating systems (*e.g.*, Windows 9*x* or NT). Windows CE fills the gap by sitting between these two very different worlds.

However, this positioning requires developers to have a broad knowledge of numerous technologies, such as assembly language programming, paging and virtual memory, interrupt handlers, and latency times as much as graphical user interfaces, object-oriented languages and class libraries, graphical user interface programming, and sophisticated operating system features. So like anyone, it took me a while to become comfortable at dealing with those two worlds.

It's one thing to realize that we need to acquire some understanding of a given subject, but it's another to identify what we need to learn. Let's face it: in an ideal world, we would all stay home seated in front of our computers, experimenting with the latest and greatest software we could get our hands on. Back to real life, we are faced with implementing something within budget and time constraints. So we need to acquire the information we need efficiently, no more and no less, in order to accomplish what is required. Regarding Windows CE, that something is, in fact, quite something. A visit to the bookstore will leave you with a book for each of the following topics: hardware reference manuals, device drivers, operating systems, C/C++, Windows, MFC, and the list can go on and on. Therefore, the issue was for me to find what I needed to know. That's also going to be your problem when, after stepping into the Windows CE world, you start to feel overwhelmed by the myriad of concepts that keep pouring on as you advance into the subject.

So I wrote this book with my past experience in mind. I identified the issues I believed were the most relevant and tried to explain them as simply as possible, leaving out the non-essential details and subtleties. I introduce each subject from the beginning, and I add enough information for you to understand the issues and find the solutions for them. This is the book I would have liked to have as a floating vest when I plunged into the Windows CE ocean.

Who Should Read This Book

This book covers three areas of interest: low-level programming (*e.g.,* hardware and device drivers), system programming (*e.g.,* processes, memory, graphics, communications, and file systems), and application programming (*e.g.,* Win32, C++, and MFC). Few programmers are working on those three levels simultaneously. Consequently, I can hardly make any assumption about your knowledge and experience. You may very well be versed in interrupt handlers, but have little experience in user interface development; it may also be the other way around.

Thus, instead of guessing what you know from what you need to know, I rather presuppose that you would be *generally* familiar with one or some of the following technologies (well, ideally all, but realistically only a few):

- Assembly language, C, and C++ programming
- Device drivers
- Operating system concepts, from real-time operating systems (RTOSs) to multiuser systems
- Windows programming
- Microsoft Foundation Classes (MFC)
- Application programming languages (*e.g.,* Basic, Java)

Don't worry if some topics sound unfamiliar or even scary! I introduce enough of these concepts for you to follow through even if you are unaccustomed to some topics. Because the book covers a vast array of topics, you will find some chapters easier than others, based on your personal background. In fact, I tried to keep chapters as independent from each other as possible, to allow you to get answers quickly, without requiring you to read the previous chapters to get the information you are looking for. Furthermore, I also suggest further readings should you need explanations that are more detailed. The suggested readings will let you know what you need to read if you are looking for more details. From that perspective, this book guides you in learning those technologies.

The Structure of the Book

The chapter order reflects the Windows CE architecture, but also the approach you would normally follow to port Windows CE to a custom board, to understand Windows CE concepts, and to develop applications. Hence, the book follows a bottom-up approach to help you build Windows CE systems from the ground up.

The only exception to this approach is Part I, which provides a general, sky-high, overview of Windows CE. It answers some of the most important questions about Windows

CE, such as how it compares with other contemporary classes of operating systems (embedded and desktop), whether it is or not a hard real time system, etc.

Then Part II explains how to get Windows CE running on a PC and a custom board. That also corresponds to understanding the lowest level of Windows CE: the hardware reference platforms, the OEM Adaptation Layer (OAL), device drivers, and Windows CE configurations.

Part III focuses on Windows CE system programming: processes and threads, virtual memory, the Graphics, Windows and Events Subsystem (GWES), the Object Store, file system, communications, and desktop connectivity.

Part IV looks at application programming using C++ and Microsoft Foundation Classes (MFC), by describing Visual C++ and the MFC, the document/view architecture, drawing, getting input, dialog boxes, windows, and advanced controls.

Finally, Part V provides more information about application development, by decribing shell programming, porting desktop applications to CE, using Visual Basic (as an alternative to Visual C++), and Windows CE profiling.

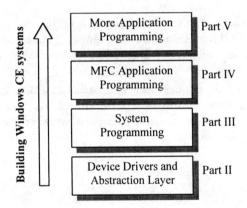

Acknowledgements

First and foremost, I am very grateful to my wife Martha, who heard "just another 15 minutes" enough to develop an allergy to it. I also thank her for her patience and encouragement, and for disabling the Dolby Digital effect on our DVD, since a shaking desk is not the ideal writing environment.

I would like to thank all the people at Annabooks, especially John and Craig Choisser, for their unconditional support and help in making this book possible. I truly appreciate the latitude they gave me throughout the writings, and their scrutiny in filtering out errors. My sincere thanks to Scott Lehrbaum from Ampro Computers, Inc., who provided me with their LittleBoard P5*i*, a PC-based platform, instead of turning me down as other manufacturers did. I also want to thank Dave Barker, from the Motorola Computer Group, who graciously and enthusiastically provided me with a PowerPC821-powered MBX821-006B target board and chassis. A sincere thanks to Sundar Krishnamurthy and Brian Sherrell from Microsoft, who helped me resolve some technical issues, and to Carolee Thompson and Carlo Latasa for their review and judicious comments. I also want to express my gratitude to "Sir" Mark Saunders, for his special humour and his Palm-size PC. Last but not least, I want to thank my good friend Jean "μC/OS" Labrosse, who inspired me to undertake a writing avenue along my career. This book would have never been completed without the collaboration and help of all these fine people.

On the other hand, I am not so grateful to my then puppy Bubba, which found countless methods to get my attention while I was trying to understand the unresolved mysteries of Windows CE. It's unbelievable how far how a dog can go to have fun with you – dog fun, that is. Its good feline buddy, Spotty, occasionally contributes in making my life miserable by walking on the keyboard and sniffing the screen (and hence, graciously presenting me his behind).

Despite our best efforts, mistakes will likely make it in the final print. For my part, I can attest that the Windows CE documentation is not always updated or clear, so I present my understandings based on my own experimentation. If you want to report bugs, along suggestions and comments, are very welcome to do so, by e-mailing me at jgareau@annabooks.com. I'll do my best to acknowledge in a timely manner every e-mail I receive. I also maintain update information about this book and various Windows CE development topics at http://www.exposecorp.com/windowsce.htm. Make sure to mark and visit this page on a regular basis.

Jean Louis Gareau
May 1999
San Diego, California

Part I

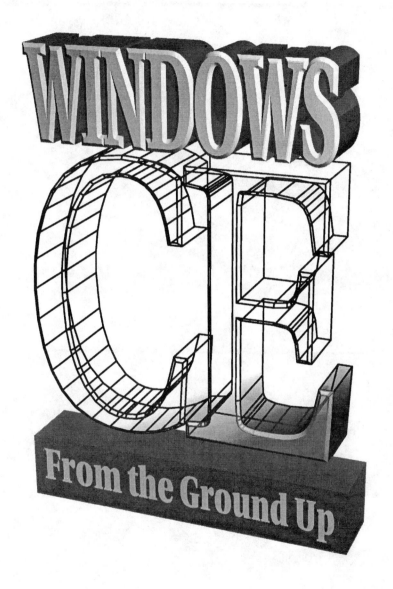

Introduction to Windows CE

Chapter 1

Windows CE Architecture

Windows CE is the latest operating system from Microsoft to have been designed from scratch. The objective was to produce a brand new, portable, modular, real time operating system to fill the market for embedded devices. This market consists of systems that are not seen by the user as a computer, such as engine controls, electronic appliances (VCRs, DVDs, etc.), fax machines, modems, mechanical control devices, as well as Personal Digital Assistants (PDAs), such as handheld computers. The other Windows operating systems are inadequate for these devices for a variety of reasons (large memory requirements, lack of real-time capabilities, higher cost, etc.)

1.1 THE WINDOWS CE ARCHITECTURE

The need for modularity led the designers to a system that is highly componentized and configurable (see Figure 1-1). That goal has been achieved by creating a set of modules that can be added or removed, so that you can produce a system that includes enough functionality to meet your specific requirements, but no more, to save space and cost.

1.2 A JOINT EFFORT

Unlike other Windows platforms, most Windows CE systems are not entirely built upon Microsoft components. As Figure 1-1 shows, there are three groups involved in the implementation of a Windows CE system:

- The lower level that directly interfaces with the hardware is written by OEMs (Original Equipment Manufacturers), like some of you. That level is the object of Section II of this book.

- The middle level consists of hardware-independent modules that implement most of the Windows CE functionality, and is entirely provided by Microsoft. Section III describes this layer in greater detail.

- The top level is written by Independent Software Vendors (ISV) *i.e.,* software developers, consultants, or, simply put, more people like you and me. Section IV explores what facilities are available to application developers.

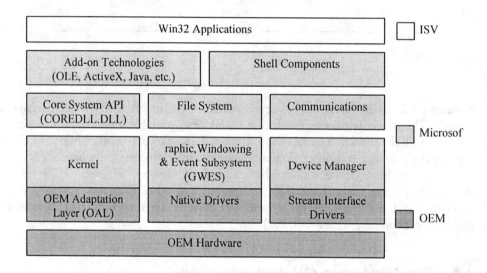

Figure 1-1: Windows CE architecture.

1.3 WINDOWS CE COMPONENTS

OEMs design, develop, manufacture, and sell Windows CE devices. Their main focus is on hardware design, such as Handheld PC (H/PC), Palm-size PC (P/PC), and Auto PC (A/PC), but also any embedded systems on custom boards, using a variety of devices.

Above the OEM hardware resides the OEM Adaptation Layer (known as the OAL), which provides the glue between the Windows CE kernel and the OEM hardware. It is a set of routines (not drivers) that provides platform initialization, interrupt service routines (ISRs), real-time clock (RTC), interval timer, debugging, interrupt enable/disable, profiling, and the like. This layer is platform-dependent, and is developed by the OEMs, along with various device drivers.

The OAL is eventually linked with the Kernel, the key component that implements the core functionality of Windows CE: process and thread management, preemptive scheduling, memory management, synchronization mechanism, debugging support, profiling, and exception handling. This component is present in all Windows CE configurations. It is written by Microsoft and is provided in object format for all supported CPUs.

The Graphical, Windows, and Events Subsystem (GWES) implements the user interface functionality and graphical capabilities. For those of you who are familiar with the other Windows architectures, it combines the functionality of the USER and GDI (Graphic Device Interface) modules. This module controls window management (windowing), message passing (events), graphical operations, and user input (keyboard, touch screen, voice, and stylus). The related devices are accessed through native device drivers.

Native device drivers control devices that are bundled with a Windows CE platform (touch screen, LED, keyboard, battery, serial port, PC Card socket, etc.) These devices cannot be removed by the user (as opposed to PC Cards, or serial devices such as printers, cameras, etc.). Each native driver has a unique, custom interface, defined by Microsoft.

The Device Manager is another subsystem that manages third-party devices, such as printers and modems. These devices are designed to be eventually added by the user, and they connect through serial, USB, or PC Card connectors. The related device drivers rely on native drivers (serial, for instance) to provide applications with a standard, common API. Since all the drivers for these "external" devices rely on a common byte-oriented API, they are called stream interface device drivers.

The Core System Interface is a dynamic-linked library (`COREDLL.DLL`) that makes the Win32 API available to applications, and reroutes each system call to the appropriate CE module. Development tools provide application libraries to use that DLL.

The File System implements persistent storage in RAM and on external devices. The Object Store is a portion of RAM dedicated for system use (*i.e.,* not to run applications), and implements a local file system, a database, and the system registry. FAT file systems are available and new file systems can be installed to provide access to external storage (Flash memory, PC Card disk, etc.)

The Communications module offers a multitude of networking protocols (*e.g.,* TCP/IP, PPP, SLIP, IrDA, IRSOCK, SMB, RAS) accessible to applications via multiple APIs (*e.g.,* WinSock, WinInet, TAPI) over various hardware (*e.g.,* serial cables, infrared transceivers, LAN). All these acronyms are explained in Part III.

The Add-on Technologies module includes OLE/COM automation, Active-X, the Visual Basic Run-Time, Java Scripts, and a subset of Microsoft Foundation Classes (MFC), all designed to enhance applications. Parts IV and V demystify these far-out acronyms.

Windows CE 2.x doesn't provide a sophisticated shell that allows the user to interact with the system. However, it provides shell components that allow you to build a customized one. Among these components are the Control Panel, the shell services API (as found on other Windows platforms), a command line console (a sort of "DOS prompt"), and a Task Manager window.

Finally, on top of this layout rest the applications, which make system calls through COREDLL.DLL to access the entire Win32 API. Parts IV and V explain how to develop applications.

1.4 WINDOWS CE AND OTHER OPERATING SYSTEMS

Windows CE is aimed at the embedded market, a battlefield of more than 50 known real-time operating systems (RTOSs), including some that have been dominant for years. Needless to say, the landing of Windows CE in that market triggered numerous debates regarding how Windows CE compared with these other RTOSs.

The first issue everybody argued about was whether Windows CE was a hard or soft real-time system. A hard real-time system is one that must process specific events (*i.e.,* interrupts) within a pre-determined period of time (usually less than a few microseconds), with potentially disastrous consequences if failing to do so. Hard real-time systems are used in life-support medical devices, braking systems, planes, etc. On the other hand, soft real-time systems don't have such time-critical or failure constraints: they are required to process events as soon as possible, without adverse effects otherwise. Soft real-time systems are used in PDAs, electronics appliances, copiers, etc. By now, almost everybody agrees that Windows CE 2.x is aimed at soft real-time systems. Nevertheless, it is expected that Windows CE 3.x will meet hard real-time requirements, by adding support for nested interrupts, better thread response, additional task priorities, and semaphores.

The next issue was the memory requirements. Traditional embedded systems only require 8- or 16-bit processing, and must fit into very small amount of ROM and RAM (sometimes less than 1 kilobyte), keeping costs low. On the other hand, Windows CE only comes in 32-bit flavors, and needs megabytes of ROM and RAM to perform adequately. Under the hood, Windows CE uses advanced virtual memory management (paging), whereas most RTOSs don't.

Finally, an issue few people focused on was the functionality within CE. Being a Windows system, Windows CE incorporates a rich application programming interface (API), namely a subset of the Win32 interface found on Windows NT. There is no official metric, but it is said than Windows CE supports about 1500 functions of the original Win32 API, and this number is expected to grow in future releases. These functions are implemented into various modules that make Windows CE scalable. But ultimately, Windows CE includes many more features than most RTOSs available today. Figure 1-2 compares the characteristics of Windows CE vs. those found on other popular RTOSs.

	Windows CE 2.11	RTOSs
Processor	32-bit	4, 8, 16 or 32-bit
Board	Standard and custom	Standard and custom
Minimum memory requirements	350+ KB	A few kilobytes
Typical memory requirements	RAM: 4MB, ROM: 4MB	Hundreds of kilobytes
ROMable	Yes	Most
Paging memory management	Yes	Few
Interrupt latency	90-170µs	<10µs
Nested interrupts	No	Most
Deterministic	No	Most
Processes[1]	Yes	Few
Kernel-mode threads[2]	Yes	Yes
Preemptive kernel	Yes	Yes
Intertask communication	Yes	Yes
Intertask synchronization	Yes	Yes
Priority scheduling	Dynamic	Fixed and dynamic
Priority inheritance	Yes	Some
Input	Keyboards, pens, touch pad, voice	Sensors, switches, analog input
Output	Screens, speakers	Embedded devices, relays, analog output
Device driver model(s)	Yes	Some
Graphical user interface	Yes	Few
File systems	Yes	Most
Networking (*e.g.*, TCP/IP)	Yes	Most
Programming API	Subset of Win32	Proprietary: most POSIX: some Win32: few
Dominant programming languages	C/C++, Basic	Assembly language, C
Source code available	No	Some
Proprietary development tools	Yes	Some
Technical support	Yes	Yes

Figure 1-2: Windows CE 2.11 and other popular RTOSs.

All these characteristics make CE the perfect operating system for Handheld PC, Palm-size PC, and Auto PC, depicted in Figure 1-3, which today feature fast 32-bit processing and

---

[1] A process is not a runnable entity; it encompasses an address space and system resources shared by its threads.

[2] A thread is a runnable entity within a process. Some RTOSs label their threads as processes.

megabytes of memory. And since Windows CE is configurable and scalable, it can be retrofitted into smaller embedded systems. It should be understood, though, that such systems share little with hard real-time embedded systems in terms of timing constraints, memory requirements, basic architecture, and the like, where a commercial RTOS is more appropriate.

(a)

(b)

(c)

(d)

Figure 1-3: Windows CE is the ideal operating system for (a) Handheld/PC Pros and Handheld PCs, (b) Palm-size/PCs, (c) Auto/PCs, and (d) some embedded systems (AMPRO P5e computer and Motorola MBX board shown here).

Windows CE also shares a lot with larger systems, such as Windows NT or UNIX. For one, it implements both notions of processes and threads, as found on NT, whereas most RTOSs implement a single-process, multiple-thread model. Memory is also managed through paging, providing advantages such as inter-process memory protection and code sharing, features usually only found on large systems. Windows CE implements numerous features, such as a database, a registry to hold system and user settings, file system, I/O systems, device drivers, etc., which make it closer to general-purpose systems than a dedicated RTOS. All in all, Windows CE is positioned closer to multipurpose operation systems than RTOSs, as shown in Figure 1-4.

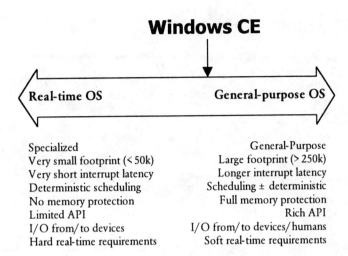

Figure 1-4: Windows CE's features make it closer to general-purpose operating systems than real-time ones.

SUGGESTED READING

Labrosse, Micro-C/OS-II The Real-Time Kernel
> Chapter 2 presents some concise and clear explanations regarding interrupt processing, scheduling and priorities, synchronization primitives, memory requirements, etc., specific to real-time systems.

Leffler, The Design and Implementation of 4.4BSD UNIX Operating System
> The first chapters present a history of BSD Unix, as well as the design goals and the architecture. For serious readers interested in operating system concepts.

Murray, Inside Windows CE
> Chapter 1 explains the origins and motivations behind the Windows CE development effort, whereas chapter 2 provides an overview of it.

Solomon, Inside Windows NT, Second Edition
> Chapters 1 and 2 give a good overview of the architecture of NT, and illustrate how design goals vary from such a system compared to a real-time one, as depicted in Labrosse's book.

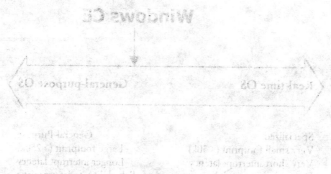

Chapter 2

Getting Started

This chapter presents what you need to know to start developing for Windows CE: development tools, workstation and target requirements, how to use Platform Builder to build Windows CE images, connecting a CE device to your workstation, building applications with Visual C++, and how to stay informed.

2.1 DEVELOPMENT TOOLS

The development tools for Windows CE fall in two categories:

- Those targeting application development for PC companions: Handheld PC (H/PC), Palm-size PC (P/PC), and Auto PC (A/PC). These devices are popular and the demand for new applications is constantly growing. Sections 2.1.1 and 2.1.3 apply to application development.

- Those targeting embedded systems onto custom boards, for OEMs porting Windows CE onto their custom hardware platforms. Sections 2.1.2 and 2.1.3 apply to embedded development.

2.1.1 Application Development on PC Companions

PC Companions are the ideal platforms for Windows CE application developers, because they usually run a full-featured version of CE. Hence, most applications run easily.

Microsoft has been providing very successful integrated development environments (IDEs) for years. It started in the early '90s with Visual Basic, which allowed developing Basic applications by designing graphical forms (*i.e.*, windows), and adding code to form components, *à la* object-oriented. Visual C++ was introduced soon after. Although it wasn't

9

form-based like Visual Basic, it still provided an easy-to-use graphical front-end to the traditional tools (compiler, linker, etc.), including an integrated debugger. The tool evolved and became Visual Studio, a host IDE supporting multiple programming languages (C++ and Java, to name a few).

Instead of providing brand new tools for Windows CE, Microsoft opted for add-on Toolkits, to be integrated into the existing IDEs, namely Visual C++ and Visual Basic. Hence, developing applications for any Windows platform is done about the same way, from a developer's perspective. Today, Microsoft provides application developers with Toolkits for Visual C++ 6.0 and Visual Basic 6.0. Although Visual J++ 1.1 was originally supported, it is no longer mentioned on the official Windows CE site (http://www.microsoft. com/windowsce as of this writing).

The toolkits have now become generic enough to work with multiple versions of CE. Specifically, they rely on Software Development Kits (SDKs), which must be installed depending on the target platform. These SDKs are also called Platform SDKs, and are available free from Microsoft's Web site. The following paragraphs explain what SDKs you need and how to get your hands on them.

Handheld PC Pro

The Handheld PC Pro is the development platform of choice: it provides a complete implementation of Windows CE 2.1x, along with various applications (Pocket Word, Pocket Excel, etc.) Microsoft tools are always first released for that platform. Note that the platform called Handheld PC is the previous release of the Handheld PC Pro. Here is the list of software you need to start developing applications, depending on the programming language you choose.

If you are targeting C++, then you need:

- *Microsoft Visual C++ 6.0 Professional or Enterprise edition.* This is the Visual C++ IDE for Windows 9x and NT. It includes an editor, compilers, linkers, loaders, debuggers, browser, online help, etc.

- *Microsoft Windows CE Toolkit for the Microsoft Visual C++ 6.0.* This is an add-on that fully integrates into Visual C++ in order to provide cross-compilers, linkers, and supplemental development tools for various versions of Windows CE. This toolkit also includes the following:

    - *Microsoft Windows CE Platform SDK for the Handheld PC Version 2.0*, which provides a software development kit (header files, libraries, and an emulator) for H/PC applications targeted to Windows CE 2.00. This SDK has been superseded by the version for the Handheld PC Pro (see below).

- *Microsoft Windows CE Platform SDK for the Palm-size PC Version 2.0*, which provides a software development kit (header files, libraries, and an emulator) for P/PC applications targeted to Windows CE 2.01.

- *Microsoft Windows CE Platform SDK for the Handheld PC Pro Version 3.0*, which provides a software development kit (header files, libraries, and an emulator) for H/PC Pro applications targeted to Windows CE 2.11. You can download this SDK free at http://msdn.microsoft.com/cetools/platform/hpcprofeatures.asp.

If you are targeting Basic, then you need:

- *Microsoft Visual Basic 6.0 Professional or Enterprise edition.* This is the Visual Basic IDE for Windows 9*x* and NT. It includes all the tools required to develop applications (editor, compilers, run-time libraries, etc.)

- *Microsoft Windows CE Toolkit for Visual Basic 6.0.* This is an add-on to Visual Basic that provides complete support for Windows CE.

Palm-size PC

Developing for the Palm-size PC is very similar to developing for the Handheld PC Pro. In fact, you need the exact same tools (Visual C++ 6.0 and the related CE Toolkit, or Visual Basic 6.0 and the related CE Toolkit). However, you need a different SDK.

Microsoft just released a new SDK for the Palm-size PCs, which now supports color screens and Windows CE 2.11. You can download that SDK for free from http://msdn.microsoft.com/cetools/platform/ppcfeatures.asp. Note that the version of this SDK is 1.2, which is confusing given that the previous Palm-size PC SDK (which targeted Windows CE 2.01) was version 2.0 ...

Auto PC

Probably because Auto PC is the most-recently supported platform, there is only support for Visual C++ 5.0 and Windows CE 2.0.

If you are targeting C++, then you need:

- *Microsoft Visual C++ 5.0 Professional or Enterprise edition.* Auto PC development is not supported yet on Visual C++ 6.0.

- *Microsoft Windows CE Toolkit for the Microsoft Visual C++ 5.0.*

- *Microsoft Windows CE Platform SDK, Auto PC Edition,* available in Beta only. Available at: http://msdn.microsoft.com/cetools/platform/autopc.asp.

2.1.2   Application and System Development on Embedded Systems

If you are an OEM, you are facing a different challenge than application developers: you are porting Windows CE onto your custom boards. You won't be relying on the Toolkits mentioned above, as these tools are solely targeted to application development. Instead, you'll rely on the following:

*   *Microsoft Windows CE Platform Builder Version 2.11.* Platform Builder is what is available to develop the bottom layer of Windows CE (the OAL and device drivers), configure Windows CE by removing unwanted components, and produce a ready-to-run CE image. Platform Builder includes tools such as cross-compilers, build utilities, ROM image builder, loaders, debuggers, etc. It actually consists of two distinct products, bundled together:

    a)   The *Windows CE Development Environment*, a Visual C++-like IDE that provides an editor, a compiler and a linker to build plain Win32 applications in C or C++ (without Microsoft Foundation Classes, though). It also allows building redistributable, customized Software Development Kits (SDKs) that match a specific platform. For instance, you may design a board with a certain set of features, and produce an SDK that strictly supports those features. More on this in Chapter 6.

    b)   The *Windows CE Operating System and Development Tools*, a set of command-line tools used for building customized Windows CE images. This set of tools was formerly known as the Embedded Toolkit (ETK) in previous versions, but its content is essentially the same. This set of tools is text-based, rather than graphical, which makes it significantly harder or more error-prone to use.

*   *Licenses.* In order to redistribute the Windows CE images, you must pay licensing fees to Microsoft, usually through licensing distributors. These fees vary depending on the CE configuration features that are to be used. More information is available at http://windowsce.microsoft.com/licensing.asp.

2.1.3   Windows CE Services

You can download Windows CE Services, which is software that runs on the host and that provides synchronization services with a CE device. This software is mainly used when end users need to synchronize contact list, appointments, etc. with the data kept on their desktop computer. Microsoft does not distribute the software itself, although it is available free from other manufacturers. Consult the following site to download the software: http://www.microsoft.com/windowsce/products/download/wceserv.asp. The current version of Windows CE Services is 2.2.

The installation is usually straight-forward, but you must re-install Windows NT Service Pack 3, specifying "No to All" when asked about replacing existing files, and reboot the workstation.

Installing Windows CE Services adds a "Mobile Devices" folder under "My Computer", accessible from the Explorer. Opening that folder automatically starts Windows CE Services if it wasn't already running, and opens a Mobile Devices window, initially empty. This window will later be used to browse a connected device (copy files and so forth).

Windows CE Services shows its presence by displaying a small icon in the tray bar, next to the clock, as displayed on Figure 2-1. Right-clicking the icon and choosing **Communications...** presents the dialog box also shown in Figure 2-1. By default, Windows CE Services can connect to a remote device through a direct serial connection (by default, COM1: at 19200 bps).

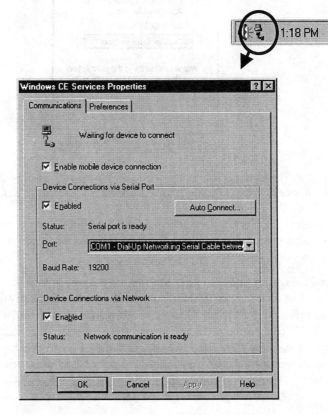

Figure 2-1: Windows CE Services indicates its presence in the tray bar. Right-clicking on it and choosing "Communications..." displays its properties.

It is a good idea to ensure that the CE device is ready to communicate with the host if you intend to use a direct serial link (that is, if you have a working CE device). On the CE device, select **Communications** from the **Control Panel**, and tap on the **PC Connection** tab. Make sure the information presented there confirms that the device is ready to connect to the host. For instance, Figure 2-2 presents the settings of a Palm-size PC (running Windows CE 2.00). Note that connection speed (19200) matches the one specified with Windows CE Services.

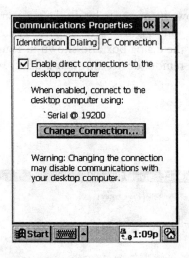

Figure 2-2: The Communication Properties on Windows CE can be checked to ensure that the device is willing to connect to Windows CE Services on a desktop computer.

With Windows CE Services waiting for a connection, simply connecting a CE device to the desktop with a serial cable activates Windows CE Services, which reacts by showing the dialog box shown on Figure 2-3.

Advanced users may choose either the first or the last option, but new users can simply click **Browse**. The dialog box is then automatically closed. Depending on the setting of Windows CE Services, the Mobile Devices window may automatically show up (if it was not already visible). If that window doesn't show up, simply double-click on the Windows CE Services icon in the tray bar. After a few seconds, an entry is displayed in the window, labeled Guest. Double-clicking **Guest** shows you the CE device's file content (see Figure 2-4). You can further explore the device, drag and drop files, etc.

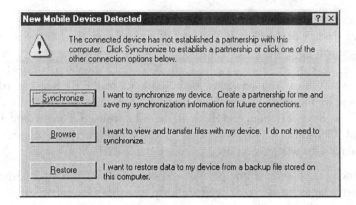

Figure 2-3: Once a connection is established between a CE device and a desktop, Windows CE Services displays this dialog box.

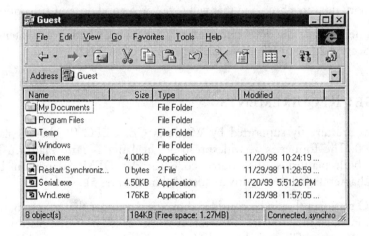

Figure 2-4: Browsing a CE device is as easy as browsing your desktop.

2.2 WORKSTATION REQUIREMENTS

Setting up a new development workstation is relatively inexpensive, but buy as much as you can afford. A reasonable configuration would a Pentium II with 128MB of RAM, a 16GB hard disk (partitioned in 4GB+ drives), NT 4.0 Workstation Service Pack 3 or 4 pre-installed, and a 19-inch monitor (about $2500, and decreasing monthly). If you're serious, invest in a Pentium III, 256MB of RAM, SCSI disks, and a 21-inch monitor (~$3500). That extra money for such a configuration pays for itself within days.

If you use an existing workstation, make sure that it runs NT 4.0 Workstation and that you have Service Pack 3 or 4 at hand. You can download free the latest Service Pack from http://www.microsoft.com/support/winnt/default.htm. Also make sure that you have at least 4GB of free disk space, including at least 2GB on a single partition (to hold a full installation). It won't hurt to have extra disk space (a few GB) because of the various configurations and applications that you will develop over time. Be aware that your life will be miserable if you have less than 64MB of RAM. Do yourself a favor and install at least 128MB of RAM. Consider stealing your boss' 21-inch monitor (who doesn't need such a screen to write daily 1-page status reports and use e-mail, after all ...)

Most PCs today have at least one parallel and one serial port. If your target is equipped with an Ethernet adapter, make sure your desktop also has one in order to speed up the connection between the two devices. On the other hand, if you intend to build and download Windows CE images on an networking-less device, it can be a good idea to invest in a second parallel port on your workstation, since one must be fully dedicated to CE development. While shopping for that parallel port, build a combo adapter that gives you a second serial port; they are cheap and that will save you a good dose of frustrations.

Then you need to add the development tools, depending whether you intend to develop applications (Section 2.1.1) or Windows CE systems (Section 2.1.2).

2.3 TARGET REQUIREMENTS

Two platforms are directly supported by Windows CE: CEPC (PC-based platforms) and Hitachi D-9000. The former is as widespread as the latter is rare. Platform Builder 2.11 provides, for both platforms, the source code for the OEM Adaptation Layer (OAL, described in Chapter 3) and device drivers (detailed in Chapter 5).

The CEPC platform should be considered by any developer that is getting introduced to Windows CE. First, all the tools from Microsoft work "as is" with that platform; all is left is to understand Windows CE and the tools (easier said than done, though). Secondly, that platform (a plain PC) is documented in many books, which makes it easier (or at least, possible) to understand the source code provided in Platform Builder. Section 2.4 details a step-by-step procedure to build a Windows CE image for a PC-based platform.

The second platform is much less popular. However, it is very versatile[3] and can be used with a variety of processors. What's more, most sample drivers are provided for that platform.

Nonetheless, Windows CE can run on a diversity of hardware, provided that a few requirements are met in terms of CPUs, memory, timer and communication ports.

---

[3] Which got it dubbed ODO, the shape-shifter thing in Star Trek Deep Space 9.

2.3.1   CPUs

To run Windows CE, the CPU must be one of those listed in Figure 2-5. All these processors feature 32-bit processing and a little-endian architecture. They all support user and kernel mode as well as paged virtual memory (with page size of 1KB or 4KB). Microsoft is adding more CPUs on a regular basis, so check out updates on the Windows CE web site (see Suggested Readings for interesting links).

Vendor	CPU	Family
ARM		
	ARM 720T	ARM
Intel		
	Intel i486, Pentium, Pentium II	X86
	DE-S1100-XX	ARM
Hitachi		
	SH-3, SH-4	SH
Motorola		
	MPC821	PowerPC
	MPC860	PowerPC
IBM		
	PPC403GC	PowerPC
NEC		
	VR4102, VR4111, VR4111A, VR4121, VR4300	MIPS
Philips		
	Poseidon v1.0 (PR31500)	MIPS
	Poseidon v1.5 (PR31700)	MIPS
Toshiba		
	TX3912	MIPS

Figure 2-5: Supported processors (Windows CE 2.11).

2.3.2   Memory

Windows CE has been tested with up to 32MB of RAM. Expansion RAM (another block of disjoint RAM) is also supported, although it requires some coding in the OAL (see Chapter 3 for details). ROM memory usually holds the Windows CE image, whose size can vary from 350KB to about 5MB. Flash memory is also supported to keep non-volatile data, such as the Windows CE image itself or the Boot Loader (~16KB), during development.

2.3.3 Timer

Windows CE requires an interval timer, which primarily serves scheduling purposes. A real-time clock is also required to maintain the system time when the system is off.

2.3.4 Communication Ports

The target board should include some communication ports in order to communicate with the desktop.

In general, all target boards should have at least one serial port. Windows CE uses the device's first serial port to output run-time messages as a debugging aid. If something goes wrong, this is where you can find a hint about the nature of the problem. If some applications are expected to use serial communications of their own, a second serial port will be required. Other communication services may require that second port as well, such as RAS (required to connect the CE device to the host when no Ethernet connection is available). This second port will appear as COM1: to the applications whereas the first serial port is hidden from them (the first serial port is only visible to CE).

If you intend to build and load Windows CE images periodically, you should equip the target board with either a parallel or an Ethernet port, as an alternative to burning PROMs each time a new Windows CE image is to be tested.

The parallel port is used for downloading images, where the debug port maintains its original role of outputting run-time messages.

An Ethernet port is the ultimate method of not only downloading a CE image, but also obtaining debug messages. If there's a DHCP server on the network, an Ethernet adapter is all you need (no serial or parallel ports are needed); on the other hand, if no such server is available, the debug serial port is still needed in order to enter the CE device's IP address, as we'll see shortly.

2.4 BUILDING WINDOWS CE IMAGES

Let's now focus on some real hands-on work. This section explains how to build a Windows CE image. To make it easier, a PC-based platform is used, because such a platform is cheap but more importantly, widely available (virtually any recent PC or x86-based SBC[4] will do). However, to broaden the picture, the build process is explained for a non PC-based platform (a Motorola MBX board).

---

[4] Single-Board Computer

2.4.1   Setting Up Your Workstation

The very first step is to ensure that the workstation requirements are met (Section 2.2) and that Platform Builder (Section 2.1.2) is installed on it.

The build process we are about to describe essentially relies on various directories, including two in particular: the platform and project directories.

The Platform Directory

The platform directory contains the code (OAL and device drivers) specific to a given platform. Platform Builder provides two directories under %_WINCEROOT%\Platform[5] that are ready to be used:

- Cepc, for PC-based platforms
- Odo, for Hitachi D9000

If your target platform matches one of those, you can simply use the corresponding directory. On the other hand, if your board (or its configuration) is different, choose the platform that closely resembles yours, and copy it using a new name (typically, your platform name). For instance, to use a PC-based platform with specific drivers under a new directory called MyPC, type the following in command window:

```
cd \Wince211\Platform
xcopy Cepc MyPC /E /V /I
```

Then, go into the new platform's directory, and rename the batch file with the previous platform name. For instance (building on the previous commands):

```
cd MyPC
ren Cepc.bat MyPC.bat
```

This batch file, called the platform batch file, contains platform-dependent environment variable settings.

The Project Directory

Building a Windows CE image based on a specific configuration constitutes a project. For instance, if you want to work on two versions of Windows CE, one with windowing and the

---

[5] A symbol that starts and ends with '%' refers to an environment variable. For instance, %_WINCEROOT% refers to the content of _WINCEROOT, as set by Platform Builder, in a command window.

other without, you would use two different projects. Each project resides in its own directory.

Platform Builder 2.11 provides seven sample projects (or configurations, described in detail in Chapter 6), one of which should serve as a base for your project. Copy the project that fits your needs using a new name, that is, your project name. That name must contain eight or fewer characters. For instance, to copy the `Maxall` project to `MyProj`, execute the following commands in a command window:

```
cd \Wince211\Public
xcopy Maxall MyProj /E /V /I
```

Then, go into the new project's directory, and rename the batch file with the previous project name. For example, building on the previous commands:

```
cd MyProject
ren Maxall.bat MyProj.bat
```

This batch file, hereafter referred to as the project batch file, contains project-dependent environment variable settings.

The Developer Directory

Each developer should have his or her own directory to keep personal settings and commands. Developers' directories are named `%_WINCEROOT%\developr\%USERNAME%` (for instance, `F:\WINCE211\developr\john` in my machine). Note that it is "`developr`", not "`developer`"[6]. The directory is not created by default, so it is a good thing to create one immediately:

```
md %_WINCEROOT%\developr
md %_WINCEROOT%\developr\%USERNAME%
```

Each developer's directory should contain a file called `Setenv.bat`. The name is important, as the file will be automatically invoked when setting a build window (the next topic). This file should contain environment variables that control build parameters.

This directory is also a good place to store your own commands that you may add over time. For instance, you can add the following batch file, called `Cleance.bat`:

---

[6] That good old 8.3 filename convention ...

```
@echo off
REM Cleance.bat

cd %_WINCEROOT%
rd /s /q %_FLATRELEASEDIR%
md %_FLATRELEASEDIR%
del %_TARGETPLATROOT%\%_TGTPROJ%.bif
```

This is the recommended method to clean up an entire project before working on another one. The use of this command is demonstrated in Section 2.4.6.

The Build Window

The next step in preparing a build environment is to set up a command prompt build window that uses your platform and project directories. This essentially consists of starting a command prompt window (CMD.EXE on NT) and running WINCE.BAT with a few parameters (CPU, platform, and project). For instance, start a new command window and type the following:

```
F:\>cd \WINCE211\public\common\oak\misc
F:\WINCE211\PUBLIC\COMMON\OAK\MISC>wince x86 i486 CE MyProj MyPC
```

WINCE.BAT sets numerous environment variables, but also executes three batch files already described:

- %_WINCEROOT%\developr\%USERNAME%\Setenv.bat
- %_WINCEROOT%\Platform\%_TGTPLAT%\%_TGTPLAT%.bat
- %_WINCEROOT%\Public\%_TGTPROJ%\%_TGTPROJ%.bat

For instance, for John's MyProj project on MyPC platform, these files would be as follows:

- \WINCE211\PUBLIC\MYPROJ\MYPROJ.BAT
- \WINCE211\PLATFORM\MYPC\MYPC.BAT
- \WINCE211\DEVELOPR\JOHN\SETENV.BAT

Invoking WINCE.BAT as shown above is error-prone and easy to forget. Instead of typing this long command all the time, Platform Builder provides shortcuts for the Minshell project for all processors. The easiest and most convenient approach is to make a copy of that shortcut and adapt it to your platform and project directories. Here's how to do it:

1. First identify the shortcut to copy. From the **Start** button, click **Programs** and **Microsoft Windows CE Platform Builder**. This first entries in the submenu are

labeled "*ProcessorFamily* Tools" (for instance, "ARM Tools", "PowerPC Tools", "x86 Tools", etc.) depending on your installation options. Selecting any of these entries shows a submenu, whose first item is "Build Minshell for *CPU*" (for instance, "Build Minshell for x86"). This is the shortcut to copy.

2. Go back to the proper "*ProcessorFamily* Tools" entry and right click on it. Then click **Explore**. This invokes the Explorer, whose right panel contains the entry of the associated menu. Select the entry **Build Minshell for ...**, and drag it down by pressing the **Ctrl** key. This copies the shortcut to a new one called "Copy of Build Minshell for ..." Right-click on it, click **Rename** and provide a name that includes your project directory name. For instance:

```
Build MyProj for x86
```

3. Press **Enter** to apply the new name. Then right-click on the entry again and choose **Properties**. This displays the properties of the shortcut, as shown in Figure 2-6. The **Target** command is already selected. The last five parameters must reflect your project's settings. These parameters are:

    *   The CPU family: ARM, SHx, MIPS, x86, or PPC.
    *   The CPU model: ARM720T, R3000, R4102, R4111, R4300, i486, PPC821, SA1100, SH3, or SH4.
    *   CE (always)
    *   The project directory name (ex.: MyProj)
    *   The platform directory name (ex.: MyPC)

    For instance, to support MyProj and MyPC for an x86 platform, the command should read as follows (as one continuous line)

```
C:\WINNT\system32\CMD.EXE /k
  g:\WINCE211\public\common\oak\misc\wince.bat
  x86 i486 CE MyProj MyPC
```

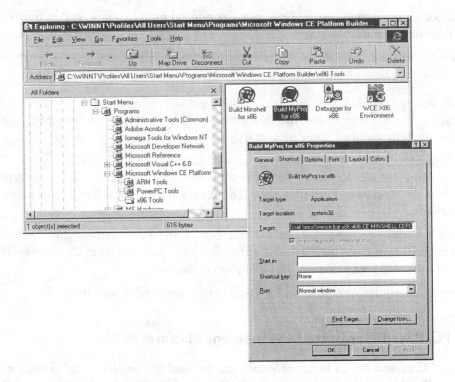

Figure 2-6: Editing the shortcut properties.

4. Click OK to apply the change and close the Explorer Window. The new command is now available from the "... Tools" command menu (see Figure 2-7)

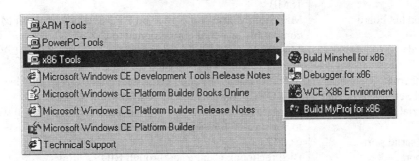

Figure 2-7: The new shortcut in place.

5. Click on that new shortcut. This open a command prompt window, that shows the following or similar messages:

```
Type 'blddemo' to build MyProj
Wince x86 i486 CE MyProj MyPC Development Environment for ...
```

If you get instead the message "The system cannot find the path specified", then review the shortcut properties and make sure the path names are properly specified. They must exactly match.

If you get "WARNING: This build window is incompatible . . ." (a four-line message, in fact), then clean up the \Wince211\Release directory, close the window and restart it again. This is caused by residual files from a previous project.

Here's a useful tip: right-click on the title bar of the command window and click **Properties** and **Layout**. Set the Screen Buffer Size Height from 25 to 1000. That will help you to scroll back to review the build process later on.

All these procedures seem tedious, but you'll quickly get familiar with them.

2.4.2   PC-Based Hardware Development Platform

About any PC using a 486 or better processor can be used to complete a full development cycle of a Windows CE project. Specifically, the configuration listed in Figure 2-8 is supported.

Hardware/Software	Notes
Boot operating system	MS-DOS 6.22
CPU	Any Intel 486 or Pentium, ISA and/or PCI bus
RAM	16MB
Mouse and keyboard	Microsoft Mouse compatible on PS/2 port or Microsoft Mouse compatible on serial port assigned to COM2:
Video cards	Most VGA-compatible video cards (S3, Cirrus, Trident, Western Digital, Tseng, Video 7, and ATI Mach64).
Debug Ethernet	SMC 9000 and NE 2000 cards with either ISA or PCI bus type.
Universal Serial Bus (USB)	Any OHCI compliant USB host controller
Debug serial port	COM1:. 16550 UART recommended; 8250 UART will work at lower speeds. It requires a null modem cable.
Standard serial port	COM2:
Parallel port	Bi-directional. Can be set through BIOS settings.
Audio	SoundBlaster AWE64 ISA PnP card

Figure 2-8: The supported PC configuration.

Although you can use your existing NT workstation to run Windows CE, by copying the Windows CE image onto a floppy disk and rebooting, it is much better to use a second PC as the target. The two devices can be connected using a null modem serial port (COM1: to COM1:) and a CEPC parallel cable (detailed below). An alternative to using the parallel port is to connect both devices to an Ethernet hub. Both methods are explained in the following pages.

Note that Platform Builder 2.11 doesn't provide host tools to download and boot a Windows CE image over a single serial connection. Consequently, connecting the two PCs with a single null modem cable is not enough.

Method 1: Using Serial and Parallel Ports

In this approach, the target's first serial port (COM1:) is used as the debug port, and the parallel port is used for downloading a Windows CE image from the host, as an alternative to burning PROMs or using Ethernet. You must consider a few important issues if you choose this approach:

- You must use a null modem serial cable. A simple pass-through serial cable will not work.

- Make sure the parallel port on both the workstation and the target support bidirectional modes, such as PS/2-compatible, Enhanced Parallel Mode (EPP) or Extended Capabilities Parallel Port (ECP). In fact, all IEEE-1284-compliant modes are supported, except the output-only mode, known as the standard PC/AT mode. Beware that some PCs are shipped with the standard PC/AT mode active by default, so you should verify (and set if needed) the mode using the BIOS setup utilities at boot time. Some modes may not work on your machine, but EPP usually works fine. Also make sure that the parallel port's IRQ is set to 7 and that the port is 378H (this is the common case).

- A custom DB25 Male to DB25 Male parallel cable is needed, also called a CEPC cable (see Figure 2-9). Note that this isn't a normal or a Laplink or a file transfer parallel cable. Platform Builder also contains the cable specification.

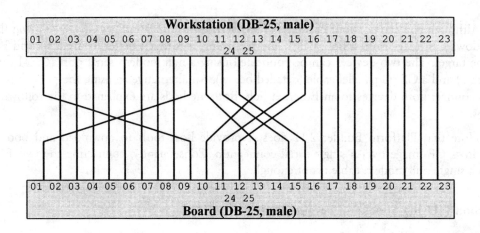

Figure 2-9: The wiring diagram of the null parallel cable needed to download a Windows CE image using CESH on the host.

- A special NT driver is required to use the parallel port for downloading CE images. This driver, called PPShell, is installed with Platform Builder and may be activated during the installation or later, manually, using the Devices applet in the Control Panel. The issue here is that this driver takes full ownership of the parallel port once active. Consequently, you can no longer print or use a removable disk connected to the parallel port, such as a Zip drive or a scanner.

  If your parallel port is already being used on your workstation (say, for printing) when installing Platform Builder, consider not activating the PPShell device automatically. Rather, identify the related drivers currently in use, as well as their state (Automatic, Boot, and so forth), by using the Devices applet in the Control Panel. For instance, the Parallel driver is typically active. To use the CEPC parallel cable, that device must be stopped and PPShell must be started. You can then connect the CEPC cable in the parallel port to use it. To print again, you must stop the PPShell driver, start the Parallel device, and connect the printer. You might have to reboot the system in order to use any extra device based on the parallel port[7]. Some devices (such as Parallel) cannot always be stopped, and also require rebooting. You might have to develop your own procedure depending on the current usage of the parallel port.

  All these problems can be avoided by connecting those parallel-based devices to a second workstation parallel port (as recommended in Section 2.2), dedicating the first one (`LPT1:`) to CE development.

---

[7] And in some cases, you might have to re-install them – no kidding.

Then follow these steps to build, transfer and run a Windows CE image.

1. Make sure the serial and parallel cables are properly connected on each machine. Next, using the Devices applet in the workstation's Control Panel, verify that the Parallel, Parport and ParVdm devices are stopped, and that the PPShell device is started (see Figure 2-10). Here's a tip to prevent fatal blue screens when trying to deactivate/activate these devices: set the startup modes of these devices to Manual, to prevent any of them from being started automatically. After booting your workstation start the proper devices depending whether you intend to use your printer (Parallel, Parport, and ParVdm) or develop CE applications (PPShell).

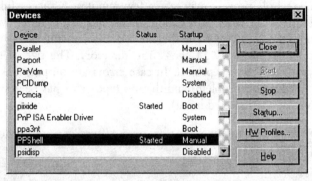

Figure 2-10: The first three devices (Parallel, Parport, and ParVdm) are stopped, whereas PPShell (the selected entry) is started. Also not that the four devices must be started manually, as indicated by "Manual" under "Startup".

2. Your environment must be set to specify which video card comes with your target. This is done by setting an environment variable (refer to Figure 2-11 to identify it) in your platform batch file (i.e., %_TGTPLAT%.bat). For instance, for a VGA adapter, the command is:

```
SET CEPC_DDI_VGA8BPP=1
```

If the wrong variable is set, the target PC's screen will remain dark.

If the target has this video adapter	Then set this environment variable
S3Trio64	(none). This is the default.
CT655X	CEPC_DDI_CT655X
Accelerated S3ViRGE	CEPC_DDI_S3VIRGE
Generic VGA	CEPC_DDI_VGA8BPP

Figure 2-11: The environment variable to set in the platform batch file, depending on the video adapter. This ultimately indicates what video device driver to use.

3. The next step is to start a build window, as explained earlier. You can use your project name, or `Maxall` to build a complete version of CE. Before going any further, right click in the window's title bar, select **Properties**, and set the screen buffer size's height to 1000 lines (if you haven't already changed that setting). This will give you enough room to scroll backward later on. You can type the **SET** command to have an idea of what the settings consist of, although don't let yourself get distracted by the multiple variables at this time. The first time this command is run, you may double-check that each variable set in the platform, project, and developer batch files are indeed listed.

4. Finally, simply type **blddemo**, which is the invocation of the batch file that builds the entire image. The whole process may take a few minutes. A successful build terminates as shown in Figure 2-12. Don't worry about the details of the build; we'll explore them later. The Windows CE image is in the file `Nk.bin`, in the `%_FLATRELEASEDIR%` directory, typically the `\WINCE211\release` directory. The size of the image should be about 4Mb for the `Maxall` project. In case errors are output, make sure your hard disk is not full (a common problem) and that no typo error has been introduced (which can happen, given all the required input).

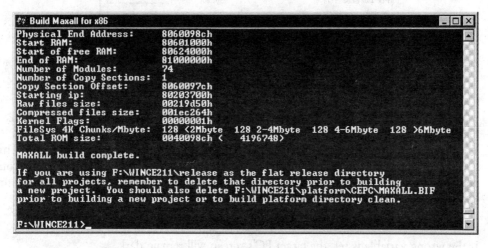

Figure 2-12: A successful build of the `Maxall` terminates like this.

5. Windows CE outputs numerous messages onto its debug port (`COM1:` on the target board). To catch all that information, start `CETERM.EXE` from the command window. Its location (`%_WINCEROOT%\PUBLIC\COMMON\OAK\BIN\I386`) is already in the path. You may also create a desktop shortcut for future access, since there is originally none.

   `CETERM` is a simple terminal emulator. Verify the communication settings by choosing **Communications**, from the **Settings** menu. Use the settings as shown in Figure 2-13.

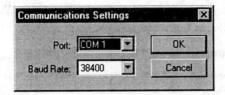

Figure 2-13: The default CETERM communication settings. If COM1: is used by another application or device, connect the null model cable onto another COM port, select that COM port, and click OK.

If your workstation is equipped with two (or more) serial communication ports, reserve the first for Windows CE Services, and use another one to run CETERM.

If you have only one port, make sure that it is not being used by another application (such as Windows CE Services, or another terminal emulator). If so, CETERM will output the message shown on Figure 2-14. Close any application using that port or use another serial port if one is available. If you choose the latter solution, reconnect the null modem and set the communication settings to reflect the port being used.

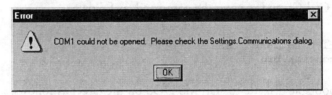

Figure 2-14: Ceterm shows this error if the COM port is busy.

An alternative to CETERM is to use HYPERTERMINAL, located in **Start, Programs, Accessories, Hyperterminal**, and **HyperTerminal**. After starting it, provide a connection name (any name) and click OK. Then, select COM1: (or another available port) in "**Connect using:**" and click OK. This shows a **COM*x* Properties** window, whose options should read **38400, 8, None, 1, Hardware**. If you get the message box shown on Figure 2-15, terminate any application using the port or use another port.

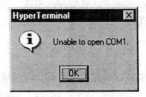

Figure 2-15: This is the error when trying to use HyperTerminal over an already busy serial COM port. Make sure no other application is trying the use the port at the same time, or use another COM port.

Leave either CETERM or HYPERTERMINAL running as is. You can minimize it to save screen space if needed.

6. Enter the following commands on the command window:

```
cd \WINCE211\release (or whatever %_FLATRELEASEDIR% is)
cesh -p cepc Nk.bin
```

If you see the error message shown on Figure 2-16, then the PPShell device isn't running. Refer to Step 1 to fix the problem. No error is shown on success.

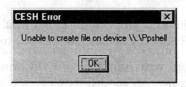

Figure 2-16: CESH output this error if PPShell is not started.

Yet, due to a bug (apparently in the PPShell driver), you must abort CESH (by pressing **Ctrl-C**) and re-enter the command, as follows

```
Press Ctrl-C to abort CESH
cesh -p cepc Nk.bin
```

7. Prepare a bootable diskette to start MS-DOS on the target as follows:

• On the host, insert a blank floppy disk in the floppy drive. Then type:

```
C:>FORMAT A: /S
```

• Then create and edit CONFIG.SYS on the floppy disk and add the following line:

```
DEVICE=a:\dos\himem.sys /testmem:OFF
```

• Locate the file Loadcepc.exe in the %_WINCEROOT%\PLATFORM\CEPC directory and copy it on the floppy disk.

8. Install the diskette in the target's floppy disk drive and reboot the target. Copy LOADCEPC.EXE onto the PC's hard disk, and execute the following command:

```
C:>loadcepc /B:38400 /C:1 /P Nk.bin
```

It then outputs the following messages and a progress bar:

```
2 PCI busses (Version 2.10) using Configuration Mechanism #1
Loading image nk.bin via parallel port
```

Downloading an image is CPU-intensive on the host, and basically prevents you from doing anything useful with your computer during that time (from a few seconds to a few minutes, depending on the size of the Windows CE image). If you are the type of person that exploits multitasking to the limit, you can prevent your system from becoming sluggish by initially reducing the priority of CESH.EXE. To do so, invoke Task Manager (press **Ctrl-Alt-Del** and click **Task Manager...**) and click the **Processes** tab to list all processes. Locate the entry labeled **CESH** and right-click on it; then choose **Set Priority** and **Low** (see Figure 2-17). This has to be repeated every time a CESH session is started. You can in fact execute this procedure immediately after (re)starting CESH.

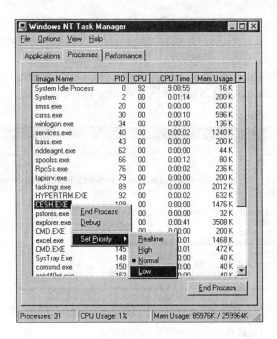

Figure 2-17: Reducing the priority of CESH.EXE, using Task Manager.

9.   After a few seconds, Windows CE starts and displays a Windows CE logo (see Figure 2-18). Other projects/platforms may display something else (or nothing at all).

Figure 2-18: The logo displayed on the Windows CE device upon start-up.

On the workstation, CESH outputs the following prompt:

```
Windows CE>_
```

Finally, CETERM (or HYPERTERMINAL) should be displaying the screen shown in Figure 2-19, indicating that Windows CE is alive and kicking.

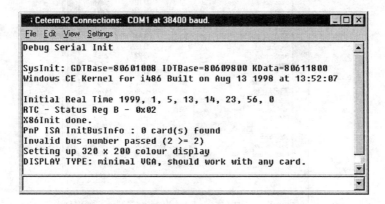

Figure 2-19: CETERM once Windows CE is running.

Here are a few tips to check if you don't see the Windows logo on the target:

- In CESH, simply press the **Enter** key; if the prompt is shown again, CE is very likely running fine. Then type the command **gi proc**, which lists all running processes:

  ```
  Windows CE>gi proc
  ```

  The output should be the following, indicating a running Windows CE system:

  ```
  PROC: Name            hProcess: CurAKY :dwVMBase:CurZone
   P00: NK.EXE          00ffefe2 00000001 02000000 00000000
   P01: filesys.exe     00ffdbda 00000002 04000000 00000000
   P02: shell.exe       20ffb436 00000004 06000000 00000000
  ```

```
P03: device.exe      00ffab76 00000008 08000000 00000000
P04: gwes.exe        00fb54f2 00000010 0a000000 00000000
P05: taskman.exe     00f5b392 00000020 0c000000 00000000
Windows CE>
```

If the output differs on column PROC and Name, then a process didn't start properly. Consult the terminal emulator, as an error message indicating the problem is likely shown. If you see the following error in the emulator, then it is very likely that the wrong video driver was chosen.

```
Exception 00e Thread=80fb5530 Proc=00fb54f2 'gwes.exe'
```

In this case, go to Step 2 and build another image using another video driver.

- If CETERM (or HYPERTERMINAL) is not displaying any sign of life at all, verify that the null modem is properly connected on both ends, in the proper ports (typically COM1: on both PCs), and that the terminal emulator is connected (as indicated by the title bar or status bar). Also make sure the communication settings is set to 38400 8-N-1.

  Then restart CE. If your device has a hard disk, you may use an alternate method which consists of first copying the image on the disk and then loading it in memory. This approach is useful in order to reuse the same image over time, because you don't have to load the image each time you reboot the target. In order to copy the Windows CE image from the host, enter the following command on the target (assuming CESH is still running):

  ```
  C:\>loadcepc -g Nk.bin
  ```

  A bar will be shown to indicate the progression. Once the file is copied, LOADCEPC exits. Invoke it again, this time to boot the copied image:

  ```
  C:\>loadcepc /B:38400 /C:1 Nk.bin
  ```

  Note that the option /P is not specified at this time. This indicates that the Nk.bin image can be used as is, without being downloaded again from the host. The image is loaded in about one second, and CE starts executing.

  If your PC-based device doesn't have a disk big enough to accommodate the image, re-execute the LOADCEPC command entered on Step 8.

Method 2: Using the Ethernet Port

Using an Ethernet port is a faster alternative when downloading a Windows CE image. For instance, a 4MB image takes about 90 seconds using the parallel port vs. 10 seconds using Ethernet (*i.e.*, almost 10 times faster). The only drawback is that the image can only be downloaded and run, not copied on the target (not a big deal, given the transfer rate).

Platform Builder 2.11 supports two Ethernet adapters: NE2000 or SMC9000. Install one of these cards on the target, and set the IRQ to 9 using the BIOS utility.

The Ethernet boot method requires a separate installation (it isn't automatically installed along with Platform Builder). The installation only takes a few minutes and is straight-forward:

1. Insert the Platform Builder Disk 1 into your CD-ROM drive, and go to the `\CEPCBoot` directory. Copy `websetup.exe` and `ebootpc.144` to your workstation, into some temporary directory.

2. Run `websetup.exe` (see Figure 2-20). Enter the Window NT directory and click **Install**. This quickly copies `webimgnt.exe` in the specified directory.

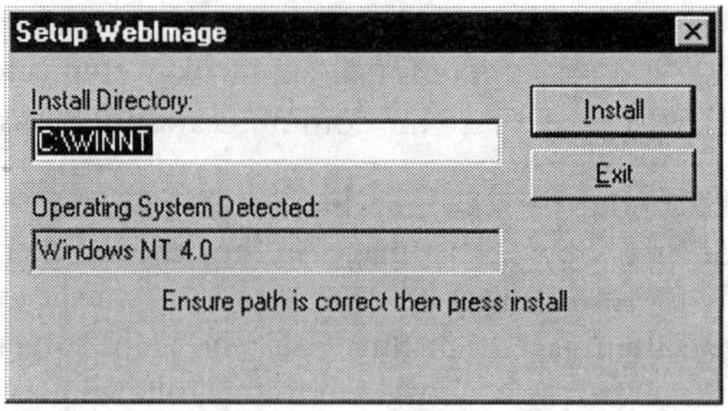

Figure 2-20: Running `webimage.exe`.

3. Then run `Ebootpc.144`, which is indeed an executable (see Figure 2-21). Insert a blank 1.44Mb diskette into the A: drive and click **A Drive** (you can also use a B: drive). A series of files will be copied to the diskette, making it bootable.

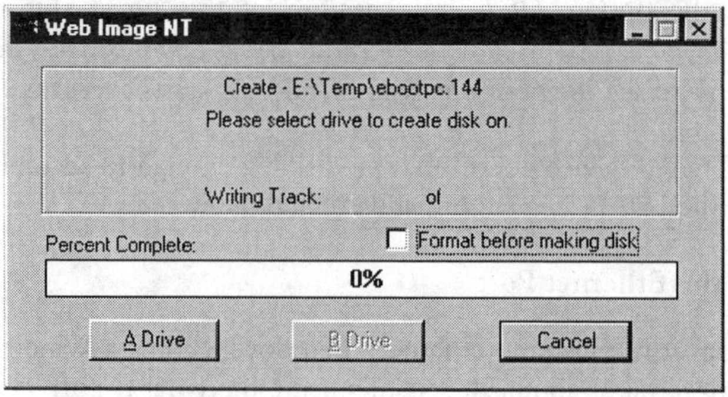

Figure 2-21: Running `Ebootpc.144`.

The diskette is configured to use an NE2000 Ethernet adapter hooked to IRQ 9. If you are using an SMC 9000 adapter, or another IRQ, you must edit `Autoexec.bat`. Line 19 originally reads as follows:

```
loadcepc /b:38400 /v /e:1:0:9 eboot.bin
```

If you are using an SMC 9000 adapter replace `/e:1:0:9` by `/e:0:0:9`. If you are using another IRQ than 9 (say 11), replace `/e:x:0:9` by `/e:x:0:b` (all numbers must be hexadecimal, x being 0 or 1).

Then, you must configure some workstation tools to connect to the device via Ethernet:

4. On the workstation, start a terminal emulator, as described in Step 5 of the previous method. The following assumes that `HYPERTERMINAL` is used (to avoid some confusion since `CETERM` will also be used later).

5. On the workstation, start `ESHELL.EXE`. The file is in `%_WINCEROOT%\Public\ Common\Oak\Bin\I386`, but you can simply run it from a command window (since the path is updated).

6. Insert the diskette into the target's A: drive and reboot. When the menu shown in Figure 2-22 appears, press **2** to boot using `boot.bin`.

```
MS-DOS 6.22 Startup Menu

  1. Boot CE/PC (local nk.bin)
  2. Boot CE/PC (ether via boot.bin)
  3. Boot CE/PC (parallel direct)
  4. Clean Boot (no commands)

Enter a choice:          Time remaining: 2
```

Figure 2-22: Booting with the diskette prepared by `Ebootpc.144`.

Note that you can copy all the files on the floppy onto your device's boot disk (assuming it normally boots MS-DOS 6.22) to speed up the boot process.

After a few seconds, messages similar to those shown below will be displayed on the target (these messages are based on an SMC Ethernet adapter):

```
File not found
SMC Detect: SMC board found at I/O base 0x300
MAC Address:00:40:53:00:4B:0D
Debug network address: SMC9000 at I/O port 0x300, IRQ 0x2
Warning A20 line already enabled
2 PCI busses (Version 2.10) using Configuration Mechanism #1
```

35

```
Total free extended memory = 15296, largest block = 15296
Block allocated at 0x110000
(Extra text not shown)
```

Some errors are displayed if something is wrong. You then have the challenging task of identifying what exactly went wrong. My first attempt failed because of an unsupported Ethernet adapter. Using an SMC9000 adapter resolved the problem. This is really the "Ethernet go/no-go" step.

7. HYPERTERMINAL will then be showing the following (output via the debug serial port):

```
Microsoft Windows CE Ethernet Bootloader 2.2 for CE/PC (Oct  9 1998)
Boot Args @ 0x1C3A6
PCI devices = 2
+SMCInit
SMC Ethernet card detected at I/O base 0x00000300
SMC Ethernet Address: 00:40:53:00:4B:0D
SMC config reg val: 000032B1
SMC Reset complete
-SMCInit
Returned MAC Address:00:40:53:00:4B:0D
Using device name: CEPC19213
(Extra text not shown)
```

The device name shown here in bold, CEPC19213 (yours will be different), is very important because it identifies your CE device to your workstation. You will need it each time you use CESH and CETERM. So it's a good thing to write it down.

8. From ESHELL, select **Manage Device List...** from the **Tools** menu. Then reboot the target device (the first boot is really to test whether the target board properly boots and to identify the PC device name). Upon booting up, ESHELL should detects the device and show its name (see Figure 2-23). Double-click on the name to transfer it in the "Controlled Devices" list, and click **Done**.

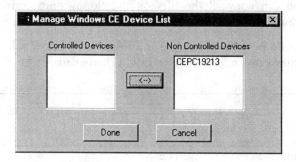

Figure 2-23: Upon rebooting the target, CESHELL detects the CE device name.

9. Still in ESHELL, from the **Options** menu, select **Automatically Download Images**. Then, from the **File** menu, click **Select Image File ...** and select the Windows CE image file, typically *drive*:\Wince211\Release\Nk.bin.

10. Start a build window (refer to Step 3 of the previous method, go to the %_FLATRELEASE% directory, and start CETERM and CESH as follows (replacing CEPC*xxx* by your device's number).

    ```
    F:\Wince211\Release>CETERM -e CEPCxxx
    F:\Wince211\Release>CESH -e CEPCxxx
    ```

11. The HYPERTERMINAL session, connected to the device's serial debug port (not the one just started), will output the following:

    ```
    You have 10 seconds to prove that you exist (via net or serial input)...
    Wait for DHCP, enter new IP address, or CR to use existing IP: _
    ```

    If there's a DHCP server on the network, an IP address will be automatically assigned to the device when it boots.

    Otherwise, you have to type in an IP address, Enter, and a submask. If in doubt, ask for an IP address from your system administrator. On an isolated network, you can safely use 192.168.*xxx.xxx* (where *xxx* is a number between 0 and 255), with a submask of 255.255.255.0. For instance:

    ```
    Wait for DHCP, enter new IP address, or CR to use existing IP: 192.168.1.4
    Enter new subnet mask or CR to use existing mask: 255.255.255.0
    ```

12. Your CE device is now connected to your workstation using debug Ethernet. From that point, you can notice the following:

- ESHELL downloads the image onto the target (a 4MB image takes about 10 seconds). ESHELL's status bar (at the bottom of the ESHELL window) indicates in percentage how much is being downloaded.

- CETERM (started on Step 10) displays debug messages. From that point, HYPERTERMINAL (or CETERM through serial connection) is no longer required.

- CESH (started on Step 10) shows the **Windows CE>** prompt, and accepts any valid command, such **gi proc**.

- If you built a debug version of Windows CE (we'll see how later), the following messages will be displayed on HYPERTERMINAL, indicating that CE is trying to connect to a host debugger (*i.e.*, WinDbg).

```
Connecting to KDBG svc...
!CheckUDP: Not UDP (proto = 0x00000001)
Timed out (retry 1)
Connecting to KDBG svc...
!CheckUDP: Not UDP (proto = 0x00000001)
Timed out (retry 2)
Connecting to KDBG svc...
```

In that case, start another command window and invoke WinDbg as follows:

C:\>**WINDBG –y % _FLATRELEASEDIR% –k CEPC udp CEPCxxx –g**

Note that WinDbg must be started when the target is trying to communicate with it; otherwise, WinDbg will no longer respond and will have to be stopped through Task Manager (invoked with **Ctrl-Alt-Del/Task Manager...**). Section 2.4.4 explains how to use WinDbg.

Here's a quick summary for the next time your start your CE device:

- Start a command prompt and execute "ESHELL", "CETERM –e CEPCxxx", and "CESH –e CEPCxxx" if they aren't already started. Also start HYPERTERMINAL (or CETERM) using COM1: at 38400 bps 8-N-1.

- Reboot your target, choose option 2 (the default). If prompted, enter the IP address and the submask in the HYPERTERMINAL window. After a few seconds, the device is connected.

2.4.3 Motorola Platform

Platform Builder provides the source code for a generic, non PC-based platform, called ODO. In the worst case scenario, you must create your own platform directory and adapt the ODO code to your own board. This is a very tedious step, which is explored in Part II.

Now that CE has been around for a few years, there is an increasingly growing number of third party companies that are providing some development kits for their boards. This section presents an overview of Motorola's kit for its family of MPC821-based systems, including the MBX821-006B embedded board (see Figure 2-24). This board is powered by a PowerPC MPC821 processor running at 40MHz, has 16MB of DRAM and 8MB of flash, a 10BaseT Ethernet connector, EIDE and floppy interfaces, an LCD panel connector, and various communication ports: infrared, two serial, and ADI (described in a second).

Figure 2-24: The Motorola MBX821 embedded board.

Motorola provides you with (under agreements) the *Motorola PowerPC Supplement for the Microsoft Windows CE Embedded Toolkit (ETK)*, version 1.3. This kit provides all the software required to run Windows CE 2.10 and 2.11 on such a target. The only hard work that might remain is to add device drivers for specific devices.

The kit is installed in the `%_WINCEROOT%` directory, blending in with your installation. The major add-on is the `motoads2` platform directory, which includes the entire source code of the kit. Additionally, two projects (`MotoDemo` and `MotoTest`) are added in the `Public` directory, along with the `extras` directory, which contains useful building tools.

What's very different from a PC-based platform is how the code is downloaded. A special PC adapter, called an ADI board (also from Motorola), must first be installed in the workstation (using an available slot). This board provides a connector that is directly wired to the MPC821-based target's ADI port using a flat ribbon cable. The image is downloaded using `MPC8BUG.EXE`, a workstation utility that communicates with the target board over the ADI connection. In this scenario, there is no need for a parallel port or an Ethernet adapter. The debug serial port is still required in order to display any life sign when CE boots, using a terminal emulator, as explained before. In this case, a regular serial cable works fine.

The supplemental commands provided in the `extras` directory supersede some of Platform Builder's, but the idea is the same: you start a command prompt, and you invoke a batch to build the Windows CE image. The commands differ, but the concept remains identical. In both cases you end up with hundreds of lines scrolling before your eyes as the system is being built.

Finally, this kit provides documentation to support custom devices and modifications.

This is one good example of the kits that are becoming available. Other companies have already announced kits to support Windows CE for their embedded platforms. This is certainly an avenue to explore, as it dramatically reduces development time.

2.4.4   Debugging

Platform Builder provides some tools and methods to help debugging a Windows CE image. The first step is to build a debug window CE image (the default settings build a retail version). Open a build window and type the following commands:

`set IMGNODEBUGGER=`	*To include debugger subsystem*
`set WINCEDEBUG=debug`	*To generate debugging info in .OBJ files*
`set WINCEREL=1`	*Allows incremental changes in the release directory*
`blddemo`	*Rebuild the image*

To rebuild a retail version, use the default build window settings or set the variables to the following:

`set IMGNODEBUGGER=1`	*To exclude the debugger subsystem*
`set WINCEDEBUG=retail`	*To prevent the generation of debugging info in .OBJ files*

Debug Zones

Debug zones identify categories of messages to output at run-time on the debug serial port. Each application can use up to 16 categories (or debug zones in CE terminology). Debug zones are typically defined in an application's header file as follows:

```
#include <dbgapi.h>

#ifdef DEBUG
// These macros are used as the first arg to DEBUGMSG
#define ZONE_INIT       DEBUGZONE(0)
#define ZONE_SECOND     DEBUGZONE(1)
#define ZONE_EXCEPT     DEBUGZONE(2)
.
.
.

#define ZONE_WARNING    DEBUGZONE(14)
#define ZONE_ERROR      DEBUGZONE(15)
#else
// For RETAIL builds, these conditionals are always 0
#define ZONE_INIT       0
#define ZONE_SECOND     0
#define ZONE_EXCEPT     0
.
.
.

#define ZONE_ERROR      0

#endif
```

Then the application must declare and initialize the variable dpCurSettings. The name is important, because it is implicitly used by the debug zone macros later on. The following example declares the variable in an application's source file:

```
#include <Dbgapi.h>


DBGPARAM dpCurSettings =
{
    // Application (or module) name (32 bytes max)
    _T("MyApp"),

    // Application-defined names (32 bytes max) for all 16
    // debug zones. Use "" for unused debug zones.
    {_T("Init"), _T("Seconds"),_T("Except"),_T(""),
     _T(""),_T(""),_T(""),_T(""),
     _T(""),_T(""),_T(""),_T(""),
     _T(""),_T(""),_T("Warnings"),_T("Errors")},

    // Initial zone settings. This is a 32-bit value. Bit 0
    // means debug zone 0 is on; bit 1 means debug zone 1 is
    // on, and so on. In the current case, debug zones 0 and
    // 15 are initially on; all others are off.
    (1 << 0) | (1 << 15)
};
```

At start-up, the application must register this variable by calling the macro DEBUGREGISTER(). It requires one parameter: NULL (when used in an application) or hModule when used in a dynamic-link library (DLL). The following example invokes the macros for an application:

```
DEBUGREGISTER(NULL);
```

From that point, a few other macros are available to associate messages to specific debug zones, and output them on the debug serial port if the related debug zone is on. The most popular macros are RETAILMSG(), DEBUGMSG(), and DEBUGCHK().

RETAILMSG() requires two parameters: an expression and a printf-like argument. If the expression is true, the second argument is formatted and output. Here are a few examples:

```
// This message shows up only if the current debug zone
// settings include ZONE_WARNING.
RETAILMSG(ZONE_WARNING, (_T("Device not connected\n")));

// This message shows up all the time because the first
// argument is always TRUE.
RETAILMSG(TRUE, (_T("Module XYZ initialized\n")));
```

The other two macros (DEBUGMSG() and DEBUGCHK()) are only effective when used in a debug Windows CE system:

- DEBUGMSG() works exactly like RETAILMSG(). The only difference is that the former is active in debug mode only, whereas the latter is active in both debug and retail mode.

- DEBUGCHK() only requires an expression. If this expression is false, the macro outputs an error message (something like "module: DEBUGCHK failed in file ... at line ...") and invokes DebugBreak(). That function causes a breakpoint exception to be raised, which is caught by WinDbg (reviewed below).

Here are a few examples using these macros. Note that the extra parentheses are required, due to the underlying macro implementation.

```
// This message shows up in DEBUG builds only, when the
// ZONE_INIT debug zone is turned on.
DEBUGMSG(ZONE_INIT, (_T("Device intialized\n")));

// If bDetected is FALSE, generate a breakpoint.
DEBUGCHK(bDetected == TRUE);
```

Let's recall that the dpCurSettings variable identifies, on an application basis, what debug zones are initially active. This setting can be changed programmatically, by setting dpCurSettings.ulZoneMask to a new mask, and manually, via CESH, as explained next.

CESH

CESH support is series of rudimentary commands to monitor and debug a Windows CE system. These commands can only be invoked when CESH is connected to a running Windows CE device:

- You can load and run EXE files on a running CE platform, by copying them in the %_FLATRELEASEDIR% directory (usually \Wince211\Release) and typing: **s** *name*. For instance, **s MyApp** starts MyApp.exe on CE.

- You can examine processes (by typing **gi proc**), threads (**gi thrd**), modules (**gi mod**) or all running entities (**gi all**). You can kill a process by typing **kp *index***, where index is obtained via gi proc.

- Debug zones can be examined or altered. For instance, **zo p 7** lists the debug zone names of process index 7; **zo m 7 0x0011** sets debug zones 4 and 0 for process 7; that last command can be entered as follows too: **zo m 7 on 4,0**; later on, debug zone 4 can be turned off by typing **zo m 7 off 4**.

- Other commands are available. Simply type **?** to get the list of all valid commands.

WinDbg

WinDbg (pronounced "Win-Debug") allows you to debug just about anything built into the Windows CE image (device drivers, bundled applications, etc). A snapshot of this debugger is shown in Figure 2-25. Note that application debugging is better done with Visual C++ or Platform Builder, since WinDbg is not as refined as those tools. WinDbg only operates on a Windows CE target system, and can rely either on the serial port or the Ethernet port.

Here are the steps to invoke WinDbg with a CEPC platform, using the serial port:

- Make sure the host and target are connected through a null modem cable, on both COM1 ports, and via a CEPC cable as well.

- Stop any terminal emulator currently running, if any. They are not required with WinDbg, since it will display output messages itself.

- Open a command prompt window on the host and start WinDbg (in drive:\wince211\Sdk\Bin\I386) as follows:

  ```
  windbg -k cepc com1 38400 -g
  ```

- Platform Builder installs shortcuts in the **Start** menu, but the initial settings are on com2 at 57600 bps, which must be changed depending on your configuration.

- Execute CESH on the host and LOADCEPC on the target to boot CE (as described in Section 2.4.2).

- The output from CE will be shown in WinDbg's output window. Refer to Platform Builder's online documentation for details about using WinDbg once connected.

If you are using an Ethernet connection instead, follow these steps:

- Start all Ethernet tools (ESHELL, CETERM, CESH) and HYPERTERMINAL, and start the CE device.

- When CE repeatedly outputs the following (in the HYPERTERMINAL window):

  ```
  Connecting to KDBG svc...
  ```

- start WinDbg (in drive:\wince211\Sdk\Bin\I386) as follows:

```
windbg -g -y %_FLATRELEASEDIR% -k cepc udp cepcxxx
```

- The output from CE will be shown in WinDbg's output window. Refer to WinDbg's online documentation for details about using WinDbg once connected.

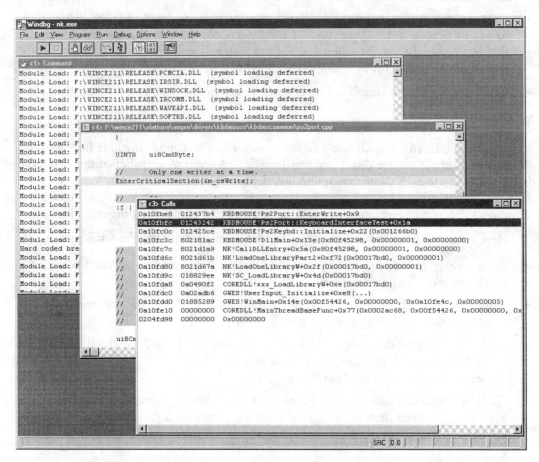

Figure 2-25: WinDbg in action. The top window overrides HYPERTERMINAL and displays the debug messages output by CE. The middle window contains the actual source code being debugged (here, the PC keyboard driver), and the bottom window shows the call stack.

From CESH, you can type the "break" command to stop the Windows CE target and use WinDbg to put various breakpoints and resume CE (**Run/Go**).

2.4.5   The Build Process in Detail

Building a Windows CE image consists of running BLDDEMO.BAT, which invokes various batch files and utilities (see Figure 2-26).

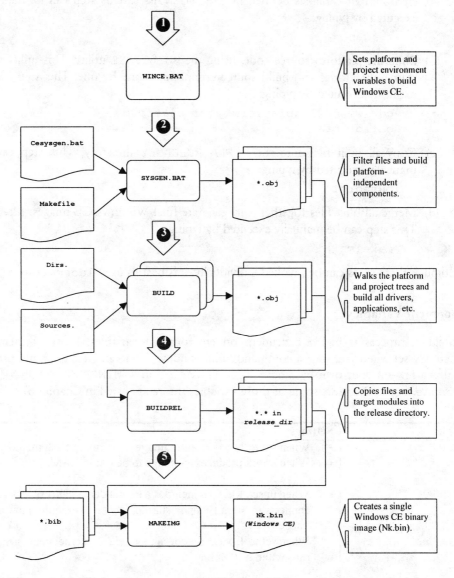

Figure 2-26: The building process of a Windows CE image. It can be invoked from a master batch file (blddemo.bat), or developers may invoke individual commands.

BLDDEMO.BAT

BLDDEMO.BAT essentially consists of four steps:

(a) Build selected Windows CE modules and components, as defined by environment variables defined in CESYSGEN.BAT. This step can be manually executed by typing:

```
sysgen
```

(b) Build the platform source code, using the BUILD.EXE utility. This utility visits source directories and build source components one by one. This step can be manually executed by typing:

```
cd \wince211\platform\your_platform
build -cfs
```

(c) Copy all built files into the %_FLATRELEASE% directory. This step can be manually executed by typing:

```
buildrel
```

(d) Merge all built files together and generate final Windows CE images: Nk.bin. This step can be manually executed by typing:

```
makeimg
```

Although these steps can be invoked individually, it is best to use blddemo.bat.

Environment Variables

The building process is highly dependent on environment variables. Most of them are automatically set when you start a command build window. You can alter the build process by setting a few on your own by modifying SETENV.BAT in %_WINCEROOT%\developr \username. Figure 2-27 lists some of those variables (more are listed in Chapter 6).

Variable	Settings
IMGFLASH	• When set to 1, produces an image to be run in flash memory. • When unset, produces an image to be run in RAM.
IMGNODEBUGGER	• When unset, Nk.bin includes a kernel debugger (Kb.lib) that connects to WinDbg upon startup. WinDbg is required to run the image. • When set to 1, Nk.bin doesn't include the kernel debugger and runs without WinDbg.
WINCEDEBUG	• When set to debug, source files are compiled with debugging information.

WINCEREL	• When set to `retail`, sources files are compiled without debugging information and are optimized.
	• When set to 1, copies built files into `%_FLATRELEASEDIR%`. • When unset, doesn't copy built files in that directory.

Figure 2-27: Some of the environment variables that control the build process.

Adding Custom Modules to the Build Process

`BLDDEMO.BAT` is designed to automatically build custom modules (programs or libraries) that you add in your project directory as the entire system is built. You can rely on this method (hereafter described) to build custom system components. However, it is easier to build applications by using Visual C++ or Platform Builder, as described in Section 2.5

`BLDDEMO.BAT` invokes `BUILD.EXE` on the project directory (`%_PROJECTROOT%`) to build some custom modules (either programs or libraries). `BUILD` internally relies on three data files:

- The `Dirs` file, which resides in the project directory, indicates what subdirectories must be visited and built.
- The `Sources` file, which resides in a program directory to build, identifies what files to build.
- The `Makefile` file indicates how to build the source file.

Here is the directory hierarchy that shows the locations of those files:

```
%_PROJECTROOT%\
    .
    .
    .
    Dirs
    MyApp\
            Makefile
            MyApp.cpp
            MyApp.rc
            Sources
```

In this example:

- `Dirs` contains one line:
    `DIRS=MyApp`

- `Makefile` contains one line that includes a much larger Makefile that provides default clauses:

      !INCLUDE $(_MAKEENVROOT)\makefile.def

- The `Sources` file contains the following:

      TARGETNAME=MyApp
      TARGETTYPE=PROGRAM
      EXEENTRY=WinMain

      COPYRES=1
      WINCETARGETFILES=$(_RELEASELIBDIR)\$(TARGETNAME).res

      TARGETLIBS=$(_COMMONSDKROOT)\lib\$(_CPUINDPATH)\coredll.lib
      SOURCES=MyApp.cpp \
          MyApp.rc

Each subdirectory specified in `Dirs` should produce one binary file (`.lib`, `.dll` or `.exe`). Programs are copied into:

    %_PROJECTOAKROOT%\Target\%_TGTCPUTYPE%\%_TGTCPU%\%_TGTOS%\%WINCEDEBUG%
(for instance: `\Wince211\Public\Maxall\Target\x86\i486\Ce\Retail`)

Also, if `%WINCEREL%` is set to 1, the file is also copied into `%_FLATRELEASEDIR%`, typically `\Wince211\Release`.

Libraries (.lib files) are copied into:

    %_PROJECTOAKROOT%\Lib\%_TGTCPUTYPE%\%_TGTCPU%\%_TGTOS%\%WINCEDEBUG%
(for instance: `\Wince211\Public\Maxall\Lib\x86\i486\Ce\Retail`)

2.4.6 Cleaning Up

As long as you work on the same project, there is no need to clean things up. You simply rebuild as required to incorporate incremental changes.

If you work on multiple projects, you have to clean up once done with a project and ready to start another one. Within a build window set to the project you're done with, simply invoke `Cleance.bat`, which is described in Section 2.4.1. Then close all build windows for that project, and open new build windows for the new project.

If you want to completely clean a project, you should also deletee the `Cesysgen` tree, directly under the project directory.

2.5   BUILDING WINDOWS CE APPLICATIONS

With a Windows CE system running, either Platform Builder or Visual C++ can be used to build Windows CE applications. Before taking a closer look at each tool, you must first ensure that a debugging connection is established between the host and the target:

2.5.1   Establishing an Application Debugging Connection

Visual C++ and Platform Builder support remote debugging using a direct serial connection. The following sections explain how to set-up that link on the workstation and the target using either REMNET.EXE or REPLLOG.EXE.

A basic rule to remember is that if the CE device has only one available serial port (the common case), either REMNET or REPLLOG - but not both - can be used at a time[8]. Which one to use depends if you intend to use Windows CE Services or RAPI on the host. If yes, you must use REPLLOG, otherwise you can use REMNET, which is easier to include in your CE image.

Using REMNET

Windows CE includes a Connection application (see Figure 2-28), invoked from the Control panel, that establishes a connection with the host. Once connected, applications running on Windows CE can use the communication APIs (*e.g.*, WinSock, WNet, etc).

The applet allows establishing a connection with a host using either Direct Cable Connection or Dial-up Networking. Direct Cable Connection uses a direct serial connection between the CE device and the host, whereas Dial-up Network connects the CE device to a network by calling a remote computer.

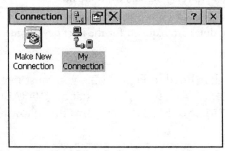

Figure 2-28: The Connection application (REMNET.EXE). "My Connection" has been added by clicking on "Make New Connection".

---

[8] This is because both use the same, unsharable access method (RAS, described in Chapter 13).

A connection setting can be configured to use a serial cable on COM1: (not to be confused with the debug serial port) at a baud rate of 38400, requesting the desktop to provide a TCP/IP address for the duration of the connection. Another connection may rely instead on an available modem (on COM2:) at a baud rate of 19200, using a predetermined TCP/IP address. Finally, another setting may be a direct connection using infrared, at a baud rate of 19200, requiring a TCP/IP address from the host.

Each setting has a name, which is listed in the **Start, Programs, Communications** menu, allowing the user to choose any one. These connections communicate with an NT desktop running a Remote Access Services (RAS) server.

REMNET also starts RNAAPP.EXE, which connects to the host workstation's Direct Cable Connection Manager (DCCMAN) socket, and echoes signals from the host.

Windows CE must be configured by including a few modules in order to communicate with the host development tools. Figure 2-29 lists each of these modules with a brief description and the default CE configurations that already include them.

Module	Description	Configurations
Toolhelp	TOOLHELP.DLL, a library to access system data.	All
Shell	SHELL.EXE, the counterpart of CESH on the host.	All
Ppp, Tcpstk	Point-to-point protocol and TCP/IP support	Mincomm Minshell Minwmgr Maxall
Remnet	REMNET.EXE, Remote networking.	Maxall
Rnaapp	RNAPP.EXE, to relay signals from the host	Maxall

Figure 2-29: These modules are required for the host development tools to work with Windows CE.

In order to use any module listed in Figure 2-29, you must make sure that they are listed in the project's CESYSGEN.BAT file. For instance, MAXALL's CESYSGEN.BAT (in \WINCE211\PUBLIC\MAXALL\OAK\MISC) contains the following lines:

```
set CE_MODULES=coredll filesys nk toolhelp shell
set CE_MODULES=%CE_MODULES% tcpstk ppp
set CE_MODULES=%CE_MODULES% pegterm termctrl rnaapp remnet
```

Using REPLLOG

REPLLOG also provides some connectivity to the host, but it additionally monitors the connection and provides data synchronization services. A Windows CE device running REPLLOG is detected by Windows CE Services on the host, whereas a device running REMNET is not. REPLLOG exclusively relies on a direct serial connection to a RAS server on NT.

REPLLOG also starts RNAAPP.EXE to relay events from the host. Furthermore, REPLLOG starts Rapisrv.exe, which enables host's applications to execute system calls on CE via the Remote API (RAPI), described in Chapter 22. REPLLOG is usually started via the Registry upon a connection drop hardware event (for instance, this is the application that is started when you drop your Palm PC into its dock).

REPLLOG cannot be included by setting some configurations. Instead, you must complete the following steps:

1. Copy Repllog.exe, Rapisrv.exe, Rra_stm.dll, Pegobj.dll and Aafobj.dll from:

    ```
    Public\Common\oak\target\CpuPath\CE\{debug|retail}
    ```
    to
    ```
    Public\Projectname\cesysgen\oak\target\Cpupath\CE\{debug|retail}
    ```

2. Edit the `Modules` section of the file `Public\ProjectName\Oak\Files\Project.bib` and add the following lines at the end of the file:

    ```
    MODULES
    ;  Name                 Path
    Memory Type
    ;  --------------       --------------------------------      -----
    ------
        repllog.exe          $(_FLATRELEASEDIR)\repllog.exe        NK
        rapisvr.exe          $(_FLATRELEASEDIR)\rapisvr.exe        NK
        rra_stm.exe          $(_FLATRELEASEDIR)\rra_stm.exe        NK
        pegobj.exe           $(_FLATRELEASEDIR)\pegobj.exe         NK
        aafobj.exe           $(_FLATRELEASEDIR)\aafobj.exe         NK
    ```

3. Start a build window for your project and run BUILDREL to copy the updated `Project.bib` and the executable files to `%_FLATRELEASEDIR%`.

4. Rebuild the Windows CE image (`Nk.bin`) by running MAKEIMG.

2.5.2 Using Platform Builder 2.11

Platform Builder provides all the tools required to write Windows applications. Before you start Platform Builder, make sure your workstation is connected to a running Windows CE platform, using a debug serial cable and either a parallel cable or Ethernet, and that CESH is running.

Building a Hello World Application

1. Start Platform Builder. Select **New** from the **File** menu, click on **Projects** and select **WCE Application**. Then enter the project name **MyApp**, in the directory of your choice. Also select the proper platform (*e.g.*, **Win32 (WCE x86)**). Click OK.

2. The WCE Application – Step 1 of 1 window is shown. Select A typical "Hello World" application and click Finish. This generates a Win32 application that displays ... you know what by now. You can see in the left panel (called the Workspace) some files being listed.

3. Select Build MyApp.exe from the Build menu, or simply press F7. The entire project is built in a few seconds and the executable (MyApp.exe) is copied in the directory specified by the %_FLATRELEASEDIR% environment variable. Note that the file is not transferred onto CE.

4. Then simply select Execute MyApp.exe from the Build menu, or simply press Ctrl+F5. The application is automatically started onto the target (see Figure 2-30). Typing **gi proc** in CESH will confirm that MyApp.exe is running.

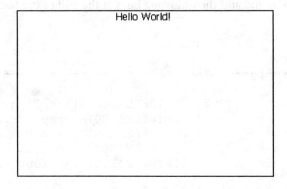

Hello World!

Figure 2-30: The Hello World application generated by Platform Builder.

If the application doesn't start, make sure that CESH has been started in the %FLATRELEASEDIR% (an essential requirement). If this is not the case, stop CESH, restart your CE device and re-run the application from Platform Builder.

5. To stop the application, invoke **gi proc** from CESH and locate the id of MyApp.exe (6 in the example below). The kill the process by typing **kp 6**, in CESH.

```
Windows CE>gi proc
PROC: Name            hProcess: CurAKY :dwVMBase:CurZone
 P00: NK.EXE          00ffefe2 00000001 02000000 00000000
 P01: filesys.exe     00ffd5ca 00000002 04000000 00000000
 P02: shell.exe       20ffad86 00000004 06000000 00000000
 P03: device.exe      00ffa512 00000008 08000000 00000000
 P04: gwes.exe        00f5ec12 00000010 0a000000 00000000
 P05: taskman.exe     00f27a3e 00000020 0c000000 00000000
 P06: MyApp.exe       20f088b6 00000040 0e000000 00000000
```

There is a subtle, yet *extremely* important detail to note here. The file MyApp.exe has not been copied onto the target. If you were to use Windows CE Services and explore the device, you wouldn't find it anywhere. And there's a good reason for that: the file is still on the host, in the %FLATRELEASEDIR% directory. This directory acts as a paging file system for the CE device. This functionality is controlled by SHELL.EXE on the device and CESH.EXE on the host. For this to work, however, CESH must be started in that directory; otherwise, it only sees the file(s) in the directory it was started from.

Hence, in order to access or run files on CE, you simply have to copy them into \WINCE211\Release. Then, to run a file for instance, you can type **s** *appname* in CESH or **Alt-Tab, Alt-R** and the application name on CE. Pretty cool, huh?

Using Remote Tools

Platform Builder includes a few remote tools to analyze the Windows CE target as it runs. The tools are listed under the **Tools** menu. For these tools to be usable, however, you must run Remote Access Service (RAS) on the host and REMNET on the target.

RAS is described in details in Chapter 13, but follow this procedure to start it on NT:

1. Identify an available COM: port. If all are being used, stop any application using one of them in order to free one. Note that CESH can still see the CE device through the parallel port or Ethernet.

2. From the **Start** menu, click Programs, **Administrative Tools (Common)** and **Remote Access Admin**. This starts the RAS control application.

3. If the message "Remote Access Service is not started on the selected server" is shown, click **Start Remote Access Service** from the **Server** menu. Confirm the host name by clicking OK. After a few seconds, RAS is running and the hostname is shown in the main window.

Then, start REMNET on CE as follows:

1. On CESH, type: **s remnet**. This displays the **Connection** window. The **Make New Connection** icon is already selected, so simply press **Enter**.

2. The **Make New Connection** window is shown. Make sure **Direct Connection** is selected and click **Next**. As an alternative to click, use the **Tab** key and press **Enter**.

3. Then make sure "**Serial Cable on COM1:**" is selected. Remember that COM1: is not the debug port, but the second serial port, and make sure that the serial cable is attached on both ends.

4. Click **Finish** to add a new connection icon, labeled "My Connection".

5. Select **My Connection** and press **Enter**. The "User Logon" window is shown. Enter a a valid logon name and password. The "Connected to My Connection" window is then shown (see Figure 2-31).

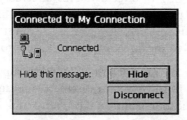

Figure 2-31: The window displayed on the target once connected to the host.

Then you can use any tool from Platform Builder. For instance, select **Windows CE Zoom** from the **Tools** menu. The application starts and connects to the target. Choose **File** and then **New**, and the image shown on the target is downloaded.

Debugging the Application

Debugging is as easy once REMNET is running on the target. By default, the MyApp project is generated in debug mode, and is ready to be debugged.

1. First make sure that MyApp is not running on the target. Press **Alt-Tab** on the target; if MyApp is listed, select **MyApp** and click **End Task** (or press **Alt-E**).

2. Back to Platform Builder, make sure MyApp.cpp is opened, and position the cursor on line 29 (the first executable line in WinMain()). Press **F9** to set a breakpoint, identified by a red dot on the left.

3. From the **Build** menu, select **Start Debug** and **Go**, or press **F5**. The operation takes a few seconds (up to 30), since it requires copying and starting a debugging process (CEMON.EXE) on the target. A yellow arrow in shown over the red dot (breakpoint), indicating that the line has been reached.

4. First note that the Build menu is replaced by the **Debug** menu, which lists numerous debugging commands. You can try any of them, although some take a few seconds to execute.

5. There are other interesting features. For instance, to see the content of a variable, move the cursor onto that variable and leave it there half a second. A tip window will appear, showing the variable's value.

6. To resume execution, select **Go** from the **Debug** menu (or press **F5**); to stop running, select **Stop Debugging** from the **Debug** menu (or press **Shift-F5**). It takes about five seconds for the debugger to fully stop.

Using Visual C++ 6.0

Using Visual C++ is similar to using Platform Builder. The procedure described below uses the H/PC Pro emulator. This approach allows you to develop a CE application without using a real target, or requiring ESHELL, CESH, CETERM, or HYPETERMINAL.

1. Start Visual C++. Select **New** from the **File** menu, click on **Projects** and select **WCE MFC AppWizard (exe)**. Then enter the project name **MyApp**, in the directory of your choice. Select the x86em platform (*i.e.*, **Win32 (WCE x86em)**) and other platform(s) if desired. Click OK.

2. The **WCE MFC Application (exe) – Step 1 of 4** window is shown. Simply click **Finish** to use all the default options. This generates a plain MFC Win32 application

3. From the **Build** menu, click **Set Active WCE Configuration**, and choose **H/PC Pro 2.11**. From the same menu, click **Set Active Configuration**, choose **MyApp – Win32 (WCE x86em) Debug**, and click OK. This ensures that the project is built for the H/PC Pro emulator.

4. Select **Build MyApp.exe** from the **Build** menu, or simply press **F7**. The entire project is built in a few seconds and the executable (MyApp.exe) is copied into the emulator's directory (on the host). Then, the emulator is automatically started (after a few seconds), and is positioned in the top left corner of the screen (and it cannot be moved).

5. Select **Execute MyApp**.exe from the **Build** menu, or simply press **Ctrl+F5**. The application is automatically started in the emulator (see Figure 2-32).

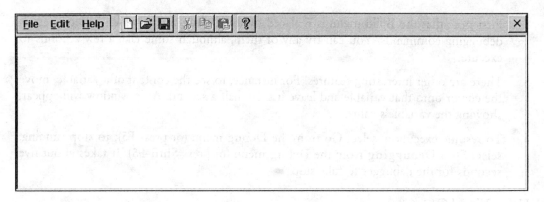

Figure 2-32: The MyApp application generated by Visual C++'s AppWizard.

If the application is to run on a real target, make sure to first start REMNET as described earlier.

6. The application can be stopped by clicking on the application Close button (**x**), in the top right corner.

7. The emulator can be stopped by clicking **Start** (in the emulator window) and **Suspend**.

2.6 HOW TO STAY TUNED

Most CE developers are initially overwhelmed by all that information. In addition, Windows CE is evolving very fast – some think too fast – and it is difficult to stay updated. Microsoft's web site is probably the best source of information, although it sometimes doesn't reflect the latest products being advertised elsewhere on the same site.

2.6.1 About Windows CE

The most up-to-date source of general information about Windows CE is on Microsoft's Web site, at http://www.microsoft.com/windowsce. Note that the site keeps changing as new information becomes available. The site has recently been reshaped, and is much easier to navigate.

Numerous magazines are taking a look at Windows CE. Keep an eye on them on a monthly basis to catch any useful articles. Here are just a few that have published Windows CE articles recently:

- Windows CE Tech Journal (http://www.cetj.com)
- Embedded Systems Programming (http://www.embedded.com)

- Microsoft Systems Journal (http://www.microsoft.com/msj)
- Dr. Dobbs (http://www.ddj.com)
- RTC (http://www.rtcgroup.com)
- And others.

2.6.2   About Hands-on Development

From a development standpoint, the Microsoft Developer Network (MSDN) provides the latest information about the Win32 API for all Windows platforms, including CE. It is available under two formats: CD-ROMs and online.

The CD-ROM version requires a 1-year subscription, which includes four CD-ROMs quarterly distributions, and is available in three formats:

- Library subscription, which includes a variety of technical programming documentation.
- Professional subscription, which includes the Library subscription, plus operating systems (98 and NT), Software Development Kits (SDKs) and Device Driver Kits (DDKs).
- Universal subscription, which includes the Professional subscription, plus Visual Studio Enterprise Edition, Office 97 Developer Edition and more.

These three subscription are respectively priced at $199, $699 and $2499, although pricing many vary. Consult http://msdn.microsoft.com/default.asp for details.

The online version is very similar to the Library subscription, and is freely accessible at http://msdn.microsoft.com/library/default.htm.

2.6.3   About This Book

Make sure you regularly visit http://www.exposecorp.com/windowce.htm. This page contains book updates (samples, links, etc.) and other useful material regarding Windows CE development.

SUGGESTED READINGS

Microsoft, http://www.microsoft.com/windowsce
> The official Windows CE's site, at Microsoft. Most of the links mentioned above can be traced from that entry point.

Microsoft, Platform Builder online documentation
> The highlighted topics below covers some of the topics mentioned in this chapter.

```
Building a Platform for Windows CE
    Adapting Windows CE for Embedded systems
        Windows CE Platform Builder
            Getting Started
            Visual Development Environment
```

RFC1918
>   This Requests for Comments identifies a range of IP addresses to use in local networks. See http://www.teknovations.net.

De Herrera, http://www.cewindows.net
>   This non-official site contains a flock of useful information about using and configuring Windows CE devices. It is constructed and maintained by Chris De Herrera, a Windows CE enthusiastic that even responds to e-mails! This site is not about programming, but just about everything else.

Part II

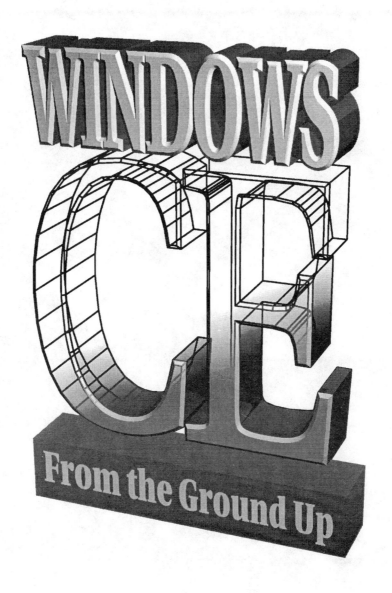

Porting Windows CE

Chapter 3

Boot Loader

The next issue, once a Windows CE image is built, is to load and run it on the target. One method is to copy the image into flash memory or burn it into PROM, and give it a try. This certainly works, but is inefficient in terms of time and resources. The Windows CE designers anticipated that situation and introduced a boot loader, a piece of software that runs on the target, that dynamically loads a CE image from the host into memory and jumps into it. That piece of software also has to be written in flash or burned in PROM (so there no way to escape the process), but it is much simpler to implement. And once it is bug-free, Windows CE images can be downloaded from the host easily during development. Once a Windows CE image is ready to go into production, that image is then burned and the boot loader is discarded. This chapter describes the boot loader provided by Microsoft and summarizes the step to implement one for a custom board.

The boot loader is the recommended approach to load and boot CE on most targets, even on the CEPC platform. But in that case, Microsoft provides LOADCEPC.EXE, an MS-DOS loader that is worth taking a close look at first.

3.1 LOADCEPC

LOADCEPC.EXE is the boot loader for MS-DOS 6.22. This is a 16-bit program, that requires a real mode compiler (*e.g.*, Visual C++ 1.5).

The program starts by parsing the arguments and initializing a BOOT_ARGS structure. That structure is important, as Windows CE uses it upon its initialization.

LOADCEPC has a dual functionality (see Figure 3-1). The first one is to act as a parallel port file system tool, that can access the host's file system. The second is to load a Windows CE image and/or boot it up.

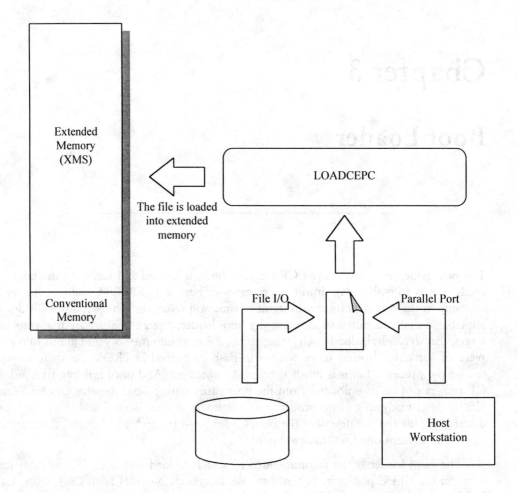

Figure 3-1: LOADCEPC can load files from a local disk or from the parallel port.

Parallel Port File System Tool

A few LOADCEPC commands consist of listing directories on the host (NT) and transferring files from the host. Those commands take place over the parallel port and require a peer on NT's side (which is CESH).

LOADCEPC uses a simple, proprietary protocol to accomplish its work. For instance, in order to list the files in the directory CESH was started, LOADCEPC transmits a small packet containing an operation code ("find first") and a mask (*e.g.,* "*.*"). CESH finds the first matching file, fills up a _finddata_t structure, and sends that structure to LOADCEPC, which displays the file's name and attributes. The process is repeated, one file at a time, until the entire directory has been displayed.

Using that method, other file-oriented commands are supported, such open, read, write, and close file(s). These operations are used to transfer files from host, such as a Windows CE image (Nk.bin).

The functions that send and receive data to and from the parallel port do so one byte at a time, through polling, by invoking OEMParallelPortGetByte() and OEMParallel PortSendByte(). Those 16-bit functions are very similar to their 32-bit twins implemented in the CEPC's OAL (described in the next chapter).

Loading and Booting using the Parallel Port

Besides listing and transferring files, LOADCEPC can load a Windows CE image in memory and jump to it. The image might have already transferred, in which case it is simply loaded in memory; otherwise, LOADCEPC can download it using the parallel port, directly in memory.

LOADCEPC is a 16-bit, real mode program, and is limited to the first MB of RAM. To access the physical memory beyond it, LOADCEPC, like many other MS-DOS programs, relies on the eXtended Memory Specification (XMS), as set of functions implemented by the HIMEM.SYS driver (hence the need for that driver to boot Windows CE). LOADCEPC terminates if that driver is not installed; otherwise it allocates and zeroes the largest chunk it can in extended memory.

LOADCEPC then starts either reading (from a file) or downloading (from the parallel port) the Windows CE image, Nk.bin. This is the image produced by MAKEIMG on NT (see Chapter 2 for details). The first bytes of the files are compared against a known signature, and the process is aborted if there's a mismatch. The signature is followed by the base address where the image is to be loaded in physical memory and the image size.

The bin files produced by MAKEIMG are composed of *sections*. A section describes a chunk of data via the address it must be copied to, the size of that data chunk and a checksum (see Figure 3-2).

In the case of Nk.bin, the first section is loaded at address 0x200000 (2MB) The last section of the image is identified by a zero address, and its size is in fact the entry point into the image. For Nk.bin, this is the OAL entry point. Chapter 4 provides more information about the load address and the OAL entry point.

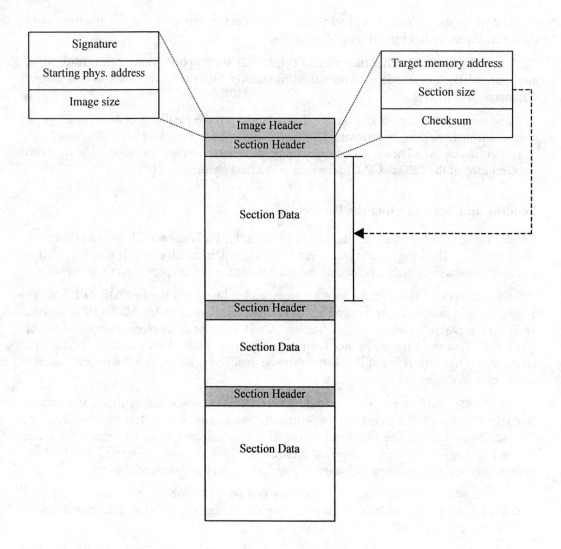

Figure 3-2: MAKEIMG's bin files are composed of sections.

Once the entire image is copied into extended memory, LOADCEPC activates the A20 address line[9], switches into protected mode, stores the address of the BOOT_ARGS structure

---

[9] In real mode, the x86 generates 20-bit addresses, but address arithmetic sometimes generates a carry bit (*i.e.*, address bit 20) On an 8086, there is no bit 20, so all addresses are 20 bits. On a 286 and up, there is an address bit 20, so PC designers introduced a twist to keep that bit off all the time. Programs that use the protected mode to access memory beyond the first MB (like XMS) must return the address line 20 to the CPU's control.

into address 0x1FFFFC (just under the 2MB mark), and jumps at the entry point address, whatever it is (an act of faith!), giving control to Windows CE.

That very same BOOT_ARGS structure will be referred to by CE upon its initialization (more details in Section 4.2).

Loading and Booting using Ethernet

Ethernet is an alternative to downloading Windows CE using a parallel port. A much faster alternative that is. As shown in Chapter 2, LOADCEPC must first load an MS-DOS Ethernet boot loader (eboot.bin) into memory, and give control to that loader. The Eboot.bin image resides with LOADCEPC (on the same disk) and doesn't have to be initially transferred from the host.

Eboot.bin is another file, like Nk.bin, produced by MAKEIMG on NT. It is read from the local disk and loaded into extended memory, as described in the previous paragraphs. The only differences are a smaller image size and a different load address (0x130000). Once loaded, LOADCEPC jumps into the entry point as indicated in the last section of file.

Eboot.bin then relies on Ethernet to communicate with Eshell on the host. It downloads the Windows CE image (Nk.bin) at 0x200000 (2MB) and jumps into it (see Figure 3-3).

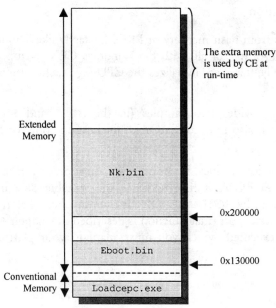

Figure 3-3: The PC memory when eboot.bin jumps into Windows CE.

3.2 BOOT LOADER

Platform Builder provides two boot loaders. The first one loads an image through the parallel port, whereas the second is Ethernet-based. The first one is described in the next section, and the second in Section 3.2.3.

3.2.1 Parallel Boot Loader

Platform Builder provides a complete example of a parallel boot loader in `Wince211\Platform\Odo\Bootload`. The code can be divided into the following modules:

- Startup and initialization
- Image download
- Parallel port I/O
- Debug serial I/O
- Flash write
- Firmware monitor

Startup and initialization

The boot loader starts from flash memory or PROM, exactly like Windows CE. The startup code will then share a lot (if not all) with the Windows CE's startup code, detailed in the next chapter. Specifically, this piece initializes the CPU (*e.g.*, caches, memory access, etc.) and then calls `main()`.

Platform Builder provides two samples (in the `Mips` and `Shx` directories, under `Bootload`), but you can also refer to the OAL initialization code for other processors. See Chapter 4 for details.

The `main()` function resides in `Bootload\Common\Main.c`. Because the code might be running from ROM, it first relocates the writable data into RAM. It uses a relocation table produced by `ROMIMAGE.EXE`. It then invokes `OEMInitDebugSerial()` to initialize the debug serial port (that function is described in Chapter 4). A series of Power-On-Self-Test is then executed, which you must adapt to your platform. On success, the image is downloaded.

Image download

Downloading an image is exactly as described with `LOADCEPC`. A boot packet is first sent to a peer running on the host (`CESH`), passing a boot packet string. The file is then sent from the host. The very first bytes are a signature, which is verified first. The program terminates if there's a mismatch.

Then the base address and the image size are read next (see Figure 3-2). That address determines whether the image is targeted to some flash or RAM memory.

If the file is to be loaded in RAM, the boot loader reads one section header (12 bytes), and then reads the section data and stores it at the location indicated in the section header. The last section contains the start address, which is passed to Launch() to execute the image. Launch() typically resides in the assembly language file that implements the start-up.

If the file is to be loaded in flash, write delays must be addressed. The issue is that writing a word in flash memory requires a certain time for the memory to settle and accept the new data. The application must query the flash memory status to determine when the write operation is completed and another word can be written into it.

As a result, it takes more time to write *n* bytes in flash than to read them from the parallel port. So it is not possible to load the data as it is done for RAM memory, *i.e.*, read a chunk of data and write it, read another chunk and write it, and so on. This approach would result a data overrun in the parallel port resulting in data loss. The situation could be different if some form of flow control was implemented between the target and the host, but this is not the case at this point.

The solution is to buffer the data as it is read from parallel port. The buffer is in fact a circular buffer (see Figure 3-4). Four pointers are used: the beginning and end of the buffer, the position to add the next byte read from the parallel port, and the position of the last byte written into flash. The first two pointers are static, but the last two move around as data is read and written.

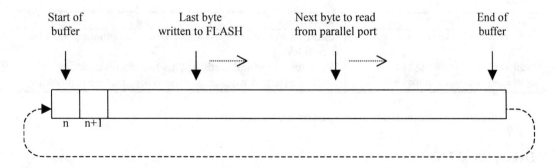

Figure 3-4: A circular buffer holds the data read from the parallel port until it gets written into flash.

To keep reading the parallel port as bytes are ready and write words in flash whenever the flash is ready to accept some, the download function is a spinning loop, which roughly goes as follows:

```
while (!done)
    if a byte can be read from the parallel port
            read it into the circular buffer
    endif

    if the circular buffer contains at least a word (two bytes)
            if the FLASH memory can accept a write
                    write two bytes into FLASH memory
            endif
    endif
endwhile
```

The function is a little bit more complex, because remember that section headers must be read to identify the target location in physical memory. So bytes are written into flash when a section has been read and data bytes are available. The loop terminates when the last section header is read (the one with an address of 0, whose size is the entry point).

The image download is pretty much platform independent and may work as is, because it relies on low-level functions to complete its work. These functions, reviewed in the next sections, are very similar to those required in the OAL (detailed in the next chapter).

Parallel port I/O

A few platform-dependent methods must be implemented in order to read and write bytes from the parallel port (see Figure 3.4).

Parallel Port Function	Description
OEMParallelPortGetStatus()	Returns a byte if ready, -1 otherwise. This function must be non-blocking.
OEMParallelPortGetByte()	Waits for a byte and reads it. This function is blocking.
OEMParallelPortSendByte()	Sends a byte and waits until done. This function is blocking.

Figure 3-4: Platform-dependent parallel port functions.

Debug Serial I/O

The download function output various information messages through the debug serial port as it progresses. If you are interested in receiving these messages on the host (using a terminal emulator), the few functions listed in Figure 3-5 are required.

Debug Serial Function	Description
OEMInitDebugSerial()	Initializes the serial port. It is recommended to set it to 38400, 8-N-1.
OEMReadDebugByte()	Waits for a byte and reads it. This function is blocking.
OEMWriteDebugByte()	Sends a byte and waits until done. This function is blocking.

Figure 3-5: Platform-dependent debug serial port functions.

Flash Memory

As explained earlier, the download image function may write into flash memory. If this approach is used, the functions listed in Figure 3-6 must be implemented. If the image is loaded into RAM, stubs can be provided, but make sure OEMFlashWriteBegin() returns a non-zero value (to indicate that flash cannot be written to).

Flash Memory Function	Description
OEMFlashWrite()	Writes data in flash memory.
OEMFlashWriteBegin()	Prepares flash memory for write access. The function must return 0 when the flash is ready to be written to, or an error code if the specified address is not in flash.
OEMFlashWriteEnd()	Completes flash memory write operations
OEMFlashWriteStatus()	Obtains the status of flash memory. This function is called to identify when flash memory is ready to accept more data.

Figure 3-6: Platform-dependent flash memory write functions.

Firmware Monitor

The boot loader can implement a firmware monitor that is activated, instead of jumping into the loaded image. For instance, once the image is loaded, the boot loader can output on the debug serial port "Do you want to start the image? (Y/N)". If the answer is no, the loader can enter into its monitor mode, where it reads commands and outputs results from and to the debug serial port.

The role of the firmware monitor is to help developers take a look at the image that had been downloaded. The purpose is *not* to debug the loaded image (*i.e.*, Windows CE), since WinDbg kicks in early for that purpose.

A standard set of commands is detailed in Platform Builder's online documentation, and Figure 3-7 lists a subset of them. However, there is no example provided to give you a head start.

Firmware Monitor Commands	Description
? or h	Displays help for all commands
r	Displays all registers. If a register is specified (i.e. "r eax") only that register is shown.
g start-address	Jumps to the specified address
mb start-address count	Dumps memory from the specified address (either a value or a register), for count bytes.
u start-address count	Unassembles instructions from the specified address (Value or register), for count bytes.
I pathname	Loads an image from the workstation

Figure 3-7:.Some of the standard commands implemented in firmware monitors.

3.2.2   Building the Boot Loader

The procedure to build the boot loader is much simpler than building a Windows CE image:

1. Create a directory named Bootrel under %_WINCEROOT% and set %_FLATRELEASEDIR% to it (*e.g.*, F:\Wince211\Bootrel). This will leave the initial release directory intact.

2. Start an ordinary command prompt (CMD.EXE) and run the following commands:

   ```
   F:\>CMD /k F:\WINCE211\public\common\oak\misc\wince.bat
       MIPS R4100 CE COMMON ODO <Enter>
   F:\>
   ```

3. Make sure WINCEREL is set to 1, in order for built files to be copied into the %_FLATRELEASEDIR% directory.

4. Go into the Bootload\Common directory and type **build –cfs**. This will build Bootload.lib. Note that a few warnings will show up.

5. Go into the %_WINCEROOT%\Platform\Odo\Bootload directory and execute **build –cfs** again. Expect warnings, even minor errors, easy to fix, though. That produces Bootload.exe, which is copied into %_FLATRELEASEDIR%.

6. Copy Bootload\%_TGTCPUTYPE%\Boot.bib into %_FLATRELEASEDIR%. This file determines the final location of the boot loader, and it must be updated as follows:

- Update the MEMORY section, which contains two lines. The first one ("BOOT") describes the ROM base address (or'd with 0x80000000) and size. The second line ("RAM") describes a RAM area to copy the boot loader's writable data.

- Update the CONFIG section by adding ROMSTART, ROMSIZE, and ROMWIDTH. Those three attributes describe the ROM area, but also cause the generation of an absolute,

70

non-relocatable image. Otherwise, the final image would have the typical BIN format, with the section headers and so forth, which is unsuitable for execution as is.

- Update the image path (last line).

  Here's an example. The MEMORY section indicates that the ROM image will be loaded at 0x9fc00000 (reset vector), and that a RAM area is located at address 0x80010000. Both memory areas measure 64KB. The CONFIG section indicates that the starting ROM address is 0x8000000 and its size, 1 MB. There are other parameters, described in Section 6.3.1.

```
; BOOT.BIB

MEMORY
;   Name        Start       Size        Type
;   -------     --------    --------    ----
    BOOT        9FC00000    00010000    RAMIMAGE
    RAM         80010000    00010000    RAM

CONFIG
    COMPRESSION=OFF
    PROFILE=OFF
    KERNELFIXUPS=ON
    ROMSTART=80000000
    ROMSIZE=100000
    ROMWIDTH=32

MODULES
;   Name            Path                                        Memory Type
;   --------------  --------------------------------------      -----------
    bootload.exe    f:\wince211\bootrel\bootload.exe            BOOT
```

7. Go in the `%_FLATRELEASEDIR%` and enter the following command:

   ROMIMAGE Boot.bib

This generates `boot.nb0`, an absolute, byte-by-byte image of the boot loader. This image can then be stored in ROM and executed.

3.2.3   Ethernet Boot Loader

Platform Builder also provides a complete sample of an Ethernet boot loader, in `%_WINCEROOT%\Platform\ODO\Eboot`, for the ARM, MIPS, PPC and SHx processors. That loader relies on two common libraries, both under `PUBLIC\COMMON\OAK\DRIVERS\ETHDBG`:

- `Eboot.lib` (in the EBOOT subdirectory), which implements the TFTP protocol for transferring file and the DHCP protocol to obtain an IP address for a DHCP server.

- `Smc9000.lib` (in the SMC9000 subdirectory), which implements low-level function to the SMC9000 Ethernet adapter.

This boot loader can be ported by adapting the functions in the CPU-specific directories.

Chapter 4

OEM Adaptation Layer

The OEM Adaptation Layer (OAL) is the glue between the hardware and the operating system. Specifically, it consists of a set of functions that are either triggered by the hardware (when interrupts are fired) or called by the operating system itself. It doesn't, however, include device drivers, which are positioned above the OAL (although it does access some devices).

Platform Builder provides OAL source code samples for the CEPC and ODO platforms, and they include all supported CPUs. This is very welcome, because developing an OAL from scratch would add weeks, if not months, to the process. Nonetheless, the code is complex and there are numerous topics that must be understood. This chapter highlights and explains those topics to help understanding the code provided by Platform Builder.

4.1   WHAT AND HOW TO BUILD

Before focusing on the implementation details of the OAL, let's explain where the OAL resides and how it is built. But first, you must know that the samples provided with Platform Builder don't call the OAL "OAL", but rather "HAL" (Hardware Abstraction Layer)[10]. So, whenever you see HAL, you can mentally substitute OAL and vice-versa.

---

[10] The HAL is to Windows NT what the OAL is to CE. Since NT has been around for a while, CE designers initially retained HAL, although they changed it later (in some places only) to OAL.

4.1.1 Platform Kernel Directories

The OAL samples are consistently laid out from one platform to another (see Figure 4-1). The `%_TARGETPLATROOT%` directory contains a directory called `Kernel`. The `Dirs` file in it tells `BUILD.EXE` – the tool to build the source code – to visit the subdirectories `Hal`, `Profiler` and `Buildexe`, in that order.

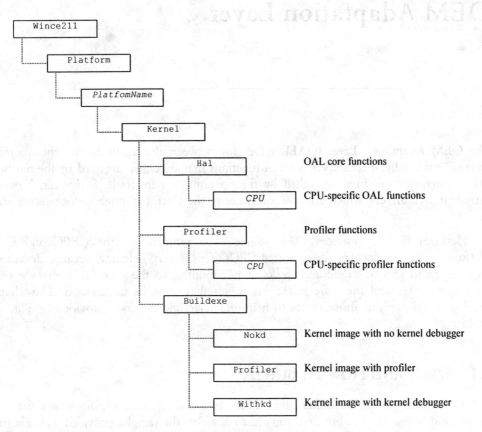

Figure 4-1: OAL directories installed with Platform Builder.

The HAL directory is where the OAL core functions reside. It contains the source files to start working with. This directory contains generic files and processor-specific subdirectories (*e.g.*, x86, ARM, etc.) to implement specialized functions, some written in assembly language. Building this directory (*i.e.*, invoking BUILD in it) builds a library called `Hal.lib`. The `Sources` file indicates what files are to be part of that library. You can add, rename and delete files, as long as your changes are reflected in `Sources`.

The `Profiler` directory implements the OAL functions that support profiling. If you intend to support profiling, you must focus on that directory. The `Sources` file specifies the files to build in order to produce `Profiler.lib`.

The `Buildexe` directory produces the kernel images (which contain the core functions of Windows CE). It has three subdirectories, which are always built regardless of the build configuration:

- `Nokd` contains a `Sources` file that links `Nk.lib` (provided by Microsoft), `Hal.lib` (yours), and other libraries (all from Microsoft) and produces `Nknodbg.exe`, a kernel image <u>without</u> the kernel debugger.

- `Withkd` is similar to `Nokd`, but it adds `Kd.lib` (Microsoft's kernel debugger library), in order to produce `Nk.exe`, a kernel image <u>with</u> the kernel debugger.

- `Profiler` is also similar to `Nokd`, but it adds `Profiler.lib` (yours) in order to produce `Nkprof.exe`, a kernel image with profiling capabilities but no kernel debugger.

Those three kernel subdirectories contain `Sources` files (as usual), and they all specify the kernel base virtual address (*e.g.*, 0x80200000 for the CEPC platform) and the target file name (*e.g.*, `Nknodbg.exe`). You can make changes here if needed.

4.1.2 Build Procedure

As mentioned earlier, the best method to port an `OAL` is to copy the platform that implements your CPU into a working platform directory (see Section 2.4.1), create a build window for that platform, and start modifying the `KERNEL\HAL` directory.

The development cycle is tedious, because it is command-line oriented and involves numerous steps:

1. Edit one or more source files.

2. Invoke `BUILD` from the `Kernel\Hal` directory to compile the files and build `Hal.lib`.

3. Invoke `BUILD` from the `Kernel` directory to link the kernel images. Expect a few surprises here. For instance, the CEPC platform must implement some undocumented functions, otherwise it doesn't link. From that standpoint, not starting from an existing OAL makes the task almost impossible.

4. Invoke `Buildrel` to copy the built files into the `%_FLATRELEASEDIR%` directory. Note that all kernel images (`Nk.exe`, `Nknodbg.exe,` and `Nkprof.exe`) are copied.

5. Invoke `Makeimg` to create an `Nk.bin`, by using one single kernel image based on the environment variables:

- If `IMGNODEBUGGER` is set, `Nknodbg.exe` is used
- If `WINCEPROFILE` is set, `Nkprof.exe` is used
- Otherwise, `Nk.exe` (which includes the kernel debugger) is used.

6. Boot the target device and download `Nk.bin`, using either the parallel port method or Ethernet.

7. Enjoy, or return to Step 1.

Step 7 usually generates tons of emotions, good and bad. Usually bad. If something goes wrong during the initialization, the board may hang or reboot within milliseconds. In either case, debug messages may not even have been transmitted on the host, so it's very hard to know *what* went wrong. Debugging is really tricky, especially during initialization. One basic trick to know whether a specific point in the code is reached is to output a trace message followed by an infinite loop. For instance, on an x86:

```
void OEMInit()
{
    // Do some tricky stuff here
    .
    .
    .

    lpWriteDebugStringFunc(_T("Tricky stuff done!\r\n"));
    __asm    jmp $

    // More tricky stuff follows
    .
    .
    .
}
```

This will hang CE, but you will at least get the message if that point is reached. Naturally there are high-tech alternatives, like In-Circuit Emulators (ICE) and the like.

Because you will have to load the CE image very often, using an Ethernet boot method really saves time. The boot process is not affected whether your code hangs or not, since it runs before your image is launched. Also, you may work on a project smaller than MAXALL, which always produces 4MB (in retail mode, 7.5MB in debug). For instance, MINKERN produces a smaller image (~350KB, retail mode), and the same OAL functions are called anyway.

Again, it is really not recommended to start developing an OAL from scratch, because it's hard to understand what things come first. One may argue that Platform Builder provides samples that are not the easiest nor the cleanest code ever written, but they w-o-r-k.

4.2 INITIALIZATION

The trickiest part is certainly the initialization. The system is not stable yet, and there's really nothing you can count on, except your understanding of what's going on. But there are only a few functions to implement, and they aren't too complicated (especially with the samples around).

Roughly, the initialization goes as follows:

- Windows CE's images are built to jump into some startup code that you write. Once done, the kernel is called for the first time.

- The kernel initializes itself, and calls OEMInitDebugSerial() to initialize the debug serial port. All other OAL functions can therefore send trace messages over the debug port.

- Those who read about LOADCEPC in Chapter 3 might recall that this loader stores at address 0x1FFFFC the address of a BOOT_ARGS structure, which contains the baud rate among other parameters. OEMInitDebugSerial() accesses that structure and initializes the COM port to the specified baud rate.

- The kernel then calls OEMInit(), which is the main OAL initialization function. This is the go/no-go OAL function, where interrupt are sets, timers are started, etc. This is the most critical OAL function.

- Once the initialization is completed, interrupts are enabled and the ball starts rolling...

These steps are described in detail in the following sections.

4.2.1 Startup Code

The startup is the entry point into the Windows CE image. The exact address is identified by the Startup label, as specified in the Sources files in the Nokd, Withkd, and Profiler directories (under the Buildexe directory). For instance, Nokd\Sources is as follows (for CEPC):

```
SYNCHRONIZE_DRAIN=1
RELEASETYPE=PLATFORM
EXEENTRY=StartUp              ← This is the entry point
EXEBASE=0x80200000
TARGETTYPE=PROGRAM
TARGETNAME=nknodbg

TARGETLIBS =           \
    $(_COMMONOAKROOT)\lib\$(_CPUDEPPATH)\nk.lib \
    $(_COMMONOAKROOT)\lib\$(_CPUDEPPATH)\ethdbg.lib \
    $(_COMMONOAKROOT)\lib\$(_CPUDEPPATH)\smc9000.lib \
    $(_COMMONOAKROOT)\lib\$(_CPUDEPPATH)\ne2kdbg.lib \
    $(_COMMONOAKROOT)\lib\$(_CPUDEPPATH)\eboot.lib \
    $(_TARGETPLATROOT)\lib\$(_CPUINDPATH)\hal.lib \
    $(_COMMONOAKROOT)\lib\$(_CPUINDPATH)\fulllibc.lib

!IF ("$(SCHEDLOG)" == "1")
TARGETLIBS=$(TARGETLIBS) $(_COMMONOAKROOT)\lib\$(_CPUDEPPATH)\schedlog.lib
!ENDIF

LDEFINES=-subsystem:native /DEBUG /DEBUGTYPE:BOTH,FIXUP

SOURCES=nokd.c

WINCETARGETFILES=dummy
```

The goal of Startup() is to bring the CPU into an acceptable running mode (32-bit, little-endian, with paging enabled), initialize control registers (if any), set up ROM and DRAM access if required, perform Power-On Self Test (POST), etc. Then it must call KernelStartup() (or KernelInitialize() on CEPC) to give the control to CE. Some implementations don't do more than disabling the interrupts and call the kernel.

Startup() is usually written in assembly language, and implemented in KERNEL\HAL*CPU*.

4.2.2   Debug Services

To make our lives easier, Windows CE initializes some debug services, even before initializing the operating system, in order for developers to output trace messages.

Serial

Soon after Startup() completes, CE calls OEMInitDebugSerial(). This function must initialize the serial port in order to transmit bytes. Some OALs hardcode the baud rate (say, to 115200 bps), but others may rely on parameters passed by the boot loader.

Three other functions must be implemented to transmit and receive data:

- `OEMWriteDebugByte()`, to transmit one byte.

- `OEMWriteDebugString()`, to transmit a string.

- `OEMReadDebugByte()`, to read one byte.

These functions poll the port in order to complete their duties, instead of being interrupt-based (ISRs are not yet installed at that point). There is no need to implement some sort of circular buffer, as all the data to output must be sent *now*.

Optionally, OAL designers may decide to use other communication ports at this point, or even keep those functions mute (*i.e.*, to prevent any data transmission).

Finally, `OEMClearDebugCommError()` is called to clear and reset the serial port.

Ethernet

As an alternative to using the serial port, debug Ethernet is a faster option. The implementation of debug Ethernet is split between the OAL and some system libraries.

The OAL must implement a few Ethernet functions to send and receive UDP (User Datagram Protocol) packets. Platform Builder provides complete samples for the ODO and CEPC platforms (in `Kernel\Hal\Halether.c`), using SMC9000 or NE2000 boards (whose drivers are respectively implemented in the `Smc9000` and `Ne2000` directories, in `Public\Common\Oak\Drivers\Ethdbg`). Those drivers are also used with some boot loaders.

Platform Builder also provides libraries for applications (on the workstation and the target) to have access to those debug Ethernet services, respectively `Edbg.dll` and `Ethbbg.lib`, and to exchange information.

Parallel port

Devices equipped with a parallel port may use it to communicate with CESH, as an alternative to using Ethernet. There is no initialization function, so the parallel port must be initialized in `OEMInit()` (described below).

Then, two functions are required to send and receive one byte: `OEMParallelPort GetByte()` and `OEMParallelPortSendByte()`. These functions also poll the port until ready to transmit and receive data, instead of relying on interrupts.

Devices that do not include a parallel port must provide stubs:

```
int OEMParallelPortGetByte(void)
{
    return -1;
}

VOID OEMParallelPortSendByte(BYTE chData)
{
}
```

Sending Trace Messages

With either the debug serial port or debug Ethernet available, functions within the OAL can output debug trace messages by calling lpWriteDebugStringFunc, a pointer that uses the active debug communication channel (either serial or Ethernet). For instance

```
lpWriteDebugStringFunc(_T("Firmware initialization started\r\n"));
```

will go either on the debug serial port or debug Ethernet depending on the boot method.

4.2.3   System Initialization

The operating system initialization takes place in OEMInit(), invoked by the kernel after the call to OEMInitDebugSerial(). OEMInit() can start by initializing the debug Ethernet and debug parallel ports first. Then, the function must initialize the following, described in the next pages.

- Interrupt Service Routines (ISRs)
- ISR management functions
- Timer
- High-resolution timer
- Real-time clock
- Detect extra memory

Interrupt Service Routines

A crucial step is to install the ISRs for all supported interrupts. This is done by calling HookInterrupt() to associate each hardware interrupt to a system-defined interrupt identifier.

Windows CE's ISR model is not to write ISRs that actually process the interrupt. The "real" ISRs are in the kernel, which call your ISRs in order to obtain the logical interrupt identifier that corresponds to the interrupt that has been raised. Windows CE defines a series of logical interrupt identifiers (see Figure 4-2).

Logical Interrupt Identifier	Description
SYSINTR_NOP	No further processing required
SYSINTR_RESCHED	Set the reschedule flag
SYSINTR_BREAK	Break into the debugger
SYSINTR_DEVICES	Base value for non-OAL system interrupts
SYSINTR_PROFILE	System profiling (= SYSINTR_DEVICES+1)
SYSINTR_TIMING	Latency analysis (= SYSINTR_DEVICES+2)
SYSINTR_RTC_ALARM	Real-time clock alarm (= SYSINTR_DEVICES+5)
SYSINTR_FIRMWARE	Base value for OAL system interrupts (= SYSINTR_DEVICES+8)
SYSINTR_MAX_DEVICES	= 32
SYSINTR_MAXIMUM	The maximum logical id (= SYSINTR_DEVICES+SYSINTR_MAX_DEVICES)

Figure 4-2: Windows CE predefined logical interrupt identifiers.

Although most OAL ISRs usually simply return a logical interrupt identifier, some perform additional processing, in particular the timer interrupt (we'll see an example later on). ISRs may also return SYSINTR_NOP when no further processing is required.

ISRs are really free to implement any behavior – as long as they return a logical interrupt identifier. ISRs can be hooked in multiple ways (see Figure 4-3):

- The same ISR may service all interrupts. That ISR must then identify the source of the interrupt (*i.e.*, the IRQ) and return the proper code based on a table previously built. The OAL for CEPC uses that approach.

- Each ISR can service one interrupt, in order to provide more direct processing.

- The two previous approaches can be mixed, too: some ISRs service one interrupt, others serve many.

ISR Management Functions

Other interrupt functions to implement in the OAL are:

- OEMInterruptEnable(), to enable a specific interrupt.

- OEMInterruptDisable(), to disable a specific interrupt.

- OEMInterruptDone(), to signal the completion of an interrupt. Some OAL implement signal the completion right in the ISR and make that function a duplicate of OEMInterruptEnable().

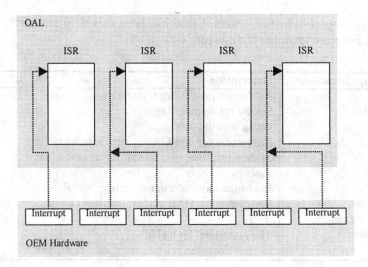

Figure 4-3: Interrupts can be hooked to shared Interrupt Service Routine (ISR), or use their own.

All these functions receive a system interrupt identifier, which must be converted into a hardware interrupt identifier (the CPU doesn't know anything about CE's interrupt identifiers). This is achieved by maintaining a logical-to-hardware interrupt table (see Figure 4-4). Each entry in that table corresponds to a logical interrupt identifier (making the size of that table SYSINTR_MAXIMUM+1), and it contains the associated hardware interrupt identifier. This table can be initialized as ISRs are hooked or whenever an logical interrupt is enabled.

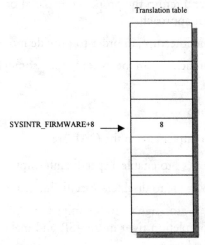

Figure 4-4: A logical-to-hardware interrupt translation table is required to implement some interrupt management functions.

For instance, consider the ISR08() handler, which handles hardware interrupt 0x28 by returning SYSTEM_FIRMWARE+08. As ISR08() is hooked to interrupt 0x28, the related entry in the translation table is set to interrupt 8:

```
void OEMInit()
{
    .
    .
    .
    // Hardware interrupt 0x28, which is the logical system
    // interrupt (SYSTEM_FIRMWARE+8) is handled by ISR08().
    HookInterrupt(0x28, ISR08);
    LogicalToHardwareIntrTbl[SYSTEM_FIRMWARE+8] = 8;
    .
    .
    .
}

ULONG ISR08()
{
    .
    .
    .
    return SYSTEM_FIRMWARE + 08;
}

VOID OEMInterruptDone(DWORD dwSysIntr)
{
    // Get the hardware interrupt no
    int    nIntrNo = LogicalToHardwareIntrTbl[dwSysIntr];

    // Signal the completion of the hardware interrupt nIntrNo
    .
    .
    .
}
```

When one of the three functions mentioned above is invoked with the SYSTEM_FIRMWARE + 08 identifier (such as OEMInterruptDone() in the previous example), the table can be directly accessed to return the hardware interrupt identifier.

Timer

CPUs that don't directly implement a timer channel (like the x86) must provide an interval timer ISR, which is triggered on a periodic frequency. This is an example of an ISR that does more than just returning a value (in this case SYSINTR_RESCHED): the OAL variables CurMSec and DiffMSec must be incremented by the number of milliseconds that have elapsed since the last SYSINTR_RESCHED was returned. For instance, if the ISR is set to a frequency of 100Hz (100 times per second, once every 10 ms), the two variables would be incremented by 10 (ms) in the ISR.

Additionally, the OAL must implement `GetTimerPeriod()`, which returns the time between two timer interrupts, and `SC_GetTickCount()`, which returns the number of milliseconds since the boot.

High Resolution Timers

Windows CE can take advantage of timers with a higher resolution than milliseconds. If such high-resolution timers are available, the OAL can implement `QueryPerformance Counter()` and `QueryPerformanceFrequency()`. For instance, if a timer provides a microsecond resolution, the first function would simply return the timer value, and the second, 1000000. Furthermore, if those functions are provided, two pointers must be set to their address, respectively `pQueryPerformance Counter` and `pQueryPerformance Frequency`. Those functions are optional.

Real-Time Clock

The OAL must implement three functions that maintain the time-of-day:

- `OEMGetRealTime()` returns the time-of-day as a `SYSTEMTIME` value.

- `OEMSetRealTime()` sets the time-of-day based on the specified `SYSTEMTIME` value.

- `OEMSetAlarmTime()` must record the specified time-of-day value; when that time is reached, the logical interrupt identifier `SYSINTR_RTC_ALARM` must be returned by some ISR. Some OALs rely on the timer ISR to implement that extra functionality.

Note that at cold boot, `Filesys.exe` calls `OEMIoControl(IOCTL_HAL_INIT_RTC)` to initialize the real-time clock. Some OAL implementations just ignore the call, since they maintain the real-time clock using a battery (as it is for the CEPC). Other devices that don't have that feature may instead just reset the clock to the specified `SYSTEMTIME` value.

Detect Extra Memory

The last operation at initialization is to detect extra DRAM memory. `Config.bib` is set to the target amount (see Chapter 6), but this feature allows taking advantage of a platform that would have more DRAM than anticipated. All there is to do is to probe memory and set the variable `MainMemoryEndAddress` to the memory limit.

Also, `OEMGetExtensionDRAM()` is called after `OEMInit()` to find out whether another disjoint bank of DRAM exists (which is not specified in `Config.bib`). The function must return `TRUE` if that's the case, along the starting address and the size, or `FALSE` if there is no extra bank. Again, this is a useful feature when running on a board with more memory than initially expected.

4.2.4 Profiling

The profiling-enabled version of the kernel relies on the OAL to obtain timing measurements. Two basic functions must be implemented:

- `OEMProfileTimerEnable()` is called to notify the OAL to start profiling. Most implementations increase the frequency of the system clock (by 100 for instance). Every time the clock interrupt is triggered, the clock ISR calls `ProfilerHit()` (a kernel function), passing the program counter at the moment of the interruption. Under profiling, the timer ISR must return `SYSINTR_RESCHED` only on the initial clock frequency. For instance, if profiling increases the frequency by 100, `SYSINTR_RESCHED` is returned once every 100 ticks; the 99 other ticks return `SYSINTR_NOP`. This function must also set the system variable `bProfile_Enabled` to `TRUE`. Windows CE sets `bProfileKCall` and `bProfileBuffer` when kernel calls and buffered profiling are enabled (see Chapter 24 for details).

- `OEMProfileTimerDisable()` disables profiling, and typically returns the timer and the normal speed. It also sets `bProfileEnabled` to `FALSE`.

Windows CE doesn't specify how often `ProfileHit()` must be called, but the more it is called, the more precise the results are. The trade-off is the overhead associated with the increased clock tick rate.

Other functions are required to conduct kernel profiling:

- `KCP_GetStartTime()` must return the value of a 32-bit timer.

- `KCP_GetElapsedTime()` must return the difference between the current 32-bit timer value and specified value. Since timers wraps, this function must add some logic to always return a positive value.

- `KCP_ScaleDown()` must return the number of microseconds corresponding to the specified value, which is expressed in units of the timer used in the two other functions. This is used to determine the frequency of the two other functions. For instance, if `KCP_GetStartTime()` and `GetElapsedTime()` use a millisecond timer (*i.e.*, 1000 ticks/sec), calling `KCP_ScaleDown` with 2 (2 ms) would return 2000 (µs), *i.e.*, (2 * 1000000 / 1000).

4.2.5 Power Management

Windows CE calls the OAL under two conditions to save energy:

- `OEMPowerOff()`, when the device is shut off.

- `OEMIdle()`, whenever there is no thread ready to run (all existing threads are blocked on some events). This function can enable the interrupts and halt the CPU, for example.

Note that some implementations do nothing, especially those that are plugged into wall outlets.

4.2.6   OEM I/O Control

Finally, the OAL must implement OEMIoControl(), a function that accepts a generic code and performs some code-dependent action. This function is primarily used to obtain system information (as requested by SystemParametersInfo()), access the debug Ethernet, and handle OEM-defined codes (though KernelIoControl()) from the kernel itself or device drivers.

A few codes are predefined by Windows CE (see Figure 4-5), but you are free to ignore some of them. The common implementation is done via a switch statement, whose default clause invokes SetLastError(ERROR_NOT_SUPPORTED). Also, most of your OAL implementations will add other internal codes for your own usage (*e.g.,* to access control registers, allocate memory, etc.)

Code	Description
IOCTL_HAL_ENABLE_SCHEDULER_LOGGING	Invokes SchedLogEnable() (see Chapter 24)
IOCTL_HAL_GET_DEVICE_INFO	Returns system information
IOCTL_HAL_GET_IP_ADDR	Retrieved network information
IOCTL_HAL_INIT_RTC	Resets the real-time clock.
IOCTL_HAL_REBOOT	Warm reboot
IOCTL_HAL_SEND_UDP	Invokes EdbgSendUDP()
IOCTL_EDBG_DEREGISTER_CLIENT	Invokes EdbgDeregisterClient()
IOCTL_EDBG_REGISTER_CLIENT	Invokes EdbgRegisterClient()
IOCTL_EDBG_REGISTER_DFLT_CLIENT	Invokes EdbgRegisterDfltClient()
IOCTL_EDBG_RECV	Invokes EdbgRecv()
IOCTL_EDBG_SEND	Invokes EdbgSend()
IOCTL_EDBG_SET_DEBUG	Invokes EdbgSetDebug()
IOCTL_SET_KERNEL_COMM_DEV	Invokes SetKernelCommDev()

Figure 4-5: Some predefined code for OEMIoControl().

4.2.7   Registry

The OAL provides two functions to store and read the registry from persistent storage: ReadRegistryFromOEM() and WriteRegistryToOEM().

The first function is called during the initialization of the registry. It is, in fact, called more than once, until it returns 0 or –1. The function cannot rely on other operating system services (such as disk access), so it must implement everything that is needed to read the data. No other operating system activity takes place during the call.

The second function is repeatedly called to store the registry, as long as it returns TRUE and more registry data has to be saved. Again, this function cannot rely on operating system services to complete.

SUGGESTED READINGS

Microsoft, Inside Windows CE

> Chapter 6 is about porting Windows CE. Major issues are summarized by those who actually wrote the code. There is no code, no details, but that is what makes it relatively easy to understand.

Chapter 5

Device Drivers

Device drivers are system software that allow Windows CE to recognize the devices attached to the platform. Device drivers also present device-related services to applications. Devices fall in two categories: built right into the device (*e.g.*, touch screen) and peripheral (*e.g.*, digital camera).

To support the variety of devices, Windows CE supports four models of device drivers.

- Native drivers, unique to CE, are described in Section 5.1.

- Stream interface drivers, also unique to CE, are described in Section 5.2.

- Universal Serial Bus (USB) drivers connect USB-compliant devices to CE platforms. They can expose a stream interface, a custom set of functions, or rely on the existing CE API (input-event system and installable file system).

- Network Driver Interface Specifications (NDIS) drivers are derived from Windows NT. They allow networking protocol (TCP/IP, IrDA) to be independent of the network interface card (NIC).

This chapter describes the CE-specific drivers (native and stream interface). It also lists important registry keys and the samples provided with Platform Builder.

5.1 NATIVE DRIVERS

Native drivers control low-level devices built-in with the CE platform: audio, battery, display, keyboard, notification LED, serial port, touch screen, and PC Card socket.

Each driver has a predefined interface because of the specialized services that it must provide, but also because of the strong ties with the operating system.

5.1.1 Architecture

There are two types of native driver (see Figure 5-1):

- A *monolithic* driver is contained in a single piece of code.
- A *layered* driver is composed of a Model Device Driver (MDD) and a Platform-Dependent Driver (PDD). Most native drivers use this type.

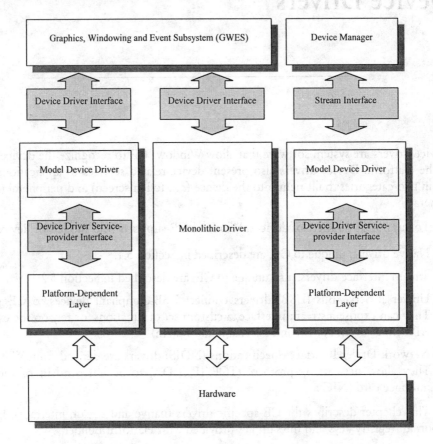

Figure 5-1: Native drivers use a custom interface or a stream interface. They can be built using a layered architecture or being monolithic.

Each native driver must export a specific set of functions, called the DDI (Device Driver Interface). Those functions are called by the GWES module at run-time.

Layered drivers internally use another interface, called DDSI (Device Driver Service-provider Interface), between the MDD and PDD. That interface is the set of PDD functions that are called by the MDD.

Microsoft provides numerous native driver samples (listed in Section 5.4) that are implemented using a layered architecture. For those drivers, the MDD implements the set of functions that must be exposed for the particular driver, and handles interrupt(s). This layer is hardware-independent, common to all platforms, and can usually be re-used as is. On the other hand, OEMs must port the PDD layer, which is hardware-dependent. The PDD can be re-written from scratch if needed, as long as it provides the same DDSI.

That layered design makes it easier to port drivers, but it adds some overhead. The only solution to eliminate that overhead is to revert to a monolithic driver, often written entirely from scratch.

Also, some native drivers use a stream interface as their DDI (*e.g.*, audio), because that interface is better suited for the device being controlled. They are in fact stream interface drivers (described later), but implemented using a layered approach, very similar to other native drivers.

5.1.2   Interrupt Handling

Devices generate interrupts to get some attention. For instance, a device driver may start a disk operation, which is to be conducted by the device asynchronously with other system activities. When the disk operation is done, the device generates an interrupt to notify the driver that it is ready to accept another operation. The alternative to using interrupt-driven notifications would be for the driver to poll (a method used by some functions in the OAL). Interrupt processing with CE is quite different that what is found in other RTOSes. In some cases, commercial RTOSes do not provide any device support at all; applications are required to install their own interrupt handler and process whatever they have to do. On the other hand, Windows CE encapsulates interrupt processing in order to simplify device driver development.

The components involved in interrupt handling in CE are the following (see Figure 5-2):

- **Event Handler** (EH), which resides in the kernel. All interrupts vector to it. When an interrupt is raised, the Event Handler disables all interrupts and calls the ISR (in the OAL) that has been hooked for that interrupt.

- **Interrupt Service Routines** (ISRs), which resides in the OAL. Those routines must perform a minimum of processing (if any) and return a logical system interrupt id to the kernel. Chapter 4 provides more details about ISRs.

- **Interrupt Service Threads** (IST), which reside in native device drivers. Each IST waits for an event object to be signaled (by the kernel) and then processes one interrupt by directly accessing the device. In a layered driver, the IST runs in the MDD layer and accesses the PDD layer through the DDSI interface. An IST is a preemptive thread, which means that it can be interrupted just about any time. Critical processing should be done by first raising the priority to `THREAD_ PRIORITY_HIGHEST` or `THREAD_PRIORITY_TIME_CRITICAL` if required (see Chapter 7 for details about priorities).

- **Interrupt Service Handler** (ISH) also resides in the kernel. Once an ISR has returned a system interrupt id, the ISH internally re-enables all interrupts – except the one about to be serviced – and signals the related event object. This unblocks the associated IST. Once the IST is done, the ISH re-enables the interrupt.

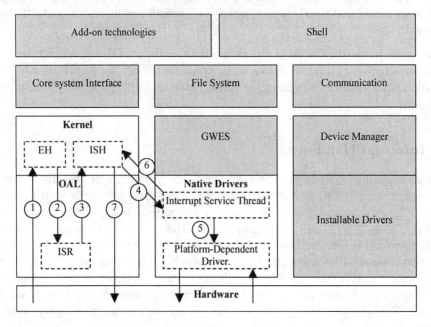

Figure 5-2: When an interrupt occurs, the Exception Handler (EH) in the kernel is first invoked ①. The Exception Handler disables all interrupts and invokes the proper Interrupt Service Routine (ISR) ② which returns a logical interrupt ID to the Interrupt Support Handler (ISH) ③. The Interrupt Support Handler re-enables all other interrupts and signals the Interrupt Service Thread ④. This thread invokes Platform-Dependent Driver routines to process the interrupt ⑤ and once completed, notifies the kernel ⑥. The Interrupt Support Handler re-enables the related interrupt by calling interrupt management functions in the OAL ⑦.

Nested Interrupts

On most systems, interrupts are not born equal: some have a higher priority than others. Those high-priority interrupts should ideally be handled as soon they are raised, even if the operating system is currently servicing a low-priority interrupt.

A system that supports nested interrupts allows exactly that: to process an interrupt while servicing another one. Windows CE 2.x is not such a system and doesn't yet support nested interrupts. What that means is that if a low interrupt is being serviced and a high interrupt is raised, that higher interrupt must wait until the low interrupt is serviced.

The advantage of preventing nested interrupts is simplified interrupt handlers: once in control, an interrupt handler cannot be interrupted. However, the disadvantage is an increase of the interrupt latency time, *i.e.*, the time the system takes to handle an interrupt. And that is an issue for high-level interrupts.

This design prevents Windows CE from being a hard real-time system, precisely because high-priority interrupts may not be serviced early enough. Fortunately though, Microsoft has already announced support for nested interrupts in forthcoming versions.

5.1.3   Interrupt Service Thread

Upon being loaded, a native driver creates a thread, the Interrupt Service Thread (IST), and an event object (see Chapter 7 for creating threads and event objects). The event object should be auto-reset, initially nonsignaled, and unnamed. For instance:

```
// Device driver initialization

void Initialize()
{
    HANDLE  hEvent;
    .
    .
    .
    hEvent = CreateEvent(0, FALSE, FALSE, NULL);
    CreateThread(NULL, 0, IST, &hEvent, 0, NULL);

    // The IST function is shown on the next page.
}
```

The driver then calls `InterruptInitialize()`, passing a system interrupt identifier and the event handle. For instance, if a touch screen's ISR generates the (`SYSINTR_FIRMWARE + 3`) interrupt identifier, the touch screen device driver would use the same value. It is common to use a `#define` directive instead of using `SYSINTR_FIRMWARE+n`, since the value is used in both the kernel (ISR) and device driver. Microsoft's platforms list all of those `#define`s is `%_TARGETPLATROOT%\Inc\Oalintr.h`. For instance:

```
// Oalintr.h
#define SYSINTR_TOUCH          (SYSINTR_FIRMWARE+3)
```

```
// Touch.c (Device Driver)

#include <Oalintr.h>

void Initialize()
{
    .
    .
    .
    InterruptInitialize(SYSINTR_TOUCH, hEvent, NULL, NULL);
}
```

```
// ISR.c (Kernel)

#include <Oalintr.h>

ULONG TouchScreenISR()
{
    return SYSINTR_TOUCH;
}
```

The IST is a thread that waits until that event object becomes signaled, by calling `WaitForsingleObject()`. The next example shows a typical IST:

```
DWORD WINAPI IST(LPVOID lpParam)
{
    HANDLE  hEvent = * (HANDLE *) lpParam;

    while (!Done())
    {
        // Wait for the kernel to signal the event object.
        WaitForSingleObject(hEvent, INFINITE)

        // Process the interrupt (by calling the DDSI API)
        ProcessIntr();

        // Indicate end of interrupt processing
        InterruptDone(dwInterruptID);
    }
}
```

When `InterruptInitialize()` is called, the kernel internally registers the system interrupt identifier and the event handle. When an ISR returns that system interrupt identifier, the Interrupt Service Handler (in the kernel) signals the event object, which unblocks the IST. As the IST starts processing the interrupt, all other interrupts are re-enabled, except the one being processed. The IST accesses the device (by calling the DDSI

API in a layered driver), and calls `InterruptDone()` once the interrupt has been serviced, which ultimately re-enables that interrupt.

An IST can de-register itself from an interrupt by calling `InterruptDisable()`. The ISH would then turn off the associated interrupt.

5.1.4   Adding Custom Native Devices

You are free to add as many native devices into your CE-based platform as needed. However, native drivers cannot be used to control those devices, because native drivers are managed by the GWES module, which is developed by Microsoft and is not extensible.

That's not really a problem though, because a native device can be implemented as a stream interface driver as well, which can be installed at any time, as explained next.

5.2   STREAM INTERFACE DRIVERS

Stream interface drivers are a generic type of driver, because they expose the same set of functions (unlike native drivers that have a unique API). They are implemented as Dynamic-Link Libraries (DLLs) and reside in the `\Windows` directory. They usually drive connectable third-party devices, such as printers, bar-code readers, GPS receivers, etc. They can also drive native devices, when a stream interface is better suited, for example, for a serial port.

A stream interface driver's goal is to present a device as being a special file. As a result, applications interacts with those devices through the file system API (`CreateFile()`, `Read()`, `Write()`, etc).

Another feature that sets them apart from native drivers is that they are loaded by either the Device Manager module or some applications, instead of by the GWES module. The details are provided in the next pages.

5.2.1   Device Names

Stream interface drivers must follow a strict name convention, to be easily identifiable when loaded at run-time by the file system. The format is three upper-case letters, followed by a single-digit index (1-9, 0 for 10), terminated with a colon. For instance, `"COM1:"` and `"GPS1:"` are valid names, whereas "MYDRIVER" or "COM12" are not.

The three letters serve as a key to access the driver functions, whereas the digit identifies specific drivers. For instance, if there's a GPS driver already installed (`"GPS1:"`), another one can be installed using `"GPS2:"`.

5.2.2 The Device Manager Module

The Device Manager module is a user-level process, not part of the kernel, that interacts with the kernel, registry and stream interface drivers (see Figure 5-3). Its primary goal is to load and unload devices as needed.

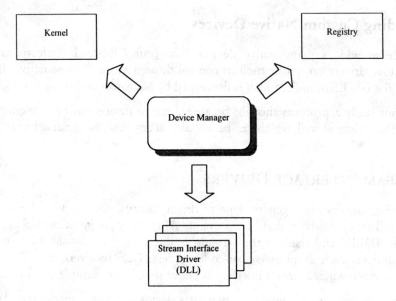

Figure 5-3: The Device Manager is a process that interacts with the Kernel, the registry and all stream interface drivers.

Loading Drivers

Stream interface drivers can be loaded under three scenarios:

1. At boot time, Device Manager loads all drivers listed under the `HKEY_LOCAL_MACHINE\Drivers\Builtin` registry key. Those drivers are typically stream interface drivers that control built-in devices.

2. When a device is connected (like a PC Card), the Device Manager calls the native socket driver to obtain a Plug and Play identifier. This id is compared against registry entries in `HKEY_LOCAL_MACHINE\Drivers\PCMCIA`. If found, the corresponding driver is loaded. Otherwise the Device Manager calls detection functions listed in `HKEY_LOCAL_MACHINE\Drivers\PCMCIA\Detect`. Those functions are implemented in stream interface drivers. If one of those functions indicates that it can handle the device, the Device Manager registers that driver for the device.

3. An application attempts to open a device only to realize that the driver is not loaded. This happens for devices that do not notify the system when being plugged in, like a digital camera connected to a serial port. The application can load the device and then open and access it. This is very useful for OEM software provided along with connectable devices (such as a photo editing software).

In the first two scenarios, the Device Manager calls `RegisterDevice()` to load and lock the driver in RAM (to prevent it from being swapped out or create page fault that would slow it down) and creates a subkey under `HKEY_LOCAL_MACHINE\Drivers\Active` to track the driver.

In the last case, the application must call itself `RegisterDevice()` to load the device.

Unloading Drivers

Similarly, drivers can be unloaded using two scenarios:

1. If the Device Manager is notified of the disconnection (for devices that provide such notifications), the corresponding entry is removed from `HKEY_LOCAL_MACHINE\Drivers\Active`. The Device Manager also calls `DeregisterDevice()` to remove the driver name from the file system and `FreeLibrary()`, to unload the DLL from memory.

2. If an application loaded a driver itself, it must unload it when done by calling `DeregisterDevice()` and `FreeLibrary()`.

5.2.3   Adding Custom Stream Interface Drivers

There are a few considerations to take into account when developing custom stream interface drivers:

- Required entry points
- Single vs. multiple accesses
- Interrupt processing
- Serial-based drivers
- PC Card-based drivers

Required Entry Points

Each driver must implement a few functions that will be called at run-time. Those functions are listed in Figure 5-4. Here's how it works: an application that needs to access the serial port (for instance) calls `CreateFile()`, specifying `T("COM1:")` and `OPEN_EXISTING`. In return, `COM_Open()` is called in the serial communication driver. This function returns an identifier to the application (a file handle), which is then used to call `ReadFile()`, passing the file handle. The system calls `COM_Read()`, within the driver, which can use the handle to identify a context if needed. When the application is done, it closes the handle by calling `CloseHandle()`, which calls the driver's `COM_Close()`.

Driver Function	Description
`XXX_Close()`	Closes the device identified by a handle.
`XXX_Deinit()`	Called by the Device Manager to de-initialize the driver.
`XXX_Init()`	Called by the Device Manager to initialize the driver.
`XXX_IoControl()`	Sends a device-defined command to the driver.
`XXX_Open()`	Opens a device for reading or writing.
`XXX_PowerDown()`	Powers down the device, if capable.
`XXX_PowerUp()`	Powers up the device.
`XXX_Read()`	Reads data from the device
`XXX_Seek()`	Moves the data pointer within the device.
`XXX_Write()`	Writes data to the device.

Figure 5-4: Stream interface drivers must implement a few standard functions.

Single vs. Multiple Access

A stream interface device driver may implement a policy of either single or multiple accesses. Multiple accesses means that multiple handles are returned for a single device to potentially multiple applications.

Which policy is being implemented depends on the returned value of `XXX_Open()`. To implement multiple access, each call to `XXX_Open()` must return a unique handle, which is passed to other `XXX` functions. This handle is a driver-defined value that maintains some context, typically a pointer to some data structures. This handle will always be specified to subsequent call to `XXX_Close()`, `XXX_IoControl()`, `XXX_Read()`, `XXX_Write()`, and `XXX_Seek()`.

To enforce a single use, `XXX_Open()` must return NULL if the device is already opened by an application. That same logic can be applied to impose a limit on the number of simultaneous openings. For instance, `XXX_Open()` can start returning NULL if the device is already opened twice. Naturally, the driver must track the `XXX_Close()` call to allow subsequent access.

Interrupt Processing

Connectable devices do not always generate interrupts, but some do. Drivers that control interrupt-driven devices must create an IST in `XXX_Init()` and call `Interrupt Initialize()`, pretty much like a native driver.

PC Card drivers receive notifications from the function `CardRequestIRQ()`, since the interrupt is handled by the native PC Card Socket driver. `CardRequesstIRQ()` allows specifying a callback to be called by the PC Card Socket driver when an interrupt occurs.

Drivers for Serial Devices

Third-party devices that are connected through a serial port can be directly driven by the native serial driver, or by an OEM driver that encapsulates some data processing.

In the first case, applications can directly open `COM1:` (for instance) and directly communicate with that device, if they can interpret the data. In the second case, an OEM driver is installed (say `COM4:`), which internally uses `COM1:`, but that also processes the data to provide applications with a simplified interface.

For instance, consider reading an image from a digital camera. If the read operation is done by an application through `COM1:`, the application must write the proper code to get the digital image, and read (and interpret) the data back. On the other hand, reading from a camera driver can return a bitmap handle, which is the equivalent of formatted data.

The advantage of accessing `COM1:` and bypassing a driver is efficiency, although serial ports are not the fastest devices around anyway. However, providing a driver that relies on `COM1:` makes it easy to present an simplified interface, to any number of applications.

Installation

Whereas native drivers are built along the CE image, stream interface drivers can be installed long after the device has been manufactured. Those drivers are typically installed from a host computer. The setup program must first connect to the CE-based platform, copy the DLLs in the platform's `\Windows` directory, and create registry keys (if needed) on that platform.

The best method to transfer a file from the desktop to CE is to use a .CAB file and transfer it using the Application Manager. The CAB wizard (`Cabwiz.exe`) creates .CAB files. It is distributed with the Palm-size PC and H/PC Pro SDKs. The Application Manager (`CeAppMgr.exe`) is a Windows CE Services application that runs on the host and that transfers files onto CE platforms. Refer to the *Windows CE Platform SDK Guide* for details about both tools. The `Load_XXX` API can be used to achieve the same results on Windows CE 1.x platforms only. That API is also described in the Platform SDK.

5.3 REGISTRY KEYS

Crucial information about drivers is stored in the registry. Driver registry keys are stored under HKEY_LOCAL_MACHINE\Drivers. The next section describes common keys.

5.3.1 Active

The Active key lists the active stream interface drivers loaded by the Device Manager. The subkeys are updated through RegisterDevice(). Each subkey is a two-digit integer. Figure 5-5 lists the values, although drivers should not expect any particular value to be present.

Name	Type	Description
Hnd	REG_DWORD	Specifies the device handle
Name	REG_SZ	Specifies the device name, such as "PGR1:".
Key	REG_SZ	Registry path to the device key in \Drivers\PCMCIA.
PnpId	REG_SZ	Plug and Play identifier (PC Card)
Sckt	REG_DWORD	PC Card socket and function. This value is the hSocket parameter passed to CardRequestIRQ() (PC Card)

Figure 5-5: Values under HKEY_LOCAL_MACHINE\Drivers\Active.

Here is an example of such an entry:

```
HKEY_LOCAL_MACHINE
    [Drivers]
        [Active]
            [03]
                Hnd  = 393592
                Key  = Drivers\BuiltIn\Serial
                Name = COM1:
```

5.3.2 BuiltIn

The BuiltIn key lists the stream interface devices to be loaded at boot time by the Device Manager (since some native devices can be driven by stream interface drivers). Figure 5-6 lists the values under that key.

Name	Type	Description
Dll	REG_SZ	Dynamic link library (DLL) implementing the driver.
Entry	REG_SZ	Alternate entry point, called by the Device Manager when the driver is loaded. This entry point must refer to a function that calls RegisterDevice(). Such a driver is not tracked by the Device Manager. This is useful to load DLLs at boot time that are not device drivers.
Keep	REG_SZ	Used with Entry, it indicates to the Device Manager not to call FreeLibrary() after having called the alternate entry point.
Order	REG_DWORD	Load order. This is useful when a driver requires other drivers being loaded in order to run. This is required for non-PC Card driver, but ignored for PC Card driver.
Prefix	REG_SZ	The driver's 3-letter prefix.
Other	Any	Other keys can be added as required.

Figure 5-6: Values under HKEY_LOCAL_MACHINE\Drivers\Builtin.

Here is an example of such an entry:

```
HKEY_LOCAL_MACHINE
    [Drivers]
        [BuiltIn]
            [Serial]
                DevConfig        = 10 00 00 00 05 00 00 00
...
                DeviceArrayIndex = 0
                DeviceType       = 0
                Dll              = Serial.DLL
                FriendlyName     = Serial Cable on COM1:
                Order            = 0
                Prefix           = COM
                Tsp              = Unimodem.dll
```

5.3.3 Display

The Display key lists installed display device drivers. Each subkey corresponds to a device name. Figure 5-7 lists the values under each subkey.

Name	Type	Description
Bpp	REG_SZ	The color-depth: either 1, 2, 4, 5, 6, 8, 15, 16, 24, or 32.
CxScreen	REG_DWORD	Screen's width, in pixels
CyScreen	REG_DWORD	Screen's height, in pixels
Dll	REG_SZ	Associated DLL.

Figure 5-7: Values under HKEY_LOCAL_MACHINE\Drivers\Active.

Here is an example of such an entry:

```
HKEY_LOCAL_MACHINE
    [Drivers]
        [Display]
            [GenericVGA]
                Bpp      = 8
                CxScreen = 0x280
                CyScreen = 0xF0
                Dll      = GENVGA.DLL
```

5.3.4   Display\Active

The Display\Active key lists the current active display driver. Figure 5-8 lists the values.

Name	Type	Description
BufferMode	REG_DWORD	One of the following: • 0: no common frame buffer • 1: the top half of the display adapter's buffer is mirrored on the built-in display. • 2: a scaled down version of the display adapter's frame buffer is mirrored on the built-in display • 3: the built-in display is turned off while this driver is active.
Dll	REG_SZ	Associated DLL.
TapMode	REG_DWORD	One of the following: • 0: tapping not supported. • 1: tap coordinates are unmodified. • 2: tap coordinates are scaled to match the display driver's coordinate space • 3: tap coordinates are undefined, but tap events are still delivered to applications, optionally with coordinates (0, 0).

Figure 5-8: Values under HKEY_LOCAL_MACHINE\Drivers\Active.

Here is an example of such an entry:

```
HKEY_LOCAL_MACHINE
    [Drivers]
        [Display]
            [Active]
                [GenericVGA]
                    BufferMode = 0
                    Dll        = GENVGA.DLL
                    TapMode    = 0
```

5.3.5   PCMCIA

The PCMCIA key lists the subkeys related to PC Cards and their stream interface drivers. Figure 5-9 lists the values.

Name	Type	Description
Dll	REG_SZ	Associated DLL.
Prefix	REG_SZ	The driver's 3-letter prefix.
Context	REG_DWORD	Passed as the dwInfo to RegisterDevice(). If absent, the registry path to the device's Active key is passed instead.
Ioctl	REG_DWORD	If present, Device Manager calls XXX_IoControl() after the device is loaded, in order for the driver to perform post-initialization functions.

Figure 5-9: Values under HKEY_LOCAL_MACHINE\Drivers\PCMCIA.

Here is an example of such an entry:

```
HKEY_LOCAL_MACHINE
    [Drivers]
        [PCMCIA]
            [RAMCard]
                Dll    = RAMCARD.DLL
                Prefix = RAM
```

5.3.6   PCMCIA\Detect

The PCMCIA\Detect key lists the subkeys that help Device Manager detect PC Cards with an unknown Plug and Play identifier or no such identifier at all. Each subkey corresponds to a device driver and a detection function. The subkey number determines the detection order. Figure 5-10 lists the values.

Name	Type	Description
Dll	REG_SZ	Associated DLL.
Entry	REG_SZ	Detection function name in the DLL.

Figure 5-10: Values under HKEY_LOCAL_MACHINE\Drivers\PCMCIA\Detect.

Here is an example of such an entry:

```
HKEY_LOCAL_MACHINE
    [Drivers]
        [PCMCIA]
            [Detect]
                [10]
                    Dll   = SERIAL.DLL
                    Entry = DetectModem
```

5.3.7 PCMCIA\Plug-and-Play-id

The PCMCIA\plug-and-play-id key lists the subkeys that load device drivers when PC Cards are inserted. Figure 5-11 lists the values.

Name	Type	Description
Dll	REG_SZ	Associated DLL.
Prefix	REG_SZ	The driver's 3-letter prefix.
Index	REG_DWORD	Specifies the device index. If absent, Device Manager assigns the lowest index available.
Context	REG_DWORD	Passed as the dwInfo to RegisterDevice(). If absent, the registry path to the device's Active key is passed instead.
Ioctl	REG_DWORD	If present, Device Manager calls xxx_IoControl() after the device is loaded, in order for the driver to perform post-initialization functions.

Figure 5-11: Values under HKEY_LOCAL_MACHINE\Drivers\PCMCIA\Plug-and-play-id.

Here is an example of such an entry:

```
HKEY_LOCAL_MACHINE
    [Drivers]
        [PCMCIA]
            [SRAMDisk]
                Dll    = SRAMDISK.DLL
                Ioctl  = 4
                Prefix = DSK
```

5.4   DEVICE DRIVER LIST

The following tables provide the complete list of device drivers provided with Platform Builder 2.11. Most drivers are under one of these directories:

- `%_WINCEROOT%\PLATFORM\CEPC\DRIVERS`
- `%_WINCEROOT%\PLATFORM\ODO\DRIVERS`
- `%_WINCEROOT%\PUBLIC\COMMON\OAK\DRIVERS`

5.4.1   Input Devices

Driver Category/Name	DLL Name	CEPC	ODO
Keyboard+Mouse Combo Driver	Kbdmouse.dll	✓	
ODO Proprietary Keyboard Driver	Keybddr.dll		✓

5.4.2   Serial Devices

Driver Category/Name	DLL Name	CEPC	ODO
Native Serial Driver	Serial.dll	✓	✓
16550 Serial UART Driver	Ser16550.lib	✓	✓
PC Card Serial Driver	Ser_card.lib	✓	✓
Proprietary ODO Serial DMA Driver	Odo_pdd.lib		✓
Dual Serial Driver	Dualio.dll	✓	✓

5.4.3   Ethernet Devices

Driver Category/Name	DLL Name	CEPC	ODO
NE2000-Compatible Native NDIS Driver	Ne2000.dll	✓	✓
Xircom CE2-Compatible NDIS Driver	Xircce2.dll	✓	✓
Proxim RangeLAN2 NDIS Driver	Proxim.dll	✓	✓
NE2000-Compatible Ethernet Debug Driver	Ne2kdbg.lib	✓	
SMC Chipset Compatible Ethernet Debug Driver	Smc9000.lib		✓

5.4.4 Storage Devices

Driver Category/Name	DLL Name	CEPC	ODO
Native PCMCIA Bus Driver	Pcmcia.dll	✓	✓
PC Card ATA Driver	Atadisk.dll	✓	✓
PC Card IDE Driver	Atadisk.dll	✓	
PC Card SRAM Driver	Sramdisk.dll	✓	✓
PC Card Linear Flash Driver	Trueffs.dll	✓	✓
RAMDisk Driver	Ramdisk.dll	✓	✓

5.4.5 Display Devices

Driver Category/Name	DLL Name	CEPC	ODO
Default Citizen Display Driver for ODO	Citizen.dll		✓
Citizen 2BPP Display Driver	Cit2bpdr.dll		✓
Citizen 4BPP Display Driver	Cit4bpdr.dll		✓
Citizen 8BPP Display Driver	Cit4bpdr.dll		✓
ODO Proprietary Display Driver	Odo2bpp.dll		✓
SED 3-3-2 Color Display Driver	Smos332.dll		✓
SED 3-3-2 Color Monochrome Driver	Smos4bpp.dll		✓
Generic VGA Driver	Ddi_vga8.dll	✓	
S3 Virge Driver	Ddi_s3v.dll	✓	
S3 Trio 64 Driver	Ddi_s364.dll	✓	
C&T Laptop Driver	Ddi_ct.dll	✓	

5.4.6 Touch Screen

Driver Category/Name	DLL Name	CEPC	ODO
Touch (native)	touch.dll		✓

5.4.7 Modem Devices

Driver Category/Name	DLL Name	CEPC	ODO
Unimodem Driver (TAPI Service Provider)	Unimodem.dll	✓	✓
TAPI Driver	Tapi.dll	✓	✓
USB Host Interface Driver	Usbd.dll	✓	
USB Host Controller Driver (Native)	Ohcd.dll	✓	
USB Mouse Client Driver	Usbmouse.dll	✓	

5.4.8   Parallel Devices

Driver Category/Name	DLL Name	CEPC	ODO
Parallel Port Driver	Parallel.dll	✓	✓

5.4.9   Printer Devices

Driver Category/Name	DLL Name	CEPC	ODO
Printer Driver	Pcl.dll	✓	✓
Parallel Port Printer OS Component	Prnport.dll	✓	✓

5.4.10   Audio Devices

Driver Category/Name	DLL Name	CEPC	ODO
Proprietary ODO Sound Driver	Wavedev.dll		✓
SoundBlaster AWE64 PNP ISA Driver	Wavedev.dll	✓	
ACM Sample Filter Driver	Msfilter.dll	✓	✓
ACM Sample PCM Driver	Pcmconv.dll	✓	✓
ACM Sample Codec Driver	Cegsm.dll	✓	✓

5.4.11   IrDA Devices

Driver Category/Name	DLL Name	CEPC	ODO
Fast IR Driver	Nscirda.dll	✓	
Serial IR Driver	Irsir.dll	✓	✓
Battery Driver	Battery.lib[*]	✓	✓
Notification LED Driver	Nleddrv.lib[*]	✓	✓

[*] Indicates a library linked to the GWES.

SUGGESTED READINGS

Microsoft, Windows CE Device Driver Kit

> This section of the Platform Builder online help provides numerous details about developing device drivers. The information provided there should be used in conjunction with the various samples.

Chapter 6

Windows CE Configuration

Unlike general purpose operating systems (like NT or Unix), Windows CE is built from a set of independent components, some of which can be left aside if not needed in order to reduce the final image's size. For instance, a system that runs graphical applications that do not need windowing (*i.e.*, windows with tool bars and the like) can simply drop the window management component. Another example is an isolated system that can let go of the entire communication module (networking, etc.). Windows CE is a scalable system that shrinks and grows as needed.

Also part of the configuration of a CE system is its content (data files, libraries, and executables), its representation in memory, its initial registry and object store, and other details that must be addressed when designing a system.

This chapter explains the modules and components that, when put together, build Windows CE, the various configuration files to prepare in order to generate the final image, and how to use existing localized versions of Windows CE.

6.1 PROJECT CONFIGURATIONS

A Windows CE system is built upon a platform, a project, and some common elements. Of those, the project specifies what modules and components will make it in the final image.

A module is a typically an executable or a dynamic-link library that usually implements self-contained functionality. Examples are the `Filesys.exe` module or the `Ppp.dll` library, which respectively implement the File System and the Point-to-Point Protocol. Modules can be broken down into components that can be replaced or removed for further customization.

The issue quickly becomes which modules and components should be used (and discarded) for a given project, when the memory requirements are strict.

6.1.1 Sysgen

The build process starts with `Sysgen.bat`, invoked from `Blddemo.bat`. `Sysgen.bat` executes `%_PROJECTROOT%\Oak\Misc\Cesysgen.bat`, a batch file that selects (or eliminates) components and modules from the desired configuration. This file is the one that you must edit to customize your system. This file enumerates multiple module and component names, not intuitive at first (ever, some say!). Luckily, Platform Builder provides some pre-tested, ready-to-use project configurations.

6.1.2 Pre-Tested Configurations

Platform Builder provides seven project configurations that have been tested and are known to work. Figure 6-1 lists those configurations. Although each configuration builds on the previous, there are many environment variables that influence the final size. Those variables can be set in your `Setenv.bat`. The size values shown in the figure have been obtained using a default configuration, for an x86 processor in both release and debug mode.

It is strongly recommended that you base new projects on one of these configurations. Once it runs, gradually refine the configuration (by editing `Cesysgen.bat`) in order to reduce the size as needed. This is a delicate step, because a system incorrectly configured may not necessarily crash immediately upon booting up. Some of those configurations can be easily be customized by using some environment variables, listed in Figure 6-12.

Configuration	Description	Components	License	Size (KB) Retail/Debug
Minkern	Minimal version of the kernel, plus a very simple application.	Kernel, CoreDLL, File System, Debug Shell, Toolhelp	Kernel	514 / 910
Mininput	Minimal version supporting user input and native driver support (e.g., display, etc.)	Kernel, CoreDLL, File System, GWES (message queues), Native Drivers, Debug Shell, Toolhelp	Kernel	409 / 813
Mincomm	Minimal version supporting communications and networking	Kernel, CoreDLL, File System, GWES, Communications, Stream Interface Drivers, Debug Shell, Toolhelp	Kernel	1252/3037
Mingdi	Minimal version supporting graphical operations (GDI), with one application.	Kernel, CoreDLL, File System, GWES (GDI support), Native Drivers, Debug Shell, Toolhelp	Limited	1431/2184

Minwmgr	Minimal version including window management, communications, COM and OLE	Kernel, CoreDLL, File System, GWES (windowing), Communications, Native Drivers, Stream Interface Drivers, Add-on Technologies, Debug Shell, Toolhelp	Full	1639/3791
Minshell	Almost-complete version of CE.	Kernel, CoreDLL, File System, GWES, Communications, Native Drivers, Stream Interface Drivers, Add-on Technologies, Shell Components, Debug Shell, Toolhelp	Full	2993/5985
Maxall	Complete version of CE (Minshell + cryptography, soft input panel, handwriting, WinINET FTP and communication applications)	Kernel, CoreDLL, File System, GWES, Communications, Native Drivers, Stream Interface Drivers, Add-on Technologies, Shell Components, Debug Shell, Toolhelp	Full	3887 / 7272

Figure 6-1: Pre-tested Windows CE configurations.

Variable	Description (when set to 1)	Minkern	Mininput	Mincomm	Mingdi	Minwgr	Minshell	Maxall
ODO_NOSERIAL	Excludes the serial driver configuration	✓	✓	✓	✓			
ODO_NOAUDIO	Excludes the wavedev driver configuration	✓	✓	✓	✓			
ODO_NOKEYBD	Excludes the keyboard driver configuration	✓	✓	✓	✓			
ODO_NONLED	Excludes the notification LED driver configuration	✓	✓	✓	✓			
ODO_NODISPLAY	Excludes the display driver configuration	✓	✓	✓	✓			
ODO_NOTOUCH	Excludes the touch-screen driver configuration	✓	✓	✓	✓			
ODO_NOPCMCIA	Excludes the PC card driver configuration	✓	✓	✓	✓			
ODO_NOBATTERY	Excludes the battery driver configuration	✓	✓	✓	✓			
ODO_NOGWES	Defines GWES macro definitions	✓	✓	✓	✓			
ODO_NOMOUSE	Defines mouse macro definitions				✓			
IMGUSB	Includes USB components						✓	✓
IMGNSCFIR	Includes NSCFIR component						✓	
MINKERN_NOFMTMSG	Removes the FormatMessage API function	✓						
MINKERN_NODATABASE	Removes database component.	✓						
MINKERN_NOPASSWORD	Removes password component	✓						
MINKERN_NOTOOLHELP	Removes the toolhelp component	✓						
MINKERN_NORAMFS	Removes the RAM-based file system component	✓						

MININPUT_NOIDLE	Removes the idle component	✓					
MININPUT_NOPOWER	Removes the power management component	✓					
MININPUT_NONLED	Removes notification LED component	✓					
MINCOMM_NOPPP	Removes PPP component. If included, it requires TCP/IP, Serdev, and TAPI components. Unimodem component is optional.		✓				
MINCOMM_NOSERDEV	Removes serial driver component.		✓				
MINCOMM_NOTAPI	Removes telephony component.		✓				
MINCOMM_NONDIS	Removes NDIS component. If included, it requires TCP/IP component.		✓				
MINCOMM_NOTCP	Removes TCP/IP component. If included, it requires either PPP or NDIS component.		✓				
MINCOMM_NOIRCOMM	Removes infrared communications component. If included, it requires IrDA component.		✓				
MINCOMM_NOIRDA	Removes IrDA (infrared port) component. If included, it requires the Serdev component.		✓				
MINCOMM_NOINETFTP	Removes FTP component. If included, it requires Wininet component.		✓				
MINCOMM_NOWININET	Removes internet component. If included, it ptionally may include Inetfp component.		✓				
MINCOMM_NOMODEM	Removes unimodem component. If included, it requires PC Card component		✓				
MINCOMM_NOPCMCIA	Removes PC Card driver component.		✓				
MINCOMM_NOSECURE	Removes security component.		✓				
MINCOMM_NONETUI	Removes network user interface component.		✓				
MINCOMM_NOREDIR	Removes network redirector component.		✓				
MINCOMM_NORASDEMO	Removes Rasdemo.exe.		✓				
MINGDI_NOTRUETYPE	Removes TrueType font component.			✓			
MINGDI_NOPRINT	Removes printing component.			✓			
MINGDI_NODRWTXT	Removes text drawing component.			✓			
MINGDI_NOPALETTE	Removes color palette component.			✓			
MINWMGR_NOIRDA	Removes IrDA (infrared port) component. If included, it requires the Serdev component.				✓		
MINWMGR_NOOLE	Removes OLE component.					✓	
MINWMGR_NOFATFS	Removes FAT file system component.					✓	
MINWMGR_NOAUDIOMGR	Removes audio manager component.					✓	
MINWMGR_NOCURSOR	Removes cursor component.					✓	
MINSHELL_NOCURSOR	Removes cursor component						✓

Figure 6-2: Environment variables that alter the pre-tested configurations

6.2 MODULES AND COMPONENTS

Once a Windows CE system works based on a pre-tested configuration, you have the option to replace or remove modules and components, if the final image doesn't meet the memory size requirements. This flexibility of adding, replacing, or removing modules and components makes Windows CE scalable and versatile.

6.2.1   Adding and Removing Modules and Components

The list of components and modules to include is determined on a per-project basis. Each project includes the batch file `Cesysgen.bat`, in the `%_PROJECTROOT%\Oak\Misc` directory. This file sets environment variables, which are used throughout the build process to include or exclude modules and components. The result is a directory called `%_PROJECTROOT%\Cesysgen`, which contains filtered system header files and libraries, based on the specified configuration. These files will later be used to produce the final modules.

Adding and Removing a Module

Adding or removing a module consists of opening the projects `Cesysgen.bat`, and add (or remove) the modules and components listed in Appendix F. It is usually not a problem to add a module, but removing one may prevent a system from being built. For instance, if a module implements some API used by some applications (or another module), builds will produce some errors. Note that a few modules are required in all configurations (`coredll` and `nk` for instance).

A module is added by including its name into the `CE_MODULES` environment variable. The following example adds the `wininet` module:

```
REM %_PROJECTROOT%\Oak\Misc\Cesysgen.bat
.
.
.
set CE_MODULES=%CE_MODULES% wininet
```

Removing a module is simpler: just eliminate the module name from `Cesysgen.bat`.

Adding and Removing Components

Components are added and removed the same way, except that specific environment variables (representing modules) must be used instead of `CE_MODULES`. Those environment variables are listed in Figure 6-3.

Module	Project's Cesysgen.bat Environment Variables
gwes	GWES_REPLACE
	GWES_REPLACE_COMPONENTS
	GWE1_COMPONENTS
	GWE2_COMPONENTS
	GWE3_COMPONENTS
	GWE4_COMPONENTS
filesys	FILESYS_COMPONENTS
fatfs	FATFS_COMPONENTS
coredll	COREDLL_REPLACE
	COREDLL_REPLACE_COMPONENTS
	COREDLL_COMPONENTS
corelibc	CORELIBC_COMPONENTS
ole32	OLE32_COMPONENTS
winsock	WINSOCK_COMPONENTS
wininet	WININET_COMPONENTS

Figure 6-3: Module environment variables, to add components.

The GWES module is broken down into four basic components (GWEn_COMPONENTS), each of which produces a specific library (gwen.lib). It apparently doesn't matter which library contains what, since all those libraries are linked together to produce GWES.EXE.

Under the Hood: Filtered Files

Once the module environment variables are set, the Makefile in %_PUBLICROOT%\ COMMON\CESYSGEN\ is executed to filter out the definitions and declarations that are not required for the given configuration. Specifically, Cefilter.exe is invoked to filter out undesirable elements from the following files:

- $(_COMMONPUBROOT)\sdk\inc*.*
- $(_COMMONPUBROOT)\oak\inc*.*
- $(_COMMONPUBROOT)\ddk\inc*.*
- $(_COMMONPUBROOT)\oak\files\common.*
- $(_COMMONOAKROOT)\lib\$(_CPUINDPATH)*.def

The filtered versions of those files are respectively copied into the following directories:

- $(_PROJECTROOT)\cesysgen\sdk\inc
- $(_PROJECTROOT)\cesysgen\oak\inc
- $(_PROJECTROOT)\cesysgen\ddk\inc
- $(_PROJECTROOT)\cesysgen\oak\files
- $(_PROJECTROOT)\cesysgen\oak\lib\$(_CPUINDPATH)

6.2.2   Customizing Modules and Components

Some modules can be customized by replacing some of their components. The next pages describe how to customize the GWES and FILESYS modules.

GWES Components

A few modules can be customized. Figure 6-4 lists the GWES components that you can rewrite.

Component	Description	Functions to implement
Oomui	Out-of-memory user interface	OomUI_CreateNotRespondingWindow() OomUI_CreateOomWindow() OomUI_FShowOomWindow() OomUI_Initialize() OomUI_NotRespondingWndProc() OomUI_OnShow() OomUI_OomWndProc() OomUI_SetWindowsInfo() OomUICallback_CloseWindow() OomUICallback_IsCritical() OomUICallback_NonClientPaint()
Startui	Startup user interface	Startup_Initialize() Startup_DlgProc() Startup_WantStartupScreen() Startup_PowerOnNotification() Startup_PowerOffWhileStartupActiveNotification() Startup_DestroyDialogCallback()
Calibrui	Calibration user interface	TouchCalibrateUI_Done() TouchCalibrateUI_DrawConfirmationScreen() TouchCalibrateUI_HandleUserInputMessage() TouchCalibrateUI_Initialize() TouchCalibrateUI_WaitForConfirmation()
Netui	Network user interface (used by the Network applet).	AdapterIPProperties() ConnectionDialog() DisconnectDialog() GetDriverName() GetIPAddress() GetNetString() GetResourcePassword() GetUsernamePassword() LineConfigEdit() LineTranslateDialog() NetMsgBox() RegisterIPClass() UnregisterIPClass()
Waveui	Wave API	waveui_AcmDlgProc() waveui_AfterDialogBox() waveui_BeforeDialogBox() waveui_DeInit() waveui_Init()

Figure 6-4: GWES components that can be re-implemented for customization.

Default fonts can also be replaced by updating the following keys in the registry file (see `Project.reg`, later in this chapter):

Font	Registry Key
System font	HKEY_LOCAL_MACHINE\SYSTEM\GDI\SysFnt
Menu bar font	HKEY_LOCAL_MACHINE\SYSTEM\GWE\Menu\BarFnt
Popup menu font	HKEY_LOCAL_MACHINE\SYSTEM\GWE\Menu\PopFnt
Out-of-memory dialog font	HKEY_LOCAL_MACHINE\SYSTEM\GWE\OOMFnt

Figure 6-5: Registry entries to modify in order to replace the default system fonts.

For each of those keys, the following values must be set as follows:

Value Name	Value Type	Value Description
Nm	REG_SZ	Font name, without the extension. The font must reside in the \Windows directory
Ht	REG_DWORD	Font height, in pixels
It	REG_DWORD	0: no italics, 1: italics
Wt	REG_DWORD	Font weight, a value between 100 (thin) and 900 (heavy black), multiple of 100. Normal is 400, and bold, 700.
CS	REG_DWORD	Character sets. Wingdi.h (in %_PUBLICROOT%\COMMON\SDK\ INC) lists all the values, among them: ANSI_CHARSET (0), DEFAULT_CHARSET (1) and OEM_CHARSET (255)

Figure 6-6: Font subkey values.

Message boxes (the `msgbox` component) can be customized as well. By default, message boxes are centered in the work area (the portion of the screen excluding the system tray). You can specify another rectangle (in the registry) within which message boxes will be centered (for instance, the top half of the screen). Here's an example that sets that rectangle to (0, 0, 480, 120):

```
[HKEY_LOCAL=MACHINE\SYSTEM\GWES]
"DlgCtr"=hex:00,00,00,00,00,00,00,00,E0,01,00,00,78,00,00,00
```

The first four digits are the left coordinates (in little endian), followed by the top, right and bottom coordinates, respectively, 0, 0, 0x1E0 and 0x78 in this example (i.e. 0, 0, 480, 240 in decimal).

File System Components

The FAT file system module (`fatfs`) is composed on the `fatmain` and `fatui` components. The latter can be customized to control the appearance of error and other messages. Only one function needs to be implemented, `FATUIEvent()`, which is called back whenever some messages are to be displayed to the user. The function receives two data structures, `FATUIDATA` and `UIPARAM`, that describe the event.

The registry can be stored and loaded by implementing two OAL functions: `WriteRegistryToOEM()` and `ReadRegistryFromOEM()`. There are some important limitations to consider, though:

- When the only file system that is mounted is the RAM file system.

- When devices being serviced by the Device Manager are not accessible (*i.e.*, PC Card)

For example, a Windows CE system can reserve a small area in flash memory (by updating `Config.bib`, described soon), and store/load the registry to/from that location. Other devices can be accessed, as long as doing so doesn't require a stream-interface driver.

6.3   CONFIGURATION FILES

Besides modules and components, a few configuration files must be carefully reviewed to determine crucial run-time attributes.

6.3.1   Bib Files

Binary Image Builder files (.bib) are used in the build process (by `Makeimg.exe`, in fact) to determine what modules and files will make it into the final Windows CE image, and the shape of that image in regard to where it will run in memory. To favor reusability, four `bib` files are being used instead of a single one:

- `Config.bib`, in `%_TARGETPLATROOT%\Files`, identifies memory configuration items, for the given platform.

- `Platform.bib`, in `%_TARGETPLATROOT%\Files`, identifies device driver files for the given platform.

- `Project.bib`, in `%_PROJECTOAKROOT%\Files`, identifies modules and data files for the given project.

- `Common.bib`, in `%_PUBLICROOT%\Common\Oak\Files`, identifies standard modules and data files for all projects on all platforms.

These bib files are re-used in most projects, with the exception of `Project.bib`, which is project-specific. A typical build combines the four `bib` files into `Ce.bib`, in `%_FLATRELEASEFDIR%`. This file ends up with four sections: MEMORY, CONFIG, MODULES, and FILES, described in the following paragraphs.

MEMORY Section

The MEMORY section determines what portion of the memory is for RAM vs. ROM, and how much RAM is available to the applications. Each entry in the file contains a unique name (any), the base address, the size (in bytes), and the type. The type can be either:

- RAM, which is a region of RAM for running processing and/or dedicated to the Object Store (Windows CE uses that region the way it needs).

- RAMIMAGE, which is a region that should be treated like ROM. It can be real ROM space, or an area of RAM to be used like ROM (useful to test a Windows CE image in RAM, which is to be later stored in ROM). Writable data in that memory region is copied into RAM and fixed up by the kernel at initialization.

- RESERVED, which prevents the system from using it. This area could correspond to some flash memory, where the registry could be stored for instance, or an area of physical memory used by some devices.

The next example describes four regions (NK, RAM, FRAMEBUF, and PCMCIABUF):

```
MEMORY

    NK              80200000   00900000   RAMIMAGE
    RAM             80b00000   00500000   RAM
    FRAMEBUF        800A0000   00020000   RESERVED
    PCMCIABUF       800D0000   00010000   RESERVED
```

Note that all addresses have the most significant bit on (0x8 ...), which indicates kernel space. The corresponding physical addresses are obtained by zeroing that bit.

The NK region starts a 0x200000 (2MB), measures 9MB and is considered ROM (to hold the CE image). The RAM region starts at 0xB00000 (11MB), occupies 5MB and is RAM (dedicated to run processes and hold the Object Stored). Two regions are reserved for OEM use: FRAMEBUF, from 0xA0000 (640KB), for 128KB (0x20000), and PCMCIABUF, from 0xD0000 (832KB), for 64KB (0x10000).

CONFIG Section

The CONFIG section is optional and is used to customize the final image. The entries are listed in Figure 6-7, and can be specified in any order.

Entry	Description	Values
AUTOSIZE	For RAM-only system, all unused IMAGERAM memory is used as RAM.	ON: Extra RAM is used OFF: Extra RAM is unused
BOOTJUMP	Write the jump to startup code at the beginning of the image	Address to jump to (hexa) NONE
COMPRESSION	Compresses all writable sections in RAM	ON (default) OFF
FSRAMPERCENT	Specifies the percentage of RAM allocated to the file system	Percentage as a 4-byte value.
IMAGESTART	Starts allocating the image at the specified address and wraps to the beginning of ROM	Address where the image begins
KERNELFIXUPS	Specifies whether the kernel relocates kernel-writable sections	ON (default) OFF
OUPUT	CE image's output directory	Path
PROFILE	Include profiler structure and symbols	ON: using abbreviated names (default) OFF ALL: like ON, but using full names
RESETVECTOR	Adds the jump to startup code at the specified address. The address must be in a RESERVE section.	Address
ROMFLAGS	Adds an additional DWORD in the table of content (pTOC), to be accessed by the kernel/OAL.	DWORD value
ROMOFFSET	Writes the image to the specified address	Address
ROMSIZE	Specifies the size of ROM. This is used with ROMSTART and ROMWIDTH in order to generate an absolute image.	Size, in bytes
ROMSTART	Specifies the start address of the ROM image	Address
ROMWIDTH	Specifies the number of data bits of each ROM and how the image is to be split.	8 16 32
SRE	Generates an .SRE file	ON OFF (default)
X86BOOT	Initial jump opcode for a boot loader	ON (adds 0xE9 to the image) OFF (default)

Figure 6-7: CONFIG entries.

The next example illustrates the use of some of those entries (for the CEPC platform).

```
CONFIG
    AUTOSIZE=ON
    COMPRESSION=ON
    PROFILE=OFF
    KERNELFIXUPS=ON
    ROMFLAGS=1
    ROMOFFSET=80000000
```

Note that this section controls the format of the final image, either a .bin file (readable by a boot loader), .sre file (Motorola's S-record format), or absolute images. The latter format is ideal for boot loader (described in Chapter 3) which can then be stored as is in ROM or flash.

MODULES Section

The MODULES section lists the modules that will be part of the final Windows CE image and the memory regions in which they will reside. Each entry consists of a name, a full path (where the module resides on the host), the memory region where the module will be located (the name must have been declared in the MEMORY section), and the type. The type is one of the following value(s):

- S for a system file

- H for a hidden file

- R to compress resources

- C to compress everything. Without this option, executables can be executed in place (XIP). If compressed, executables must be paged in RAM to run, which is a little bit slower. Compression is not recommended for executables, unless space is an issue.

For example:

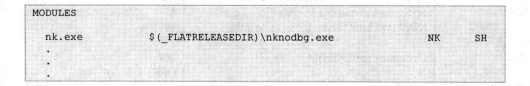

```
MODULES
    nk.exe           $(_FLATRELEASEDIR)\nknodbg.exe          NK      SH
    .
    .
    .
```

FILES Section

The FILES section lists data files to include in the Windows CE image. Entries in this section are identical to those in the MODULES section, except for the type, which can be one of the following value(s):

- S for a system file

- H for a hidden file

- U to keep the file uncompressed. By default, all files are and should be compressed. Files that are used very often (like True Type fonts) should remain uncompressed for increased performance. Most of these files are static (read-only), since writable files (*i.e.*, application data files) will reside in the Object Store, in RAM.

```
FILES
    initobj.dat        $(_FLATRELEASEDIR)\initobj.dat              NK      SH
```

6.3.2 Registry Files

Similar to `bib` files, registry files are combined together into `Reginit.ini` during the build to produce the initial registry:

- `Common.reg`, in `%_PUBLICROOT%\Common\Oak\Files`, contains common registry settings.

- `Platform.reg`, in `%_TARGETPLATROOT%\Files`, contains hardware settings.

- `Project.reg`, in `%_PROJECTOAKROOT%\Files`, contains project-specific settings.

These files must contain everything that must be present in the registry at cold boot time. The best strategy to build the initial registry for a given project is to naturally start from the existing samples, and customize the entries. Unfortunately, not all entries are documented, since some entries are used by esoteric and undocumented applications.

Here's an example of such entries:

```
; System font
[HKEY_LOCAL_MACHINE\SYSTEM\GDI\SYSFNT]
     "Nm"="Tahoma"
     "Ht"=dword:e
     "It"=dword:0
     "Wt"=dword:190
     "CS"=dword:0

; Registry values for the TCP/IP stack
[HKEY_LOCAL_MACHINE\Comm\Tcpip\Parms]
   "IpEnableRouter"=dword:1

; PCMCIA detection function for RAM disk card.
[HKEY_LOCAL_MACHINE\Drivers\PCMCIA\Detect\99]
   "Dll"="SRAMDISK.DLL"
   "Entry"="DetectSRAMDisk"
```

Launching Applications

You can edit the `project.reg` file to specify executables to run at the initialization. Consider the following example:

```
[HKEY_LOCAL_MACHINE\init]
"Launch10"="MyApp.exe"

"Launch20"="MyApp2.exe"
"Depend20"=hex:0A,00
```

The `Lauchnn` entry corresponds to an application to launch. The `nn` index provides a launch order. You can specify that some applications be launched after others by adding a `Depend` entry. In the previous example, Depend20 is associated with Launch20 (because of the "20"); that Depend entry specifies that launch 0x000A (*i.e.*, Launch10, "MyApp") must be completed in order to launch MyApp2.

Setting Windows CE's Gateway

Some communication services rely on TCP/IP computer names. Windows CE does not include a `Hosts` file in its `\Windows` directory (unlike 9*x* and NT), nor does it provide any name servers (DHCP or WINS). As a result, when Windows CE is connected to a host using PPP (via a serial direct link or a modem), its TCP/IP stack must be configured to use this host's IP address as a default gateway. The entries are specified in `Config.reg` (in `%_PUBLICROOT%\COMMON\OAK\FILES`). The host in this case doesn't have to run Windows NT Server, nor does it have to run any name server. For instance, Windows NT Workstation works fine.

```
[HKEY_LOCAL_MACHINE\Comm\Tcpip\Parms]
    "IpEnableRouter"=dword:1

[HKEY_LOCAL_MACHINE\Comm\ppp\Parms\TcpIp]
    "DefaultGateway"="192.168.1.1"
    .
    .
    .
```

The IP address shown above (192.168.1.1) is an example of a host workstation address. Use the **Network** applet in the workstation's Control Panel to identify the IP address. Look in **Protocols**, select **TCP/IP Protocol**, and click **Properties**. Unless your workstation obtains its IP address from a DHCP server, the address will be shown.

If your workstation is indeed relying on DHCP, then the address may change each time your start your computer, forcing you to update the Windows CE's registry quite often. Instead, uncheck the DHCP option, and enter the following IP address: 192.168.1.1.

RFC1918 reserves class B networks 192.168.x.x to local networks (see Suggested Readings at the end of this chapter for details). Hence, you can use any address between 192.168.1.1 and 192.168.255.255, with a subnet mask of 255.255.255.0, for your NT and CE devices.

It is a good idea to ensure that the address is not already used on the network by trying to ping it first. For instance, if the following NT command produces roughly the same result, then the address is already taken by another computer:

```
C:\WINNT>ping 192.168.1.1

Pinging 192.168.1.1 with 32 bytes of data:

Reply from 192.168.1.1: bytes=32 time<10ms TTL=128
Reply from 192.168.1.1: bytes=32 time<10ms TTL=128
Reply from 192.168.1.1: bytes=32 time<10ms TTL=128
Reply from 192.168.1.1: bytes=32 time<10ms TTL=128
```

6.3.3 Data Files

The initial content of the RAM file system (at cold boot) is determined by three .dat files, combined into Initobj.dat:

- Common.dat, in %_PUBLICROOT%\Common\Oak\Files

- Platform.dat, in %_TARGETPLATROOT%\Files

- Project.dat, in %_PROJECTOAKROOT%\Files

Consider the following example:

```
root:-Directory("My Documents")
root:-Directory("Program Files")

Directory("\Program Files"):-Directory("My Stuff")
Directory("\Program Files"):-Directory("Accessories")
Directory("\Program Files"):-Directory("Communication")

Directory("\My Stuff"):-File("My App",
"\Windows\MyApp.exe")
```

The root keyword refers to the system's root directory ("\Windows"). The first line creates the "My Documents" directory under \Windows (*i.e.*, "\Windows\My Documents"). The third line creates "My Stuff" directory under "\Windows\Program Files". The last line copies MyApp.exe from ROM ("\Windows") into the "My Stuff" directory, which makes the file writable.

6.3.4 Database Files

The initial content of the object store database is determined by `Initdb.ini`, which is the combination of three `.db` files:

- `Common.db`, in `%_PUBLICROOT%\Common\Oak\Files`
- `Platform.db`, in `%_TARGETPLATROOT%\Files`
- `Project.db`, in `%_PROJECTOAKROOT%\Files`

Consider the following example:

```
Database: "Email Database" : 10 : 2 : 4001001f : 2 :
4002001f : 2
Record :
Field : 4001001f : John Doe
Field : 4002001f : john@doe.com
End
Record :
Field : 4001001f : Jane Doe
Field : 4002001f : jane@doe.com
End
.
.
.
End Database
```

The first line contains a database definition: its name, its type identifier (hexadecimal), the number of sort orders, and as many pairs of field/sort-order as there are sort numbers. These values are described in detail in Section 10.3, and summarized below:

- The type identifier is any number that identifies the database from a programming standpoint, especially when searching database using the `CeFindFirstDatabase Ex()` API.

- Each field is composed of a 16-bit property identifier and a 16-bit data type, combined together. For instance, 0x0001001f means property identifier 0x0001 and data type 0x001f. Property identifiers are simple consecutive numbers, whereas data types are listed in Figure 6-8.

Data Type	Value (hex)
2-byte integer	0x0002
4-byte integer	0x0003
string	0x0001f

Figure 6-8: Field data types and values.

- The sort order is 0 for ascending, case sensitive and unknown values last, or a combination of the values listed in Figure 6-9 (which can be combined together by adding them):

Sort Order	Description
0x01	Descending order
0x02	Case insensitive
0x04	Unknown values first.

Figure 6-9: Sort order description.

In this case, the database name is "Email Database", the database number is 0x10, there are two sort orders, based on the property identifier 0x0001, of type 0x001f (string), and property identifier 0x0002, also of type 001f, respectively sorted using an ascending, case insensitive, unknown values last order (2).

Then each record follows, delimited by a "Record"/"End" line pair. In between, each property is described by a line starting with "Field", followed by the property identifier (such as those listed in the sort order or others) and the associated value, either a number (hexa) or a string.

Again, Chapter 10 provides details about CE databases.

6.3.5   Adding MFC/OLE/ATL to a Configuration

You must install the MFC, OLE, or ATL dynamic-link libraries on your target platform if you intend to use applications that rely on these technologies. These libraries are distributed with the Platform SDKs. For instance, the latest revision (for the H/PC Pro) of MFC is 2.11. Figure 6-10 lists the files of interest.

Technology	Debug DLL	Release DLL
MFC	Mfcce211d.dll Mfcce211d.pdb	Mfcce211.dll
OLE	Olece211d.dll Olece211d.pdb	Olece211.dll
ATL	n/a	Atlce211.dll

Figure 6-10: Development DLLs. Note the PDB files are required when using debug DLLs.

Follow these steps in order to install these libraries onto your target system:

- Copy the files into `%_PUBLICROOT%\%_TGTPROJ%\Cesysgen\Oak\Target\ %_TGTCPUTYPE%\%_TGTCPU%\%_TGTOS%`. For instance (for the retail version of MFC):

```
F:\WINCE211\PUBLIC\MAXALL\cesysgen\oak\target\x86\i486\CE\retail
```

- Then, edit `Project.bib` and add the file name(s). For instance:

```
MODULES
; Name               Path
Memory Type
; --------------     --------------------------------    -----
------
   mfcce211.dll      $(_FLATRELEASEDIR)\mfcce211.dll      NK
SH
   .
   .
   .
```

- Then, type the following commands:

```
Buildrel
Makeimg
```

You're done.

6.4 LOCALIZATION

Windows CE can run in languages other than English. For instance, Figure 6-11 shows a French version.

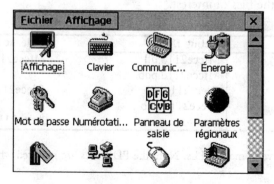

Figure 6-11: Windows CE ... in French.

Platform Builder directly supports a few languages (see Figure 6.12). All there is to do to use one of those country codes is to set the COUNTRY environment variable, and run Makeimg.exe. For instance, the French version has been obtained by typing the following:

```
F:\WINCE211>set COUNTRY=FRANCE
F:\WINCE211>makeimg
```

Language	Country Code
Brazilian Portuguese	BRAZIL
Dutch	NLD
English (default)	USA
French	FRANCE
German	GERMANY
Italian	ITALY
Japanese	JAPAN
Spanish	SPAIN
Swedish	SVE

Figure 6-12: Development DLLs. Note the PDB files are required when using debug DLLs.

However, your applications won't get localized automatically. The best method to localize your application is to make a copy of the resource file (for backup purposes), and localize all resources as required (translating strings and dialog boxes, using adequate colors in bitmaps and icons, etc.).

128

Part III

System Programming

Chapter 7

Processes and Threads

Processes form the core of any operating system. They are the applications – the programs – that the user runs. Everything else in the operating system centers on the notion of process.

Equally important is the notion of thread, which is a running abstraction, a flow of execution within a process. What makes them truly interesting is the ability to have many threads per process.

This chapter explores the implementation of processes and threads in Windows CE, and explains how to use the related application programming interfaces (APIs).

7.1   USING PROCESSES AND THREADS

Windows CE inherits most process and thread calls that are available in the original Win32 API. The next sections review these calls.

7.1.1   Processes

Each individual application runs as an individual *process* under Windows CE. The term process refers to a collection of resources (code, data, stack, heaps, dynamic-link libraries, threads, mutex objects, event objects, and files), not a running entity. This approach has been popularized by all Unix systems and most general-purpose operating systems, including Windows 9*x* and NT.

This design provides each process with its own address space and resources, as if it was the sole application running on the system (address space is discussed in Chapter 8). This scheme restricts a process to its own code and data, and prevents it from accessing the code and data of other processes (see Figure 7-1). This provides many advantages from a programming standpoint, as developers do not need to worry about co-existing with other applications. Each process is restricted to its own environment, preventing a faulty process from destroying code and data belonging to other processes[11]. Furthermore, a process that crashes does not affect the other processes in the system. This insures a greater system stability and consistency. Such a design also helps the operating system to identify faulty applications by pinpointing instructions that violate the privacy of each application (such as accessing a wrong address). This feature allows debuggers to identify the exact line that causes a process to crash. The main disadvantages are the heavy memory management and extra overhead that must be set in place to ensure this process control and privacy. This overhead can not only be measured in size (additional code in the kernel), but also in time (executing that extra code in the kernel). Most RTOS manufacturers reject such a design because the objectives of their real-time systems are to be very small and very fast, but not very secure[12].

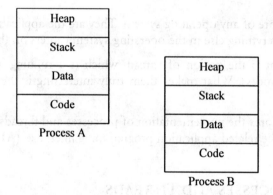

Figure 7-1: Processes are isolated from each other in Windows CE.

Windows CE limits the number of processes to 32. Although many modern systems do not limit the number of processes, CE designers opted to impose a limit due to the memory limitation commonly found on small devices.

---

[11] In Windows 3.x, an application could easily erase another application's data, since all applications were sharing the same address space. This is no longer possible in recent Windows operating systems, including CE.

[12] Most RTOSs do not implement the notion of processes, but rather multiple threads within one single context. There is no protection, so one faulty thread can bring the entire system to a halt. On the plus side though, some of these systems are extremely compact and usually very fast.

7.1.2 Threads

Threads are the entities within a process that execute the code and access the data. In contrast to processes, they do not hold resources; they only use the CPU when they run. Windows CE internally maintains for each thread a set of register values. When a thread is given the opportunity to run, its set of values are copied in the CPU registers for that thread to run. When that thread is suspended, the CPU registers are stored in the thread's register value set, and they are reloaded with another thread's register value set.

When a process is created, an initial thread is automatically created. This thread, called the primary thread, starts executing the code at the entry point specified in the .EXE file, usually `WinMain()`. This thread executes the code, and reads and/or writes the data that is part of its parent process (the process to which the thread belongs).

Most applications are single-threaded: only the primary thread runs at any time in those applications. But the primary thread can create additional running threads, making the application a multithreaded application. Multithreading is the solution to running asynchronous operations. For instance, consider a terminal emulator application that needs to read from a serial line as well as from the keyboard. A single-threaded implementation would consist of a loop that first peeks at the serial line and displays whatever comes from it, then peeks at the keyboard, displaying whatever the user has typed (see Figure 7-2-a). These operations must be repeated until the user closes that application. Note that the application peeks at the input devices; it does not sit and wait, because it has to look at both. Peeking can be achieved by using non-blocking calls, a feature described later. Nevertheless, the problem with that application is the waste of CPU cycles: if nothing is received from the serial line or the keyboard, the application keeps spinning in the loop. To reduce that problem, one may introduce some delays (sleep) instead of rapidly looping. But doing so makes the application less responsive: if the user presses a key while the thread is sleeping, the key will only be shown after a certain delay, which may annoy the user. Simply remember how frustrating it was to use old systems where you would type 10 letters before seeing them appearing one by one ...

On the other hand, a multithreaded application can take advantage of the two distinct operations, by creating one thread to read from the serial line and another thread to read from the keyboard (see Figure 7-2-b). Each thread sits and waits for some input, without using any extra CPU cycles. When some input is received from either or both sources, it gets displayed on the screen (extra processing can be done with the data as well).

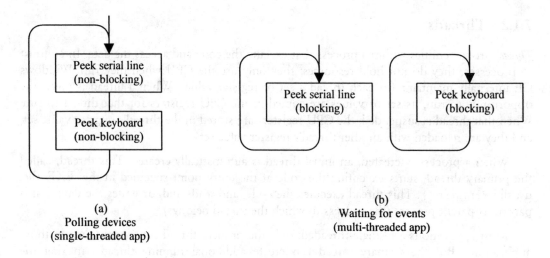

Figure 7-2: A terminal emulator application, implemented with one single thread (a) and with multiple threads (b). The first approach uses most available CPU cycles, whereas the second uses almost none, which is preferred.

Multithreading brings its share of problems though, as concurrency issues may surface. Simply consider what happens when the two threads in the above example display what they received at roughly the same time: the text would be interlaced and unreadable. But multithreading systems, including CE, provide various synchronization resources that we'll explore later to prevent those problems.

7.1.3   Creating a Process

Processes are created by applications, or by the shell when a program is invoked by the user (such as double clicking a program icon). Creating a process is done by calling `CreateProcess()`. The process that makes a call to `CreateProcess()` is called a parent process, whereas the newly created process is called a child process. The call returns immediately (it doesn't wait until the new process is created to return). The next example demonstrates how a child process is created.

```
void foo()
{
    PROCESS_INFORMATION    ProcInfo;     // Process information structure
    BOOL                   rc;

    rc = CreateProcess(
            TEXT("Hello.exe"),           // Application name
            NULL,                        // Command line arguments
            NULL,                        // No process attributes on CE
```

```
          NULL,                    // No thread attributes on CE
          FALSE,                   // No handle inheritance on CE
          0,                       // No special flags
          NULL,                    // No environment on CE
          NULL,                    // No current directory on CE
          NULL,                    // No startup info on CE
          &ProcInfo);              // Get info about that process

     // rc is TRUE if the process has been created, FALSE otherwise

     . . .

}
```

The first parameter is the application name, and is not case sensitive. The second argument contains the command arguments if any. The sixth parameter indicates special flags; set to 0 to run graphical applications, or to CREATE_NEW_CONSOLE to run a console application apart. A console application (introduced with CE 2.1x) supports stdio calls and runs in a character-based window. All other parameters but the last are ignored under CE, and are simply set to NULL. The last parameter (&ProcInfo) gathers information about the process being started. This structure is defined as follows:

Type	Member	Description
HANDLE	hProcess	Process handle
HANDLE	hThread	Primary thread handle
DWORD	dwProcessId	Process identifier
DWORD	dwThreadId	Primary thread identifier

Figure 7-3: The PROCESS_INFORMATION structure.

The process handle and identifier can be used with other Win32 functions, described later. The structure also holds the primary thread handle and identifier, automatically created along with the process. These handles are required with subsequent Win32 calls. Nonetheless, if the process and thread handles are not needed anymore, they can be closed by calling CloseHandle(). This does not terminate the process or thread, but simply helps the system cleans up resources.

A process can subsequently query its own handle and identifier by respectively calling GetCurrentProcess() and GetCurrentProcessId(). This is useful to specify itself when a process handle or identifier is required, or to print a debug message, such as the following:

```
printf("Process (%x, %x) entering WaitForInput()\n",
    GetCurrentProcessId(), GetCurrentProcess());
```

Also, `OpenProcess()` returns the handle of a process, given its identifier. This call can be used by debuggers to access a process's address space (refer to section 8.1.2 for more details and examples about reading and writing process address space). The following example obtains a process handle based on `nProcId`, the target process's identifier[13]:

```
HANDLE hProcess = OpenProcess(
                NULL,          // Always ignored on CE
                FALSE,         // Always FALSE on CE
                nProcId);      // Process identifier

// hProcess is non NULL on success, NULL on error.

// Perform some processing over that process (more in Chapter 8).
. . .

// Once the handle is no longer required, it must be closed.
CloseHandle(hProcess);
```

7.1.4 Creating a Thread

As mentioned earlier, the primary thread is automatically created, so you don't have to worry about it. Secondary threads are created by calling `CreateThread()`:

```
DWORD WINAPI ReCalc(LPVOID pParam);

void foo()
{
    DWORD    nThreadId;
    int      nParam = 1000;              // Param to thread

    HANDLE hThread = CreateThread(
            NULL,                        // No thread attributes on CE
            0,                           // No specific stack size on CE
            ReCalc,                      // Start address
            &nParam,                     // Unique parameter
            0,                           // No special creation flags
            &nThreadId);                 // Thread id

    // Upon successful creation of the thread, hThread contains the thread
    // handle and nThreadID contains its identifier. On error, hThread is
    // NULL and nThreadId is undefined.
    printf("Thread (id=%x, handle=%x) started\n", nThreadId, hThread);

    // Because the thread handle is not required anymore, close it. This
    // does not affect the running thread.
    CloseHandle(hThread);
```

---

[13] Process identifiers can be obtained by using calls such as `Module32First()` and `Module32Next()`. These calls are part of `Toolhelp.dll`, which must be present on the target CE system.

```
}

// Working thread.

DWORD WINAPI ReCalc(LPVOID pParam)
{
    int             nCount = * (int *) pParam;

    // Do something with nCount

    return 0;
}
```

Thread security attributes don't exist on CE, so the first parameter is simply set to NULL. Since CE always assigns the stack size as indicated in the .EXE, no stack size is required. The third parameter is the entry point: a function that accepts a LPVOID parameter and returns an integer. The next parameter is the argument to be passed to the thread. It can be any value: a constant, a literal, a pointer, anything, as long as the called thread casts it to the proper type. The creation flag can be used to create a thread in a suspended state (CREATE_SUSPENDED) to prevent the thread from starting immediately; otherwise the value is 0. The last argument is the address of an integer that will hold the thread id upon successful completion. The call returns the thread handle, or NULL on error.

If successful, the new thread starts executing at the address specified by the third parameter. Upon returning from that function, the thread is automatically terminated. Note that if the primary thread calls that very same function, returning from it does not terminate it.

Threads are always created with the THREAD_PRIORITY_NORMAL priority. Section 7.2 explains priorities in details.

If the thread handle is not required beyond that call, it should be closed by calling CloseHandle(), as shown in the example above. This does not terminate the thread, but simply helps CE in performing internal housekeeping duties.

Subsequently, a thread can query its own handle and identifier by respectively calling GetCurrentThread() and GetCurrentThreadId(). This is useful to specify itself when a thread handle or identifier is required.

The number of threads is unlimited, and each thread can create as many threads as required, in addition to the primary thread. It is common for the main thread to create extra threads to accomplish dedicated tasks, leaving the main thread focused on windowing operations. Naturally, threads can continue to be created as long as CE has enough memory to manage them.

7.1.5   Process and Thread Termination

A process terminates when the primary thread terminates, regardless of the other threads and their status, if any. Hence, the primary thread should make sure that the other threads are not in the middle of some work when it terminates. A thread (primary or secondary) terminates by calling ExitThread():

```
ExitThread(0);      // 0 is the exit code. Any user-defined value is fine.
```

Again, if the specified thread is the primary thread, the process is also terminated (a process in CE cannot run if its primary thread is terminated or exits). Note that the primary thread terminates when it returns from WinMain(), even if it doesn't explicitly call ExitThread(). A process also terminates if any of its threads attempts to execute an illegal instruction, such as using an invalid address or overwriting executable code (which is read-only).

The call accepts one parameter: an exit code. A secondary thread's exit code can be queried by any other thread by calling GetExitCodeThread(). This function requires a terminated thread handle and a pointer to a DWORD (to hold the exit code). If the thread is still running, the function returns an error code. GetExitCodeThread() is usually invoked after the thread is known to be terminated.

A thread can be unconditionally and abruptly terminated by calling TerminateThread(). This method is not recommended, because the thread has no chance to perform any clean up. Its stack is not deallocated either. Furthermore, if that thread owns a critical section object (Section 7.3.2), the critical section is not released, preventing any other thread from owning it afterwards. Hence, use TerminateThread() only as a last resort, when everything else has failed.

A process can also be brutally terminated by calling TerminateProcess(). Again, this is not the recommended method, because the process does not have a chance to perform some in-house cleanup. Besides, associated DLLs may be left in an inconsistent state. The child processes remain active, however.

Finally, make sure you close the handles (via CloseHandle()) of all processes and threads that you terminate or that exit, in order to let the system clean up internal resources.

7.2   SCHEDULING AND PRIORITIES

Windows CE is a *preemptive* system. Preemptive means that in order to give the illusion that multiple threads run at the same time, Windows CE executes each thread one after the other, letting each of them run for a very short period of time (on the order of milliseconds).

Once a given thread has run for that period of time, CE preempts – or interrupts – it regardless of what the thread was doing. Then CE selects another thread to run. That thread runs until the same period of time elapses, and so on. From the user standpoint, all those threads seem to be running simultaneously, whereas they run in reality for very brief periods one after the other. This rapid succession of threads is fully handled internally by Windows CE; you rarely need to be concerned about the details of it.

Among those threads that are competing to run, some are more important than others and must run more often. Consider, for instance, a handwriting recognition thread compared with another thread that is downloading a large file from the Internet. If these threads were running one after the other, the handwriting thread would not have a chance to fully recognize the user's input, but would only detect a series of short inputs. That would likely produce erratic recognition (see Figure 7-4). Hence, the recognition thread must be given more importance, or a higher priority, over the file-download thread, to ensure that it can run as long as the user is writing something.

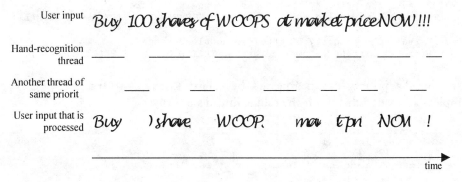

Figure 7-4: A handwriting recognition thread competing for the CPU against another thread would only read some of the user input, unless it gets access to more CPU time.

Whereas it makes sense to give that thread a higher priority, it does not make sense to lower it. If the priorities were reversed (giving more priority to the browser), the user's input would be ignored until the file is loaded. No one would be happy with such a system. Windows CE gives you the ability to change priorities, but it is ultimately your responsibility to assign them judiciously.

7.2.1   Priorities

Processes do not have priorities (or priority classes as in NT); threads do. Windows CE supports eight levels of priority, as shown in Figure 7-5. The first of these priorities are used by the most critical threads, that must run as soon as they are ready. Threads are always created with the `THREAD_PRIORITY_NORMAL` priority.

Level	Priority	Some Typical Usage
Highest	THREAD_PRIROTITY_TIME_CRITICAL	Burst processing by real-time applications
	THREAD_PRIROTITY_HIGHEST	Device drivers
	THREAD_PRIROTITY_ABOVE_NORMAL	Very responsive applications
	THREAD_PRIROTITY_NORMAL	Most applications
	THREAD_PRIROTITY_BELOW_NORMAL	Secondary, less important threads
	THREAD_PRIROTITY_LOWEST	Low-priority (backup, file download, etc.)
	THREAD_PRIROTITY_ABOVE_IDLE	Disk maintenance utilities, etc.
Lowest	THREAD_PRIORITY_IDLE	Rarely used

Figure 7-5: The priorities in Windows CE.

A thread can increase or decrease its priority by calling `SetThreadPriority()`:

```
// Increase the priority of the hand recognition thread
SetThreadPriority(hHandRecognitionThread, THREAD_PRIORITY_ABOVE_NORMAL);

// Decrease the priority of the file download thread.
SetThreadPriority(hFileDownloadThread, THREAD_PRIORITY_BELOW_NORMAL);
```

A thread's priority can be queried by calling `GetThreadPriority()`. The next example is a function that prints the calling thread's priority:

```
void DisplayPriority()
{
    printf("The current thread priority is: ");

    switch (GetThreadPriority(GetCurrentThread()))
    {
    case THREAD_PRIORITY_TIME_CRITICAL:
        puts("THREAD_PRIORITY_TIME_CRITICAL");
        break;

    . . .

    case THREAD_PRIORITY_IDLE:
        puts("THREAD_PRIORITY_IDLE");
        break;
    }
}
```

It is important to realize that despite the range of priorities that are available, most application threads do not require special needs, and therefore can run at `THREAD_PRIORITY_NORMAL`. What priority to assign to your threads largely depends on your application needs. Device drivers (seen in Chapter 5) must run very quickly; it's a good idea to set their priority to `THREAD_PRIORITY_HIGHEST`, or higher if required. Long lasting operations, such as performing disk housekeeping activities, should be set at `THREAD_PRIORITY_BELOW_NORMAL`, if not lower. It should be noted that real-time systems really make use of a broader range of priorities, because they handle a myriad of events of various significance. For these applications, Windows CE may not offer enough priorities. But for most applications, usually the use of one or two priorities are enough to meet the requirements.

7.2.2 Scheduling

As mentioned earlier, CE runs a thread for a short period of time, and then selects another thread to run. That selection is called scheduling. It consists of identifying the next thread that should be given the opportunity to run.

Internally, CE maintains a list of threads per priority, as seen in Figure 7-6. Each list contains the threads that are ready to run. Threads that are not ready to run (say, waiting for some input) are maintained in a different list not related with scheduling. The ready lists are scanned from top to bottom when the scheduling takes place. Here's how it works. When a thread has run for its time period, CE rotates the thread from the head of the list to the end. Then, CE scans each list, from the first to the last, looking for the first list containing a thread. For instance, CE looks at the first list, which is associated with the `THREAD_PRIORITY_TIME_CRITICAL`. If there is a thread in that list, that thread is chosen to run. If the list is empty (there is no thread of that priority that needs to run), CE looks for a thread on the following list (which is associated with the `THREAD_PRIORITY_HIGHEST`), and so on.

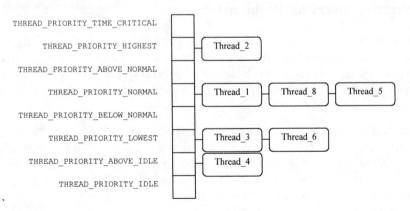

Figure 7-6: CE maintains a list of threads ready to run, per priority. Ready threads, from all processes, are managed through that list.

That list is scanned whenever another thread must be given a chance to run. This happens when the current thread has been running for long enough, but also when some external events awake some higher-priority threads. Let's review the previous hand-recognition thread example. Whenever the user writes something, that hand recognition thread is awakened and placed in its ready list. The running thread (which is downloading a file from the Internet) is preempted, the scheduler is called, and the control is given to the high priority hand recognition thread. And all this happens very quickly (less than one millisecond).

In case there is no thread to run at all (whenever the system is very inactive or all threads are awaiting external events), CE runs a system thread called the idle thread. This thread does nothing but loop[14]. Whenever another thread becomes ready, even a low-priority thread, that idle thread is preempted to let that other thread run.

Within any priority level but one (the highest), scheduling takes place on a fair basis: each thread runs for a short period of time, and the next thread is selected, and so on. This is called *round-robin scheduling* and each thread receives about the same amount of time. That way, if a thread enters a very long process, the other threads of same priority still have their fair share of scheduling.

The highest-priority thread (with the THREAD_PRIORITY_TIME_CRITICAL) is never interrupted. They run until they explicitly relinquish the CPU, either by terminating or by awaiting external events. That high priority is ideal when some work must be absolutely completed as soon as possible. These threads are usually designed to perform some very short processing and then return into a waiting state. If they run for too long, they monopolize the system.

7.2.3 Priority Inversion Problem

Real-time systems take priorities quite seriously. Consider an anti-lock braking system that detects under braking conditions that one wheel is locked. The system immediately awakes a thread, whose purpose is to gradually release the braking pressure on the wheel until it becomes unlocked. That series of events must take place as soon as some conditions are detected (*i.e.,* when the wheel locks).

It sounds quite natural to assign a very high priority to that thread, for it to accomplish its task when needed. But suppose that the thread shares some data with some other thread, using a critical section object to control the access to that data (more about critical sections in Section 7.3.2). If the thread is awakened to release a locked wheel, only to be blocked over the critical section object because a low-priority thread is using it, the system ends in a situation where a high-priority thread is blocked by a low-priority thread. Should a medium-priority be ready to run, it would be given the CPU, bypassing the high-priority thread. This problem is called priority inversion.

---

[14] In fact, that thread halts the CPU in order to preserve the batteries until an interruption is raised.

Windows CE automatically detects and prevents this situation: should a high-priority thread becomes blocked because of a low-priority one, that low-priority thread's priority is temporarily boosted to the same level as the high-priority thread, until the resource is freed and the pending high-priority thread executes. The other thread returns to its low priority afterward. Hence, Windows CE manages priority inversion internally.

7.2.4   Controlling Thread Execution

A thread can suspend and restart another thread of any priority by respectively calling `SuspendThread()` and `ResumeThread()`. Suspending a thread will not succeed if the thread is executing a system call, so `SuspendThread()` might have to be called more than once depending on the thread activity. The next example suspends another thread in order to conduct some high-priority work:

```
void bar(HANDLE hSecondaryThread)
{
    DWORD   dwCount = 0;

    // Suspend the thread. If it does not work, sleep 10 ms and retry.
    // Sleeping prevents eating CPU cycles uselessly.
    while (SuspendThread(hSecondaryThread) == 0xFFFFFFFF)
            Sleep(10);

    // Conduct high-priority work
    . . .

    // Then resume the suspended thread.
    ResumeThread(hSecondaryThread);
}
```

The call to `Sleep()` suspends the calling thread for the specified interval, expressed in milliseconds. `Sleep()` only works on the calling thread. If the main thread needs to suspend another thread for a period of time, a third thread must be created, which will first suspend the second thread, then sleep for the specified time, and then resume that second thread. Hence, the third thread simply controls the second thread's execution and terminates.

You must be very careful when suspending threads, especially when resources are shared among threads. Section 7.3 explores the issues related to thread synchronization.

7.2.5   Thread Running Time

`GetThreadTimes()` is useful to determine how long a thread has been running since its creation. Only one of the four parameters is meaningful in CE, however (the others are not supported, nor NULL values, either). The following example displays the running time of the current thread:

```
void DisplayThreadTime(HANDLE hThread)
{
    FILETIME       UserTime;           // Running time
    FILETIME       DummyTime;          // Required for GetThreadTimes()
    __int64        t64;                // 64-bit integer (Microsoft C)

    GetThreadTimes(
            GetCurrentThread(),         // Current thread
            &DummyTime,                 // No creation time on CE
            &DummyTime,                 // No exit time on CE
            &DummyTime,                 // No kernel time on CE
            &UserTime);                 // Total execution time on CE

    // Convert FILETIME into a 64-bit integer.
    t64 = ((__int64) (UserTime.dwHighDateTime) << 32) |
          UserTime.dwLowDateTime;

    // FILETIME stores time in 100-ns unit. Convert it is to ms.
    t64 /= 10000;

    printf("The thread has been running for %I64d ms\n", t64);
}
```

7.3 SYNCHRONIZATION

Whereas each process is independent from one another, all threads within a single process compete for the same resources. Threads within a process can be compared to kids in a kindergarten class: they all want the same toys at the same time. The same is almost true with threads.

Since threads have an equal access to their process's resources, problems occur when two or more threads want to access the same resource (a shared memory variable for instance) or want to execute the same piece of code. This often degenerates into race conditions[15] because you cannot control the moment where preemption takes place.

Here is an example that illustrates the problem. Consider the following typical C++ code, which simply inserts a node into a linked list.

```
void CList::InsertNode(CNode * pNode)
{
    if (m_pHead == NULL)
```

---

[15] A race condition is an erratic situation where a piece of code produces inconsistent results due to the simultaneous execution of two or more threads.

```
    {
            m_pHead = pNode;                // Set the head on the node.
            m_pTail = pNode;                // Set the tail on the node.
    }
    else
    {
            m_pTail->m_pNext = pNode;       // Last item points on the node.
            m_pTail = pNode;                // The node is also the tail.
    }

    pNode->m_pNext = NULL;
}
```

Let's see how this simple piece of code can degenerate into multiple problems. Refer to Figure 7-7 for the following description. Suppose thread 1 initially calls `CList::InsertNode()`. Because there is no node in the list, the *then* clause gets executed. The head is set to the node, but then, thread 1 gets interrupted (by Windows CE), before the tail is initialized (Figure 7-7-a). You probably start to have an idea of what will go wrong. Then thread 2 executes, and also calls `CList::InsertNode()`. Because the head is not null, the *else* clause is executed. But at this point, the expression `m_pTail->m_pNext` may either corrupt some memory or crash the application[16]. Assuming the first scenario (memory corruption, not a crash), the tail is set to point to the node (see Figure 7-7-b). Thread 2 is then interrupted. Thread 1 regains control where it was interrupted and sets the tail to the node thread 1 inserted earlier. At this very moment, the node inserted by thread 2 does not appear in the list!

These problems are the result of (1) two threads accessing the same code and the same data without checking what the other is doing, and (2), threads being interrupted at any moment by the operating system. That situation leads to missing data or inconsistent execution, and is not obvious to detect at first. Even experienced developers overlook race conditions on some occasions. In some cases, many hours (if not days!) must be spent to pinpoint and fix the problem.

---

[16] This instruction would go through if `m_pTail` were uninitialized and (wrongly) pointing to some existing memory. If it is NULL however, the instruction will crash the application.

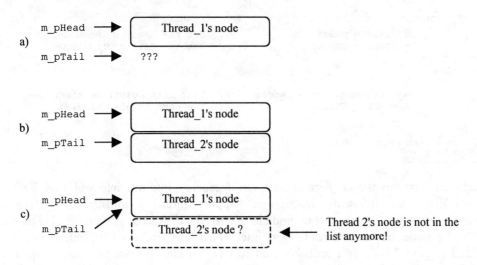

Figure 7-7: A three-step race condition problem when two threads insert an item in a linked list.

The solution consists of serializing the access to sensitive resources by allowing only one thread *at a time* to execute sensitive code. Only when that thread is done should another thread be allowed to proceed. Windows CE offers multiple resources to implement such a solution, namely:

- Critical section objects
- Mutex objects
- Event objects
- Interlock functions

Before describing these resources, let's review how Windows CE internally manages system objects.

7.3.1 System Objects

System objects (processes, threads, event objects, mutex objects, heaps, etc.) are kept within internal data structures, and are represented by handles. A handle is a value whose content is only meaningful to CE; applications strictly use handles as resource identifiers. Windows CE maintains a handle table per process, to prevent a thread from using another process's resource by "guessing" handles. A resource shared by two processes has a different handle for each process (see Figure 7-8).

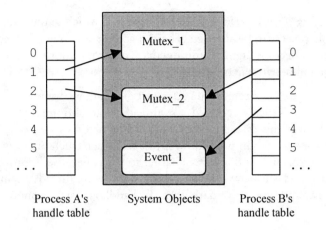

Figure 7-8: Each process has its own handle table. System objects are either private or shared, but handles are meaningful on a process-basis only.

System Object States

Some system objects have two states: *signaled* and *nonsignaled*. The exact meaning of the state depends on the object. Objects are initially nonsignaled (usually); they become signaled upon various conditions, as described in Figure 7-9.

System Object	Signaled When	See Section
Process	The process terminates	7.1.4
Thread	The thread terminates	7.1.4
Mutex	It is not owned by any thread	7.3.3
Event	`SetEvent()` or `PulseEvent()` is called	7.3.4

Figure 7-9: System objects and their signaled state

Waiting on System Objects

The Win32 API offers three system calls to wait for an object to become signaled. The first is `WaitForSingleObject()`, which takes an object handle and a time-out value as arguments. This call blocks the calling thread (*i.e.,* the thread that called `WaitForSingleObject()`) until the designated object becomes signaled or the time-out expires, whichever occurs first. `WaitForSingleObject()` returns a code indicating whether the object has been acquired (and is in a nonsignaled state) or not (due to timeout or some error). The calling thread must check that returned value to ensure it successfully acquired the object.

147

The second call is `WaitForMultipleObjects()`, which allows waiting, as its name implies, on multiple objects to be signaled. The call accepts an array of object handles; it can wait on any handle to become signaled (disjunctive synchronization), or it can wait for all to become signaled (conjunctive synchronization).

The last one, `MsgWaitForMultipleObjects()`, allows waiting on multiple objects and window messages. This is required for threads that also manage windows (usually primary threads). Should this thread be waiting on some objects to become signaled, it must return to its main loop to pump window messages when such message is ready to be processed. However, this makes that thread harder to write, because it must later on still wait on the initial object(s). It is usually simpler to keep windowing threads dealing with windows and messages only, and use secondary threads handling asynchronous events through waiting.

7.3.2 Critical Section Objects

A critical section object protects a critical section of code, by allowing one thread at a time to go in and execute it (such as the `CList::InsertNode()` method seen earlier), regardless of the preemption. Each process can have any number of critical section objects, which are equally shared among its threads. However, critical sections are not sharable among processes.

Critical sections are created and deleted once through `InitializeCritical Section()` and `DeleteCriticalSection()` respectively. A sensitive piece of code can be protected by surrounding it with `EnterCriticalSection()` and `LeaveCriticalSection()`. Any instruction between these two calls is guaranteed (by Windows CE) to be executed by at most one thread (see Figure 7-10).

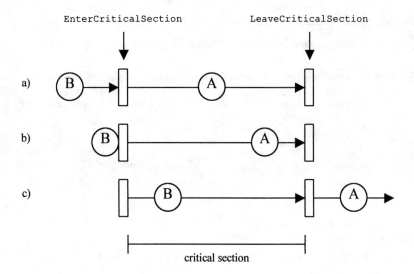

Figure 7-10: Acquiring a critical section object. In (a), Thread A has been allowed to enter the critical section because no one else was in it. In (b), as Thread A progresses in the critical section, thread B is blocked and cannot enter the already-occupied critical section. In (c), thread B is allowed to enter the critical section as soon as thread A leaves it.

Consider the following example, based on the linked list insertion seen earlier.

```
class CList
{
    CRITICAL_SECTION        m_CritSect;     // Critical section object.
    . . .
};

CList::CList()
{
    m_pHead = m_pTail = NULL;

    // Initialize the critical section object.
    InitializeCriticalSection(&m_CritSect);
}

CList::~CList()
{
    // Release the system object
    DeleteCriticalSection(&m_CritSect);
}

void CList::InsertNode(CNode * pNode)
{
    // Wait until clear
```

```
    EnterCriticalSection(&m CritSect);

    // Only one thread executes this code at a time.

    if (m_pHead == NULL)
    {
            m_pHead = pNode;                // Set the head on the node.
            m_pTail = pNode;                // Set the tail on the node.
    }
    else
    {
            m_pTail->m_pNext = pNode;       // Last item points on the node.
            m_pTail = pNode;                // The node is also the tail.
    }

    pNode->m_pNext = NULL;

    // Done. Let another thread go in.
    LeaveCriticalSection(&m_CritSect);
}
```

The linked list's constructor initializes a critical section object, whereas the destructor releases it. These two events happen once for that list. Inserting a node first consists in *acquiring* that critical section. Since a critical section can only be acquired by one thread at a time, any other thread is prevented from acquiring it. If it is already acquired, the thread is automatically blocked until the critical section object is released. Once the node is inserted in the list, the critical section object is released, allowing another thread to acquire it. If a thread was already waiting, that thread is now allowed to acquire the object and execute the sensitive code.

Such a linked list implementation has other sensitive pieces of code, such as removing an object from the list. Because the list uses the same data to insert and delete objects (*i.e.*, the list head and tail pointers, and the nodes), only one of any of these operations should be executed at any time. Hence, the list uses one critical section object, and could use it with CList::DeleteNode() (not shown). This ensures that one function at a time accesses sensitive data. On the other hand, if that list had other sensitive pieces of code, but unrelated to the list itself (such as allocating memory for a new node), another critical section object should be used to allow concurrency between two unrelated operations.

Also note that this implementation hides the critical section object from the application, which is a plus. Application developers do not need to use any special synchronization objects, as the CList object takes care of that internally. Also, once a thread owns a critical section object, it may repeatedly call EnterCriticalSection() on the same critical section object without blocking. This allows a thread to repeatedly call a function that internally uses a critical section object without blocking on itself (a problem known as a deadlock, which is usually fatal). However, the thread must call LeaveCritical Section() for each EnterCriticalSection() call. Since these two functions are always implemented in pairs, this does not cause any problem.

7.3.3 Mutex Objects

A mutex is a system object very similar to a critical section object: its goal is to provide some mutual exclusion by allowing one thread at a time to execute a sensitive piece of code such as the node insertion function seen earlier. Here's how it works: in order to execute some sensitive code, a thread must own a mutex by calling WaitFor...Object(). Mutexes are initially in a signaled state (*i.e.,* available). Once acquired, the mutex enters the nonsignaled state. Any other thread that tries to own that mutex will have to wait until the first thread releases it. Once a thread is finished with a mutex, it calls ReleaseMutex() which sets the mutex to a signaled state. Internally, Windows CE maintains a list of waiting threads on the mutex. When the mutex becomes signaled, one and one thread only becomes the owner and is allowed to proceed.

One of the differences between a mutex object and a critical section object is that the former can be used among threads and processes, whereas the latter is restricted to the threads of a single process. Also, the waiting time can be controlled with mutexes, but not with critical sections.

Mutex objects are created through CreateMutex(). The calling thread may require immediate ownership, and may also associate a name with it, which is useful for inter-process synchronization (more on this later). CreateMutex() returns a mutex object handle, which can be used by all threads within a process to wait on it.

The following example demonstrates a linked list object that internally uses a mutex object to prevent some race conditions from occurring:

```cpp
class CList
{
    HANDLE  m_hMutex;                       // Mutex object.
    . . .
};

CList::CList()
{
    m_pHead = m_pTail = NULL;

    m_hMutex = CreateMutex(                 // m_hMutex is declared as HANDLE
            NULL,                           // No security attributes on CE
            FALSE,                          // Not owned by any thread
            NULL);                          // Used within this process only
}

CList::~CList()
{
    CloseHandle(m_hMutex);                  // Release the system object
}

void CList::InsertNode(CNode * pNode)
```

```
{
    // Wait for the mutex to be signaled (available, not owned)
    WaitForSingleObject(m_hMutex, INFINITE);

    // Only one thread executes this code at a time.

    if (m_pHead == NULL)
    {
            m_pHead = pNode;                    // Set the head on the node.
            m_pTail = pNode;                    // Set the tail on the node.
    }
    else
    {
            m_pTail->m_pNext = pNode;           // Last item points on the node.
            m_pTail = pNode;                    // The node is also the tail.
    }

    pNode->m_pNext = NULL;

    ReleaseMutex(m_hMutex);                     // Let another thread go in.
}
```

The third argument of CreateMutex() is the mutex object name (which is case-sensitive). If a mutex object is to be used within the process, no name is required (NULL must then be specified). But the real advantage of using mutex objects is to synchronize threads that belong to different processes. Consider two applications that need to access the same file: to ensure consistency, their threads may synchronize themselves on each other by using a single, global mutex object. This can be achieved simply by naming the mutex, by attributing to it a unique name. The first thread that calls CreateMutex() with the name will create the mutex object within Windows CE. Other threads in other process that subsequently call CreateMutex() with the very same name simply gain access to the very same mutex. Hence, calling CreateMutex() with the name of an existing mutex object simply returns a handle to it.

The only issue has to do with the name itself. In order to prevent other applications from mistakenly use your mutex, make sure you use a rather unique name, such as CompanyAppnameType, where:

- Company is your company name
- Appname is the name of the application
- Type is a name that describes the code protected by the mutex

For example, "AcmeReportgenPrint" would be the name of the mutex object that protects some printing code, in the ReportGen application, of Acme, a fictitious company no one has ever heard of!

7.3.4   Event Objects

A thread uses an event object to indicate that a specific condition did occur. Like a mutex object, it has signaled and nonsignaled states. Embedded systems usually use multiple event objects while monitoring various conditions.

An event object is created with the `CreateEvent()` call. The call specifies the initial state (signaled or nonsignaled) and whether it is a manual-reset or an auto-reset event object. The first case requires system calls to change the state of the event, whereas the second type, once signaled, automatically returns to the nonsignaled state when a thread acquires it.

Manual-reset event objects require calling `SetEvent()` to set the state to signaled and `ResetEvent()` to set it to nonsignaled.

`PulseEvent()` can also be used to set an event and reset it after threads have been released.

The **Slbridge** example on the CD-ROM simulates a single-lane bridge by using event flags. This example is based on [Ripp89].

Like mutex objects, event objects can be shared among processes by naming them with unique names. Given an event object name, the first call to `CreateEvent()` creates the event object within CE whereas subsequent calls simply return a handle to it.

7.3.5   Interlock Functions

We saw earlier an example of how sensitive some code can be (the linked list insertion). An experienced programmer can quickly detect these situations and use a synchronization object accordingly. But there are other situations that are not that easy to detect, and that are, in fact, so simple that using a synchronization object involves too much overhead, relatively speaking.

Consider the following simple, yet troublesome piece of code, assumed to be executed by more than one thread:

```
int nCount = . . .;

void EndProcessing()
{
        if (--nCount == 0)              // nCount is a global variable
            ResetController();
}
```

On an x86, the corresponding assembly language code is as follows:

```
_EndProcessing PROC NEAR
; Line 12
    mov     eax, DWORD PTR _nCount ; Store nCount into the EAX register
    dec     eax                    ; Decrement EAX
    mov     DWORD PTR _nCount, eax ; Store EAX back to nCount
    jne     SHORT $L1              ; if EAX is not zero, jump to $L1
; Line 13
    jmp     _ResetController      ; Optimized call to ResetController()
$L1:
; Line 14
    ret     0                     ; Exit the function
_EndProcessing ENDP
```

Hence, the statement "if (--nCount == 0)" actually accounts for four assembly language statements. Now let' suppose that nCount is 2 and thread 1 executes that code. nCount (whose value is 2) is stored in EAX (a 32-bit general purpose register), which is then decremented to 1. Then thread 1 is preempted and thread 2 comes in to execute the same code: nCount (still 2) is assigned to EAX, which is decremented to 1 and stored back to nCount. Thread 1 comes back again (with its own registers, including EAX, which is 1). EAX is stored in nCount. Since its value is 1, ResetController() is not called. Back to Thread 2, which was interrupted before the comparison (the jne instruction). nCount being 1, thread 2 does not call ResetController() either. Bottom line: preemption strikes again! nCount, originally 2, has been decremented twice, yet its value is still 1!

One should note that this situation does not *always* occur, but is rather *susceptible* to occurring. But susceptible is usually not acceptable. And worse, that'snot the only potential pitfall with that code. In the optimized code above, a conditional jump can be executed after assigning a value, without executing a comparison instruction. But a less optimized version could add an extra instruction, as follows:

```
_EndProcessing PROC NEAR
; Line 12
    mov     eax, DWORD PTR _nCount ; Store nCount into the EAX register
    dec     eax                    ; Decrement EAX
    mov     DWORD PTR _nCount, eax ; Store EAX back to nCount
    cmp     DWORD PTR _nCount, 0   ; is nCount equals to 0?
    jne     SHORT $L1              ; No, jump to $L1
; Line 13
    jmp     _ResetController      ; Optimized call to ResetController()
$L1:
; Line 14
    ret     0                     ; Exit the function
_EndProcessing ENDP
```

This introduces another pitfall. Let's reset nCount to 2 and have thread 1 running that code again, up to the "cmp" instruction (nCount and EAX are both 1). Then thread 1 is preempted and thread 2 executes that same code, also up to the 'cmp' statement. At that point nCount and EAX are both 0 (so far so good). Back to thread 1, EAX is still 1, but nCount is now 0! The "cmp" instruction goes through, and because nCount is 0, ResetController() is called. Back to thread 2, and because nCount is 0, ResetController() is called again! Hence, ResetController() has been called twice whereas it should have been called once!

What's the conclusion? Unless the operating system assists to prevent these erratic behaviors, applications cannot provide a safe implementation of such simple code, which can degenerate into race conditions.

Luckily, Windows CE offers some functions to solve these race condition problems. The problem we just saw (decrementing and checking a variable) and the twin problem of incrementing and checking a variable can be solved by respectively calling InterlockedDecrement() and InterlockedIncrement(). Hence, the following code snippet solves the problem on CE:

```
void EndProcessing()
{
    if (InterlockedDecrement(&nCount) == 0)          // If (--nCount == 0)
            ResetController();
}
```

A brief look into the assembly code of InterlockedDecrement() reveals that on an x86, the subtraction and the memory move of EAX to nCount is done within a single instruction:

```
InterlockedDecrement:

    mov     ecx,dword ptr [esp+4]        ; ECX is &nCount
    mov     eax,0FFFFFFFFh               ; EAX is -1
    lock    xadd dword ptr [ecx],eax     ; Store the content of ECX
                                         ; (nCount) into EAX and add
                                         ; -1 to the content of ECX
                                         ; (i.e. nCount--)
    dec     eax                          ; Also decrement EAX
    ret     4                            ; Restore stack, return to caller
```

This works because in the same operation, EAX is set to nCount and nCount is decremented by one. Because EAX is part of the calling thread's context, it can be safely decremented later and returned as the new nCount value. If a thread is interrupted after the 'lock xadd' instruction, the return value (EAX) of that function will still be nCount minus one, as it should appear to that thread.

InterlockedDecrement() and InterlockedIncrement() are implemented in similar ways on other processors, and can safely be used across the supported processors.

Finally, the last case involving shared variables that may cause some problems is swapping two (shared) variables. This causes a problem because a third temporary variable is required to do so. For example, if you have one glass of milk and one glass of water, and you want to exchange their content, you temporarily need a third recipient (other than your stomach!). Same scenario for shared variables, except that your stomach is definitely not an option. The potential race condition consists in one thread overwriting that temporary variable before it gets assigned to one of the two shared variables. To prevent that situation, `InterlockedExchange()` takes a variable and a new value, and returns the previous value, which can be assigned to another variable. For example:

```
nVar1 = InterlockedExchange(&nVar2, nVar1);        // nVar1 ⇔ nVar2
```

Again, that function works on all supported processors.

SUGGESTED READING

Intel, Pentium Processor Family Developer's Manual, Volume 3

> For those in need of some x86 assembly language background to understand Section 7.3.5, about interlocked functions. This manual combines a complete and accurate programmer's guide and an instruction set reference sections.

Labrosse, Micro-C/OS-II The Real-Time Kernel

> Chapter 2 covers more important real-time concepts, including multitasking, scheduling, reentrancy, priorities, mutual exclusion, synchronization, priority inversion, etc. with a lot of examples and diagrams.

Ripp, An Implementation Guide to Real-Time Programming

> Ripp provides multiple, concise chapters on synchronization primitives. Numerous examples are provided to illustrate their use.

Tanenbaum, Modern Operating Systems

> Chapter 2 reviews processes, inter-process communication (IPC), classical IPC problems and process scheduling. It explores some concepts not directly found on CE (*e.g.*, event counters, monitors), but that can be implemented using existing synchronization objects. By the way, Tanenbaum's style is legendary.

Chapter 8

Virtual Memory

A fundamental characteristic of an operating system is its memory management approach. Today's 32-bit processors support virtual memory, a feature that provides a uniform and large address space, which simplifies application development. In this chapter, we will explore Windows CE's particular adaptation of that popular concept.

8.1 ADDRESS SPACE LAYOUT

The word 'virtual' is commonly used in today's conversations: virtual memory, virtual reality, virtual this, virtual that. Virtual means artificial: it *only* appears to exist; it does not exist as such. In the case of virtual memory, it means that each application is under the illusion that it solely occupies a very large, zero-based, pool of physical memory. In reality, each application only occupies a few KB of physical memory (see Figure 8-1).

32-bit processors offer a virtual address space of 4GB for each process. General-purpose systems (Unix, OpenVMS, Windows 9x, and NT, to name a few) adopted this approach to provide ample room for applications. Should applications ask for more physical memory than what is available, these systems just save some occupied portions of physical memory onto a special disk file (called the swap space), freeing some physical memory that can then be allocated to satisfy the actual memory demand.

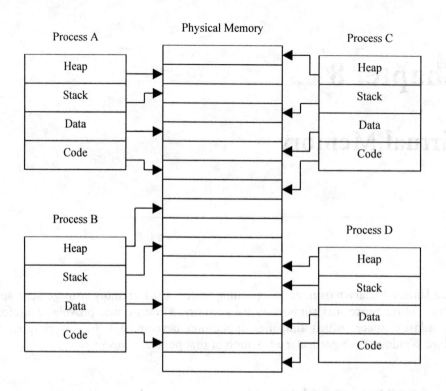

Figure 8-1: Virtual memory vs. physical memory

But with CE, it doesn't make much sense to give so much for limited devices. After all, large applications should be targeted for NT for instance, not CE! Hence, CE designers came up with an ingenuous scheme: instead of providing each application with 4GB, the entire system is given 4GB of virtual memory, and everything has to fit in it. "Fine, but how can this make sense in a device equipped with only 8MB of RAM and no disk?" you may ask.

There are various reasons to use virtual memory on CE devices:

- Simplicity. Virtual memory shields applications from any physical memory dependency. On CE, each application runs under the illusion that is uses a linear address space of 32MB, starting from address 0. This simplifies application and tool development.

- Efficient use of physical memory. Thanks to virtual memory, an application does not have to be fully loaded in memory to run. In fact, only the code being executed and the related data need to be loaded; the rest can stay on external storage (or, in Windows CE, compressed). Hence, as an application executes, only a small subset of the entire application in maintained in memory. This allows running more applications, whose total size would otherwise far exceed the physical memory capacity.

- Code and data sharability among processes. For instance, running the same application twice results in the code being loaded once, reducing memory needs while providing each application with the illusion that it owns the code. Another example: applications can share large amounts of data easily, again without any physical memory dependency. All this contributes to reduce the system's appetite for physical memory and allows running more applications.

- Protection. Virtual memory allows setting some protection on an application's code and data sections. For instance, an application's code section is marked as read-only; if an application attempts to modify it, an exception notifies the operating system, which automatically shuts down the faulty application before the damage is done. Another aspect of that protection is to isolate applications from each other, preventing any application from accessing other application's code and data. This improves overall robustness and data confidentiality.

There are also a few drawbacks when using virtual memory, such as increased overhead within the kernel. But they are usually negligible, especially when measured against the advantages they provide.

8.1.1   System Address Space

A device running Windows CE has 4GB of virtual memory to play with, laid out as depicted in Figure 8-2.

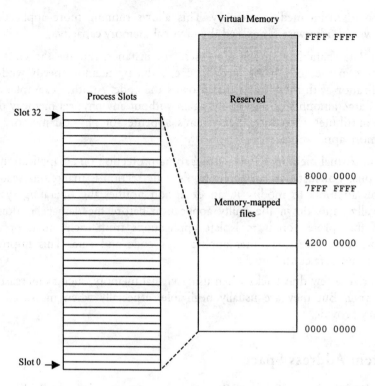

Figure 8-2: Windows CE virtual address space layout

Windows CE occupies the top portion of the address space, and applications have neither read nor write access to it. That is another example of protection: if an application attempts to access that top region, the CPU raises an exception, inciting the operating system to stop the faulty application before the access is done. Quite interestingly, Windows CE resides in ROM, so the occupied top portion of the address space is said to be *mapped* to ROM memory. Whenever the CPU is executing some code at address 0x8 ... (*i.e.,* in the top portion), it is in fact running code in ROM. Mapping is achieved through paging, described later.

The lower end of the system address space is dedicated to processes. The bottom contains 33 slots of 32MB each. All these slots are dedicated to processes (one process per slot, plus an extra slot, explained in just a moment).

In between, there is a 992MB virtual area that accommodates memory-mapped files, which are shared among all processes. Memory-mapped files are explored in detail in Chapter 12.

8.1.2 Process Address Space

Each process occupies a specific 32MB slot until it terminates. A slot contains roughly the following sections, from top to bottom (see Figure 8-3):

- Dynamic-link libraries (from ROM) used by the process
- Dynamic-link libraries (from RAM) used by the process
- Extra heaps and stacks
- Local heap
- Primary thread's stack
- Application data (read-only and read-write static data, and resource data)
- Application code (executable and read-only)
- 64KB reserved area (that the process cannot use)

As mentioned before, a process only uses a fraction of its address space. It is important to note that the threads within a given process can also access memory beyond the process address space (more on this later).

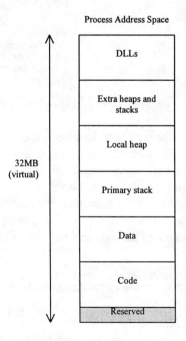

Figure 8-3: Process address space. Each section (code, data, stack, heaps, and DLLs) occupy a varying amount of space

However, because Windows CE does not implement any form of security, a process can read and write another process' memory by calling `ReadProcessMemory()` and `WriteProcessMemory()`. `ReadProcessMemory()` requires five arguments: the handle of the process to read from, a base address within that process, a buffer to store data (in the calling process), a byte count, and the address of a `DWORD`, which will contain the actual number of bytes read. Similarly, `WriteProcessMemory()` requires the handle of the process to write to, a base address, a buffer address, a size, and the address of `DWORD`, which will contain the actual number of bytes written.

These calls are useful for a debugger to control a child process being debugged. It is not recommended using this approach to share memory, as this practice is tricky: it requires knowing the identifier of the process to read from and/or write to, as well as the exact memory address of the area(s) to access. The next example demonstrates how to read a 4-byte variable at address pointed to by `pData`, from the process whose handle is `hDebugProc`. It is assumed that the calling process has some method of initializing `pData` (which must be cast into an `LPCVOID` data type) and `hDebugProc`[17].

```
    BOOL    rc;                         // Return code
    int     nVar;                       // To store data to be read
    DWORD   dwCount;                    // Byte count

    rc = ReadProcessMemory(
            hProcess,                   // Handle of process to read from
            (LPCVOID) pData,            // Address to read from
            &nVar,                      // Buffer to store read data
            sizeof(nVar),               // Buffer size
            &dwCount);                  // Byte count read.

    // rc is non zero on success, zero (FALSE) on error.
```

A better method to exchange data with another process is to send the `WM_COPYDATA` message to that process, via `SendMessage()` (described in Chapter 9). This method requires knowing the target process's main window handle[18], and is ideal to pass a block of data. The following example implements a function that sends some data to another process using `WM_COPYDATA`. It requires five parameters: the handle of the window sending the message (obtained from the `WindowProc()`, see Chapter 9), the target window handle, a code to identify the data, a pointer to the data and the size of the data.

```
LRESULT SendDataToWnd(HWND hWndFrom, HWND hWndTo, DWORD dwCode,
                      LPVOID pData, DWORD dwSize)
{
    COPYDATASTRUCT cds;                 // WM_COPYDATA uses this struct.
```

---

[17] A debugger can start or open a process (see Chapter 7 for details) to debug and obtain its process handle. It can also consult the target process' symbol table to obtain relevant data addresses.
[18] Functions like `FindWindow()` or `GetWindow()` can be used to identify and obtain such a handle.

```
    cds.dwData = dwCode;              // User-defined code (optional)
    cds.cbData = dwSize;              // Data size (in bytes)
    cds.lpData = pData;              // Pointer to data
    // Send WM_COPYDATA to the target window. Note that the third and
    // fourth params are respectively cast into WPARAM and LPARAM.
    return SendMessage(
            hWndTo,
            WM_COPYDATA,
            (WPARAM) hWndFrom,
            (LPARAM) &cds);
}
```

8.1.3   The 33ʳᵈ Slot: Slot 0

Why is a 33ʳᵈ slot required whereas only 32 processes are supported? The answer has to do with the tools to develop Windows CE applications.

Development tools of a given platform (Unix, NT, etc.) must generate code that exactly fits the memory management style of the underlying system. For instance, a DOS C compiler generates a program designed to run at some relocatable, segmented, real mode physical address (there is no virtual memory on DOS). On the other hand, a Windows NT C compiler generates a program expected to run in a flat address space, from virtual address 0, independently of its physical location in memory.

On NT, the format of an executable as generated by a linker is called PE (Program Executable) and is also used on Windows 9x. Using the same format on both platforms allows the use of the same development tools. CE designers also opted for the same file format to let you rely on the tools you already know.

However, there is a problem. On NT, each process has its own address space starting from 0, so the PE format perfectly fits the picture. But on CE, since a single 4GB virtual address space is split among 32 processes, only slot 0 starts at virtual address 0; slot 1 starts a virtual address 32MB; slot 2 starts at virtual address 64MB, and so on. As a result, the PE format, with its base address of 0, does not fit the picture that well for slots (processes) other than 0.

Hence, slot 0 is reserved for the active process, whichever it is. That means that whenever a process runs, it is copied from its reserved slot back to slot 0, to be run there (see Figure 8-4-a). When another process is chosen to run, the process in slot 0 is copied back to its reserved slot, and the next process is copied into slot 0 (see Figure 8-4-b).

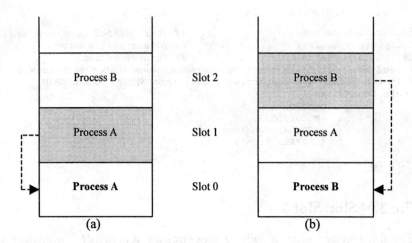

Figure 8-4: Running various processes in slot 0, one at a time. In (a), process A is run from slot 0. In (b), Process A is returned to slot 1 and process B is copied from slot 2 to slot 0

Although that seems to be an awfully large overhead, it turns out that this process swapping activity can be implemented via a few quick operations. Thanks to paging, process address space is simply *remapped* to slot 0 (and back to their original slot). Remapping consists in updating a few internal virtual memory tables, not copying the actual process code and data. As a result, with almost no performance penalty, the PE format is supported on CE.

One may ask why using this apparent complexity instead of just using the NT approach of giving 4GB of virtual memory to each process? Simply because doing so would add more memory management overhead in terms of size and performance within CE. Although the retained approach does not eliminate all overhead, it greatly reduces it and provides an acceptable memory management framework for the kind of applications for which Windows CE is targeted.

8.1.4   Under The Hood: Paging

All the memory management magic that takes place in Windows CE is based on one technique: paging. As a matter of fact, Windows CE requires a CPU to support paging in order to run. The CPU is involved because each instruction or data address is virtual, not physical. Considering that each application runs from slot 0, and uses addresses in the range 0 to 32MB, some form of address translation must take place to "reroute" instructions and data access to the application's code and data in physical memory (see Figure 8-5). That translation consists of transforming a virtual address, as seen by an application, to the corresponding physical address, as seen by Windows CE. This translation is what paging is all about, and is implemented deep in Windows CE; applications are completely unaware of it.

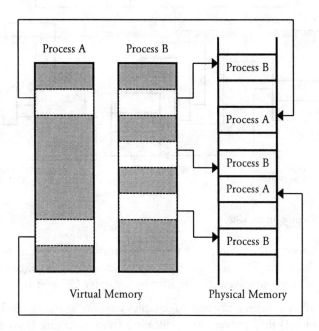

Figure 8-5: Although each application uses the same addresses (0 to 32MB), the corresponding physical addresses differ from application to application, thanks to paging

Each process is under the illusion that it has a zero-based, 32MB, flat address space. In reality, paging breaks that address space into a multitude of small physical pages, as illustrated in Figure 8.5. The size of a page is determined by the CPU (Windows CE requires page size to be either 1KB or 4KB). Of these pages, only those that contain actual code and data have to be in physical memory; the other pages are ignored. Unused code and data pages can remain compressed in CE to reduce memory requirements. As memory is needed by a process (due to the growth of the heaps and stacks), more pages are transparently allocated by CE; at the end, a process only uses the pages it needs. This technique considerably reduces memory waste compared with other techniques such as segmentation.

On an x86, a 32-bit logical address is broken up into three parts (see Figure 8-6). The left portion is an index into a page directory table; the middle portion is another index to a page table; and finally, the right portion is an index into a page frame, containing actual code or data. At the end of that transformation, the original 32-bit logical address is translated into a 32-bit physical address.

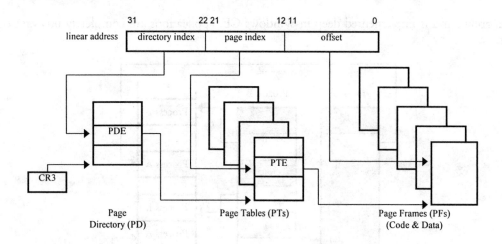

Figure 8-6: Paging on an x86

The page directory, page tables, and pages are constructed by CE as applications are loaded in memory and run. This is a very dynamic operation, all managed internally by CE. Again, processes are never involved in page management; it's CE's business.

Each entry in the page directory and page tables contains some control bits. The role of these bits is two-fold: 1) they prevent an application from accessing beyond its slot and the memory-mapped file area and 2) they prevent an application from overwriting its own code or trying to execute its own data. Simply put, they ensure that an application behaves properly.

8.2 MEMORY ALLOCATION

Applications work with data structures; Windows CE works with pages. Hence, an API is required to provide some abstraction that shields intricate details of physical memory. Nonetheless, some applications (especially embedded applications) might in fact want to work directly on a page level, to bypass all of the overhead generated by that abstraction.

Therefore, Windows CE provides two APIs to manage memory: heap and page allocation. But first, let's review how data is stored in applications by compilers and linkers.

8.2.1 Storing Application Data

Each programming language provides various means to allocate data, without even relying on the Windows CE API (at least, directly):

- Global variables
- Stacks
- Dynamic memory allocation

Let's review each of them.

Global Variables

Global variables are typically declared outside any function, and live during the entire application scope. Static variables (in C and C++) are also global, despite a reduced access scope. They can be accessed at any time, through the programming language syntax and semantic.

Today's tendency, though, is to minimize their use in order to prevent side effects, the cause of numerous bugs. Object-oriented language also contributes to reduce global variables, by moving them into classes. It is interesting to note that some data is marked global without being declared as such (*e.g.,* string literals).

Stacks

A stack is a finite pool of memory, reserved for a given thread. Stacks are used to temporarily store local variables (as opposed to global variables) and function call return addresses. A stack works on a last-in-first-out basis. Imagine a stack of dishes: the last one you put on the stack is the first one that you can remove (unless you try to impress your friends by removing the very first one at the bottom).

Each thread has its own stack, initially set to one page. The stack automatically grows up, as needed. The stack is usually implicitly managed by the programming language you use (one notable exception being when you write in assembly language, where you have to manage the stack yourself). There is no special system call to manage memory on the stack.

By default, stacks are limited to 58KB (the stack is actually slightly bigger, but some of it is reserved to detect overflow or underflow). Linker options can change that limit by reserving more space; doing so affects the stack of all threads of that application, not one in particular. Reserving more space in itself does not take up more physical memory.

Regardless of its size, accessing memory beyond a stack causes an exception and shuts down the application, regardless of which thread committed the fault. Very large objects can be instead allocated through dynamic allocation, described hereafter.

Dynamic Memory Allocation

Consider an application that needs to read a certain amount of data from a file. Since the amount of data to read is initially unknown, neither global nor local data (stack data) can be used. Hence, the application must allocate memory to store the data as it reads it.

Obtaining memory to store data at run-time is called dynamic memory allocation (as opposed to global data whose size is static at run-time). It is usually based on a large pool of memory, under the control of a few memory management functions. The standard C library includes its own memory management functions: `malloc()` and `free()`. So does the C++ language with the `new` and `delete` operators.

Most application developers simply rely on these functions/operators to obtain and release dynamic memory. Some applications, especially those under real-time constraints, can often not tolerate the delay incurred by using these functions, and prefer manage memory themselves. Also, using dynamic memory with blocks of various sizes may lead to fragmentation, which results in poor memory utilization. For those who need a better control over dynamic allocation, Windows CE provides heaps, the topic of the next section. Note that `malloc()` and `free()`, as `new` and `delete`, likely rely on a heap internally.

8.2.2   Heaps

A heap is another finite pool of memory, managed by Windows CE, available for the process to use. It allows applications to allocate memory at run-time via some system calls. Heaps grow up as your application requires more dynamic memory from them, but they may not necessarily shrink (there is no automatic memory compaction). Heap sizes are only limited to physical and virtual memory availability[19].

Local Heap

Each process has initially a default heap, called the local heap[20]. Its size is initially set to 384KB (virtual) the first time it is accessed and grows as required. Windows CE internally uses fragments of the local heap when the application creates and uses resources.

A thread can allocate dynamic memory from the local heap by calling `LocalAlloc()`. Once that memory is no longer required, it can be freed by calling `LocalFree()`, as shown below.

---

[19] The documentation mentions that heaps are limited to 1MB, but this is no longer true.
[20] The concept of *local* heap is purely historical. Previous Windows platforms also had a *global* heap, but this concept disappeared with the arrival of 32-bit Windows systems.

```
struct SOME_DATA_STRUCT
{
    . . .
};

void DoSomething()
{
    // Allocate a block to hold a variable of type SOME_DATA_STRUCTURE
    SOME_DATA_STRUCT *     ptr;

    ptr = (SOME_DATA_STRUCT *) LocalAlloc(
            LPTR,                           // Initialized to zero
            sizeof(SOME_DATA_STRUCTURE)); // Size, in bytes

    // The memory can be accessed through ptr.
    . . .

    // Release the memory pointed to by ptr.
    LocalFree((HLOCAL) ptr);
}
```

You may wonder why all these cast operators are required in this example. The original Win32 API local heap allocation functions can either allocate fixed or moveable blocks. In the first case, the return value is the address, which must be cast to the appropriate data type. In the second case, the return value is a handle (not an address) that identifies the block. Moveable blocks are not supported on CE; hence, LocalAlloc() always returns an address, which requires casting to pass the compiler's syntax checking. Similarly, CE's version of LocalFree() truly accepts the address of a block, but it requires some casting.

Two other local heap functions are available, as shown in Figure 8-7.

Function	Description
LocalRealloc()	Changes the size of a previously allocated block, given its address and a new size. The function returns the new address.
LocalSize()	Return the size of a previously allocated block, given its address.

Figure 8-7: Extra local heap functions

The local heap functions internally implement some mutual exclusion, making them reliable when used in a multithread environment.

Supplemental Heaps

As with dynamic allocation using programming languages, the issue with a heap is the fragmentation. Allocating and deallocating numerous blocks of various sizes result in holes in the heap. These holes are often too small to satisfy subsequent allocation requests, but taken together, they may represent a significant amount of wasted memory (see Figure 8-8-a).

To help circumvent the problem, Windows CE allows processes to support supplemental heaps. For instance, the default heap can be used for small blocks of data, whereas another heap could be used for large blocks only. Using such an approach would help reduce fragmentation within each heap, resulting in less wasted memory and better overall memory management (see Figure 8-8-b). And that is the real advantages of using heaps over programming language when allocating dynamic memory: to reduce fragmentation.

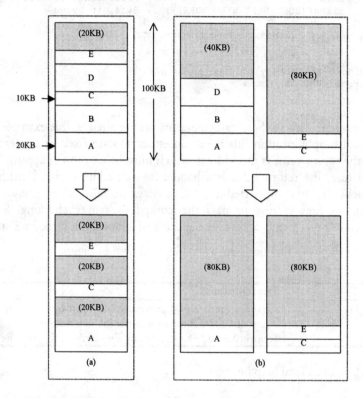

Figure 8-8: Using multiple heaps reduces fragmentation. In (a), five blocks have been allocated in one single heap. If blocks B and D are removed, the largest block that can be allocated cannot exceed 20KB, even if 60KB are available. In (b), two heaps have been used (one for large blocks, the other for small blocks); freeing B and D leaves 80KB in the first heap.

An extra heap is allocated through `HeapCreate()`. The call requires a minimum and maximum sizes, but these values are actually ignored[21]: 384KB is reserved when the first memory block is allocated from the heap, and the heap automatically expands (its size is restricted only by the available virtual and physical memory).

`HeapCreate()`, like most supplemental heap functions, accepts a flag parameter that determines whether some mutual exclusion should be retained or not when allocating and deallocating memory. It turns out that despite what's suggested by the documentation, mutual exclusion always takes place.

Memory is allocated and freed from a heap by calling `HeapAlloc()` and `HeapFree()`. Both functions accept a heap handle and a flag to turn off serialization (if the heap access is serialized and it makes sense for the application to turn it off). The first call requires the amount of memory to allocate; the second requires the address of the data block to free. These functions work in pairs, as you would expect. An existing block's size can be obtained by calling `HeapSize()`, whereas blocks can be resized by calling `HeapRealloc()`.

Here is an example of an application that creates and uses an extra heap for large block allocations:

```
HANDLE      hLargeBlockHeap;

struct LARGE_STRUCT
{
    . . .
};

// Initialize the application. This function is called once.

void Initialize()
{
    // Allocate an extra heap for large block allocation.
    hLargeBlockHeap = HeapCreate(
        0,                      // No special flag
        512 * 1024,             // Initial size (512KB), although unused.
        0);                     // No maximum size on CE

    // Make sure the heap has been allocated
    if (hLargeBlockHeap == NULL)
        Error("Unable to allocate the extra heap");
}

// Perform some processing. This may be executed by more than one thread,
// so all heap operations must be serialized (they are by default) to
// prevent any race conditions.

void ProcessSomething()
{
    // Allocate a small object (initialized to zero) from the extra heap
```

[21] Perhaps future versions on CE will take into account the minimum size, however.

```
LARGE STRUCT * p = (LARGE STRUCT *) HeapAlloc(
        hLargeBlockHeap,          // Heap to allocate from
        HEAP_ZERO_MEMORY,         // Initialize the memory to zero
        sizeof(LARGE_STRUCT));    // Requested size

// Make sure some memory has been allocated
if (p == NULL)
{
        Error("Unable to allocate memory from the extra heap");
        return;
}

// Use p
p->. . .

// Release p once done
HeapFree(
        hLargeBlockHeap,          // Heap to release to
        0,                        // No special flag
        p);                       // Block to release
}

// Clean-up the application. This function is called once.

void Cleanup()
{
    // Destroy the extra heap
    if (hLargeBlockHeap != NULL)
        HeapDestroy(hLargeBlockHeap);
}
```

The `HeapAlloc()`, `HeapRealloc()` and `HeapFree()` functions can also be used on the local heap, by using `GetProcessHeap()` as the first argument. `GetProcessHeap()` returns the handle of the local heap; hence, the following calls, which allocate a zeroed 128 bytes from the local heap, are equivalent:

```
LocalAlloc(LPTR, 128);
HeapAlloc(GetProcessHeap(), HEAP_ZERO_MEMORY, 128);
```

8.2.3 Page Allocation

Very large blocks can also be allocated by calling `VirtualAlloc()`. This function is the lowest memory function offered by CE (it is internally used by `CreateHeap()`). `VirtualAlloc()` works in terms of virtual pages (*e.g.*, either 1KB or 4KB depending on the CPU). Thus, you can use that call to allocate a certain number of pages within a process address space.

Pages can be either reserved or committed. An application can reserve a group of virtual pages with the intent of using them later, in order to store data. Reserved pages are guaranteed not to be used by heaps or stacks. The space is reserved in the calling process's virtual memory address space, not in physical memory. But to be accessible, virtual pages must be committed, *i.e.*, associated with some physical memory. Hence, an application may commit already-reserved pages before accessing them, or may simply commit them upon calling `VirtualAlloc()` (instead of reserving them). You may legitimately wonder at this point the advantages of reserving memory ... After all, why not allocate and commit memory at once? The answer is: to preserve physical memory.

Consider a Calendar application, where the user may enter daily appointments and notes. That data can hypothetically be kept into a data structure, one for each day. The application could manage these data structures through some linked list (via `HeapAlloc()`), an efficient memory-management technique. However, accessing a specific day requires iterating through the list, which is slow. A faster method would be to use a 365-day array, but this would result in wasted memory, as users may enter data for some days only (the general case). To prevent that waste, the application can reserve enough space to store the entire array, but only commit pages as the user enters information. Hence accessing a specific day requires committing memory if it is not already committed, and making a simple array access.

But a big plus on CE is that `VirtualAlloc()` also supports auto-commit pages, which are initially reserved, but automatically committed on access. Referring back to the Calendar example, the array could be allocated as auto-commit pages. The array is initially reserved, but whenever an array element is accessed, Windows CE automatically commits the underlying page(s), freeing the application from doing so. This implementation is easier and simpler than using a linked list, and uses less memory than using an array.

Specifically, `VirtualAlloc()` can be called to reserve, commit and/or auto-commit memory, by specifying an allocation flag, whose values are the following.

- `MEM_RESERVE`. When reserving memory, the requested size is rounded up to the next 64KB. The exact value can be found in the `dwAllocationGranularity` field of the `SYSTEM_INFO` structure, as described in Section 8.3.3. This only consumes virtual memory, not physical memory. Reserved pages can be committed by invoking `VirtualAlloc()` with `MEM_COMMIT`.

- `MEM_COMMIT`: When committing virtual memory, the requested size is rounded up to the next physical page (either 1KB or 4KB, depending on the processor) and physical memory is used. `VirtualAlloc()` also accepts a parameter that describes the page protection to apply (read-only, read-write, execute, no cache, etc.)

- `MEM_AUTO_COMMIT`: same as `MEM_RESERVE`.

Remember that memory must be committed to be accessed. Otherwise, any attempt to access memory that is only reserved (either by simply reading) results in a fatal error and shuts down the entire application.

Pages can be uncommitted or freed (*i.e.,* de-allocated) by calling `VirtualFree()` and passing the address of a virtual block. `VirtualFree()` requires three parameters: a base address, a size, and a mode (uncommit or release).

When releasing pages (making them unreserved), the first parameter must the address of a block as returned by a previous call to `VirtualAlloc()`. The size must be 0, as the entire block (as specified to `VirtualAlloc()`) is released. The mode (the third parameter) must be `MEM_RELEASE`. But there is one catch: all pages must be in the same state: reserved. If the block contains some committed pages, `VirtualFree()` will fail to release any page! Consequently, committed pages must be uncommitted first.

Pages can be uncommitted by setting the first parameter to a committed page address, setting the size of the committed area and specifying `MEM_DECOMMIT`. The issue here is to identify the addresses of the pages that are committed in the block. An application can use some various techniques to identify these pages, or rely on the method presented below.

The next example allocates a pool of 128KB of virtual memory, in auto-commit mode, by calling `VirtualAlloc()`. Each page is committed automatically (as it is accessed), and is both readable and writable. Then, committed pages in that pool (whichever they are) are uncommitted by calling `UncommitMemory()`, declared below. Finally, the pool is released by calling `VirtualFree()`. This example is implemented in the **VirtMem** sample, on the CD-ROM.

```
#define MEM_POOL_SIZE      (128 * 1024)    // 128KB

void UseSomeVirtualMemory()
{
    BOOL    rc;
    LPVOID  pMemPool;

    // Allocate a pool of 128KB memory, using auto-commit,
    // read/write pages. Return if the allocation fails.
    pMemPool = VirtualAlloc(
                NULL,
                MEM_POOL_SIZE,
                MEM_RESERVE | MEM_AUTO_COMMIT,
                PAGE_READWRITE);

    if (pMemPool == NULL)
    {
        printf("Couldn't allocate memory\n");
        return;
    }

    // Use that pool by reading from and writing  to it,
    // through pointer references. For example:
    //      Reading: DWORD dwData = * (LPDWORD) pMemPool;
    //      Writing: * (LPDWORD) pMemPool = 0;
    .
    .
```

```
     .
      // Uncommit committed pages (whichever they are). The pages
      // must remain reserved though for VirtualFree() to work.
      UncommitMemory(pMemPool, MEM_POOL_SIZE);

      // Release all (reserved) pages from the memory pool.
      // All pages from the pool must be (and are) reserved, not committed.
      rc = VirtualFree(pMemPool, 0, MEM_RELEASE);

      if (!rc)
            printf("Couldn't free memory\n");
}

// Scans a block of memory, specified by a starting address and
// a size. Uncommit each range of pages that are marked committed.

void UncommitMemory(LPVOID pAddr, DWORD dwSize)
{
    LPVOID pMaxAddr = (LPVOID) ((DWORD) pAddr + dwSize);

    do
    {
          // Get info about the first range of pages.
          MEMORY_BASIC_INFORMATION       mbi;

          VirtualQuery(pAddr, &mbi, sizeof(mbi));

          // If that range is committed, uncommit it.
          // Otherwise, ignore the range.
          if (mbi.State & MEM_COMMIT)
                VirtualFree(
                      mbi.BaseAddress,
                      mbi.RegionSize,
                      MEM_DECOMMIT); // Uncommit, do not release yet

          // Go beyond the range.
          pAddr = (LPVOID) ((DWORD) mbi.BaseAddress + mbi.RegionSize);

    } while (pAddr < pMaxAddr);              // Loop while within the block
}
```

VirtualQuery() returns information about a consecutive range of pages sharing common attributes. Based on the address specified as the first parameter, it fills a structure of type MEMORY_BASIC_INFORMATION. Essentially, VirtualQuery() identifies the page containing the address, and returns the number of pages with the same attribute (committed, freed, mapped, private, or image). UncommitMemory() scans the entire block of memory, and uncommits committed pages.

VirtualProtect() is another available function. It changes the protection already associated to a region of committed pages. That type of protection is the same as the one that can be specified when committing pages with VirtualAlloc() (*e.g.*, read-only, read-write, etc.)

Managing pages at that level seems to be a lot of trouble, but it is sometimes the only choice. Consider using `VirtualAlloc()` to implement a proprietary memory allocation scheme. Real-time applications do not have the luxury of waiting for `malloc()` or `new` to succeed, and may instead implement a fixed-size memory management algorithm, whose allocation and deallocation is deterministic. This approach typically requires a large memory pool to work with. This pool can initially be reserved by using `VirtualAlloc()`, to ensure that this memory will not be used for anything else (stacks or heaps, for instance). Pages can be set to auto-commit whenever they are accessed. If some protection scheme is desired (to detect invalid access, for instance), pages can initially be set to reserved, only to be committed when "allocated"; an invalid pointer that wrongly references a reserved page (not committed) would then fail.

8.2.4   Memory Allocation Summary

Boy, who thought that would be that complicated! At the end, one may wonder what approach should be used. It is not obvious how these multiple features can be used optimally. Figure 8-9 summarizes these methods, from the easiest to the hardest to use.

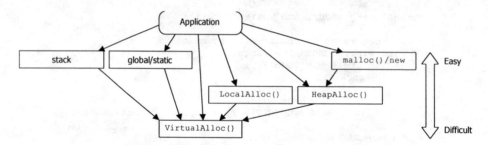

Figure 8-9: Memory allocation techniques, from the easiest to the most difficult to use

Here are some suggestions:

- If your main concern is the ease of use, rely on some programming language features for dynamic memory (*e.g.,* `malloc()` in C, `new` in C++), stacks for temporary data, and global/static variables for permanent data.

- For random-sized items that are allocated and deallocated at runtime, use the local heap. To improve memory usage by reducing fragmentation, use various heaps to hold data items of similar sizes. This is most useful when the data item size range is significant. It is somehow more complicated than using the previous approach (*e.g.,* `malloc()` and `free()`), but it helps reducing memory needs and improves performance.

- Rely on `VirtualAlloc()` to have a precise control over your address space, to allocate large blocks, or to adjust page protection. This requires working (and thinking) in terms of pages, and is without a doubt more difficult. Using map files generated by the linker can also help maximize page uses (see Section 8.3.2 for details).

Finally, one important recommendation: always check the returned value of any memory allocation function. In the worst scenario, your application will be launched with little memory available. The application may face the eventuality where there will not be enough memory to perform what it has been designed to do. The best defensive strategy is to allocate ahead everything you need (if that is possible); if there is a memory shortage, the application can politely notify the user, and release the already-allocated memory and other related resources if any.

8.2.5 Thread Local Storage

Despite the fancy memory allocation schemes that Windows CE supports, there are some situations that still present complications. These problems are inherent to multithreading.

All C/C++ compilers must provide an ANSI C library, which most of you are accustomed to. The original C library hasn't been developed with multithreading in mind, though. Consider `localtime()`, which returns a pointer to an internally `tm` structure, defined in `<time.h>`. This function used to be typically implemented as follows:

```
struct tm * localtime(const time_t * timer)
{
    static struct tm tm = {0};

    // Converts timer into tm.
    .
    .
    .

    return &tm;
}
```

Now suppose that thread A invokes that function, and starts accessing the structure through the pointer that has been returned. Then, the thread is preempted and thread B (in the same process) is given its chance to run. Thread B also invokes `localtime()`, passing a different timer, resulting in the `tm` structure being updated differently. Eventually, the control returns to thread A. Since both thread A and B are using the same structure (because `localtime()` uses one single `tm` structure within the application), thread A ends up with thread B's date ... Simply put, this version of `localtime()` is not thread-safe.

Some people suggested that another version of the function should be provided, which would need two parameters: the timer and a `tm` buffer (as shown below). This approach is thread-safe as long as each thread uses its own `tm` buffer. That's a solution that works, but it hasn't been retained[22].

```
void localtime2(const time_t * _time, struct tm * tm)
```

Windows CE provides a mechanism to retain the `localtime()` as is, yet making it thread-safe: thread local storage (TLS), that is, storage allocated on a per-thread basis. There are two implementations: static (easiest) and dynamic. Let's start with the easiest.

Static Thread Local Storage

Microsoft's C/C++ compiler implements extended storage class attributes, which are extensions to the C language. These extensions are not portable. One of these extensions allocates variables on a per-thread basis. Consider the following thread-safe (although not portable) implementation of `localtime()`:

```
struct tm * localtime(const time_t * timer)
{
    __declspec(thread) static struct tm tm = {0};

    // Converts timer into tm.
    .
    .
    .

    return &tm;
}
```

The addition of `__declspec(thread)` to the `tm` variable declaration means that each thread has its own copy of the variable. If two threads invoke that function (at the same time or not, it doesn't matter) each thread *automatically* sees its own copy of it. This nicely solves the multithreading issue while preserving the original API.

There are just a few restrictions to bear in mind when using static thread local storage:

- It may increase the loading time of dynamic-link libraries that uses it. As the library is attached to an application, space is automatically allocated and reserved for each thread.

- This storage only applies to static and global data, not local variables or function declarations. For example:

```
__declspec(thread) int MyFunction()      // Error (function declaration)
{
    __declspec(thread) int nCount;        // Error (local variable)
```

---

[22] Many people worked on that problem, but it was somewhat preferred to keep the standard intact.

```
          .
          .
          .
}
```

- The address of this type of variable is not considered constant, and cannot be used to initialize a static pointer variable in C. There is no such restriction in C++ though.

```
void MyFunction()
{
    __declspec(thread) static int nCount;

    static int * pnCount = &nCount;      // Error (not constant)
    int * pnCount2 = &nCount;            // OK (evaluated at run-time)
}
```

- Thread local storage, when used in dynamic-link libraries explicitly loaded at run-time (through `LoadLibrary()`), may not be properly initialized, and accessing it may result in access violation. This doesn't happen when dynamic storage (explained below) is used.

Dynamic Thread Local Storage

Applications may get one step further and precisely control how and when the storage is allocated. Internally, Windows CE maintains a local storage array for each thread. The size of each element is four bytes, and the size of the arrays is guaranteed to be at least `TLS_MINIMUM_AVAILABLE`, which is 64 on Windows CE.

The goal is to associate the same element of all threads' arrays to the same storage purpose. For instance, consider using a `DWORD` value on a per-thread basis (see Figure 8-10). Elements at index 0 within all arrays can be reserved for that purpose. Whenever a thread needs that value, the related array is accessed, and the element at index 0 is used as the value. Additionally, let's say that a second `DWORD` must be also used on a per-thread basis. Then, elements at index 1 within all arrays can be used for that purpose: when a thread accesses that second `DWORD`, it in fact accesses the element at index 1 of its related array.

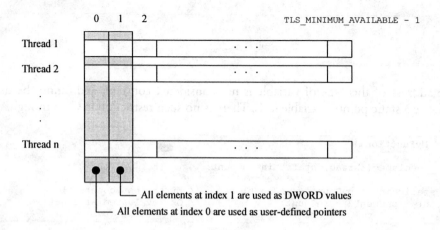

Figure 8-10: Using Thread Local Storage (TLS)

The implementation is far less magical than with static thread local storage seen earlier, and relies on a few functions. Let's start with an example to illustrate their use in a dynamic-link library (a common scenario).

```
DWORD         dwTlsIndex;

BOOL WINAPI DllMain(HINSTANCE hInstDll, DWORD dwReason, LPVOID lpReserved)
{
    switch (dwReason)
    {
    case PROCESS_ATTACH:
            // Obtain and reserve a TLS index (once).
            dwTlsIndex = TlsAlloc();

            if (dwTlsIndex == TLS_OUT_OF_INDEXES)
                    return FALSE;
            break;

    case PROCESS_DETACH:
            // Release the TLS index (once)
            if (dwTlsIndex != TLS_OUT_OF_INDEXES)
                    TlsFree(dwTlsIndex);

            break;
    }
}

// The following function is called by any thread to process something.

void DoSomething()
{
    // Perform some calculation and store the result in the storage
    // at index dwTlsIndex
    DWORD   dwValue = CalculateSomeValue();
```

```
    TlsSetValue(dwTlsIndex, (LPVOID) dwValue);
}

// The following function is called by any thread to perform some
// processing based on the actual value in the storage, at index
// dwTlsIndex.

void DoSomethingElse()
{
    DWORD   dwData;

    dwData = (DWORD) TslGetValue(dwTlsIndex);

    ProcessData(dwData);
}
```

When the DLL is attached to a process, it requests from Windows CE an available index, not used by any other application or DLL, by calling `TlsAlloc()`. Conversely, upon terminating, it releases the index, making it available to other modules, by invoking `TlsFree()`. Indices are system-wide: once an index has been reserved and is being used, subsequent `TlsAlloc()` (within the same or another process) will always return another (free) index (or `TLS_OUT_OF_INDEXES` when all of them are already reserved).

When a given thread invokes `DoSomething()`, it sets the proper element in its own array by calling `TlsSetValue()`. The function requires the index (to specify what element to access in its array), and the new 4-byte value. That value is simply written in the array, at the specified position. Since each thread has its own array maintained by Windows CE, any thread can safely invoke that function, without affecting any other thread.

Similarly, `DoSomethingElse()` simply reads the value by calling `TlsGetValue()`. The function also requires the index, and returns the associated `DWORD` value. `TlsGetValue()` automatically uses the proper internal array, associated with the calling thread.

Applications or DLLs can use more than one index, by repeatedly calling `TlsAlloc()`. The call succeeds as long as at least one index is available system-wide. Furthermore, although the threads' arrays store 4-byte values, they can be treated as pointers to larger structures. `TlsAlloc()` not only reserves an index, but it also initializes the corresponding element in all arrays to `NULL`. Hence, a thread can test the value returned by `TlsGetValue()` against `NULL`, and allocate a structure if so.

```
void ProcessSomething()
{
    struct MyData * p = TlsGetValue(dwTlsIndex);

    if (p == NULL)
    {
            p = LocalAlloc(LPTR, sizeof(struct MyData)
```

```
            TlsSetValue(dwTlsIndex, p);
    }

    p->. . .
}
```

Deallocating the structure may present an issue, though. If the dynamic-link libraries are unloaded through `FreeLibrary()`, threads do not get a chance the release the memory they allocated. That would require the library to manage itself as to what is allocated to whom.

Is It Worth The Trouble?

This is a question we may legitimately ask, especially regarding the dynamic thread local storage and the related API.

In the case where you design and implement new code, the answer is probably no. An application and/or library can be made thread-safe by using local variables instead of global or static ones (such as the `localtime2()` function mentioned before). It makes the code easier to maintain, especially for subsequent developers who may not be familiar with the concept of thread local storage.

However, when making legacy code thread-safe, under the constraint where the API cannot be changed (because it would require modifying too much code), thread local storage might be the only solution. In this case, it is easier to use static thread local storage, because the compiler and Windows CE inherit the responsibility of managing the storage for each thread. In some other cases, it might better to control that duty programmatically, and hence rely on the dynamic thread local storage API.

8.3 MEMORY SHORTAGE

Memory being a finite resource, the system may eventually run into the situation where there is just not enough available physical memory to satisfy applications' needs. For instance, any of the following may fail under memory shortage:

- Allocating memory through direct system calls (`HeapAlloc()` or `Virtual Alloc()`)
- Executing a system call that internally requires memory (such as mapping a file)
- Increasing the stack. This problem is nasty because it suspends the application until a page becomes available. During that period, the application does not execute.

8.3.1   Managing Low Memory conditions

Windows CE monitors memory usage to detect low memory conditions. When the amount of available memory falls below the threshold of 128KB[23], Windows CE enters a low-memory state and performs the following actions to prevent the memory from deteriorating any further:

- It sends `WM_HIBERNATE` to applications for them to release memory, eventually followed by `WM_ACTIVATE` when the application is asked to run again. Windows may also send `WM_CLOSE` (instead of `WM_ACTIVATE`), if the user chooses to close the application. Upon receiving `WM_HIBERNATE`, an application should release as much data (including resources) as possible, and reload it when either `WM_ACTIVATE` or `WM_CLOSE` is received.

- Memory allocation requests become restricted to small blocks as memory becomes scarce. Hence, calling `VirtualAlloc()`, `LocalAlloc()`, `HeapAlloc()` or a programming language allocation function, such as `malloc()`, may fail.

At some point, Windows CE will display the low-memory dialog box, prompting the user to close some applications. Applications are not aware of that event.

8.3.2   Identifying Static Memory Needs

Even before running an application, you can identify the exact memory needs of an application, by analyzing the output of some development tools. The methods we are about to see report how much memory an application initially occupies in memory, if it is fully loaded. This memory is called static to contrast with the dynamic memory allocated at run time.

The DumpBin Utility

The code and the data of an executable image (`.EXE`) are grouped into sections, based on their attributes. By carefully examining the size of each section, one can establish how much data is wasted due to page alignment.

Each section starts at the beginning of a page. Because of that alignment, the last page of a section is only partially used. For instance, on a system supporting 4KB pages, a 6KB section will occupy two pages, but the second page will only be half-used. Since there are a few sections in an image, there are a few pages that are underutilized. Developers can take a close look at the sections to identify how much space will be wasted, and perhaps make a few programming changes to reduce that waste.

---

[23] This value can be configured in the `HKEY_LOCAL_MACHINE\system\hibernate` registry entry.

The DUMPBIN utility lists all sorts of information about executable file (.EXE, .DLL), particularly the virtual address and size of each section. The following shows the output of a simple application; comments are shown in italic, whereas information of special interest, described below, is highlighted in bold. Also note that all numbers are in hexadecimal.

```
F:\CEProjects\MEM\WMIPSREL>dumpbin /headers mem.exe
Microsoft (R) COFF Binary File Dumper Version 5.11.7351
Copyright (C) Microsoft Corp 1992-1997. All rights reserved.


Dump of file mem.exe

PE signature found

File Type: EXECUTABLE IMAGE

FILE HEADER VALUES
         166 machine (R4000)                  ; CPU type
           4 number of sections               ; Number of sections
(truncated)

OPTIONAL HEADER VALUES
         10B magic #
        5.11 linker version                    ; Linker version
         400 size of code                      ; Code section size (rounded)
         600 size of initialized data          ; Data section size (rounded)
           0 size of uninitialized data        ; Usually 0
        10B8 address of entry point            ; Entry point in the program
        1000 base of code                      ; Code location in virtual memory
        2000 base of data                      ; Data location in virtual memory
       10000 image base
        1000 section alignment                 ; Section alignment in virtual memory
         200 file alignment                    ; Section alignment in the file (.EXE)
        4.00 operating system version          ; Host OS version (NT 4.0 in this case)
        0.00 image version
        2.00 subsystem version
           0 Win32 version
        5000 size of image                     ; Full image size in virtual memory
         400 size of headers
           0 checksum
           9 subsystem (Windows CE GUI)        ; Targeted system (Windows CE in this case)
           0 DLL characteristics
      100000 size of stack reserve             ; Reserved stack size
        1000 size of stack commit              ; Initial stack size
      100000 size of heap reserve              ; Reserved local heap size
        1000 size of heap commit               ; Initial local heap size

(truncated)

SECTION HEADER #1
   .text name                                  ; .text section: instructions
         298 virtual size                       ; Size (in bytes)
        1000 virtual address                    ; Relative address in virtual memory
         400 size of raw data                   ; Occupied space (in bytes) in the .EXE file
(truncated)
    60000020 flags
           Code                                ; Code
           Execute Read                        ; Will be marked as executable and read-only

SECTION HEADER #2
   .rdata name                                 ; .rdata section: read-only data
          86 virtual size                       ; Size (in bytes)
```

```
    2000 virtual address              ; Relative address in virtual memory
     200 size of raw data             ; Occupied space (in bytes) in the .EXE file
     800 file pointer to raw data
(truncated)
40000040 flags
         Initialized Data             ; Data
         Read Only                    ; Will be marked as read-only

SECTION HEADER #3
    .data name                        ; .data section: read-write data
     188 virtual size                 ; Size (in bytes)
    3000 virtual address              ; Relative address in virtual memory
     200 size of raw data             ; Occupied space (in bytes) in the .EXE file
(truncated)
C0000040 flags
         Initialized Data             ; Data
         Read Write                   ; Will be marked as read-write

SECTION HEADER #4
    .pdata name                       ; .pdata section: pointers (DLL)
      78 virtual size                 ; Size (in bytes)
    4000 virtual address              ; Relative address in virtual memory
     200 size of raw data             ; Occupied space (in bytes) in the .EXE file
(truncated)
40000040 flags
         Initialized Data             ; Data
         Read Only                    ; Will be marked as read-only

  Summary                             ; Occupied space (in bytes) in virtual memory
                                      ; for each section
    1000 .data
    1000 .pdata
    1000 .rdata
    1000 .text
```

Note that there are five headers listed in this listing: the File header, the Optional header, and four Section headers. Figure 8-11 lists the most common sections.

Section	Description
.text	Executable machine code instructions
.data	Initialized and uninitialized data (global and static variables)
.rdata	Read-only data (literal strings, constants)
.rsrcn	Resource data, from the .RES file (produced by the resource compiler over the application .RC file)
.debug	Debug information

Figure 8-11: The most commonly sections output by linkers.

This output helps identify how many bytes are wasted between sections. The Optional header reveals that the "section alignment" is 1000h (a page on an x86 CE target, which is used in this example), which means that each section starts on a multiple of 1000h. By looking at the "virtual size" value of each section, you can establish how many bytes are wasted for each. For instance, the .data section occupies 392 (0x188) bytes. Since the alignment is 4096 bytes, 3704 bytes are wasted (4096 – 392). Regarding the `.rdata` section, which occupies 134 (0x86) bytes, 3962 bytes are lost (4096 – 134).

If memory is at an absolute premium, carefully moving variables from one section to another may help use pages to their maximum and reduce waste. In order to identify what variables can be moved and where, we need to rely on the `.MAP` file, described hereafter.

MAP Files

A map file is a text file that lists the name, address, and section of all symbols (functions and global variables) found in an application's `.EXE` file. It doesn't only list the symbols defined in the program, but also any other symbols imported from specified libraries that are required to build the `.EXE`.

A map file helps in identifying what sections variables are assigned to. Each language has its own interpretation of variables (for example, C and C++ constant variables are treated differently). Whereas the `DUMPBIN` utility reveals the exact size of the read-write and read-only section, the map file reveals the exact content of each of these sections.

The most common section names output by compilers are listed in Figure 8-12. Note that these names are just industry standard, used internally by compilers and linkers, and have no impact at all on the application at run-time.

Section	Description
`.text`	Machine code instructions
`.data`	Initialized data (global and static variables)
`.bss`	Uninitialized data (global and static variables). The loader initialized that section to zero
`.rdata`	Read-only data (literal strings, constants, some debug information)
`.rsrcn`	Resource data, from the .RES file (produced by the resource compiler over the application .RC file)
`.idata`	Imported function table
`.idata$n`	Portions of an imported function table, from an import library
`.CRT`	Tables of initialization and shutdown pointers, used by the C++ runtime library
`.CRT$XXX`	Tables of initialization and shutdown pointers, found in .OBJ.
`.debug`	Debug information

Figure 8-12: The most common sections output by compilers.

You might notice that multiple sections exist for data. Linkers combine some of these sections together (as seen earlier in Figure 8-11).

Map files are generated by specifying some option to the linker. For instance, Microsoft Linker generates a map file if the option /map:filename is specified. Consider the following code example:

```
// Mem.c

#include <windows.h>

int         nMin = 3;              // Read-write data     ie .data section
const int   nMax = 10;             // Read-only data      ie .rdata section
int         nAvg;                  // Uninitialized data ie .bss section


int WINAPI WinMain(HINSTANCE hInstance, HINSTANCE hPrevInstance,
    LPTSTR lpCmdLine, int nCmdShow)
{
    static int nSize = 8;          // Read-write data     ie .data section

    MessageBox(                    // Instructions        ie .text section
            NULL,
            TEXT("Hi!"),           // Read-write data     ie .data section
            TEXT("Windows CE"),    // Read-write data     ie .data section
            MB_OK);

    return 1;                      // Instructions        ie .text section
}
```

The following is the map file corresponding to the example shown above. The DumpBin output seen earlier is also based on the same program and corresponds to that map file.

```
Mem

(truncated)

    Preferred load address is 00010000

    Start           Length      Name                 Class
    0001:00000000 0000038cH .text                    CODE
    0002:00000000 00000058H .rdata                   DATA
    0002:00000058 00000014H .idata$2                 DATA
    0002:0000006c 00000014H .idata$3                 DATA
    0002:00000080 0000000cH .idata$4                 DATA
    0002:0000008c 00000028H .idata$6                 DATA
    0002:000000b4 00000000H .edata                   DATA
    0003:00000000 0000000cH .idata$5                 DATA
    0003:0000000c 00000004H .CRT$XCA                 DATA
    0003:00000010 00000004H .CRT$XCZ                 DATA
    0003:00000014 00000004H .CRT$XIA                 DATA
(truncated)
    0003:00000030 00000034H .data                    DATA
    0003:00000064 0000000cH .bss                     DATA
    0004:00000000 000000b4H .pdata                   DATA
```

```
    Address           Publics by Value              Rva+Base    Lib:Object

 0001:00000000        WinMain                       00011000 f  Mem.obj
 0001:00000058        MessageBoxW                   00011058 f  coredll:COREDLL.dll
 0001:00000068        WinMainCRTStartup             00011068 f  LIBCd:pegwmain.obj
 0001:000000c4        _cinit                        000110c4 f  LIBCd:crt0dat.obj
 0001:00000110        exit                          00011110 f  LIBCd:crt0dat.obj
 0001:00000144        _exit                         00011144 f  LIBCd:crt0dat.obj
 0001:00000178        _cexit                        00011178 f  LIBCd:crt0dat.obj
 0001:000001a8        _c_exit                       000111a8 f  LIBCd:crt0dat.obj
 0001:0000037c        ExitThread                    0001137c f  coredll:COREDLL.dll
 0002:00000054        nMax                          00012054    Mem.obj
 0002:00000058        __IMPORT_DESCRIPTOR_COREDLL 00012058     coredll:COREDLL.dll
 0002:0000006c        __NULL_IMPORT_DESCRIPTOR      0001206c    coredll:COREDLL.dll
 0003:00000000        __imp_ExitThread              00013000    coredll:COREDLL.dll
 0003:00000004        __imp_MessageBoxW             00013004    coredll:COREDLL.dll
 0003:00000008        \177COREDLL_NULL_THUNK_DATA 00013008      coredll:COREDLL.dll
 0003:0000000c        __xc_a                        0001300c    LIBCd:crt0init.obj
 0003:00000010        __xc_z                        00013010    LIBCd:crt0init.obj
(truncated)
 0003:00000030        nMin                          00013030    Mem.obj
 0003:00000058        _exitflag                     00013058    LIBCd:crt0dat.obj
 0003:0000005c        _C_Termination_Done           0001305c    LIBCd:crt0dat.obj
 0003:00000064        nAvg                          00013064    <common>
 0003:00000068        __onexitbegin                 00013068    <common>
 0003:0000006c        __onexitend                   0001306c    <common>

 entry point at       0001:00000068


Static symbols

 0001:000001d8        doexit                        000111d8 f  LIBCd:crt0dat.obj
 0001:00000304        _initterm                     00011304 f  LIBCd:crt0dat.obj
```

The first part lists all the sections obtained from the object files (OBJ) that were linked together. Sections sharing some attributes (such as read-only or read-write) are grouped together, using a 4-digit section number. For instance, all sections that start with 0002:xxxxxxxx will be grouped into one single block. In this listing, numbers 0001 to 0004 are being used, meaning that all these sections have been grouped into four "super sections". Note that, indeed, four sections are reported by the DUMPBIN utility.

Below the section list, the map file contains all public symbols. The MEM.C program variables have been highlighted (WinMain, nMin, nAvg, and nMax). One can see that nMax is part of section 0002. DUMPBIN reveals that section 2 is a read-only section. Hence, nMax is stored in a read-only section (which makes sense given its const declaration). Conversely, nMin and nMax reside in section 3, which is a read-write section.

Let's recall that the objective is to use full pages, not fractions of them, by moving variables from one section to another. Say DUMPBIN reveals that the size of the read-only section is 1004 bytes (*i.e.,* 1 page plus 4bytes), moving a 4-byte read-only variable to the read-write section would save one memory page. This move can be achieved by making that read-only variable a non-constant variable, moving it into the read-write section. Here are a few suggestions to re-arrange your data to optimize page usage:

- Global and static data can perhaps be moved onto heaps, in order to prevent wasting most of a data page (assuming the heap is already used for some other purpose; otherwise there is no gain).

- Read-write data that is never modified can perhaps be moved to the read-only section by making them constant.

You may legitimately wonder if all this trouble is worth the effort ... Well, it all depends on the environment in which your application is expected to run. If the requirements are quite strict and your applications must fit within what you have no matter what, doing that tedious work may become a necessity. Conversely, if you are targeting an H/PC with 8MB of RAM, saving a page here and there is no big deal, so spending a few hours arranging your variables might not be justified.

8.3.3   Identifying Memory Needs at Run Time

The static memory an application occupies is often only half of the story: applications may very well allocate memory at run time that far exceeds its initial, static size. Here are a few methods to determine how greedy an application really is at run time.

Querying Windows CE

The first thing an application can do is to ask Windows CE how much memory is available, both virtual (*i.e.*, in the address space) and physical. Windows CE offers two system calls that return some memory information.

First, `GlobalMemoryStatus()` returns information about the current physical and virtual memory availability. It requires a structure `MEMORYSTATUS`, detailed below:

Type	Field	Description
DWORD	dwLength	Equal to `sizeof(MEMORYSTATUS)`
DWORD	dwMemoryLoad	Memory utilization, in percentage
DWORD	dwTotalPhys	Total physical memory size, in bytes
DWORD	dwAvailPhys	Available physical memory size, in bytes
DWORD	dwTotalPageFile	Always 0 on CE
DWORD	dwAvailPageFile	Always 0 on CE
DWORD	dwTotalVirtual	Total virtual memory size, in bytes
DWORD	dwAvailVirtual	Available virtual memory size, in bytes

Figure 8-13: The MEMORYSTATUS structure

Two fields are particularly interesting:

- `dwAvailPhys` reveals how much RAM is available to run programs. It does not include the size allocated to the Object Store, and varies depending on the user's memory settings. This value is highly volatile, as the system allocates and frees memory to conduct some internal operations.

- `dwAvailVirtual` indicates how much virtual memory remains available in the current process. Most of the time, though, processes are really bound by how much physical memory remains, as they typically occupy a fraction of their address space.

Second, `GetSystemInfo()` queries the system and returns the `SYSTEM_INFO` structure describing the current system. The structure is `SYSTEM_INFO` and is depicted below:

Type	Member	Description
WORD	wProcessorArchitecture	Processor architecture constant (e.g. PROCESSOR_ARCHITECTURE_INTEL)
DWORD	dwPageSize	Page size, as used by `VirtualAlloc()`
LPVOID	lpMinimumApplicationAddress	Lowest memory accessible by applications
LPVOID	lpMaximumApplicationAddress	Highest memory accessible by applications
DWORD	dwActiveProcessMark	Mask of configured processors
DWORD	dwNumberOfProcessors	Number of processors
DWORD	dwProcessorType	Obsolete (backward compatibility)
DWORD	dwAllocationGranularity	Memory allocation granularity with `VirtualAlloc()`.
WORD	wProcessorLevel	Architecture-dependent processor level
WORD	wProcessorRevision	Architecture-dependent processor revision

Figure 8-14: The `SYSTEM_INFO` structure.

The field `dwPageSize` indicates the size of a page on that system (either 1KB or 4KB). `dwAllocationGranularity` is the minimum allocation size returned by `VirtualAlloc()`. The other members are not of interest regarding memory management.

The Remote Heap Walker Utility

An application's heaps (local and supplemental) can be scrutinized at run-time by using the Remote Heap Walker utility, as shown in Figure 8-15.

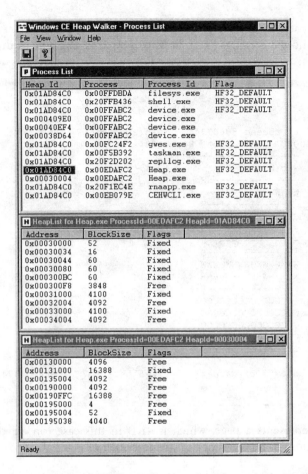

Figure 8-15: The Remote Heap Walker utility reveals all heaps in the system.

In this example, the application "Heap.exe" uses two heaps. The first one (highlighted) is the local heap, as indicated by the flag HF32_DEFAULT in the right column. The entry that follows (whose identifier is 0x00030004) is a supplemental heap.

By double clicking on each entry, each heap is exploded in its own window: the middle window details the local heap, whereas the bottom window reveals the supplemental heap. One can note that although the Heap application does not use its local heap directly, the system still allocated some memory out of it to execute other system calls.

Memory Information through CESH

Finally, the CESH utility provides some very valuable information about the system memory. The command mi full (memory information, full) dumps a map of all running processes' address space. By analyzing the one related to your process, you can have an exact snapshot of the memory it is using. The following is a partial example of that command:

```
Windows CE> mi full

. . .

Memory usage for Process 80607344: 'Heap.exe' pid 7
Slot base 10000000  Section ptr 80ec1000
   10000000(1): -----r----------
   10010000(0): -ccrWW-
   10020000(0): --------------SS
   10030000(0): WWWWW-----------
   10090000(0): --------------S
   100a0000(0): --------------S
   10100000(0): --------------S
   10110000(0): --------------S
   10120000(0): --------------S
   10130000(0): WWWWWWWWWWWWWWWW
   10190000(0): W----W----------
   101a0000(0): ----------------
   11aa0000(0): -CCCCCCCCCCCCCCC
   11ab0000(0): CCCCCCCCCCCCCCCC
   11ac0000(0): CCCCCCCCCCCCCCCC
   11ad0000(0): CCCCCCCCWrrrrrrr
   11ae0000(0): rrrrrrrrrrrrrrr
   11af0000(0): --
Page summary: code=57(2) data r/o=0 r/w=51 stack=7 reserved=374

. . .
```

Each symbol represents a page, which is 4KB in this case (on an x86). The symbols indicating how memory pages are allocated are described in Figure 8-16:

Symbol	Description
C	Code page, in ROM
R	Read-only page, in ROM
c	Code page, in RAM
W	Read-write page, in RAM
r	Read-only page, in RAM
S	Stack page
O	Object Store
P	Pending commit
–	Reserved, ready for commitment

Figure 8-16: Symbols representing page allocation in CESH.

In this example, the page summary indicates that the application has consumed the following:

- 57 pages of code, of which two are from the application's code, the rest from the system DLLs (*e.g.,* COREDLL.DLL);

- 51 pages of data. The summary groups all data pages together (read-only and read-write).

- 7 pages for stacks: two for the primary thread and one for each supplemental thread.

- 374 pages are reserved for the application (stack and heap space). The map does not show all reserved pages, though.

This example illustrates the memory map of a multithreaded application called "Heap", which uses an extra heap. We can immediately notice that five extra stacks have been allocated (one per thread) in the address range of 0x10090000 to 0x10130000. Interestingly enough, each of these stacks is limited to 64KB (the default), since they don't have room to expand beyond (they would spill over other memory pages otherwise).

Using the Heap Walker utility, one can notice that the local heap starts at 0x10030000, and the supplemental heap at 0x10130000.

8.3.4 Dealing with Low Memory Conditions

Embedded developers are very accustomed to saving space by whatever means they can think of. On the other hand, programmers with a desktop programming background are not used to concentrating on these issues.

What to do when memory is short largely depends on your target device and the environment in which your applications will run. Let's explore what can be done to reduce memory needs.

- Review the map file and the output of the Dumpbin utility to determine if moving data from one section to another can improve memory usage (by using full pages instead of partial ones).

- Move as much data as possible into the read-only section. Read-only pages can be easily discarded by Windows CE when memory is short. This is not the case for read-write data pages, which must stay in memory.

- When working with data files, load them only when needed, and write the data back as soon as possible. When the data is not used, your application has more memory to work with.

- Large amounts of data can be saved into temporary files (which are compressed in the Object Store), and loaded only when needed.

- Resist using too many bitmaps, and implement your own compression-decompression scheme.

- Use `GlobalMemoryStatus()` and `GetStoreInformation()` to determine the availability of the program area and the Object Store respectively. This helps identify potential problems; the application can warn the user about it, which may make more room.

- Process the `WM_HIBERNATE` message, which is received when Windows CE detects a low memory condition.

- During development, keep an eye on the dynamic memory needs to detect unusually large amounts of data or memory leaks (heap data not released).

SUGGESTED READING

Microsoft, Windows CE Programmer's Guide

> Chapter 29 is called "Writing Memory-Efficient Applications" and provides tips to make your applications thinner.

Pietrek Mark, "Peering Inside the PE: A Tour of the Win32 Portable Executable File Format"
> Mark Pietrek is well known for providing "under the hood" information. This article details the Win32 PE file format, and provides detailed explanations about sections. He also included the source of `PEDUMP.EXE`, a program that dumps more information that `DUMPBIN.EXE` regarding PE and OBJ files

Pietrek Mark, "Remove Fatty Deposits from your Applications Using Our 32-bit Liposuction Tools"

> In this article, Pietrek provides various tips to reduce the application's appetite for memory. He also provides a program called `LIPO32` that analyzes PE executables and reports their fitness.

Chapter 9

Graphics, Windowing, and Events Subsystem

The Graphics, Windowing and Events Subsystem (GWES) manages the interaction with the user. Specifically, it controls the following functionality:

- Windowing: window-management activities, such as creating windows, moving them, etc.
- Events: managing the message-based interaction among windows.
- Graphics: all graphical operations, such as managing device contexts, drawings, etc.

The GWES can be fairly large because that triple functionality includes a lot of code. The Windows CE designers recognized the situation and made sure that this module would be highly componentized: you can include just what you need, and keep the size of your system in check (Chapter 6 explores system configuration in detail).

Because this subsystem interacts with the user, efficiency was not only a requirement: it was primordial. Given the context CE is used for (memory-constrained devices), much of the graphical functionality found on larger Windows systems (9x and NT) could not be simply brought in; it had to be smaller and simplified. Non-essential functionality, such as non-client messages, has simply been discarded. This helped producing a leaner, smaller and faster graphical engine. In order to eliminate extra threads and layers, user input drivers (e.g., keyboard, touch screen) have been merged within the GWES process, instead of being run in separate processes.

Above all, the designers had to stay in line with the trend of following as closely as possible the Win32 API. The final result is a system that carries a subset of what is found on NT, and that is well understood by Windows developers.

195

This chapter reviews the core features of the user interface. The API implemented in this module is so vast that it is not presented in this chapter, but rather in Part IV, over multiple chapters, using object-oriented libraries.

9.1 WINDOWING

It's no big mystery that a Windows operating system is about managing windows. What is less obvious though, is what the term "window" encompasses. Everybody is familiar with a traditional window, such as the one shown in Figure 9-1-a. A CE window, such as the one depicted, typically has a command bar (new to CE) which combines a menu and a toolbar. It also includes the client area, *i.e.*, the area where the application's data is displayed. Some applications may also display a title bar, above the command bar, displaying the application name. But such a window turns out to be the parent of many other, smaller windows.

Consider the command bar buttons of an application. Although they appear as small push buttons, they are internally handled as windows, with their own properties. One of those properties is to be a *child window*, that is, to belong to a parent window, such as an application main window or a dialog box. This parent-child relationship is an important concept in Windows CE, as we will explore later. Suffice it to say at this point that child windows are also called *controls*. Examples of controls are illustrated in Figure 9-1-b.

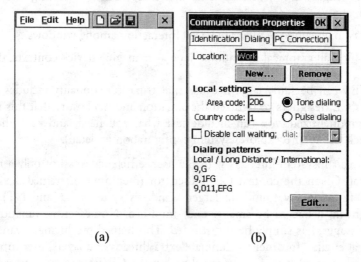

(a)   (b)

Figure 9.1: A plain application window (a), and one with a few controls, such as buttons (b)

Windowing refers to the management of all these windows and controls: creation and destruction, moving and resizing, painting, responding to events, and so forth. Given the broad definition of the term "window", windowing implies a very rich functionality indeed.

9.1.1 Event-Driven Programming

Graphical programs are quite different than console applications (also called text-based) commonly found on MS-DOS, Unix, OpenVMS, etc. Graphical programs display many input controls on the screen: radio buttons, check boxes, push buttons, lists, edit fields, etc. The user can usually select anyone of them and perform an action on it (click on it, enter text, etc.) Such an action results in an *event* being delivered to the application (more on this later). Furthermore, other events the application is looking for can take place: mouse movements, keystrokes, redrawing the entire client area surface, etc. What is common with these events is their order, or the lack thereof: they are all random. Any event can be delivered at any time, and an application must respond to them in the order they have been received. Consequently, Windows applications are labeled "event-driven". This is very different from a console application, that usually offers one selectable action at a time, such as reading from the keyboard ("Press ENTER to continue...").

9.1.2 Window Procedures

In order to be notified of these events, Windows CE sends *messages* to each application in response to the events that take place. For instance, when the user clicks a push button, CE creates a message (no more than a simple data structure) and sends it to the application. The word "send" is abstract: it means that CE calls a specific function in the application to process the message. Because this function is defined in the application, but called by Windows CE, that type of function is dubbed a *callback procedure* (*i.e.,* called back by CE). Each window has a callback function, defined as follows:

```
LRESULT CALLBACK WndProc(          // LRESULT is long, CALLBACK is __stdcall
    HWND hWnd,                     // Window this message is targeted to
    UINT uMsg,                     // Message identifier
    WPARAM wParam,                 // 1st message-dependent parameter
    LPARAM lParam)                 // 2nd message-dependent parameter
{
    ...
}
```

Window procedures are often called *Window Proc*, or *WndProc* for short[24]. This procedure is really a function, since it returns a value.

---

[24] WndProc() is usually the name programmers retain to name that procedure.

The message data structure created by Windows CE is translated into generic parameters to the callback procedure (see Figure 9-2), which is called to process any message the window receives. One of these parameters is the message identifier (messages are numbered individually). For instance, the "left button down" mouse message is WM_LBUTTONDOWN (0x0201). As a result, the procedure is implemented as a big switch statement (when coded in C or C++). The larger the application is, the longer and complex the switch is.

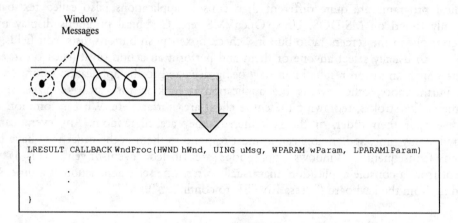

Figure 9-2: Messages are broken up and passed as arguments to window procedures

Applications only have to process messages of interest to them (*e.g.*, mouse movements and painting, to name a few), although unprocessed messages must be passed back to Windows. This is done by calling DefWndProc(), which internally handles these unwanted messages. The following illustrates the use of that function:

```
LRESULT CALLBACK WndProc(HWND hWnd, UINT uMsg,
WPARAM wParam, LPARAM lParam)
{
    switch (uMsg)
    {
    case WM_PAINT:                          // Process WM_PAINT
        . . .                               // Paint something
            return 0;

    case WM_DESTROY:                        // Process WM_DESTROY
            PostQuitMessage(0);
            return 0;
    }

    // Unwanted message come here: back to Windows for default processing
    return DefWindowProc(hWnd, uMsg, wParam, lParam);
}
```

Message passing is a core feature of the Windows operating system. All window activities, even non-graphical ones (*e.g.*, timers), take place with messages.

9.1.3 More About Windows

Windows' behavior is governed by the window procedure. But a window has other important attributes that directly impact its appearance and reactions: its class and style.

Classes

Windows are created based on some window templates, called *window classes*. The name *class* is misleading. Class here does not refer to any object-oriented concept (such as a C++ class). A better name would be *category*. The name had been introduced long before object-oriented languages became popular.

A window class defines the skeleton of a window implementation and is implemented using a WNDCLASS structure (see Figure 9-3)

Type	Field	Description
UINT	style	Class style e.g. if double-clicks are sent to the window, whether the window is repainted when resized, etc. These styles mostly affect the behavior of the window.
WNDPROC	lpfnWndProc	The address of a window procedure (i.e. the *WindowProc*)
int	cbClsExtra	Number of extra bytes to allocate following the window class structure.
int	cbWndExtra	Number of extra bytes to allocate following the window structure.
HANDLE	hInstance	Application instance
HICON	hIcon	Application icon
HCURSOR	hCursor	Application cursor
HBRUSH	hbrBackground	Application background color
LPCTSTR	lpszMenuName	Menu identifier
LPCTSTR	lpszClassName	Name of this class.

Figure 9-3: The WNDCLASS structure defines a window class.

Applications create their own classes by initializing a WNDCLASS structure and passing it to RegisterClass(). This function registers the class inside CE, but does not create any window. When writing C applications, developers always create their own class and their own window procedure when writing a new application. The following typical example registers a window class and uses it to create the application window:

```
LRESULT CALLBACK WndProc(HWND, UINT, WPARAM, LPARAM);

int WINAPI WinMain(HINSTANCE hInstance, HINSTANCE hPrevInstance,
    LPTSTR pszCmdLine, int nCmdShow)
{
    MSG             msg;
    WNDCLASS        wc;
    HWND            hWnd;

    // Register a class
    wc.style          = CS_HREDRAW | CS_VREDRAW;
    wc.lpfnWndProc    = WndProc;
    wc.cbClsExtra     = 0;
    wc.cbWndExtra     = 0;
    hInstance         = hInstance;
    wc.hIcon          = 0;
    wc.hCursor        = NULL;
    wc.hbrBackground  = (HBRUSH) GetStockObject(WHITE_BRUSH);
    wc.lpszMenuName   = NULL;
    wc.lpszClassName  = TEXT("MyClass");

    RegisterClass(&wc);

    // Create the main application window, using the registered class.
    hWnd = CreateWindow(TEXT("MyClass"), TEXT("App"), WS_VISIBLE, 0, 0,
            CW_USEDEFAULT, CW_USEDEFAULT, NULL, NULL, hInstance, NULL);

    // Pump and dispatch messages to windows.
    . . .

    return msg.wParam;              // wParam is the exit code.
}
```

Upon creation, a window inherits all the attributes of the specified class. Perhaps the most important attribute is the window procedure, which determines how the window is going to process messages. What is interesting is that multiple windows can be created based on the same class, and therefore inherit the same window procedure. If you remember the window procedure prototype, the first parameter is a window handle. Since multiple windows can be managed by the same window procedure, Windows makes sure that the handle refers to the proper window whenever the window procedure is called. Let's take an example to illustrate that concept. Consider two push buttons, labeled OK and Cancel. Whenever the user clicks on OK, a message (WM_LBUTTONDOWN) is sent to the OK button. The push button's window procedure (within Windows) is invoked. Whatever processing that takes places uses hWnd, which is the handle of the OK button in this case. If the user clicks Cancel, the same processing take place (in the same window procedure), but using the Cancel button handle instead.

Several predefined classes already exist within Windows; Figure 9-4 lists a few. Application programmers use them profusely, giving their applications a standard Windows look and feel. For instance, creating a window based on the "BUTTON" class creates a standard button, familiar to all users. These predefined classes rely on multiple window procedures, already within Windows. For instance, the "STATIC" class refers to the window procedures that implement static controls. As a result, programmers can use standard windows and controls with very little coding.

Class	Description
BUTTON	Push button, radio button, check box button, groupbox
STATIC	Text, frames, images
SCROLLBAR	Vertical or horizontal
EDIT	To display or enter text
LISTBOX	To list a series of values

Figure 9-4: A few control classes. These classes are the original controls, introduced with the first release of Windows. Starting with Windows 95, new controls have been added.

Style Attributes

A window can have a different appearance and behavior than the other windows based on the same class by having a different *style*. Each window has a style attribute associated with it. It is a 32-bit value, where each bit controls a specific attribute. Consider all the buttons supported in Windows: check boxes, radio buttons, and push buttons. They are all based on the same window class: "BUTTON". Nonetheless, each of them has a unique attribute set, which makes them appear and behave differently. Figure 9-5 lists a few button-specific style attributes.

Style	Description
BS_AUTORADIOBUTTON	Creates a radio button, except that when the user selects it, all other buttons in the same group become unselected.
BS_CHECKBOX	Creates a check box button.
BS_ICON	Specifies that the button displays an icon instead of text.
BS_OWNERDRAW	Creates an owner-drawn button that is, a button drawn by the application.
BS_PUSHBUTTON	Creates a push button.
BS_RADIOBUTTON	Creates a radio button.

Figure 9-5: A few button attributes.

A few styles are more generic, and can be equally applied to windows and controls. For instance, WS_VISIBLE makes the window visible (when set) or invisible (when unset). Window styles are explored in Chapter 15.

These attributes are specified when a window is created, and they can later be changed by calling `SetWindowLong()`. For instance, to ensure a window is visible, an application can first obtain the current style by calling `GetWindowLong()` and then update the style, as shown in the following example:

```
DWORD dwStyle;

dwStyle = GetWindowLong(hWnd, GWL_STYLE);      // Get current style
dwStyle |= WS_VISIBLE;                          // Set visible on
SetWindowLong(hWnd, GWL_STYLE, dwStyle);        // Set current style
```

`SetWindowLong()` can also be called later to change other attributes (such as the window procedure).

As mentioned earlier, the style is a 32-bit value. Because Windows designers eventually ran out of style bits, they introduced an extended 32-bit style attribute. Extended attributes are specified upon creation too, via `CreateWindowEx()`. They can also be updated through `SetWindowLong()`, but using the `GWL_EXSTYLE` parameter instead of `GWL_STYLE`. Figure 9-6 lists a few extended style attributes that are supported on CE:

Style	Description
WS_EX_CLIENTEDGE	The window has a border with a sunken edge.
WS_EX_NOACTIVATE	The window cannot be activated nor receive the focus.
WS_EX_NOANIMATION	Does not show animated exploding and imploding rectangle and does not have a button in the taskbar.
WS_EX_STATICEDGE	The window has a three-dimensional border that indicates that it does not accept user input.
WS_EX_WINDOWEDGE	The window has a border with a raised edge.

Figure 9-6: A few common extended window style attributes

9.1.4 Dialog Boxes

Dialog boxes are another type of window. The main advantage over plain windows is that their appearance is built using a graphical dialog box editor, such as the one provided with Visual C++. This method simply requires dragging controls in various positions, making it trivial to align and size them. This is much easier than using plain windows, whose controls must be explicitly created with hard-coded positions and sizes, requiring numerous attempts to achieve the desired layout.

Dialog boxes are created, displayed, run, and destroyed by a dialog manager within the GWES. As a result, using dialog boxes is fairly straightforward from an application standpoint. This contrasts with a normal window, which muct be explicitly created, along a new class (in some cases) and all its controls.

There are two types of dialog boxes: modal and modeless. A modal dialog box is displayed on top of the application, and must be closed for the application to continue to run. As long as the dialog box is shown, the application is "frozen". This is useful to stop whatever processing that is taking place in order to gather some information from the user. An example is a "File Open" dialog box, which requires a filename to go further. On the other hand, a modeless dialog box runs in parallel with the application. The programmer must explicitly create and destroy the dialog box, although its controls are automatically created. The typical example of a modeless dialog box is a "Find and Replace" dialog box in a word processor. Dialog boxes, both modal and modeless, are explored in detail in Chapter 18.

Message boxes are a variant of the dialog boxes. They display an icon, a message, and a few standard buttons, such as OK/Cancel, or Yes/No/Cancel. Message boxes are very easy to use (see Chapter 18 for details), as they are also created, displayed and destroyed by the GWES.

9.1.5   Controls are Windows

Controls (or child windows) are windows and also are message-based. Likewise, they are internally implemented through `switch` statements. In fact, apart from their appearance and a few properties, controls are not much different that application windows. From a programming standpoint, they are essentially the same: they react to messages. What makes a control different than an application window is that the former belongs to the latter. When you move an application window, all the child controls it contains automatically move in it as well. Child controls also have a unique identifier within their parent window. The exact value of an id is not important, as long as it is unique within a window.

There is a parent-child relationship between an application window (the parent) and the controls (the children), as shown in Figure 9-7. And to be consistent with the nature of Windows, that relationship is based on messages (what else?).

When a button control is clicked upon, the button (not the application window) receives the `WM_LBUTTONDOWN` message. The button redraws – or repaints, in the Windows terminology – itself with a "pushed down" look, to provide some feedback to the user that it has been clicked upon. Then, the button sends the `BN_CLICKED` *notification* – a child control message for "button clicked" – to its parent window, the application main window. That window then takes action upon that notification. For instance, if the button is labeled *Print*, the window can show another window asking for the print parameters (number of copies, etc.) As far as the application window is concerned, the button notification is just another message to be processed in the `switch` statement. When the parent window receives a notification, the control id bundled within identifies who sent it. Hence, using the id, the parent may know if the BN_CLICKED notification has been sent by the *Print* button, or the *OK* button, etc.

The parent also sends messages to its child controls whenever it has to do so. For example, to add a string is a list box control, a parent sends an "add string" message to the list box.

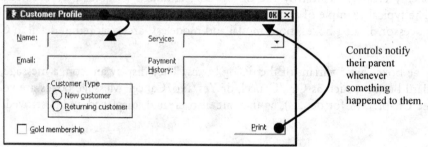

Figure 9-7: Parent-child relationship: when a control is clicked upon, it notifies its parent. The parent can also send messages to a control to alter its appearance (such as changing its text).

Although clicking a button seems to generate a lot of work, this approach is very advantageous. First, it must be recognized that the "dirty work" of sending messages and receiving them is all handled internally by Windows. Also, because each control has a well-defined interface (the messages it sends and processes), each control/window can be developed independently. Finally, because messages can be sent and received by any window or control, it is easy to mix-and-match them together, like Lego blocks[25]. For instance, if you develop your own control, say a round button, you can easily reuse it in many of your future applications with little coding effort. Documentation is the key here: it is important to know what messages are processed and what messages are sent under what circumstances.

Besides, this is a true object-oriented approach, right in the guts of Windows CE. To make programming even better, application programming languages such C++ (detailed in Part IV) add other object-oriented layers of functionality. Chapters 19 and 20 review each control and explain how to use them.

---

[25] This does <u>not</u> intend to imply that developing Windows applications is child's play!

9.1.6   Console Applications

The first releases of Windows CE only supported graphical applications. However, because numerous developers (especially those that have been involved in embedded system development for years) are not necessarily familiar with these windowing concepts, the GWES provided with Windows CE 2.1 introduced support for console, text-based applications. MS-DOS and Unix developers will be delighted to read that the good old stdio functions (*e.g.,* printf(), gets(), etc.) are readily available, in plain ASCII.

There is also a command-line utility, called CMD.EXE (see Figure 9-8), that provides basic command shell capabilities, more in line with MS-DOS's COMMAND.COM. Command-line fans will hence feel at home with CE.

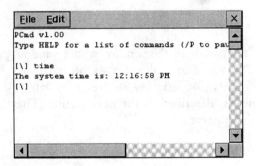

Figure 9-8: Windows CE includes a command line utility called CMD.EXE.

9.2   EVENT MANAGER

It cannot be overstated that message passing is the core processing of the user interface on any Windows operating system. Paradoxically, Windows CE can be configured not to include any user interface components (imagine a system connected to various sensors that output ASCII HTML pages). Hence, all user interface components of such a system could be eliminated, resulting a smaller CE system which would not require message passing!

But systems that implement user interfaces – most Windows applications in fact – must rely on message passing to achieve the adequate responsiveness users expect from any Windows system, big or small.

An event is either a message or a thread synchronization object that changes state. Both are managed by the event manager, within the GWES. Messages are explained below, and synchronization objects are explained in Chapter 7.

9.2.1 Messages

A message is an `MSG` structure that describes an event. That data structure is defined as follows:

Type	Field	Description
HWND	hWnd	Target window handle
UINT	message	Message identifier
WPARAM	wParam	First generic parameter
LPARAM	lParam	Second generic parameter
DWORD	time	Time when this message was sent/posted
POINT	pt	Cursor position

Figure 9-9: The `MSG` structure.

The `hWnd` handle is the handle of the window whose window procedure is invoked to process the message. The `message` identifier is an unsigned 32-bit integer, usually represented by some constants (for instance, `WM_HELP` is 0x0053). `wParam` and `lParam` are 32-bit generic parameters, described in the next section. The `time` and `pt` fields are usually of no interest to the applications.

Message Parameters

The names `wParam` and `lParam` originate from older Windows systems. `wParam` was then a 16-bit `WORD` value, whereas `lParam` was (and still is) a 32-bit `LONG` value. In CE, both are 32-bit values.

The exact content of `wParam` and `lParam` is message-dependent. Let's take the case of `WM_KEYDOWN`, which is sent to the window with the focus when a non-system key is pressed. The `wParam` parameter is a virtual key code (*e.g.*, `VK_F1` for the F1 key), whereas `lParam` contains some flags encoded in 32-bit (repeat count, scan code, etc.). Sometimes, one or both parameters are irrelevant. For instance, `WM_CLOSE` (sent when an application should terminate) has no parameter, whereas `WM_PAINT` (sent when an application should redraw itself) only contains one meaningful parameter (`wParam`). In other circumstances, the parameters are pointers to a variable-size data structure. With the `LVM_ITEMCHANGING` message, sent from a view control to its parent when one of its items is changing, `lParam` is a pointer to an `NMLISTVIEW` structure, defined in Windows (and `wParam` is undefined).

Hence, processing each message requires understanding what parameters are relevant and what they contain. Windows itself does not assist in analyzing messages, but some application programming languages do. Needless to say, processing a message requires double-checking the exact meaning of `wParam` and `lParam`.

Message Classification

Messages can be classified into two general categories:

- System messages, defined in the range of 0 to 0x3ff. There are more than 700 system messages (including control notifications) in Windows CE.

- User-defined messages, defined in the range 0x400 to 0x7fff. User-defined messages are not interpreted by the system and are not passed back to `DefWindowProc()`. Be careful to choose unique message identifiers to avoid potential message mismatches within an application. The function `RegisterWindowMessage()` can be used to obtain a system-wide unique message id.

One never uses the identifiers directly (*e.g.,* 0x402). Windows headers files are provided with development tools (*e.g.,* `Windows.h` with Visual C++) that define symbols that are easier to remember (*e.g.,* `WM_CREATE`, `WM_MOUSEMOVE`, etc.)

System messages are divided into about 40 categories. Each category has its own acronym (*e.g.,* `BN` for <u>b</u>utton <u>n</u>otification). These acronyms are prefixed to messages. For instance, the button click notification is `BN_CLICKED`. Figure 9-10 lists all message prefixes.

Prefix	Description
BM	Button message
BN	Button notification
CB	Combo box message
CBN	Combo box notification
CDM	Common dialog box message
CDN	common dialog box notification
CPL	Control panel message
DB	Object store message
DM	Dialog box default push button message
DTM	Date time picker and HTM viewer message
DTN	Date time picker notification
EM	Edit control message
EN	Edit control notification
HDM	Header control message
HDN	Header control notification
IMN	Input context message
LB	List box control message
LBN	List box control notification
LINE	Line device message
LVM	List view message
LVN	List view notification
MCM	Month calendar message
MCN	Month calendar notification

NM	General notification message
PBM	Progress bar message
PSM	Property sheet message
PSN	Property sheet notification
RB	Rebar message
RBN	Rebar notification
SB	Status bar message
SBM	Scroll bar message
STM	Static bar message
STN	Static bar notification
TB	Toolbar message
TBM	Trackbar message
TBN	Trackbar notification
TCM	Tab control message
TCN	Tab control notification
TVM	Tree view message
TVN	Tree view notification
UDM	Up-down control message
UDN	Up-down control notification
UM	General user-defined message
WM	General window message

Figure 9-10: Message prefixes

9.2.2 Message Queue

Every thread that creates one or more application windows (or control), that is, every thread that calls CreateWindow() or CreateWindowEx(), has a private message queue to receive messages (see Figure 9-11). A thread will not receive any message for a window it did not create itself.

Because of the event-driven nature of Windows programming, the message queue must be periodically queried. The core of the application consists of a main loop that gets and processes messages. This loop is often referred to as the *message pump*. If messages are not pumped, an application will appear to be "frozen" and will not respond to user interaction.

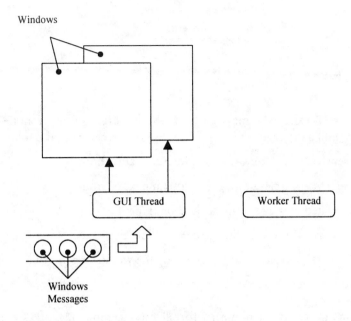

Windows

GUI Thread

Worker Thread

Windows
Messages

Figure 9-11: Each thread that creates windows has its own message queue. Threads that do not create windows do not have a message queue.

In a single-threaded application, WinMain() contains the message loop. In a multithreaded application, any thread that creates a window must also contain a message loop.

Message Loops

Here's a typical message loop in WinMain(), the heart of a Windows CE application:

```
int WINAPI WinMain(HINSTANCE hInstance, HINSTANCE hPrevInstance,
    LPTSTR pszCmdLine, int nCmdShow)
{
    MSG             msg;

    // Register a class
    . . .

    // Create the main application window
    . . .

    // Pump messages
    while (GetMessage(&msg, NULL, 0, 0))
            if (!TranslateAccelerator(hWnd, hAccel, &msg))
```

```
        {
                TranslateMessage(&msg);
                DispatchMessage(&msg);
        }

    return msg.wParam;              // wParam is the exit code.
}
```

GetMessage() extracts a message from the message queue. If none are there, the function blocks until a message is received. Messages are received in the following order:

1. Messages sent via SendMessage() (more in next section)

2. Messages sent via PostMessage() (more in next section)

3. User input-related messages (mouse, keyboard, pen)

4. WM_QUIT message (placed in the queue by calling PostQuitMessage())

5. WM_PAINT messages (placed in the queue by the windowing system)

6. WM_TIMER messages (placed in the queue by the timer system)

GetMessage() returns a non-zero for all messages but WM_QUIT, in which case it returns zero and ends the loop. TranslateAccelerator() and Translate Message() are two functions that filter some messages in order to simplify their processing. These functions are discussed later. Finally, DispatchMessage() takes a message and invokes the related window's callback window procedure. Since an application can create more than one window, DispatchMessage() redirects messages to various windows. Figure 9-12 illustrates message processing from an application's standpoint.

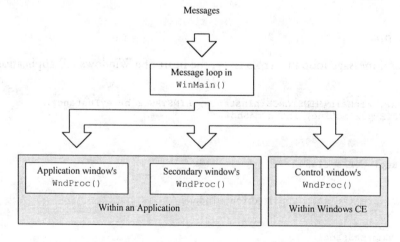

Figure 9-12: An application's main loop receives messages and distributes them to the proper window procedure, either within the applications or within Windows.

Such a message loop is extremely common. In fact, all C-based programs are based on it, although some don't call `TranslateAccelerator()`.

Posting vs. Sending a Message

Messages can either be posted or sent. Posting a message is done by calling `PostMessage()` and consists of adding the message to the target window's message queue. `PostMessage()` does not wait for that message to be processed; it simply deposits the messages in the queue and returns immediately. The message will eventually be processed by the target window procedure. Posting is useful to simply notify a window of an event. For instance, consider when you use the Windows Explorer and you single-click on a directory name on the left panel. That tree view control may post a message to its parent (the main application window) to let it know that the right panel does have to be refreshed. But this doesn't have to happen *now*, especially if other messages are already in the queue in order to be processed. Once the message is posted (but not necessarily processed by the target window), the sender continues to execute.

Sending a message is achieved via `SendMessage()`. This call adds the message in the message queue of the thread that created the target window, and waits until the message is processed. Sending is useful when a notification must be processed immediately. Reconsider the Windows Explorer example. When the user expands a directory (by clicking the [+] next to the directory name, the tree control must *immediately* display the subdirectory names. For arbitrary design considerations, obtaining the list of directories might be implemented in the parent window (*i.e.*, the application window, which also manages the directory content on the right panel). Hence, the view control must query the application window *at once* in order to expand itself and show the subdirectories. By sending a message, the tree view control will be blocked until the message is processed by the parent. Assuming the parent processes the message by inserting items in the tree view, the control can safely assume that the data has been inserted when `SendMessage()` returns.

Both functions take the same arguments: the handle of the window the message is sent to, a message identifier (system- or user-defined), and `wParam` and `lParam` (both message-dependent).

Control Notifications

If you were unfamiliar with the messaging aspect of Windows, you might be surprised by the number of messages that are sent from one window to another when using an application. Section 9.1.5 explained how a button notifies its parent window when it is clicked upon. The same strategy is used by all controls to communicate with their parents.

In earlier versions of Windows, there were only six predefined controls (static controls, buttons, edit controls, list boxes, and scrollbars). These controls send notifications through

WM_COMMAND messages, storing in wParam both the notification code and the control's own identifier, and the control's own handle in lParam. This used to be adequate, except when additional information had to be sent. For instance, a scroll bar needs to specify by how much it has been scrolled and in what direction. Since there are only a few situations requiring passing more information, the chosen solution consisted of introducing new messages, namely WM_VSCROLL and WM_HSCROLL, to allow passing that extra information in wParam and lParam. These controls still work that way under CE for Win32 compatibility reasons.

But with the introduction of the common controls with Windows 95 (list view, tree view, spin controls, etc.), using additional messages would have become a burden. These controls were fancier and had more things to say more often to their parent. Since a unified, generic message was desired over a myriad of new messages, WM_NOTIFY was introduced as the solution. With this message, wParam holds the control's own identifier and lParam is a pointer to NMHDR structure. That structure is defined as follows:

Type	Field	Description
HWND	hwndFrom	Control handle
UINT	idFrom	Control Id
UINT	code	Notification code

Figure 9-13: The NMHDR structure

In fact, the common controls use lParam as a pointer to a control-defined structure, whose first element is NMHDR. Using specific structures allows controls passing as much information as required. Consider the NMLVKEYDOWN structure that is passed by a list view control to its parent when it detects that a key has been pressed:

Type	Field	Description
NMHDR	hdr	General notification data
WORD	wKey	Virtual key code
UINT	flags	Flags

Figure 9-14: The NMLVKEYDOWN structure. Note the first element, an NMHDR structure. All other items are specific to that structure.

The parent can safely use lParam as a pointer to an NMHDR structure, since <u>all</u> notification messages have NMHDR as their first member. Based on the notification code in NMHDR, the parent can determine the exact structure type and interpret it accordingly.

To summarize, some notifications rely on WM_COMMAND, others use a few WM specific messages and finally, others send WM_NOTIFY messages. New controls will certainly use

WM_NOTIFY. If you develop your own custom control, make sure all your notifications are done through WM_NOTIFY for increased flexibility. Custom controls are discussed in Chapter 20.

User Input System

The user interacts with an application using input devices: keyboard, mouse, pens, or voice. These devices are controlled by their respective device drivers, actually managed by the GWES system. These drivers work hand in hand with the GWES to send events (messages) to applications.

For instance, when the user taps on a window with a pen, the window ultimately receives a WM_LBUTTONDOWN message. Internally, the touch video driver detected the tap and notified the GWES, which stored the message in the message queue of the thread that created the window. That's a lot of action, but from an application standpoint, only a simple message is received. The same processing occurs with the keyboard and the mouse. There, an input thread within the GWES runs the drivers, which results in various messages being posted to applications.

Keyboard input is sent to the window that has the focus, generally a control, within the foreground application. The control with the focus identifies itself with a fine dotted line. The focus is usually moved by clicking on another control or, in a dialog box, by pressing the Tab key. Mouse events are sent to the window under the mouse. Hence, tapping on a window internally involves the user input thread (to run the touch video device driver) and the window manager (to identify the window that has been tapped upon).

9.3 GRAPHICS

Drawings are handled by functions commonly referred to as the Graphical Device Interface (GDI)[26]. These functions can arbitrarily be grouped in the following categories:

- Device contexts
- GDI objects: bitmaps, brushes, fonts, palettes, pens, and regions
- Drawing and printing primitives: rectangles, ellipses, text, etc.

The following paragraphs summarize those items, whereas Part IV describes how to use them in details.

---

[26] In other Windows operating systems, these functions are implemented in a DLL called GDI.EXE. In CE, they are all part of GWES.EXE.

9.3.1 Device Contexts

Device contexts are the heart of the graphics model within CE. A device context can be seen as a drawing board that applications use for rendering graphics. Internally, the drawing board is output on a screen or on a printer, through the relevant driver (see Figure 9-15).

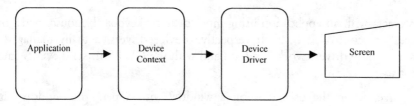

Figure 9-15: An application draws on a device context, whose output is sent to a device through the proper device driver.

Windows CE supports as many device contexts as required, limited only by the available memory. Applications typically use only one device context, but some may use many to speed graphics rendering.

Device contexts have many attributes that are used implicitly with graphics primitives. Applications must first set the device context and then invoke these primitives. Not doing so would require specifying too many parameters for each primitive.

9.3.2 GDI Objects

The GDI supports six types of objects to perform drawing operations:

- **Pens** are used for drawing individual lines and the outline of shapes. In the latter case, pens can be null to prevent drawing the outline.

- **Brushes** fills the interior of shapes. For instance, to draw a red rectangle, one must create a red brush, select it in the device context and call the `Rectangle()` primitive.

- **Fonts** designates the glyphs to output text (note that pens are not used for text). Windows CE supports raster and TrueType fonts, but one a time. Specifically, fonts are implemented in two different font modules (`mgrast`, for raster fonts, and `mgtt`, for TrueType fonts), where each module implements the same font API. Hence only one module can be used in a given Windows CE configuration, because using both would generate "duplicate symbol" errors. Since applications simply rely on the API, using one font type or another (that is, using one font module or another) makes no difference from a programming standpoint.

- **Regions** are rectangular areas that can be combined with each other, used for controlling the appearance of special shapes.

214

- **Palettes** allow an application to manage colors on a device with a limited number of colors. For instance, some devices can display 256 colors, but only 16 at a time. By using palettes, applications can control the 16 colors being used.

- **Bitmaps** are a binary representation of images. They are objects because they are intimate with some device contexts. For instance, when creating a memory device context, one must select a bitmap of a certain width, height, and depth to adjust the memory device context accordingly.

These GDI objects are used with graphic primitives in order to render graphics. For instance, to draw a line, one must create a pen carrying the desired attribute (thickness, color), select it in the device context, and call a primitive that draws a line on the device context.

Because objects are used by many primitives, selecting an object in the device context simplifies the call to these primitives. For instance, by selecting a red pen, an application can output a red line and a rectangle with red edges, without having to specify the red pen explicitly each time.

9.3.3 Drawing Primitives

The drawing primitives can be invoked once a device context's attributes have been set to application-defined values. There are a few primitives, which can be categorized as follows:

- Lines and curves
- Shapes (rectangle, ellipse, etc.)
- Images (bitmaps, icons)
- Text

    These graphics primitives are easier to use with Microsoft Foundation Class (MFC), and are detailed in Chapter 16.

9.4 OTHER FUNCTIONS

Besides managing graphics, windows and events, the GWES also provides other important functions:

- It keeps track of the amount of time the system has been running, and shuts off the device after three minutes of idle time.

- It displays the out-of-memory dialog box when the system memory becomes low.

- It displays the optional startup screen.

- It contains the code to calibrate the screen (the video driver is incorporated within the GWES).

- And others.

As mentioned at the beginning of the chapter, the GWES is highly componentized. For instance, the window manager can be reduced to very simple configuration, just enough to create windows, pass them messages, but without any graphical support; just event handlers. This is useful to implement window timers for instance. These timers require a message queue and a window procedure to be processed. Using window core functionality (message queue and window proc) is all it takes to support them.

SUGGESTED READING

Inside Windows CE

> The people who designed Windows CE at Microsoft discuss design goals and a few implementation issues.

Chapter 10

Object Store

Like any other computer, a Windows CE device needs what is called persistent storage, an area where data can be stored and retrieved afterwards. Most computers (desktops, servers, etc.) simply rely on hard disks of various capacities. But most Windows CE devices do not have the luxury of a hard disk (to reduce size and cost). This has greatly influenced the design of these devices and CE itself.

Windows CE implements a storage area, called the Object Store, right into RAM. Whereas traditional RAM loses its content when the device is shut down, this RAM is required to remain battery-powered. Hence, a Windows CE device is never fully shut down; it is merely suspended.

On that assumption, Microsoft designers decided to split the RAM into two areas (see Figure 10-1):

- The program area, that holds applications' code and data, to run programs. This is the "traditional" use of RAM.

- The Object Store, which roughly assumes the functionality of a virtual hard disk. It provides storage for the Registry, a file system, and the system Database, all explained in the following sections.

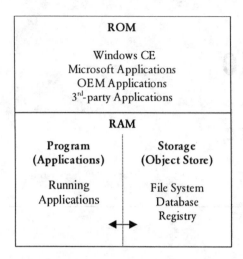

Figure 10-1: The RAM memory is divided in two areas in Windows CE: the program area and the Object Store. The user can usually control the ratio of the two memory spaces.

The Object Store stores objects (what else!) of various types: files, directories, databases, and records. Each object has its own object store id, of type CEOID (a 32-bit value). An application can obtain more information about an object by calling CeOidGetInfo() and specifying an object store id (OID). It fills a structure of type CEOIDINFO, detailed in Figure 10-2.

Type	Field	Description
WORD	wObjType	The type of object (file, directory, database or record)
DWORD	dwSize	sizeof(CEOIDINFO)
WORD	wPad	Padding to align the following on a DWORD boundary
union		The following is part of an union
CEFILEINFO	infFile	Information about a file
CEDIRINFO	infDirectory	Information about a directory
CEDBASEINFO	infDatabase	Information about a database
CERECORDINFO	infRecord	Information about a record in a database.

Figure 10-2: The CEOIDINFO structure.

Examples of using of this function will be demonstrated later on in this chapter, as the Registry and Databases are scrutinized. But let's explore the Object Store by reviewing the file system it implements.

10.1 FILE SYSTEM

Because of the memory constraints, Windows CE designers chose not to adopt existing file systems such FAT or NTFS. These file systems are designed to operate on a hard disk where information is split into fixed-sized clusters (*e.g.,* 4KB on an NTFS file system). This is efficient to store information on large media, but it results in some wasted space on small devices. To avoid losing precious bytes of RAM, Windows CE implements a new, proprietary file system.

Chapter 11 details the API available to conduct I/O operations, including accessing files for any file system, including the one implemented in the Object Store.

10.2 REGISTRY

The Registry is a memory area that centralizes various applications and system settings. Former Windows systems used to rely on AUTOEXEC.BAT, CONFIG.SYS, multiple .INI files and the like, all scattered throughout the hard disk. It eventually became clear that a standard and centralized solution was required. That solution was the Registry, introduced with Windows 95, and brought into CE. The Registry is a single and unique entity that stores the same type of information (*i.e.,* settings). The original Win32 API has about 25 Registry functions; about half are supported on CE, but they essentially cover the same functionality.

The Registry is stored as a hierarchy. The Windows CE Registry Editor is useful to explore the branches and leaves of a CE device registry (see Figure 10-3).

Each element in the left pane is called a key, whether it is a "branch" or a "leaf" (branch keys have subkeys, that is, every non-leaf and non-root key is a subkey).

A leaf key is called a key, whereas a non-leaf item is called a subkey. Individual keys and subkeys are often expressed in a way similar to path names (see the Locations key example above).

Each key (and subkey) has one default value and optional extra values associated with it. Each value has a name (except the default one) and optionally a value associated with it. In the previous Registry snapshot, the Dial key is a subkey of the key ControlPanel and it has three values: its default value (whose data is not set), CurrentLoc, whose data is 0, and HighLocID, whose data is 2.

Note that the right pane only contains the selected key's values, not subkey(s) if any. For instance, Locations, which is a subkey of Dial, does not appear in the right pane.

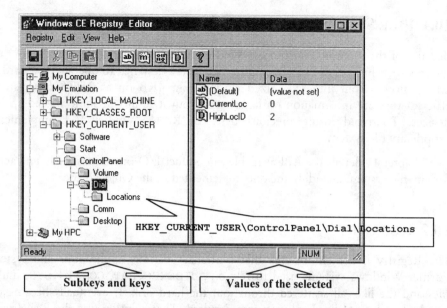

Figure 10-3: A Registry snapshot using the Windows CE Registry Editor.

A Registry has up to four *roots*, or predefined keys, listed in Figure 10-4. The purpose of these keys is to provide some standard locations to store settings. For instance, settings related to the current device should be stored under HKEY_LOCAL_MACHINE, whereas settings for the user should reside in HKEY_CURRENT_USER. These two roots are commonly used in applications that make use of the Registry.

Predefined Keys	The Child Keys Define
HKEY_LOCAL_MACHINE	The physical characteristics of the computer (e.g. CPU, bus) and installed hardware and software.
HKEY_USERS	The default user configuration as well as the current user.
HKEY_CURRENT_USER	The preferences of the current user. These preferences include the settings of environment variables, data about program groups, colors, printers, network connections, and application preferences. This key is in fact a subkey of HKEY_USERS if present.
HKEY_CLASSES_ROOT	The types and properties of supported documents. COM and shell components heavily rely on the information under this key. This key merges HKEY_LOCAL_MACHINE and HKEY_CURRENT_USER)

Figure 10-4: The predefined, primary root keys in a Registry.

10.2.1 Creating, Opening, Closing, and Deleting Keys

A key is created in the Registry by calling `RegCreateKeyEx()`. The following example creates the key `TheApp`, without any associated values, under the key `HKEY_CURRENT_USER\oftware`:

```
LONG        rc;                         // Return code
HKEY        hKey;                       // New key handle
DWORD       dwDisp;                     // Disposition code

rc = RegCreateKeyEx(
            HKEY_CURRENT_USER,          // Predefined key handle
            TEXT("Software\\TheApp"),   // Subkey string
            0,                          // Reserved (must be 0)
            NULL,                       // Object type
            0,                          // No options on CE
            0,                          // No security access on CE
            NULL,                       // No security on CE
            &hKey,                      // New key handle
            &dwDisp);                   // Disposition

// rc contains ERROR_SUCCESS (0) on success, non-zero on error
```

`RegCreateKeyEx()` requires as the first argument a valid key handle. It can be an already-opened key handle, or one of the predefined keys (see Figure 10-4). The second argument is the key name, relative to the specified handle. The name can include subkeys, which will be automatically created if required. The third argument is a reserved value and is always 0. The next parameter is the class type, usually set to NULL. The next three parameters are simply 0 (or NULL), as they are unsupported on CE. The next to last parameter is the returned key handle. Finally, the last parameter is the disposition code; since creating an already existing key simply opens it, that code indicates whether the key has been created (`REG_CREATED_NEW_KEY`) or opened (`REG_OPENED_EXISTING_KEY`). A created key's default value is undefined and there are no extra values associated with that key either.

`RegCreateKeyEx()` creates a key (or opens an existing key) and returns a key handle, which is used in subsequent registry operations.

Similarly, `RegOpenKeyEx()` opens a key and returns its handle. Unlike `RegCreate KeyEx()` though, the key is not created if it does not already exists. In that case, an error code is returned.

The following example opens the key `HKEY_CURRENT_USER\Software\theApp`:

```
LONG        rc;                         // Return code
HKEY        hKey;                       // Key handle

rc = RegOpenKeyEx(
            HKEY_CURRENT_USER,          // Predefined handle.
```

```
         TEXT("Software\\TheApp"),   // Subkey string
         0,                          // Reserved (must be 0)
         KEY_ALL_ACCESS,             // Permissions
         &hKey);                     // Returned handle

// rc is ERROR_SUCCESS on success, or a nonzero value on error.
```

The first three arguments to RegOpenKeyEx() match those of RegCreateKeyEx(). The next argument is the required permission. KEY_ALL_ACCESS grants access to read, write, create subkeys, enumerate subkeys, set values, create link, and notify operations. Fewer access rights can be chosen if required. Finally, the last parameter returns the key handle, which can be used in subsequent key operations.

Note that RegOpenKeyEx() requires specific access permission and potentially limits which operations can later be applied on the key. On the other hand, opening or creating a key through RegCreateKeyEx() grants all access.

Once a key is no longer required within an application, it must be closed by calling RegCloseKey(). The following example demonstrates the use of that call:

```
LONG      rc;

rc = RegCloseKey(hKey);              // hKey is a valid key handle.
```

A key and all its values (that is, the default value and any extra values) can be deleted by calling RegDeleteKey(). Note that a key cannot be deleted if it is opened or has any subkeys (each of the existing subkeys must be deleted first individually). The following example deletes a key (assuming that it has been closed).

```
// Delete the key TheApp from HKEY_CURRENT_USER\Software.

rc = RegDeleteKey(
         HKEY_CURRENT_USER,          // Predefined key handle
         TEXT("Software\\TheApp"));   // Subkey string
```

Querying, Setting and Deleting Key Values

Using an opened key handle and a value name, RegQueryValueEx() retrieves the associated type and data. A key value can be queried if the key has been opened with the KEY_QUERY_VALUE access.

RegQueryValueEx() requires a valid key handle (either predefined or opened), the name of the value under that key (or NULL for the default key), and a few pointers to store return values: the type (see Figure 10-5), the value's data, and the size (in bytes) of the value's data. Note that the very last parameter must initially contain the size (in bytes) of the buffer to store the value's data.

Registry Data Type	Description
REG_BINARY	Binary data (i.e. anything)
REG_DWORD	A DWORD value
REG_DWORD_LITTLE_ENDIAN	Little-endian DWORD value (same as REG_DWORD)
REG_DWORD_BIG_ENDIAN	Big-endian DWORD value
REG_EXPAND_SZ	A null-terminated string that refers to environment variables and that needs to be expanded when interpreted (example: "%LIB%")
REG_LINK	A Unicode symbolic link (used internally)
REG_NONE	No defined value type
REF_RESOURCE_LIST	A device-driver resource list
REG_SZ	A null-terminated string

Figure 10-5: Supported key data types REG_DWORD and REG_SZ are the most common.

Conversely, RegSetValueEx() updates one value of a key (either the default or an extra key), using a handle to that key and a value name. The default key is used when that name is NULL. The function also requires the value's data type (which can later be changed) and the value's data. The key requires the KEY_SET_VALUE access for this function to succeed. The value is created if it does not already exist.

The following example loads the value Color from the key HKEY_CURRENT_ USER\Software\TheApp into an application variable. It is then assumed that some processing changes the value. Then, upon terminating, that value is stored back in the Registry:

```
HKEY        hKey;                        // Key handle
DWORD       dwColor;                     // The value to store
DWORD       dwType;                      // Data type
DWORD       dwDataLen;                   // Data length
LONG        rc;

// Open the key HKEY_CURRENT_USER\Software\TheApp into hKey.
// Use the KEY_ALL_ACCESS access to query and set the value.
rc = RegOpenKeyEx(HKEY_CURRENT_USER, TEXT("Software\\TheApp"),
        0, KEY_ALL_ACCESS, &hKey);

// Read the "Color" value from the Registry.
dwDataLen = sizeof(dwColor);            // Set size of data buffer

rc = RegQueryValueEx(
        hKey,                           // Opened key handle
        TEXT("Color"),                  // Value
        0,                              // Reserved (must be 0)
        &dwType,                        // Pointer to type
        (LPBYTE) &dwColor,              // Pointer to data
        &dwDataLen);                    // Exact data length is returned
```

```
// Perform some processing, which might alter dwColor.
.
.
.

// Store the value upon terminating into the Registry.
rc = RegSetValueEx(
        hKey,                       // Opened key handle
        TEXT("Color"),              // Value
        0,                          // Reserved (must be 0)
        REG_DWORD,                  // This is a 32-bit value
        (LPBYTE) &dwColor,          // Pointer to data
        sizeof(dwColor));           // Size of Data

// Close the key.
rc = RegCloseKey(hKey);
```

Here are a few notes about setting a value:

- Although value's data can have any arbitrary length, it is recommended that the length be kept under 1KB. Longer data should be stored in a file, whose name is stored in the Registry.
- If the value's name contains a \ (as in "Color\\Screen"), this will not create a subkey Screen; instead, that will create a value whose name is Color\Screen.

A value (name and data) can be deleted from a key by calling RegDeleteValue(), which requires a key handle and the value name. If the name is NULL, the default value is removed. The key itself is not changed. This call requires the key handle to have a KEY_SET_VALUE permission. The following example removes the value Color from the key hKey, previously opened on HKEY_CURRENT_USER\Software\TheApp with the KEY_ALL_ACCESS access.

```
rc = RegDeleteValue(
        hKey,                       // Opened key handle
        TEXT("Color"));             // Value name
```

10.2.2 Obtaining More Key Information

Information about an opened key is obtained by calling RegQueryInfoKey(). The call can return the number of subkeys, the length of the longest subkey name, the number of values and the length of the longest value name, among others. This is very useful to enumerate the content (subkeys and values) of the given key.

RegEnumKeyEx() enumerates all the subkeys of an opened key. It simply requires an opened key handle, a subkey index (zero-based), and a key name buffer. All subkeys of an opened key can be identified by repeatedly calling that routine and specifying a valid subkey index. The number of keys and the size of the buffer to receive the subkey name is obtained by RegQueryInfoKey().

Similarly, RegEnumValue() enumerates all the values of an opened key. It requires a zero-based index and returns the value name, the value type and the value data. Similarly, the number of values and the size of the buffer to receive the value name can be obtained by RegQueryInfoKey(). However, there is no method to know ahead the maximum size for the value's data. Hence, applications must use a large buffer (1KB is usually adequate).

The following example shows all the values of the opened key HKEY_CURRENT_USER\Software\TheApp:

```
const int   MAX_DATA_SIZE = 1024;        // In bytes

LONG        rc;                          // Return code
DWORD       i;                           // Iterator
HKEY        hKey;                        // Key handle
DWORD       dwSubkeyCount;               // Subkey count
DWORD       dwLenKeyName;                // Key name's length
DWORD       dwValueCount;                // Value count
DWORD       dwLenValueName;              // Value name's length
LPTSTR      pszName;                     // Name pointer
DWORD       dwNameLen;                   // Value name length
DWORD       dwType;                      // Value type
BYTE        Data[MAX_DATA_SIZE];         // Data buffer
DWORD       dwDataSz;                    // Data size

// Open the key
rc = RegOpenKeyEx(HKEY_CURRENT_USER, TEXT("Software\\TheApp"),
    0, KEY_ALL_ACCESS, &hKey);

// Query the number of subkeys and values from the key.
// Note that the subkey count and the longest subkey name's parameters
// could be NULL if not required. They are queried here for demonstration
// purpose only.

rc = RegQueryInfoKey(
        hKey,                           // Opened key handle
        NULL,                           // No class name required
        NULL,                           // No class name size
        NULL,                           // Reserved on CE
        &dwSubkeyCount,                 // Subkey count
        &dwLenKeyName,                  // Longest subkey name's length
        NULL,                           // Longest subkey class' length
        &dwValueCount,                  // Value count
        &dwLenValueName,                // Longest value name's length
        NULL,                           // Not used on CE
        NULL,                           // Not used on CE
        NULL);                          // Not used on CE

// Allocate space to store the name.
pszName = (LPTSTR) LocalAlloc(LMEM_FIXED, dwLenValueName);
```

225

```
// Get information about all values.
for (i = 0; i < dwValueCount; i++)
{
    dwNameLen = dwLenValueName;           // Set to initial length
    dwDataSz = sizeof(Data);              // Set to initial size

    RegEnumValue(
            hKey,                         // Key handle
            i,                            // Value index (first is 0)
            pszName,                      // Name buffer (name is returned)
            &dwNameLen,                   // Name length (returned)
            0,                            // Reserved (must be 0)
            &dwType,                      // Value type (returned)
            Data,                         // Value's data (returned)
            &dwDataSz);                   // Value's data size

    // Display the name (pszName), the type (dwType) and
    // the associated data (Data).
    DisplayKeyInfo(pszName, dwType, Data, dwDataSz);
}

// Free the buffer
LocalFree(pszName);

// Close the key
rc = RegCloseKey(hKey);
```

The **Regdemo** sample also shows how to enumerate subkeys and values.

10.2.3 Registry Tips

It's one thing to know the API, but it's another to use it judiciously. The Registry holds an application's settings. The settings can be initially created by a SETUP program, but every application should expect keys not to be there, and if possible, provide default values.

For instance, suppose an application starts and need to find the path of some data file. If the Registry entry is missing, perhaps the application can use a default set of values and move on. On the other hand, if the file is absolutely required no matter what (say it holds some encrypted passwords to let the user perform some actions), the application must display a message ("Consult your system administrator") and exit.

The Registry is commonly used for storing user's settings. Say an application displays some graph, using three colors. Initially, the three colors are set to pre-defined values, hard-coded in the application. During the use of the application, the user may change these colors through a typical Options dialog box. Hence, upon closing, the application would store the three colors under the `HKEY_CURRENT_USER\\Software\\{Company}\\{AppName} \\Colors` for instance. The next time the application is started, the colors are read back from the Registry. If for some reason the values aren't there, the application reverts to the hard-coded values (but this scenario is only likely to happen the first time the user runs that application). This approach is implemented in the **Regdemo** sample.

Here are a few suggestions when using the Registry:

- User's settings (such as color, screen position, last files opened, anything that has to do with the way the user used the application) should be kept under the following key: HKEY_CURRENT_USER\Software*Company**AppName**SettingItem*.

- When reading user's settings, always use default values if keys are not found. Don't bother to notify the user; mentioning Registry will probably only remind them to balance their checkbook[27].

- Application's settings (installation directory, extra files/tools locations, system-wide configuration parameters, anything related with what the application needs to run, independently of the user using it) should be stored under the key HKEY_LOCAL_MACHINE\Software*Company**AppName**SettingItem*

- Setup applications should store the initial application settings if they are required for the application to run.

10.3 DATABASES

Windows CE offers a feature not found on other Windows platforms: an integrated database. The purpose is to provide a consistent API to store and retrieve simple information, such as names, telephone numbers, e-mail addresses, and so on. This is traditionally accomplished by using data files. The CE database is a central data repository that can be accessed through a few Win32 operations. Databases are stored in the Object Store and on mounted volumes. Volumes have been introduced with Windows CE 2.10, and they required some changes to the Database API. This new, modified API is reviewed in the next sections. Also, most calls are implemented in the **DB** sample, on the CD-ROM.

A few words of caution though: the term "database" refers to an agglomeration of data rather than a Database Management System (DBMS) powered by a relational database engine. In fact, databases offer a convenient way to store and retrieve data, but no more.

There is little in common with a real database system. In particular, it suffers from the following limitations, compared to a traditional database:

- There is no SQL[28] around here. All access operations are done through API calls.

---

[27] That's at least what I thought myself...

[28] SQL is the language of choice to access and manipulate relation database, such as Oracle, SQL Server, etc.

- There is no centralized locking mechanism. If a database is to be shared among applications (or threads), synchronization primitives (described in Chapter 7) must be coded right into each application.

- There is no concept of database transactions, which ensures consistency in case of errors. Consider the case where $100 is transferred from your checking account to your savings account. If everything goes fine, the money is transferred. If an error happens during the transfer, both accounts should remain in their initial state (without the money transferred). Database transactions can ensure such consistent states; Windows CE databases cannot. The Object Store implements some transactions, but these transactions operate on a lower level: individual operations are monitored, but not *groups* of operations.

- There is no primary key, or foreign keys, and hence, no support for referential integrity, which is another relational database feature that promotes data integrity and consistency.

- The terminology differs. Those of you familiar with DBMSs will have to adjust your vocabulary. Figure 10-6 summarizes these differences.

Relational Database Term	What It Is	How It Is Called Under Windows CE
Database	A collection of tables	Volume
Table	A collection of rows	Database
Tuple, record	A table row	Record
Attribute	A table column	Property
Index	A method to quickly access rows	Sort order

Figure 10-6: Terminology used with relational databases and with the CE databases

10.3.1 Windows CE Databases

A Windows CE database consists of *records*, and each record is composed of *properties*. Each property refers to a property identifier, a data type, and a data value. Here's an example that stores a list of contact people (name, e-mail address, and daytime telephone number). The database's name is "Contacts", each contact is stored as a record (*i.e.*, one row) and each record contains three properties (or three columns): a name, an e-mail address, and a telephone number (see Figure 10-7).

Name	eMail	Phone
Jane Doe	Jane@Doe.com	123-456-7890
John Doe	John@Doe.com	123-456-7890
.		

Figure 10-7: A Windows CE database can be viewed as a table that stores records (rows), and properties (columns).

Unlike commercial databases, Windows CE imposes very few restrictions regarding data organization. For instance, a database's format is not defined anywhere, making its content heterogeneous. For a given table, the first record can contain two properties (name and address), the second record can contain other properties (telephone and city), etc. This is advantageous because it makes the implementation simpler and faster (no need for validation), but in return, applications must be very careful when manipulating the records and properties, as the content format and structure is unpredictable.

Before Windows CE 2.10, databases were exclusively confined to the Object Store. Now, they can also live in volumes. A database volume is a file that contains one or more databases, and a log. A volume has a name, which must be unique among volumes, and can reside on any storage. Within a volume, databases have their own name. The portion of the Object Store that holds databases is considered a single volume too.

Windows CE databases support the most common data types, which is enough for most applications: integers and doubles, character strings, file date and time (FILETIME), and variable-length arrays of bytes, also called Binary Large Objects (BLOB). We'll explore these types in detail later.

The maximum size of a record is defined as CEDB_MAXRECORDSIZE, whereas the maximum size of a property is CEDB_MAXPROPDATASIZE, respectively 128KB and (64KB - 1) under Windows CE 2.11.

Each database can support up to four sort orders, which are usually defined upon database creation. Each sort order is defined upon a property. A sort order allows retrieving records in a specific order, based on the values of one property (*e.g.,* names, dates, etc.) It is best to keep the sort orders to a minimum to avoid taking too many system resources.

10.3.2 Mounting and Unmounting Volume Databases

File volumes must be *mounted* - opened - in order to be accessed, by calling CeMountDBVol(). The first parameter is a pointer to a globally unique volume identifier

(GUID), of type CEGUID (an opaque structure whose content is irrelevant for applications). This identifier is initialized within the function, and is used in subsequent calls. The second parameter is the volume name (any valid file name, including UNC names, will do). Finally, the last parameter is a series of flags, listed in Figure 10-8. You will certainly note that these flags bear resemblance to those used with CreateFile().

Flag	Description
CREATE_NEW	Create a new database volume, and fail if it already exists.
CREATE_ALWAYS	Create a new database volume. If it already exists, truncate it.
OPEN_EXISTING	Open the database, fail if it does not exist
OPEN_ALWAYS	Open the database. If it does not exist, create it.
TRUNCATE_EXISTING	Open and truncate the database, fail if it exists.

Figure 10-8: The flags used as the second parameter to CeMountDBVol(), to mount databases.

On success, the function returns TRUE, and the first parameter (the globally unique identifier) is initialized. On error, the function returns FALSE. The following mounts the file volume "\MyVolume":

```
CEGUID      guid;                         // Globally unique Identifier
BOOL        rc;

rc = CeMountDBVol(
            &guidObjStore,                // Pointer to GUID
            TEXT("\\MyVolume"),           // File name
            OPEN_ALWAYS);                 // Opening mode

// rc is TRUE if the volume has been mounted, FALSE otherwise
```

The Object Store doesn't have to be mounted, but an application will still need a GUID to access database within. The macro CREATE_SYSTEMGUID() is provided to initialize a GUID that identifies the Object Store. Hence, an application use this macro to use the Object Store or calls CeMountDBVol() to use a file volume. Here's an example that creates a GUID for the Object Store:

```
CEGUID      guid;                         // Globally unique Identifier
CREATE_SYSTEMGUID(&guidObjStore);
```

Subsequent operations on mounted databases that write data are not automatically flushed; they are cached until explicitly flushed, the system becomes low in memory, or the volume is unmounted. Hence, if an application crashes, the last bytes written in a mounted database might be lost.

Once a file mounted database is no longer needed, the volume can be unmounted by calling CeUnmountDBVol() and specifying the GUID. Note that more than one application can mount a volume (Windows CE internally maintains a mount counter to keep things in order). The Object Store volume never has to and cannot be unmounted.

10.3.3 Creating and Deleting Databases

A volume database is created by calling CeCreateDatabaseEx(). The first argument is a valid GUID. The second parameter is a pointer to a CEDBASEINFO structure, defined in Figure 10-9.

Type	Member	Description
DWORD	dwFlags	Specifies the valid member of the structure
WCHAR	szDbaseName[]	Database name.
DWORD	dwDbaseType	Type identifier.
WORD	wNumRecords	Number of records
WORD	wNumSortOrder	Number of active sort orders
DWORD	dwSize	Total size, in bytes
FILETIME	ftLastModified	Time of last modification
SORTORDERSPEC	rgSortSpecs[]	The sort order specification array (of size wNumSortOrder)

Figure 10-9: The CEDBASEINFO structure.

The first member, dwFlags, identifies which remaining members are valid. For creation, this value is simply set to CEDB_VALIDCREATE. The next member is the database name (any unique name will do). The third member is an arbitrary type identifier. This is an application-defined value, used with other database calls within the application. We'll see more about this value with CeFindFirstDatabaseEx(). wNumSortOrder is the total number of sort orders that will be maintained on the database at all times. A maximum of four sort orders can be maintained on each database; hence, wNumSortOrder can vary from zero to four. The next two members (dwSize and ftLastModified) are ignored for creation. Finally, rgSortSpecs is an array of four SORTORDERDESC structures. Each structure specifies a property to sort the database upon. It is best to determine and specify ahead how the database will be sorted, rather than adding a sort order later on (an operation that could take a few minutes). The SORTORDERDESC structure is defined as follows:

Type	Member	Description
PEGPROPID	propid	Property identifier
DWORD	dwFlags	Sort flags

Figure 10-10: The SORTORDERDESC structure.

231

The property identifier is an application-defined value, unique for a given database. We'll see shortly how to use this identifier when opening a database. It is common to simply use zero-based values (0 for the first, 1 for the second, etc.) represented by constants or #defines. Once a database is created, property identifiers cannot be changed; they become as permanent as the database name. Throughout the database examples, we will use four properties (always the same), which are defined as follows:

```
const      CEPROPID PROPID_NAME  = MAKELONG(CEVT_LPWSTR, 0);
const      CEPROPID PROPID_EMAIL = MAKELONG(CEVT_LPWSTR, 1);
const      CEPROPID PROPID_TEL   = MAKELONG(CEVT_LPWSTR, 2);
const      CEPROPID PROPID_AGE   = MAKELONG(CEVT_I2,     3);
```

A property identifier consists of a 16-bit data type and a 16-bit property identifier combined together. The macro MAKELONG(*data type, property identifer*) makes that formatting easy. The valid data types are listed in Figure 10-17. In the example above, the name property (PROPID_NAME) is an Unicode string (CEVT_LPWSTR) and its identifier is 0.

The sort flag (dwFlags) specifies the sort order. The default is CEDB_SORT_ GENERICORDER (which is 0), which implies an ascending, case sensitive order, with records containing an unknown value for the property at the end. The sort order can be altered by specifying a combination of the following self-explanatory flags: CEDB_SORT_ DESCENDING, CEDB_SORT_CASEINSENSITIVE, and CEDB_SORT_UNKNOWNFIRST.

OK, let's see how to use these data structures. The following example creates a database called "Contacts". It is assumed that guid is a valid GUID; the database will be created within the related volume.

```
CEDBASEINFO        CEDBInfo;              // Database info
CEOID              oidDB;                 // Database object identifier

// Set the flags to indicate that all the fields required for the creation
// are set: name, type, and sort order.
CEDBInfo.dwFlags = CEDB_VALIDCREATE;

// Set the database name
_tcscpy(CEDBInfo.szDbaseName, TEXT("Contacts"));

// Database type (a user-defined value)
CEDBInfo.dwDbaseType = 0;

// Number of active sort order
CEDBInfo.wNumSortOrder = 1;

// The unique sort order is based on the name and uses the default order.
CEDBInfo.rgSortSpecs[0].propid  = PROPID_NAME;
CEDBInfo.rgSortSpecs[0].dwFlags = CEDB_SORT_GENERICORDER;

// Create the database.
```

232

```
oidDB = CeCreateDatabaseEx(
         &guid,
         &CEDBInfo);

// oidDB is non-null on success or NULL on error.
```

On success, CeCreateDatabaseEx() returns an database identifier, or NULL on error. This object identifier is of type CEOID. Creating a database does not grant an application access to it. A database must be opened to be accessed.

A database can be deleted by calling CeDeleteDatabaseEx(). The first parameter is a GUID, the very same that was specified with CeCreateDatabaseEx(). The second parameter is the database identifier, as returned by CeCreateDatabaseEx().

10.3.4 Opening and Closing Databases

A volume database is opened by calling CeOpenDatabaseEx(), and specifying either the database identifier - if known, such as after calling CeCreateDatabaseEx() - or its name.

The first parameter is invariably a GUID, as obtained from CeMountDBVol() or CREATE_SYSTEMGUID(), but you can also use an identifier created with CREATE_INVALIDGUID() to search all the volumes (starting with the Object Store) for a specific database.

The second parameter is a database identifier pointer, and the third parameter is the name of the database. Only one of the two is required to open the database:

- If the database identifier is known, specify it as the second parameter, and specify NULL as the database name (the third parameter). The next example opens a database using its identifier. It assumes that oidDB is a valid identifier (returned from CeCreateDatabaseEx() for instance); the other parameters are explained below.

```
HANDLE      hDB;                        // Database handle

hDB = CeOpenDatabaseEx(
          &guid,                        // GUID
          &oidDB,                       // Valid database identifier
          NULL,                         // Unknown database name
          PROPID_NAME,                  // Primary key (property id)
          CEDB_AUTOINCREMENT,           // Action flag
          NULL);                        // No notification

// hDB is nonzero if the database has been opened, or
// INVALID_HANDLE_VALUE on error.
```

- To open a database using its name, set the second parameter as the address of a zero CEOID value and specify the name of an existing database as the third parameter. The next example opens a database using its name; this method of opening a database is very common, since database names are usually known, whereas object identifiers aren't unless the database is created within the same application.

```
CEOID        oidDB;
HANDLE       hDB;

oidDB = 0;                              // The database id is unknown
hDB   = CeOpenDatabaseEx(
             &guid,                     // GUID
             &oidDB,                    // Unknown database identifier
             TEXT("Contacts"),          // Database name
             PROPID_NAME,               // Primary key (property id)
             CEDB_AUTOINCREMENT,        // Action flag
             NULL);                     // No notification

// If the database has been opened, hDB is nonzero and oidDB contains the
// database identifier. On error, hDB is set to INVALID_HANDLE_VALUE.
```

The fourth parameter to CeOpenDatabaseEx() is the property identifier, used for sorting the database; this order will become apparent as records are read. The property identifier must match one of those specified when the database was created with CeCreateDatabaseEx(). In the database creation example given earlier, the property identifier was set to PROPID_NAME; hence, the same value is used when opening the database. Any active sort order (either specified when the database was created or set later on) can be specified, but only one at a time. The same database can be opened multiple times if many sort orders are to be required, resulting in many database handles to work with.

The fifth parameter is an action flag that is used in conjunction with the sort orders. CEDB_AUTOINCREMENT means that, after reading a record (explained in Section 10.3.6), the current record seek position is moved to the next record, based on the sort order specified in the previous parameter. As an alternative, 0 indicates that the seek position must be moved "manually", using CeSeekDatabase(), described in Section 10.3.8.

The sixth and last argument indicates whether the application should be notified when the database is modified by another application as it is opened. For instance, consider that the user is using an application that lists all the records of the Contacts database on its main window. Now suppose the user downloads from the desktops new contacts. The first application can be notified of the new records being are added in the Contacts database, by requesting notification messages to be sent to its main window (see Figure 10-11).

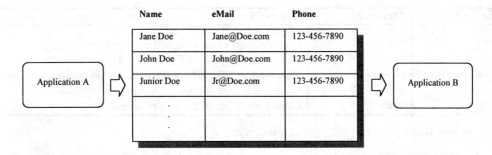

Figure 10-11: Applications can be notified of database changes performed by other applications.

Specifically, this argument is a pointer to a CENOTIFYREQUEST structure, listed in Figure 10-12. A NULL value indicates that the application is not interested in receiving notifications. On the other hand, a valid pointer results in notifications being delivered (listed in Figure 10-13), along a CENOTIFY structure (listed in Figure 10-14); the application process a notification by updating its internal data.

Type	Member	Description
DWORD	dwSize	sizeof(CENOTIFYREQUEST)
HWND	hWnd	Window to send notifications to
DWORD	dwFlags	0: send messages only (CE 1.0 up to 2.0)
		CEDB_EXNOTIFICATION: send a CENOTIFICATION structure as well (2.1 and up)
HANDLE	hHeap	Heap handle to allocate the CENOTIFICATION structure from.
WORD	wNumSortOrder	Number of active sort orders
DWORD	dwParam	User-defined value stored in the dwParam field of the CENOTIFICATION structure when sent.

Figure 10-12: The CENOTIFYREQUEST structure.

Flag	Description
DB_CEOID_CREATED	An object has been created.
DB_CEOID_DATABASE_DELETED	A database has been deleted on a volume
DB_CEOID_RECORD_DELETED	A record has been deleted in a database.
DB_CEOID_FILE_DELETED	A file was deleted (for OEM replication process only)
DB_CEOID_DIRECTORY_DELETED	A directory was deleted (for OEM replication process only)
DB_CEOID_CHANGED	An object was modified

Figure 10-13: Notification types, sent through the CENOTIFY structure.

Type	Member	Description
DWORD	dwSize	sizeof(CENOTIFICATION)
DWORD	dwParam	User-defined value assigned in CENOTIFYREQUEST.
UINT	uType	Notification type (see Figure 10-13)
CEGUID	guid	Volume identifier where the notification applies.
CEOID	oid	Object identifier where the notification applies
CEOID	oidParent	Object identifier of the parent object.

Figure 10-14: The CENOTIFICATION structure.

On success, CeOpenDatabaseEx() returns a valid handle, which can be used with other database operations (such as reading and writing records). On error, the handle is INVALID_HANDLE_VALUE. Applications can call GetLastError() to determine the exact nature of the error. Three self-explaining error codes can be returned: ERROR_INVALID_PARAMETER, ERROR_FILE_NOT_FOUND (no database with the specified name), or ERROR_NOT_ENOUGH_MEMORY.

Once an application is finished with a database, it must close it by calling CloseHandle() with the database handle. Do not confuse CloseHandle() with CeCloseHandle(); the latter can only be invoked from a host (desktop) computer.

10.3.5 Writing Records

An application calls CeWriteRecordProps() to create or update a record. The function writes property values within one single record. The call uses a CEPROPVAL array, which identifies the data type and value of each property to write. The CEPROPVAL structure is described in Figure 10-15. The value is stored in the val member, which is the CEVALUNION union. Finally, Figure 10-16 lists the valid data types, their corresponding variable in the CEVALUNION union, and their C/C++ representation.

Type	Field	Description
CEPROPID	propid	Property identifier (high 16-bit) and data type (low 16-bit)
WORD	wLenData	Unused
WORD	wFlags	Property flags
CEVALUNION	val	Property value (see following table)

Figure 10-15: The CEPROPVAL structure.

Type	CEVALUNION Member	C/C++ Data Type	Description
CEVT_BLOB	blob	CEBLOB structure	Binary large object
CEVT_BOOL	boolVal	BOOL	Boolean value
CEVT_FILETIME	filetime	FILETIME type	File time
CEVT_I2	iVal	short	16-bit signed integer
CEVT_I4	lVal	long	32-bit signed integer
CEVT_LPWSTR	lpwstr	LPWSTR	Null-terminated string
CEVT_R8	dblVal	double	8-byte real
CEVT_UI2	uiVal	USHORT	16-bit unsigned integer
CEVT_UI4	ulVal	ULONG	32-bit unsigned integer

Figure 10-16: Valid database property types, along their associated CEVALUNION field and their C/C++ representation. For instance, a CEVT_UI2 property is a USHORT whose value is stored in the uiVal variable of the CEVALUNION union.

Here's an example to clarify the use of these tables. The following code example creates a new record in the "Contacts" database:

```
CEOID       oidRec ;                    // Record identifier
CEPROPVAL   PropVal[4];                 // Four property values

// Initialize the property values to zero
memset(PropVal, 0, sizeof(PropVal));

// Initialize each property, specifying the property id combined with
// the property data type, and the related value.
PropVal[0].propid     = PROPID_NAME;
PropVal[0].val.lpwstr = TEXT("Doe, John");

PropVal[1].propid     = PROPID_EMAIL;
PropVal[1].val.lpwstr = TEXT("john@doe.com");

PropVal[2].propid     = PROPID_TEL;
PropVal[2].val.lpwstr = TEXT("(123) 456-7890");

PropVal[3].propid     = PROPID_AGE;
PropVal[3].val.iVal   = 25;

// Write the property. Because a record id of 0 is specified as the
// third parameter, a record is created. If a record id was instead
// specified, that record would be updated.
oidRec = CeWriteRecordProps(
            hDB,                         // Database handle
            0,                           // Create record
            4,                           // Four properties to write
            PropVal);                    // Property data

// oidRec is non-zero on success. In this case, it is the record is of
// the newly created record. On error, oidRec is zero.
```

Since four properties are inserted, an array of four CEPROPVAL items is declared (PropVal[4]). This structure is initialized to zero. Specifically, the wLenData and wFlags fields are set to 0. The first property to be inserted is the contact name ("Doe, John"). The propid field must contain both the property identifier (declared earlier as a const) and the data type. Depending on the data type, the proper field of the CEPROPVAL's val union field must be chosen and initialized with the data. Refer to Figure 10-16 to identify the member to use in the union depending on the data type.

Finally, calling CeWriteRecordProps() requires four arguments. The first is a valid database handle, obtained from CeOpenDatabase(). The second argument is a record id to update (assuming one is known) or 0 to create a record. The remaining two arguments are the number of properties to insert and the CEPROPVAL array.

The free-format of the Windows CE databases allows specifying properties in any order, for the same table (the order being established by the CEPROPVAL array). For instance, an application may insert the name, e-mail, and telephone properties (in that order), whereas another application may insert the name, telephone, and e-mail. Furthermore, within the same table, records do not have to contain the same number of properties. For instance, in the Contacts database, a record containing the usual four properties plus a fax phone number could be inserted. This has an impact on reading records as well, which is described in the next section.

In order to update a record, the second parameter to CeWriteRecordProps() must be a valid record identifier, such a the one returned by the call itself. We'll soon see another method to get record identifiers. Suffice it to say that given an existing record identifier, writing exiting properties updates them. New properties are simply added within the same existing record.

10.3.6 Reading Records

Reading records closely resembles writing them. After having opened the database, one can invoke CeReadRecordProps() to obtain the first record. This record is returned as a CEPROPVAL array, in the same format that is used for writing. More on this in a second. The next call to CeReadRecordProps() depends on how the database has been opened. Let's recall that CeOpenDatabase() takes an optional sort order, which determines the order in which records are successively returned. It also takes an optional flag (0 or CEDB_AUTOINCREMENT), which determines whether the internal file pointer is automatically moved or not on the next record, based on the sort order. Using CEDB_AUTOINCREMENT is common when applications need to load the entire table. We'll see later why this flag is sometimes not specified.

Records are returned in a buffer that contains a CEPROPVAL array, optionally followed by extra data, such as strings or blobs (see Figure 10-17). The size of the array directly depends on the number of properties that have been returned. An application may read specific properties or all of them. The application can allocate the buffer itself, but it is best to let the system do so, for two reasons:

- When reading strings (which is very common), the size of the string to read is unknown. Ditto when reading blobs. Using predefined buffers, say a 1KB buffer, may not be enough.

- Since the number of properties can vary from one record to another, an application cannot establish ahead how much memory it will need.

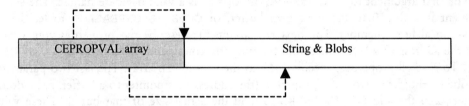

Figure 10-17: Records are returned in a buffer that contains an array of CEPROPVAL structures, followed by strings and blobs, if any.

The next examples illustrate how to use CeReadRecordProps(). It reads all properties, with system-allocated buffers. This is the easiest and safest method to read some or all properties.

```
CEIOD       oidRec;                      // Record identifier
WORD        wPropCount;                  // Property count
LPBYTE      pBuffer = NULL;              // Record buffer
DWORD       dwBufferSz = 0;              // Buffer size

// Read all records, one by one
while (1)
{
    // Get all properties of the first/next record, depending on the sort
    // order. The database has been opened with CEDB_AUTOINCREMENT.
    oidRec = CeReadRecordProps(
                hDB,                     // Database handle
                CEDB_ALLOWREALLOC,       // Use local heap memory
                &wPropCount,             // Property count on return
                NULL,                    // Retrieve all properties
                &pBuffer,                // Buffer (indirect pointer)
                &dwBufferSz);            // Buffer size (in/out)

    if (oidRec == 0)
            break;

    // At this point, pBuffer points on some local heap memory, whose
    // size is in dwBufferSz. Subsequent calls will re-use that memory.
```

```
      DisplayRecord(wPropCount, pBuffer);   // Display the record
}

// Applications should make sure that GetLastError() returns
// ERROR_NO_MORE_ITEMS, which is a normal. Anything else is an error.
if (GetLastError() != ERROR_NO_MORE_ITEMS)
    Error(. . .)

// Free the buffer if not NULL. It refers to some local heap memory.
if (pBuffer)
    LocalFree(pBuffer);
```

The first argument to CeReadRecordProps() is a valid database handle. The second argument is a flag: 0 to use your own buffer, or CEDB_ALLOWREALLOC to let the call allocate local heap memory. The next two arguments describe the properties you want to read: the address of a WORD that hold the property count, and the address of a CEPROPID array. To read all properties, specify NULL as the CEPROPID array. The last two parameters describe the buffer to store the properties (the address of a pointer to a buffer, *i.e.*, a double pointer), and the address of a DWORD to hold the actual size of that buffer. These values must be initialized before making the call, and they are updated when returning from it.

The next example reads a specific number of properties. This method has the advantage that only expected properties are returned; extra properties, known or unknown to the application, are ignored. Because some records may not have the requested properties, so the application must test for their presence in the returned buffer. The wFlags field of CEPROPVAL contains CEDB_PROPNOTFOUND if the requested property has not been found. This example still relies on local heap memory.

```
CEIOD       oidRec;                    // Record identifier
WORD        wPropCount;                // Property count
LPBYTE      pBuffer = NULL;            // Record buffer
DWORD       dwBufferSz = 0;            // Buffer size
CEPROPID    PropIDs[2];                // Property identifiers

// Set the property identifier array, specifying the data type and the id.
PropIDs[0] = PROPID_NAME;
PropIDs[1] = PROPID_AGE;

// Set the property count variable.
wPropCount = sizeof(PropIDs) / sizeof(CEPROPID);

while (1)
{
    // Read the two properties. Let the system allocate memory.
    oidRec = CeReadRecordProps(
                hDB,                   // Database handle
                CEDB_ALLOWREALLOC,     // Use local heap memory
                &wPropCount,           // Property count
                PropIDs,               // Retrieve the two properties
                &pBuffer,              // Buffer (indirect pointer)
                &dwBufferSz);          // Buffer size (in/out)
```

```
        if (oidRec == 0)
            break;

    DisplayRecord(wPropCount, pBuffer);   // Display the record
}

// Applications should make sure that GetLastError() returns
// ERROR_NO_MORE_ITEMS, which is a normal. Anything else is an error.
if (GetLastError() != ERROR_NO_MORE_ITEMS)
    Error(. . .)

// Free the buffer if not NULL. It refers to some local heap memory.
if (pBuffer)
    LocalFree(pBuffer);
```

The last example illustrates how to interpret the resulting buffer. This is the implementation of `DisplayRecord()`, used in the previous two examples. This function is very generic; you might want to adapt it to your exact need (for instance, when using specific properties).

```
void DisplayRecord(WORD wPropCount, LPBYTE pBuffer)
{
    TCHAR        szData[1024];
    TCHAR        szNumber[16];
    PCEPROPVAL   pPropVal;
    int          i;

    for (i = 0, pPropVal = (PCEPROPVAL) pBuffer;
            i < wPropCount;
            i++, pPropVal++)
    {
        // Extract the property id. The order depends on how they
        // have been written in the record.
        switch (pPropVal->propid)
        {
        case PROPID_NAME:
                _tcscpy(szData, TEXT("PROPID_NAME: "));
                break;

        case PROPID_EMAIL:
                _tcscpy(szData, TEXT("PROPID_EMAIL: "));
                break;

        case PROPID_TEL:
                _tcscpy(szData, TEXT("PROPID_TEL: "));
                break;

        case PROPID_AGE:
                _tcscpy(szData, TEXT("PROPID_AGE: "));
                break;

        default:
                _tcscpy(szData, TEXT("(Unknown property): "));
```

```
                          break;
            }

            // Make sure a value is specified.
            if (!(pPropVal->wFlags & CEDB_PROPNOTFOUND))
            {
                    // Format the output based on the data type.
                    switch (LOWORD(pPropVal->propid))
                    {
                    case CEVT_I2:            // (short)
                            _itow(pPropVal->val.iVal, szNumber, 10);
                            _tcscat(szData, szNumber);
                            break;

                    case CEVT_LPWSTR:        // (LPWSTR)
                            _tcscat(szData, pPropVal->val.lpwstr);
                            break;

                    // Process other data types.
                    . . .
                    }
            }
            else
                    // No value for this property.
                    _tcscat(szData, TEXT("No value"));

            // Display the string szData (or insert it in a list, etc.)
            . . .
    }
}
```

10.3.7 Deleting Properties and Records

At some point, it might be desirable to delete a property from a record. Deleting a property is not the same as setting its value to 0 (or NULL). Deleting a property means that there is no value for that property, or that the value is unknown; setting a property to NULL means that the property has a known value, and that value is 0 (whatever it means to the application).

A property can be deleted through CeWriteRecordProps(), by specifying the flag CEDB_PROPDELETE in the wFlags field of the CEVALUNION structure. For instance, the following example deletes the name property of the specified record (oidRec).

```
CEPROPVAL    PropVal[1];                    // One property values

memset(PropVal, 0, sizeof(PropVal));        // Initialize to zero

PropVal[0].propid     = PROPID_NAME;        // Property to delete
PropVal[0].wFlags     = CEDB_PROPDELETE;    // Delete this property

oidRec = CeWriteRecordProps(
            hDB,                            // Database handle
            oidRec,                         // Update record
```

```
        1,                              // One property
        PropVal);                       // Property data
```

Deleting a record is straightforward: simply call `CeDeleteRecord()`, passing a valid database handle and a record identifier, such as those returned by `CeRead RecordProps()`. Here's an example (which assumes that `hDB` and `oidRec` are valid, as shown in the previous examples).

```
BOOL        rc;

rc = CeDeleteRecord(hDB, oidRec);

// rc is TRUE on success, FALSE on error. Call GetLastError() if needed.
```

10.3.8 Seeking Databases

So far, the examples simply needed to read records sequentially, using a sort order when opening the database. But on some occasions, the application might have to directly jump to a record.

In order to navigate within the database, an application calls `CeSeekDatabase()`. Based on the specified arguments, this function returns the identifier of the record that has been sought. It should be noted that `CeSeekDatabase()` always operates on the current sort order. For instance, using `CEDB_SEEK_BEGINNING` returns the first record, based on the current sort order. If another order is desired, the database must be re-opened with the proper order.

`CeSeekDatabase()` works with four parameters. The first is, as usual, a database handle. The second is the seek access; see Figure 10-18 for the possible values, and how they impact the third parameter, a `DWORD` value. The last parameter contains an index relative to the start of the database upon returning.

Seek Access Type	Seeking The Record ...	The Third Parameter Is
CEDB_SEEK_CEOID	Using the specified record identifier	Record identifier
CEDB_SEEK_VALUESMALLER	Having the immediate previous value. If none, move to end of database	A pointer to CEPROPVAL
CEDB_SEEK_VALUEFIRSTEQUAL	Matching the specified value. If none, move to end of database	A pointer to CEPROPVAL
CEDB_SEEK_VALUENEXTEQUAL	By moving forward by one record. If that record does not match the specified value, move to end of database	A pointer to CEPROPVAL

CEDB_SEEK_VALUEGREATER	Having the immediate next value. If none, move to end of database.	A pointer to CEPROPVAL
CEDB_SEEK_BEGINNING	At the nth position from the beginning	n i.e. the number of records
CEDB_SEEK_CURRENT	At the nth position from the current position	n i.e. the number of records
CEDB_SEEK_END	At the nth position from the end	n i.e. the number of records

Figure 10-18: Seek access types.

If the seek operation completes successfully, the sought record's identifier is returned; otherwise, zero is returned. Some access types also move to the end of the database (the CEDB_SEEK_VALUExxx types).

10.3.9 Listing Databases

The database API offers three calls to sequentially enumerate the Object Store databases, similar to the file search API. An application first calls CeFindFirstDatabaseEx(), specifying a GUID and a database type. The GUID can be a valid GUID or NULL to search all volumes. The type is a user-defined value, the same in fact as the second parameter of CeCreateDatabase(). An application can use 0 to search all databases within the specified volume(s). The function returns an enumeration handle, or INVALID_HANDLE_VALUE on error. No database is returned yet.

Armed with a valid handle and a GUID, an application repeatedly calls CeFindNextDatabaseEx(). Each call returns a database object id (or zero after the last database has been reached). An application can query more information about each database by calling CeOidGetInfoEx() and using the returned object id. Figure 10-2 lists the CEOIDINFO returned by CeOidGetInfo(). The infDatabase field of that structure is relevant for databases, and contains the information shown in Figure 10-9.

When the search is over, the enumeration handle must be closed by calling CloseHandle(). The following code example enumerates the name of all databases found.

```
void ListDatabases(CEGUID& guid)
{
    HANDLE          hEnum = CeFindFirstDatabaseEx(&guid, 0);

    if (hEnum == INVALID_HANDLE_VALUE)
            return;

    CEOID           oidDB;
    CEOIDINFO       oidInfo;
```

```
      while ((oidDB = CeFindNextDatabaseEx(hEnum, &guid)) != 0)
            if (CeOidGetInfoEx(&guid, oidDB, &oidInfo))
                   _putws(oidInfo.infDatabase.szDbaseName);
      else
                 puts("Unable to obtain database information.");

      if (GetLastError() != ERROR_NO_MORE_ITEMS)
            puts("Unable to find more databases.");

      CloseHandle(hEnum);
}
```

10.3.10 Changing Database Attributes

CeSetDatabaseInfoEx() can alter the attributes of a database, such as its name or the property sort order. It requires a GUID, a database identifier, and a pointer to a CEDBASEINFO structure, listed in Figure 10-9. Of that structure, wNumRecords is not used (*i.e.*, the content of the database is not altered by that call). The function returns TRUE on success, FALSE otherwise.

Changing the sort order (*i.e.* using the fields wNumSortOrder and rgSortSpecs) may take a few minutes on large databases. An application that intends to change the order should notify the user and ask whether he/she wants to go ahead anyway.

The following example renames a database, assuming its GUID and identifier are known. A CEDBASEINFO structure is initialized with the new name and CeSetDatabase InfoEx() is called.

```
CEDBASEINFO          DBInfo;
BOOL                 rc;

// Zero the structure, then set the flag and the new name.
memset(&DBInfo, '\0', sizeof(DBInfo));
DBInfo.dwFlags = CEDB_VALIDDBFLAGS | CEDB_VALIDNAME;
_tcscpy(DBInfo.szDbaseName, pszNewName);

// Set the database name. The function returns TRUE on success.
CeSetDatabaseInfoEx(&guid, oidDB, &DBInfo);
```

10.3.11 Tips on How to Write Database Applications

The previous examples work well because the database has been opened with the flag CEDB_AUTOINCREMENT. This is ideal to load a database into memory. Consider an application that presents a list of contacts, as found in the Contacts database, into a list box, and lets the user browse that list box. The application could present three push buttons to respectively create, modify, and delete a record.

At first, that application must read records one by one and store them in memory. Since the buffers used by CeReadRecordProps() are overwritten for each call, the application needs extra buffers to store each record. Each call also returns the record identifier, which the application can hold. All this information can be kept in a list box and presented to the user, who may browse it at will.

Adding a record consists of gathering new information and calling `CeWrite RecordProps()`, using a null record id and the entered properties. If it is successful, the information is also added in the list box as a single row.

Modifying a record consists of gathering the new values and calling `CeWrite RecordProps()`, passing the record identifier initially read and the modified properties. On success, the corresponding row in the list box is also updated to reflect the changes.

Finally, deleting a record consists of calling `CeDeleteRecord()`, using the corresponding record identifier initially read. The corresponding row in the list box is then destroyed.

As you can see, the strategy is to execute the database operation first, and update the list box on success. On error, an error message can simply be shown.

Another type of application might simply perform some updates not directly triggered by the user. Consider merging two contact databases, one on the desktop and one on the CE device. When a desktop record is read, the application must determine if it already exists, because simply adding it could result in duplicates. In that case, using the property the order is based upon, the application may seek a record with the same property. For instance, the application may seek to discover whether a record with the name "Smith, John" already exists. If so, that record can be read and compared to see if all fields are equal. Alternatively, the application may show both to the user and let him/her decide. The strategy here is to seek potentially matching records, instead of reading all of them sequentially.

10.3.12 The Original Database API

Prior to Windows CE 2.10, databases were exclusively residing in the Object Store. Consequently, that was no notion of volumes or GUIDs. The original API resembles the one described earlier, minus the "Ex" suffix. The most important difference compared with the actual API is the lack of GUIDs in the original API.

Unless you are specifically targeting a version of Windows CE 2.10 prior to 2.10, you should use the current API described in the previous pages, giving you access to volumes.

SUGGESTED READING

Date, "An introduction To Database Systems"

> This is for those of you who are serious about databases. Few of the concepts presented here directly apply to Windows CE databases, but it might give you ideas about how to split information among tables and prevent data inconsistencies.

Chapter 11

File System

A file system is an operating system module that controls the organization of files on various devices. Each file system has its own characteristics and implementation, such as how files are named, stored and accessed by application. For instance, the FAT (File Allocation Table) file system, implemented on MS-DOS, supports a naming convention dubbed "8.3", an 8-letter file name and 3-letter extension, and relies on a sequential allocation table to store files. On the other hand, NTFS (NT File System) supports longer file names, and implements an efficient scheme to store files. It even supports disk restoration upon system failure. Windows CE, like most general-purpose operating systems, supports multiple file systems.

What is of interest to developers, though, is the fact that any of the available file systems can be accessed through a common API, regardless of the underlying implementation. It is up to CE to provide a level of abstraction that shields applications from most file system implementation-specific details. That API allows not only manipulating files, but also the ability to conduct input/output operation on files and system devices. We'll explore all these topics in this chapter.

11.1 THE OBJECT STORE VS. STORAGE CARDS

Windows CE's primary file system controls the portion of the Object Store where files reside. In particular, that's where the Windows directory (\Windows) is to be found. This file system supports long file names as found on other recent Windows platforms, but a few features have been dropped:

- There is no security (such as file ownership or access permissions) whatsoever.

- There is no notion of drives such as "A:", "C:", etc. Everything is accessible from the Object Store's root directory *i.e.*,"\".

- There is no concept of current directory, requiring each application to access files through their full path name.

The Object Store is limited in size to 16MB, although internal file compression increases the effective amount of bytes being be stored in there.

A Windows CE device can expand the Object Store in order to accommodate more files, by adding storage cards. Such a card is an external storage device such as an ATA flash card. Windows CE has the ability to detect these extra storage devices; when connected, they appear under the directory "\StorageCardx", where x is a sequential number ranging from 1 to 255. For instance, if two storage devices are detected, they will be accessible under "\StorageCard1" and "\StorageCard2", respectively. Names are attributed based on the order of detection.

An application can query the size of a storage device (including the Object Store's file portion) by calling GetDiskFreeSpaceEx(). This call requires a directory path, whose related device is identified by the system. The next three arguments are pointers to ULARGE_INTEGER (a 64-bit union type), respectively the total number of free bytes available to the calling thread, the disk total byte capacity, and the total number of free bytes on the disk. The next example queries these values for the Object Store. Any path related to the Object Store will do, although the example simply uses the root directory of it.

```
void PrintDiskSpace()
{
    ULARGE_INTEGER nFreeBytesAvailableToCaller;
    ULARGE_INTEGER nTotalNumberOfBytes;
    ULARGE_INTEGER nTotalNumberOfFreeBytes;

    GetDiskFreeSpaceEx(_T("\\"),             // Object Store
            &nFreeBytesAvailableToCaller,
            &nTotalNumberOfBytes,
            &nTotalNumberOfFreeBytes);

    printf("Free bytes available to caller: %I64d\n",
            nFreeBytesAvailableToCaller);

    printf("Total number of bytes        : %I64d\n",
            nTotalNumberOfBytes);

    printf("Total number of free bytes   : %I64d\n",
            nTotalNumberOfFreeBytes);
}
```

Note that this example makes uses of Microsoft's C/C++ __int64 type, as well as of the I64 size prefix in printf() to print 64-bit values (other compilers may not support these non-ANSI features).

11.2 FILE AND DEVICE INPUT/OUTPUT

Most programmers are accustomed to reading and writing bytes from and to files. But the same concept applies to some other devices. Consider reading bytes from a serial port, for instance. Windows CE implements a common API to access files and devices, as found on Windows NT. This section explains how to use this API to access and store data in files and devices.

Bear in mind, though, that there are a few subtle differences whether a file or a device is being accessed. For instance, files can be created, but not device (since they already exist). These differences are highlighted throughout the sections that follow.

11.2.1 Creating and Opening Files

A file is created by calling `CreateFile()`. This call is very flexible and accepts numerous options. For instance, when creating a file, one can instruct `CreateFile()` to return an error if the file already exists or to simply discard the previous version and create a new, empty one.

That same call is also used when opening a file: it simply requires different options. Hence, `CreateFile()` is used for both creating and opening files. The call returns a file handle that can be used with the other file-oriented Win32 calls. The following example opens the file `"MyFile.txt"` for read and write access, and creates it if it doesn't exist:

```
HANDLE      hFile;

hFile = CreateFile(
    TEXT("MyFile.txt"),                // Unicode file name
    GENERIC_READ | GENERIC_WRITE,      // Desired access
    FILE_SHARE_READ,                   // Shared access is READ
    NULL,                              // No security attrib. on CE
    OPEN_ALWAYS,                       // Open existing or create
    FILE_ATTRIBUTE_NORMAL |            // This is a normal file
    FILE_FLAG_RANDOM_ACCESS,           // Use random access caching
    NULL);                             // NULL on CE

// hFile is a valid handle on success or INVALID_HANDLE_VALUE on error.
```

The first argument is the Unicode file name. This must be a zero-terminated string. The backslash (\) is used as a directory delimiter; don't forget to double it in C and C++ (*e.g.,* "\\MyFile.txt"), due to its special meaning in these languages. Filenames cannot include characters whose Unicode value is less than 32, nor any other characters not supported by the targeted file system. For instance, a FAT file system does not support the following characters in file names, although another file system theoretically could: / \ : * ? " < > |.

The second argument is the desired access. This access can be either 0 (to query or set file information; more in Section 11.2.6), GENERIC_READ, GENERIC_WRITE or a combination of the last two (a common situation). In the latter case, use the logical "or" operator (|) to combine both modes.

The third parameter indicates how the same file can be shared with other threads or applications when the file is opened. Use 0 for an exclusive access, or a combination of FILE_SHARE_READ and FILE_SHARE_WRITE. Subsequent CreateFile() calls fail if the requested access violates the share access of an opened file. For instance, if an application tries to open a file with FILE_SHARE_READ sharing mode and the file is already opened for writing, the call fails; similarly, specifying the FILE_SHARE_WRITE share mode when opening a file already opened for reading fails.

The fourth parameter is NULL on CE. The next parameter indicates what action to take if the file does or does not exist (see Figure 11-1). The sixth parameter sets the file flags and attributes (listed in Figure 11-2 and Figure 11-3). The flags specify some access modes, whereas the attributes specify the file's type. But pay attention here: whereas the flags are considered in both creating and opening files, the attributes are only used when creating them, not opening them. Furthermore, upon creating a file, the attributes are always merged with FILE_ATTRIBUTE_ARCHIVE, and they establish the initial attributes of the file. Finally, the last parameter is always NULL.

Disposition Mode	Description
CREATE_NEW	Creates a new file and fails if it already exists.
CREATE_ALWAYS	Creates a new file and truncates it if it already exists.
OPEN_EXISTING	Opens a file and fails if it does not exist.
OPEN_ALWAYS	Opens the file, creates it if it does not exist.
TRUNCATE_EXISTING	Opens the file and truncates its length. It fails if the file does not exist.

Figure 11-1: The supported creation disposition modes. They indicate what action to take whether the file does or does not exist.

File Flags	Description
`FILE_FLAG_WRITE_THROUGH`	Write operations are unbuffered and go directly to the disk.
`FILE_FLAG_RANDOM_ACCESS`	Indicates subsequent random access and helps optimizing cache use.

Figure 11-2: The flags indicate some access modes. They are specified along the file attributes. They are always taken into account, and strictly impact performance (specifically, cache operations).

File Attributes	Description
`FILE_ATTRIBUTE_NORMAL`	Normal file, i.e., no special attribute. Effective when specified alone only. When combined with other flags, it is ignored[29].
`FILE_ATRTIBUTE_ARCHIVE`	An attribute used by backup software.
`FILE_ATTRIBUTE_HIDDEN`	The file is hidden and normally doesn't show up in directory listing.
`FILE_ATTRIBUE_READONLY`	Read-only file. Such a file cannot be written to, nor deleted.
`FILE_ATTRIBUTE_SYSTEM`	System file, used by the operating system. It normally doesn't show up in directory listing.
`FILE_ATTRIBUTE_TEMPORARY`	Not supported by the native file system, it indicates directories that are storage devices.

Figure 11-3: The attributes indicate some the file types. They are specified along the file flags. They are only taken into account when creating a file; they are ignored when opening a file.

11.2.2 Opening Devices

Applications must open devices to access them. However, devices can only be opened, not created, since they already exist. Likewise, they cannot be deleted, whereas files can (see Section 11.3.3 regarding deleting files).

Applications rely on `CreateFile()` to open devices, using parameters as shown in Figure 11-4.

---

[29] The value of `FILE_ATTRIBUTE_NORMAL` is zero, whereas all other flags are non-zero values.

CreateFile() Parameter	Value to Use With Devices
lpFilename	The device name e.g. _T("COM1:").
dwDesiredAccessMode	Usually GENERIC_READ | GENERIC_WRITE
dwShareMode	Usually 0
lpSecurityAttributes	NULL
dwCreationDisposition	OPEN_EXISTING
dwFlagsAndAttributes	Usually 0
hTemplateFile	NULL

Figure 11-4: CreateFile() should be called with these parameters in order to open devices.

Refer to Section 11.2.7 for an example showing how to open a device.

11.2.3 Reading and Writing Files and Devices

Two system calls are provided to read and write files and devices: ReadFile() and WriteFile().

ReadFile() reads the bytes from a file or device. With a file, bytes are read from the current file pointer position, which is then moved after the last byte is read, ready for the next operation to be executed. For devices, ReadFile() obtains the next available bytes.

ReadFile() requires five parameters: a file handle, a buffer, the size of that buffer (in bytes), a pointer to a DWORD to store the byte count on success, and NULL. The function returns non-zero on success, or 0 (FALSE) on error. Reading beyond the end of file marker returns success, but the byte count (as specified by the fourth parameter) is zero.

Don't forget that a Unicode character occupies two bytes. Hence, reading two characters requires a four-byte buffer. The next example reads some Unicode characters from a file or device. Note that nCharCount, the Unicode character count, is multiplied by two to get the equivalent byte count. And upon returning, the Unicode character count is half the value specified by dwBytesRead. The following example reads an Unicode string from a file.

```
BOOL ReadFromFile(HANDLE hFile, LPTSTR pBuffer, int nCharCount)
{
    BOOL    rc;                          // Status code
    DWORD   dwBytesRead;                 // Read bytes count

    rc = ReadFile(
            hFile,                       // Valid file/device handle
            pBuffer,                     // Buffer address
            nCharCount * 2,              // Number of bytes to read
            &dwBytesRead,                // Number of bytes read
            NULL);                       // No overlap on CE
```

```
    // rc is non-zero on success, FALSE on error
    return rc;
}
```

`WriteFile()` writes some bytes into a file or device. When used with a file, the operation is done from the current file pointer position, which is moved after the last written byte. For devices, `WriteFile()` sends the bytes to the device. `WriteFile()` essentially requires the same arguments as `ReadFile()`.

Again, remember that Unicode characters require two bytes each. Hence, when writing a string of an unknown length, rely on `_tcslen()` * 2 instead of `strlen()` to get the exact byte count (and add 2 to include the NULL character if required). The next example writes a null-terminated string. The NULL characacter is also written.

```
BOOL WriteToFile(HANDLE hFile, LPCTSTR pszBuffer)
{
    BOOL    rc;                         // Status code
    DWORD   dwBytesWritten;             // Written bytes count

    rc = WriteFile(
            hFile,                      // Valid file handle
            pszBuffer,                  // Buffer address
            _tcslen(pszBuffer) * 2 + 2, // Number of bytes to write
            &dwBytesWritten,            // Number of bytes written
            NULL);                      // No overlap on CE

    // rc is non-zero on success, FALSE on error
    return rc;
}
```

`WriteFile()` writes data into an internal buffer, which CE flushes to the appropriate file system or device on a regular basis. `FlushFileBuffers()` can by used by applications to force an immediate flush of these buffers. This is useful if an application requires the data to be stored in a file system at a given moment (to let another application read the same data from the same file, for instance). `FlushFileBuffers()` simply requires a file handle, and is usually used immediately after calling `WriteFile()`, as follows:

```
rc = FlushFileBuffers(hFile);          // Flush buffers

// rc is non-zero on success, FALSE on error
```

11.2.4 File and Device Seeking

Files are accessed via two methods: sequentially or random.

253

A file is essentially a stream (or a series) of bytes. Most applications, upon startup, repeatedly call `ReadFile()` to load data, in a sequential order. Similarly, upon terminating, those same applications invoke `WriteFile()` multiple times to save the data, again in a sequential order. Most applications rely on this approach because it is simple and adequate.

Other applications, though, do not need to read an entire file to use it. For instance, a phone dialer application does not need to load the entire list in memory, it simply needs to locate where the desired phone number is and read it. Data within these files is usually organized in records, and applications only need to access some specific records. That kind of access is called random access (as opposed to sequential access). It involves moving the current file pointer and read or write a certain record (see Figure 11-5). Random access files are harder to manipulate, because when overwriting an existing record, an application must be careful not to overwrite the following record. If a record is modified in a way that results in it containing more information, the record must be written at the end of the file, and the previous location must be marked as "vacant", ready to be used eventually by another record that will fit in there.

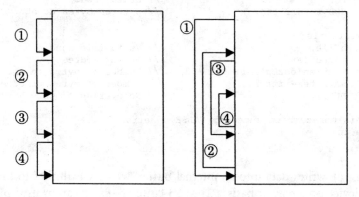

Figure 11-5: Most applications sequentially read or write files from top to bottom (a). Other applications use a random access technique to manipulate files, by moving the file pointer (b).

Random access is supported on Windows CE by calling `SetFilePointer()`. It simply consists of moving the current file pointer by an offset (expressed in bytes). This offset can be negative (to move backward, toward the beginning of the file) or positive (to move forward, toward the end of the file). Additionally, the offset is applied from one of three possible starting positions: the beginning of the file, the end-of-file-position, or the current file pointer position.

The offset can be expressed either as a 32-bit value (for files less than 2GB in size) or 64-bit value (for files larger than 2GB). Local files are unlikely to be that big, but remote files, accessible through the network (as described in Section 12.2.3), may be that huge.

The following example demonstrates how to position the file pointer on the 65th byte (offset 64), from the beginning of the file, using a 32-bit byte offset. This offset is specified as the second parameter. Passing NULL as the third parameter indicates that the offset is a 32-bit value. As a result, SetFilePosition() returns a 32-bit value, which is the new file pointer position.

```
LONG          nPosition;

nPosition = SetFilePointer(
              hFile,                    // File handle
              64,                       // Offset (low-order 32 bits)
              NULL,                     // Offset (high-order 32 bits)
              FILE_BEGIN);              // Start from beginning of file

// The new file pointer is dwPosition, expressed as a 32-bit value.
```

If you truly need to specify a 64-bit value (to specify an offset greater than 2GB), the third parameter must be a pointer to a DWORD containing the high-order 32 bits. The contents of that pointer, plus the second parameter (not a pointer itself) are combined to form the 64-bit offset. In that case, upon returning, the new file pointer position is equally expressed as a 64-bit value; the high 32-bit DWORD in stored in the value pointed by the third parameter, and the low 32-bit DWORD is the value returned by the call. Here is an example of using a 64-bit offset:

```
// Move to position 0x100000000 (1 with 8 zeroes)

LONG          nHighPos = 0x1;          // Upper 32-bit
LONG          nLowPos = 0;             // Lower 32-bit

nLowPos = SetFilePointer(
              hFile,                    // File handle
              nLowPos,                  // Passed by value
              &nHighPos,                // Passed by address
              FILE_BEGIN);              // Start from beginning of file

// The new file pointer it at (nHighPos:dwLosPos), a 64-bit value.
```

Unless files are accessed across the network (on large file servers), 32-bit offsets are enough.

11.2.5 Setting the End of File

A file can be truncated or extended by calling SetEndOfFile() (see Figure 11-6). This sets the actual end of file marker to the current file pointer position. For instance, if a 100-byte file is opened and the file pointer is moved on the 50th byte, followed by a call to

`SetEndOfFile()`, the file's length is truncated to 50 and the extra 50 bytes is discarded. If later on, the file pointer is moved 20 bytes beyond the 50th byte, followed by a call to `SetEndOfFile()`, the new file length becomes 70 bytes. The content of these 20 extra bytes is undefined.

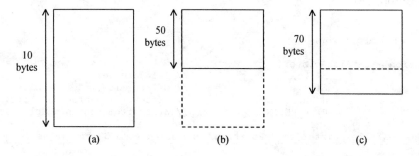

(a)   (b)   (c)

Figure 11-6: A file can be truncated or extended by moving the end of file marker. In this figure, the original file (a) is truncated by 50 bytes (b), to be later extended by 20 (c).

This call is useful with random access files, containing a series of records. In cases in which last records would be deleted, moving the end of file marker would release the now-unoccupied space.

11.2.6 Getting File Information

A few Win32 functions are available to query more information about files, listed in Figure 11-7.

Function	Description
`CeOidGetInfo()`	Returns the Object Store id of the file (see Chapter 10)
`GetFileAttributes()`	Returns the attributes of a file, the same as explained earlier (`FILE_ATTRIBUTE_...`). that functions requires a file name.
`GetFileInformationByHandle()`	Returns a `BY_HANDLE_FILE_INFORMATION` structure about a file. This structure is a superset of `WIN32_FIND_DATA`, described in Section 11.4.3. The function requires a file handle (not a file name).
`GetFileSize()`	Returns the size of a file. The function requires a file handle.
`GetFileTime()`	Returns the creation, last accessed and last modified times, as `FILETIME` structures. FAT and NTFS file systems maintain these values, but other file systems may not.

SetFileAttributes()	Sets the file attributes to those specified. The function requires a file name.
SetFileTime()	Sets the creation, last accessed and last modified times. The function requires a file handle and FILETIME structures. The outcome of this function depends whether the underlying file supports the time values.

Figure 11-7: A few system calls to query or set file information.

Be careful, because some of these functions require a file handle (which can be obtained by calling CreateFile()), whereas others require an Unicode file name.

11.2.7 Device Input/Output Control

External devices may support some functionality that is not available through the API we've seen in the previous sections. Consider accessing a digital camera. An application can call CreateFile() to access the device, WriteFile() to store pictures in binary format, ReadFile() to read them back, and CloseHandle() when terminating. But what if the camera supports a rewinding function? How could it be invoked? One might use SetFilePointer(), using an offset of 0 as the first picture, 1 as the second, and so on. But the semantic of SetFilePointer() is to move the file pointer to a byte offset, not a picture offset.

In order for applications to exploit the full functionality of any type of device, Windows CE implements DeviceIOControl(). This function makes use of a driver-specific code, which is passed "as is" to the device, without being interpreted by CE. The call also accepts input and output buffers, in case any data is required (in and out) to complete the call (see Figure 11-8). The format and content of these buffers are driver- and service-specific.

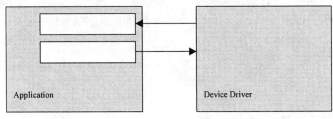

Figure 11-8: An application can specify input and output buffers when invoking a device driver-specific function. The driver can directly access this buffer to read parameters and return results.

Here's an example. Let's assume that a digital camera driver returns the number of pictures taken with code 1. The application could obtain that number by passing a buffer to an integer, as shown below:

```
#include "cam.h"                        // Camera header
file

DWORD GetPictureAvailCount()
{
    HANDLE hCam;

    hCam = CreateFile(
            _T("CAM1:"),                 // Camera device driver
            GENERIC_READ | GENERIC_WRITE,
            0,                           // Exclusive access
            NULL,                        // No security attributes
            OPEN_EXISTING,               // Must use OPEN_EXISTING
            0,                           // No overlapped I/O on CE
            NULL);                       // NULL for comm devices

    if (hCam == INVALID_HANDLE_VALUE)
            return -1;

    // Invoke I/O Control 1 on the driver.
    BOOL    rc;
    DWORD   dwCount;
    DWORD   dwBytesReturned;

    rc = DeviceIoControl(
            hCam,                        // Camera device handle
            CAM_GET_PICTURE_COUNT,       // Driver-specific code
            NULL,                        // Input buffer (none here)
            0,                           // Input buffer size
            &dwCount,                    // Output buffer
            sizeof(dwCount),             // output buffer size
            &dwBytesReturned,            // Count of bytes returned
            NULL);                       // No overlapped I/O on CE

    if (!rc)
            dwCount = -1;

    CloseHandle(hCam);

    return dwCount;
}
```

You must consult the driver's documentation to know what codes can be used, and whether input and/or output buffers are required, as each driver is free to support any functionality through that function. Drivers should also be shipped with some header files (cam.h in the previous example), which would contain any data type and/or function declarations.

11.2.8 Closing Files and Devices

When a file or device is no longer needed, the associated file handle must be closed by calling CloseHandle() and specifying the handle.

11.3 DISK AND FILE OPERATIONS

Besides supporting functions to perform input/output, Windows CE provides a few convenient routines to manipulate files as a whole.

11.3.1 Copying Files

A file can be copied to a new one by calling CopyFile(). It takes the name of the source file (to copy from), the name of the target file (to copy to), and a flag indicating what to do if the target file exists (overwrite it or return an error). The flag attributes (see Figure 11-8) are copied as well. The following copies the file "MyFile.txt" to "MySecondFile.txt":

```
BOOL        rc;                         // Return code

rc = CopyFile(
        _T("\\MyFile.txt"),             // File to copy from
        _T("\\MySecondFile.txt"),       // File to copy to
        FALSE);                         // Do not fail if the file exists

// rc is non-zero on success, FALSE on error
if (!rc)
    . . .
```

11.3.2 Moving and Renaming Files

A file can be renamed or moved to another directory, on the same or different volume, by calling MoveFile(). A directory (and its files) can be moved as well, but on the same volume. The call takes source and target file names. The new name must not already exist. The following example moves the file "MyFile.txt" to the parent directory:

```
BOOL        rc;                             // Return code

rc = MoveFile(
    _T("\\MyFile.txt"),                     // File to move
    _T("\\Windows\\MyFile.txt"));  // New location and name

// rc is non-zero on success, FALSE on error
if (!rc)
    . . .
```

11.3.3 Deleting Files

DeleteFile() removes a file. It requires one argument: the file name (not the handle), and returns an error if the file is opened (by the same or another application) or if it does not exist. The following example deletes a file:

```
BOOL         rc;                          // Return code

rc = DeleteFile(_T("\\MyFile.txt"));     // File to delete

// rc is non-zero on success, FALSE on error
if (!rc)
    . . .
```

11.4 DIRECTORY OPERATIONS

Windows CE also supports functions to create, browse, and delete directories.

11.4.1 Creating and Deleting Directories

Windows CE includes two directory-specific functions to create and delete directories.

The first is CreateDirectory() and is simple to use: it requires the new directory name, and a NULL parameter (some security attributes that are meaningful on other Windows platforms only).

The second is RemoveDirectory() and is even simpler: it only requires a path name. This must be the name of an empty directory: the call does not automatically destroy the directory's content. To do so, an application must navigate through its files and sub-directories (as described in Section 11.4.3), deleting everything it encounters.

11.4.2 Temporary Directories

Windows CE defines a temporary directory, that applications use to store temporary files. The temporary name can be obtained by calling GetTempPath(). The function requires two arguments: a buffer size and a buffer address. It returns the size (in Unicode characters) of the buffer. Indeed, the path is returned as a null-terminated Unicode string.

The next example invokes GetTempPath(). Note the use of %S (instead of %s) to print an Unicode string in a console application.

```
TCHAR        szTempPath[MAX_PATH];        // Unicode string
DWORD        dwCount;

dwCount = GetTempPath(sizeof(szTempPath), szTempPath);

printf("dwCount = %d, [%S]\n", dwCount, szTempPath);
```

11.4.3 File Searching

Windows CE includes some functions that we'll call the file search API, to search for a file or, more generally, to list the content of some directories. Such a search is based on a file *mask* specification. A mask is a path name, whose purpose is to identify matching file names. A mask usually contains *wildcards* as its last file element. Two wildcards are supported: the star (*), which means any sequence of characters, and the question mark (?), which can be substituted for any one character. Figure 11-9 shows a few examples of using these wildcards.

Mark	Description	Examples
.	All files, with or without an extension	Makefile, P1.doc, P2.doc, Projects, People, Project1.xls, Project2.xls
*	Same as *.*	Makefile, P1.doc, P2.doc, Projects, People, Project1.xls, Project2.xls
*.	All files, without an extension	Makefile, Projects, People
P*.*	All files starting with P with or without an extension	P1.doc, P2.doc, Projects, People, Project1.xls, Project2.xls
P*	Same as P*.*	P1.doc, P2.doc, Projects, People, Project1.xls, Project2.xls
P*.	All files starting with P, without an extension	Projects, People
ake	All files with "ake" in it, with or without and extension	Makefile
P?.doc	All files starting with P, following by any character, whose extension is "doc".	P1.doc, P2.doc

Figure 11-9: Description and examples of file masks.

The WIN32_FIND_DATA Structure

File searches rely on a WIN32_FIND_DATA structure, which is filled up for each matching file. That structure is defined in Figure 11-10:

Type	Member	Description
DWORD	dwFileAttributes	File attributes
FILETIME	ftCreationTime	Time of creation
FILETIME	ftLastAccessTime	Time of last access
FILETIME	ftLastWriteAccess	Time or last write operation

DWORD	nFileSizeHigh	High-order 32-bit file size
DWORD	nFileSizeLow	Low-order 32-bit file size
DWORD	dwOID	Object Store Identifier
TCHAR	cFileName[MAX_PATH]	Full file name
TCHAR	cAlternateFileName[14]	Filename, using the 8.3 format.

Figure 11-10: The WIN32_FIND_DATA structure.

The first member, dwFileAttributes, identifies the file attributes. In addition to those listed in Figure 11-3, a few others might be returned as well (see Figure 11-11).

File Attributes	Description
FILE_ATTRIBUTE_COMPRESSED	The file is compressed.
FILE_ATTRIBUTE_DIRECTORY	The file is in fact a directory.
FILE_ATTRIBUTE_ENCRYPTED	The file is encrypted
FILE_ATTRIBUTE_INROM	The file is stored in ROM
FILE_ATTRIBUTE_OFFLINE	The data is not immediately available.
FILE_ATTRIBUTE_ROMMODULE	This file executes directly from ROM.

Figure 11-11: Some file attributes from the WIN32_FIND_DATA structure.

The next three members are the creation, last access, and last write times, stored as FILETIME structures. Because they are expressed in Coordinated Universal Time (UTC), the values must first be converted to local time by calling FileTimeToLocal FileTime(). A resulting FILETIME structure contains a 64-bit value, which it is best converted into a SYSTEMTIME value by calling FileTimeToSystemTime(). A SYSTEM TIME structure is easier to interpret and is defined as follows:

Type	Member	Description
WORD	wYear	4-digit year
WORD	wMonth	Month (1 is January)
WORD	wDayOfWeek	Day of week (0 is Sunday)
WORD	wDay	Day
WORD	wHour	Hour
WORD	wMinute	Minute
WORD	wSecond	Seconds
WORD	wMilliseconds	Milliseconds

Figure 11-12: The SYSTEMTIME structure is easier to interpret than the plain 64-bit FILETIME.

The next two members of Win32_FIND_DATA (nFileSizeHigh and nFileSize Low) indicate the file size when combined together as a 64-bit value.

The original file name is stored in cFileName. It is also stored in cAlternate FileName, in the "8.3" format. This format is the old MS-DOS file name format and might be required when working with FAT file systems.

Finding Files

The search starts by invoking FindFirstFile(), passing a file mask specification and a pointer to a WIN32_SEARCH_DATA structure. The function searches for the first matching file. If found, the WIN32_SEARCH_DATA structure is filled with information about that file, and the function returns a search handle that can be used for continuing the search. On the other hand, if no file is found, the returned value is INVALID_HANDLE_VALUE and the search is over.

The next matching file is returned by calling FindNextFile(). The call requires the search handle and a pointer to the WIN32_SEARCH_DATA structure. The same or another pointer can be used; if the same is used, its content is overridden. FindNextFile() returns a Boolean: non-zero means that another file has been found whereas 0 (or FALSE) indicates that no more file matches the mask.

As long as a file is found, FindNextFile() can be called again and again to find the next files, one by one. This method does not visit sub-directories automatically. If an application needs to list the entire content of a directory, including its sub-directories, the file attribute of each matching file must be compared against FILE_ATTRIBUTE_DIRECTORY. If this attribute is set, then the entire search cycle (FindFirstFile(), FindNextFile(), and FindClose()) must be repeated.

Call FindClose() (not CloseHandle()) with the handle when the search is over.

The following example (which is implemented in the **ListFile** sample, on the CD-ROM) finds the files in the "\Windows" directory, and prints some information about each file. The method implements a recursive call to list sub-directories as well. It can be invoked by executing:

```
    ListFiles(0, _T(""));
```

to list all files.

```
void ListFiles(int nLevel, LPCTSTR pszDirName)
{
    HANDLE              hSearch;
    TCHAR               Buffer[MAX_PATH];
    LPTSTR              pszBuffer;
    WIN32_FIND_DATA     FileData;
```

```
        // Set the mask specification by appending "\*.*"
        _stprintf(Buffer, _T("%s\\*.*"), pszDirName);

        // Find first file, return if none.
        hSearch = FindFirstFile(Buffer, &FileData);

        if (hSearch == INVALID_HANDLE_VALUE)
                return;

        // Add indentation spaces to the buffer.
        pszBuffer = Buffer;

        for (int i = 0; i < nLevel; i++)
                *pszBuffer++ = _T(' ');

        do
        {
                // Format and display file information
                FormatFileInfo(FileData, pszBuffer);
                _putts(Buffer);

                // If this is a directory, list its contentas well
                if ((FileData.dwFileAttributes &
                        FILE_ATTRIBUTE_DIRECTORY) != 0)
                {
                        // Format the complete name of the directory
                        _stprintf(pszBuffer, _T("%s\\%s"),
                                pszDirName, FileData.cFileName);

                        // And list it.
                        ListFiles(nLevel + 1, pszBuffer);
                }

        } while (FindNextFile(hSearch, &FileData));

        FindClose(hSearch);
}

void FormatFileInfo(WIN32_FIND_DATA& FileData, LPTSTR pszBuffer)
{
    FILETIME        LocalTime;
    SYSTEMTIME      SystemTime;

    FileTimeToLocalFileTime(&FileData.ftLastAccessTime, &LocalTime);
    FileTimeToSystemTime(&LocalTime, &SystemTime);

    _stprintf(pszBuffer, _T("%s\t%02d/%02d/%d %02d:%02d"),
            FileData.cFileName,
            SystemTime.wMonth,
            SystemTime.wDay,
            SystemTime.wYear,
            SystemTime.wHour,
            SystemTime.wMinute);
}
```

11.5 MEMORY-MAPPED FILES

Windows CE supports memory-mapped files, as implemented on other Windows platforms. Memory-mapped files are exactly that: they are mapped into memory, making them easily accessible through plain pointers (see Figure 11-13). Applications no longer need to allocate buffers to read or write data, nor execute I/O operations, such as calling `ReadFile()` or `WriteFile()`, etc. Another big plus is the ability to share memory-mapped files among processes, as we will see soon.

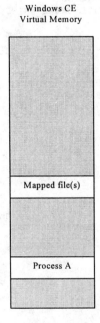

Windows CE
Virtual Memory

Mapped file(s)

Process A

Figure 11-13: Memory-mapped files become part of a process's address space. In this case, process A has access to its slot and all files it maps.

Memory-mapped files in fact increase a process address space. Let's recall that a process originally has a virtual address space of 32 MB (see Chapter 8 for details). Mapping a 4MB file increases that address space to 36MB, although the extra 4MB is not contiguous to the initial 32MB. Memory-mapped files always reside in a predetermined address range.

Memory-mapped files are so convenient that Windows CE uses them internally to run applications and load dynamic-link libraries.

11.5.1 Using Mapping Files

Mapping a file requires making three calls, as shown in the following example.

```
void SomeFunction()
{
    HANDLE hFile, hMap;
    LPVOID pFile;
    LPTSTR pStr;

    // Open the file. In this case, the file is required to exist.
    hFile = CreateFileForMapping(          // A variant of CreateFile()
            pszFileName,
            GENERIC_READ | GENERIC_WRITE,
            FILE_SHARE_READ | FILE_SHARE_WRITE,
            NULL,
            OPEN_EXISTING,                 // Open existing, fail otherwise
            FILE_ATTRIBUTE_NORMAL,
            NULL);

    // Return if the file couldn't get opened
    if (hFile == INVALID_HANDLE_VALUE)
            return;

    // Create the file mapping object.
    hMap = CreateFileMapping(
            hFile,                         // Opened file handle
            NULL,                          // No security attributes on CE
            PAGE_READWRITE,                // Pages will be read-write
            0,                             // Size (high): use file's size
            0,                             // Size (low):  use file's size
            NULL);                         // Unnamed mapping

    // On error, return.
    if (hMap == NULL)
    {
            CloseHandle(hFile);
            return;
    }

    // Create the mapping view. This returns a pointer to the mapped file.
    pFile = MapViewOfFile(
            hMap,                          // File mapping object
            FILE_MAP_WRITE,                // Read-write access
            0,                             // Offset (high): start of file
            0,                             // Offset (low) : start of file
            0);                            // Size: the whole file

    // On error, return
    if (pFile == NULL)
    {
            CloseHandle(hFile);
            CloseHandle(hMap);
            return;
    }

    // From that point, pFile points at the mapped file. The generic
    // pointer is cast into a TCHAR pointer, and the file's second
    // Unicode character is output.
    pStr = (LPTSTR) pFile;
```

```
    tprintf( T("p[1] = %c\n"), pStr[1]);

    // Unmap the file.
    UnmapViewOfFile(pFile);
    CloseHandle(hMap);
    CloseHandle(hFile);
}
```

`CreateFileForMapping()` works exactly like `CreateFile()`. As a matter of fact, the other Windows platforms use `CreateFile()` for this step, but another call was required for Windows CE to process mapped files properly. Nonetheless, the same parameters can be used as with `CreateFile()`. The function returns a file handle as usual, or `INVALID_HANDLE_VALUE` on error.

`CreateFileMapping()` creates a file-mapping object and associates it with the specified opened file. The first argument is the file handle returned by `CreateFileForMapping()`. The second argument is simply `NULL`. The following argument indicates the page protection associated with the area. Common values are either `PAGE_READONLY` or `PAGE_READWRITE`. Note that the access rights specified in `CreateFileForMapping()` must match (for instance, `PAGE_READWRITE` requires `GENERIC_READ|GENERIC_WRITE` access mode). The next two parameters are the maximum size of the file-mapping object, the high-order 32 bits first, followed by the low 32 bits. Use zeroes for both to use the actual file size. Finally, the last parameter is the name of the mapping object (more in Section 11.5.2); `NULL` means that the mapping object is unnamed. The function returns a file mapping handle, or `NULL` on error.

Finally, `MapViewOfFile()` maps the file in memory. The first argument is the mapping object handle, as returned by `CreateFileMapping()`. The second parameter specifies the map access mode, such as `FILE_MAP_READ` or `FILE_MAP_WRITE`. Again, the mode must match the access modes of the two previous calls. The next three parameters control which portion of the file is to be mapped. Use zeroes to map the entire file. However, to map a portion of it, specify the starting point and the size. The starting point is a 64-bit value specified by the third and fourth parameters (respectively the high 32-bit and low 32-bit offset values); the size is the byte count and is specified using the sixth parameter. The call returns a generic pointer (`LPVOID`), which can be cast and interpreted as required.

Then, the fun really begins: you can read and write the file through simple pointers. No more `ReadFile()` nor `WriteFile()`, even less `SetFilePointer()`! As shown in the example above, the generic pointer (`LPVOID pFile`) is cast into an adequate pointer to handle the data (in this case, `LPTSTR`).

Once you're done working with the file, you must unmap the file, and close both the mapping object handle and the file handle, as shown in the example.

You can verify that the file is mapped beyond the process's address space by simply taking a look at the value returned by `MapViewOfFile()`:

```
    printf("pFile = %#x\n", pFile);
```

which, for instance, outputs:

```
pFile = 0x43200000
```

This address is beyond the last process slot, in the range reserved for file mapping (*i.e.,* 0x42000000 to 0x80000000). This address also indicates that other files are mapped as well between 0x42000000 and 0x43200000.

11.5.2 Sharing Memory Through Memory-Mapped Files and Objects

Once a file is mapped within a process, all threads have equal access to the mapped file. However, Windows CE does not serialize any access to the area, exposing the threads to race conditions. It is important to identify any possibility in which two or more threads might attempt to read and modify the same data. Consider using synchronization objects (explained in Chapter 7) to prevent these nasty and unpleasant effects.

Sharing a memory-mapped file among processes is best done through memory-mapped objects, which do not require any physical file to act as a physical page repository. Instead, this method relies on named file mapping objects, and memory internally allocated by Windows CE. Because no file is involved with this approach, there is no need for any process to call CreateFileForMapping().

The first argument to CreateFileMapping() becomes 0xFFFFFFFF, instead of a file handle. This value indicates that Windows will provide the physical pages to back the mapped area (instead of using a file)[30]. Let's also recall that this function requires the size of a mapping object. Whereas specifying zero is acceptable with mapped files (meaning that the size is the file size), a non-zero size must be specified.

The last parameter to CreateFileMapping() is an optional name (a Unicode string). The previous example used NULL, leaving the file mapping unnamed (there was no advantage to name it in that case). But if a name is specified, Windows CE tries to identify any existing file-mapping object with the same name. The first time the name is used, a new mapping object is created (and named), whose handle is returned to the caller. If another process invokes CreateFileMapping() using the same name, the same mapping handle is returned. Then, for both processes, MapViewOfFile() will return a pointer on the same area, at the same virtual address in fact. Furthermore, when the mapping object already exists, GetLastError() returns ERROR_ALREADY_EXISTS, which in this case is not an error, but a hint.

---

[30] On 9*x*/NT, the pages are committed on the paging file; on CE, somewhere in RAM.

Sharing memory through name memory-mapped objects using this method is very efficient. It is also very safe, since the memory remains mapped until all processes unmap it.

The following example lists a function that many processes could use to share some of memory by executing:

```
SharedMemory(_T("MAP1"), 0x10000);
```

Note the first two functions, which implement the 64-bit C++ version of the HIWORD and LOWORD macros.

```
DWORD HIDWORD(__int64 nValue)
{
    return (DWORD) (nValue >> 32);
}

DWORD LODWORD(__int64 nValue)
{
    return (DWORD) (nValue & 0xFFFFFFFF);
}

void SharedMemory(LPCTSTR pszName, __int64 nSize)
{
    // This example assumes (for the sake of simplicity) that
    // (_tcslen(pszName) > 0) and (nSize > 0).

    HANDLE  hMap;
    LPVOID  ptr;

    // Create/open the file mapping object, using the specified name
    hMap = CreateFileMapping(
            reinterpret_cast<HANDLE>(0xFFFFFFFF),
            NULL,
            PAGE_READWRITE,
            HIDWORD(nSize),             // Non-zero size (high)
            LODWORD(nSize),             // Non-zero size (low)
            pszName);                   // Null-terminated string

    if (hMap == NULL)
            return;

    ptr = MapViewOfFile(
            hMap,
            FILE_MAP_READ | FILE_MAP_WRITE,
            0,
            0,
            0);

    if (ptr == NULL)
    {
            CloseHandle(hMap);
            return;
    }
```

```
    // Access the share memory area. One method is to cast the
    // pointer to some expected data structure. Example:
    // LPSOMEDATASTRUCT pData = (LPSOMEDATASTRUCT) ptr;
    // pData->. . .

    // Unmap the file.
    UnmapViewOfFile(ptr);
    CloseHandle(hMap);
}
```

11.5.3 A Few Observations

Memory-mapped files and objects are very convenient, but using caution is required. Here are a few things to keep in mind:

- The mapped memory is not protected against other processes. In the example above, it turned out that the file was mapped at address 0x43200000. Any other process can access that area as well, simply by doing something like this:

```
LPTSTR p = (LPTSTR) 0x43200000;
_tprintf(_T("p[1] = %c\n"), p[1]);
```

  Of course, this requires the other process to know the address and how many bytes are being mapped there, because using an incorrect address (where no file is mapped) will result in a fatal fault. But the risk is there.

- By default, when two processes map the same file, MapViewOfFile() will return a different address to each process if the file mapping objects are unnamed (or named differently). Nevertheless, because the same file is mapped, a change done by a process is visible by the other. Hence, this method is valid for sharing memory-mapped files.

- When using named file mapping object, only the first call to CreateFile Mapping() shapes the mapped area. Subsequent calls to CreateFile Mapping() referring to the same object will not alter its size or change the pages being used to back the mapped area. Consider a named area of 64KB, object-based. If another process uses the same file mapping name, but uses a valid file handle (instead of 0xFFFFFFFF) and a size of 128KB, the mapping area remains object-based (not file-based) and its size stays at 64KB (it does not increase to 128KB).

Suggested Reading

Richter, Advanced Windows Programming

Chapter 8 describes memory-mapped files in great detail for Windows 95 and NT. Chapter 14 provides a detailed explanation of file system management on the same platforms. Chapter 15 provides the complete NT API to execute device and file I/O operations.

Chapter 12

Communications

Windows CE's ability to communicate with remote devices, desktops, and the Internet is a key design goal. This essential feature gives users the ability to send and receive e-mails, browse the Web, access files and printers on desktops and servers, use terminal emulators when accessing with remote systems, and so forth. Three modes of communications are supported (see Figure 12-1):

- Developers use serial communications, fundamental to Windows CE, to communicate with their desktops and other devices in close proximity. Communications can be achieved through serial cables or infrared. Serial communications are described in Section 12.1.

- Networking allows a Windows CE device to be connected to a local area network (LAN) or the Internet, and access any available resource. Multiple APIs and protocols are supported, all described in Section 12.2

- Telephony is modem-based and allows Windows CE applications to send information over telephone lines. This is the topic is described in [Sells 98].

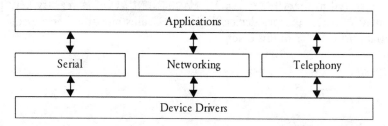

Figure 12-1: Windows CE supports serial, networking and telephony communications.

12.1 SERIAL COMMUNICATIONS

Serial communication is a very popular form of transmitting and receiving data. It is not as fast as other technologies (such as Ethernet), but it works well to connect a myriad of devices to each other, and is cheap to implement. Windows CE makes no exception and supports serial communication in its API. In fact, it is almost as easy to use a serial port than it is to read and write from files. Figure 12-2 illustrates the basic steps, which are detailed in the following sections.

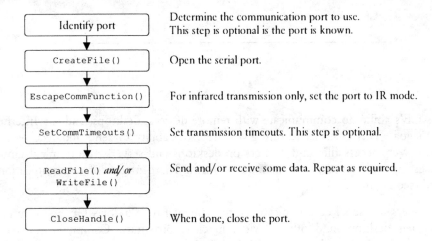

Identify port	Determine the communication port to use. This step is optional is the port is known.
CreateFile()	Open the serial port.
EscapeCommFunction()	For infrared transmission only, set the port to IR mode.
SetCommTimeouts()	Set transmission timeouts. This step is optional.
ReadFile() *and/or* WriteFile()	Send and/or receive some data. Repeat as required.
CloseHandle()	When done, close the port.

Figure 12-2: The steps to follow in order to use serial communications.

12.1.1 Identifying a Serial Port

The first step to establish a serial link with a device is to identify the port (*e.g.,* COM1, COM2). This step is optional if an application is designed to use, say, COM1. However, generic applications may first let the user choose from all available ports.

Ports are stored in the \HKEY_LOCAL_MACHINE\Drivers registry key. There is one subkey (named 00, 01, etc.) per device. Figure 12-3 illustrates the entry associated with an infrared serial port (COM3: in this case).

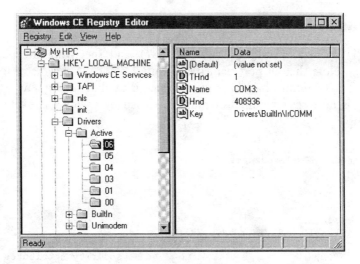

Figure 12-3: The list of device drivers present on a particular device.

The `Key` value indicates where, in the registry, more information can be found for that driver. In this case, the value of that key is `Drivers\Builtin\IrCOMM`. Figure 12-4 lists the content of that key. Note its `FriendlyName` value ("`Infrared Port`"), which is what should be displayed to the user when listing that port.

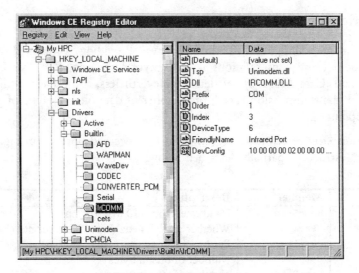

Figure 12-4: The description of a specific device is found in the registry.

Refer to Chapter 10 to access these keys in the registry.

12.1.2 Opening a Serial Port

A serial port is opened by calling `CreateFile()` and specifying the port name (*e.g.,* `_T("COM1:")`). Note that all port names end with a colon, as they refer to devices, not files. `CreateFile()` returns handle as usual, which is used in subsequent I/O operations. Once the port is no longer required, it must be closed by calling `CloseHandle()`. The following example opens `COM1`:

```
HANDLE OpenCom(LPCTSTR pszComPort)
{
    HANDLE  hCom;

    hCom = CreateFile(
            pszComPort,
            GENERIC_READ | GENERIC_WRITE,
            0,                              // Exclusive access
            NULL,                           // No security attributes
            OPEN_EXISTING,                  // Must use OPEN_EXISTING
            0,                              // No overlapped I/O on CE
            NULL);                          // NULL for comm devices

    // hCOM is INVALID_HANDLE_VALUE on error.

    return hCom;
}
```

12.1.3 Configuring a Serial Port

Serial ports can be configured in various ways. Providing a detailed and thorough explanation about these configurations is well beyond the scope of this book (refer to [Labrosse 95] and [Campbell 193] for details). Nevertheless, some basic configurations are usually required: the transmission speed, the number of data bits, the type of parity, and the number of stop bits.

The function `SetCommState()` configures the specified port according to the second argument, a `DCB` structure, partially described below:

Type	Member	Description
DWORD	BaudRate	Baud rate, from 110 to 256K bps.
DWORD	fParity	Whether parity is enabled (TRUE) or not (FALSE)
BYTE	Parity	Parity scheme to use
BYTE	ByteSize	Number of bits in bytes
BYTE	StopBits	Number of stop bits to use

Figure 12-5: The DCB structure. Only a few members are listed.

The structure contains numerous other fields. Instead of filling the entire structure from scratch, an application can query a port's current settings by calling `GetCommState()`. Then only the values of interest are changed. The new configuration takes effect by calling `SetCommState()`. The following example sets the port transmission to 19200, 8-bit, no parity, 1 stop bit:

```
BOOL ConfigPort(HANDLE hCom)
{
    DCB      dcb;

    // Get the current configuration.
    if (!GetCommState(hCom, &dcb))
          return FALSE;

    // Fill in the DCB:
    // baud=19200, 8 data bits, no parity, 1 stop bit.
    dcb.BaudRate   = CBR_19200;          // Baud rate
    dcb.ByteSize   = 8;                   // 8-bit
    dcb.fParity    = FALSE;               // No parity
    dcb.Parity     = NOPARITY;            // No parity
    dcb.StopBits   = ONESTOPBIT;          // 1 stop bit

    // Set the state
    return SetCommState(hCom, &dcb);
}
```

Serial device drivers can also be configured by calling `DeviceIOControl()`, which is used for sending driver-specific commands, as described in Chapter 11.

12.1.4 Infrared Transmissions

Windows CE supports two methods to use infrared IR transceivers: raw IR and IrComm.

Raw IR treats the IR transceiver as a serial cable. The data is not processed by the system, and it requires applications to control errors (collision, loss of data, etc.) An application can identify the port number by looking into the registry (`\HKEY_LOCAL_MACHINE\Comm\IrDA\Port`). Then it must place the port in IR mode by calling `EscapeCommonFunction()`, as follows:

```
EscapeCommFunction(hSerial, SETIR);
```

The second method uses the IrDA protocol, part of the network stack. Windows CE provides a serial emulator over that protocol, dubbed "IrComm". From an application standpoint, this emulator acts as its own `COMn`: it's named and works like one, but it takes care of transmission problems such as collisions. IrComm is much easier to use than raw IR transmissions. Since it is an emulator, applications do not have to call `EscapeCommFunction()` on it, nor can they configure it through `SetCommSate()`.

12.1.5 Setting Timeouts

Timeouts can be applied on read and write operations if required. For instance, if you write a single-threaded graphical application that reads data from the serial port, short timeouts must be specified to prevent the thread from waiting on the serial port (because while it waits, it cannot process Windows messages and the application appears frozen).

On the other hand, a multithreaded application can have its main thread processing Windows messages, while having a worker thread that only deals with the communication port. In that case, it may be perfectly acceptable for that thread to simply sit and wait on the communication port if no data is available.

This step is optional, as each driver uses default values.

Read and write time-outs can be set by calling `SetCommTimeouts()` and passing a `COMMTIMEOUTS` structure, listed in Figure 12-6. An application can query the driver to obtain the actual settings by calling `GetCommTimeouts()`.

Type	Member	Description
DWORD	ReadIntervalTimeout	Timeout (ms) between two characters
DWORD	ReadTotalTimeoutMultiplier	Read operation multiplier
DWORD	ReadTotalTimeoutConstant	Read operation constant
DWORD	WriteTotalTimeoutMultiplier	Write operation multiplier
DWORD	WriteTotalTimeoutConstant	Write operation constant

Figure 12-6: The COMMTIMEOUTS structure, which controls time-outs.

The first value, `ReadIntervalTimeout`, is an interval time-out. During a `ReadFile()` call, characters are read and stored in the buffer specified in the call. If `Readfile()` does not receive any character within that timeout (expressed in milliseconds), it returns whatever characters have already been received, if any. A value of 0 means no time-out (*i.e.*, infinite wait).

The second and third values, `ReadTotalTimeoutMultiplier` and `ReadTotalTimeoutConstant`, are combined to together using the following formula to form a total time-out:

```
Total Timeout = ReadTotalTimeoutConstant +
    (ReadTotalTimeoutMultiplier * number_of_bytes_to_read)
```

When `ReadFile()` is called, the specified number of bytes is applied to the formula and establishes the total time-out period (in milliseconds) to read all the requested characters. By using a multiplier, this formula takes into account the number of characters to read (it naturally takes more time to read 100 characters than 10). And because it also uses a constant, applications can establish a minimum no matter how many characters are expected.

The following table summarizes how read operations are impacted by the interval and total time-out values:

Interval	Total	ReadFile() Returns
0	0	When all bytes have been read.
0	n	When all bytes have been read or after n milliseconds.
m	0	When all bytes have been read or after m milliseconds following the reception of the last character.
m	n	When all bytes have been read or after n milliseconds or after m milliseconds following the reception of the last character.

Figure 12-7: How time-out values affect ReadFile().

The last two values, `WriteTotalTimeoutMultiplier` and `WriteTotalTimeout Constant`, are combined together in a similar fashion and are applied to `WriteFile()`. This is useful to detect a blocked transmission when sending data.

The following example first queries the driver to initialize the `COMMTIMEOUTS` structure. Then it sets the interval timeout to two seconds, and the reading multiplier factor to $1/10^{th}$ of a second.

```
BOOL SetTimeout(HANDLE hCom)
{
    COMMTIMEOUTS    ct;

    if (!GetCommTimeouts(hCom, &ct))       // Query the driver first.
         return FALSE;

    ct.ReadIntervalTimeout       = 2000; // 2 sec.
    ct.ReadTotalTimeoutMultiplier = 100;  // 1/10th sec.

    return SetCommTimeouts(hCom, &ct);     // Set the time-out values.
}
```

12.1.6 Reading and Writing Data

Reading and writing data is done by respectively calling `ReadFile()` and `WriteFile()` (introduced in Chapter 11). The time-out values are applied and prevent the operations from taking too long to complete, if required.

The following example writes an ASCII string (not Unicode) over a previously-opened serial port. Immediately after, it reads back data from it. Both operations are subject to time-outs.

```
void WriteAndReadData(HANDLE hCom)
{
    PCHAR   pszText = "Hello, from Windows CE";
    DWORD   dwBytesWritten;

    CHAR    InBuffer[32];
    DWORD   dwBytesRead;

    if (!WriteFile(hCom, pszText, strlen(pszText), &dwBytesWritten, NULL))
        return;

    printf("WriteFile() wrote %d bytes\n", dwBytesWritten);

    if (!ReadFile(hCom, InBuffer, sizeof(InBuffer), &dwBytesRead, NULL))
        return;

    printf("ReadFile() read %d bytes\n", dwBytesRead);
}
```

Other functions are also available (see Figure 12-8).

Function	Description
TransmitCommChar()	Transmit one character ahead of any pending data.
PurgeComm()	Discard any pending data
FlushFileBuffers()	Flushes the transmit buffer.
SetCommBreak()	Suspends character transmission
ClearCommBreak()	Restores character transmission

Figure 12-8: Various serial data transmission functions.

12.1.7 Monitoring Communication Events

Applications can monitor the serial ports for specific events to take place. This is the basis to use serial ports asynchronously. Here are a few events of interest:

Function	Description
EV_RXCHAR	A character has been received and placed in the input buffer.
EV_TXEWMPTY	The last character in the output buffer has been sent.
EV_BREAK	A break was detected on input.

Figure 12-9: Events that can be monitored over a serial connection.

An application calls `SetCommMask()` to indicate what events are to be monitored. `GetCommMask()` returns the current mark.

Once a set of events is specified, the application calls `WaitCommEvent()`, which waits until an event is triggered. It returns only when an event has occurred (there is no timeout). Note that a windowing application's main thread should not call `WaitCommEvent()`, because the application will not respond to user's command until an event is triggered (the application will appear frozen). In this case, `WaitCommEvent()` should be best handled by a separate working thread, leaving the user interface thread handling user's input.

The following example waits until the EV_RXCHAR (character reception) event is received.

```
void WaitUntilInputReady(HANDLE hCom)
{
    DWORD   dwEventDetected;
    BOOL    rc;

    // Specify an event mask containing: EV_RXCHAR.
    SetCommMask(hCom, EV_RXCHAR);

    // Wait until the event occur.
    rc = WaitCommEvent(
            hCom,                       // Serial port
            &dwEventDetected,           // Mask of events that occurred
            NULL);                      // NULL on CE.

    // rc is zero on error, non-zero on success.

    // Since the mask was set to EV_RXCHAR, dwEventDetected can
    // only contain the same bit. But this variable could be used
    // to identify what event took place if more than one event
    // were monitored.
}
```

12.1.8 Closing Serial Ports

Once an application is done with a serial port, it simply has to close the handle by calling `CloseHandle()`:

```
    CloseHandle(hCom);
```

12.2 NETWORKING

Networking capabilities give Windows CE the ability to communicate with other computers – or nodes, in network terminology – on a LAN or even the Internet. All Windows platforms support various network protocols, and Windows CE is no exception. The box labeled "Network" in Figure 12-1 can be further enhanced, as depicted in Figure 12-10.

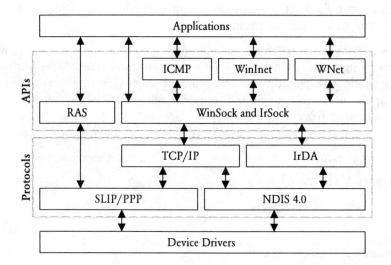

Figure 12-10: Windows CE networking supports many programming APIs and protocols.

Let's summarize this alphabet soup in order to provide a general understanding of what Windows CE networking is all about. The following sections will push that description further.

- Internet browsing (via HTPP and FTP) and access to remote files and printers are generally done through two high-level Win32 APIs: WinInet and WNet.

- Pinging – looking for a specific computer on the network – is achieved through the high-level ICMP API, which relies onto a protocol of the same name to conduct its work.

- Connectivity with remote devices can be achieved via the Remote Access Service (RAS) API. Windows CE supports RAS client, allowing connections to RAS servers (such as desktop computers). The connection can be established over a serial connection or a dial-up modem connection.

- WinSock and IrSock provide access to the TCP/IP protocol family, as well as the Infrared Data Association (IrDA) communication protocol. These protocols implement the core functionality of sharing information with other computers.

- The Serial-Line Interface Protocol (SLIP) and Point-to-Point (PPP) protocols specify how to transmit information across serial lines, and both are implemented in Windows CE.

- Windows CE also supports Ethernet and IrDA miniport drivers that conform to the Network Driver Interface Specifications (NDIS) 4.0.

Windows CE also supports the following low-level protocols, which are mostly used internally:

- PAP (Password Authentication Protocol) to connect to an Internet Service Provider (ISP). This protocol does not encrypt data, such as passwords, and is less desirable than CHAP.

- CHAP (Challenge Handshake Authentication Protocol), which also allows connecting to an ISP, but uses encrypted data.

- Dynamic Host Configuration Protocol (DHCP), which allows obtaining a TCP/IP address from a server.

- Address Resolution Protocol (ARP), which allows identifying a computer's Ethernet address based on its Internet address.

- Remote API (RAPI), which allows a RAPI client (a desktop computer) to execute function calls to a RAPI server (a Windows CE device)[31]. This API is described in Chapter 13.

Before exploring these topics in detail, let's introduce some essential networking concepts.

12.2.1 Communication Protocols and APIs

Networking allows two computers to communicate with each other. But a few questions must be answered up front for that communication to be successful:

- How do applications establish communications?

- How do computers identify themselves to each other?

- What information do applications exchange and in what format?

- Is the data encoded or encrypted? What character set is going to be used (ASCII, Unicode)?

- How is a programmer going to code an application that requires networking communications?

- And so forth.

The answers to those questions are to be found in:

---

[31] This is conceptually a Microsoft implementation of Remote Procedure Call (RPC), popular on other platforms, such as Unix.

- *Communication protocols*, which establish how the communication takes place between two computers and/or applications, what information is exchanged, and the format of that information.

- *Communication APIs*, which provide applications with function calls to use those protocol(s).

There are various protocols, and various layers of protocols. The International Standard Organization (ISO) introduced a communication protocol model dubbed the Open System Interconnection (OSI) model, which depicts protocols as being built on top of each other, like a stack[32] (see Figure 12-11).

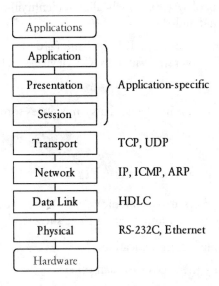

Figure 12-11: ISO's 7-layer OSI protocol model.

This model consists of seven functional layers that offer guidelines in order to implement a network stack in any system:

1. The Application layer implements application-level protocols. When two programs exchange data, they must agree on what information is sent and what is expected. This format is typically described as plain data structures.

2. The Presentation layer regroups functionality that could be used by many applications, such as text compression.

---

[32] Hence the use of "protocol stack", sometimes referred to as a "TCP/IP stack".

3. The Session layer is the applications' interface to the network, and it controls how connections are established with other computers (usernames, passwords, etc.)

4. The Transport layer splits application messages into smaller units, passes them to the Network layer, and ensures that they arrive to their destination.

5. The Network layer controls the operations of the network. One of the primary functions is to bring packets to their destination by establishing a route across many intermediate computers if required.

6. The Data Link layer manages a raw transmission medium into a line that appears error-free.

7. The Physical layer transmits bits of information over a communication channel.

Each layer implements its own protocol to manage a specific functionality, relying on the other layers to control other aspects of the communication (see Figure 12-12). For instance, the Physical layer is strictly concerned in transmitting bits over a communication medium, whereas the Network is concerned about transmitting information to the proper host across the network. Breaking this complex networking functionality into multiple layers makes the implementation easier.

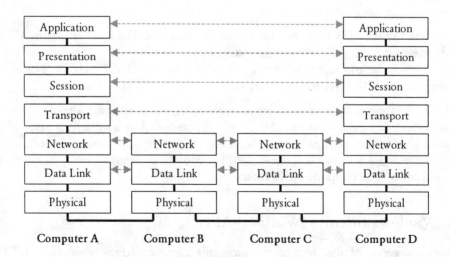

Figure 12-12: Sending data through network stacks. Each layer has the illusion that it communicates directly with its peer (shown by the grayed arrow), whereas the actual communication is done with adjacent layers (except for the physical layers, which are connected to each other).

Note that this is only a model; most protocols blur the distinction between the layers, or simply group various layers together. For instance, the TCP/IP protocol suite and related applications do not use the Application and Session layers, blurring the distinction between layers from 5 to 7.

Here is an example that demonstrates how these layers interact with each other. Consider two applications, on two different computers (A and D), that exchange information using TCP/IP over an Ethernet connection. The first application sends some data (for instance, a customer profile), based on an application-specific protocol that dictates what information is sent (essentially a data structure). This application-level protocol lets the recipient know how to interpret the information when received. The information is passed to the underneath layer (TCP), which breaks the application data into TCP packets. Each of these packets contains a TCP header, followed by the application data. The header is used by the remote computer to control packet sequencing. These packets are in turn passed to the underneath layer (IP), which wraps each packet with its own IP headers. These headers provide routing information. Finally, the IP packets are passed to the Ethernet drivers, which further breaks down the packets into Ethernet packets, and transmits them to another, reachable computer. When the Ethernet packets reach the destination computer, they are reassembled into IP packets, and passed to the IP layer. Then the packets are reassembled into TCP packets and passed to the TCP layer. Finally, the original data is passed to the application. As packets are reassembled, error-checking of all kinds is performed to ensure error-free transmission; when errors are detected at a specific layer, this layer communicates with its peer to correct the problem.

There are various APIs to access these multiple protocols. The most common API is the socket-based WinSock API, which provides access to almost any protocol, although applications typically use high-level protocols only (such as TCP or UDP). Furthermore, Windows provides high-level APIs that are easier to use than WinSock.

All in all, applications are concerned with APIs, not with the details of network implementation. Nonetheless, protocols cannot be discarded as easily, because it must be established ahead what protocol(s) will be retained for two applications to communicate. Once the protocol(s) are known, a relevant API is chosen, and developers typically focus on that API in order to develop the applications.

12.2.2 Windows Internet (WinInet) API

With the emergence of the Web, some protocols became extremely popular: HTTP, to download web pages, and FTP, to perform remote file operations. These two protocols are well-documented (see Suggested Readings for details) for those interested in the details. These two protocols are based on the TCP/IP protocol suite, which implements the foundation of the Internet we know today.

A developer that needs to develop an application using either or both protocols could do so by using WinSock, which is the Windows base network API (detailed in Section 12.2.5). However, because some developers might not be very motivated in understanding and using WinSock and these protocols, Windows CE implements a high-level API called the WinInet API, also called the Win32 Internet API. This API sits on top of WinSock and provides a simplified interface to HTTP and FTP. A developer simply has to know how the Web can be accessed from the current location (via a proxy or not) and the remote page or file name to access. This API is quite easy to use (see Figure 12-13). The next sections demonstrate three methods to use it. The **Inet** sample on the CD-ROM implements those methods.

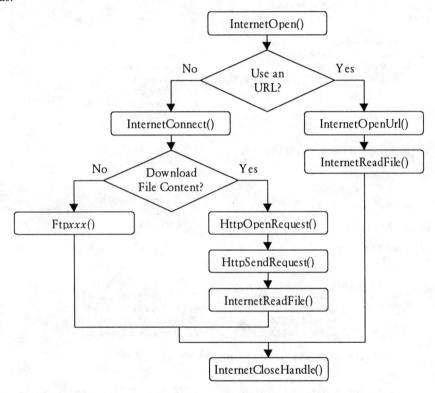

Figure 12-13: Choosing the proper WinInet API depends on what information is needed.

Method 1: Downloading a File With a URL

If you want to download the content of a remote file by using a URL (such as `http://yoursite.com/index.html`, you can use `InternetOpenUrl()`. This function analyzes the specified URL and uses the proper protocol (HTTP or FTP). You can then repeatedly call `InternetReadFile()` to read the file content and store it in a buffer or in a file.

The next example implements a function that loads an html page. It could be further enhanced to process the page content (by displaying it for instance), and deal with errors.

```
BOOL LoadHtmlPage(LPCTSTR pszUrl)
{
    HINTERNET       hNetSession;
    HINTERNET       hNetConnection;
    BOOL            rc;
    DWORD           dwBytesRead;
    BYTE            buffer[4096];

    // Open a session
    hNetSession = InternetOpen(
            TEXT("MyApp"),                  // Agent name
            INTERNET_OPEN_TYPE_DIRECT,      // Access type
            NULL,                           // Proxy name
            NULL,                           // Proxy bypass (NULL on CE)
            0);                             // Flags

    // Open the URL
    hNetConnection = InternetOpenUrl(
            hNetSession,                    // Session handle
            pszUrl,                         // Complete URL
            NULL,                           // Header
            -1,                             // Header length
            0,                              // Flags
            0);                             // Context

    // Load the page
    while (1)
    {
            rc = InternetReadFile(
                    hNetConnection,         // Connection Handle
                    buffer,                 // Buffer to store data
                    sizeof(buffer),         // Size of buffer
                    &dwBytesRead);          // Byte read count

            if (rc == FALSE || dwBytesRead == 0)
                    break;

            // Store data in a file, memory-mapped file or memory block.
            . . .
    }

    // Clean up
    InternetCloseHandle(hNetConnection);    // Close connection handle
    InternetCloseHandle(hNetSession);       // close session handle

    return rc;
}
```

That function is typically invoked as follows:

```
LoadHtmlPage(_T("http://CALIFORNIA/expose/index.htm"))
```

This example relies on a direct access to the computer running the web server (as specified with `InternetOpen()`). However, if the web was only accessible through a proxy (a common case in business organizations), the call to `InternetOpen()` would then become:

```
hNetSession = InternetOpen(
        TEXT("MyApp"),
        INTERNET_OPEN_TYPE_PROXY,        // Use a proxy
        TEXT("internet"),                // Proxy name
        NULL,
        0);
```

Then, the following would go through:

```
LoadHtmlPage(_T("http://www.some-external-site.com/index.htm"));
```

Method 2: Explici

An alternate metho   en passing information
using HTTP (whe   t consists of invoking
`InternetConnec`   to connect to a remote host (e.g. www.somesite.com) and
`HttpOpenReques`   sually GET), a file name
(e.g., index.html   (usually 1.0). That request must then
be sent through   eaders and parameters.
Again, the result i

The next exa   an HTTP request, specifying some parameters gathered via a
form. There is no

```
BOOL LoadPag
{
    HINTERNE
    HINTERNE
    HINTERNET      hNetRequest;
    BOOL           rc;
    DWORD          dwBytesRead;
    BYTE           buffer[4096];

    // Open a session (direct access)
    hNetSession = InternetOpen(
        TEXT("MyApp"),
```

```
                INTERNET OPEN TYPE DIRECT,
                NULL,
                NULL,
                0);

// Connect to the web site (specified by pszWebSite)
hNetConnection = InternetConnect(
        hNetSession,                     // Session handle
        pszWebSite,                      // Server name
        INTERNET_DEFAULT_HTTP_PORT,      // Server port
        NULL,                            // Username (use default)
        NULL,                            // Password (use default)
        INTERNET_SERVICE_HTTP,           // Service to access (HTTP)
        0,                               // Flags
        0);                              // Context

// Open a request handle
hNetRequest = HttpOpenRequest(
        hNetConnection,                  // Connection handle
        TEXT("GET"),                     // Verb
        pszFile,                         // Object name (file to access)
        TEXT("HTTP/1.0"),                // HTTP version
        NULL,                            // Referer
        NULL,                            // Accept all types
        INTERNET_FLAG_RELOAD,            // Flags
        0);                              // Context

// Send the request
HttpSendRequest(
        hNetRequest,                     // Request handle
        NULL,                            // Headers (none in this case)
        -1,                              // Header length
        NULL,                            // Optional data (none)
        -1);                             // Optional data length

// Read the page
while (1)
{
        rc = InternetReadFile(
                hNetRequest,
                buffer,
                sizeof(buffer),
                &dwBytesRead);

        if (rc == FALSE || dwBytesRead == 0)
                break;

        // Store data in a file
}

// Clean up
InternetCloseHandle(hNetRequest);      // Close request handle
InternetCloseHandle(hNetConnection);   // Close connection handle
InternetCloseHandle(hNetSession);      // close request handle

return rc;
}
```

Method 3: Performing FTP Operations

The previous methods cannot perform file operations, such as renaming remote files, creating a remote directory, or copying local files to a remote directory and vice-versa.

If what you need is a program that can accomplish those operations, you're still in good hands with WinInet. The API contains a few functions that implement the complete FTP protocol. The functions are listed in Figure 12-14 below.

WinInet FTP Function	Description
FtpGetCurrentDirectory()	Returns the current directory on the remote server.
FtpSetCurrentDirectory()	Sets the current directory on the remote server.
FtpCreateDirectory()	Creates a directory on the remote server.
FtpFindFirstFile()	Returns the first file matching the specified file mask. Conceptually, this is the same as executing FindFirstFile() on the remote server.
InternetFindNextFile()	Returns the next file matching the specified file mask. Conceptually, this is the same as executing FindNextFile() on the remote server.
FtpRenameFile()	Renames a file on the remote server.
FtpDeleteFile()	Deletes a file on the remote server.
FtpPutFile()	Copies a local file on the remote server.
FtpGetFile()	Copies a remote server's file on the local system.

Figure 12-14: The FTP functions of WinInet.

The following example demonstrates how to copy a file from a remote FTP server, via an FTP get command). The function requires the FTP site, the remote file name and the local file name. Both file names can accept existing directory names. The example uses FtpGetFile(), which the WinInet API function that implement the FTP get command:

```
BOOL LoadFileViaFTP(LPCTSTR pszFtpSite, LPCTSTR pszRemoteFilename,
    LPCTSTR pszLocalFilename)
{
    HINTERNET      hNetSession;
    HINTERNET      hNetConnection;
    BOOL           rc;

    // Open a session
    hNetSession = InternetOpen(
            TEXT("MyApp"),                  // Agent name
            INTERNET_OPEN_TYPE_DIRECT,      // Access type
            NULL,                           // Proxy name
            NULL,                           // Proxy bypass
            0);                             // Flags

    // Opn an FTP session
```

```
    hNetConnection = InternetConnect(
        hNetSession,                    // Session handle
        pszFtpSite,                     // Server name
        INTERNET_DEFAULT_FTP_PORT,      // Server port
        _T("john"),                     // User name (use your own)
        _T("gareau"),                   // Password (use your own)
        INTERNET_SERVICE_FTP,           // Service
        0,                              // Flags
        0);                             // Context

    // Get the remote file and copy it onto the local drive.
    rc = FtpGetFile(
        hNetConnection,                 // FTP session handle
        pszRemoteFilename,              // Remote file name
        pszLocalFilename,               // Local file name
        FALSE,                          // Do not fail if file exists
        FILE_ATTRIBUTE_NORMAL,          // New file attributes
        FTP_TRANSFER_TYPE_ASCII,        // Flags
        0);                             // Context

    // Close all handles.
    InternetCloseHandle(hNetConnection);
    InternetCloseHandle(hNetSession);

    return rc;
}
```

This function would typically be invoked as follows:

```
LoadFileViaFTP(_T("192.168.1.1"), _T("c:\\sm.log"), _T("\\sm.log"));

// or

LoadFileViaFTP(_T("California"), _T("c:\\sm.log"), _T("\\sm.log"));
```

12.2.3 Windows Networking (WNet) API

Windows CE supports an API to access remote disks and printers on other Windows platforms (currently Windows 9x and NT). It allows attaching remote devices locally, allowing the user to access remote files and printing on remote printers. The API is called WNet, and is conceptually independent of the physical network implementation. However, Windows CE supports WNet on a Microsoft Networking LAN only. A subset of the full WNetAPI is supported, but it is sufficient to implement the core functionality.

Before jumping into the API, let's review some features about WNet resources. There are three types of such resources (see Figure 12-15):

- Disks, which are connectable devices.
- Printers, which also are connectable devices.

- Containers (such as a remote server computer), which aren't connectable devices, but that form a hierarchy: they hold disks, printers and ... containers.

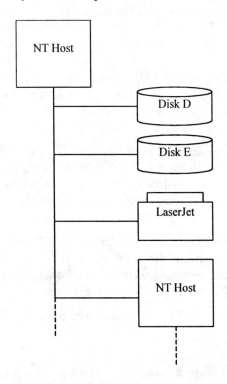

Figure 12-15: WNet resources are maintained through a hierarchy.

A remote resource is attached – mapped, in WNet terminology – to a local resource to be accessible. For instance, a remote disk appears as a local disk once mapped. Such local resources are said to be *redirected* to remote resources. Hence, Windows CE includes a redirector (implemented in REDIR.DLL and NETBIOS.DLL), that internally implements the WNet functionality.

Some WNet calls require the scope of the desired resources to be specified. From a Windows CE device standpoint, disk and printer resources exist in three scopes:

- Devices can be *connected* to the system, through some system calls we are about to see.

- Upon being connected, a device name can be stored in the Registry, making it *remembered* by CE. If the connection is dropped (because the user disconnected from the resource or because of some network failures), and the user attempts to access that same resource again, Windows CE will automatically attempt to reconnect. Unlike other Windows platforms, Windows CE does not automatically reconnect to remembered devices when the user logs in, but only when the user attempts to access them and they are not already connected.

- Any device that is on the network is said to be *global*.

Devices and containers are identified using the Universal Naming Convention (UNC), using the format `\\servername\sharename\path\file`. For instance, `\\CALIFORNIA\D` is the shared D: drive on the CALIFORNIA computer, `\\CALIFORNIA\D\MyFile.txt` is the host file `D:\MyFile.txt`, and `\\CALIFORNIA\LaserFax` identifies the printer `LaserFax` managed by the server CALIFORNIA. UNC names are not case sensitive.

Disks and printers must initially be made sharable on their respective hosts. For instance, on Windows NT, using the Explorer, right-clicking a disk or a printer presents a context menu that includes an item labeled "Sharing...". Clicking on that item presents a dialog box that is used for making the device shared. Once shared, a Windows CE device can "see it".

On CE, redirected resources appear under the `\NETWORK` directory. For instance, mapping `\\CALIFORNIA\D` using the local name `D_Drive` makes it available under `\NETWORK\D_Drive`. There are no drive-letters on CE (*e.g.*, `C:`), and names can contain up to 64 characters. Names are not case sensitive on CE, either.

The **Wnet** sample on the CD-ROM implements the calls explained in the following sections.

Determining Available Remote Resources

An application can obtain the list of available resources (disks and printers) on the network by calling `WNetOpenEnum()`, `WNetEnumResource()`, and `WNetCloseEnum()`. These functions enumerate the resources.

`WNetOpenEnum()` is called once and initializes the enumeration. The first argument determines the scope of the enumeration: connected, remembered, or global. The second argument determines whether disks, printers, or both types are to be enumerated. The third argument selects whether connectable devices (disk and printers) or containers are to be enumerated. The fourth parameter indicates the location where to start the search. This is mostly useful to identify the root of the network when looking up all network devices or a container; otherwise it can be NULL. The last parameter is a handle to be used with subsequent functions.

With a valid handle, the application repeatedly calls `WNetEnumResource()`. This function returns an array of NETRESOURCE structures (detailed in Figure 12-16), each of which describe a single resource.

Type	Member	Description
DWORD	dwScope	Scope: connected, remembered, or global
DWORD	dwType	Disk, printer, or any (shared)
DWORD	dwDisplayType	Domain, generic, server, or share
DWORD	dwUsage	Connectable devices or containers
LPTSTR	lpLocalName	Local device name (if connected)
LPTSTR	lpRemoteName	Remote device name (in UNC format)
LPTSTR	lpComment	Provider-specific comments
LPTSTR	lpProvider	Provider name

Figure 12-16: The NETRESOURCE structure

Note that the last four items are pointers, not arrays. Since the structure in itself is not large enough to contain all the returned information, one cannot pass an array of NETRESOURCE to WNetEnumResource(), because the function needs more space to store strings as well. The solution is to call WNetEnumResource() with a sufficiently large buffer (Microsoft recommends 16K bytes). The function will use the space to store an array of NETRESOURCE structures and extra strings (see Figure 12-17).

The first parameter to WNetEnumResource() is the handle returned by WNetOpenEnum(). The second parameter is the address of a variable that indicates how many resources are to be returned in the buffer. A value of -1 (which is common) indicates as many as possible. The third argument is the buffer to store the data, and the fourth argument is the buffer size, in bytes.

Assuming that the requested number of resources is -1, WNetEnumResource() stores as many entries as possible in the buffer. Since the exact count may vary from one call to another, that second parameter is set to the exact count when the function returns.

The function normally returns NO_ERROR, which indicates that the enumeration can continue. Applications must check for that value and call the function all over again. If the same buffer is used again, the data is overwritten; hence, applications should either process the data within each iteration or store it somewhere else. When the enumeration is done, the function returns ERROR_NO_MORE_DATA, which is not an error, but simply an indication that nothing more can be returned. Finally, any other error value indicates some failure; the exact code can be retrieved by calling GetLastError().

Once the enumeration is over, the application must call WNetCloseEnum(), by passing the enumeration handle.

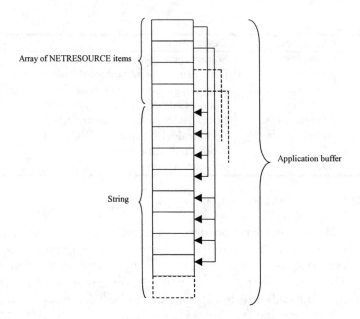

Figure 12-17: The buffer used by `WNetEnumResource()`.

The following example enumerates all accessible resources on the network. Refer to Section 6.3.2 ("Setting Windows CE's Gateway") to ensure that you first have a working connection with the host workstation.

```
#include <Winnetwk.h>

void ListResources(LPTSTR pszRemoteName)
{
    DWORD           rc;                 // Return code
    DWORD           nCount;             // Entry count
    DWORD           nBufferSize;        // Buffer size
    HANDLE          hEnum;              // Enumeration handle
    BYTE            Buffer[16384];      // Buffer (size as recommended)
    NETRESOURCE     nr;                 // Container to enumerate

    // Specify the container to enumerate as the host
    memset(&nr, '\0', sizeof(NETRESOURCE));
    nr.lpRemoteName = pszRemoteName;
    nr.dwUsage      = RESOURCEUSAGE_CONTAINER;

    // Open an enumeration handle
    rc = WNetOpenEnum(
            RESOURCE_GLOBALNET,     // List all available resources
            RESOURCETYPE_ANY,       // Type : all (disk & print)
            0,                      // Usage: all (connectable & container)
            &nr,                    // Container description
            &hEnum);                // Returned handle
```

```
    if (rc != NO ERROR)
    {
            puts("WNetOpenEnum failed()");
            return;
    }

    // Get all the information
    while (1)
    {
            LPNETRESOURCE  pnr;

            nBufferSize = sizeof(Buffer);
            nCount = 0xffffffff;   // Get as many entries as possible.

            rc = WNetEnumResource(
                    hEnum,           // Enumeration handle
                    &nCount,         // Requested entry count
                    Buffer,          // Buffer to store results
                    &nBufferSize);   // Buffer size

            if (rc != NO_ERROR)
                    break;

            // The beginning of the buffer is an array of
            // NETRESOURCE. There are nCount items in it.
            pnr = (NETRESOURCE *) Buffer;

            for (unsigned i = 0; i < nCount; i++)
            {
                    // Print the available information (as Unicode strings)
                    printf("Remote name: %S\n", pnr->lpRemoteName);

                    if (pnr->lpLocalName)
                            printf("Local name : %S\n", pnr->lpLocalName);

                    if (pnr->lpComment)
                            printf("Comment    : %S\n", pnr->lpComment);

                    if (pnr->lpProvider)
                            printf("Provider   : %S\n", pnr->lpProvider);

                    pnr++;           // Next resource.
            }
    }

WNetCloseEnum(hEnum);

// Make sure that the enumeration stopped because there was nothing
// else to show, not because of some sort of errors.
if (rc != ERROR_NO_MORE_ITEMS)
{
        puts("WNetEnumResource() failed");
        return;
}
}
```

Hence, in order to list the resources on the \\CALIFORNIA computer, the previous function can be invoked as follows (note that each "\" is doubled, a C/C++ requirement):

```
ListResources(_T("\\\\CALIFORNIA"));
```

On the other hand, if only the connected resources were to be listed, the call to WNetOpenEnum() could be replaced with:

```
rc = WNetOpenEnum(
        RESOURCE_CONNECTED,     // Connected resources only
        RESOURCETYPE_ANY,       // Any type
        0,                      // Usage
        NULL,                   // No container description
        &hEnum);
```

Connecting to Remote Resources

There are two functions to attach remote devices locally: WNetConnectionDialog1() and WNetAddConnection3().

WNetConnectionDialog1() prompts the user by showing the dialog box in Figure 12-18. This dialog box doesn't allow the user to browse the network; the names of the container and the resource must then be known.

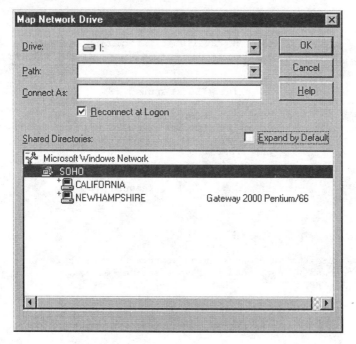

Figure 12-18: The connect dialog box (in the emulator).

The call requires a single parameter, a CONNECTDLGSTRUCT structure, which must be initialized as follows:

Type	Member	Value
DWORD	cbStructure	Size of this structure, in bytes *i.e.,* sizeof(CONNECTDLGSTRUCT)
HWND	hwndOwner	The handle of an existing window or NULL to center the window on the screen
LPNETRESOURCE	lpConnRes	A pointer to a NETRESOURCE structure. Of that structure, only dwType must be set to either RESOURCETYPE_DISK or RESOURCETYPE_PRINT; all other parameters must remain NULL.
DWORD	dwFlags	0 or CONNDLG_RO_PATH. This flag shows a read-only path, and does not allow the user to type in it.
DWORD	dwDevName	The number of devices connected to, if the call is successful.

Figure 12-19: The CONNECTDLGSTRUCT structure.

The following illustrates the use of WNetConnectionDialog1():

```
#include <winnetwk.h>

void ConnectToResources()
{
    CONNECTDLGSTRUCT        cds;
    NETRESOURCE                  nr;

    memset(&nr, '\0', sizeof(NETRESOURCE));
    nr.dwType = RESOURCETYPE_DISK;

    cds.cbStructure = sizeof(CONNECTDLGSTRUCT);
    cds.hwndOwner = NULL;
    cds.lpConnRes = &nr;
    cds.dwFlags = 0;
    cds.dwDevNum = 0;

    WNetConnectionDialog1(&cds);
}
```

The second call, WNetAddConnection3(), runs without prompting the user. The first parameter is NULL. The second parameter is a pointer to a structure NETRESOURCE, seen in the previous section, which must be initialized as follows:

NETRESOURCE Member	Value
dwType	RESOURCETYPE_DISK or RESOURCETYPE_PRINTER.
lpLocalName	The local name of the device, once connected. Note that Windows CE does not support drive letters (*e.g.*, A:). It should be instead any unique name (up to 64 characters). That name will show up as a folder in the \Network directory.
lpRemoteName	The remote name of the device, in UNC format.
Other fields	0 or NULL

Figure 12-20: The NETRESOURCE fields that must be initialized with WNetAddConnection3().

The third parameter to WNetAddConnection3() is the user's password, or NULL to use the default password associated with the username, as specified by the fourth parameter. The username can also be NULL to use the default user name. Finally, the fifth parameter is a flag, which can either be 0 or CONNECT_UPDATE_PROFILE; using this flag makes the connection remembered. The function returns NO_ERROR on success. Otherwise, an application can obtain the exact error code by calling GetLastError().

The following example uses WNetAddConnection3() to attach a remote directory:

```
BOOL Connect(LPTSTR pszRemoteName, LPTSTR pszLocalName)
{
    NETRESOURCE    nr;
    DWORD          rc;

    memset(&nr, '\0', sizeof(NETRESOURCE));
    nr.dwType       = RESOURCETYPE_DISK;
    nr.lpLocalName  = pszLocalName;
    nr.lpRemoteName = pszRemoteName;

    rc = WNetAddConnection3(NULL, &nr, NULL, NULL, 0);

    // Optionally, process rc is different than NO_ERROR.

    return (rc == NO_ERROR);
}
```

For instance, in order to map \\CALIFORNIA\D_drive under \NETWORK\D_Drive, this function could be called as follows:

```
Connect(_T("\\\\CALIFORNIA\\D_Drive"), _T("D_Drive"));
```

Disconnecting from Remote Resources

There are three methods to disconnect from remote devices: WNetDisconnectDialog(), WNetDisconnectDialog1() and WNetCancelConnection2().

WNetDisconnectDialog() displays a simple dialog box that allows the user to select one device and disconnect from it upon closing the dialog. WNetDisconnectDialog() is easy to use:

```
WNetDisconnectDialog(
    NULL,                      // A window handle or NULL
    NULL);                     // Ignored on CE
```

The second call, WNetDisconnectDialog1(), is a variation of the previous call[33]. This function requires a DISCDLGSTRUCT structure, defined as follows:

Type	Member	Value
DWORD	cbStructure	Size of this structure, in bytes *i.e.*, sizeof(CONNECTDLGSTRUCT)
HWND	hwndOwner	The handle of an existing window or NULL to center the window on the screen
LPTSTR	lpRemoteName	The network resource to disconnect from.
LPTSTR	lpLocalName	The local name of a network resource.
DWORD	dwFlags	0 or DISC_NO_FORCE. If set, the user will be informed if any device are being used by some applications and will have the choice to go ahead or cancel.

Figure 12-21: The DISCDLGSTRUCT structure.

The following example illustrates using WNetDisconnectDialog1():

```
BOOL Disconnect(LPTSTR pszRemoteName, LPTSTR pszLocalName)
{
    DISCDLGSTRUCT   dss;
    DWORD           rc;

    memset(&dss, '\0', sizeof(dss));
    dss.cbStructure   = sizeof(dss);
    dss.hwndOwner     = NULL;
    dss.lpRemoteName  = pszRemoteName;
    dss.lpLocalName   = pszLocalName;
    rc = WNetDisconnectDialog1(&dss);

    // Optionally, process rc is different than NO_ERROR.

    return (rc == NO_ERROR);
}
```

---

[33] Now you know why some WNet functions are suffixed by 1, 2, 3 and so on: they are just variations of some other basic functions. Note that only a few variations are supported on CE.

For instance, in order to unmap \\CALIFORNIA\D_Drive from \NETWORK\ D_Drive, this function could be called as follows:

```
Disconnect(_T("\\\\CALIFORNIA\\D_Drive"), _T("D_Drive"));
```

The last call, WNetCancelConnection2(), detaches connected devices, but it can also erase remembered devices from the registry. The first parameter is the device name, either local or remote. The second parameter is a flag, either 0 or CONNECT_UPDATE_ PROFILE. If set, this flag also erases the entry in the registry, making the device no longer remembered. The third argument is a Boolean value that indicates if the call should proceed even if some applications are using the device. If TRUE, the call proceeds no matter what; if FALSE, the call fails if the device is in use.

The following illustrates two equivalent calls to WNetCancelConnection2() in order to disconnect \\CALIFORNIA\D_Drive from \NETWORK\D_Drive. Only one is required:

```
// The first parameter can be the remote name...
WNetCancelConnection2(_T("\\\\CALIFORNIA\\D_Drive"), 0, TRUE);

// -- or --

// it can be the local name.
WNetCancelConnection2(_T("D_Drive"), 0, TRUE);
```

Obtaining Network Information

A few functions are available to query information about the network (see Figure 12-22):

Function	Descripton
WNetGetUniversalName()	Returns either the UNC name or remote name of a remote device based on a local name.
WNetGetConnection()	Returns the name of a remote device based (as a string) based on a local name. This is simpler to use.
WNetGetUser()	Returns the name of the user that established a connection based on a local name.

Figure 12-22: Various functions to obtain miscellaneous networking information.

Printing Over the Network

Remote printers are simply remote devices, which can be attached locally by calling WNetAddconnection3(), as explained before.

A file is sent to a printer by calling CopyFile(), which requires the file name to print and the printer name, which can either be local or remote; in the latter case, an UNC name is required. The third parameter (to fail the copy if the destination file already exists) is irrelevant and can simply be set to FALSE.

The following example prints the file MyFile.txt on the printer LaserFax, which is redirected to \\CALIFORNIA\LaserFax using the remote and local names:

```
// First method: use the remote name (UNC format)
CopyFile(
    _T("\\Temp\\MyFile.txt"),           // File to print
    _T("\\\\CALIFORNIA\\LaserFax"),      // Printer's remote name
    FALSE);

// Second method: map the printer and print using the local name.
// This approach relies on Connect() and Disconnect() introduced earlier.

Connect(_T("\\\\CALIFORNIA\\LaserFax"), _T("LaserFax"));

CopyFile(
    _T("\\Temp\\MyFile.txt"),           // File to print
    _T("LaserFax"),                      // Printer's local name
    FALSE);

Disconnect(_T("\\\\CALIFORNIA\\LaserFax"), _T("LaserFax"));
```

An alternate method to print is to call CreateFile(), using the printer name (local or remote), followed by a series of call to WriteFile(). Upon calling CloseHandle(), the data will be submitted. These calls are detailed in Chapter 11.

12.2.4 Internet Control Message Protocol (ICMP) API

The TCP/IP protocol family includes the ICMP (Internet Control Message Protocol), which is a low-level protocol to control packet flow, among other things. One of its best known uses, though, is to determine if a given node is reachable (or not). In fact, the famous PING utility simply relies on ICMP to complete its duty, by sending a few packets and waiting for an echo of these packets to be sent back from that target node.

The ICMP API

WinSock 1.1 does not provide applications direct access to the ICMP protocol[34]. Instead, Windows CE includes the ICMP API, listed in Figure 12-23.

---

[34] Other socket implementations (on Unix systems, for instance) allow direct access to ICMP.

ICMP Function	Description
IcmpCreateFile()	Creates an ICMP handle to use with other ICMP functions.
IcmpSendEcho()	Sends an echo request and waits for replies.
IcmpCloseHandle()	Closes an ICMP handle.

Figure 12-23: ICMP functions.

The first and last functions do not require arguments, and respectively create and delete a handle to use with `IcmpSendEcho()`. This function does what its name implies; it sends an ICMP echo packet to the specified node and waits for the reply.

`IcmpSendEcho()` needs the target node's IP address, expressed as an `IPAddr` value (which is a long integer). Node addresses such as 192.168.1.1 or `California` can respectively be converted to an `IPAddr` by respectively calling `inet_addr()` or `gethostbyname()`. The next two parameters identify some data to send (anything meaningful to the application) and the length of that data. The call also accepts some optional parameters, not required, though, to implement a basic ping. Replies will be stored in the specified buffer, along with the total length. Replies consist of a series of `ICMP_ECHO_REPLY` structures, each providing information about the nodes between the local system and the target node. Finally, the last parameter holds a time-out limit, to prevent the call from remaining blocked should the target node being unreachable.

The next example demonstrates how to use this API to determine if a given host is reachable and the round-trip packet time (in milliseconds). Note that building an application using this example requires a few modifications to your linker settings, detailed below.

```
#include <icmpapi.h>
#include <winsock.h>

BOOL Ping(LPCTSTR pszIpAddr, int * pnRoundTripTime)
{
    HANDLE  hIcmp;                  // ICMP handle
    int     nReplyCount;
    long    Data = 0;
    char    bszIpAddr[16];
    BYTE    Reply[sizeof(ICMP_ECHO_REPLY) + 8];

    // Create an ICMP handle.
    hIcmp = IcmpCreateFile();

    if (hIcmp == INVALID_HANDLE_VALUE)
            return FALSE;

    // Convert the Unicode address into an Ascii string,
    // since inet_addr() works in Ascii only.
    wcstombs(bszIpAddr, pszIpAddr, 15);

    // Send a request and wait for the reply.
```

```
    nReplyCount = IcmpSendEcho(
        hIcmp,                            // ICMP handle
        inet_addr(bszIpAddr),             // Where to send
        &Data,                            // Data to send
        sizeof(Data),                     // Size of data to send
        NULL,                             // No special options
        Reply,                            // Reply buffer
        sizeof(Reply),                    // Size of reply buffer
        3000);                            // Wait at most 3 seconds (in ms)

    IcmpCloseHandle(hIcmp);               // Always close handle

    if (nReplyCount == 0)                 // Return FALSE if no reply
        return FALSE;

    // Extract the round-trip time from the first reply packet.
    *pnRoundTripTime = ((ICMP_ECHO_REPLY *) &Reply)->RoundTripTime;

    return TRUE;
}
```

That function could be invoked as follows:

```
    int     nRoundTrip = 0;

    /* Ping a remote device */
    Ping(_T("192.168.55.99"), &nRoundTrip);
    printf("Round trip (ms) = %d\n", nRoundTrip);

    /* Ping the local device */
    Ping(_T("127.0.0.1"), &nRoundTrip);
    printf("Round trip (ms) = %d\n", nRoundTrip);
```

Compiling and Building ICMP Applications

Compiling and running the previous example is not straightforward, because the Windows CE SDK is not quite up to date with these functions. Although the documentation references Icmpapi.h, it might not be part of your SDK's distribution (it wasn't part of mine). For those in this situation, simply use the following version of Icmpapi.h. Note that this is not the *official* version, simply the result of my understanding of what it must contain; hence, Microsoft's implementation may differ.

```
/*
 * Icmpapi.h
 *
 * This file defines structures and declares prototypes to use
 * the ICMP functions in Icmplib.lib. Unfortunately, this file is
 * not distributed with the Windows CE SDK (up to 2.11).
 *
 * Use this file if your application needs it and your version of
```

```
 * the Windows CE SDK does not provide it.
 *
 * Note that the Microsoft's implementation (when available!) may
 * somewhat differ.
 *
 * This file can be included by C and C++ source files.
 */

#pragma once

#ifdef __cplusplus
extern "C" {
#endif

typedef DWORD       IPAddr;

typedef struct ip_option_information
{
    unsigned char       Ttl;
    unsigned char       Tos;
    unsigned char       Flags;
    unsigned char       OptionsSize;
    unsigned char *     OptionsData;

} IP_OPTION_INFORMATION, * PIP_OPTION_INFORMATION;

typedef struct icmp_echo_reply
{
    IPAddr Address;
    unsigned long       Status;
    unsigned long       RoundTripTime;
    unsigned short      DataSize;
    unsigned short      Reserved;
    LPVOID              Data;
    IP_OPTION_INFORMATION Options;
} ICMP_ECHO_REPLY;

HANDLE WINAPI       IcmpCreateFile(VOID);

DWORD WINAPI        IcmpSendEcho(HANDLE IcmpHandle, IPAddr
                        DestinationAddress, LPVOID RequestData,
                        WORD RequestSize, PIP_OPTION_INFORMATION
                        RequestOptions, LPVOID ReplyBuffer, DWORD
                        ReplySize, DWORD Timeout);

BOOL WINAPI         IcmpCloseHandle(HANDLE IcmpHandle);

#ifdef __cplusplus
}
#endif
```

Furthermore, you must include `Icmpapi.lib` part of the linker settings. You might also have to add `Winsock.lib`, if you use any Winsock function (such as `inet_addr()`). Both libraries are part of all CE SDK distributions. Finally, I had to turn on the linker option "Ignore all default libraries" (which corresponds to `/nodefaultlib`) in order to be able to successfully link the application. The **Icmp** sample on the CD-ROM implements the complete ping utility.

12.2.5 Windows Sockets (WinSock) API

The APIs we've seen so far are fairly easy to use because their functionality is limited. Consequently, they don't support a broad range of services. For instance, if two applications must directly share some information (through some sort of common channel), those APIs are inadequate.

This section will focus on the lowest communication API available on Windows CE: the socket API. Sockets are not particularly hard to use, but they require more effort to work with. In return, they offer a broader range of functionality to meet most communication requirements.

Other socket programming topics are discussed in Chapter 14.

Socket Programming Concepts

A socket is simply a communication end point in an application. It can be used to send and receive data (*i.e.*, bytes), but this only works if the socket is connected to another socket from another application (see Figure 12-24). To make an analogy, consider that a socket is a telephone handset. It naturally takes two people and two telephones to make a conversation. Likewise, it takes two applications, each with its own socket, to exchange information.

Figure 12-24: Each application needs a socket in order to communicate. Sockets are bi-directional *i.e.*, they can send and receive bytes.

Like telephone conversations, one of the two applications initiates a call to another application. The caller is said to be a client application and the callee, the application that is being called, is said to be a server application. Hence, applications that use sockets implement what is called the client-server paradigm. This paradigm was originally based on the assumption that servers would be faster computers than clients. Although this is not always true today, servers play important role by centralizing and providing information to various clients. For instance, servers are commonly used with databases and Web servers.

The basic idea of a client-server system is to have a client sending a request to a server. That request is fully application-dependent; it can be a form to process, a web site address, an application-defined data structure, etc. Upon receiving the request, the server conducts some specific work (such as accessing some files or databases). Once the work is done, the server returns a reply to the client. Note that clients and servers may exchange additional information before a final reply is returned.

To illustrate this concept, let's see how a browser (a client application) downloads an HTML page from a Web site (a server application):

1. The Web site server is initialized. It opens a socket and waits for any incoming connection over that socket.

2. A user starts a browser and enters a URL (Uniform Resource Locator) to download a page (*e.g.*, http://www.yoursite.com/index.htm)

3. The browser creates a socket and sends a request to the server (identified by the name: www.yoursite.com).

4. The server accepts the connection and creates a socket dedicated to that client, resulting in the client being directly connected to the server through their respective sockets.

5. The client sends the name of the page to download ("index.htm") to the server.

6. The server locates the file and returns it to the client.

7. The client stores the file content in memory (or in a local file) as it is received (*i.e.*, read from the socket).

8. Once the file is fully transmitted, the server and client close their respective sockets. From now on, the server can handle requests from any other clients.

9. The client displays the HTML page on the screen.

This appears to be different that what we've seen earlier with the WinInet API, simply because WinInet is a high-level API. However, this is the scenario that takes place at the socket level.

In real-world situation, though, servers are multithreaded and are implemented slightly differently, but the concept remains the same from the socket point of view. Needless to say, the client-server paradigm is extremely popular today, largely due to Web servers and databases.

Windows Sockets

The Windows socket API has its origins in the Unix BSD socket implementations (see [McKusick 96] for more info about BSD). A few years ago, Microsoft adapted that BSD API for Windows 3.x, making necessary fixups in the process to make it work on its platforms, including changing its name to WinSock. Today, Windows CE caries the most important Winsock 1.1 functions, and two transport protocols:

*   TCP/IP is a family of protocols, originally called the "DARPA Internet Protocol Suite", introduced in the early 1980s. This protocol family successfully spread across the world and supports the Internet that you and I use everyday.

*   IrDA is an infrared protocol that allows devices within close proximity to exchange information. Infrared has been used for years with remote TV commands, etc.

    The remainder of this section focuses on TCP/IP, whereas Section 12.2.6 focuses on IrDA.

Client Socket Programming

A client application, such as the browser seen earlier, only needs a few WinSock calls to establish a connection, send a request, and read back a reply. Figure 12-25 illustrates these calls, detailed in the following paragraphs.

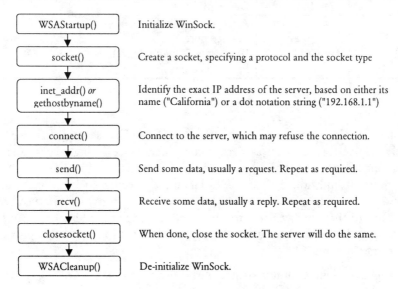

WSAStartup()	Initialize WinSock.
socket()	Create a socket, specifying a protocol and the socket type
inet_addr() *or* gethostbyname()	Identify the exact IP address of the server, based on either its name ("California") or a dot notation string ("192.168.1.1")
connect()	Connect to the server, which may refuse the connection.
send()	Send some data, usually a request. Repeat as required.
recv()	Receive some data, usually a reply. Repeat as required.
closesocket()	When done, close the socket. The server will do the same.
WSACleanup()	De-initialize WinSock.

Figure 12-25: The sequence of WinSock calls as implemented in a client application.

WSAStartup() must be the first WinSock() call made by the application. It initializes the application to use WinSock.

Then, the application creates its own socket by calling socket(). The call takes three arguments:

- The address formats. It must be AF_INET for TCP/IP.

- The socket type, either SOCK_STREAM (for a reliable connection-based link) or SOCK_DGRAM (for a non-reliable, connectionless link). The former type is by far the most popular.

- The exact protocol, usually set to 0. WinSock chooses the proper protocol based on the first two arguments.

A socket identifier is returned if socket() succeeded; otherwise the returned value is INVALID_SOCKET. The application can execute WSAGetLastError() to determine what went wrong.

The application is then ready to establish a connection. To do so, it must first obtain the address of the server it wants to connect to. The address of a node depends on the protocol. TCP/IP specifies that an address is a 4-byte value, represented using a dot notation string (*e.g.,* "192.168.1.1"). A computer may also have a name (*e.g.,* "California") associated with that 4-byte value, which is easier for users to remember. WinSock defines the structure SOCKADDR_IN to represent a TCP/IP address:

Type	Member	Description
short	sin_family	Always AF_INET
unsigned short	sin_port	Service port
IN_ADDR	sin_addr	IP address (a long integer)
char	sin_zero[8]	Padding zeroes

Figure 12-26: The SOCKADDR_IN structure.

The first field, sin_family, is always AF_INET. The second field, sin_port, indicates what service to access on a specific computer. Since a single computer may run many applications (clients and servers), each of them potentially using one or more sockets, each socket must be individually accessible. Hence, a specific socket on a computer is identified by a port number, which is a 16-bit value. Some ports are reserved for system services, but most of them are available for developers. The third field, sin_addr, contains the IP address encoded in a 32-bit value. Finally, the last field, sin_zero, provides some padding that can be ignored.

A client application must fill this structure in order to connect. WinSock provides a few conversion functions to translate a host name or dot notation string into a 32-bit value of type `IN_ADDR`. The two most common functions are `gethostbyname()` and `inet_addr()`, which respectively convert a name or a dot notation string into an 32-bit IP address. Applications usually query the user to obtain the name (or dot notation) of the computer to connect to.

The port number must also be known to connect to a server. Since developers often write both the client and server applications, the port number can easily be known.

With an initialized `SOCKADDR_IN` structure, the client simply calls `connect()` to establish a communication link with the server application, which must be already running[35]. Note that the server may accept or reject the connection. In the latter case, `connect()` returns `SOCKET_ERROR`.

Once connected, an application can send data by calling `send()`, which requires the socket handle, a pointer to some data, the length of the data pointed to, and some flags. Similarly, the application can receive data by calling `recv()`, which requires the socket handle, a buffer to store data, the buffer length, and some flags. The same socket can be used to send and receive data. The only issue is really to know what to send and what to receive, and the underlying format. The client and the server must have been written to use the same application protocol. This protocol can be user-defined as well. For instance, if a client sends a file name, it may first send a 4-byte integer indicating the length, followed by the name itself. The server would then expect a 4-byte integer, allocate a buffer of the proper size, and read the name in it.

Once the client is done, it must call `closesocket()` to close the socket and `WSACleanup()` to let WinSock perform some housekeeping cleaning.

The next example illustrates a client application that sends a string to a server (on system "192.168.1.1", port 5000). The server is expected to read the Unicode string, convert it in uppercase, and return it back (this is demonstrated later). The **SockCli** sample on the CD-ROM implements a client application, targeted to run on CE, that works with the **SockSvr** sample (described later).

```
#include <winsock.h>            // Use Winsock 1.1 (requires winsock.lib)
#include <stdio.h>
#include <ctype.h>

const int  PORT = 5000;         // Port no: 5000

BOOL CvtString(LPCTSTR pszServer, LPTSTR pszString)
{
    char           bszRemoteHost[15];
    WSADATA        wsaData;
    SOCKADDR_IN    SockAddr;
    SOCKET         so;
```

---

[35] Indeed, server applications must always be started before client applications.

```
       int            nLength;

// Initialize the WinSock library.
if (WSAStartup(MAKEWORD(1, 1), &wsaData) != 0)
       return FALSE;

// Identify the Internet address of that host. The name must first
// be converted in ASCII to use some WinSock functions.
wcstombs(bszRemoteHost, pszServer, sizeof(bszRemoteHost));

if (_istdigit(pszServer[0]))
{
       // Dot notation, use inet_addr to convert into a 32-bit int.
       SockAddr.sin_family      = AF_INET;
       SockAddr.sin_addr.s_addr = inet_addr(bszRemoteHost);
}
else
{
       // Server name. Use gethostbyname() to get more information.
       HOSTENT *      pHost;

       pHost = gethostbyname(bszRemoteHost);

       SockAddr.sin_family = pHost->h_addrtype;
       memcpy(&SockAddr.sin_addr, pHost->h_addr, pHost->h_length);
}

// Set the PORT value.
SockAddr.sin_port = PORT;

// Open a TCP/IP, connection-oriented socket.
if ((so = socket(AF_INET, SOCK_STREAM, 0)) == INVALID_SOCKET)
       return FALSE;

// Try to connect to the remote server.
if (connect(so, (SOCKADDR *) &SockAddr, sizeof(SockAddr)) ==
       SOCKET_ERROR)
{
       closesocket(so);
       return FALSE;
}

// Connected! Send a string and read it back. This assumes that the
// server on the other side expects Unicode strings!
nLength = wcslen(pszString) * sizeof(TCHAR);

if (send(so, (const char *) pszString, nLength, 0) == SOCKET_ERROR)
{
       closesocket(so);
       return FALSE;
}

if (recv(so, (char *) pszString, nLength, 0) == SOCKET_ERROR)
{
       closesocket(so);
       return FALSE;
}
```

```
    // Close the socket.
    closesocket(so);

    // Cleanup
    WSACleanup();

    return TRUE;
}
```

This function could be called as follows:

```
void main()
{
    TCHAR   szMyString[32];              // An Unicode string

    _tcscpy(szMyString, _T("this is in lowercase"));

    if (!CvtString(_T("192.168.1.1"), szMyString))
            return 0;

    // Output the string, using %S (for Unicode)
    printf("The converted string is \"%S\"\n", szMyString);
}
```

A few observations about this example:

- The `Winsock.lib` library must be explicitly specified to the linker.
- `WSAStartup()` and `WSACleanup()` only have to be called once within an application. Hence, the two function calls could be moved in the main function of an application.
- Note the use of `_istdigit()`, the Unicode version of `isdigit()`.
- The length is calculated in bytes, since `send()` and `recv()` use byte counts. These two functions return the number of bytes sent/received, which can be less than requested in some cases. non-blocking only
- The server must expect Unicode strings. Otherwise, either none or the first character only will be converted (depending on the processor's endian mode).
- A commercial application would display error messages when things go wrong (instead of simply returning `FALSE`).

Server Socket Programming

The main difference between a client and a server is that a server typically uses one socket to wait for incoming connection and another socket to establish a link with a specific client. The server uses the following functions, described below.

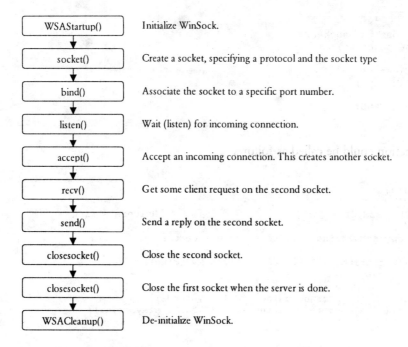

WSAStartup()	Initialize WinSock.
socket()	Create a socket, specifying a protocol and the socket type
bind()	Associate the socket to a specific port number.
listen()	Wait (listen) for incoming connection.
accept()	Accept an incoming connection. This creates another socket.
recv()	Get some client request on the second socket.
send()	Send a reply on the second socket.
closesocket()	Close the second socket.
closesocket()	Close the first socket when the server is done.
WSACleanup()	De-initialize WinSock.

Figure 12-27: The sequence of WinSock calls as implemented in a server application.

Like any other application using WinSock, a server must first call WSAStartup(), and create a socket by calling socket(). This socket must be bound to an exact port number, which will be used by the clients to connect (remember that both client and server applications must initially agree on the port number). Binding is done by calling bind() and requires an initialized SOCKADDR_IN structure. The socket is then placed in a "listening mode" by calling listen(). This indicates WinSock that the socket will receive incoming connections from some clients.

The server then typically enters a loop that will only end upon the application shutdown. Within that loop, the application calls accept(), which waits until an incoming connection is received from a client application. accept() returns a new socket, which is connected to the client. The initial socket (*i.e.*, the listening socket) remains undisturbed and continues to monitor incoming client connections.

That second socket is used for exchanging information, using recv() and send(), as seen before. The server has two options here: it can directly exchange with the client, or it can start a separate thread and let that thread handle the communication with the client.

In the first case, the server must complete the dialogue with the current client before accepting another connection. This is fine for lightweight servers whose exchange with a client is kept minimal. On the other hand, for a heavyweight server that handles multiple clients simultaneously, where each client request may take a while to process (a Web server or a database server for example), it is best to start a thread per client. This leaves the main thread ready to accept any incoming clients. Hence, clients are served immediately, independently of the work being done with other clients. A multithread design proves to be much more efficient and is commonly used in large server systems.

Here is an example of a lightweight server that receives a string, converts it to uppercase, and returns it. It works fine with the previous client example. The **SockSvr** sample on the CD-ROM implements a server application, intended to run on NT, that works with the **SockCli** sample.

```c
#include <windows.h>
#include <winsock.h>
#include <stdio.h>
#include <string.h>

const int  PORT = 5000;                   // Port number

void StringConverter()
{
    WSADATA       wsaData;
    SOCKET        so;
    SOCKADDR_IN   SockAddr;

    // Initialize the WinSock 1.1 library.
    if (WSAStartup(MAKEWORD(1, 1), &wsaData) != 0)
         return;

    // Create a socket to listen to incoming connections.
    if ((so = socket(AF_INET, SOCK_STREAM, 0)) == INVALID_SOCKET)
         return;

    // Bind to a specific port (i.e. PORT)
    SockAddr.sin_family      = AF_INET;
    SockAddr.sin_port        = PORT;
    SockAddr.sin_addr.s_addr = INADDR_ANY;

    if (bind(so, (SOCKADDR *) &SockAddr, sizeof(SockAddr)) == SOCKET_ERROR)
         return;

    // Listen for any incoming connections from any client
    if (listen(so, 5) == SOCKET_ERROR)
         return;

    while (1)
    {
         // Wait until a client attempts to connect.
         SOCKADDR_IN   SockAddr2;

         int           SockLen = sizeof(SockAddr2);
         SOCKET        so2;
         int           nLen;
         TCHAR         szString[128];
```

```
              printf("\nListening...");

              if ((so2 = accept(so, (SOCKADDR *) &SockAddr2, &SockLen)) ==
                  INVALID_SOCKET)
              {
                      printf("\naccept() failed\n");
                      continue;
              }

              // A connection has been established with the client over so2.
              // The structure SockAddr2 contains the host address and port
              // of the local/remote client. It is displayed for demo only;
              // the port is used in some applications to identify the
              // client type.
              printf("\nConnection received from host %s, port %d\n",
                      inet_ntoa(SockAddr2.sin_addr), SockAddr2.sin_port);

              // At this point, this server program could start
              // another thread/process to handle the
              // communication with the client. Because the work
              // involved here is trivial, the processing takes
              // place right here.

              // Use the second socket to read an Unicode string, convert
              // it to uppercase and return it.
              nLen = recv(so2, (char *) szString, sizeof(szString), 0);
              _wcsupr(szString);

              printf("Sending \"%S\"\n", szString);
              send(so2, (const char *) szString, nLen, 0);

              // Then close that second socket. That does not
              // affect the listening socket, which remains opened.
              closesocket(so2);
      }

      // This point is never reached, but if the previous
      // loop should ever terminate, close the listening socket.
      closesocket(so);
}
```

Note the following about this example:

- Error recovery is very minimal, but fortunately, these calls fail very rarely. One exception is bind(), which will return an error if the port is already occupied. For example, this application cannot be run twice, as the second instance would not bind on the port 5000, which would already be bound to the first instance.

- This example uses an infinite loop. Normally, a server will monitor some exit conditions, or will be terminated by users. The **SockSvr** sample has an exit condition.

- This example assumes that the client sends Unicode strings, hence the use of _wcsupr() instead of strupr().

Some Helper Functions

WinSock provides a few helper functions to help you identify addresses and ports, as well as translate Internet addresses into strings and vice versa:

Helper Function	Description
inet_addr()	Translates a dot notation string into a 32-bit IP address
gethostbyname()	Returns information about a host given its name, including its IP address.
getservbyname()	Returns information about a service given its name, including its port number.

Figure 12-28: Some helper WinSock functions.

In addition, here is another function that transforms a host name (in dot notation or not) into an IPADDR value:

```
BOOL StringToIpAddr(LPCTSTR pszIpAddr, struct in_addr * pIpAddr)
{
    char    pszIpAddrA[32];

    // The string must be converted in ASCII in order to
    // use inet_addr and gethostbyname().
    wcstombs(pszIpAddrA, pszIpAddr, sizeof(pszIpAddrA));

    // Assume a dot notation and try inet_addr(). If it fails,
    // then the address is a name and requires gethostbyname().
    if ((pIpAddr->s_addr = inet_addr(pszIpAddrA)) == INADDR_NONE)
    {
        PHOSTENT       pHost = gethostbyname(pszIpAddrA);

        // If name couldn;t be resolved, return FALSE.
        if (pHost == NULL)
            return FALSE;

        // Copy the IP address into *pIpAddr.
        memcpy(&pIpAddr->s_addr, pHost->h_addr, pHost->h_length);
    }

    return TRUE;
}
```

12.2.6 Windows Infrared Sockets (IrSock) API

WinSock is a generic interface that can potentially work with multiple protocols, not only TCP/IP. In Windows CE, WinSock can also be used with the IrDA protocol. An application is said to use the IrSock API when it uses WinSock for IrDA.

From a WinSock programming standpoint, there are very few differences when using the WinSock API for TCP/IP or for IrDA. The main difference between the two protocols is the address naming convention. Whereas TCP identifies a communication end point using a 32-bit IP address and a port (represented under WinSock as SOCKADDR_IN), IrDA devices within range are identified by an ID and a name. Applications are directly impacted by that change. In particular, functions like gethostbyname() are meaningless with IrDA because they are exclusively designed for TCP/IP. Hence, using IrDA instead of TCP/IP requires the following modifications:

- The client and server must use a SOCKADDR_IRDA instead of SOCKADDR_IN. There are no 32-bit IP addresses or port numbers to work with, but only service ids and names. A SOCKADDR_IRDA is defined as follows:

Type	Member	Description
u_short	irdaAddressFamily	Always AF_IRDA
u_char	irdaDeviceID[4]	
char	irdaServiceName[25]	

Figure 12-29: The SOCKADDR_IRDA structure.

- The client must poll for any device that is ready to accept a connection. Remember that IrDA is used by portable devices that "come and go". Since any device may be around, the client must not only poll the devices, but it must also determine whether the specific device it wants to talk to is there. For instance, to transfer information from your Palm-size PC to your desktop PC, you must be sure that your PC is around, not a coworker's PC, or a VCR!

Microsoft provides a client-server example on its CE site. The location keeps changing but look for IrSock.zip.

SUGGESTED READINGS

Campbell, C Programmer's Guide to SerialCommunications

> An entire book (almost 1,000 pages) dedicated to everything related to serial communciations.

McKusick, *et. al.*

This is THE book that describes the guts of 4.4 BSD Unix, including the socket implementation. Written by the authors of BSD.

Tanenbaum, Computer Networks

An in-depth coverage of today's networking technology, covering both software and hardware.

Chapter 13

Desktop Connectivity

Most people that use a portable Windows CE device on a daily basis (Handheld PC, Palm-size PC) maintain the core of their information on a desktop. Hence, it is vital that Windows CE devices be able to exchange information with desktops easily.

The core of the connectivity between a desktop and a CE device is implemented using Remote Access Services, commonly called RAS. This facility establishes a link between the two devices, allowing applications on either side to "see" each other and exchange information. It even allows a CE device to become part of a LAN and access other remote nodes.

This chapter starts by introducing RAS, the basis of desktop connectivity. Our focus then shifts onto the desktop, by describing some APIs that allow desktop applications to access resources on CE devices in some interesting ways.

Some of the APIs described in this chapter rely on the Common Object Model, which is described in Appendix B.

13.1 REMOTE ACCESS SERVICES (RAS)

Remote Access Services (RAS) is a Windows NT service that allows remote users (a Windows CE device in this case) to connect to a desktop or an entire network. The connection is established through a RAS-capable device, such as a wired serial connection or a modem, and supports various protocols (*e.g.*, TCP/IP) (see Figure 13-1).

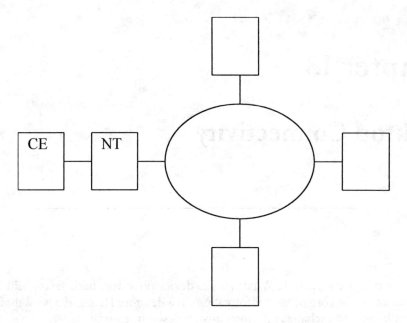

Figure 13-1: RAS allows a Windows CE device, connected to a desktop via a serial cable or a modem, to communicate with applications on the desktop or the entire network, as if it was directly connected to the network.

The Windows CE device is called a RAS client[36], and it usually connects to a RAS server (on the desktop) using PPP/SLIP. Once a connection is established, the CE device has its own IP address, and becomes part of the network. Applications on CE can use various communication APIs (such as WinSock) to send and receive information to remote applications.

Both `Remnet` and `Repplog` (distributed with CE and described in Chapter 2) use RAS. In fact, writing a `Remnet`-like application is quite easy, given the RAS API that is available on CE.

13.1.1 Phone Book

RAS connections are based on phone book entries, which reside in the registry. Windows CE only supports a few basic functions to access those entries. In particular, most functions that display some dialog boxes are not available on CE, forcing applications to manage the user interface themselves.

---

[36] Windows CE does not support RAS server capability such as NT.

Phone Book Entry

A phone book entry is defined by the RASENTRY structure, which contains the following information:

- Various connection option flags, which indicate how the connection is to take place (use a phone number, use a specific IP address when connected, use IP header compression, etc.)

- The phone number to dial, along with country code and area code. These values are required if the connection is to be established with a modem (they are unused when using a direct serial cable for instance).

- The name of the device being use to make the connection. This name is the "friendly name" of the related devices, such as "Serial Cable on COM1:" or "Infrared Port", listed in the registry under HKEY_LOCAL_MACHINE\ Drivers.

- The protocols to use when connected (*e.g.*, TCP/IP).

- Dial and disconnect options, if applicable.

- And so forth.

Enumerating Phone Book Entries

Applications can use RasEnumEntries() to list all entries in the phone book. This function is normally called twice: first to determine how many entries are to be retrieved, and second to effectively retrieve those entries at once. The information is returned as an array of RASENTRYNAME, a structure that contains a size (DWORD dwSize) and an entry name (TCHAR szEntryName[]). For each entry that is returned, more information is available by calling RasGetEntryProperties(). This call fills up a RASENTRY structure (which we just described).

The next example uses these functions to list the name and the associated device of each RAS entry.

```
void EnumRasEntries()
{
    LPRASENTRYNAME pRasEntries = new RASENTRYNAME[1];
    DWORD          dwSize      = sizeof(RASENTRYNAME);
    DWORD          dwEntries;
    DWORD          rc;

    // The size of the first entry must be initially set.
    pRasEntries[0].dwSize = sizeof(RASENTRYNAME);

    // Get the first entry and the entry count.
    rc = RasEnumEntries(
            NULL,                              // Reserved
            NULL,                              // Use the registry (on CE)
```

```
            pRasEntries,              // Entries to fill up
            &dwSize,                  // Size needed (returned)
            &dwEntries);              // Entry count (returned)

    // If there is more than one entry, use a larger array.
    if (rc == ERROR_BUFFER_TOO_SMALL || dwSize > sizeof(RASENTRYNAME))
    {
            delete [] pRasEntries;

            pRasEntries = new RASENTRYNAME[dwSize / sizeof(RASENTRYNAME)];

            pRasEntries[0].dwSize = sizeof(RASENTRYNAME);

            // Get all entries at once this time.
            rc = RasEnumEntries(
                    NULL,
                    NULL,
                    pRasEntries,
                    &dwSize,
                    &dwEntries);
    }

    // Obtain the RASENTRY information for each entry.
    RASENTRY        RasEntry;                 // Entry information buffer

    RasEntry.dwSize = sizeof(RASENTRY);   // Set the size
    dwSize          = sizeof(RASENTRY);

    for (DWORD i = 0; i < dwEntries; i++)
    {
            // Get the information about the ith entry.
            RasGetEntryProperties(
                    NULL,                     // Use the registry
                    pRasEntries[i].szEntryName,
                    (LPBYTE) &RasEntry,       // Entry buffer
                    &dwSize,                  // Entry buffer size
                    NULL,                     // No device configuration info.
                    NULL);                    // No device configuration info

            // Print the entry name and the associated device name.
            // Note that those names are in Unicode (hence %S with printf).
            printf("%S, %S\n",
                    pRasEntries[i].szEntryName,
                    RasEntry.szDeviceName);
    }

    delete [] pRasEntries;
}
```

Managing Phone Book Entries

A few functions are available to add, modify, delete and rename entries in the phone book. A graphical application could present dialog boxes to provide the user with a simple interface. These functions are listed in Figure 13-2 and are easy to use. Note that the first parameter, the name of the file containing the phone book to use, must always be set to NULL on CE, as the phone book can only reside in the registry.

Function	Description
RasSetEntryProperties()	Adds or modifies an entry
RasValidateEntryName()	Validates a potential entry name
RasDeleteEntry()	Deletes an entry
RasRenameEntry()	Renames an entry.

Figure 13-2: Phone book management functions.

13.1.2 Connecting to a RAS Server

The purpose (and the fun part) of the RAS API is to establish a connection. With a valid phone book entry, it is quite easy to connect to a RAS server.

Making a Connection

A RAS connection is established by obtaining the dial parameters of a book entry and dialing the call. "Dialing" shouldn't be taken literally here; it rather means to establish a connection (there is no dialing when using a direct serial connection).

The dial parameters can be obtained by calling RasGetEntryDialParams(), specifying the book entry name, a pointer to a RASDIALPARAMS structure (see Figure 13-3), and a pointer to a Boolean. That Boolean is TRUE if the structure contains a valid password; if FALSE, the application should prompt the user for one.

Type	Member	Description
DWORD	dwSize	sizeof(RASDIALPARAMS)
TCHAR	szEntryName[]	Phone book entry name
TCHAR	szPhoneNumber[]	Phone number
TCHAR	szCallbackNumber[]	Call back number
TCHAR	szUserName[]	User name
TCHAR	szPassword[]	Password
TCHAR	szDomain[]	NT domain

Figure 13-3: The RASDIALPARAMS structure. Most members are null-terminated strings.

Note that the very first time a book entry is used, all the members are NULL; in that case, an application must query the user beforehand.

The next example implements a function that takes a phone entry name and establishes a RAS connection. For the sake of simplicity, the name, password, and domain are set to a hard-coded value. A real-world application would rather query them through a dialog box, and store them using `RasSetEntryDialParams()`. The function returns a RAS connection handle on success, NULL on error.

```
HRASCONN DialRasEntry(LPCTSTR pszRasEntry)
{
    RASDIALPARAMS  rdp;

    rdp.dwSize = sizeof(RASDIALPARAMS);
    _tcscpy(rdp.szEntryName, pszRasEntry);

    BOOL           bPassword;
    DWORD          rc;

    rc = RasGetEntryDialParams(
            NULL,
            &rdp,
            &bPassword);

    if (rc)
    {
            printf("Unable to retrieve the entry dial parameters\n");
            return NULL;
    }

    // bPassword is 1 if the password is known, 0 otherwise. In that
    // case, the application should ask for it. Also, the first time
    // the RAS entry is used, a name, password and domain must be
    // entered. For the sake of clarity, these fields here are
    // set to a known combination for the NT server to connect to.
    _tcscpy(rdp.szUserName, _T("john"));  // Username
    rdp.szPassword[0] = _T('\0');         // No password on that account
    rdp.szDomain[0] = _T('\0');           // No domain either

    HRASCONN             hRasConn;        // Value to return

    rc = RasDial(
            NULL,                         // No extension on CE
            NULL,                         // No phonebook (only Registry)
            &rdp,
            0xffffffff,                   // Always that on CE
            NULL,                         // No notification window handle
            &hRasConn);                   // Set on return

    // On success, rc is 0. On error, rc is an error code listed
    // in Raserror.h. A common error is 602 (port already opened).

    // Return the connection handle on success, NULL on error.
    return (rc == 0) ? hRasConn : NULL;
}
```

Once a connection is established, applications running on Windows CE can use the communication API (described in Chapter 12), such as WinSock, WNet, WinInet, etc.

Also, when using a direct serial connection, the serial ports on both the windows CE device and the host cannot be used by other applications, as long as the RAS connection is active. On NT, the server side of the RAS connection is implemented via Rassrv.exe. The *Remote Access Admin* applet (see Figure 13-4) can be used to display information about the connection. The applet is accessible from the Start menu, Programs and Administrative Tools (Common). Windows CE Services also uses Rassrv.exe, starting it and stopping it when required.

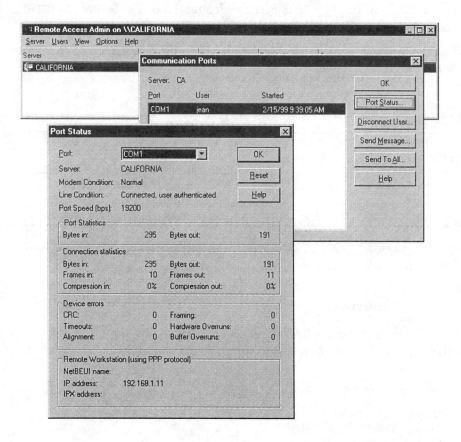

Figure 13-4: The Remote Access Admin applet on NT displays the status of RAS connections.

Monitoring a RAS Connection

The example above uses `RasDial()` synchronously: the call completes when the connection is established or when an error is detected. There's an alternate method that involves using `RasDial()` asynchronously. This approach is such that `RasDial()` immediately returns; the application receives messages as the call is being made (the `Remnet` application uses that approach and displays various messages boxes as the connection goes through).

The next to last parameter is in fact a window handle. By using `NULL` (as shown above), `RasDial()` is instructed to work synchronously. On the other hand, by specifying a valid window handle, `RasDial()` immediately returns and sends `WM_RASDIALEVENT` notification messages to that window as connection events unfold.

When this message is received, `wParam` describes the actual state of the connection, whereas `lParam` is an error code if non zero. The most common states are listed in Figure 13-5.

RAS Connection State	Description
RASCS_ConnectDevice	The device is about to be connected
RASCS_DeviceConnected	The device is connected
RASCS_Authenticate	The authentication process has started
RASCS_Authenticated	The user has been authenticated
RASCS_Connected	Successfully connected
RASCS_Disconnected	Disconnection or failed connection

Figure 13-5: Some of the connection states specified by the `wParam` parameter when `WM_RASDIALEVENT` is received.

Terminating a Connection

In order to disconnect from the RAS server, an application calls `RasHangUp()`, passing the connection handle. The next example disconnects a RAS connection.

```
void HangUp(HRASCONN hRasConn)
{
    if (hRasConn != NULL)
            RasHangUp(hRasConn);
}
```

Once the RAS session is terminated, other applications can no longer communicate with the RAS server.

13.2 RAPI

Windows CE supports the Remote Application Programming API (RAPI), an interface that allows a desktop application to call a specific function on a Windows CE device. The desktop computer is called a RAPI client and the Windows CE device, the RAPI server. Internally, the communication is Winsock-based and relies on RAS. The API described in this section is called by desktop applications, not CE applications. In fact, in most cases, there is nothing to do on CE to use RAPI.

RAPI is composed of a set of functions that have direct equivalents on Windows CE. For instance, the RAPI function `CeCreateDirectory()` is the RAPI version of Windows CE's `CreateDirectory()` function. Hence, a desktop application that invokes `CeCreateDirectory()` turns out to invoke `CreateDirectory()` on the connected Windows CE device (see Figure 13-6).

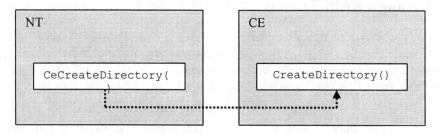

Figure 13-6: Invoking `CeCreateDirectory()` on the desktop results in the invocation of `CreateDirectory()` on Windows CE.

All RAPI functions are in fact prefixed with "Ce", making them easy to identify on the desktop. Note that a few Windows CE functions start with the same prefix; for instance, `CeCreateDatabase()` is both the name of RAPI function and a Windows CE native function. However, there is no issue as to which one to link against; there is only one available for each platform (the desktop or the CE device) in their respective application library.

The concept is not new, as it rings a bell to those of you familiar with Remote Procedure Calls (RPCs); see the Suggested Readings section for more information). But it is available now and very easy to use.

RAPI is very useful, because it allows managing a Windows CE device from a desktop. Consider a large application that only needs to be run occasionally on CE. Installing that application on CE would permanently use memory (to hold the application). On the other hand, implementing that same application using RAPI and running it from a host can provide the same functionality, yet without consuming space on the CE device.

13.2.1 Initial Setup

Using RAPI requires setting up both the workstation and the Windows CE device.

On the workstation, your application needs to have access to `Rapi.h` and `Rapi.lib` at compile and link time. The two files, along `Rapi.dll`, are installed with the C++ Toolkit (see Chapter 2 for details about the Toolkits). `Rassrv.exe` must also be running as the RAS server (it is automatically started with Windows CE Services).

On the Windows CE device, `Repllog.exe` and the associated modules (including `Rapisvr.exe`) must be running to implement the client-side of the RAS connection (see Chapter 2 about building a configuration including those modules). In particular, running `Remnet.exe` on the target will not do the trick[37].

13.2.2 Starting a RAPI Session

A RAPI session is started by calling either `CeRapiInit()` or `CeRapiInitEx()`. Both calls initialize underlying communication layers between the desktop and the CE device. A RAS connection must already have been established via Windows CE Services (on the desktop) and `Repllog.exe` (on the CE device) for RAPI to initialize. On CE, `Repllog.exe` starts `Rapisvr.exe`, which is used by the calls we are about to examine.

`CeRapiInit()` takes no argument and is synchronous: it blocks until a connection is made. `CeRapiInitEx()` is asynchronous: it immediately returns, and sets an event flag when completed (see Chapter 7 about event flag objects). `CeRapiInitEx()` requires a `RAPIINIT` structure (see Figure 13-7).

Type	Member	Description
DWORD	cbSize	Always `sizeof(RAPIINIT)`
HANDLE	heRapiInit	Handle to an event flag object, created by RAPI (not by the application), which is set when RAPI is initialized.
HANDLE	hrRapiInit	Result of the connection, available when `heRapiInit` is signaled.

Figure 13-7: The `RAPIINIT` structure. Only `cbSize` needs to be initialized.

The following example demonstrates a helper function that combines the two initialization functions. It takes a time-out (in milliseconds), and invokes `CeRapiInit()` if the time-out is `INFINITE` or `CeRapiInitEx()` if it is something else. The function

---

[37] Specifically, `Rapisvr.exe` requires `Repllog.exe` and does not work along `Remnet.exe`.

returns a Boolean (non-zero on success, 0 on error). Note that a graphical application would use `MsgWaitForMultipleObjects()` instead of `WaitForSingleObject()`.

```
BOOL StartRapi(DWORD dwTimeOut)
{
        RAPIINIT          ri;

        if (dwTimeOut == INFINITE)
                return SUCCEEDED(CeRapiInit());

        ri.cbSize = sizeof(RAPIINIT);

        if (FAILED(CeRapiInitEx(&ri)))
                return FALSE;

        if (WaitForSingleObject(ri.heRapiInit, dwTimeOut) == WAIT_TIMEOUT)
        {
                CeRapiUninit();
                return FALSE;
        }

        return SUCCEEDED(ri.hrRapiInit);
}
```

This function can be invoked as follows to wait until the connection is established.

```
BOOL    rc;

rc = StartRapi(INFINITE);
```

Or it can be called as follows to wait at most one second:

```
rc = StartRapi(1000);
```

The latter approach is preferred, as it ensures that the application doesn't block indefinitely if the desktop is not physically connected to the device.

13.2.3 Terminating a RAPI Session

When the desktop application is finished with making RAPI calls, it de-initializes RAPI by calling `CeRapiUninit()`, allowing the system to perform some internal clean-up.

```
CeRapiUninit();
```

13.2.4 RAPI Functions

Most other RAPI functions are simply the host counterpart of some Windows CE Win32 functions. These functions are listed in the following figures, with the corresponding CE function or some description. Figures 13-8 to 13-12 lists RAPI functions regarding databases, files and Object Store, the registry, windows, and the system.

RAPI Function	Corresponding Windows CE Call – or – Description
CeCreateDatabase()	CeCreateDatabase()
CeDeleteDatabase()	CeDeleteDatabase()
CeDeleteRecord()	CeDeleteRecord()
CeFindAllDatabases()	This RAPI function lists all databases on CE. See Section 13.2.5 for details.
CeFindFirstDatabase()	CeFindFirstDatabase()
CeFindNextDatabase()	CeFindNextDatabase()
CeOpenDatabase()	CeOpenDatabase()
CeReadRecordProps()	CeReadRecordProps().
CeSeekDatabase()	CeSeekDatabase()
CeSetDatabaseInfo()	CeSetDatabaseInfo()
CeWriteRecordProps()	CeWriteRecordProps()

Figure 13-8: RAPI database functions. Most RAPI functions share their name with their equivalent on CE.

RAPI Function	Corresponding Windows CE Call – or – Description
CeCloseHandle()	CloseHandle()
CeCopyFile()	CopyFile()
CeCreateDirectory()	CreateDirectory()
CeCreateFile()	CreateFile()
CeDeleteFile()	DeleteFile()
CeFindAllFiles()	This RAPI function lists all files on CE. See Section 13.2.5 for details.
CeFindClose()	FindClose()
CeFindFirstFile()	FindFirstFile()
CeFindNextFile()	FindNextFile()
CeGetFileAttributes()	GetFileAttributes()
CeGetFileSize()	GetFileSize()
CeGetFileTime()	GetFileTime()
CeGetStoreInformation()	GetStoreInformation()
CeGetTempPath()	GetTempPath()
CeMoveFile()	MoveFile()
CeOidGetInfo()	CeOidGetInfo() *i.e., same name*
CeReadFile()	ReadFile()
CeRemoveDirectory()	RemoveDirectory()
CeSetEndOfFile()	SetEndOfFile()
CeSetFileAttributes()	SetFileAttributes()
CeSetFilePointer()	SetFilePointer()
CeSetFileTime()	CeSetFileTime()
CeWriteFile()	CeWriteFile()

Figure 13-9: RAPI files and Object Store management functions.

RAPI Function	Corresponding Windows CE Call – or – Description
CeRegCloseKey()	RegCloseKey()
CeRegCreateKeyEx()	RegCreateKeyEx()
CeRegDeleteKey()	RegDeleteKey()
CeRegDeleteValue()	RegDeleteValue()
CeRegEnumKeyEx()	RegEnumKeyEx()
CeRegEnumValue()	RegEnumValue()
CeRegOpenKeyEx()	RegOpenKeyEx()
CeRegQueryInfoKey()	RegQueryInfoKey()
CeRegQueryValueEx()	RegQueryValueEx()
CeRegSetValueEx()	RegSetValueEx()

Figure 13-10: RAPI registry functions.

RAPI Function	Corresponding Windows CE Call – or – Description
CeGetClassName()	GetClassName()
CeGetWindow()	GetWindow()
CeGetWindowLong()	GetWindowLong()
CeGetWindowText()	GetWindowText()

Figure 13-11: RAPI windows functions.

RAPI Function	Corresponding Windows CE Call – or – Description
CeCheckPassword()	CheckPassword()
CeCreateProcess()	CreateProcess()
CeGetDesktopDeviceCaps()	GetDeviceCaps()
CeGetLastError()	GetLastError()
CeGetSpecialFolderPath()	Returns the path to the special shell folder
CeGetSystemInfo()	GetSystemInfo()
CeGetSystemMetrics()	GetSystemMetrics()
CeGetSystemPowerStatusEx()	GetSystemPowerStatusEx()
CeGetVersionEx()	GetVersionEx()
CeGlobalMemoryStatus()	GlobalMemoryStatus()
CeSHCreatreShortcut	SHCreateShortcut()
CeSHGetShortcutTarget()	SHGetShortcutTarget()

Figure 13-12: RAPI system functions.

13.2.5 Using RAPI Functions

Most of the functions listed above plainly correspond to their CE equivalent, and are used the same way. There are however a few functions that are specific to RAPI (*i.e.*, running on the host, with no direct equivalent on CE).

The first one is CeRapiGetError(), which returns RAPI-related error codes, if relevant.

The other functions are related to finding information on CE. CeFindAllFiles() searches for files, starting from the specified directory, and fills an array of CE_FIND_DATA structures (see Figure 13-13). The array is allocated by the system, and must be freed by calling `CeRapiFreeBuffer()`.

Type	Member	Description
DWORD	dwFileAttributes	File attributes
FILETIME	ftCreationTime	Time of creation
FILETIME	ftLastAccessTime	Time of last access
FILETIME	ftLastWriteAccess	Time of last write access
DWORD	nFileSizeHigh	High-order file size
DWORD	nFileSizeLow	Low-order file size
DWORD	dwOID	Object Store identifier
WCHAR	cFileName[MAX_PATH]	File name

Figure 13-13: The `CE_FIND_DATA` structure, used with `CeFindAllFiles()`. The total size of the file is obtained as follows: `(nFileSizeHigh * MAXDWORD) + nFileSizeLow`.

Similarly, `CeFindAllDatabases()` fills up an array of `CEDB_FIND_DATA` structures (see Figure 13-14), for each database that can be matched to the specified type. The array must be freed using `CeRapiFreeBuffer()` as well. Speaking of databases, `CeReadRecordProps()` also uses system memory, which must be freed via `CeRapiFreeBuffer()`.

Type	Member	Description
CEOID	OidDb	Object Store identifier
CEDBASEINFO	DbInfo	Information about database

Figure 13-14: The `CEDB_FIND_DATA` structure, used with `CeFindAllDatabases()`.

The next example lists all the files in the root directory (`L"\\*.*"`, which must be specified in `Unicode`), as well as all databases of type 0 in the Object Store. Only the names are retrieved and displayed (as `Unicode` strings). This example can be found in the **Rapidemo** sample.

```
void ListFilesAndDBs()
{
    // List all files
    DWORD          i, dwCount;
    LPCE_FIND_DATA pCefd;

    CeFindAllFiles(
        L"\\*.*",                   // File mask (in Unicode)
        FAF_NAME,                   // Info. to retrieve
        &dwCount,                   // Count (a DWORD)
        &pCefd);                    // Ptr to CE_FIND_DATA array,
```

```
                                    // automatically allocated

    for (i = 0; i < dwCount; i++)
         printf("%S\n", pCefd[i].cFileName);

    CeRapiFreeBuffer(pCefd);            // Release system memory

    // List all databases of type 0.
    WORD                  wCount;
    LPCEDB_FIND_DATA      pCeDbfd;

    CeFindAllDatabases(
         0,                            // Database type
         FAD_NAME,                     // Info. to retrieve.
         &wCount,                      // Count (a WORD this time)
         &pCeDbfd);                    // Ptr to CEDB_FIND_DATA array,
                                       // automatically allocated

    for (i = 0; i < wCount; i++)
         printf("%S\n", pCeDbfd[i].DbInfo.szDbaseName);

    CeRapiFreeBuffer(pCeDbfd);         // Release system memory
}
```

13.2.6 User-Defined Functions

In addition to the predefined functions described in the previous sections, RAPI allows invoking user-defined functions on Windows CE from the desktop. Developers must write these functions and store them in a regular dynamic link library (DLL). The remote call is initiated via `CeRapiInvoke()` on the desktop, resulting in the specified function to be invoked in the specified DLL on the target (see Figure 13-15). Data can be passed in both directions, either in block or stream modes (we'll see the details in a second). You must code both the desktop call invocation and the function in the DLL on Windows CE.

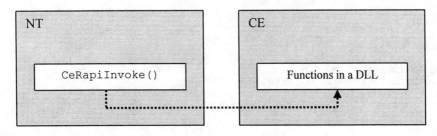

Figure 13-15: A desktop application can invoke a user-defined function on Windows CE that resides in a dynamic-link library (DLL).

Target Side Implementation

The first step is to develop a DLL that contains the function(s) that will be remotely invoked. Any tool listed in Chapter 2 can generate a Windows CE DLL skeleton. For instance, Platform Builder 2.11 generates a customizable skeleton that exports a variable, a function and a class.

The documentation is unclear as to what arguments are passed and returned from and to the desktop. Luckily, a look into `Rapi.h` reveals that information:

```
// Rapi.h

.
.
.

// RAPI extension on Windows CE (e.g., MyFunctionFOO) called
// via CeRapiInvoke should be declared as:
// EXTERN_C RAPIEXT MyFunctionFOO;
typedef  HRESULT (STDAPICALLTYPE RAPIEXT)(
              DWORD         cbInput,           // [IN]
              BYTE          *pInput,           // [IN]
              DWORD         *pcbOutput,        // [OUT]
              BYTE          **ppOutput,        // [OUT]
              IRAPIStream   *pIRAPIStream      // [IN]
              );

.
.
.
```

The next example (`MyCeDll.dll`) exports one function (`GetTime()`), which will later be invoked from the desktop.

```
// MyCeDll.h

#include "CeRapi.h"

#ifdef MYCEDLL_EXPORTS
#define MYCEDLL_API __declspec(dllexport)
#else
#define MYCEDLL_API __declspec(dllimport)
#endif

EXTERN_C MYCEDLL_API RAPIEXT GetTime;            // Must be exported.
```

```
// MyCeDll.cpp

#include "stdafx.h"
#include "MyCeDll.h"
```

```
BOOL APIENTRY DllMain(HANDLE hModule,
                      DWORD  ul_reason_for_call,
                      LPVOID lpReserved)
{
    return TRUE;
}

HRESULT GetTime(DWORD cbInput, BYTE * pInput,
    DWORD * pcbOutput, BYTE ** ppOutput, IRAPIStream * pIRAPIStream)
{
    LPSYSTEMTIME pst;

    // Allocate a SYSTEMTIME buffer to return the result. If memory
    // is unavailable, return FALSE to caller.
    pst = static_cast<LPSYSTEMTIME>(LocalAlloc(LPTR, sizeof(SYSTEMTIME)));

    if (pst == NULL)
    {
            *pcbOutput = 0;                         // Nothing to return
            return FALSE;
    }

    GetLocalTime(pst);                              // Get local time

    *pcbOutput = sizeof(SYSTEMTIME);                // Data count to return
    *ppOutput = reinterpret_cast<BYTE *>(pst);      // Data to return

    return TRUE;
}
```

Desktop Side Implementation

Once RAPI is initialized, a desktop application simply calls CeRapiInvoke() to execute a function remotely. The prototype of that function is as follows:

```
#include "Rapi.h"

HRESULT CeRapiInvoke(
         LPCWSTR pDllPath,
         LPCWSTR pFunctionName,
         DWORD cbInput,
         BYTE *pInput,
         DWORD *pcbOutput,
         BYTE **ppOutput,
         IRAPIStream ** ppIRAPIStream,
         DWORD dwReserved);
```

The first argument is the DLL name where the function resides. That DLL may contain one or many functions, and they may include other functions for other purposes than being invoked remotely (helper functions, for instance). The name must be specified in Unicode.

The second argument is the function name, which must also be specified in Unicode.

The third and fourth arguments are input parameters (size and content), passed from the desktop to the target. Any input data on the desktop must be allocated from the local heap (via `LocalAlloc()`), which is later automatically freed by the system.

Similarly, the fifth and sixth arguments are output parameters (pointers to size and content), passed from the target to the desktop. The output data is automatically allocated by the system on the local heap, which the application must release (by calling `LocalFree()`).

The next argument is a pointer to an `IRAPIStream` interface. This value indicates whether the call is done in block mode (`NULL`) or stream mode (non-`NULL`). In block mode, the remote call is done synchronously: the input data is passed to the remote function, which executes and returns output data. The caller (on the desktop) remains blocked until the remote function terminates, whose return value is also returned by `CeRapiInvoke()`. In stream mode, `CeRapiInvoke()` immediately returns, and any input/output data is passed back and forth via the `IRAPIStream` interface. We're just about to see an example of each approach, also found in the **Rapidemo** sample , on the CD-ROM. This demo requires **MyCeDll.dll**, also on the CD-ROM, to be installed on CE, in the `\Windows` directory..

Finally, the next parameter is reserved and should be zero.

Block Mode Example

Here is an example that remotely invokes the function `GetTime()` in `MyCeDll.dll`, on CE. Remember that this code runs on the host.

```
#include "rapi.h"

void CeGetLocalTime()
{
    HRESULT         hr;
    LPSYSTEMTIME    pst;
    DWORD           nBytesOut;

    hr = CeRapiInvoke(
            L"MyCeDll",             // DLL is "MyCeDll.dll"
            L"GetTime",             // Function name
            0,                      // Size of input
            NULL,                   // No input parameter
            &nBytesOut,             // Size of output
            (BYTE **) &pst,         // Pointer to SYSTEMTIME
            NULL,                   // Block mode
            0);                     // Reserved

    if (SUCCEEDED(hr))
    {
            printf("Date on CE is %02d/%02d/%d\n",
                    pst->wMonth, pst->wDay, pst->wYear);

            printf("Time on CE is %02d:%02d:%02d\n",
```

```
                pst->wHour, pst->wMinute, pst->wSecond);

        LocalFree(pst);                    // Free output buffer memory
    }
}
```

Stream Mode Example

The previous method blocks the caller until the call has been completed on the CE side. During that wait, the caller can't do anything by itself, such as providing some feedback to the user. An alternative is to use a COM-based object, in which case the invocation of the remote function does not block. Appendix B provides an overview of COM if you unfamiliar with that tehcnology. For the sake of simplicity, let's just say that the object to use, IRAPIStream, exposes two methods (interfaces): Read() and Write(), which can be used as their names suggest.

Using this approach, both the caller and callee obtain a pointer to an IRAPIStream interface, and they can dynamically exchange information with it: whatever is written on one end can be read on the other end. The data being transferred is not interpreted. In fact, the only thing that matters is the caller and callee to agree on what to read and write.

The next example illustrates GetFormattedTime(), another exported function in MyCeDll.dll (on CE). It obtains the local time, formats it in a predefined format, and writes it trough an IRAPIStream interface. Specifically, the length is sent first (as a DWORD), followed by the string in Unicode, including the terminating NULL.

```
// CE RAPI method that returns a formatted string containing the
// local data and time. This code runs on CE.

HRESULT GetFormattedTime(DWORD cbInput, BYTE * pInput,
    DWORD * pcbOutput, BYTE ** ppOutput, IRAPIStream * pIRAPIStream)
{
    SYSTEMTIME    st;
    TCHAR         szTime[64];
    DWORD         nLen;
    ULONG         nByteCount;

    GetLocalTime(&st);

    nLen = wsprintf(szTime,
        _T("Date: %02d/%02d/%d - Time: %02d:%02d:%02d"),
        st.wMonth, st.wDay, st.wYear,
        st.wHour, st.wMinute, st.wSecond);

    nLen++;                        // Add one for the final NULL.

    pIRAPIStream->Write(&nLen, sizeof(DWORD), &nByteCount);

    nLen *= sizeof(TCHAR);         // Character count, in bytes
```

```
        pIRAPIStream->Write(szTime, nLen, &nByteCount);

        return TRUE;
    }
```

On the desktop side, the invocation is slightly different than in block mode: the next to last parameter is a pointer to an IRAPIStream object, instead of NULL. The object is created by the system, not by the application.

```
// Host function that invokes GetFormattedTime() on CE.
// This code runs on the host.

void CeGetFormattedTime()
{
    HRESULT      hr;
    DWORD        nBytesOut;
    LPBYTE       pOut;
    IRAPIStream * pIRAPIStream;              // Pointer to interface

    hr = CeRapiInvoke(
            L"MyCeDll",
            L"GetFormattedTime",
            0,
            NULL,
            &nBytesOut,
            &pOut,
            &pIRAPIStream,
            0);

    if (SUCCEEDED(hr))
    {
            ULONG   nByteCount;
            DWORD   nLen;
            LPTSTR  pszTime;

            // Get the length (in characters)
            pIRAPIStream->Read(&nLen, sizeof(DWORD), &nByteCount);

            // Allocate a buffer to hold an Unicode string.
            nLen   *= sizeof(WCHAR);
            pszTime = new TCHAR[nLen];

            // Get the string, print it, and delete it.
            pIRAPIStream->Read(pszTime, nLen, &nByteCount);

            printf("%S\n", pszTime);

            delete [] pszTime;

    }
}
```

13.3 CONNECTION NOTIFICATIONS

Desktop applications can be automatically notified whenever CE devices connect and disconnect from the host. Two methods are available: via the Registry, or by using a COM interface.

13.3.1 Registry-Based Notifications

By simply adding specific entries in the host Registry (on NT), desktop applications can be started whenever a Windows CE device is connected or disconnected. These entries are:

```
HKEY_LOCAL_MACHINE\
   SOFTWARE\
      Microsoft\
         Windows CE Services\
            AutoStartOnConnect
            AutoStartOnDisconnect
```

The entry `AutoStartOnConnect` must contain a value that identifies an application (`.EXE`), which is to be started whenever a connection is established. Each value must be identified by a unique name (*e.g.*, company name, product) and the data must be the application path, including arguments if any. Figure 13-16 shows an actual entry in the Registry: the name is "Microsoft SChannel RNG" and the data is the program `Secrng.exe`.

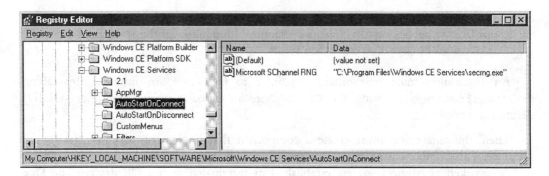

Figure 13-16: An actual registry `AutoStartOnConnect` entry.

The entry `AutoStartOnDisconnect` must also contain a string value that identifies an application (`.EXE`), which is to be started whenever a connection is dropped.

You can add these entries using the Registry editor (`Regedit.exe`), use some Win32 registry calls, or better, use the CEUTIL API, described in Section 13.4.

13.3.2 COM-Based Notifications

Windows CE Services implements a connection manager that displays an icon in the system tray, next to the time, in the task bar. (That icon shows two connected computers when a CE device is connected.) This connection manager implements the `IDccMan` interface, which sends connection notifications to registered applications.

An application must implement a component that implements the `IDccManSink` interface, and lets the connection manager be aware of that component (see Figure 13-17). The concept is simple, but the implementation is non-trivial for those unfamiliar with COM. If this is your case, it is strongly recommended that you read Appendix B before continuing; it will make the time spent reading what follows much more worthwhile.

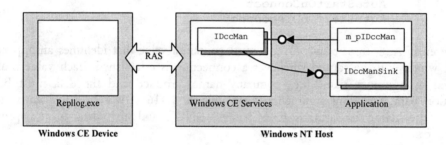

Figure 13-17: Windows CE Services' device manager implements the `IDccMan` interface. An application that creates a component that implements the `IDccManSink` interface will be notified of connection events.

An application must first obtain a pointer to the `IDccMan` interface, by calling `CoCreateInstance()`, using the `CLSID_DccMan` globally unique identifier (GUID) defined in `dccole.h`.

Then, the application must create a component that implements the `IDCCManSink` interface. This component must implements up to eight methods (see Figure 13-18), which will be invoked as connections are established or terminated with a CE device. The **Dcc** sample, on the CD-ROM, demonstrates those concepts, which are detailed on the next pages.

IDccManSink Method	Description
OnLogActive()	Called when a connection is established between the client application and the connection manager.
OnLogAnswered()	Called when the Windows CE connection manager has detected the communications interface.
OnLogDisconnection()	Called when the connection manager has terminated the connection between the desktop computer and the Windows CE-based- device.
OnLogError()	Called when the connection manager failed to start communications between the desktop computer and the Windows CE-based device.
OnLogInactive()	Called upon a disconnection, or disconnected state, between the desktop computer and the Windows CE-based device.
OnLogIpAddr()	Called when an Internet Protocol (IP) address has been assigned to a Windows CE device
OnLogListen()	Called when a connection is waiting to be established between the desktop computer and the Windows CE-based device.
OnLogTerminated()	Called when the Windows CE connection manager has been shut down.

Figure 13-18: `IDccManSink` methods that are called as CE devices connect and disconnect. Only a few are actually called on NT.

The example that illustrates this approach is more complicated than the previous, because it cannot simply be implemented using a console application unless the application implements a message pump. Therefore, a graphical application is required. An example of the output is shown on Figure 13-19; it consists of a plain window that contains a list box, filled with the notifications that are received as a CE device connected and disconnected.

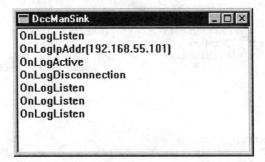

Figure 13-19: The output of DccManSink. In this example, a CE device received the IP address 192.168.55.101 upon connection. The entry OnLogDisconnection showed up when the CE device disconnected (specifically, when `Repllog.exe` on CE terminated).

The example uses an API not covered yet: the Microsoft Foundation Classes (MFC). Using it makes the example simpler than writing it in C. Although MFC is fully described in Part IV, the code contains extra comments for newcomers to MFC to help understand the core functionality.

The example consists of two source files and their respective header file:

- `Dcc.cpp` implements the application's main window, which essentially consists of a list box. This code heavily relies on MFC.

- `DccManSink.cpp` implements the `IDccManSink` interface. Whenever a method is called by the device manager (which resides outside the application), it sends a message to the main window in order to add a string in the list box. Figure 13-19 shows a few strings. This code is a COM interface implementation, detailed in Appendix B.

Also, these source files must be linked against `wsock32.lib`, because of the WinSock call to `inet_ntoa()`.

Dcc.h

```
#include "afxwin.h"

// The main application class definition. There must be one instance
// in the application. Its role is essentially to pump and dispatch
// messages to the main window.
class CTheApp: public CWinApp
{
public:
    virtual BOOL    InitInstance();
    virtual BOOL    ExitInstance();
};


// The main window class definition.
class CMainWnd: public CFrameWnd
{
    DWORD           m_dwDccContext;         // Required by IDccMan
    IDccMan *       m_pIDccMan;
    IDccManSink *   m_pIDccManSink;
    CListBox        m_cListBox;             // Application's list box

public:
    CMainWnd();

protected:
    // Standard message handlers
    afx_msg int  OnCreate(LPCREATESTRUCT lpcs);         // WM_CREATE
    afx_msg void OnDestroy();                           // WM_DESTROY
    afx_msg void OnSize();                              // WM_SIZE

    // User-defined message handler (sent by CDccManSink)
    afx_msg void OnDccNotify(WPARAM, LPARAM);           // WM_DCCNOTIFY

    DECLARE_MESSAGE_MAP()
};
```

Dcc.cpp

```cpp
#include "afxwin.h"
#include "objbase.h"
#include "initguid.h"
#include "dccole.h"
#include "Dcc.h"
#include "DccManSink.h"

CTheApp       ThisApp;                       // Only one instance required

BOOL CTheApp::InitInstance()
{
    CoInitialize(NULL);                      // Initialize COM

    m_pMainWnd = new CMainWnd;               // Create main window
    m_pMainWnd->ShowWindow(m_nCmdShow);      // Make it visible...
    m_pMainWnd->UpdateWindow();              // ... now

    return TRUE;
}


BOOL CTheApp::ExitInstance()
{
    CoUninitialize();                        // Say goodbye to COM
    return CWinApp::ExitInstance();
}

// Window's message map, which invokes handlers in response
// to window messages.
BEGIN_MESSAGE_MAP(CMainWnd, CWnd)
    ON_WM_CREATE()                           // Invokes OnCreate()
    ON_WM_DESTROY()                          // Invokes onDestroy()
    ON_MESSAGE(WM_DCCNOTIFY, OnDccNotify) // Invokes OnDccNotify
END_MESSAGE_MAP()

CMainWnd::CMainWnd()
{
    m_pIDccMan = NULL;
    m_pIDccManSink = NULL;

    // Create a visible window by calling CWnd::Create(). This method
    // stores the handle of the created window into CWnd::m_hWnd;
    Create(NULL, "DccManSink");

    // Make sure the window was successfully created. Display an
    // assertion failure message box otherwise.
    ASSERT(m_hWnd != NULL);
}

// Handler to WM_CREATE.
// It must return 0 to continue the creation, -1 to abort it.

int CMainWnd::OnCreate(LPCREATESTRUCT lpcs)
{
    HRESULT        hr;
```

```
      // Obtain a pointer to IDccMan, return -1 on error.
      hr = CoCreateInstance(CLSID_DccMan, NULL, CLSCTX_SERVER,
            IID_IDccMan, (void **) &m_pIDccMan);

      if (FAILED(hr))
            return -1;

      // Create an instance of IDccManSink by using an IUnknown interface
      IUnknown *      pIUnknown = CDccManSink::CreateInstance(m_hWnd);

      pIUnknown->QueryInterface(IID_IDccManSink, (void **)&m_pIDccManSink);
      pIUnknown->Release();

      // Notify IDccMan of the existence of our IDccManSink. From now on,
      // IDccManSink's methods are automatically called depending on the
      // connection status with the CE device.
      hr = m_pIDccMan->Advise(m_pIDccManSink, &m_dwDccContext);

      if (FAILED(hr))
      {
            m_pIDccManSink->Release();
            m_pIDccMan->Release();

            return -1;
      }

      // Create the list box, the size of the client area.
      CRect    rect;
      GetClientRect(rect);
      m_cListBox.Create(WS_VISIBLE, rect, this, 1);

      return 0;
}

// Handler to WM_SIZE.
// Whenever the window is resized (that happens at creation time too),
// also resize the list box to fully cover the client area.

void CMainWnd::OnSize()
{
    CRect    rect;

    GetClientRect(rect);
    m_cListBox.MoveWindow(rect);
}

// Handler to WM_DCCNOTIFY.
// The IDccManSink method send WM_DCCNOTIFY messages when invoked.
// This message is handled here: wParam is assumed to be a string,
// which is appended to the list box.

void CMainWnd::OnDccNotify(WPARAM wParam, LPARAM)
{
    m_cListBox.AddString(reinterpret_cast<LPCTSTR>(wParam));
}
```

```
// Handler to WM DESTROY.
// When the application terminates, notify IDccMan that we no longer
// want to receive notifications, and release the interfaces.

void CMainWnd::OnDestroy()
{
    m_pIDccMan->Unadvise(m_dwDccContext);
    m_pIDccManSink->Release();
    m_pIDccMan->Release();
}
```

DccManSink.h

```
#ifndef DEFINE_GUID
#include "objbase.h"
#include "dccole.h"
#endif

// Message to send to parent window.
const int   WM_DCCNOTIFY = WM_USER + 100;

class CDccManSink: public IDccManSink
{
    long        m_nRef;                 // Reference count
    HWND        m_hWnd;                 // Window to notify

public:
    CDccManSink(HWND hWnd);            // Constructor
    ~CDccManSink();                    // Destructor

    // IUnknown interface
    virtual HRESULT __stdcall         QueryInterface(const IID& iid,
                                                     void ** ppv);
    virtual ULONG   __stdcall  AddRef();
    virtual ULONG   __stdcall  Release();

    // IDccManSink interface
    virtual HRESULT __stdcall  OnLogActive();
    virtual HRESULT __stdcall  OnLogAnswered();
    virtual HRESULT __stdcall  OnLogDisconnection();
    virtual HRESULT __stdcall  OnLogError();
    virtual HRESULT __stdcall  OnLogInactive();
    virtual HRESULT __stdcall  OnLogIpAddr(DWORD dwIpAddr);
    virtual HRESULT __stdcall  OnLogListen();
    virtual HRESULT __stdcall  OnLogTerminated();

    // Component creation method
    static IUnknown * CreateInstance(HWND hWnd);

private:
    void    ShowMessage(LPCTSTR pszMsg);
};

inline void CDccManSink::ShowMessage(LPCTSTR pszMsg)
{
```

```
        // Send the user-defined message WM DCCNOTIFY to the window.
        // wParam is the string to show, lParam is always NULL.
        SendMessage(
                m_hWnd,
                WM_DCCNOTIFY,
                reinterpret_cast<WPARAM>(pszMsg),
                NULL);
}
```

DccManSink.cpp

```cpp
#include "DccManSink.h"

CDccManSink::CDccManSink(HWND hWnd)
{
    m_nRef = 0;
    m_hWnd = hWnd;
}

CDccManSink::~CDccManSink()
{
}

IUnknown * CDccManSink::CreateInstance(HWND hWnd)
{
    IUnknown * pI = static_cast<IDccManSink*>(new CDccManSink(hWnd));
    pI->AddRef();
    return pI;
}

HRESULT __stdcall CDccManSink::QueryInterface(const IID& iid, void ** ppv)
{
    if (iid == IID_IUnknown || iid == IID_IDccManSink)
            *ppv = static_cast<IDccManSink *>(this);
    else
    {
            *ppv = NULL;
            return E_NOINTERFACE;
    }

    reinterpret_cast<IUnknown*>(*ppv)->AddRef();
    //AddRef();
    return S_OK;
}

ULONG __stdcall CDccManSink::AddRef()
{
    return InterlockedIncrement(&m_nRef);
}

ULONG __stdcall CDccManSink::Release()
{
    if (InterlockedDecrement(&m_nRef) == 0)
    {
            delete this;
```

```
            return 0;
    }

    return m_nRef;
}

HRESULT __stdcall CDccManSink::OnLogActive()
{
    ShowMessage("OnLogActive");
    return S_OK;
}

HRESULT __stdcall CDccManSink::OnLogAnswered()
{
    ShowMessage("OnLogAnswered");
    return S_OK;
}

HRESULT __stdcall CDccManSink::OnLogDisconnection()
{
    ShowMessage("OnLogDisconnection");
    return S_OK;
}

HRESULT __stdcall CDccManSink::OnLogError()
{
    ShowMessage("OnLogError");
    return S_OK;
}

HRESULT __stdcall CDccManSink::OnLogInactive()
{
    ShowMessage("OnLogInactive");
    return S_OK;
}

HRESULT __stdcall CDccManSink::OnLogIpAddr(DWORD dwIpAddr)
{
    TCHAR          szMsg[32];
    struct in_addr in_addr;

    in_addr.S_un.S_addr = dwIpAddr;
    wsprintf(szMsg, "OnLogIpAddr (%s)", inet_ntoa(in_addr));

    ShowMessage(szMsg);
    return S_OK;
}

HRESULT __stdcall CDccManSink::OnLogListen()
{
    ShowMessage("OnLogListen");
    return S_OK;
}
```

13.4 CEUTIL

Windows CE Services extensively uses the Registry to store various settings, which may sometimes be used by desktop applications. To provide an easy access to these settings, an new desktop API is available: the CEUTIL API. Useful type definitions and prototypes are listed in `Ceutil.h`. Note that this API is only valid on host Windows platforms, not on CE. This API is essentially a front-end to some Registry functions.

13.4.1 CEUTIL Logical Subkeys

A set of logical subkey constants have been introduced to simplify access to the Windows CE Services Registry entries. Figure 13-20 lists the constants that reside under `"HKEY_LOCAL_MACHINE\Software\Microsoft\Windows CE Services"`, whereas Figure 13-21 lists those under `"HKEY_CURRENT_USER\Software\Microsoft\Windows CE Services"`.

Logical Subkey	Registry Keys	Description
CESVC_ROOT_MACHINE	.	Root
CESVC_FILTERS	Filters	Filters root
CESVC_CUSTOM_MENUS	CustomMenus	Custom menu root
CESVC_SERVICES_COMMON	Services	Services root
CESVC_SYNC_COMMON	Services\Synchronization	Synchronization root

Figure 13-20: CEUTIL constants for keys under `"HKEY_LOCAL_MACHINE\Software\Microsoft\Windows CE Services"`.

Logical Subkey	Registry Keys	Description
CESVC_ROOT_USER	.	CE Services Root
CESVC_DEVICES	Partners	Individual device root
CESVC_DEVICESX	Partners*dev_id*	Particular device root
CESVC_DEVICE_SELECTED	Partners*selected_dev_id*	Selected device root
CESVC_SERVICES_USER	Partners*dev_id*\Services	Particular device services root
CESVC_SYNC	Partners*dev_id*\Services\Synchronization	Synchronization root for a particular device.

Figure 13-21: CEUTIL constants for keys under `"HKEY_CURRENT_USER\Software\Microsoft\Windows CE Services"`.

13.4.2 Accessing CEUTIL Subkeys

A desktop application can open a particular key by calling `CeSvcOpen()`. The call accepts four parameters: a logical subkey constant (as shown in Figures 13-20 and 13-21), a key name, a Boolean that indicates whether the key should be created if is doesn't already exist, and a pointer to a key handler, returned by the call. The next example opens the AutoStartOnConnect key, under CESVC_ROOT_MACHINE:

```
HRESULT     hr;
HCESVC      hSvc;

hr = CeSvcOpen(CESVC_ROOT_MACHINE, "AutoStartOnConnect", TRUE, &hSvc);

// Use SUCCEEDED(hr) or FAILED(hr) to determine the outcome of the call.
```

Using the returned key handle, a few calls are available to get or set values (see Figure 13-22). These functions require a key handle, a value name and value data.

CEUTIL Function	Description
CeSvcGetDword()	Gets the DWORD value of a key
CeSvcSetDword()	Sets the DWORD value of a key
CeSvcGetString()	Get the string value of a key
CeSvcSetString()	Set the string value of a key
CeSvcGetBinary()	Get the binary data value of a key
CeSvcSetBinary()	Set the binary data value of a key

Figure 13-22: CEUTIL functions to access CE Services registry keys.

In additionally, other functions are available given a valid key handle. These functions can be used along the other registry functions found in the Win32 API.

CEUTIL Function	Description
CeSvcOpenEx()	Opens a nested subkey of an already-opened key
CeSvcDeleteVal()	Deletes a named value for a given key
CeSvcGetDeviceId()	Returns the Id if the currently connected device. 0 means error, whereas −1 means a guest device.
CeSvcGetSelectedDeviceId()	Returns the Id if the currently selected device. 0 means error, whereas −1 means a guest device

Figure 13-23: CEUTIL functions to access CE Services registry keys.

Finally, CeSvcClose() closes a previously-opened key.

13.4.3 Enumerating CE Devices

One final CEUTIL function, CeSvcEnumProfiles(), allows scanning the entries under CESVC_DEVICES. Each invocation returns a profile (a DWORD value), which describes one connected device. That profile can be passed to CeSvcOpen(), when called with CESVC_DEVICEX, to have access to the values describing it. Among those values is "DeviceName", the name of the device.

The next example lists all connected devices by their name.

```
// A routine that lists connected CE devices. This runs on 9x/NT.

#include <windows.h>
#include <ceutil.h>                      // Requires Ceutil.lib
#include <stdio.h>

void ListConnectedDevices()
{
    HCESVC  hSvc = NULL;
    int     nDevCount = 0;
    DWORD   dwProfile;

    while (SUCCEEDED(CeSvcEnumProfiles(&hSvc, nDevCount, &dwProfile)))
    {
        HCESVC  hKey;
        char    szName[64];

        CeSvcOpen(CESVC_DEVICEX,         // Open a specific device key
            (LPTSTR) dwProfile,          // Profile of the device
            FALSE,                       // No need to create
            &hKey);                      // Returned key

        CeSvcGetString(hKey,             // Device key
            "DisplayName",               // Value name
            szName,                      // Buffer for value data
            sizeof(szName));             // Size of buffer

        printf("Name: %s\n", szName);

        CeSvcClose(hKey);                // Close the device key
        nDevCount++;                     // Next device
    }
}
```

SUGGESTED READINGS

Stevens, UNIX Network Programming, Volume 2

> Part 5 of Stevens' book describes RPC in detail.

Part IV

MFC Application Programming

Chapter 14

Visual C++ and Microsoft Foundation Classes

Windows application development has been known to be extremely tedious. Just a few years ago, developers had to expect a six-month learning curve to *start* to be comfortable with the vast API that is Win32. Today, new tools that drastically simplify the work are widely available. This chapter focuses on the most popular of those tools: Visual C++, and the Toolkit for Windows CE. It also highlights the benefits of plunging into C++ and the Microsoft Foundation Class (MFC) library, rather than developing in C using Win32.

14.1 VISUAL C++

Visual C++ is the most popular development tool for Windows CE, closely followed by Visual Basic (which is discussed in Chapter 23). This section presents an overview of the features found in Visual C++.

An Integrated Development Environment

Microsoft's Visual C++ 6.0 (also called VC++ 6.0) is an Integrated Development Environment (IDE), a tool that unifies everything you need to build applications: source code and resource editor, compiler, linker, debugger, source browser, and online help. As detailed in Chapter 2, Visual C++ requires the Microsoft Windows CE Toolkit for Visual C++ (dubbed VCCE 6.0), which adds cross-development tools. Together, they form a single, unified development tool, shown in Figure 14-1.

For the sake of clarity, the text that follows uses "Visual C++" when referring to Visual C++ 6.0 *and* the Windows CE Toolkit for Visual C++ 6.0.

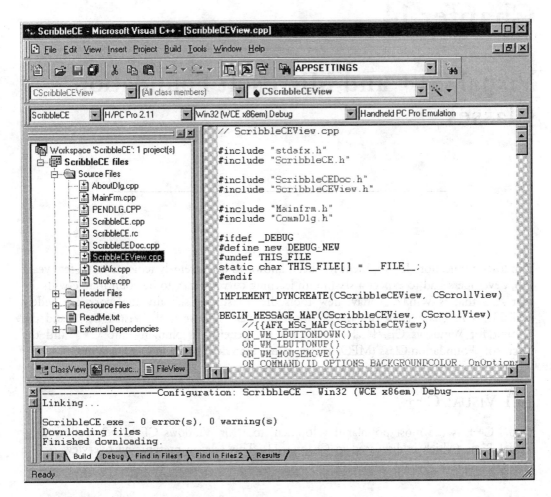

Figure 14-1: Microsoft Visual C++ 6.0, including its Windows CE Toolkit.

Windows CE Development

As explained in Chapter 2, the Windows CE Toolkit for Visual C++ 6.0 includes Software Development Kits (SDKs) for various Windows CE versions. Developers should also visit Microsoft's Windows CE web site for new revisions of those SDKs (such as the H/PC Pro Version 3.0). Visual C++ detects the SDKs being installed and allows users targeting their applications to another Windows CE configurations on-the-fly.

Connection to Windows CE devices is now achieved through the Platform Manager, within Visual C++, which lists all known platforms (or devices). Users can precisely control how connectivity takes place between Visual C++ and those devices. For instance, Figure 14-2 lists three platforms (H/PC Pro 2.11, H/PC 2.00 and Palm-size PC 2.01), and shows the properties of the default Palm-size device.

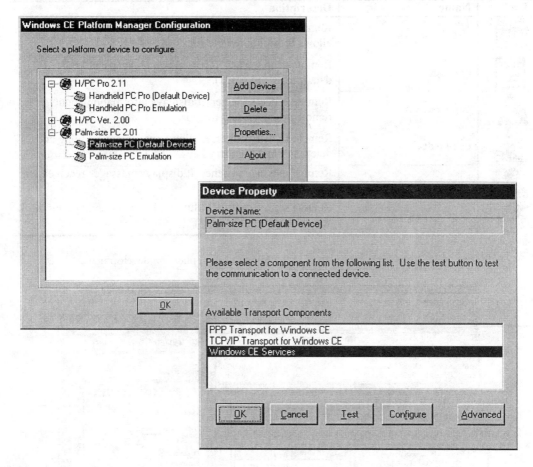

Figure 14-2: The Visual C++ Platform Manager.

Remote tools

Visual C++ also comes with separate diagnostic tools, directly callable from within the IDE or via the *Start* menu. Of these tools, a few are provided for Windows CE (see Figure 14-2).

Those tools now use Platform Manager to connect and transfer helper files on the target devices.

On-line documentation is available for each tool, although they are easy to use. Figure 14-4 illustrates a few of those tools.

Tool	Name	Description
	`Cefilevw.exe`	Remote file viewer. This is an explorer-like utility that allows browsing remote files.
	`Ceheapwk.exe`	Remote heap walker. It lists allocated heaps and related data (process id, flags).
	`Cepview.exe`	Remote process viewer. It displays information about remote processes and threads.
	`Ceregedt.exe`	Remote registry editor. It allows entering, modifying and deleting remote registry keys.
	`Cespy.exe`	Remote message watcher. It displays messages received by remote applications.
	`Cezoom.exe`	Remote screen capture utility. It allows retrieving remote screen snapshot.

Figure 14-3: Visual C++ remote tools for Windows CE application development.

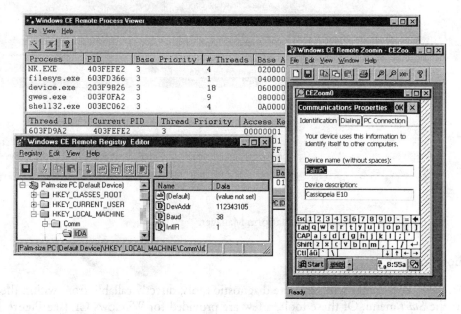

Figure 14-4: A few remote tools provided with Visual C++.

14.1.1 Projects

Visual C++ is based on application *projects*. A project is essentially a binary *makefile*. The concept of makefiles appeared on Unix many years ago, as a method to establish dependencies among files and provide instructions to automatically build programs. Back then, developers had to maintain makefiles manually, and edit them whenever the project structure was changed (when a file was added, moved, renamed, or deleted). Today, all these activities remain under the control of Visual C++, and you no longer edit the makefile manually. What's left is a very simple user interface that allows you to forget *how* to build a project.

The project is shown in the Workspace window (the file hierarchy on the left of Figure 14-1). This window is used when adding, renaming, etc. files within a project. What's more, projects can include subprojects (when an application consists on a client and a server for instance). All in all, the interface is intuitive and works well.

14.1.2 A First Application

In this section, we'll see how to use visual C++ to generate, yes, generate an application. Well, this is an application skeleton, but you will be surprised as what you get quite easily if you are new to Visual C++.

Developing an application starts by using the application wizard, dubbed AppWizard. It is invoked from the New dialog box (invoked via File/New), choosing "WCE MFC AppWizard (exe)", and entering a project name and location. This is a series of four screens that determine your application's main requirements and generate the appropriate application skeleton. Figure 14-5 shows AppWizard's steps.

The first step determines the application architecture, which can either embrace the document/view architecture supported in MFC or be dialog-based. The former choice allows developing an application whose content will be drawn (such as a text editor), whereas the latter choice is ideal for an application like a calculator, whose user interface is essentially a dialog box.

The second step determine some user interface features: whether the application will have a command bar or not, whether it supports online help, etc.

The third step indicates whether AppWizard (and ClassWizard, described later) automatically generate some comments in the source code to guide developers. This is highly recommended, even for experienced developers, since those comments provide hints as to where to insert code into the generated skeleton. Developers can also specify whether MFC should be statically or dynamically linked. This option can be changed later, but it is important to remember that if the latter option is chosen, the corresponding DLLs must be copied onto the target device (see Section 6.3.5 for details). The DLL to choose depends on the targeted platform. The three most common choices are listed in Figure 14-6.

Finally, the fourth and last step controls the names of the classes to be generated, as well as their parent class. This step is used by advanced developers to fine-tune their applications.

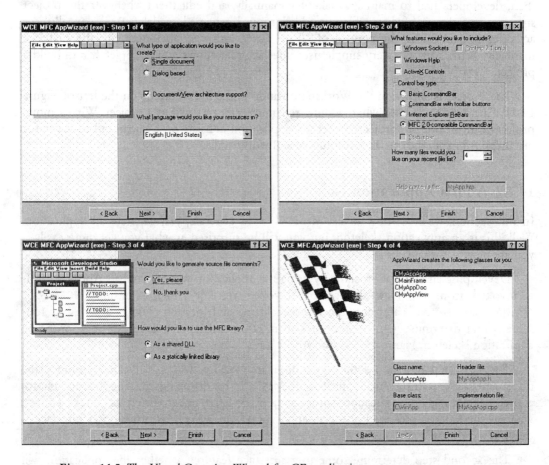

Figure 14-5: The Visual C++ AppWizard for CE applications.

If you are targeting:	Then use the following release and debug DLLs:
H/PC 2.0	mfcce20.dll (506Kb) and mfcce20d.dll (1184Kb)
P/PC 2.01	mfcce201.dll (487Kb) and mfcce201d.dll (1196Kb)
H/PC Pro 2.11	mfcce211.dll (525Kb) and mfcce211d.dll (1263Kb)

Figure 14-6: The MFC dynamic link libraries. The sizes are for the MIPS processor.

What AppWizard generates depends directly on the choices entered before. Generating a project based on default values (such as those shown in Figure 14-5) generates a flock of files, quite intimidating for newcomers. In addition to numerous header and source code files, there are also some control files, internally managed by Visual C++. The files of interest are described in Chapter 15.

The source files are automatically added into the project's workspace, and the entire project can be built by choosing **Rebuild All** from the **Build** menu, or pressing **F7**. There are menu items and toolbars to select Windows CE devices, choose between debug and release modes, etc. Visual C++ responds by using the relevant compiler and linker options. If required, you can also directly control those options, but this is rarely required.

You can also use the integrated debugger to set breakpoints, inspect variables, dump memory, and even analyze registers.

Another wizard is available, called ClassWizard. This is a tool that you can use to add member variables and methods within their classes, or to generate brand new classes. It doesn't support everything one might imagine, but it simplifies a whole lot of otherwise tedious and error-prone activities.

Windows CE Emulators

A very neat feature of the Toolkit is the Windows CE emulators it provides (see Figure 14-7). Those emulators (for H/PC, P/PC, and H/PC Pro) run on Windows NT (not 9x) and allow you to start developing applications without having a real device running CE. Note that those emulators emulate PC Companions with fully-loaded versions of Windows CE. They are not as adequate when developing an application for a custom configuration of Windows CE (this ultimately requires the exact configuration with the real target device to develop).

The H/PC 2.00 emulator is now superseded by the H/PC Pro 2.11 emulator, which provides a larger screen by default, and more embedded tools. You should now use the H/PC Pro instead of H/PC. The P/PC emulator has recently been upgraded to support Windows CE 2.11.

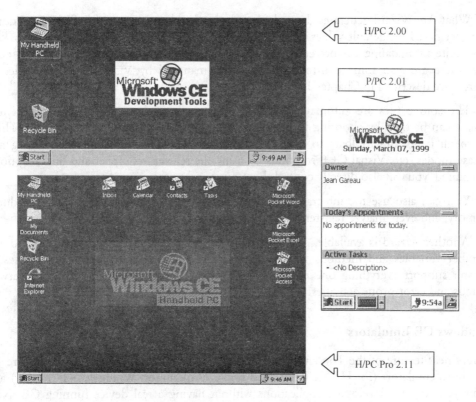

Figure 14-7: The Windows CE emulators under Windows NT.

14.2 MICROSOFT FOUNDATION CLASSES

Microsoft Foundation Classes – MFC for short – have been introduced in the early '90s, to simplify application development in C++. This is an alternative to plain C programming using Win32, specifically, the Platform Software Development Kit (Platform SDK)[38].

Windows programs were initially developed in C, using no more than a compiler, linker, resource compiler, and binder (whose purpose is to integrate compiled resources into the final image). This approach worked, but it was tedious because writing a graphical application is demanding without modern tools. Drawing things and gathering user input is easier said than done.

---

[38] The Platform SDK is simply another name for the Win32 API for all Windows platforms. Some of that API is naturally not supported on Windows CE to keep the system small.

In the early 1990s, a few companies (Borland and Microsoft) pioneered commercial object-oriented programming with integrated development environments. Today, hundreds of thousands of developers have adopted C++ and MFC as their programming language of choice for Windows application development.

The goal of MFC is to free you from application implementation details as much as possible, and to help you focus on the application functionality, rather than how to implement it. Additionally, MFC provides what is called a framework, that is, a structure of components that are reused from one project to another, and that are extended to meet specific application requirements. Chapter 15 describes this framework in great detail.

MFC 2.11 for Windows CE is a set of 146 C++ classes, portable across Windows platforms. Chapter 24 reviews the major changes between MFC 6.0 (for 9x/NT) and MFC 2.11 for CE.

It is natural for newcomers to feel overwhelmed with 146 classes to learn. Indeed, it takes a few weeks, if not months, to master most of those classes. But the object-oriented nature of MFC allows developing simple applications in just a few days. In fact, only a few classes must be understood to start developing applications. And as you gain experience in using some advanced features, you may revisit your applications and extend them as much as you want.

MFC is not a simple jacket around the Win32 SDK. Over the years, MFC grew in size to include classes or methods that do not have a counterpart in the SDK. This will become more and more obvious as you progress in MFC, especially if you have some experience using the SDK.

To illustrate how easy it is to use MFC compared with the SDK, let's compare two similar applications, illustrated in Figure 14-8. At first glance, these two applications are almost identical (they only differ by the text in the client area). The differences in their implementation is highlighted in the following paragraphs.

(a)

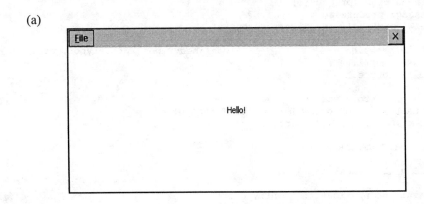

(b)

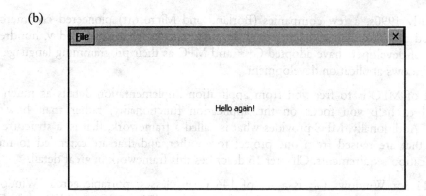

Figure 14-8: Two nearly identical Windows programs, one using the SDK and C (a), the other, using MFC and C++ (b). The major differences are under the hood.

14.2.1 A Simple Win32 Application

The following code example illustrates the implementation of the application shown in Figure 14-8 (a). The code is written in C and uses plain Win32 calls. If you are familiar with C programming in Windows, this is nothing new to you. For those not familiar with Windows programming, this program essentially creates a normal application window that displays a vertically- and horizontally-centered "hello".

```
// This application demonstrate a C Windows application skeleton.
// Topics of interest are:
//  - WinMain() as the entry point (i.e. not main())
//  - Predefined types (LRESULT, WNDCLASS, etc.)
//  - Programming convention (hWnd, szAppName)
//  - Window class
//  - Message loop (a.k.a. "message pump")
//  - Window proc (procedure)
//  - Message processing
//  - DefWindowProc() and a message bucket.

#include <windows.h>              // Predefined types, prototypes, etc.
#include <commctrl.h>
#include "resource.h"

// Window proc prorotype.
LRESULT CALLBACK WndProc(HWND hWnd, UINT message,
    WPARAM wParam, LPARAM lParam);

const int  IDC_CMDBAR = 101;

HINSTANCE g_hInstance;

// WinMain: the application's entry point.
int WINAPI WinMain(HINSTANCE hInstance, HINSTANCE hPrevInstance,
```

```
    LPWSTR lpszCmdLine, int nCmdShow)
{
    INITCOMMONCONTROLSEX  cc;
    static TCHAR          szAppName[] = TEXT("Sample1");
    WNDCLASS              wc;
    HWND                  hWnd;
    MSG                   msg;

    // Register common control classes.
    cc.dwSize = sizeof(cc);
    cc.dwICC  = ICC_BAR_CLASSES | ICC_COOL_CLASSES;
    InitCommonControlsEx(&cc);

    // Store the application instance (required later).
    g_hInstance = hInstance;

    // Register a Windows class (note that this has nothing to do with
    // a C++ class). It describes the basic behavior of a category of
    // windows.
    wc.style = CS_VREDRAW | CS_HREDRAW;    // Class style(s)
    wc.lpfnWndProc = (WNDPROC) WndProc;    // Window proc (se below)
    wc.cbClsExtra = 0;                     // Extra bytes after wnd class.
    wc.cbWndExtra = 0;                     // Extra bytes for the window.
    wc.hInstance = hInstance;              // Instance handle.
    wc.hIcon = NULL;                       // Icon handle
    wc.hCursor = NULL;                     // Cursor handle
    wc.hbrBackground = (HBRUSH) (COLOR_WINDOW + 1);      // Background
    wc.lpszMenuName = NULL;                // Menu name
    wc.lpszClassName = szAppName;          // Class name

    RegisterClass(&wc);

    // Create a window, specifying the window class just registered.
    // Most parameters are left to default values.
    hWnd = CreateWindow(
    szAppName,                             // Class name (just registered)
    szAppName,                             // Application caption (title)
    WS_VISIBLE,                            // Initial style(s)
    CW_USEDEFAULT,                         // Initial X position
    CW_USEDEFAULT,                         // Initial Y position
    CW_USEDEFAULT,                         // Initial width
    CW_USEDEFAULT,                         // Initial height
    HWND_DESKTOP,                          // Parent window handle
    NULL,                                  // Menu handle
    hInstance,                             // Application's instance handle
    NULL);                                 // Window-creation data.

    // Show the window and paint it *immediately*.
    ShowWindow(hWnd, nCmdShow);
    UpdateWindow(hWnd);

    // Get messages from the message queue and process them.
    // GetMessage() returns 0 when WM_QUIT is retrieved.
    while (GetMessage(&msg, NULL, 0, 0))
    {
        TranslateMessage(&msg);
        DispatchMessage(&msg);
```

```
        }

        return msg.wParam;
    }

// Window proc. Windows calls this function in order to process
// the messages related to the window. Messages that do not require
// specific procesing are returned to Windows (via DefWindowProc()),
// to be internally processed.

LRESULT CALLBACK WndProc(HWND hWnd, UINT message,
    WPARAM wParam, LPARAM lParam)
{
    PAINTSTRUCT    ps;                  // Required to process WM_PAINT.
    HDC            hDC;                 // Required to process WM_PAINT.
    RECT           rcClient;
    static HWND    hWndCB;

    switch (message)
    {
    case WM_CREATE:
            // On creation, add a command bar with
            // the application menu and a close button.
            hWndCB = CommandBar_Create(g_hInstance, hWnd, IDC_CMDBAR);
            CommandBar_InsertMenubar(hWndCB, g_hInstance, IDM_MAINMENU, 0);
            CommandBar_AddAdornments(hWndCB, 0, 0);
            return 0;

    case WM_PAINT:
            // Draw "Hello!", using the default font, on the screen,
            // vertically and horizontally centered.
            hDC = BeginPaint(hWnd, &ps);

            GetClientRect(hWnd, &rcClient);
            DrawText(hDC, TEXT("Hello!"), -1, &rcClient,
                    DT_VCENTER | DT_CENTER | DT_SINGLELINE);

            EndPaint(hWnd, &ps);
            return 0;

    case WM_DESTROY:
            PostQuitMessage(0);
            return 0;
    }

    // Reroute message to Windows for default processing.
    return DefWindowProc(hWnd, message, wParam, lParam);
}
```

The core concepts found in this example have been explained in Section III. If you have already read that section, you can skip the following. For those who haven't, here's how it goes.

The very first step consists of initializing common controls, in order to use the command bar, a new control for Windows CE. The command bar is the gray bar that holds the menu and the close (X) button. Then the application instance is stored in a global variable (all of them prefixed with g_, according to the Microsoft's coding convention, listed in Appendix E).

Then an application-specific window class is registered. The term class here is synonymous to category, and has nothing to so with object-oriented concepts. The class defines basic behavioral characteristics of the window. Then the window is shown.

What follows is the heart of any Windows application: the message loop, also known as the "message pump". Windows is a message-based system, so the application interacts with the system and the user through messages. The loop analyzes messages and dispatches them to WndProc(), which follows. The application terminates when the loop exits.

WndProc() handles all messages for the application window. Many messages are sent to every application, but only three are handled in this case: WM_CREATE, WM_PAINT, and WM_DESTROY. All others are handled through default processing, by calling DefWindowProc().

WM_CREATE is sent and processed during the creation of the main window, after it has internally been created but before it is visible. This is the ideal moment to create the command bar, which is set to contain a basic menu (a resource) and a close button.

Whenever the application needs to be painted (drawn), i.e., upon creation, but also after it has fully or partially been hidden by another window, Windows sends WM_PAINT. The size of the client area (the white surface below the bar) is established and the string "Hello!" is drawn in the middle of it. The exact position must be calculated precisely to center the text.

Finally, when the user wants to quit, Windows deletes the window and sends WM_DESTROY to perform some cleanup. The usual procedure is to call PostQuitMessage(0), which terminates the message loop. Not doing so would keep the application running in the background indefinitely, although no window would be displayed.

This example is as simple as a Windows application can get. If you are new to Windows programming, this may seem quite intimidating. Luckily, MFC is here to help.

14.2.2 A Simple MFC Application

The following example illustrates essentially the same application (see Figure 14-8-b), but using C++ and MFC. It uses two classes: CMyApp, which is a C++ class that receives and dispatch messages, and CMainWindow, which represents the main window. This example could be split into a .H and .CPP files for clarity, as is commonly the case. This example has not been generated by AppWizard, but has instead been developed by hand in order to produce a minimal application[39].

```
#include <afxwin.h>
#include "resource.h"

// Application class.
class CMyApp: public CWinApp
{
    public:
    virtual BOOL    InitInstance();
};

// Main window class.
class CMainWindow: public CFrameWnd
{
public:
    CMainWindow();

protected:
    afx_msg void    OnPaint();
    afx_msg void    OnFileClose();
    DECLARE_MESSAGE_MAP()
};

// One instance if the application class. This instance pumps messages
// and passes them to windows through their message maps.
CMyApp      MyApp;

// Upon initialization, create the main window and display it.
BOOL CMyApp::InitInstance()
{
    m_pMainWnd = new CMainWindow;
    m_pMainWnd->ShowWindow(m_nCmdShow);
    m_pMainWnd->UpdateWindow();
    return TRUE;
}

// Main window's message map. This table is internally used by MFC
// to identify the function to call in response to specific messages.
// In this case, ON_WM_PAINT() implies that upon receiving WM_PAINT,
// the CMainWindow::OnPaint() method is invoked.
BEGIN_MESSAGE_MAP(CMainWindow, CFrameWnd)
    ON_WM_PAINT()
    ON_COMMAND(ID_FILE_CLOSE, OnFileClose)
END_MESSAGE_MAP()

// In the main window's constructor, create a visible window and
// add the Close button.
CMainWindow::CMainWindow()
{
    Create(NULL, TEXT("MFC Application"), WS_VISIBLE, rectDefault,
        this, MAKEINTRESOURCE(IDM_MAINMENU));
```

---

[39] AppWizard generates applications with more components because it better fits the types of applications built by developers.

```
    AddAdornments(0);
}

// When painting, draw the string "Hello again!", vertically
// and horizontally centered.
void CMainWindow::OnPaint()
{
    CPaintDC        dc(this);
    CRect           rect;

    GetClientRect(rect);
    dc.DrawText(TEXT("Hello again!"), -1, &rect,
            DT_SINGLELINE | DT_VCENTER |  DT_CENTER);
}

// Come here when the user chooses File/Close
void CMainWindow::OnFileClose()
{
    PostQuitMessage(0);                // Force the app to terminate.
}
```

The CMyApp class essentially creates the application, pumps messages, and terminates the application. InitInstance() sets m_pMainWnd to an instance of CMainWindow, and then creates the main window and displays it. There is an important distinction to make here. The class CMainWindow is not the visible window; it is merely a C++ object that internally manages a window through its handle, which strictly exists within Windows. We'll review that primordial concept in the following chapter.

Then comes CMainWindow's message map, a feature introduced with MFC. The SDK example seen earlier used a switch statement to handle messages. An MFC application uses a message map, which lists a message and a handler; that handler is called whenever the related message is received. In this example, CMainWindow catches WM_PAINT and WM_COMMAND. If an entry is not found in the message map, the message is passed to the parent class, and so on. Although the exact process is described in Chapter 15, we'll mention here that if no class in the hierarchy is interested in a particular message, MFC internally passes it to DefWindowProc(). Developers typically use ClassWizard to add entries in message maps.

CMainWindow's constructor is invoked when a CMainWindow object is instantiated, as it is in CMyApp::InitInstance(). A window is created by calling Create() (CFrameWnd::Create() that is).

What follows are the handlers for WM_PAINT and the one invoked when the user chooses File/Close. There is no handler when the application is closed through the Close button (X) in the command bar, nor is there any processing for WM_DESTROY. Those handlers are already implemented in CMainWindow's parent class (CFrameWnd); that processing doesn't have to be duplicated again.

One of the advantages of using MFC over the SDK is that many details are internally handled, freeing you from having to remember them. Considering that Win32 for Windows

CE has more than 1000 functions, with each having, say, an average of four parameters (coordinates, flags, etc.), it easy to realize that you can be overwhelmed rather quickly. In my experience, using MFC cuts development time by 2 to 5 times.[40]

All this seems confusing only at the beginning. Very quickly, this becomes as easy to read as C code, if this is not already the case. Experienced C programmers will notice some familiar names: `GetClientRect()`, `DrawText()`, etc. as well as totally new tokens: `CFrameWnd`, `BEGIN_MESSAGE_MAP`, etc. The next chapter introduces the major elements of MFC that simply don't exist as such in Win32.

14.3 SOME USEFUL CLASSES

MFC provides more than just a few classes to simplify Win32 application development. It implements a whole application model promoting code reusability and simplicity. While the next chapters delve into MFC's guts, this section details a few useful classes that can be used in all sorts of applications, graphical and non-graphical (console). It is not necessary to master these classes at this point; you may very well visit them later, as needed.

14.3.1 CObject

`CObject` is the root class of about 80% of the classes in MFC. It provides various features, inherited into all its descendants. Some of that functionality can be customized for each object by using some macros, as described later.

Features

`CObject` implements three types of features: diagnostics, identification, and serialization.

1. **Diagnostics.** Two virtual methods are available to provide some diagnostics regarding an object. These methods are declared as `const` so they cannot alter the object itself. Also, these functions are really useful in debug mode only, so they should be surrounded by `#ifdef _DEBUG/#endif`. You can invoke either method at any moment.

    a) `AssertValid()` validates the object's internal state and asserts when inconsistencies are found. The validation that takes place is user-defined, and consists of making sure that member variables have valid values. For instance:

```
#ifdef _DEBUG
void CMyObject::AssertValid() const
```

---

[40] And this is very conservative! Since this is arguable, e-mail me your thoughts on that.

```
{
    CObject::AssertValid();                    // Call parent first.
    ASSERT(m_XCoord >= 0 && m_XCoord < 80);
    ASSERT(m_YCoord >= 0 && m_YCoord < 24);
}
#endif
```

b) `Dump()` displays the content of the object. For instance:

```
#ifdef _DEBUG
void CMyObject::Dump(CDumpContent& dc) const
{
    CObject::Dump(dc);        // Call parent
    dc << "X Coordinate = " << m_XCoord;
    dc << "Y Coordinate = " << m_YCoord;
}
#endif
```

2. **Identification.** Two methods are available to return run-time information about a class:

a) `GetRuntimeClass()` fills a `CRuntimeClass` structure that provides all sorts of information about the object: class name, size (in bytes), base class, etc. There is no need to override this function; it works "as is".

```
void foo()
{
    CMyObject        MyObject;
    CRuntimeClass * prtc = MyObject.GetRuntimeClass();

    ASSERT(_tcscmp(prtc->m_lpszClassName, _T("CMyObject") == 0);
}
```

`GetRuntimeClass()` is also invoked on some objects by MFC to obtain information about how to create them at run-time, a process called dynamic creation.

b) `IsKindOf()` returns `TRUE` if the object is the same object type as specified by the `CRuntimeClass` parameter. Although this method can occasionally be useful, its usage is not recommended, since it defeats polymorphism. The alternative is to use virtual methods.

```
void foo()
{
    CMyObject        MyObject;

    ASSERT(MyObject.IsKindOf(RUNTIME_CLASS(CMyObject)));
}
```

Note that the macro RUNTIME_CLASS returns a CRuntimeClass pointer describing the specified class.

Identification requires the use of DECLARE_DYNAMIC/IMPLEMENT_DYNAMIC or DECLARE_SERIAL/IMPLEMENT_SERIAL macros, described in a minute.

3. **Serialization**. Two methods are available to work with serialization, *i.e.*, loading and storing the object from persistent storage:

a) IsSerializable() returns a Boolean that indicates whether the object can be serialized (described in a second). This method works "as is" (*i.e.*, no need to override it).

b) Serialize() is the function to load/store data from/to a data source. The process of serialization is initiated in a CDocument-derived class (more in Chapter 15), which invokes Serialize() on each object of that class. From a programming standpoint, Serialize() must be coded to either load or store the object. The parameter to the function is a CArchive object that usually represents a file. As we will see in Chapter 15, you don't need to create the CArchive object, you simply have to use it. This object supports the << and >> operators to load and store data from/into it. For instance:

```
// Assuming CMyObject contains two member variables (m_XCoord and
// m_YCoord) load them from the archive of store them into it whether
// the method is called to load or store.

void CMyObject::Serialize(CArchive& ar)
{
    // Query the archive object to know whether this has been called
    // to store or load information.
    if (ar.IsStoring())
    {
        // Store the member variables in the archive.
        ar << m_XCoord;
        ar << m_YCoord;
    }
    else
    {
        // Load the member variables from the archive.
        ar >> m_XCoord;
        ar >> m_YCoord;
    }
}
```

Serialization requires the use of the DECLARE_SERIAL and IMPLEMENT_SERIAL macros, described below.

Macros

By default, a plain `CObject` doesn't support identification and serialization. Macros must be added for an object to support them. Figure 14-9 summarizes what macros can be used.

Macro	Identification	Dynamic creation	Serialization
No macro	✗	✗	✗
DECLARE_DYNAMIC & IMPLEMENT_DYNAMIC	✓	✗	✗
DECLARE_DYNCREATE & IMPLEMENT_DYNCREATE	✓	✓	✗
DECLARE_SERIAL & IMPLEMENT_SERIAL	✓	✓	✓

Figure 14-9: Macros that control `CObject` features.

The `DECLARE` macro must appear in the class definition (typically, in a the .h file), whereas the `IMPLEMENT` macro must appear outside of it (in the .cpp file). Here's an example of a class declaration and implementation that need to support serialization:

```
// MyClass.h
void CMyClass: public CObject
{
    DECLARE_SERIAL(CMyClass);
public:
    CMyClass();
 .
 .
 .
};
```

```
// MyClass.cpp
IMPLEMENT_SERIAL(CMyClass, CObject, 1);

CMyClass::CMyClass()
{
 .
 .
 .
}

// Other CMyClass methods could follow ...
```

Chapter 15 provides more information regarding serialization and the `SERIAL` macros.

14.3.2 CString

CString is MFC's variable-length Unicode string implementation, with plenty of operators and methods to make using strings quite easy – certainly easier than plain null-terminated character arrays. The best way to use CString is to use it as a string value, and not try to take advantage of its implementation (which has improved over the revisions by sharing buffer space). CString offers numerous methods, listed in Figure 14-10.

Method	Description
GetLength()	Returns the number of Unicode characters.
IsEmpty()	Returns TRUE if the string is empty.
Empty()	Empties the string.
GetAt()	Returns the Unicode character based on the specified index.
SetAt()	Sets the Unicode character based on the specified index.
operator []	Allows using a CString like an array.
operator LPCTSTR	Casts the CString into an LPCTSTR. This means that you can pass a CString to any function that requires an LPCTSTR.
+, =, +=, ==, <, >, etc.	Many operators are supported, allowing using a CString as a value, without worrying about its implementation.
Left(), Mid(), Right()	Extracts a substring.
MakeUpper(), MakeLower()	Converts to uppercase or lowercase.
Format()	printf-like formatting.
Find()	Finds a character or a substring.
GetBuffer(), ReleaseBuffer()	Provides direct access to the internal buffer.

Figure 14-10: Some CString methods.

Most methods are easy to use. Those not so obvious are the last two listed, which are required in order to obtain a non-const pointer (of type LPTSTR) to the internal character buffer (as opposed to the LPCTSTR operator that returns a const pointer). Here's an example:

```
CString    s;

LPTSTR p = s.GetBuffer(128);

// Access p

s.ReleaseBuffer();
```

14.3.3 CPoint

CPoint is derived from the POINT structure, commonly used in Win32. Being derived from the POINT structure, it inherits x and y, both integers, and can be used wherever POINT is used.

CPoint implements one method, Offset(), which adds values to the x and y member. This method accepts the offsets either as two integers, a POINT structure or a SIZE structure.

CPoint also implements various operators, which makes it as easy to use as an integer: ==, !=, +=, -=, +, and -.

14.3.4 CRect

CRect is derived from the RECT structure, commonly used in Win32, and inherits its left, right, top, and bottom integer members. It provides various operators to make it easier to use than a RECT. CRect can be used wherever a RECT structure is required.

As a developer, you must ensure that the rectangle object is normalized, *i.e.*, that (left <= right) and (top <= bottom); otherwise, many functions using CRect (or RECT) won't work properly. Most applications are designed to use normalized rectangles, but it's a good idea to call CRect::NormalizeRect() when the rectangle's content is unknown (such as when read from a data source).

CRect implements a flock of methods and operators, all very easy to use. Figure 14-11 lists a few of them:

Operator/Method	Description
Width()	Returns the rectangle's width.
Height()	Returns the rectangle's height.
Size()	Returns the rectangle's size.
IsRectEmpty()	Tests for a width and height of 0.
IsRectNull()	Tests for all coordinates being 0.
PtInRect()	Returns TRUE if the specified POINT is in the rectangle.
InflateRect()	Enlarges the rectangle (higher and wider).
NormalizeRect()	Normalizes the rectangle.
IntersectRect()	Sets the rectangle to the intersection of two RECT structures.
operator LPCRECT	Returns an LPCRECT. This means that a CRect object can be passed as is where a LPCRECT is required.
operator LPRECT	Same as before, but for LPRECT. This is the same as passing the address of the rectangle (i.e. &MyRect).
=	Assignment operator.
==, !=	Equality and inequality operators.
+, -, +=, -=	Adds or subtracts operators.
&=, &, |=, |	Intersection (&) and union (|) operators.

Figure 14-11: Some CRect methods.

14.3.5 CSize

CSize is derived from the SIZE structure, commonly used in Win32, and inherits its cx and cy integer members. It provides various operators to make it easier to use than a SIZE. CSize can be used wherever a SIZE structure is required.

CSize implements a few operators: ==, !=, +=, -=, +, and -.

14.3.6 CTime

CTime encapsulates the time_t data type and represents an absolute date and time. It provides numerous functions (most inline) to manipulate it (see Figure 14-12)

Operator/Method	Description
GetCurrentTime()	A static method that initialize this object to the current time.
GetTime()	Returns the time_t value.
GetYear()	Returns the year.
GetMonth()	Returns the month (1 to 12).
GetDay()	Returns the day (1 to 31).
GetHour()	Returns the hour (0 to 23).
GetMinute()	Returns the minutes (0 to 59).
GetSecond()	Returns the minutes (0 to 59).
GetDayOfWeek()	Returns the day of week (1 for Sunday, 2 for Monday, etc.)
GetAsSystemTime()	Converts into a SYSTEMTIME structure.
Format()	Formats in user-readable string.
=	Assignment operator.
+, -, +=, -=	Adds or subtracts CTimeSpan objects.
==, !=, <, >, <=, >=	Comparison operators.

Figure 14-12: Some CTime methods.

14.3.7 CTimeSpan

CTimeSpan is a companion class to CTime, and represents a relative time (as opposed to CTime that represents an absolute time). For instance, a CTimeSpan may represent five seconds, which could be added to a CTime object to obtain the time of that CTime object plus five seconds. CTimeSpan can be positive or negative.

CTimeSpan is usually used with CTime's operators, but it can also be used with other CTimeSpan objects (*e.g.*, adding two CTimeSpan objects). Also, since it keeps the time span in seconds, a few methods are provided to convert the span into days, hours, minutes, and seconds. For instance, `GetHours()` returns the number of hours within the current date (-23 to 23), whereas `GetTotalHours()` returns the number of complete days.

14.3.8 CArchive

`CArchive` is used for object serialization. Developers that use the document/view architecture described in Chapter 15 (the vast majority of developers do) are only concerned with storing and retrieving data from the archive (see Figure 14-13). Other methods are available for advanced operations, but only occasionally used.

Operator	Description
`operator >>`	Loads objects (`CObject*`) and primitive types (`BYTE`, `WORD`, `int`, `LONG`, `DWORD`, `float` and `double`) from the archive. Any other type must be broken down into these types.
`operator <<`	Stores objects and primitive types in the archive.

Figure 14-13: The two most popular `CArchive` methods.

14.3.9 Arrays

MFC includes collection classes, whose purpose is to group items together. The first type of collection is a dynamic array.

Arrays are ideal to store items that need to be accessed on a random basis (*i.e.*, in any order), since the access time is independent of the number of items. On the other hand, arrays are not so good at inserting or removing items, as items must be shifted (*i.e.*, copied), which is a slow operation.

MFC Array Classes

The initial MFC implementations introduced a series of dynamic array classes that can grow as required. Each class is built to support a specific data type (see Figure 14-14). As we'll see shortly, using these arrays is now discouraged.

Array	Data Type
`CByteArray`	`BYTE`
`CDWordArray`	`DWORD`
`CObArray`	Pointer to `CObject`-derived objects, such as user-defined classes.
`CPtrArray`	Generic pointers (to user-defined data structures).
`CStringArray`	`CString` objects
`CUIntArray`	`UINT`
`CWordArray`	`WORD`

Figure 14-14: The various MFC arrays.

CObArray and CPtrArray are arrays of pointers, as opposed to the other arrays that are an array of data (for instance, a CDWordArray internally contains an array of DWORDs). The main difference between CObArray and CPtrArray is that the former contains pointers to CObjects, and supports serialization; the former contains pointers to data structures or objects not derived from CObjects, and doesn't support serialization.

All these classes share the exact same methods, adapted to the supported data type. Figure 14-15 lists some popular methods.

Method	Description
GetSize()	Returns the number of elements.
GetUpperBound()	Returns the largest valid index.
SetSize()	Sets the number of elements.
RemoveAll()	Removes all elements. This doesn't delete the data pointed to, in a CPtrArray or CObArray.
GetAt()	Returns the element at the specified index.
SetAt()	Sets the element at the specified index.
SetAtGRow()	Same as SetAt(), but automatically grows the array if required.
ElementAt()	Returns a reference to a given element.
Add()	Appends an element by growing the array if required.
Append()	Appends another array and grows the array if required.
Copy()	Copies another array into the array by overwriting the elements and grows the array if required.
InsertAt()	Adds an element at a specific position and shifts outward the elements from that position to make room.
RemoveAt()	Removes an element from a specific position and shifts inward the following item. No memory is released.
operator []	Sets or gets an element at the specified index. This allows using an array class like a real array.

Figure 14-15: Some CObArray methods.

Here are a few examples using arrays:

```
CObArray MyArray;

MyArray.Add(new CMyObject());                            // Element 0
MyArray.Add(new CMyObject());                            // Element 1

ASSERT(MyArray.GetUpperBound() == 1);                    // Largest index
ASSERT(MyArray.GetSize() == 2);                          // Count

CMyObject * pMyOb;

pMyOb = reinterpret_cast<CMyObject *>(MyArray[0]);       // operator []
pMyOb = reinterpret_cast<CMyObject *>(MyArray.GetAt(0)); // Element 0
```

```
// Set pOb as a reference to &array[0]. pObj becomes an l-value.
CMyObject *& pOb = reinterpret_cast<CMyObject *&>(MyArray.ElementAt(0));

// Add a new element at position 0, right-shifting all others.
MyArray.InsertAt(0, new CMyObject());

// Remove the first element, left-shifting all others.
MyArray.RemoveAt(0);

// Remove all elements and frees the array. The objects pointed to are
// not freed though.
MyArray.RemoveAll();
```

Although these array classes work fine, they are adapted for specific data types, not user-defined classes or data structures. To use user-defined data types, you can use a CObArray or CPtrArray and cast elements in and out, but this approach is not type-safe (due to the explicit cast). Consider the following:

```
CObArray       MyArray;
CMyObject *    pMyObject;
CWnd *         pWnd;

// Store a CMyObject object at position 0.
MyArray.Add(new CMyObject());

// This statement compiles and runs fine.
pMyObject = reinterpret_cast<CMyObject *>(MyArray[0]);

// This statement compiles but is incorrect at run-time.
pWnd      = reinterpret_cast<CWnd *>(MyArray[0]);
```

From the compiler standpoint, this code is perfectly acceptable, but the execution will certainly go wild, since MyArray[0] points to a CMyObject, not a CWnd. The problem comes from the fact that the [] operator returns a pointer to a CObject, which must be cast (and that's where the problem is). The solution would be to have an array whose [] operator would return a pointer to a CMyObject object (or any other user-defined type, as required). This would eliminate the need to cast and it would help detect wrong assignments.

With the increasing popularity of C++ templates, recent revisions of MFC now rely on templates to generate user-defined type arrays (templates are a perfect fit for that need).

There are two array templates, CTypedPtrArray and CArray, built around a specific data type. The former is an array of pointers to the specified data types, whereas the latter is an array of elements of the specified data type (see Figure 14-16). CArray is usually used with small data types, whereas CTypedPtrArray is more suited to holding larger data types. These templates are defined in afxtempl.h (which you must include).

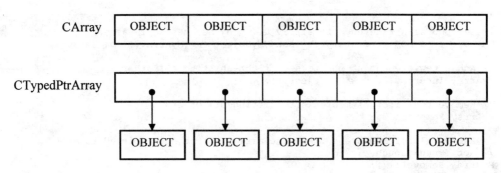

Figure 14-16: The implementation of `CArray` vs `CTypedPtrArray`.

CTypedPtrArray Template

`CTypedPtrArray` is pretty much like a `CObArray` or a `CPtrArray`, with the important difference that the methods are defined to accept any specific type. Consider the following:

```
#include <afxtempl.h>

// Array of CMyObject *
CTypedPtrArray<CObArray, CMyObject*>     MyObjectPtrArray;

// Array of SMyStruct *
CTypedPtrArray<CPtrArray, SMyStruct*>    MyStructPtrArray;
```

The first template parameter is either `CObArray` or `CPtrArray`, whether the data pointed to are objects derived from `CObject` or anything else (objects not derived from `CObject` or non-objects data types). Only the former type supports serialization. The second template parameter is the data type pointed to, and must be a pointer.

Once declared, you can use any array methods listed in Figure 14-15, and those operations are type-safe, *i.e.*, adapted to the data type specified as the second template parameter, eliminating the need to cast. For instance:

```
CTypedPtrArray<CObArray, CMyObject *> MyArray;
MyArray.Add(new CMyObject());           // Store a CMyObject object

CMyObject * pMyObject = MyArray[0];      // OK (and no need to cast)
CWnd *      pWnd      = MyArray[0];      // ERROR
```

Assigning `MyArray[0]` to a `CMyObject` pointer can now be done without a cast. Also, the wrong assignment to the `CWnd` pointer variable is now detected by the compiler, making the array type-safe.

CArray Template

A `CArray` is declared as follows:

```
#include <afxtempl.h>

CArray<LONG, LONG> MyLongArray;            // Array of LONG
CArray<CMyObject, CMyObject&> MyObArray;  // Array of CMyObject
```

The first template parameter is the data type directly stored in the array and returned by methods such as `GetAt()`. The second template parameter is the type of data passed to methods such as `SetAt()`. The second parameter is usually a reference to the first type (especially for user-defined types).

Note that adding or returning elements involves copying them. For instance:

```
CMyObject MyObject;
MyObArray.Add(MyObject);                    // Copies MyObject in the array
```

For that reason, `CArray` is often used with small data types. Larger data types are held in a `CTypedPtrArray`, which only copies pointers.

Hard to read?

Since those template declarations are sometimes hard to read, you can use `typedef` to increase the readability. For instance, instead of declaring types and variables at once:

```
#include <afxtempl.h>

CArray<CMyObject, CMyObject&>               MyObjectArray;
CTypedPtrArray<CObArray, CMyObject*>        MyObjectPtrArray;
```

declare new types and use them to declare variables:

```
#include <afxtempl.h>

typedef CArray<CMyObject, CMyObject&>            CMyObjectArray;
typedef CTypedPtrArray<CObArray, CMyObject*>     CMyObjectPtrArray;

CMyObjectArray     MyObjectArray;
CMyObjectPtrArray  MyObjectPtrArray;
```

14.3.10 Lists

The second type of collection MFC supports is a doubled-linked list. A list is advantageous when you expect to insert or remove a lot of items, since those operations can be done very efficiently. On the minus side, accessing a specific item is directly proportional to its position, as the access must start from the first list item, until the target item is reached. On average, the access time is $n/2$, where n is the number of items.

MFC List Classes

MFC initially introduced three list classes, shown in Figure 14-17.

List	Data Type
CObList	Pointer to CObject-derived objects, such as user-defined classes.
CPtrList	Generic pointers (to user-defined data structures).
CStringList	CString objects.

Figure 14-17: The MFC lists.

The main difference between CObList and CPtrList is that the former only supports serialization. The implementation is otherwise almost identical. Figure 14-18 lists some popular methods found on those classes. Many methods are based on a "position", a concept explained next.

Method	Description
Head/Tail Insertion	
AddHead()	Adds an element at the head of the list.
AddTail()	Adds an element at the tail of the list.
Head/Tail Removal	
RemoveHead()	Removes the element at the head of the list.
RemoveTail()	Removes the elements at the tail of the list.
RemoveAll()	Removes all elements from the list. Note that for a CObList and CPtrList, you must also delete the items pointed to.
Head/Tail Access	
GetHead()	Returns the head element of the list.
GetTail()	Returns the tail element of the list.
Position-Based Iteration	
GetHeadPosition()	Returns the position of the head element.

`GetTailPosition()`	Returns the position of the tail element.
`GetNext()`	Given a position, returns the element pointed to, and moves the position on the following element. This method is used to iterate from head to tail.
`GetPrev()`	Given a position, returns the element pointed to, and moves the position on the previous element. This method is used to iterate from tail to head.
Position-Based Access	
`GetAt()`	Returns an element at a given position.
`SetAt()`	Sets the element at a given position.
`RemoveAt()`	Removes the element at a given position.
`InsertBefore()`	Inserts an elements before the specified position.
`InsertAfter()`	Inserts an element after the specified position.
Position-Based Searching	
`Find()`	Returns the position of an element given a value.
`FindIndex()`	Returns the position of an element given its index in the list (0 is head).
`Status`	
`GetCount()`	Returns the number of elements in the list.
`IsEmpty()`	Returns TRUE is the list is empty, FALSE otherwise.

Figure 14-18: Some `CObList` methods.

Lists internally uses `CNode` objects (see Figure 14-19). Specifically, a list is a doubled-linked list of `CNode` objects, each referring to `CObject`-derived objects (for a `CObList`) or to some user-defined structures (for a `CPtrList`).

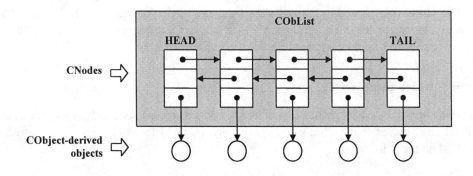

Figure 14-19: A `CObList` internally relies on `CNodes`, each of which points to a `CObject`-derived object.

A "position" is a pointer to a CNode. Specifically, position-based methods listed in Figure 14-18 use the POSITION data type, defined as follows:

```
typedef CNode * POSITION;
```

Let's see an example of how iteration takes place using POSITIONs:

```
POSITION pos = MyList.GetHeadPosition();

while (pos != NULL)
{
    CMyObject * pMyObject;

    // Obtain the object pointed to by 'pos'. Note that this requires
    // a cast, since the returned value is 'CObject *' by default.
    pMyObject = reinterpret_cast<CMyObject *>(MyList.GetNext(pos));

    // pMyObject points onto an object of type CMyObject,
    // whereas pos points on the following CNode.
}
```

CObList::GetNext() requires a POSITION parameter, passed as a reference, which points to a CNode. The method returns the object (or data) pointed to by that CNode, but it also moves the POSITION parameter onto the next CNode. This is initially confusing, because one would very likely believe that CObList::GetNext() returns the next element. Remember that it returns the current element, and then moves to the next. Similarly, CObList::GetPrev() returns the current element, and moves the position to the previous CNode.

Those lists have the same problem as the MFC array classes: they are ill-suited for user-defined types, since they require explicit casting, which opens the door to bugs. In the previous example, casting the returned value of CObList::GetNext() into the wrong object would lead to some bugs, but the compiler can't help. The solution is, again, found in templates, which implement a list directly based on user-defined types, eliminating the need for casting and making them type-safe.

CTypedPtrList Template

A CTypedPtrList holds pointers to objects or data types, pretty much like a CObList or a CPtrList, except that such a list is specifically designed to work with the specified data type. Consider the following:

```
#include <afxtempl.h>

CTypedPtrList<CObList, CMyObject *>  MyList1; // List of ptr to CMyObject
CTypedPtrList<CPtrList, SMyStruct *> MyList2; // List of ptr to SMyStruct
```

The first template parameter is either `CObList` or `CPtrList` (and nothing else). Use `CObList` when each node is to point to a `CObject`-derived object, or `CPtrList` for any other data type. The second template parameter is the object or data type pointed to. Note that this type must be a pointer. Remember that lists that are based on `CObList` support serialization, whereas those based on `CPtrList` do not.

CList Template

Whereas a `CTypedPtrList` holds pointers to objects, a `CList` directly holds objects. A `CList` is a template whose `CNodes` directly contain an object (or data type), instead of pointing to it (see Figure 14-20). This is similar to a `CStringList`, which directly contains `CStrings`, except that a `CList` explicitly works for the specified data type.

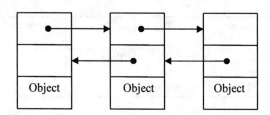

Figure 14-20: A `CList` implements a doubled-linked list template that directly holds objects or data types, instead of pointing on them.

Here is the declaration of a list:

```
#include <afxtempl.h>

CList<CMyObject, CMyObject&> MyList;
```

Such a `CList` declaration makes `MyList` a doubled-linked list that directly holds `CMyObject` objects. The first template argument is the data type directly stored into each node; `CMyObject` in this case. The second template argument is the data type of the method arguments and return values. For instance:

```
CMyObject& GetAt(POSITION pos) const;
void SetAt(POSITION pos, CMyObject& newElement);
```

Most of the time, the second template argument is a reference to the data type specified as the first template argument. Like CArrays, CList copies objects when they are added or returned. For that reason, a CList should be used with small data types, whereas a CTypedPtrList is more appropriate for large data structure.

Maps

MFC also supports table maps, which associates some values to others, like WORDs to PTRs. It also now provides a template implementation (CMap) for type-safe maps. Maps are much less popular than arrays or lists, although MFC uses various maps internally (to map window handles to CWnd objects, for instance).

14.3.11 Synchronization Classes

A few classes (CCriticalSection, CEvent, and CMutex) encapsulate the synchronization objects discussed in Chapter 7. They are all derived from a common pure class, CSyncObject, which defines the Lock() and Unlock() methods.

Figures 14-21, 14-22, and 14-23 highlight some methods respectively found in CCriticalSection, CEvent, and CMutex.

CCiticalSection Method	Description	Implementation
Lock()	Acquires the resource. The call blocks until the resource is available.	::EnterCriticalSection()
Unlock()	Releases the critical section.	::LeaveCriticalSection()

Figure 14-21: CCriticalSection methods.

CEvent Method	Description	Implementation
Lock()	Acquires the resource. The call blocks until the event is available, i.e., signaled.	::WaitForSingleObject()
SetEvent()	Sets the event flag to an available, signaled state, unblocking any thread blocked on it.	::SetEvent()
PulseEvent()	Sets the event flag to an available, signaled state, unblocks any thread blocked on it and resets the event to an unavailable, unsignaled state.	::PulseEvent()
ResetEvent()	Resets the event flag to an unavailable, unsignaled state.	::ResetEvent()
Unlock()	Releases the event object.	*nothing*

Figure 14-22: CEvent methods.

CMutex Method	Description	Implementation
Lock()	Acquires the mutex. The call blocks until the resource is available.	`::WaitForSingleObject()`
Unlock()	Releases the mutex.	`::ReleaseMutex()`

Figure 14-23: `CMutex` methods.

14.3.12 Sockets

The WinSock API, described in Chapter 12, is ideal when used in console applications, but it doesn't fit well the event-driven nature of a graphical application. For instance, reading from a socket is a blocking operation; doing so in a graphical application would simply freeze the application. Luckily, MFC for CE provides a class to support socket programming in an event-driven context.

On other Windows platforms, MFC provides `CAsyncSocket`, whose operations are non-blocking, and which implement overridable call back methods. For instance, `CAsyncSocket::OnReceive()` is called when some data can be read from the socket. It is then possible to call `CAsyncSocket::Receive()` to obtain that data. Calling `Receive()` in other circumstances would likely return an error code indicating that nothing is available at that moment. MFC also implements `CSocket`, derived from `CAsyncSocket`, which implements blocking operations. For instance, calling `CSocket::Receive()` at any moment blocks until all bytes have been read. However, Windows messages are normally processed during the wait, preventing the application from freezing[41].

Those two classes rely on network event notifications, which are not found on CE. Instead, MFC for CE implements a new class, called `CCeSocket`, which internally uses monitoring threads to simulate those events. As a result, you must use `CCeSocket` (instead of `CAsyncSocket` or `CSocket`) in a graphical application.

14.4 FASTEST PATH TO MFC

Don't let yourself get intimated if MFC seems a strange new world to you. That's the nature of software programming anyway: it constantly evolves, even within months (that's especially true with the Windows CE development tools). Thank yourself of taking the step of learning that amazing technology *now*. You'll live happy and productive.

---

[41] CSocket is an asynchronous socket that keeps processing Windows messages until the event it's looking for arrives.

The best way for you to learn MFC is to become familiar with core C++ concepts, if you are not already at ease with that language. For those of you in that situation, Appendix A reviews the most important features of C++, for C programmers.

If you are also new to C, I highly recommend you grab the book from Prata (see Suggested Readings, below) and understand most of it (give yourself a few weeks). Then move on to C++ (see Appendix A).

Once acquainted with C++, jump into the next chapters, which explore MFC. Feel free to share your learning experience by e-mailing me (what you knew, what path you followed, what you learned, and how long it took you. Thanks).

SUGGESTED READINGS

Microsoft, Windows CE Toolkit for Visual C++ 6.0 online help

> This help file, provided with the toolkit, explains how to create, build and customize an application. It also explains how connect to a remote device and how to use the Windows CE remote tools.

Microsoft, Visual C++ 6.0 online help

> The help provided within Visual C++ 6.0 contains detailed explanations about the tool itself and developing applications. It includes tutorials, programmer's and reference guides, etc. Very complete and accurate.

Stroustrup, The C++ Programming Language

> This is the complete description of C++, by its author, Bjarne Stroustrup. It is naturally very complete (it has to be), but hard for beginners.

Prata, C Primer Plus

> In my opinion, definitely the best book to learn C. It assumes no programming knowledge, and presents the concepts as they are, without fluff and useless abstraction. A must.

Chapter 15

Document/View Architecture

___

Since its introduction, MFC has been proposing its own model of what an application should be: a group of specific classes that support some well-defined functionality. The goal is to break up an application into a few components that are easier to develop than a monolithic block. Over the years, this model evolved to become less rigid and more adapted to actual developers' needs. This chapter presents the basic model of MFC: the document/view architecture. It also introduces its major components: windows, views, documents, frames, and message routing. A few alternate architectures are also presented at the end of the chapter. If you are new to Windows programming, you should consider getting familiar with some basic concepts explained in Chapter 9.

15.1 THE DOCUMENT/VIEW ARCHITECTURE

A few years ago, Microsoft started to push for a document-centric paradigm, for the user to work with documents (*i.e.*, files), not applications. For instance, in order to open a document, a user would simply double-click on the document instead of starting the application and open the document from within that application. That's a subtle difference, but it made Windows a little bit easier to use for beginners. This led MFC designers to introduce the document/view architecture. This architecture dictates that an application is essentially composed of four objects, each of which has its very own role (see Figure 15-1):

- The *application object* implements the application initialization, the message loop, and termination. There's no window associated with it, but it works hand in hand with the other objects described below. This class really drives the application.

- The *main frame* object implements the main window, also called the application window. This is the window that features the title bar, the command bar, a client area, and a status bar, if any. However, the user interaction with the command bar is also redirected to the other classes by this main frame object.

- The *view* object implements a window that entirely covers the main frame's client area. The sole purpose is to implement the application's user interface by displaying the application's data (text, graph, etc.)
- The document object implements all the data structures required to hold the application data. It is not concerned with the representation of that data because that's the purpose of the view object. The document may internally access various data repositories (files, databases, the network, etc.) to load and store the application's data, and the exact implementation does not need to be known by the other classes.

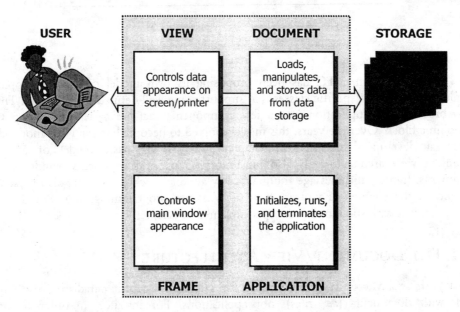

Figure 15-1: The four main classes of an MFC application. The document contains the code to store and manipulate the data when the application runs, the view displays that data, the frame implements a complete application window, and the application class pumps and dispatches messages to windows.

Taken individually, each class is not enough to implement a whole application. But joined together, they constitute a complete application (see Figure 15-2). You can focus on one object at a time, which is simpler than to work on the entire application as a whole, as it was required with traditional C and SDK Windows programming.

Furthermore, each of these objects implements some mechanics that need to be implemented in every Windows application. By reusing these objects (that is, the MFC classes), you can directly benefit from already-tested code, giving you more time to focus on the unique functionality of your own applications. Reusability is a key concept of MFC programming.

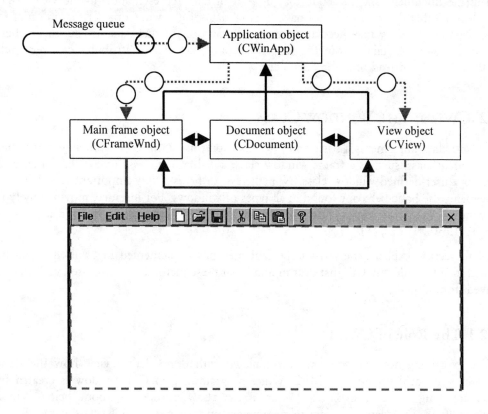

Figure 15-2: The main four classes of an MFC application (the names in parentheses are the MFC base class names). There are other architectures available, which use other classes. A solid line indicates a direct access between two classes. Windows messages (WM_xxx) are represented by small circles, and the dotted lines indicate the basic message flow (which is enhanced within MFC).

Ideally, the view does not rely on any implementation details of the document. A well-designed document fully encapsulates the data and presents generic methods to access that data (refer to Appendix A regarding encapsulation and other essential object-oriented design and programming features). Should the document's internal implementation change, a clean interface will keep the view independent of the changes (*i.e.*, no need to change or adapt the view). Countless projects have already obtained the benefits of this approach.

As far as you are concerned, the core of the functionality (about 80-90% of the application) is typically implemented in the view and the document. There is no strict rule as to what goes where. The rule of thumb is to put the code that deals with the application's data in the document and the code that deals with data representation in the view. That doesn't mean that the view does not have internal data of its own. Consider that in order to draw a graph, the view may need to maintain all sorts of internal data structures: brushes, pens, user's settings (taken from the Registry), colors, etc. These attributes can very well reside in the view instead of in the document.

15.2 CWND: THE WINDOW CLASS

The CWnd class implements a basic window. You don't use a CWnd class directly, but rather a descendant class, such as a frame window class, a dialog box class, a view class, a control class, or a user-defined window class. Nonetheless, CWnd is a very important class, since it implements the basic behavior found in all types of windows. For instance, moving any type of window (such as those just enumerated) is done by calling a CWnd method (CWnd::MoveWindow()).

This section explains the most important methods implemented in CWnd that can be applied to any window in CE. Just bear in mind that these methods are also used with classes derived from CWnd.

15.2.1 The Role of CWnd

Before explaining how windows are manipulated with CWnd, let's review how the same operations are achieved outside MFC. When programming in C, a window is created by either invoking ::CreateWindow() or ::CreateWindowEx(), both being Win32 system calls. Both accept a variety of parameters, including a window class name. Recall from Chapter 9 that a window class is a structure that defines some basic attributes of the window: the window's background color and the window procedure, among others[42]. Both calls return a window handle, which is, from an application standpoint, the window identifier. Any subsequent Win32 call referring to a window (to alter its appearance and behavior, for instance) requires the window's handle.

In MFC, developers do not access windows using their handles (as they do in C), but by using a specific CWnd class instance, which encapsulates the related handle. As a result, a CWnd class is *not* a window; it only *represents* a window by maintaining the corresponding window handle in a public member variable, called m_hWnd (see Figure 15-3).

---

[42] The use of the term "class" in "window class" is unfortunate and has nothing in common with a C++ class. You can use the expression "window category" if you prefer.

CWnd also provides numerous member functions, which in turn invoke Win32 calls by relying on this handle. Consider this extract from `Afxwin2.inl`, which implements a flock of various inline CWnd methods. In particular, note that the internal handle (m_hWnd) is always validated (by calling `::IsWindow()`) and passed to the Win32 call (which is prefixed with `::`) that corresponds to the invoked method:

```
_AFXWIN_INLINE void CWnd::GetWindowRect(LPRECT lpRect) const
    { ASSERT(::IsWindow(m_hWnd)); ::GetWindowRect(m_hWnd, lpRect); }

_AFXWIN_INLINE void CWnd::UpdateWindow()
    { ASSERT(::IsWindow(m_hWnd)); ::UpdateWindow(m_hWnd); }

_AFXWIN_INLINE BOOL CWnd::IsWindowVisible() const
    { ASSERT(::IsWindow(m_hWnd)); return ::IsWindowVisible(m_hWnd); }
```

These methods are called "wrappers" or "jackets", because they simply wrap a Win32 system call into a C++ method. However, CWnd provides numerous methods that are much more than plain jackets. For instance, CWnd implements the window's window proc, which processes messages as they are received (more on this in Section 15.3).

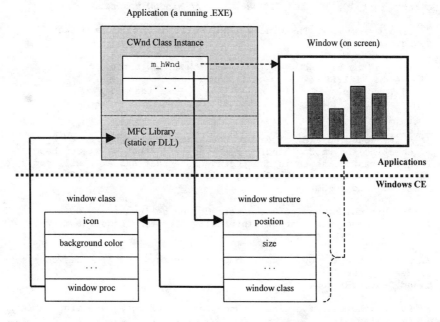

Figure 15-3: A CWnd (or a class derived from it) is not a window, but a C++ class that encapsulates a window handle (of type HWND). This window handle refers to some internal data structure that describes that same window. One of the members of that structure points to the related window class, specified when the window was created. This window class contains a pointer to the window proc, which points into the MFC library, linked to the application (either statically or dynamically).

Internally, Windows CE has no knowledge of the C++ classes being used in a given application. When a window is created, Windows maintains an internal structure describing that window (its window class, its position, its size, whether it is visible or not, the current font, etc.) All an application knows of that information is the handle returned when the window was created. Whether a C++ class within the application encapsulates this handle or not is unknown to Windows.

15.2.2 Creating and Destroying Windows

A window is created and destroyed by calling `CWnd::Create()` and `CWnd::Destroy Window()`, respectively. Let's see an example of these methods:

```
void SomeFunction()
{
    // Instantiate a CWnd class. This only creates a C++ object and invokes
    // the related constructor. In particular, it does not create a window.
    CWnd    MyWnd;
    CRect   rect(10, 10, 100, 100);      // Window position

    // Create a window. The window handle will be stored in m_hWnd.
    MyWnd.Create(
        _T("MyWndClass"),                // Window class
        _T("My Window"),                 // Window title
        WS_VISIBLE,                      // Style
        rectWnd,                         // Position and size
        NULL,                            // No parent
        0);                              // No ID

    // As a debugging-aid, make sure the window has been created by
    // checking the window handle. NULL indicates that no window has
    // been created, which is unexpected. Note that ASSERT() will pop
    // up a window within the debugger is the condition is FALSE.
    ASSERT(m_hWnd != NULL);

    // At this point, various CWnd methods can be invoked to work
    // on the underlying window. Internally, these methods use m_hWnd.
    MyWnd.GetWindowRect(rect);

    // Destroy the window by calling CWnd::DestroyWindow(). This does not
    // destroy the C++ instance MyWnd.
    MyWnd.DestroyWindow();

    // By leaving this function, MyWnd goes out of scope and its destructor
    // is called.
}
```

Declaring a CWnd instance only creates a C++ object by calling its constructor. It's very important to realize that that doesn't create any window. You can use the constructor to allocate and initialize data (such as memory, brushes, pens, etc.), but you can't call any method that relies on a window, since none exists at this time. For instance, calling `CWnd::MoveWindow()` in the constructor fails miserably, since there is no window to move yet.

A window is created by calling `CWnd::Create()`. This method is reviewed in detail in the next section. Internally, this method invokes the Win32 call `::CreateWindowEx()` and the returned window handle is stored into `m_hWnd`, a public member variable of `CWnd`. At some point during the creation (*i.e.*, after the call to `CWnd::Create()` but before it has returned), `CWnd::PreCreateWindow()` is invoked, which allows the class to override creation parameters. We'll see later how this feature is very useful when extending classes. Also, still within the creation process, the `WM_CREATE` message is sent to the window, before it is made visible. This message can be processed to initialize the window further. Although messages are deferred until Section 15.3, let's mention that when `WM_CREATE` is sent, a window has been created (*i.e.*, `m_hWnd` is valid), and `CWnd` methods can be invoked.

`CWnd::Create()` returns non-zero on success, 0 on error. An application may also test `m_hWnd` for a non `NULL` value. On success, the application can invoke other `CWnd` methods (such as `CWnd::SetWindowText()`).

Once the window is no longer required, it is destroyed by calling `CWnd::Destroy Window()`, which destroys the window, but not the C++ instance. Within the destruction process, `WM_DESTROY` is sent to the window to allow some clean-up. Note that `CWnd`'s destructor also calls `CWnd::DestroyWindow()` if required, so you don't have to explicitly destroy any window.

As mentioned earlier, you will rarely use `CWnd`, as it implements a plain and boring window. Instead, you may use other `CWnd`-derived classes, or derive your own classes. The latter approach consists of extending the `CWnd` class by deriving from it and adding extra functionality (such as painting something useful).

15.2.3 Creation Parameters

`CWnd::Create()` is an important method that deserves some explanation. You will rarely use it (since derived classes typically implement a simpler `Create()` method), but understanding it is essential.

The first parameter is an existing class name, which defines the basic characteristics of the window. The class name can be `NULL` to use a default class (transparently provided by MFC) or an application-defined class name obtained by registering one via `AfxRegister ClassName()`. Chapter 9 details class names and class registration.

The second argument is the window name or text. This is generally the title of the window.

The third argument is the style bits, to give a distinct personality to the window. WS_VISIBLE alone is normally used to create the application window. Figure 15-4 lists the most common styles, whereas Appendix C lists them all. Also note that CWnd::CreateEx() accepts extended styles, also listed in Appendix C.

Attribute Style	Description
WS_BORDER	Creates a window with a border
WS_CAPTION	Creates a window with a caption
WS_CHILD	Creates a child window. A child window is attached to a parent window; when the parent moves, the child window moves as well. Furthermore, child windows sends notifications to their parent window.
WS_DLGFRAME	Creates a window with a frame used with dialog box.
WS_HSCROLL	Creates a window with an horizontal scroll bar
WS_POPUP	Creates a popup, floating window
WS_TABSTOP	Used with controls, this styles makes it possible to navigate to the control using the Tab key.
WS_VISIBLE	Creates a visible window. If not set, the window is initially invisible. **The most commonly used style.**
WS_VSCROLL	Creates a window with a vertical scroll bar.

Figure 15-4: The most common attributes when creating a window.

The next parameter is a reference to a CRect, which defines the position and size of the window, in client coordinates of the parent window. Coordinates are explained in Chapter 16. If you want to create a window based on a desired client area size, you can call CalcWindowRect() to calculate the total size of the window, including title, border, etc. The resulting rectangle can be directly passed to CWnd::Create(). The following example uses that function to establish the window size to hold a client area measuring 100x75:

```
CRect        rect(0, 0, 100, 75);        // Target client size: 100x75

MyWnd.CalcWindowRect(rect);              // Make rect application size

rect.OffsetRect(30, 50);                 // Move the rect to (30, 50).

MyWnd.CreateWnd(..., rect, ...);         // Create the window using rect
```

Following the rectangle position is a pointer to the parent window. This parameter is NULL when creating an application window. It is non-NULL when creating child controls (described in Chapter 19).

The last two parameters are the control identifier, or 0 for an application window (more on this on Chapter 19), and a pointer to a CCreateContext class, which defaults to NULL if not specified (the common case).

The method returns a nonzero value on success, 0 otherwise. From that point, the CWnd object can be used in order to perform operations on that window. Hence, calling CWnd::SetWindowText() this time does work .

An alternative to CWnd::Create() is to call CWnd::CreateEx(), which takes a slightly different set of parameters (extended styles, etc.). Internally, CWnd::Create() calls CWnd::CreateEx().

15.2.4 Mixing Window Handles and CWnd

You can still use non-MFC functions with CWnd classes. Say you wrote a C function five years ago that creates a window (*e.g.,* that internally calls ::CreateWindow()), and that returns the window handle. You can wrap the handle with a CWnd by calling CWnd::Attach(). The window can then be accessed through the CWnd object. Once you no longer need the CWnd class, simply call CWnd::Detach(). The original window handle remains valid and can be used for other purposes. For instance:

```
HWND        hWnd = SomeOldFunctionThatReturnsAWindowHandle();

CWnd        MyWnd;
MyWnd.Attach(hWnd);                 // Attach the handle to a CWnd object

// From that point, you can access hWnd through MyWnd.
. . .

MyWnd.Detach();                     // Detach the handle from the CWnd object

// From that point, MyWnd is not associated to any window, but hWnd
// remains valid.
```

If you suspect that a window handle is already attached to a CWnd object, you can call CWnd::FromHandle(), which is a static function within CWnd:

```
CWnd *      pTmpWnd = CWnd::FromHandle(hHwnd);
```

If there wasn't any CWnd object already attached, a temporary object is created and its address is returned. The pointer is valid until the function returns but not after[43]; as a result, you cannot store that pointer in a member variable and use it in another method. If the

---

[43] Specifically, when the application becomes idle, all temporary objects are deleted.

handle was already attached to a CWnd object, that object is returned. This is made possible because MFC maintains an internal table that associates window handles and CWnd objects (see Figure 15-5).

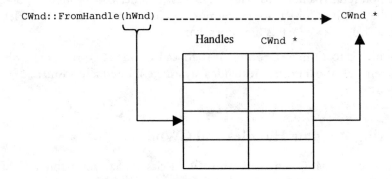

Figure 15-5: MFC maintains a table that associates CWnd objects and window handles. Various CWnd methods rely on that table.

CWnd::FromHandlePermanent() also returns the associated class given a window handle; but it returns NULL if there is no CWnd object already attached (instead of creating a temporary one).

Finally, given a CWnd object pointer, you can access the window handle by calling CWnd::GetSafeHwnd(): it returns the window handle if the pointer is non-null. The implementation is (deceptively) simple:

```
_AFXWIN_INLINE HWND CWnd::GetSafeHwnd() const
    { return this == NULL ? NULL : m_hWnd; }
```

15.2.5 Common CWnd Methods

I mentioned earlier that CWnd implements some core methods that are used with every window within an application. Figure 15-6 lists some methods that are commonly used. Refer to the Visual C++ online help (and search "CWnd Class Members" for the complete list).

Category/Method	Description
Styles	
GetStyle()	Returns the style attributes.
GetStyleEx()	Returns the extended style attributes.
ModifyStyle()	Sets the style attributes.
ModifyStyleEx()	Sets the extended style attributes.

State

EnableWindow()	Enables or disables the window.
GetFocus()	A static method that returns the current window with the input focus.
GetIcon()	Return the window's icon.
IsWindowEnabled()	Returns TRUE if the window is enabled.
SetFocus()	Moves the input focus to the current window.
SetIcon()	Sets the window's icon

Size and Position

BringWindowToTop()	Moves the window to the top of the Z order.
CenterWindow()	Centers the window against its parent.
GetClientRect()	Returns the size of the client area. The top left coordinate is always (0,0).
GetWindowRect()	Returns the size of the window. The top left coordinate is always (0,0).
MoveWindow()	Moves the window to the specified coordinates.
SetWindowPos()	Moves the window to the specified coordinates and along the Z order.

Access

FindWindow()	Finds a window based on a class name and window name (title) and return a pointer to a CWnd object.
GetDescendantWindow()	Searches all descendant of the window for the one with a matching identifier. If found, a pointer to CWnd is returned.
GetNextWindow()	Returns the next (or previous) window based on the window manager's list.
GetParent()	Returns the parent window (as a pointer to a CWnd object)
GetParentFrame()	Returns the parent frame window (as a pointer to a CWnd object)
SendMessageToDescendants()	Sends a given message to all descendant windows.

Text

GetFont()	Returns the window's default font.
GetWindowText()	Returns the window text.
GetWindowTextLength()	Returns the lengths of the window text.
SetFont()	Sets the window's default font.
SetWindowText()	Sets the window text.

Timer

KillTimer()	Stops a timer.
SetTimer()	Starts a timer based on an time-out expressed in milliseconds. Each time a time-out occurs, either the system calls the specified handler or (if NULL) sends WM_TIMER.

Alert

MessageBeep()	Emits a .beep'.
FlashWindow()	Flashes the window.

Message Passing

PostMessage()	Adds a message to window's message queue. The function immediately returns, whether the message has been processed or not.
SendMessage()	Adds a message to window's message queue. The function waits until the message has been processed

Figure 15-6: Common CWnd methods, which can be applied to any derived class as well. Many methods are not shown (for instance, those related to painting), because they are introduced in subsequent chapters.

Before closing on the subject of CWnd, keep in mind that you will use MFC objects *derived* from CWnd, not CWnd objects as such. But everything that is true for a CWnd is also true for a CWnd-derived object (as long as that object does not override it, which is very rare anyway).

15.3 MESSAGE MAPS

Windows are message-driven. About everything that happens within an application is triggered by messages sent to its windows. As a recall from Chapter 9, Windows sends messages to an application whenever events take place (mouse movement, painting, etc.) As a result, each window receives messages, one at a time, which are processed by the window's callback window procedure, as specified in the window class. Whereas developers programming in C has to code the entire functionality of message processing by hand; this is now buried in MFC. Gone is the window procedure and the traditional 10-page long switch statement. MFC has updated that approach by using message maps. What's more, the mechanics are fully buried within MFC; developers are only concerned with message maps and handlers.

The message map implements the equivalent of the switch statement developers had to code themselves in C. A message map in no more than a static structure associated with a given C++ class that is to receive and process Windows messages. The message-map logic is largely implemented in CCmdTarget; this class is the parent class of CWnd and other classes that can receive message. In practice, developers never use CCmdTarget, nor CWnd, but they use classes derived from them, hence inheriting the functionality found in those classes.

A message map contains entries that associate a message identifier to a method – or handler – defined in the class. Message maps are implemented through macros to make them easier to use. Consider the following message map for the class CMyWnd, derived from CWnd (itself derived from CCmdTarget), and illustrated in Figure 15-7:

```
BEGIN_MESSAGE_MAP(CMyWnd, CWnd)
    //{{AFX_MSG_MAP(CMyWnd)
    ON_WM_PAINT()
    ON_WM_DRAWITEM()
    ON_WM_MEASUREITEM()
    ON_COMMAND(IDM_ABOUT, OnAbout)
    //}}AFX_MSG_MAP
    ON_MESSAGE(WM_USER1, OnUser1)
END_MESSAGE_MAP()
```

Every non-commented line is a macro. The first line defines internal message map data, and associates the map with the CMyWnd class. The value next to CMyWnd must be the parent class, which indicates which message map to look up if a given message is not found in the current map. MFC automatically provides a default message map for CWnd and its parent, CCmdTarget.

The second line is a special comment, added by ClassWizard, a Visual C++ tool that helps manage message maps using a simple user interface. Section 17.1.2 shows how to use ClassWizard to manipulate messge maps. The entries between that comment and `//}}AFX_MSG_MAP` should not be edited manually. These entries are message map entries, implemented as macros. They internally contain a message identifier, the signature of the handler (*i.e.*, what type of parameters is expected and what type of value it returns) and the handler name, among other things. For instance, `ON_WM_PAINT()`, a predefined message map entry, is implemented as follows in `Afxmsg_.h`:

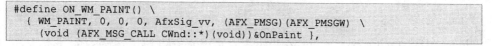

```
#define ON_WM_PAINT() \
  { WM_PAINT, 0, 0, 0, AfxSig_vv, (AFX_PMSG)(AFX_PMSGW) \
    (void (AFX_MSG_CALL CWnd::*)(void))&OnPaint },
```

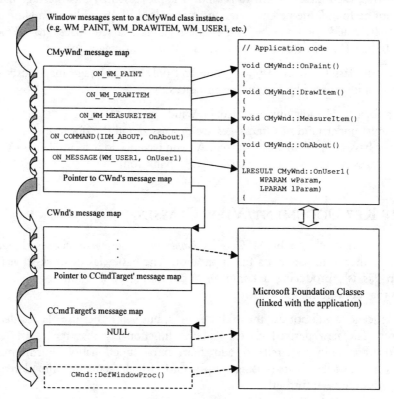

Figure 15-7: Message map of `CMyWnd`. Whenever a window message is sent to any `CMyWnd` object, `CMyWnd`'s message mapped is looked up in order to find a matching entry. If one is found, the corresponding `CMyWnd` method is invoked, and *this* is the target window. If none is found, the parent's class message map is looked up and so on. If no entry at all can be matched, `CWnd::DefWindowProc()` is invoked, which provides default processing for that message.

The first value is the message identifier, WM_PAINT, in this case. The fourth parameter is the handler signature: a void method that accepts no parameter in this case. The last parameter is the handler name: OnPaint(). Hence, ON_WM_PAINT associates WM_PAINT to the OnPaint() method in CMyWnd. That means that is CMyWnd receives the WM_PAINT message, its method OnPaint() (if present) will be called to handle it.

Any entry following \\}}AFX_MSG_MAP has been added manually, and is directly managed by the developer, not ClassWizard. This is occasionally required since ClassWizard does not support all messages, not user-defined messages.

Finally, END_MESSAGE_MAP marks the end of the message map.

Under MFC, each message sent to a window is processed by this message map logic. If entries cannot be found, the parent's message map is looked up, and so on. Ultimately, if no entries at all could be matched, the message is passed back to Windows via CWnd::Default(), for default processing (essentially a message bin).

For a given class (such as CMyWnd), one and only one message map exists within the application, and it is shared by all CMyWnd instances.

All this logic is already implemented in Windows, in CWnd and CCmdTarget to be exact. You must understand how messages are processed and the purpose of message maps, but you never have to implement it yourself. All you have to do is to implement the handlers to those messages (which is still quite challenging, thank you).

15.4 THE KEY DOCUMENT/VIEW CLASSES

The most important add-on by MFC is its *framework*, a series of classes designed to be connected together to implement a full application. The basic classes work so well that they can be run "as is", producing a complete and running application together ... but an application that does nothing.

Real applications will not use those classes as is, but will rather use classes derived from those classes. The new derived classes add the functionality that makes the application unique. You are only required to add that extra functionality. Furthermore, MFC applications are usually created using AppWizard, which generates the derived classes, simplifying your life even further!

The following sections will review in detail the key classes that compose the basis of MFC's framework: CDocument, CView, CFrameWnd, and CWinApp.

15.4.1 CDocument: The Document Class

The purpose of the document class is to hold the application data. It is not associated with a window (it is not derived from CWnd) and exists solely in memory. It provides other classes (within the application) with user-defined methods to access the data, but also includes predefined methods to load and store data from and to the data source (file, database, etc.), dump itself for debugging purposes, and so forth. The document usually plays a passive role, kind of like a data server: its methods are invoked by other classes at some point in time to perform specific actions.

Implementing a Document

Developers extend the basic CDocument class by adding encapsulated data structures to hold the application data (arrays, lists, etc.), providing methods to access that data, and implementing a few specific CDocument methods to handle the initialization, loading and storing the data, and termination.

The most important concept when designing the document is data encapsulation. The ultimate objective is to hide (from any other classes) *how* the data is implemented. Say you need to maintain a series of integers (the daily sales for a given month). If you use an array, and you make that array public, other classes will likely be coded to directly access that array. Should the implementation change (by replacing the array with a linked list), those other classes will not even compile.

To avoid those kinds of problems, the data structures that are retained must be fully encapsulated (*i.e.*, made private and protected), and various implementation-independent methods must be publicly provided. For instance, in our sales example, these methods could be GetFirstSales(), GetNextSales(), GetSalesForDay(), etc., all of which can be implemented over arrays or lists. The implementation can then be changed, as long as the public methods remain syntactically and semantically the same (*i.e.*, they are used the same way and the provide the same result). At the end , the toughest challenge is to come up with a neat interface that provides access to the data in an efficient manner, while remaining flexible enough to evolve over time. Add to that the fact that other developers may eventually derive classes from that one, forcing you to think what methods should be virtual, and you have all the best reasons in the word to take the time *it takes* to define a well-defined document[44].

Let's now explore the most important predefined methods that are typically overridden, to add some spice to the basic CDocument behavior. In the paragraphs that follow, I'll be

---

[44] Now if you have to justify to your "knowledgeable" manager why it takes so long, simply explain that you are conducting a "feasability" study on the "potential growth" of the "flagship" class of your application, which could lead to very interesting "return-on-investment". That should do it...

using `CDocument` when referring to the base class, and `CYourDocument` when referring to your implementation derived from it.

Creating a Document

Whenever an application is started, MFC automatically creates one document instance. That is, it creates an instance of the `CYourDocument`-derived class that either AppWizard generated (if you used AppWizard) or the one you coded (if you didn't use AppWizard). The document's constructor is then invoked.

The document's constructor typically initializes some member variables, as required. For instance, the constructor may allocate some buffers, initialize arrays, reset counters, etc. It is not uncommon to have an empty constructor, as initialization can take place in other methods, as we are about to see.

Then, `CYourDocument::OnNewDocument()` is called. Unlike the constructor, this method is also called whenever the user chooses File/New from the command bar (assuming such a menu item is available). This method should initialize any data that must be reset for each new document. The parent implementation should be called first (*i.e.*, `CDocument::OnNewDocument()`), to ensure consistency within the parent class. The parent's implementation invokes `CDocument::DeleteContents()`. This is a virtual method that you must implement yourself (the default does nothing). `CYourDocument::DeleteContents()` is the place to release the resources you used for that document (GDI resources, memory, etc). The parent invokes that method to ensure that the document starts clean.

To make it bullet-proof, make sure that your implementation of `DeleteContents()` can be called twice in a row. What that means is that as you release resources, keep some indicators for you to know if they have been deleted on not, and use them to determine if they must be deleted. For instance:

```
void CMyDocument::DeleteContent()
{
    // Only close the connection is it is opened.
    if (bConnectionOpened)
    {
        CloseConnection();           // Closes the connection
        bConnectionOpened = FALSE;   // Prevents closing again
    }
}
```

Once `OnNewDocument()` terminates, MFC creates the frame and the view, which will eventually access the data and possibly update the document.

Opening a Document

If the user selects File/Open, MFC automatically displays the Open dialog box for the user to enter a file name (this behavior can be altered in the `CFrameWnd` class). Provided that a name has been entered, MFC calls `CYourDocument::OnOpenDocument()` with the file name to open. There is usually no need to implement this method in your own document if your application is file-based. The default implementation (in `CDocument`) calls `CYourDocument::DeleteContents()` to clean-up the data of the previous document (if any) and `Serialize()`, to load the data from a file. Serialization is explained in Section 15-7. Hence, for file-based applications, unless you have to perform some initialization immediately after having read the data, there is no need to implement `OnOpenDocument()` in your document.

On the other hand, for non file-based data sources, you have to implement your own `OnOpenDocument()` to load the data yourself. The next example loads data from some remote data server:

```
BOOL CMyDocument::OnOpenDocument(LPCTSTR lpszServerName)
{
    // lpszServerName is in this case a server name. This requires a
    // modification in the frame class.

    // Do not call CDocument::OnOpenDocument() because  it is file-based.

    // First, delete the current data (this is essential)
    DeleteContents();

    // Open a connection to the server
    if (OpenConnection(lpszServerName))
    {
        bConnectionOpened = FALSE;     // For futur DeleteContents()
        return FALSE;                  // To indicate error
    }

    // Load data from that connection into member variables.
    . . .

    // Perform extra initialization if required
    . . .

    // Reset the modified flag
    SetModifiedFlag(FALSE);

    // Everything went OK, return TRUE.
    return TRUE;
}
```

From that point, the document is loaded with some data. The view will eventually be created, and will access the document to obtain and display that data.

Accessing and Updating a Document

The view class accesses the document's data to display them to the user. For instance, when the view receives the WM_PAINT message to show itself, it first accesses the document to obtain the data to show and then executes drawing primitives to show that data. Chapter 16 explores the details of WM_PAINT message and drawing.

In a well-designed application, the view will rely on some document methods (added by the developer) to access the data buried within the document.

The view also typically responds to user events (mouse clicks, menu commands), although other classes, such as the document itself, can do too (more in Section 15-6). For instance, if the application has an Option menu item, which shows a dialog box that allows the user to alter some color settings, that view could be a good place to handle this event. Once the dialog box is closed, the view uses document to update the document's data; then it repaints itself, again by accessing the document (which now contains updated data).

One may legitimately wonder at this point why the application should access the document twice (to store the data, and to read the data back), Why not simply keep the data in the view, which is simpler and faster, isn't it?

The simple answer is because such an approach leads toward a monolithic implementation, which is harder to maintain and evolve over time. It is easier to separate the data implementation from its representation, by respectively using two specialized classes to do so (the document and the view). However, it is true that maintaining a high degree of performance is important. In particular, it shouldn't add significant overhead to use such an approach. Hence, the document must provide data access methods that are as efficient as if they would be directly coded in the view. In practice, this is not always feasible, because the document is under the constraint of encapsulating the data, to allow easy maintenance and future derivations. Again, designing an efficient document is a real challenge in large applications. But this is definitively possible (by using inline functions for instance), as it is a skill you will gain with experience.

As mentioned earlier, documents can also handle user events. For instance, the document could handle that color setting dialog box. Once the user has entered his/her new preferences, the document could internally update its data, which is perhaps faster than the previous approach. In this scenario then, the document must be notified to refresh itself, *i.e.*, to apply the changes. The document does not have a pointer to the view; it can instead use CDocument::UpdateAllViews() to notify the view that some data changed. When invoking that method, the view's OnUpdate() method is invoked (we'll describe that method in the next section). UpdateAllViews() can also pass two user-defined values, which can serve as a hint for the view to know what has changed, and redraw accordingly. More on that later.

Finally, whenever a document's method updates data that should be eventually saved by the user, CDocument::SetModifiedFlag(TRUE) should be called. This sets an internal flag that will be used to prompt the user if he/she is attempting to close the application without having saved the data first. This flag is internally reset to FALSE in CDocument::OnNewDocument() and CDocument::OnOpenDocument(). If you override these methods and do not call the parent's implementation, make sure you call SetModifiedFlag(FALSE).

Saving a Document

When the user selects File/Save, MFC calls OnSaveDocument() with the file name to save the data to. MFC also handles the File/Save As by prompting the user with the name of the file to use. This behavior can be altered by modifying CFrameWnd.

For file-based applications, the default implementation in CDocument creates a CArchive object and calls Serialize() to store the data in the file, and resets the modified flag. Hence, for file-based applications, there is usually no need to implement OnSaveDocument() in your document.

For non file-based documents, implement this handler to store data back to their data source, as shown in the following example:

```
BOOL CMyDocument::OnSaveDocument(LPCTSTR lpszServerName)
{
    // lpszServerName is in this case a server name.

    // Do not call CDocument::OnSaveDocument() because it is file-based.

    // Store into member variables by writing to the connection
    . . .

    // Reset the modified flag
    SetModifiedFlag(FALSE);

    // Everything went OK, return TRUE.
    return TRUE;
}
```

Closing a Document

Upon File/Exit or termination, SaveModified() is called. This method does nothing if the modified flag hasn't been set. But if it has, it displays a dialog box, prompting the user whether changes should be saved or discarded. You can override this function if you need to change the message box layout, for instance. The method must return TRUE to continue and save the document, or FALSE to keep the document opened.

If `SaveModified()` returns `TRUE`, `OnSaveDocument()` is invoked, yours if you implemented one. After, `OnCloseDocument()` is called. The default implementation deletes the frame and the view, and calls `DeleteContents()`. You may override `OnCloseDocument()` to perform some final clean-up, such as disconnecting from a database. If you elect to do so, first call the base class implementation. Applications usually do not override this method, since clean-up is already handled in `DeleteContents()`. Then MFC frees its own resources, invoking the document's destructor, and the application terminates.

The scenario is different if the user chooses File/New. In that case, MFC still invokes `SaveModified()`, but `OnCloseDocument()` is not called nor is the document object deleted (the destructor is not invoked), and the application is not terminated. Instead, `OnNewDocument()` is invoked, as described earlier.

CDocument Method Summary

Figure 15-8 summarizes the document's methods that are invoked on specified events.

Event	Document's Methods Invocation

Application start-up	Document's constructor
	`OnNewDocument()`
	`DeleteContents()`

File/New	`SaveModified()`
	    `OnSaveDocument()`
	        `Serialize()`
	`OnNewDocument()`
	`DeleteContents()`

File/Open	`SaveModified()`
	    `OnSaveDocument()`
	        `Serialize()`
	`OnOpenDocument()`
	`DeleteContents()`

File/Save	`OnSaveDocument()` `Serialize()`

File/Exit –or–
application termination
	`SaveModified()`
	    `OnFileSave()`
	        `Serialize()`
	`OnCloseDocument()`
	`DeleteContents()`
	Document's destructor

Figure 15-8: Document's methods that are called upon specified events. You typically override some of them.

15.4.2 CView: The View Class

The view is the class that sits between the user and the document. It accesses data from the document and displays it to the user, in addition to respond to user commands.

We saw earlier that the application data resides in the document. The view may also implement some internal member variables, required to perform its operations. These variables are implementation-specific to the view, and are distinct from the data kept in the document. For instance, the document class of a word processor holds the text the user is entering, as well as some attributes, such as fonts, colors, spacing, etc., whereas the view, whose job is to display that text, uses internal variables to control the positioning and the alignment of the text. If the user zooms into the application, the document does not change at all, but the view has to recalculate some internal variables to redraw properly.

Developers must override a few important methods in their `CView`-derived class (methods that we are about to see), as well as adding command handlers. Additionally, because the view is associated with a window, it receives numerous window messages.

Application Start-up

Upon application startup, the view's constructor is invoked. This is the place to initialize any internal variables, if any. Since views commonly use GDI resources (pens, brushes, etc.), this is a good location to initialize them. But at this point, the document is not accessible.

Then, a call to `PreCreateWindow()` follows. We mentioned earlier that the purpose of this method is to override the parameters specified when creating the view. Here's why: since MFC creates the view (developers do not call the `CView::Create()` method themselves, MFC does), developers do not control the creation attributes of the view, which might have to be set to some specific values. Consequently, `PreCreateWindow()` has been introduced as a virtual method to allow developers customizing the creation attributes of their view. Thinking of it, this makes sense: since the framework controls the application's start-up and termination, the framework is in a better position to create and destroy the view (and the document); nonetheless, virtual methods are provided for developers to customize those operations, without being directly involved in some framework "physics". The net result is that you simply have to worry about the creation parameters at this point.

`PreCreateWindow()` receives a structure that contains the creation parameters, before the view is created. One of the most common operation is to alter the window class in order to specify a custom background color and to call the parent class. By default, the window class name is `NULL`. Your implementation of `PreCreateWindow()` can register a new class by calling `AfxRegisterWndClass()` and set the name in `cs.lpszClass`. It is also a good practice to call the parent's implementation, typically `CView::PreCreate Window()`. This method has been designed to supply a default class name only if none has already been specified. This default name is `_afxWndFrameOrView`, which sets the background color to COLOR_WINDOW (usually white), and uses a default icon and an arrow cursor.

The following example creates a new class registration for a red background.

```
CMyView::CMyView()
{
    // Create a pale yellow background brush.
    // m_bkgndBrush is a private member variable declared as
    // "CBrush m_bkgndBrush;" in the class definition.

    m_bkgndBrush.CreateSolidBrush(RGB(255, 255, 215));
}

BOOL CMyView::PreCreateWindow(CREATESTRUCT& cs)
{
    // If no class is specified, use a class with a special brush
    if (cs.lpszClass == NULL)
            cs.lpszClass = AfxRegisterWndClass(
            CS_DBLCLKS,              // No redrawing when resized
            NULL,                    // No cursor
            HBRUSH(m_bkgndBrush),    // New background color
            (HICON) 0);              // No icon

    // Call the base-class version. It will use its own class name
    // only if cs.lpszClass is NULL.
    return CView::PreCreateWindow(cs);
}
```

The same way CView gives you the courtesy of not overriding your class name if you provide one, make sure that you do the same toward derived class. If a developer one day derives a new class from yours, and implements PreCreateWindow() to provide a new background color and then calls the parent's implementation (*i.e.*, your PreCreate Window()), it wouldn't be polite to simply override the class name with your own. Extend the courtesy to derived classes, just as MFC does for you, by providing a class name only if none has been provided yet.

Because the view is associated with a window, Windows CE sends WM_CREATE to the view after is has been created but before it is made visible. Add the following highlighted predefined entry in your view's message map to handle this message in OnCreate():

```
BEGIN_MESSAGE_MAP(CScribbleCEView, CView)
    //{{AFX_MSG_MAP(CScribbleCEView)
    ON_WM_CREATE()
    ON_WM_ERASEBKGND()
    ON_WM_SIZE()
    ON_WM_LBUTTONDOWN()
    ON_WM_LBUTTONUP()
    ON_WM_MOUSEMOVE()
    //}}AFX_MSG_MAP
```

```
END MESSAGE MAP()

int CScribbleCEView::OnCreate(LPCREATESTRUCT lpCreateStruct)
{
    if (CView::OnCreate(lpCreateStruct) == -1)
         return -1;

    // Add your specialized creation code here. This is a good location
    // to create child controls, if any.

    return 0;
}
```

The OnCreate() handler is a good location to create child controls if you have to, although this is unusual (MFC supports dialog-based views, which are easier to use when dealing with controls). At this point, any CWnd method can be called, but the document is not available yet. If you process WM_CREATE, remember to call the parent's implementation, which updates some internal data within the framework.

Once OnCreate() returns, the document is created and CYourView::OnInitial Update() is called. This is the ideal spot to perform some view-related initialization that requires access to the document's data. For instance, the view might create supplemental GDI resources (fonts, brushes, etc.) based on the document's precise content. The default implementation (in CView) calls OnUpdate(), which will explore soon.

Painting

The view is responsible for painting the application's client area that the user sees. Because the view is a window, Windows sends the WM_PAINT message as required (see Chapter 16 for details about WM_PAINT). Your view doesn't have to handle this message directly, as it is already handled in CView. CView::OnPaint() creates a device context object and calls the virtual method OnDraw(), that is, CYourView::OnDraw().

You implement OnDraw() by adding drawing instructions specific to the application. For instance, if your application displays a graph, CYourView::OnDraw() must call some drawing primitives to do so, based on the data that resides in the document. Drawing is the subject of the next chapter.

Accessing the document is done by calling GetDocument(), which returns a pointer to the CYourDocument object. Using this pointer, the view simply invokes methods that return the data the view is looking for. Since developers code both the view's and the document's methods, they have full control over the data access.

Here is an example of a view that renders a graph. In this example, the document provides the sales for a given month, which is passed to DisplaySales(), a view's private method that draws a bar corresponding to the amount.

```
void CMyView::OnDraw(CDC * pDC)
{
    CMyDocument * pDoc = GetDocument();

    for (int nMonth = 0; nMonth <= pDoc->GetLastMonth(); nMonth++)
        DisplaySales(nMonth, pDoc->GetMonthSales(nMonth));
}

void CMyView::DisplaySales(int nMonth, int nAmount)
{
    .
    .
    .
}
```

In real-life applications that render elaborate graphics, OnDraw() calls numerous private (or protected) methods to display the data. In fact, the view typically largely consists of private methods that are called from OnDraw().

Your OnDraw() will be called whenever Windows decides that you application needs to be repainted. That happens at the initialization, but also if your application was obscured by another application that has moved away. Consequently, OnDraw() is a generic method that must handle different painting situations. Furthermore, it should be optimized to execute as fast as possible. We'll see some elaborate tricks to do so.

Updating the View

We saw that CView::OnInitialUpdate() is called immediately after the document has been created, whose default implementation is to call OnUpdate(). We also saw that OnUpdate() is called by CDocument::UpdateAllViews(), whenever the document wants to notify the view about changes in the application's data.

The default implementation of OnUpdate() in CView is to invalidate the entire client area. Invalidating a window (partially or entirely) places WM_PAINT in the application's message queue, which is eventually delivered to the window to repaint the invalidated area. The same logic applies to the view. Hence, OnUpdate() is closely (but not necessarily immediately) followed by a call to OnDraw() to repaint everything. In simple applications, this is often enough, because OnDraw() will get the new data from the document and repaint accordingly, making the changes visible.

For complex applications though, this solution does not work as well. Consider an application that needs to draw 1000 geometric figures. Let's say the user, via an Options dialog box, changes the color of some figures, resulting in five figures having to be repainted. Assuming the document handled the change, it notifies the view by calling UpdateAllViews(). A default implementation of OnUpdate() in the view result in repainting the entire client area, i.e., 1000 figures. Not quite efficient.

When calling `UpdateAllViews()`, the document can pass two user-defined parameters: an `LPARAM` value and a `CObject` pointer. The two values are passed "as is" to `OnUpdate()` in the view. These parameters are respectively 0 and `NULL` when `OnUpdate()` is invoked from `OnInitialUpdate()`. The document and the view must agree on the meaning of these parameters and act accordingly. For instance, the document can instead pass 1 and a pointer to an array of figures to update. The view can use that array to update only the figures are required, instead of redrawing *all* figures.

It is important to realize that `OnUpdate()` doesn't draw, since it is already `OnDraw`'s job to paint invalid areas (painting in `OnUpdate()` would essentially duplicating `OnDraw()`). `OnUpdate()` should strictly focus on invalidating some areas, and let `OnDraw()` handle the rest. Let's review again the color setting example, where the user changes some colors by using a dialog box. When that dialog box is closed, the corresponding area in the view must be repainted. Hence, Windows posts a `WM_PAINT` message for that purpose. Then the document issues the call to `UpdateAllViews()`, which results in `OnUpdate()` invalidating five small areas (for instance). When `OnDraw()` finally runs in order to process `WM_PAINT`, it not only has to repaint those five areas, it must also paint the area formally covered by the dialog box (see Figure 15-9). The rule to remember is that regardless of what `OnUpdate()` invalidates, no one can predict what `OnDraw()` is precisely called for. Consequently, `OnDraw()` must be designed to redraw any invalidated areas. We'll explore in Chapter 16 how to identify the invalid areas when drawing.

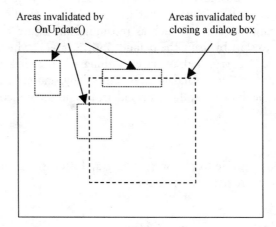

Figure 15-9: When closing a dialog box, `OnDraw()` must repaint the corresponding area in the view, in addition to other areas invalidated by `OnUpdate()`.

There are other, simpler strategies. Instead of invalidating numerous small areas, `OnUpdate()` may invalidate a rectangle large enough to cover all areas to redraw (see Figure

15-10). When OnDraw() is called, it may retrieve the invalid area and redraw everything in it. This approach is acceptable if it doesn't significantly add overhead.

Areas to invalidate in OnUpdate()

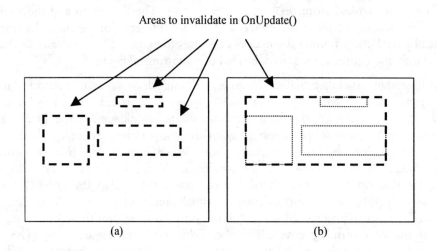

(a)   (b)

Figure 15-10: When some of the view needs to be updated, specific areas can be invalidated (a), or the tightest rectangle bounding those areas can be invalidated (b).

Drawing is a serious business. It's what users see and what they use to judge the application. The challenge is to ensure that OnDraw() paints enough regardless of the circumstances it is being called upon, such as repainting the entire client area or just some parts of it. It is easier to start by using the default OnUpdate(), which invalidates the entire client area, and have OnDraw() redrawing everything when called. Once this works, you may introduce OnUpdate() to invalidate a few areas only, and enhance OnDraw() to first identify what needs to be drawn (*i.e.*, those invalid areas) and draw accordingly.

Handling Events

The view has an important role to play in receiving and processing mouse events and menu commands. These topics are detailed in Chapter 17.

15.4.3 CFrameWnd: The Frame Class

The frame is the application's main window that implements the title (if one is visible), the command bar, and the borders (if any). The frame creates the view and is its parent. The view is managed by the frame in a way that is always fully covers the frame's client area.

Because the view covers the frame's client area, the frame does not have to paint. Hence, only the view is concerned with painting. There is in fact little to do with the frame. A default frame, as generated by AppWizard, needs few changes. As a matter of fact, only `PreCreateWindow()`, the command bar, and status bar usually require some changes.

Creation of the Frame

It is possible to override `CFrameWnd::PreCreateWindow()` to alter the style, position and size of the application window.

Then, half-way during the creation process, the frame receives `WM_CREATE`. The default MFC implementation handles that message and creates a command bar and a status bar. You can modify the handler if you need to modify this behavior.

Modifying the Command Bar

AppWizard generates a default menu template and a default toolbar, both combined into a command bar. Both resources can be individually updated using the Visual C++ resource editor.

If the toolbar is changed, through, you might also have to update a data structure in the frame, shown below. This structure corresponds to the toolbar shown in Figure 15-11.

```
static TBBUTTON g_tbSTDButton[] = {
    {0, 0,                TBSTATE_ENABLED, TBSTYLE_SEP,    0, 0, 0,  0},
    {0, ID_FILE_NEW,      TBSTATE_ENABLED, TBSTYLE_BUTTON, 0, 0, 0, -1},
    {1, ID_FILE_OPEN,     TBSTATE_ENABLED, TBSTYLE_BUTTON, 0, 0, 0, -1},
    {2, ID_FILE_SAVE,     TBSTATE_ENABLED, TBSTYLE_BUTTON, 0, 0, 0, -1},
    {0, 0,                TBSTATE_ENABLED, TBSTYLE_SEP,    0, 0, 0, -1},
    {3, ID_EDIT_CUT,      TBSTATE_ENABLED, TBSTYLE_BUTTON, 0, 0, 0, -1},
    {4, ID_EDIT_COPY,     TBSTATE_ENABLED, TBSTYLE_BUTTON, 0, 0, 0, -1},
    {5, ID_EDIT_PASTE,    TBSTATE_ENABLED, TBSTYLE_BUTTON, 0, 0, 0, -1},
    {0, 0,                TBSTATE_ENABLED, TBSTYLE_SEP,    0, 0, 0, -1},
    {6, ID_APP_ABOUT,     TBSTATE_ENABLED, TBSTYLE_BUTTON, 0, 0, 0, -1},
    {0, 0,                TBSTATE_ENABLED, TBSTYLE_SEP,    0, 0, 0,  0}
};
```

Figure 15-11: The default command bar generated by AppWizard.

If you add, update, or delete buttons in the toolbar bitmap, make sure to update the previous table in the frame accordingly.

Also, in `OnCreate()`, the frame calls `CFrameWnd::AddAdornments()` with 0 in order add the Close button (**X**) in the command bar. You can alter the call and pass either `CMDBAR_HELP`, `CMDBAR_OK` or both to add extra buttons (see Figure 15-12).

Figure 15-12: Parameters to `CFrameWnd::AddAdornments()` alter the rightmost buttons of the command bar. In a) the help button is added whereas in b) the OK button is also added.

If you have to, you can obtain a pointer to the document and the view from the frame, but this is rather unusual:

```
void CMyFrame::SomeMethod()
{
    CMyDocument *  pDoc = GetActiveDocument();
    CMyView *      pView = GetActiveView();
    . . .
}
```

From a developer's standpoint, the frame is of little interest otherwise, and is rarely extensively modified.

15.4.4 CWinApp: The Application Class

The final key class of the document/architecture model is the application class, derived from `CWinApp`. The role of this class it to initialize the application, pump and dispatch messages, and terminate the application. The default application class generated by AppWizard rarely needs more than a few changes.

Registry Settings

Upon termination, it is common for applications to store settings such as user's preference, the last files opened, the position of the application window, etc., in the registry, and use them the next time the application is opened. These are application-specific settings, not associated with documents as such. As a result, these settings are handled by the application class, not the document class.

One approach to handle these settings is to load them in InitInstance() and store them in ExitInstance(), both detailed in a second. The setting themselves can be kept in a structure (or a class) within the application class, made available to the other classes. The easiest approach is perhaps to provide a method that returns a reference to that structure. The next example demonstrates this approach.

```
// MyApp.h

// A structure containing the application-specific registry settings.
struct APPSETTINGS
{
    COLORREF        m_BkgndColor;
    COLORREF        m_DefaultColors[16];
    .
    .
    .
};

// The application class definition
class CMyApp: public CWinApp
{
    APPSETTINGS     AppSettings;            // Application settings
public:
    MyApp(LPCTSTR lpszAppName);             // Default constructor

    APPSETTINGS&    GetAppSettings();       // To return the settings

    .
    .
    .
};

// Make CMyApp::GetAppSettings inline for efficiency

inline APPSETTINGS& CMyApp::GetAppSettings()
{
    return AppSettings;
}

// Also provide a global helper function to return a pointer to the
// current application class without having to cast it.

inline CMyApp * AfxGetThisApp()
{
    extern CMyApp  theApp;
    return &theApp;
}
```

Then the other classes within the application can access the application settings (to read or modify them) by executing the following:

```
CMyView::CMyView()
{
    // Create background brush based on application settongs
    APPSETTINGS&  AppSettings = AfxGetThisApp()->GetAppSettings();
    m_bkgndBrush.CreateSolidBrush(AppSettings.m_BkgndColor);
}
```

Application Initialization

Almost immediately after the application is loaded, `CWinApp::InitInstance()` is called. AppWizard generates the following code (the comments have been stripped out):

```
BOOL CMyApp::InitInstance()
{
    SetRegistryKey(_T("Local AppWizard-Generated Applications"));

    LoadStdProfileSettings();

    CSingleDocTemplate* pDocTemplate;
    pDocTemplate = new CSingleDocTemplate(
            IDR_MAINFRAME,
            RUNTIME_CLASS(CMyDoc),
            RUNTIME_CLASS(CMainFrame),          // main SDI frame window
            RUNTIME_CLASS(CMyView));
    AddDocTemplate(pDocTemplate);

    CCommandLineInfo cmdInfo;
    ParseCommandLine(cmdInfo);

    if (!ProcessShellCommand(cmdInfo))
            return FALSE;

    m_pMainWnd->ShowWindow(SW_SHOW);
    m_pMainWnd->UpdateWindow();

    return TRUE;
}
```

`CWinApp::SetRegistryKey()` is first called to establish the parent key of the application's registry keys. Make sure that your application name is passed to `SetRegistryKey()`, not the default string `_T("Local AppWizard-Generated Applications")`. The call is followed by a call to `LoadStdProfileSettings()`, which reloads the list of the recently-used files, which will be eventually shown in the File menu.

If you have any settings to read from the Registry, you can read them by using a few `CWinApp` methods (`GetProfileInt()`, `GetProfileString()` and `GetProfile Binary()`) in `InitInstance()`. They accept default values if the corresponding keys are not found, which happens the very first time an application is run.

Then a `CSingleDocTemplate` is created and added to the framework. This class is the link between the frame, the view, and the document. This is not really of interest to developers; this is more related to the internals of MFC. This code is generated in the application (instead of being buried somewhere in MFC) because the application-specific class names are required.

Then command line arguments are parsed (if any) into a `CCommandLineInfo` instance. This class contains a few public member attributes that are set depending on standard command-line arguments. If you want to handle specific command-line options, derive a class from `CCommandLineInfo`, and add extra member variables to reflect the command-line arguments. Also implement `ParseParam()` within that class, which is called for each individual command-line argument by `ParseCommandLine()` in `InitInstance()`. Your implementation should set the member variables you added based on the command-line arguments, but importantly, it shouldn't process them as such.

Then `ProcessShellCommand()` is called. The default implement creates new instances of the frame, view and document. `CWinApp::m_pMainWnd` is set on the frame instance, which is the application's main window. You can directly use `m_pMainWnd` (it is public), or you can call `AfxGetMainWnd()`.

If no arguments were specified, such as when the application is started by double-clicking on it, the document's `OnNewDocument()` is invoked as explained in Section 15.4.1. If the application has been invoked with a document name (by double-clicking on a data file), the document's `OnOpenDocument()` is instead called.

Then, using `m_pMainWnd`, the frame is made visible (`CWnd::ShowWindow()`) and is immediately repainted (`CWnd::UpdateWindow()`), resulting in a call to the view's `OnDraw()`.

You can change the application's title by calling `CWnd::SetWindowText` using either `m_pMainWnd`, or `AfxGetMainWnd()`, both approaches being equivalent::

```
AfxGetMainWnd()->SetWindowText("New Title");
```

Application Execution

After the initialization is completed, `CWinApp` starts pumping messages and dispatching them to the frame window or the view. Until the user terminates the application, what follows strictly depends on how the user interacts with the application.

Application Termination

When the application terminates, after the document's OnCloseDocument() has been executed, CWinApp::ExitInstance() is called. The default implementation (in CWinApp) saves internal registry settings. If you loaded some settings from the registry in InitInstance(), you can save them in ExitInstance() by calling the corresponding CWinApp methods: WriteProfileInt(), WriteProfileString() and Write ProfileBinary(). Otherwise, there is no need to override ExitInstance().

The application normally terminates when the uses chooses File/Exit or presses the Close button (**X**) in the command bar. Alternatively, you can force the termination by executing the following, anywhere in your application:

```
AfxGetMainWnd()->SendMessage(WM_CLOSE);
```

Other Member Variables and Methods

CWinApp() provides numerous methods that can be called by the other classes. First, those classes can call AfxGetApp() to obtain a pointer to the CWinApp-derived class:

```
void CMyView::SomeMethod()
{
    CMyApp * pApp = AfxGetApp();
    . . .
}

void CMyDoc::SomeMethod()
{
    CMyApp * pApp = AfxGetApp();
    . . .
}
```

Note that once you get a pointer to the application class, you can access the frame (m_pMainWnd), the view (GetActiveView()) and the document (GetActive Document()) from any point in your application.

Figure 15-13 lists some of the member variables and methods CWinApp offers:

CWinApp Member Variable or Method	Description
m_pszAppName	The name of the application
m_pszExeName	The module name of the application
m_pszHelpFilePath	The help file path
m_pszRegistryKey	The root registry key for this application
LoadCursor()	

`LoadStandardCursor()`	
`LoadOEMCursor()`	
`LoadIcon()`	
`LoadStandardIcon()`	
`LoadOEMIcon()`	
`HideApplication()`	Hide the application before closing the document
`PreTranslateMessage()`	Filters messages before dispatching them to windows
`DoWaitCursor(0`	Turns the wait cursor on and off. Very useful when performing some lengthy processing.
`WinHelp()`	Show the help file.

Figure 15-13: Some members of CWinApp.

15.5 ALTERNATIVE ARCHITECTURES

Besides the architecture so far explained, MFC is flexible enough to support alternatives. Specifically, MFC supports applications:

- with splitter windows
- with/without a view and a document
- dialog-based

These different architectures are explored in the following paragraphs.

15.5.1 Splitter Windows

MFC includes a class called `CSplitterWnd`, which allows splitting a window into panes, each of which implement a view. An example of a split window is the Windows Explorer, split with a vertical splitter bar (see Figure 15-14). A window can be split vertically, horizontally or both. A pane can itself be split further, and so on.

Splitter window is a nice MFC add-on, with no direct equivalent in Win32 programming. Moreover, splitter windows are fully integrated within the document/view architecture. When using splitter windows, an application ends up with multiple views attached to one document. A document can update all views by calling `UpdateAllViews()`, resulting in each view's `OnUpdate()` being called. So, besides initializing the splitter window, there are no new issues to worry about. Is MFC fun or what?

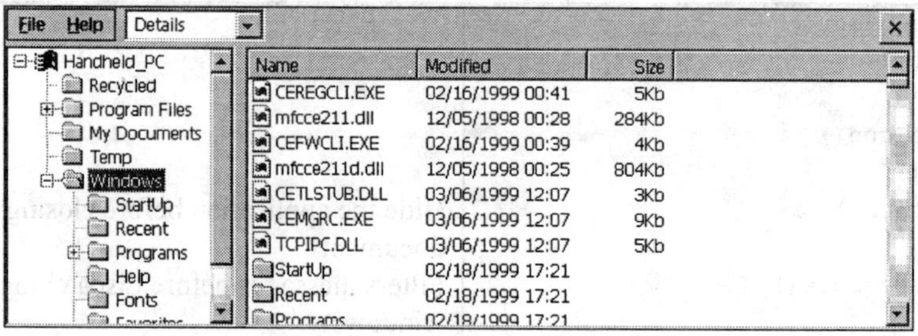

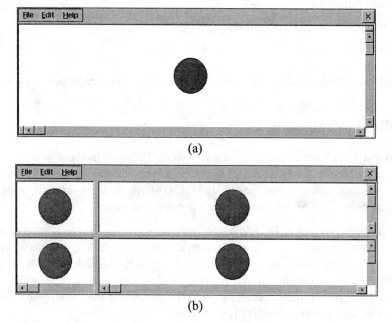

Figure 15-14: Windows Explorer contains a split window, resulting in left and right panes.

There are two types of splitter windows: dynamic and static. Each has its own properties and initialization method.

Dynamic Splitters

Dynamic splitter windows may or may not be split into two panes. The user can drag the splitter bar close to one of the window's edges to eventually remove the bar, resulting in the window no longer being split. When removed from the window, the splitter bar adds a small button on scroll bar, which is where the user can drag the bar back onto the window to split it again (see Figure 15-15).

(a)

(b)

Figure 15-15: A dynamic splitter window shows by default one view (a). The user may however drag splitters and split the view into up to four panes (b).

Dynamic splitters are usually used with the same type of views. For instance, most word processors or code editors support dynamic splitters (normally deactivated), which can be activated to see two parts of the same file simultaneously.

Splitting a window using a dynamic splitter results in two panes that share scroll bars. For instance, when splitting a window using an horizontal splitter bar, each pane has its own vertical scroll bar, but the unique horizontal scroll controls the two panes (see Figure 15-16 a). The corresponding behavior can be observed when using vertical splitter bars, in which case the two panes share the vertical scroll bar (see Figure 15-16 b).

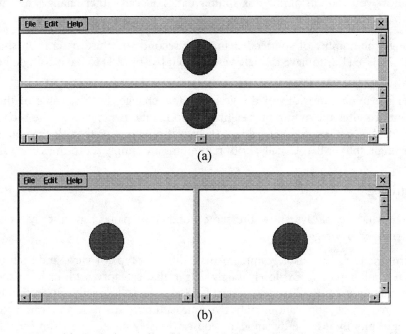

Figure 15-16: (a) A window split with an horizontal splitter bar results in two panes that share the horizontal scroll bar. (b). Splitting the same window vertically results in the two panes sharing the vertical scroll bar.

Splitter windows must be added manually (although they can be automatically generated for desktop applications by AppWizard). The procedure is simple enough, provided that the application is based on the document/view architecture:

- A protected CSplitterWnd member variable is added in the frame class definition.

- The virtual OnCreateClient() method is overridden to create the dynamic splitter window. By default, the window supports an horizontal and vertical splitter bars, and sets the minimum size of each pane to 10 pixels. Should one pane become smaller than that, the pane is removed. This method is shown below:

```
BOOL CMainFrame::OnCreateClient(LPCREATESTRUCT /*lpcs*/,
    CCreateContext* pContext)
{
    return m_wndSplitter.Create(this,
            2, 2,                   // Adjust the number of rows, columns
            CSize(10, 10),          // Adjust the minimum pane size
            pContext);
}
```

Here's how you can customize this splitter bar. You can either change the number of splitters and/or change their minimum size:

- To change the number of splitters, change the second and third parameter, shown as 2 and 2 (2,2). Use (1,2) to have a single vertical split bar or (2,1) to have a single horizontal one.

- To alter the minimum width of the vertical pane, change the first value of the CSize argument. To alter the minimum height of a horizontal pane, change the second value. Note that MFC asserts if either value is 0, even if only one of them is meaningful when using a single splitter bar. Usually, both minimums are simply set to the same value.

Static Splitters

Static splitter windows always show the same number of panes. Specifically, splitter bars cannot be removed by dragging them.

Furthermore, each pane usually implements a different type of view, and each pane may have its own scroll bars. The Explorer exactly falls in that category, with its left pane being a tree view and its right pane, a list view. Visual C++ 6.0 doesn't directly support adding static splitter windows to an application, only dynamic splitters. Instead, you can add a static splitter bar and modify it to be dynamic, or you can simply create one from scratch. Here's how to proceed from scratch to create a static vertical splitter (one row, two columns):

- Since different views are typically used, you need to create at least another view (assuming you will be using the view already created by AppWizard). Within Visual C++, choose the Insert menu, and click New Class. The New Class dialog box shows up. Enter the view class name (e.g., COtherView). Choose CView as the base class, or any other class derived from it (CTreeView, CListView, CEditView are popular among others). Click OK. This adds the class in your project.

- In MainFrm.h, first add the views' header files. You will have to add first the document's header file. Then, add a handle for OnCreateClient(), and implement the following code:

```
BOOL CMainFrame::OnCreateClient(
```

```
        LPCREATESTRUCT /*lpcs*/,
        CCreateContext* pContext)
{
        // Create the static splitter (1 row, 2 columns).
        if (!m_wndSplitter.CreateStatic(this, 1, 2))
            return FALSE;

        // Set the view for the first pane (row 0, column 0).
        // This view in this case is the original view.
        if (!m_wndSplitter.CreateView(
                0,                              // Row 0
                0,                              // Column 0
                RUNTIME_CLASS(CMyView),         // CView's runtime class info
                CSize(100, 0),                  // Initial width: 100 pixels
                pContext))                      // Default context
                return FALSE;

        // Set the view for the second pane (row 0, column 1).
        // This view in this case is the view just added.
        if (!m_wndSplitter.CreateView(
                0,                              // Row 0
                1,                              // Column 1
                RUNTIME_CLASS(COtherView),      // COtherView's runtime info
                CSize(0, 0),                    // Initial size: default
                pContext))                      // Default context
                return FALSE;

        // Everything went fine, return OK
        return TRUE;
}
```

The call to CSplitter::CreateStatic() essentially determines the number and orientation of the panes. The example above specifies one row, two columns, *i.e.*, one single vertical splitter bar. Use 2 and 1 to have two rows and one column (*i.e.*, a single horizontal bar), or 2 and 2 to have two rows and two columns (one vertical and one horizontal bar).

You must create as many views as required (either two or four) by calling CSplitterWnd::CreateView(), and specifying the pane location (in row and column numbers). For instance, in the example, the left most pane is at row 0, column 0. The rightmost pane is at row 0, column 1.

The views must support dynamic creation via the macros DECLARE_DYNCREATE() and IMPLEMENT_DYNCREATE() (they do by default). This allows the use of the RUNTIME_CLASS() macro, required with CSplitterWnd::CreateView().

The width (the fourth parameter to CSplitterWnd::CreateView()) specifies the initial size. In the case of the leftmost pane, only the cx value of the size is meaningful (*i.e.*, the width of the pane), since the height of the pane is set to the parent window's height. Hence, the cy value of the size is 0 (*i.e.*, default). With the left pane's width set, the right pane's width will automatically be set to the remaining portion of the parent window's width. Hence, the width for the right pane is 0, as well as for the height, *i.e.*, default size.

Finally, the last argument when creating the view is the second parameter to OnCreateClient(). This associates both views to the same document.

15.5.2 Removing the View and/or the Document

In Visual C++ 6.0, AppWizard presents a check box in Step 1 (see Figure 14-5) to remove the traditional view and document class (on step 1, uncheck "Document/View architecture support"). This results is an application that contains an application class, a main frame, and child view class. This latter class is a child of the main frame, but is derived from CWnd (instead of CView). This class implements PreCreateWindow() and OnPaint() by default. There is no document class, nor view class.

Alternatively, you can completely bypass AppWizard and write your own application that only includes an application class and a main frame. Such an application has been introduced in Section 14.2.2. Again, no view, no document.

Either approach helps reduce the size of an application, although it also throws away the inherent modularity found in the document/view architecture. Still, this might be the best approach for an application that has a simple user interface and that performs some background processing, which is non-document based (such as a mini Web server). Such an application does not really need a view nor a document: the main frame window (or its child if any) can directly implement the background functionality and render some output.

Such an application can also let go of the main window and simply install an icon in the tray bar (see Figure 15-17). This method also provides the user with a direct access to the application. Using the tray bar is explained in Chapter 21.

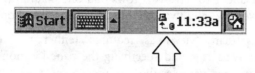

Figure 15-17: Applications that can run in the background may simply display an icon in the tray bar. Windows CE Services uses that approach.

15.5.3 Dialog-Based Applications

AppWizard also supports an option to generate a dialog-based application (in Step 1). This results in two classes: an application class, and a CDialog-based class. Again, no view, no document, even no frame! A default dialog box is generated, which must be edited according to the application's requirement specifications.

This method is ideal for a simple application whose main window is a dialog box. For instance, Calc.exe (for Windows CE) is such an application (see Figure 15-19). Because those applications are rather specific, there is no real need to add support for a view and a document.

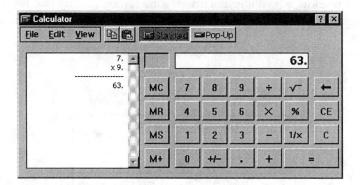

Figure 15-19: A dialog-based application, in this case, Calc.exe on an H/PC Pro 2.11

However, large applications, still dialog-based, can use the document/view architecture, if required. They do so by using a normal document/view application, but with a view derived `CFormView` instead of `CView`. `CFormView` is a view that shows a dialog box. It's very easy to generate an application using a `CFormView`-based view: in AppWizard, on the last step, specify that the view's base class is `CFormView` (instead of `CView`). A default dialog box will be generated, and you end up with full support for the document/view architecture, for a dialog-based application. Visual C++'s online help also explains how to convert an existing CView-based application into one that uses a `CFormView` (look at *CFormView Overview* in the MFC online documentation).

15.6 COMMAND ROUTING

Once all the classes have been created and the application class starts pumping messages, the application reacts to the user's actions. The application is in fact fully event-driven. Under normal conditions, the application sits and waits. Any action from the user is internally translated into a message, sent either to the frame or the view windows. For instance, menu commands result in `WM_COMMAND` being sent to the frame window; moving the mouse over the frame's client area sends mouse messages to the view.

Let's recall that whichever `CWnd`-derived window (in this case, the frame or the view) receives a message, its message map is scanned to find a handler. If none is found, its ancestors' maps are looked up as well. Unprocessed messages end up being passed to `::DefWindowProc()`.

Menu and command bar button messages are handled differently. They all send the same window message (WM_COMMAND) along their unique identifier. For instance, File/New sends WM_COMMAND and ID_FILE_NEW.

The command messages that originate from the command bar are sent to the bar's owner, the frame window, which implements very interesting routing (see Figure 15-20). The purpose is to give a chance to many classes, including non-window classes, to handle commands.

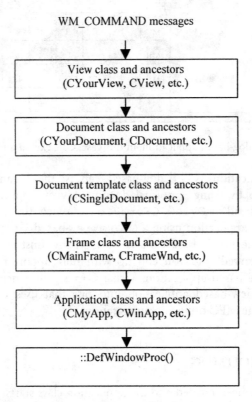

WM_COMMAND messages

↓

| View class and ancestors |
| (CYourView, CView, etc.) |

↓

| Document class and ancestors |
| (CYourDocument, CDocument, etc.) |

↓

| Document template class and ancestors |
| (CSingleDocument, etc.) |

↓

| Frame class and ancestors |
| (CMainFrame, CFrameWnd, etc.) |

↓

| Application class and ancestors |
| (CMyApp, CWinApp, etc.) |

↓

| ::DefWindowProc() |

Figure 15-20: WM_COMMAND messages (from the command bar) are routed through the key classes of every MFC application.

What that means is that you have the choice of handling command messages in your application almost wherever it makes sense to do so. Here are a few examples:

- From the "View" menu, the user chooses the "Zoom In" menu item. The command should be handled in the view, because it only impacts how the data is displayed. Note that the zoom factor can also be stored in the application class, in order to be saved (and later restored) in the registry.

- From the "File" menu, the user chooses the "Properties" menu item. This could be handled by the document class, which has all the information about the data being shown. The document class can also query supplemental details if required.

- From the "Help" menu, the user chooses the "About" menu item. Since this is a very general command (not specific to the view, the document, nor the frame), the application can handle it.

There is no rule as to where command messages have to be processed: you decide. The goal is to handle the message as close as possible to the data it impacts. Personally, I handle most commands in the view, because I mentally position the view between the user and the document. I consider that the view drives the application in a certain sense, so I let it implement what to do with most user commands. There are of course exceptions to this approach, but when in doubt, handle command messages in the view. The view can always access the document by calling GetDocument(), and the document can force the view to be updated by calling UpdateAllViews(). Over time, you will develop your own preference.

Once a class is chosen, all you need to do is to add an entry in the message map and a handler in the class. For instance, in order to handle the item Colors from the Options menu in the document (assuming the menu item has the id ID_OPTIONS_COLORS), add the following in the document file:

```
BEGIN_MESSAGE_MAP(CMyDoc, CDocument)
    //{{AFX_MSG_MAP(CMyDoc)
    .
    .
    .
    ON_COMMAND(ID_OPTIONS_COLORS, OnOptionsColors)
    //}}AFX_MSG_MAP
END_MESSAGE_MAP()

void CMyDoc::OnOptionsColors()
{
    .
    .
    .
}
```

Whenever the user chooses that menu item, the handler is automatically called. If you later decide to move that handler to another class, remove the entry in the message map and add it into the new class' message map. Then, copy and paste the function into the new class, making necessary changes.

ClassWizard, a Visual C++ tool, can manage all message maps as long as the application has been generated by AppWizard. As a result, handlers can be added and removed in a snap.

15.7 SERIALIZATION

Document/view applications have been designed to handle files. You can still use a document for non-file data sources, but you have to control access to that data source yourself.

Most MFC classes are derived from CObject, which implements serialization, the ability for an object to load and store itself from and to some storage (as you may recall from Chapter 14).

In MFC, object serialization works hand in hand with *archives*, represented by the CArchive class. A CArchive is an intermediary between a file or a socket, as shown on Figure 15-21.

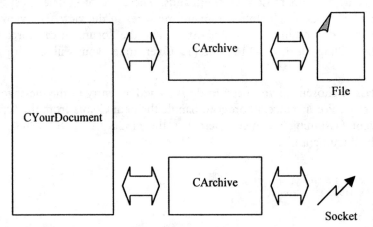

Figure 15-21: Documents allow your archive to load and store CObject-derived objects. The archive can be connected to a file or a socket.

15.7.1 Storing Data

Let's see how this is used when a document is saved for the first time. We'll assume for the sake of clarity that the document only contains three strings. When the user chooses File/Save, MFC prompts the user for a file name and invokes OnSaveDocument(). The default implementation (in CDocument) creates a CArchive object, associates it with the file name, and then passes it to Serialize(). This virtual method must be overridden in your document in order to store the application's data into the archive. Here's an example:

```
void CMyDoc::Serialize(CArchive& ar)
{
    if (ar.IsStoring())
```

```
    {
            ar << m_sString1;
            ar << m_sString2;
            ar << m_sString3;

            // This could equally be written as follows:
            // ar << m_sString1 << m_sString2 << m_sString3;
    }
    else
    {
            // More on this later
    }
}
```

A CArchive object overloads the << operators and accept these value types: BYTE, WORD, int, LONG, DWORD, float, double, and CString. Internally, the CArchive writes the data into a file.

Structures must be broken down into those types. For instance, to save a structure containing an integer and a float, one must code the following:

```
void CMyDoc::Serialize(CArchive& ar)
{
    if (ar.IsStoring())
    {
            // Store each member of a structure
            ar << m_sMyStruct.m_nCount;
            ar << m_sMyStruct.m_dAvg;
    }
    else
    {
            // More on this later
    }
}
```

Any CObject-derived class can (and should) implement its own Serialize() method. The method accepts a reference to an archive object, the very ones created by the document. For instance, if a document contains a CMyObject variable, you can serialize this object in your document by calling Serialize() on the object:

```
void CMyDoc::Serialize(CArchive& ar)
{
    if (ar.IsStoring())
    {
            // Delegates serialization
            m_MyObject.Serialize(ar);
    }
    else
    {
            // More on this later
    }
}
```

In turn, `CMyObject::Serialize()` would contain some code to serialize its own member variables.

```
void CMyObject::Serialize(CArchive& ar)
{
    if (ar.IsStoring())
            ar << m_Var1 << m_Var2;
    else
            ar >> m_Var1 >> m_Var2;
```

15.7.2 Loading Data

Now let's see what happens when the same file is later opened. When the user selects File/Open, MFC shows the Open dialog box to obtain a file name, and passes the file name to `CDocument::OnOpenDocument()`. This method internally creates a `CArchive` object and associates it with the specified file name. Then, `CDocument::OnOpenDocument()` calls `Serialize()`, passing a reference to that archive. the same virtual method overridden earlier is invoked, this time to load the data. You can identify whether `Serialize()` is called to load or store the data by executing `CArchive::IsStoring()` on the archive object. Here's an example that demonstrates a complete `Serialize()` method (the bold part is the one that loads the data).

```
void CTempDoc::Serialize(CArchive& ar)
{
    if (ar.IsStoring())
    {
            // Store the data into the archive (on File/Save)
            ar << m_sString1;
            ar << m_sString2;
            ar << m_sString3;

            ar << m_sMyStruct.m_nCount;
            ar << m_sMyStruct.m_dAvg;

            m_MyObject.Serialize(ar);
    }
    else
    {
            // Load the data from the archive (on File/Open)
            ar >> m_sString1;
            ar >> m_sString2;
            ar >> m_sString3;

            ar >> m_sMyStruct.m_nCount;
            ar >> m_sMyStruct.m_dAvg;

            m_MyObject.Serialize(ar);
    }
}
```

Here are a few important observations:

- The expression ar.IsStoring() is automatically TRUE when writing to the archive (*i.e.*, File/Save) and FALSE when reading from it (*i.e.*, File/Open).

- The order is which data is stored is not important, as long as the very same order is respected when the data is read, and vice-versa. If you store m_sString1, m_sString2, and m_sString3 in that order, you must read them in that very same order. Naturally, the exact same number of variables must be stored and loaded.

- The data is saved in binary format. Hence, if you take a look at the data file created from Serialization(), you will see gibberish. The file content is not human-readable at all.

Besides implementing your Serialize() methods, there are still a few other things you must implement to ensure a flawless compilation and execution.

First, only CObject-derived classes can be serialized. Hence, in the example above, the class CMyObject must have been derived from CObject. This is usually not a problem.

Secondly, remember that CObject-derived object are indeed serializable, but not by default. Deriving a class from CObject is not enough; you must include the macro DECLARE_SERIAL in the class definition and you must add the macro IMPLEMENT_SERIAL in the implementation file. Here is the declaration of CMyObject, followed by its implementation:

```
// In MyObject.h

class CMyObject: public CObject          // Must derive from CObject
{
    DECLARE_SERIAL(CMyObject)            // Make the class serializable

    . . .                                // Some private data

public:

    CMyObject();
    void    Serialize(CArchive& ar);     // Its own Serialize()
};
```

```
// In MyObject.cpp

IMPLEMENT_SERIAL(CMyObject, CObject, 1)  // Serialization implementation

CMyObject::CMyObject()
{
    . . .
}
```

```
void CMyObject::Serialize(CArchive& ar)    // Called from the document
{
    if (ar.IsStoring())
            ar << . . .                    // Store data in the archive
    else
            ar >> . . .                    // Load data from the archive
}
```

DECLARE_SERIAL() only requires the class name, and it must appear in the class declaration.

IMPLEMENT_SERIAL() requires the class name, the parent class name and an arbitrary revision number. As your object "evolves", you can increase the version number to differentiate old class implementations in old data files[45]. The macro must appear outside any method.

15.8 AN MFC APPLICATION EXAMPLE

Boy, that's a lot of material to grasp! Luckily, you'll get accustomed to it very quickly. To help put the blocks in place, take a look at the ScribbleCE sample, on the CD-ROM (see Figure 15-22). This is an adaptation of the popular Scribble tutorial (provided with Visual C++).

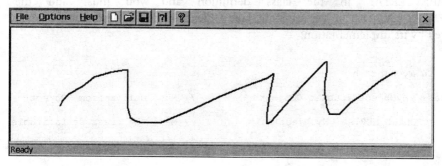

Figure 15-22: ScribbleCE's main window.

The core of the project is composed of four source files (.cpp) and corresponding header, each of which implement a key class.

- The document is implemented in ScribbleCEDoc.cpp and ScribbleCEDoc.h.

- The view is defined in ScribbleCEView.cpp and implemented in Scribble CEView.cpp.

---

[45] Although this is drastic: files containing an older revision number than the current can no longer be read!

- The frame can found in `MainFrm.cpp` and `MainFrm.h`.

- The application class resides in `ScribbleCE.cpp` and `ScribbleCE.h`.

Among the points of interest:

- The user can set the background color to his/her preference. Hence, the view handles the `WM_ERASEBKGND` message (sent by `CPaintDC` just before processing `WM_PAINT`). The color itself is kept in the registry (between executions) by the application class.

- The frame implements a status bar, not generated by default.

- As found in the original implementation, the document uses a list of `CStroke` objects, using a MFC link list template (`CTypedPtrList`), detailed in Chapter 14. The linked list is not fully encapsulated in order to minimize the differences with the initial implementation.

SUGGESTED READINGS

Microsoft, Inside Windows CE

> Design goals and implementation issues are discussed by the people who designed Windows CE right at Microsoft.

Microsoft, Visual C++ online help

> The "Visual C++ Tutorials" section contains the Scribble tutorial, which served as the basis for the ScribbleCE application described in this chapter.

Chapter 16

Drawing

Drawing is often the most rewarding aspect of Windows programming: you can directly contemplate the results of your efforts. Although drawing makes it easy for the user, it is another story for developers. This chapter presents how to draw within an application. Specifically, it presents the Graphics Device Interface (GDI) and the device contexts (DC).

16.1 DRAWING CONCEPTS

Drawing presents a dilemma: it makes applications much simpler to use than their console-based counterparts[46], but it requires much more work to implement. As a result, too many applications implement a trade-off: they implement some graphical elements, but not fancy enough. The result: applications with poorly designed user interfaces[47]. The problem is the difficulty of developing well-designed graphical applications, as well as the artistic talent it requires (a problem too many project managers refuse to recognize). Drawing graphics has to be taken seriously and is not easy. But by following a few guidelines, almost any developer can implement adequate drawing algorithms. This section focuses on how drawing should be approached. It does not focus on how to produce images from a mathematical standpoint (3D matrix transformations and so on), but rather what it takes to draw on Windows CE.

---

[46] I'm sure that there are hordes of Unix developers ready to argue, but users have the final word on that issue.

[47] That's what Unix gurus are ready to argue about, but I already agree with them, so ...

16.1.1 Drawing Is A Serious Business

First and foremost, you must recognize that drawing is not easy and that it must be taken quite seriously under Windows. Not that drawing as such is particularly difficult: most programmers are able to draw after little training. Yet, if the *mechanics* behind drawing is not well understood, applications suffer accordingly. And they are easy to identify:

- When resizing a window, the screen repeatedly flickers (it gets constantly redrawn for no apparent reason), whereas the content of the screen itself does not change.

- An application displays some animation, but what you notice the most is that annoying flickering again.

- While using a scroll bar to see a graph larger than the screen, the visible graph portion does not redraw quickly enough, resulting in the scroll bar not being responsive.

- Overall drawing is slow (drawing a complex image takes minutes!), and freezes the application (which temporarily does not respond to user commands when redrawing).

This section explains basic drawing concepts and efficient related techniques which, when applied, greatly enhance responsiveness.

16.1.2 When To Draw

There are three situations when an application must draw (or paint, in Windows terminology):

- When Windows tells the application to do so.
- When something must be drawn *now*.
- When some changes in the application data need to be shown.

Let's explore the first case. First, you must know that Windows is taking a closer look to the screen (internally), and knows which application is on top of others. If closing or moving an application uncovers parts or all of another application, that other application is instructed, by Windows, to redraw itself (see Figure 16-1). Windows does not cache window contents; instead, Windows sends one single message (WM_PAINT) to an application to refresh themselves, whether the window must be displayed fully (such as upon creation) or partially (when uncovered). From an application standpoint, that message can be received at any point, depending on the user's activity. Thus, the application code that processes WM_PAINT must be able to repaint the exact appearance of the application at *any* moment. Applications do not have to repaint their controls, as they take care of themselves (being windows themselves, they do receive WM_PAINT as required too).

There is an important Windows concept that lies under that approach: the invalid rectangle theory. Any area that must be repainted is marked as *invalid* by Windows CE. For instance, whenever a part or the entire application becomes visible, the regions that need to be repainted are said to be invalid. Whenever a window region is invalid, WM_PAINT is added to the message queue for that window. If other regions become invalid before WM_PAINT is processed, they will simply accumulate, but only one WM_PAINT will remain in the queue. That message has a low priority: it is processed when there is no other message in the queue. That allows your application to respond to more important messages (such as mouse movements) and paint the final representation of the data when everything is quiet.

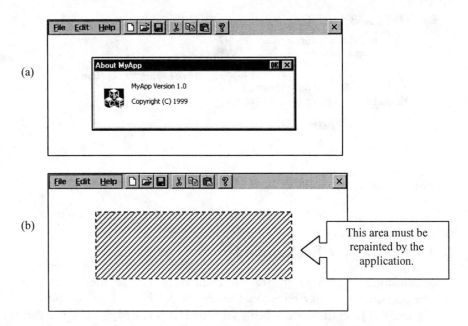

Figure 16-1: In (a), an application window is partially covered by a dialog box. In (b), when the dialog box is removed, the underneath area must be repainted ... by the application itself.

The second case where you have to paint is when some graphics must be shown *now*. Consider the case when the user is drawing a line using the mouse. The drawing occurs when processing mouse messages; no WM_PAINT message is directly involved. Instead, painting then occurs in the processing of the mouse messages.

Applications can also use the invalid rectangle approach to refresh themselves. For instance, if an application displays the status of some mechanical process, it might force a full refresh every 15 seconds. Instead of having a function to refresh and another to process WM_PAINT, the application can invalidate some or all of its client area every 15 seconds. Self-invalidating is done by calling InvalidateRect() and specifying a rectangle to invalidate. Windows then places a WM_PAINT message in the message queue, which will be processed eventually by the application (usually almost instantaneously, depending on the system load). If painting must occur *immediately* after invalidating the rectangle, you can call UpdateWindow(). This function forces WM_PAINT to be processed instantly if there is a pending WM_PAINT message in the message queue (there is one after calling InvalidateRect()). Here is an example:

```
// Called every 15 seconds
void CMyWnd::Refresh()
{
    RECT    rect;

    // Get full client area size
    GetClientRect(&rect);

    // Invalidate the client area and force the background
    // to be repainted (TRUE).
    InvalidateRect(&rect, TRUE);

    // Force WM_PAINT to be processed immediately (in OnPaint(), below)
    UpdateWindow();
}

// WM_PAINT handler.
void CMyWnd::OnPaint()
{
}
```

16.1.3 Erasing the Background

Self-invalidating is perhaps the easiest method to update the screen from within the application, since it simply relies on the WM_PAINT handler to complete. By default, the invalid area will be erased before being repainted. It is erased in the sense that it is repainted with the background brush found in the window class.

An erased background is often very convenient, since the application can redraw from scratch. Not erasing the background would superimpose drawing, which is often an undesired effect[48]. But erasing has one drawback: flickering. When scrolling an image, or performing some animation, a rapid succession of erasing-painting-erasing-painting is noticable to the user, and degrades the application.

The best way to prevent flickering is not to erase the background when invalidating. This is achieved by calling CDC::InvalidateRect(), specifying some rectangle coordinates and FALSE (instead of TRUE) to prevent erasing. But this method works well

---

[48] You can always claim that this is a *feature* instead of a bug.

only when the window's client area is static and never changes (otherwise you end up with superimposition), a case where few applications qualify.

In Section 16.3.8 we'll see a few real world, applicable techniques to reduce flickering to levels that make it almost unnoticeable.

16.2 GRAPHICAL DEVICE INTERFACE

Drawings are handled by functions commonly referred to as the Graphical Device Interface (GDI)[49]. These functions can be arbitrarily grouped into the following categories.

- Device contexts (introduced in Chapter 9)
- GDI objects: bitmaps, brushes, fonts, palettes, pens, and regions
- Drawing primitives: rectangles, ellipses, text, etc.
- Printing primitives
- Device capabilities

    These categories are reviewed in the following sections

16.2.1 Device Contexts

A device context (DC, for short) is an internal structure that governs how drawing operations take place on a specific device. Three device types are supported:

- Display, *i.e.*, video adapters and monitors
- Printer
- Memory (to perform some drawing in memory, a technique known as double-buffering).

Device contexts provide an abstraction layer by shielding from the applications the exact details of the physical devices they draw upon. Consequently, applications do not need to be concerned about the video adapter that is present, nor the exact printer they intend to print to. Applications "draw" through a device context, which in turn outputs the graphics on the device (see Figure 16-2).

One can picture a device context as a window drawing board. A device context is always associated with a window (soon we'll see how), and graphical operations performed on that device context are rendered within the associated window.

---

[49] In other Windows operating systems, these functions are implemented in a DLL called GDI.EXE. In CE, they are all part of GWES.EXE.

In C, applications must acquire a device context in order to draw in a window, and must release it when done[50]. For instance, an application acquires one device context in order to process a WM_PAINT message and releases it when done. That same acquire-release approach must be repeated for subsequent WM_PAINT messages.

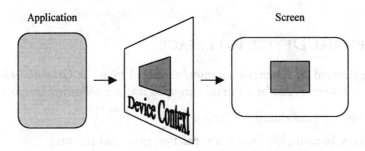

Figure 16-2: Applications draw using a device context, which in turn displays the output on the device (through device drivers).

With MFC, applications simply need to instantiate a CDC-derived class. CDC is itself a pure abstract class that solely defines an interface. There are three derived classes that implement that interface, and they must be used under specific circumstances: CPaintDC, CClientDC, and CWindowDC.

CPaintDC

CPaintDC can only be used to process WM_PAINT. Its constructor requires the window to paint into. Consider the following example:

```
void CMyWnd::OnPaint()
{
    // Instantiate a CPaintDC object, passing 'this' as the window
    // to paint into.
    CPaintDC       dc(this);

    // Use dc to paint with the 'this' window.
    .
    .
    .
}
```

Under the hood, CPaintDC's constructor and destructor call Win32 functions: BeginPaint() and EndPaint(), respectively. The first function initializes the device context in a way such that any graphical primitive that draws outside invalid areas is simply discarded (since there is no need to draw over areas already valid). The second function

---

[50] Historically, there were only a few device contexts, shared among all the applications.

notifies Windows that the painting is completed, which removes WM_PAINT from the message queue. This is very important; otherwise, the paint handler would be called all over again.

CClientDC

CClientDC can only be used for drawing within the client area when processing a message other than WM_PAINT, typically mouse messages. For instance it is used by ScribbleCE (introduced in Chapter 14) as the user draws. Its constructor also requires the window to paint into, typically this. Consider the following example:

```
void CMyWnd::OnMouseMove(UINT uFlags, CPoint pt)
{
    CClientDC        dc(this);

    // Use dc to paint
    .
    .
    .
}
```

Another approach to obtain a device context given a CWnd-derived object is to call CWnd::GetDC(), which returns a generic pointer to a CDC-derived object. This pointer can be used to render graphics, by calling CDC methods. When done, the application must call CWnd::ReleaseDC(), passing that pointer. For instance, the following example is equivalent to the previous one:

```
void CMyWnd::OnMouseMove(UINT uFlags, CPoint pt)
{
    CDC *   pDC;

    pDC = GetDC();                       // Obtain a DC using 'this'

    // Use pDC to paint
    .
    .
    .

    ReleaseDC(pDC);                      // Release the DC
}
```

Under the hood, those two CWnd methods invoke their Win32 equivalent: ::GetDC() and ::ReleaseDC, respectively. But interestingly enough, CClientDC's constructor and destructor rely on those very two methods as well, making the two approaches equivalent.

CWindowDC

CWindowDC is almost equivalent to a CClientDC. The only difference is that it allows drawing anywhere over the window, not only within the client area. Hence, an application could draw over its title bar if desired. Few applications use CWindowDC, but it's good to know that it's there.

In an MFC application using the document/view architecture, drawing is usually done in the view, a window in itself. When painting in the view, using either ClientDC or a CWindowDC makes no difference because the view has no border or title bar; the client area is the same as the window area. However, painting in the main frame using a CWindowDC allows painting anywhere in the window, including over the title and the borders (if present), whereas using a CClientDC allows painting in the client area only.

Common Pitfalls

As you can see, there are two device context class types, and they have to be used in their respective contexts. Choosing the proper device context is extremely important. Here are three common mistakes to watch for.

1. Using CClientDC instead of CPaintDC when processing WM_PAINT.

    CPaintDC's destructor notifies Windows that the area is now valid. It's only upon that notification that WM_PAINT is truly removed from the message queue. CClientDC's destructor does not exhibit that behavior; if CClientDC is used, WM_PAINT remains in the queue, and forces the paint handler to be called over, indefinitely in fact. The application will remain a little responsive because WM_PAINT is a low-priority message. But the whole system will slow down because the CPU will be 100% busy all the times. So when processing WM_PAINT, use CPaintDC.

2. Using CPaintDC instead of CClientDC when drawing in a handler other than the one processing WM_PAINT.

    When a device context is obtained via a CPaintDC, graphical operations that are performed outside invalid areas are automatically discarded by Windows (for efficiency considerations). For instance, if a small area is invalidated, but the WM_PAINT handler repaints the entire window, only the graphic primitives that draw within that small area is truly executed; the others are discarded. If the entire window is valid (*i.e.*, no invalid area), any graphic primitives executed via CPaintDC will be discarded, and nothing will be drawn. At best, only the primitives over the invalid areas will be shown, very unlikely the desired result. On the other hand, using a CClientDC ensures that all graphical primitives are rendered on the screen, independently of the invalid area(s), if any.

3. Using CWindowDC instead of CClientDC when drawing in a handler (other than the one processing WM_PAINT). The coordinate (0,0) is a CWindowDC is the top left corner of the window, whereas it is the top left corner of the client area when using a CClientDC. Hence, the image is not drawn at the proper place. Coordinates are described below.

Coordinate System

A coordinate system establishes how graphical coordinates are interpreted when drawing within a device context. Specifically, it identifies where the point of origin (0,0) is located, the orientation of the x and y axes, and how to translate logical to physical coordinates. For instance, when drawing a rectangle using the coordinates of (20, 20, 50, 30), the coordinate system dictates where the rectangle is drawn.

For instance, the following example produces the output shown in Figure 16-3:

```
void CMainWindow::OnPaint()
{
    CPaintDC        dc(this);

    dc.Rectangle(20, 20, 30, 50);
}
```

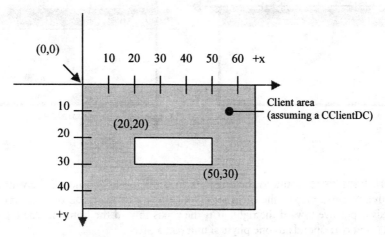

Figure 16-3: A coordinate system determines the origin and orientation of a Cartesian system. This figure demonstrates the MM_TEXT coordinate system using a CClientDC.

All Windows operating systems (CE, 9x, and NT) have two types of coordinate space. The first one is *logical* and measures 2^{32} units high and 2^{32} units wide; the second is *physical* (also called *device* coordinate space), and measures 2^{27} units high by 2^{27} units wide. Applications always draw using <u>logical</u> coordinates, which are internally translated into physical (or device) coordinates. The active *mapping mode*, specified in the device context, determines how that translation happens. There is always a mapping mode active within a device context. Windows CE supports only one mapping mode: MM_TEXT. Other Windows platforms support other mapping modes, allowing applications to work with logical coordinates expressed in inches, millimeters, etc.

MM_TEXT is an inverted Cartesian system (as shown in Figure 16-3):

- The origin (0,0) is the upper left corner of the area associated with the device context. This area is the window when using a CWindowDC, or the client area when using either a CClientDC or CPaintDC. Figure 16-4 illustrates coordinate systems depending on the type of device context being used.

- The y-axis is inverted, as its units increase toward the bottom. The inversion has been retained because that is how Western people read text (hence the name MM_TEXT): from left to right, top to bottom.

- One logical unit equals one physical unit (*i.e.*, one pixel). Hence, there is a direct map between the logical system and the physical device. For instance, drawing a rectangle from the logical coordinates (20,20) to (50,30) produces a rectangle 30 pixels wide and 10 pixels high.

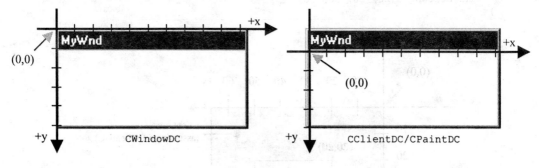

Figure 16-4: MM_TEXT positions the origin (0, 0) at the top left corner of the window area (with a CWindowDC) or the client area (with either a CClientDC or CPaintDC). The x-axis is positive toward the right, as is the y-axis toward the bottom. One logical MM_TEXT unit corresponds to one physical unit (*i.e.*, a pixel).

The device context classes we've seen so far provide numerous drawing methods to draw shapes, text, etc., using coordinates based on MM_TEXT. Section 16.3 details those methods.

It is important to remember that each device context interprets coordinates based on a specific window, and independently of the other device contexts in the system. For that reason, a window (a CWnd pointer, in fact) must always be specified as an argument when constructing a CDC-derived object (as shown in the previous code examples). In addition, the drawing area is being limited (depending on the device context), a process known as clipping, described in a few pages.

An application can query the size of its client area by calling CWnd::GetClient Rect(). The returned coordinates are relative to the client area, making the top-left corner (0,0) and the bottom-right corner (width,height). CWnd::GetWindowRect() returns the coordinates of the entire window (including title bar, borders and scroll bars, if any) in screen coordinates. You can use CWnd::CalcWindowRect() in order to determine the size of a window based on a desired client area size (this is useful when creating a window of a given client area size). An application can call GetDeviceCaps() in order to retrieve device-dependent information but this is rarely required. The use of those functions will be demonstrated later.

You've certainly noticed that some coordinates are sometimes expressed in client coordinates, sometimes in window or even screen coordinates. The coordinate system is the same (MM_TEXT), but the origin differs. There are many cases where applications must mix and match coordinates with different origins. Here are two examples:

- When processing a mouse message (such as a stylus tap), the coordinates that are passed to the handler are always relative to the window (not the client area); but in order to draw using a CClientDC (the common case), coordinates must be relative to the client area (although this doesn't make a difference for a view);

- When showing a pop-up menu (also called a context menu, described in Chapter 17), the position of the menu must be specified in screen coordinates (*i.e.*, relative to the top-left corner of the screen). However, applications typically determine those coordinates using the client area.

Fortunately, MFC (and Win32) provides some conversion functions (listed in Figure 16-5), used in the subsequent chapters.

Conversion function	Description
CWnd::ClientToScreen()	Translates a point or a rectangle, initially in client coordinates, into screen coordinates.
CWnd::ScreenToClient()	Translates a point or a rectangle, initially in screen coordinates, into client coordinates.

CWnd::MapWindowPoints()	Translates window coordinates into another window's window coordinates. These functions will be used in subsequent chapters.

Figure 16-5: Coordinate conversion functions available in MFC.

Viewport

We've seen so far that a device context is a "drawing board" with a coordinate system to draw graphics. Remember that the logical coordinate system defined within the device context is very large (2^{32} by 2^{32}) and only a fraction of it is shown on the screen; that visible surface is called the *viewport*. You can mentally picture the viewport as a twin coordinate system on top of the logical coordinate system, as shown on Figure 16-6. The viewport uses the same coordinate system (*i.e.*, MM_TEXT), and its origin is directly mapped onto the origin of the coordinate system.

The interesting aspect of the viewport is that it floats on top of the coordinate system. In fact, the viewport is always fixed; it's the logical coordinate system that can be moved against it. This is very useful for scrolling, as we'll see shortly.

As shown in Figure 16-6, the origin of the viewport is aligned on top of the origin of the logical coordinate system. Win32 (but not MFC) provides a call to change that alignment, and position the origin of the coordinate system onto another viewport's coordinate. That call is ::SetViewportOrgEx() and requires four arguments: a device context handle, an x and y coordinate within the viewport, and a pointer to a POINT structure, to hold the previous alignment point. Consider this WM_PAINT handler:

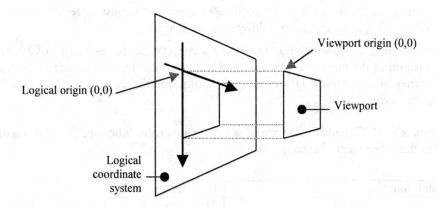

Viewport origin (0,0)

Logical origin (0,0)

Viewport

Logical coordinate system

Figure 16-6: The viewport is the visible area of the very large coordinate system.

```
void CMainWindow::OnPaint()
{
    CPaintDC      dc(this);
    CPoint        pt;

    // Align the coordinate system to the viewport coordinate (0,20)
    ::SetViewportOrgEx(dc.m_hDC, 0, 20, &pt);

    dc.Rectangle(20, 20, 50, 30);
}
```

The output of that function *without* the call to SetViewportOrgEx() is shown in Figure 16-3; the output *with* the call is shown in Figure 16-7. The viewport is the visible area, and the rectangle shown on Figure 16-7 is kind of shifted downward compared to Figure 16-3, despite that the logical coordinates remain *identical*. Internally, the GDI automatically translates all logical coordinates taking into account the new origin specified by SetViewportOrgEx().

As mentioned earlier, this is a very convenient feature to scroll, since the GDI applies the transformation, not the application. Once the scrolling amount is known, an application simply has to adjust the viewport origin, and draw as usual, using the exact same coordinates, and the output turns out to be scrolled. The alternative to that method would be to maintain the initial origin alignment, but recalculate all drawing coordinates before calling drawing methods, a more tedious approach.

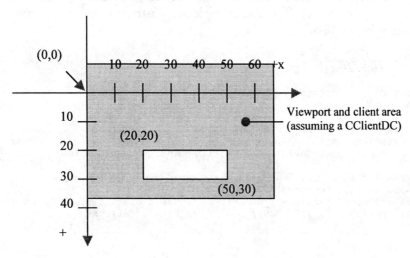

Figure 16-7: Relocating the logical origin of the coordinate system against the viewport (the grayed area) kind of slides the viewport around. In fact, it's the logical coordinate system that is moved. The viewport is the area the user sees.

Clipping

The device context not only determines the coordinate system, it also enforces some drawing boundaries, summarized in Figure 16-8. Windows CE makes sure that any graphical operations stay within the default boundaries. For instance, drawing a huge rectangle in a CClientDC will only be visible within the associated window, not outside of it.

When using	Graphics are clipped (or limited to)	The largest drawing area is
CClientDC	The client area	CWnd::GetClientRect()
CPaintDC	The invalid areas	CDC::GetClipBox()
CWindowDC	The whole window	CWnd::GetWindowRect()

Figure 16-8: Device contexts also limit the extent of graphical operations. The functions on the right indicate how to obtain the largest drawing surface given a device context.

Clipping is a fundamental computer graphic concept. It is used by Windows CE for performance considerations, and by applications to draw complex images (or to make drawing easier in some cases).

Consider an application that wants to draw the upper half of a circle. Whereas it is difficult to draw such an object precisely, it can easily be done by creating a region that establishes the drawing boundaries, and selecting that region as the clip region by calling CDC::SelectClipRegion(). The next example demonstrates exactly that, producing the window shown in Figure 16-8.

```
void CMyWnd::OnPaint()
{
    CPaintDC        dc(this);
    CRgn            rgn;

    // Define the clip region as a rectangle.
    rgn.CreateRectRgn(30, 30, 130, 80);    // Create a rectangular region
    dc.SelectClipRgn(&rgn);                // Apply the clip area

    // Draw a circle. Only the part that is in the clip rectangle
    // will in fact be shown.
    dc.SelectStockObject(BLACK_BRUSH);     // Use a black filling brush
    dc.Ellipse(30, 30, 130, 130);          // Draw an ellipse
}
```

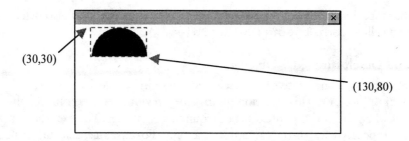

Figure 16-8: Drawing a circle using a clip region (the dotted line) makes it easy to draw only half of a circle. Without the clip or a specialized call, this is difficult to achieve.

Applications can also take advantage of clipping regions to improve drawing (more in Section 16.3.8).

16.2.2 GDI Objects

The GDI supports six types of objects to perform drawing operations: bitmaps, brushes, fonts, regions, palettes, and pens. They are used with graphic primitives in order to render graphics. For instance, to draw a line, you must create a pen carrying the desired attribute (thickness and color), select it in the device context, and call a primitive that draws a line.

To makes things more complicated, only one object per type can be selected, or active, at any time. For instance, to draw another line having different attributes, another pen must be created and selected before calling the line drawing primitive. The motivation has to do with the graphic primitives themselves: they rely on the currently selected objects to draw. For instance, the line drawing primitive implicitly uses whatever pen object is selected.

Creating and Deleting GDI Objects

MFC provides a class for each type of GDI object, all derived from CGdiObject: CBitmap, CBrush, CFont, CRgn, CPalette, and CPen. It is important to realize that each of those object is simply a C++ class that encapsulates a handle; the real graphical objects reside within Windows[51]. Hence, it is not sufficient in some cases to create an instance of a GDI object class. The application must also create the object by invoking a creation method. For instance, a pen is created not by instantiating a CPen object, but by calling either CPen::CreatePen() or CPen::CreatePenIndirect(). Each object is carefully reviewed in the following sections.

Once no longer required, these objects must be destroyed. By default, the destructor of the classes enumerated above delete the associated GDI object. This is important on small-

---

[51] This is the same concept as the one used with CWnd versus a window handle.

scale systems since it would result in memory leaks otherwise. You may also delete an object "manually" by calling `CGdiObject::DeleteObject()`.

Selecting and Deselecting GDI Objects

A GDI object is made active (or selected) within a device context by calling `CDC::SelectObject()`. This function returns the previous selected object, which should be re-selected when the device context is not required any further. The exact return value is a pointer to a temporary class of the same resource type. For instance, selecting a pen returns a temporary `CPen` object, representing the previously selected pen.

Consider the next example (see Figure 16-10): it selects a red pen and draws a red line. Then it selects a green pen and draws a green line. Finally, it restores the initial pen into the device context and returns. This application has been generated without a document, and only the modified methods are shown.

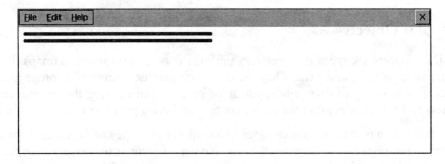

Figure 16-10: The output of the example that follows.

```
// ChildView.h

class CChildView: public CWnd
{
    CPen    m_RedPen;
    CPen    m_GreenPen;


    .
    .
    .

};
```

```
// ChildView.cpp
// Only the modified methods are listed below

const COLORREF RED      = RGB(255, 0, 0);
const COLORREF GREEN    = RGB(0, 128, 0);

CChildView::CChildView()
{
```

```
    // Create the two pens. They will destroy themselves when
    // this view goes out of scope.
    m_RedPen.CreatePen(PS_SOLID, 5, RED);
    m_GreenPen.CreatePen(PS_SOLID, 5, GREEN);
}

void CChildView::OnPaint()
{
    CPaintDC dc(this);

    // Select the red pen, and keep a pointer to the
    // previously selected one. The CPen object pointed to
    // is temporary and cannot be used outside this method.
    CPen * pPrevPen = dc.SelectObject(&m_RedPen);

    // Draw a red line
    dc.MoveTo(10, 10);
    dc.LineTo(300, 10);

    // Then select the green pen. SelectObject() returns
    // a pointer to m_RedPen, which is not needed.
    dc.SelectObject(&m_GreenPen);

    // Draw a red line.
    dc.MoveTo(10, 20);
    dc.LineTo(300, 20);

    // Select the initial previous pen.
    dc.SelectObject(pPrevPen);
}
```

You can determine the objects currently selected in a device context by calling one of the following methods:

- `CDC::GetCurrentBitmap()`
- `CDC::GetCurrentBrush()`
- `CDC::GetCurrentFont()`
- `CDC::GetcurrentPen()`.

The current palettes and regions are obtained differently as seen later.

Finally, Windows stores default GDI objects that can be retrieved through `CDC::GetStockObject()`. Figure 16-11 lists the available parameters to that function.

Stock object value	Description
BLACK_BRUSH	Solid black brush
DKGRAY_BRUSH	Solid dark gray brush
GRAY_BRUSH	Solid gray brush
HOLLOW_BRUSH	Hollow brush
LTGRAY_BRUSH	Light gray brush

NULL_BRUSH	Null brush. Ideal to make the interior of shapes transparent.
WHITE_BRUSH	Solid white brush
BLACK_PEN	Solid, 1-pixel wide black pen
NULL_PEN	Transparent pen. Ideal to make the outline of shapes transparent.
WHITE_PEN	Solid, 1-pixel wide white pen
DEVICE_DEFAULT_FONT	Device-dependent default font
SYSTEM_FONT	System font
DEFAULT_PALETTE	Default color palette, consisting of 20 static colors.

Figure 16-11: The stock objects available via CDC::SelectStockObject().

The next example draws a transparent circle, whose outline is black.

```
// Select a null brush, otherwise the circle will be filled with
// the currently selected brush.
dc.SelectStockObject(NULL_BRUSH);

// Select a black pen for the outline.
dc.SelectStockObject(BLACK_PEN);

// Draw the circle.
dc.Ellipse(10,10, 100, 100);
```

CPen

A CPen encapsulates a pen, an object to draw individual lines and shape outlines. Pens are created by the constructor, or by calling either CDC::CreatePen() or CDC::CreatePen Indirect(). The former accepts a style, a width, and a color, whereas the latter requires the same parameters to be specified in a structure of type LOGPEN.

The style is either PS_SOLID for a plain line, PS_DASH for a dashed line, or PS_NULL to create an invisible pen. The width is expressed in pixels. The smallest width is 1, and is also the fastest to draw. Note that dashed lines with a width larger than one are drawn solid (a limitation in CE). Finally, the color is a COLORREF value.

Also remember that Windows CE internally stores a few stock pens, which can be created through CGdiObject::CreateStockObject().

The following example creates a few pens:

```
// First pen: dash blue line
CPen        Pen1(PS_DASH,  1, RGB(0, 0, 128));

// Second pen: solid, 2-pixel thick, red line
CPen        Pen2(PS_SOLID, 2, RGB(128, 0, 0));

// Third pen: dash green line
```

```
CPen        Pen3;

Pen3.CreatePen(PS_DASH, 1, RGB(0, 128, 0));

// Fourth pen: solid 4-pixel thick, red line
CPen        Pen4;
LOGPEN      lp;

lp.lopnStyle    = PS_SOLID;
lp.lopnWidth.x  = 4;
lp.lopnColor    = RGB(128, 0, 0);

Pen4.CreatePenIndirect(&lp);

// Fifth pen: a standard black pen
CPen        Pen5;

Pen5.CreateStockObject(BLACK_PEN);
```

CBrush

A brush is a graphic object to fill the interior of closed shapes, and is represented by a CBrush in MFC. For instance, drawing a red rectangle is done by selecting a red brush and calling CDC::Rectangle(). The outline is the rectangle is determined by the current pen.

Brushes can be color- or bitmap-based. The easiest method to create a custom brush is to call CBrush::CreateSolidBrush(), which takes a color as input (such as RGB(255, 0, 0) for red). An application can create a brush based on system colors by calling CBrush::CreateSysColorBrush(), and passing a system color index (such COLOR_3DFACE, COLOR_3DHIGHLIGHT, COLOR_ACTIVEBORDER, COLOR_DESKTOP, COLOR_WINDOW, etc.) For instance, using COLOR_WINDOW returns a brush with the current window background color, whatever it is.

Use CBrush::CreatePatternBrush() for bitmap-based brushes, which requires a bitmap object as input, or CBrush::CreateDIBPatternBrush(), which requires a device-independent bitmap handle or a BITMAPINFO pointer followed by an array of bytes defining the pixels of the bitmaps. Bitmaps are described next.

The CBrush object has two overloaded constructors, which accepts either a COLORREF color or a pointer to a CBitmap object, respectively creating a solid colored or a bitmap brush.

The following example creates a few brushes:

```
// Brush 1: a solid red brush.
CBrush      Brush1(RGB(255, 0, 0));

// Brush 2: same as Brush 1.
CBrush      Brush2;
```

```
Brush2.CreateSolidBrush(RGB(255, 0, 0));

// Brush 3: a COLOR_WINDOW brush
CBrush       Brush3;
Brush3.CreateSysColorBrush(COLOR_WINDOW);

// Brush 4: a bitmap brush.
CBitmap      Bitmap;
Bitmap.LoadBitmap(IDB_BITMAP1);

CBrush       Brush4(&Bitmap);

// Brush 5: same as Brush 4
CBrush       Brush5;
Brush5.CreatePatternBrush(&Bitmap);

// Brush 6: a standard NULL brush.
CBrush       Brush6;
Brush6.CreateStockObject(NULL_BRUSH);
```

CBitmap

A bitmap is a series of bits that produce an image when mapped on a device. Although there are device-dependent bitmaps and device-independent ones, most of the bitmap operations use the latter format. Windows CE supports many depths: 1, 2, 4, 8, 16, 24, and 32 bits per pixel (bpp). Compressed bitmaps (such as Run-Length Encoded) are not supported. Applications are encouraged to compress their bitmaps in order to reduce memory needs.

CBitmap objects can be created by setting individual bits in it, but usually they are simply loaded from a resource, which is built using a graphical editor. The following example illustrates how easy it is to use a bitmap resource:

```
CBitmap      Bitmap;
Bitmap.LoadBitmap(IBM_MYBITMAP);
```

Beyond that point, bitmap support is not as trivial as one would expect. For instance, there is no drawing primitive to take a bitmap handle and draw it on the screen (something like DrawBitmap()). Displaying a bitmap requires loading the bitmap and selecting into a memory device context, and copying it from the memory device context to a physical device context.

Here are two helper functions to display bitmaps. The first one, DrawBitmap(), displays a bitmap "as is", whereas the second, DrawTransparentBitmap(), makes all pixels of a given color (typically the background color) transparent.

```
void DrawBitmap(CDC * pDC, WORD BitmapID, POINT pt)
{
    CBitmap Bitmap;
```

456

```
    CDC      MemDC;
    BITMAP  bm;

    // Load the bitmap and gets its width and height.
    Bitmap.LoadBitmap(BitmapID);
    Bitmap.GetBitmap(&bm);

    // Create a memory device context and selects the bitmap in it.
    MemDC.CreateCompatibleDC(pDC);
    MemDC.SelectObject(&Bitmap);

    // Copy the bitmap from the memory device context onto pDC.
    pDC->BitBlt(
          pt.x, pt.y,                   // Position in pDC
          bm.bmWidth, bm.bmHeight,      // Size to copy from MemDC
          &MemDC,                       // DC to copy from
          0, 0,                         // Position in MemDC
          SRCCOPY);                     // Copy operation
}

void DrawTransparentBitmap(CDC * pDC, WORD BitmapID, POINT pt,
    COLORREF TransparentColor)
{
    CBitmap Bitmap;
    CDC            MemDC;
    BITMAP  bm;

    Bitmap.LoadBitmap(BitmapID);
    Bitmap.GetBitmap(&bm);

    MemDC.CreateCompatibleDC(pDC);
    MemDC.SelectObject(&Bitmap);

    ::TransparentImage(
          pDC->m_hDC,                   // Destination device context
          pt.x, pt.y,                   // Position in destination dc
          bm.bmWidth, bm.bmHeight,      // Size in destination dc
          MemDC.m_hDC,                  // Source device context
          0, 0,                         // Position in source dc
          bm.bmWidth, bm.bmHeight,      // Size is source dc
          TransparentColor);            // Transparent color
}
```

Those functions could be called as follows:

```
const COLORREF RED = RGB(255, 0, 0);

void CMyView::OnPaint()
{
    CPaintDC dc(this);

    // Draw the bitmap IDB_BITMAP1 at (10, 10).
    DrawBitmap(&dc, IDB_BITMAP1, CPoint(10, 10));

    // Assuming the background color is RED, transparently draw
```

```
      // the same bitmap at (100, 10)
      DrawTransparentBitmap(&dc, IDB_BITMAP1, CPoint(100, 10), RED);
}
```

`DrawBitmap()` uses `CDC::BitBlt()` to copy a bitmap from one device context to another. `CDC::BitBlt()` simply transfers pixels from coordinates in a source device context to other coordinates, in the same or other device context. The last parameter is called the raster operation code and alters the bits as they are copied. In the previous example, `SRCOPY` indicates to simply copy the bits as is (*i.e.*, they remain unaltered). Three other modes are listed in Figure 16-12. The `CDC` class also defines other functions, listed in Figure 16-13, to manipulate bitmaps.

Raster operation code	Description
SRCAND	Combines the source and destination images using a logical AND
SRCINVERT	Combines the source and destination images using a logical XOR
SRCPAINT	Combines the source and destination images using a logical OR

Figure 16-12: Raster operations while copying bitmaps.

CDC Bitmap Method	Description
CDC::GetPixel()	Retrieves the color at a specific coordinate
CDC::MaskBlt	Copies a bitmap by combining its color to the destination area
CDC::PatBlt()	Copies a bitmap by combining its color to the device context's default brush
CDC::SetPixel()	Sets the color of a specific pixel.
CDC::StrecthBlt()	Copies and resizes a bitmap (the final bitmap can be either shrunk or enlarged)

Figure 16-13: A few CDC methods that copy bitmaps while applying some interesting effects.

Font Objects

A font, implemented as a `CFont` in MFC, designates a collection of glyphs (symbols, characters) that share a common design, based on three attributes:

- Typeface: width, height, spacing, etc.

- Style: normal, bold, italic, etc.

- Size: expressed in points (1 point is roughly 1/72 inch, or 72 points is about one inch high). A common point size is 12.

Windows supports two types of fonts: TrueType and Raster. A TrueType font describes each glyph in terms of vectors and can be used at any size. A Raster font represents each glyph as a small bitmap for specific sizes. Using a TrueType font at any size produces a very good quality because each glyph is constructed using the vector specifications. On the other hand, a Raster font will be displayed well if the size is directly supported, but when scaled to other sizes, some distortion is introduced and produces a lower quality. TrueType fonts are implemented in .FOT and .TTF files, whereas Raster fonts are stored in .FON files. Windows CE supports both types, but one a time.

A font is created by calling either CFont::CreateFont(), CFont::CreateFont Indirect() or CFont::CreatePointFont(). Those names are misleading: they do not create a font as such, they merely make it accessible to the calling applications. If an application is requiring a font not directly supported (*e.g.,* "Tahoma" on a system that does not have it), the system will arbitrarily chose another "matching" font. Hence, those methods invariably return a font, albeit not always the one requested.

Of those three methods, CFont::CreatePointFont() is the easiest to use: it requires a point size (in tenth of a point), a typeface, and a device context. This method internally fills up a LOGFONT structure and invokes CFont::CreateFontIndirect(), by passing that LOGFONT structure and a device context. That device context is internally used to calculate the exact size of the font to match the desired point size, given the number of pixels per inch.

Applications can fill a LOGFONT structure and make the call themselves too. The other function, CFont::CreateFont(), requires a battery of arguments, essentially the same contained in the LOGFONT structure. Section 16.3.7 provides a method to calculate the exact size of a font based on the actual number of device pixels per inch.

An alternative is to invoke one of the logical fonts readily available, by calling CGdiObject::CreateStockObject(). For instance, specifying SYSTEM_FONT returns a proportional font used by Windows to display window titles, menu names and dialog box text.

Here are a few example of creating fonts:

```
// Font 1: Tahoma, 12 points
Font1.CreatePointFont(120, _T("Tahoma"));

// Font 2: Times Roman, 14 points
LOGFONT      lf;

memset(&lf, '\0', sizeof(lf));
lf.lfHeight    = -14;
lf.lfWeight    = FW_HEAVY;
lf.lfItalic    = TRUE;
lf.lfUnderline = TRUE;
_tcscpy(lf.lfFaceName, _T("Times Roman"));
```

```
Font2.CreateFontIndirect(&lf);
```

`CDC::GetTextMetrics()` retrieves a font's physical dimensions, whereas `CDC::GetTextExtent()` returns the height and width of a specific string given the currently selected font. These functions are useful when aligning text strings.

As it is with other GDI resources, the chosen font must be selected (by calling `CDC::SelectObject()`) as the current font before a text drawing primitive is invoked.

Finally, the Win32 function `::EnumFontFamilies()` allows an application to obtain the list of all installed fonts. This is useful to present a dialog box that lets the user chose a specific font (such as in a word processor).

Palette Objects

Palettes manage colors. So first, let's explain how colors are presented. Colors are represented by the COLORREF type, a 32-bit integer. The macro RGB() can be used for initializing a variable of that type. That macro accepts red, green, and blue intensities (in that order), ranging from 0 to 255. Here are a few examples:

```
RGB(255, 0, 0)          // Red
RGB(0, 255, 0)          // Green
etc.
```

The macros `GetRValue()`, `GetGValue()` and `GetBValue()` extract the intensity for the red, green, and blue colors respectively, from a 32-bit color value.

Colors are then displayed through display devices. But display devices have different capabilities: some can display a few colors, whereas other can accommodate millions of them. The ability of displaying colors depends on the number of bits that is available for each pixel, commonly called *bits per pixel* (bbp). For instance, a monochrome system displays consist of one bit per pixel. Hence a pixel can either be black (0) or white (1). Today's display adapters provide up to 24, even 32, bits per pixel, hence offering billions of colors. Windows CE must support a variety of display capabilities. Hence, CE directly supports pixel depths of 1, 2, 4, 8, 16, 24, and 32 bits per pixel (bbp).

But that's half of the story. Some display devices support multiple bits per pixels, but can only represent a certain number of colors at any time. For instance, a display device may support 8 bits per pixel (for a total of 256 colors), but can only display 16 at any time. A color palette is an array that contains the colors that can be shown. In this example, that array would consist of 16 colors. Note that display drivers that can represent all colors do not need a palette. If the above display device can display its full 256 colors, it does not need any palette.

460

Windows creates a palette each time an application creates a device context. The palette is based on the underlying device's capabilities. When an application specifies a color (using the RGB() macro, which returns a color as a 32-bit value), the closest match is identified in the palette and is the color used on the display.

The best-case scenario is a display that supports 32 bits per plane and that can represent any 32-bit color. In the worst case scenario, the palette would be quite limited and would prevent the application from creating supplemental palettes, to have access to other sets of colors. Only one palette can be selected at a time in the device context.

An application can call GetDeviceCaps() to identify the underlying graphical capabilities. For instance, the parameter NUMCOLORS returns the number of supported colors; BITXPIXEL returns the number of bits per pixel; etc.

Applications can modify existing palettes (to customize them), or they can create alternate palettes to use very specific colors (such as subtle shades of blue), when the color adapter can only render a limited number of colors.

Region Objects

Regions, implemented in MFC using CRgn, are one or more rectangular areas that may or not overlap. What makes them interesting is that they can be used with numerous graphical operations such as clipping and drawing to obtain interesting effects.

Regions are created by calling either CRgn::CreateRectRgn() or CRgn::Create RectRgnIndirect(). The former takes the top-left and bottom-right coordinates of a rectangle, whereas the latter accepts a pointer to a RECT structure. Windows CE imposes a limit about region coordinates: they must be expressed as 16-bit values.

Here are a few examples of creating regions:

```
CRgn          rgn1;

rgn1.CreateRectRgn(10, 10, 100, 50);

CRgn          rgn2;
CRect         rect(10, 10, 100, 50);

rgn1.CreateRectRgnIndirect(&rect);
```

Two regions can be combined together and form a third region by calling CRgn::CombineRgn(). The call requires a parameter that specifies how that combination should take place. Figure 16-14 lists the possible values

Combine Mode	The Created Region Is
RGN_AND	The intersection of the two specified regions.
RGN_COPY	A copy of the first region.
RGN_DIFF	The part of the first region that does not intersection with the second.
RGN_OR	The combination of the two regions.
RGN_XOR	The combination of the two regions except the parts that intersect.

Figure 16-14: The various region combine modes.

CRgn implements various methods to manipulate regions, listed in Figure 16-15.

Rectangle Functions	Description
CRgn::EqualRgn()	To determine if two regions are equal in size and shape.
CRgn::GetRgnBox()	Returns the tightest rectangle around a region.
CRgn::OffsetRgn()	Offset all parts of a region.
CRgn::PtInRegion()	Returns TRUE if the specified point is in the region.
CRgn::RectInRegion()	Returns TRUE if the specified rectangle is in the region.

Figure 16-15: The most common CRgn methods.

The last two functions are particularly useful to determine whether some graphical objects are part of a given region. PtInRegion() and RectInRegion() return TRUE if the specified point or rectangle lies, partially or entirely, in the specified region.

Graphics Mode

The operations explained earlier are conducted using default graphics mode, which render them as one would expect. But the default graphics mode can be altered to introduce special effects.

The background mode alters text and dashed pens operations. By default, it is set to OPAQUE: the background is rendered using the default window background color, as specified in the window class. The background color can be changed by setting it with CDC::SetBkColor() and specifying an RGB color. Alternatively, the background mode can be set to be transparent, by calling CDC::SetBkMode() with TRANSPARENT, in which case, the background color is ignored. It is very common to call SetBkMode() with TRANSPARENT when outputting text. We'll see some examples shortly.

The foreground mode combines pen and brush operations with the color already in the window. There are 16 possible permutations, essentially binary operations, which can be set by calling CDC::SetROP2(). Figure 16-16 lists the most common.

Foreground Mode	The Result of a Pen or Brush Operation Is
R2_BLACK	Black, regardless of the colors used with the pen and/or the brush
R2_COPYPEN	The pen color
R2_NOT	The inverse of the window color, on a pixel basis
R2_XORPEN	An XOR combination of the pen and window color.

Figure 16-16: A few foreground mode set with CDC::SetROP2().

16.3 DRAWING PRIMITIVES

Once a device context is available and GDI objects have been created, an application can finally draw. This section simply presents an overview of the most useful methods. If you're curious about more details, you should definitely browse the CDC online documentation. Also Petzold's book remains the ultimate Win32 reference in this regard. The **Drawing** sample, on the CD-ROM, demonstrates many calls explained in this section.

16.3.1 Line Drawing

Lines are drawn using the current pen object in the device context, using the default foreground mode. If two lines of different colors must be painted, two pens are required and must be selected one at a time. Lines can be drawn individually or along shapes.

In the first case, an application can call CDC::MoveTo() to set a current position, and then call CDC::LineTo() to draw from that point up to the specified point, which then becomes the new current position. The application could then repeatedly call CDC::LineTo() to draw a series of connected lines. Another method, CDC::Poly line(), takes an array of points and the number of points in that array, and draws a series of connected lines. All those calls use the currently selected pen.

The next section (about shapes) explains how to use pen to draw shape outlines.

16.3.2 Shapes

Shapes are geometric forms (*e.g.*, circles, rectangles, etc.) that are filled with the current brush and outlined with the current pen of a given device context. Figure 16-17 lists the most common functions that output shapes. These functions are easy to use and simply require a device context handle and coordinates.

Methods	Description
CDC::Draw3dRect()	Draws a three-dimensional rectangle.
CDC::DrawDragRect()	Erases and draws a rectangle. This is ideal to provide feedback when the user is dragging the stylus.
CDC::DrawEdge()	Draws rectangle edge with special effects (sunken, etc).
CDC::DrawFocusRect()	Draw a focus rectangle (using a dotted pen). Very useful with custom controls to indicate that they have the focus.
CDC::DrawIcon()	Draws an icon.
CDC::Ellipse()	Draws an ellipse based on the specified top-left and right-bottom coordinates. Circles are a simple case of ellipse. Ellipse() is slow and should be called sparingly.
CDC::FillRect()	Fills a rectangle without drawing a line around it. It also simply requires a color (a 32-bit value) instead of a brush handle.
CDC::FillRgn()	Fills an area as defined by a region.
CDC::FillSolidRect()	Fills a rectangle with a COLORREF color.
CDC::FrameRect()	Draws a border around a rectangle.
CDC::InvertRect()	Inverts the content of a rectangle.
CDC::Polygon()	Draws a polygon connected by straight lines.
CDC::Polyline()	Can also draw a rectangle with the four corner coordinates.
CDC::Rectangle()	Draws a rectangle using the current pen and current brush.
CDC::RoundRect()	Outputs a rectangles whose corners are rounded instead of squared. This function is also drawn slowly and should be used as seldom as possible.

Figure 16-17: CDC's shape-drawing methods.

You can select null object to achieve "transparent" effects. For instance, if you don't want the shape outline to be drawn, you can select a null pen by calling CDC::GetStockObject() with NULL_PEN. Similarly, if all you want is the shape outline, leaving the interior of the shape transparent, you can select a null brush by calling the same function, with the argument NULL_BRUSH.

16.3.3 Text

Text designates character strings to ouput. Text is rendered through fonts, not pens. The only fonts that can be used are those already installed on the particular CE system the application is running on.

Text can be formatted by setting the device context accordingly. The text color can be changed by calling `CDC::SetTextColor()`, whereas `CDC::GetTextColor()` returns the current color. The text is drawn in a rectangle whose color is the background color; however, text is very commonly drawn using a transparent mode (by calling `CDC::SetBkMode()` with TRANSPARENT).

Finally, the two methods that draw text are `CDC::DrawText()` and `CDC::ExtTextOut()`. The former offers more options, such as left, center, and right alignment within a rectangle area, whereas the latter simply output characters from the specified coordinates. `CDC::DrawText()` is very popular thanks to its numerous options.

Some methods are also available to align text, by calculating the space a string occupies given the current font. `CDC::GetTextExtent()` accepts a string and returns a `CSize` object that holds the width and height in pixels.

16.3.4 String Table

Unicode strings can be directly hard-coded into an application, or they can be stored as a resource. The second approach is recommended because strings can be changed without altering the source code. Resource strings also make it easier to translate an application into another language: only the resource strings have to be changed. The following shows an example of a string table in a resource script. Applications usually use one string table, but they may use as many as they want.

```
STRINGTABLE DISCARDABLE
BEGIN
    ID_FILE_NEW              "Create a new document"
    ID_FILE_OPEN             "Open an existing document"
    ID_FILE_CLOSE            "Close the active document"
    ID_FILE_SAVE             "Save the active document"
    ID_FILE_SAVE_AS          "Save the active document with a new name"
    ID_FILE_PAGE_SETUP       "Change the printing options"
    ID_FILE_PRINT_SETUP      "Change the printer and printing options"
    ID_FILE_PRINT            "Print the active document"
    ID_FILE_PRINT_PREVIEW    "Display full pages"
END
```

Resource strings can be accessed in a read-only mode, or they can be loaded into an application buffer. In the next example, the first call to `CString::LoadString()` loads a string in a buffer, which can later be modified, whereas the second call returns a read-only pointer directly to the resource. The first approach is required only if the string is expected to be modified; otherwise, the second approach is faster.

```
CString     sString;              // Read-write CString
TCHAR       sBuffer[128];         // Read-write buffer
LPCTSTR     pszString;            // Read-only pointer

// Load a resource string into sString
sString.LoadString(IDS_MY_STRING);

// Load a resource string into sBuffer
LoadString(AfxGetInstanceHandle(), IDS_MY_STRING, sBuffer, 128);

// Get a pointer to a read-only resource string.
pszString = LoadString(AfxGetInstanceHandle(), IDS_MY_STRING, NULL, 0);
```

Once a string is loaded, you can process it like any other string.

16.3.5 Images

There are various methods to draw images. You can use a combination of the shape methods explained above. An easier method is to rely on resources, respectively icons and bitmaps, described in the following paragraphs.

Icons

An icon is a small image that represents an application, file, or other object. They are very interesting because their background is transparent. They come in two sizes: 16x16 and 32x32, but they can be enlarged and shrunk quite easily as we are about to see. An icon is kept in a single .ICO file and it can contain the two icon formats. The resource file (.rc) associates an identifier with an icon file name as follows:

```
IDI_MYICON          ICON               "myicon.ico"
```

Here are a few examples of icon use:

- The application icon (32x32) is typically shown in the About dialog box (activated from the Help menu).

- Applications (.exe) contain a default application icon, which is displayed in the *Start* menu, in the Explorer and so on. Windows automatically extracts that icon and displays it. Either size is used, depending on the user's preferences.

- An application can also load display icons in arbitrary locations on the client area. Because their background is transparent, they are a convenient way to display small

466

images just about anywhere. Both CWinApp::LoadIcon() and ::LoadImage()
load an icons; the former loads the default icon size[52], and the latter allows you to
specify the desired size (width and height), a very convenient feature. Loading an icon
means gaining a handle to it, which must be eventually released. The following example
loads an icon, displays it and destroys it:

```
class CChildView : public CWnd
{
    HICON            m_hIcons[4];
    .
    .
    .
};

CChildView::CChildView()
{
    // Load the IDR_MAINFRAME icon (size: 16x16)
    m_hIcons[0] = static_cast<HICON>(::LoadImage(AfxGetInstanceHandle(),
          MAKEINTRESOURCE(IDR_MAINFRAME), IMAGE_ICON, 16, 16, 0));

    // Load the IDR_MAINFRAME icon (size: 20x20)
    m_hIcons[1] = static_cast<HICON>(::LoadImage(AfxGetInstanceHandle(),
          MAKEINTRESOURCE(IDR_MAINFRAME), IMAGE_ICON, 20, 20, 0));

    // Load the IDR_MAINFRAME icon (size: 32x32)
    m_hIcons[2] = static_cast<HICON>(::LoadImage(AfxGetInstanceHandle(),
          MAKEINTRESOURCE(IDR_MAINFRAME), IMAGE_ICON, 32, 32, 0));

    // Load the IDR_MAINFRAME icon (size: 40x40)
    m_hIcons[3] = static_cast<HICON>(::LoadImage(AfxGetInstanceHandle(),
          MAKEINTRESOURCE(IDR_MAINFRAME), IMAGE_ICON, 40, 40, 0));
}

CChildView::~CChildView()
{
    for (int i = 0;i < 3; i++);
          ::DestroyIcon(m_hIcons[i]);
}

void CChildView::OnPaint()
{
    CPaintDC dc(this);

    // Draw the four icons at various locations. CDC::DrawIcon() requires
    // the icon's top left corner position when drawing.
    dc.DrawIcon(CPoint(10,  10), m_hIcons[0]);
    dc.DrawIcon(CPoint(30,  10), m_hIcons[1]);
    dc.DrawIcon(CPoint(60,  10), m_hIcons[2]);
    dc.DrawIcon(CPoint(100, 10), m_hIcons[3]);
}
```

---

[52] That size can be obtained by calling GetSystemMetrics() with SM_CXICON and SM_CYICON.

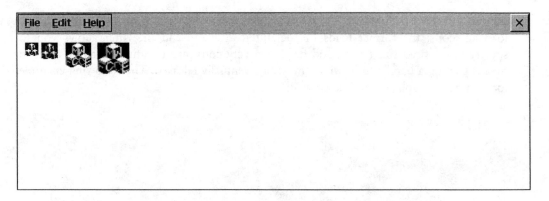

Figure 16-18: Loading and displaying icons. These four icons are actually based on one single icon, stored in the 16x16 and 32x32 formats. Windows automatically chose the proper size and enlarge/shrunk the icon to match the desired size.

Bitmaps

A bitmap is an image stored into its own file. Being a resource, that file is merged within the application .EXE, and is accessible by using its identifier. The following shows a bitmap resource script:

```
IDB_MYBITMAP        BITMAP  DISCARDABLE     "mybitmap.bmp"
```

Section 16.2.2 explained how to load and use bitmaps using CBitmap objects.

16.3.6 Device Capabilities and System Metrics

An application can query the capabilities on a specific device by calling CDC::GetDevice Caps(). That function requires an index parameter and returns some related values. For instance, one can query the exact size of the screen, the number of planes per pixels, and whether some graphical functions are supported or not (such as bitmaps, drawing lines, etc.). One common use of this function is to determine the *exact* size of a font based on the desired point:

```
int GetExactFontHeight(CDC * pDC, int nPoint)
{
    return -(pDC->GetDeviceCaps(LOGPIXELSY) * nPoint / 72);
}
```

In this example, the returned value could directly be used with CDC::CreateFont().

Applications can obtain some system metrics (width and height, in pixels) of various windows graphical elements, by calling ::GetSystemMetrics(), and passing an index of the desired metric. These metrics are useful to render precise graphics, and to align visual components. Figure 16-24 lists some common indices used with that function.

Metric	Description
SM_CXBORDER, SM_CYBORDER	Width and height of a window border
SM_CXCURSOR, SM_CYCURSOR	The size of a cursor, when a mouse cursor is supported.
SM_CXSCREEN, SM_CYSCREEN	Size of the primary display

Figure 16-24: Some of the valid metrics to request via GetSystemMetrics().

16.3.7 Efficient Painting Techniques

Painting is too often neglected in terms of optimization. Yet, this is what users notice the most. An application that performs efficient painting is usually well appreciated by its users. There are a few techniques that can be applied to speed up painting.

Calculate Once, Paint Multiple times

The first technique is straight-forward: when processing WM_PAINT, paint and paint only. That means that this is not the place to calculate where each graphical object should appear on the screen. You will certainly agree that it is much more efficient to calculate things once and draw numerous times, than repeatedly calculate *and* draw! Here's an example to illustrate the idea. The following piece of code draws a rectangle centered in the window. A quick and dirty implementation would perform the calculation right in the processing of WM_PAINT. A better approach is to calculate the position when the window is resized (WM_SIZE) – the message is also sent at creation – and simply use the position in WM_PAINT:

```
class CChildView : public CWnd
{
    CRect   m_rect;
    .
    .
    .
};

void CChildView::OnPaint()
{
    CPaintDC        dc(this);
    .
    .
    dc.FillSolidRect(m_rect, RGB(255, 0, 0));
```

```
}

void CChildView::OnSize(UINT nType, int cx, int cy)
{
    CRect   rcClient(0, 0, cx, cy);

    m_rect.SetRect(0, 0, 30, 20);
    m_rect.OffsetRect((cx - 30) / 2, (cy - 20) / 2);
}
```

I agree that the quick and dirty method in that example is not going to bring the system to its knees in terms of performance degradation. But the concept remains the same in larger applications, which do make a differece to the system performance. Always remember that WM_PAINT is placed in the application queue at any point in time, independently of what your application is doing. Calculating everything ahead will make your paint function much leaner and more important, faster. Users will *love* it!

Identify Objects to Paint

The second technique is more demanding. We know that WM_PAINT is sent whenever your application, or a portion of it, needs repainting. And Windows knows internally what parts of your application are valid from those that are not. To speed things up, all graphical operations that you perform on valid regions are internally discarded by Windows. Hence, your application might uselessly consume (precious) CPU cycles executing these graphical commands that will not be rendered anyway. Consider an application that displays a large graphic, larger than the screen. Obviously, only the screen portion needs to be drawn. So your application should determine beforehand if the objects to draw truly require being drawn.

We saw earlier that Windows CE maintains for each window an internal list of invalid areas to redraw when WM_PAINT is delivered. Whenever a CPaintDC object is instantiated, the device context's clipping area is set to those invalid areas; graphical operations that fall outside this clipping area are internally discarded by Windows (it's faster to discard them than to draw graphics over valid areas that do not need to be painted).

An application can obtain the tightest rectangle around all invalid areas within a window by calling CDC::GetClipBox(), and repaint in that area only. If only a fraction of the window needs repainting, the application will not waste CPU cycles repainting valid window area.

For a better painting control, an application may determine whether each object needs (or not) to be repainted. All you need is to be able to identify the smallest rectangle that surrounds each object (by calculating and keeping the coordinates of each object internally). Then, when processing WM_PAINT, call CDC::RectVisible() for each object; that method returns non-zero if part of that rectangle intersects with the clipping region and hence, needs repainting. If the returned value is 0, that object does not need repainting at all. Consider Figure 16-25, which shows an application that draws a certain number of rectangles of various sizes and colors, also implemented in the **Rects** sample, on the CD-ROM.

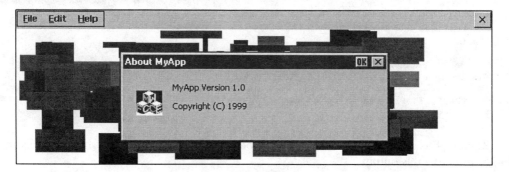

Figure 16-25: A rectangle-drawing application. Moving this dialog box requires repainting of some rectangles.

Here's the non-optimized implementation:

```
const int   OBJ_COUNT = 100;

class CChildView : public CWnd
{
    CRect        m_rect[OBJ_COUNT];       // Rectangles
    COLORREF     m_color[OBJ_COUNT];      // Colors
    .
    .
    .
};

// An inline function that returns a random number between nMin and nMax.
inline int RandomNumber(int nMin, int nMax)
{
    return rand() % (nMax - nMin + 1) + nMin;
}

// Initialize the rectangle and color arrays.
CChildView::CChildView()
{
    for (int i = 0; i < OBJ_COUNT; i++)
    {
        m_rect[i].left   = RandomNumber(0, 500);
        m_rect[i].top    = RandomNumber(0, 150);
        m_rect[i].right  = m_rect[i].left + RandomNumber(5, 100);
        m_rect[i].bottom = m_rect[i].top  + RandomNumber(5, 50);
        m_color[i]       = rand();
    }
}
```

```
// Paint all rectangles. The use of 'nCount' is to indicate how many
// objects are being painted each time OnPaint() is invoked.
void CChildView::OnPaint()
{
    CPaintDC        dc(this);
    int             nCount = 0;              // To gather statistics

    for (int i = 0; i < OBJ_COUNT; i++)
    {
            dc.FillSolidRect(m_rect[i], m_color[i]);
            nCount++;
    }

    TRACE(_T("Painted %d objects\n"), nCount);
}
```

Running this application and moving the About MyApp dialog box (as shown on Figure 16-25) produces this output:

```
Painted 100 objects
Painted 100 objects
Painted 100 objects
Painted 100 objects
Painted 100 objects
Painted 100 objects
Painted 100 objects
Painted 100 objects
    . . .
```

This implementation of OnPaint() can be significantly optimized by using CDC::RectVisible(), as follows:

```
// Paint rectangles that need to be drawn
void CChildView::OnPaint()
{
    CPaintDC        dc(this);
    int             nCount = 0;              // To gather statistics

    for (int i = 0; i < OBJ_COUNT; i++)
            if (dc.RectVisible(m_rect[i]))
            {
                    dc.FillSolidRect(m_rect[i], m_color[i]);
                    nCount++;
            }

    TRACE(_T("Painted %d objects\n"), nCount);
}
```

This implementation produces the following debug output while dragging the About MyApp dialog box:

```
Painted 100 objects
Painted 23 objects
Painted 22 objects
Painted 19 objects
Painted 26 objects
Painted 6 objects
Painted 8 objects
Painted 9 objects
Painted 6 objects
Painted 1 objects
Painted 2 objects
. . .
```

As a result, fewer objects are being drawn. This strategy can be pushed further: when an object has been identified as needing some repainting, it might be worth it to identify what part of the object needs repainting. That can be useful in the case of a very complex graphical object. However, it is not always judicious to push that approach too far, as your application will spend more time identifying what to paint, rather than painting. For instance, in the previous example, it is simpler just to output whole rectangles, than using CPU cycles to identify what parts to draw instead.

Use Multiple Device Contexts

If an application uses many resources, it may be constantly selecting various GDI resources in it (pens, brushes, etc.). An application can get more than one device context (by using additional device contexts). Each device context can be set to a particular setting. The application then executes graphic primitives using the proper device context. The application releases each of the device contexts it used.

Also, instead of selecting back previous resources, an application can first save the state of a device context by calling CDC::SaveDC(). Later on, after having modified that device context, the application can restore it to the saved state by calling CDC::RestoreDC(). The context is in fact stored in a context stack within CE. Using these two calls relieves an application from restoring an heavily altered device context.

Here's an example using these calls:

```
void CChildView::OnPaint()
{
    CPaintDC dc(this);

    // Save this entire device context.
```

```
    int     nSavedDC = dc.SaveDC();

    // Alter the device context as much as needed. When selecting objects,
    // there is no need to store the previous objects and restore them.
    .
    .
    .

    // Restore the device context to its initial state.
    dc.RestoreDC(nSavedDC);
}
```

Create GDI Objects Ahead

If the same GDI objects are used every time WM_PAINT is called (and this is often the case), it is best to create those GDI objects upon application initialization, and destroy them upon the application termination. Whereas GDI objects were limited in previous versions of Windows, this is not really a concern today (unless you use zillions of them). Painting gets faster as GDI objects simply have to be selected and deselected, not repeatedly created and deleted.

SUGGESTED READINGS

Fowler, GUI Design Handbook

> This book is essentially a reference guide that reviews all existing GUI items that are available in today's operating systems: check boxes, combo boxes, entry field, menus, etc. What's interesting is that each item is described in terms of what it is good for, how to test its usability, and further references.

Galitz, The Essential Guide to User Interface Design

> The book proposes design guidelines for building clear and easy to understand user interface applications, such as selecting the proper type of windows, menu, controls, colors, icons, etc.

Microsoft, Windows Interface Guidelines for Software Design

> This is the book Microsoft would like each of us to meticulously adopt. It describes all aspects of user interface issues, not from a programming standpoint, but from a usability standpoint. Given the success of Microsoft, this is a very valid source of information.

Petzold, Programming Windows, Fifth Edition

This monstrous book (now almost 1500 pages – 2.5-inches thick!) contains a complete description of the Win32 API. There nothing about MFC, but most CDC calls translate directly to Win32 calls. There are numerous chapters about drawing all sorts of things. A must for over-enthusiastic developers.

Chapter 17

Getting Input

All PC companions and other systems running Windows CE can be configured to support a variety of input devices, such as keyboard, stylus (pen) or mouse, touch screen, and voice. Windows CE internally manages the interaction between the user and those devices, and accordingly sends various messages to running applications.

Windows also provides controls (described in Chapter 19) that can directly manage a lot of input themselves, freeing the application from having to do so. It is in fact common for applications to strictly rely on controls to gather input.

This chapter presents how applications can receive and process user's inputs.

17.1 MENUS

Most developers are familiar with menus. In Windows CE, the command bar displays a *menu bar*, which exposes the high-level functionality of the application. Each menu bar item, when tapped, displays a *dropdown menu*, which consists of menu items. Menu items, when tapped, usually carry some actions onto the application, but they can also display *cascading* menus. Figure 17-1 shows those menu types:

- The menu bar consists of "File Edit View Format Tools". Microsoft recommends that the following menu items, when used, be shown in that order:

    File, Edit, View, Insert, Format, Tools, Window

    This doesn't mean that all items are required, nor that others items can't be inserted between two of them. For instance, Figure 17-1 doesn't have **Insert** nor **Window**.

- The menu displayed under "View" is a dropdown menu.

- The menu displayed next to "Zoom" is a cascading menu.

Dropdown and cascading menus are also called pop-up menus and their items are displayed vertically. The application menu bar isn't a pop-up menu, and its items are displayed horizontally.

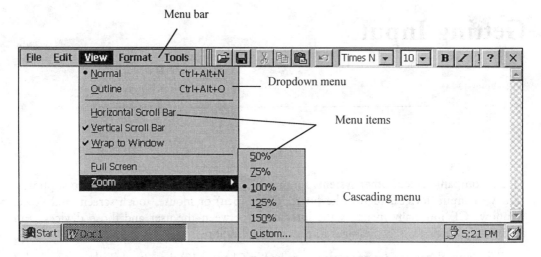

Figure 17-1: Several menu types are available on CE.

17.1.1 Designing Menus

Menus are designed using a resource editor (see Figure 17-2). The top horizontal bar is the menu bar. Clicking on a menu bar item (*e.g.*, File) reveals an empty dropdown menu. Note that in both the menu bar and the dropdown menu, there is always one empty slot (indicated by the thin dotted line rectangle) to add a new item. That empty slot is not shown in the final menu, though. Items can be moved around simply by dragging them; their order is only relevant from an user interface standpoint (not from a programming standpoint).

Each item (whether in the menu bar or dropdown menu) has a set of properties, the minimum being a caption and some style attributes. One of these styles is Pop-up, which is normally set for all the menu bar's items. Pop-up means that clicking on that item reveals another menu. Pop-up can also be applied to a drop-down menu item, in order to show a cascading menu.

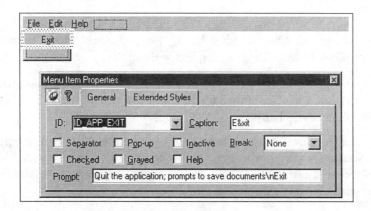

Figure 17-2: Menus are built using a resource editor.

Another style is "`Separator`", which makes the item a horizontal line, useful to visually group related menu items. Other styles can be set in the resource editor (checked, grayed, etc.) but it is often best to handle those attributes right in the application, at run-time, as described on a following page.

Other menus items are commands, and have a command identifier associated with them. Selecting such a menu item sends the `WM_COMMAND` message to the application window, with the menu item identifier in it. The application simply has to handle the command; Windows fully manages the menu otherwise, by highlighting selected menu items, hiding and displaying drop-down menus, and so on.

A command menu item has three important attributes:

- The **command identifier**, which uniquely identifies the menu item. By convention, each identifier is named *ID_menu_item* (*e.g.*, `ID_FILE_OPEN`, `ID_HELP_ABOUT`) or *IDC_menu_item* (*e.g.*, `IDC_VIEW_GRAPH`). The resource editor provides a series of default identifiers to choose from (*e.g.*, `ID_FILE_NEW`, `ID_EDIT_CUT`), but it is best to use custom identifiers with custom menus, *i.e.*, the menu items you add. For instance, in Figure 17-1, the menu item labeled "`50%`" could be `IDC_VIEW_ ZOOM_50`. This is the command identifier sent to the application when the menu item is selected.

- The **caption**, which is the text displayed in the menu. Each item must have a single-letter mnemonic for shortcuts. For instance, within the application, pressing `Alt-F` shows the <u>F</u>ile's drop-down menu and then, pressing 'x' activates the E<u>x</u>it menu item. The letter must be unique within each menu (*i.e.*, menu bar, dropdown menu, etc.) You specify a mnemonic letter by preceding it with '`&`' (*e.g.*, "`&Zoom`" produces "<u>Z</u>oom", '`Z`', or '`z`' being the mnemonic).

Also, by convention, the caption must be followed by an ellipsis (. . .) if clicking on the item requires further user input to conduct an action. For instance, the "`File/Open`" menu item's caption is "Open..." because a file name has to be entered by the user for the file to be opened. On the other hand, "Help/About" doesn't have an ellipsis, because it displays the help About dialog box without requiring any further input[53].

- The **prompt**, which is stored as a resource string using the same command identifier, and that is displayed in the status bar's left pane by CFrameWnd. See Chapter 20 for more details about status bar properties.

Internally, the resource editor generates the corresponding menu template in the application's resource file (.rc), which can simply be ignored. The next example illustrates a simple menu. Note that each MENUITEM line that is not a separator ends with its command identifier (themselves listed in resource.h)

```
IDR_MAINFRAME MENU PRELOAD DISCARDABLE
BEGIN
    POPUP "&File"
    BEGIN
        MENUITEM "E&xit",                      ID_APP_EXIT
    END
    POPUP "&Edit"
    BEGIN
        MENUITEM "&Undo\tCtrl+Z",              ID_EDIT_UNDO
        MENUITEM SEPARATOR
        MENUITEM "Cu&t\tCtrl+X",               ID_EDIT_CUT
        MENUITEM "&Copy\tCtrl+C",              ID_EDIT_COPY
        MENUITEM "&Paste\tCtrl+V",             ID_EDIT_PASTE
    END
    POPUP "&Help"
    BEGIN
        MENUITEM "&About Bar3...",             ID_APP_ABOUT
    END
END
```

AppWizard names the application menu IDR_MAINFRAME. By having this name, that menu is automatically loaded by CFrameWnd as the default application's menu. Hence, there is no need to load or unload the menu; the framework does it for us.

17.1.2 Command Handlers

As mentioned earlier, menu item commands are sent using the WM_COMMAND messages. These messages are sent to the owner of the menu bar: the main frame. The main frame politely re-routes those command messages to the other key classes, namely the view, the

---

[53] It is important not to confuse the need for an ellipsis between gathering further user input and displaying a dialog box (a common misinterpretation). A menu item whose sole action is to display a dialog box (and nothing else) doesn't need an ellipsis.

document, the application class, and then itself (Section 15.6 has the details). What that means is that those command messages can be handled in any of those classes.

Furthermore, ClassWizard has been designed to let you add handlers in a snap. Invoke ClassWizard, choose a class name, a command identifier (any), the COMMAND message, and simply click "Add Function". Figure 17-3 shows ClassWizard being used for adding a command handler in the child view for ID_TOOLS_OPTIONS (*i.e.*, the Options menu item of the Tools menu). Note that the Objects IDs list box contains all command identifiers valid for that class within that application.

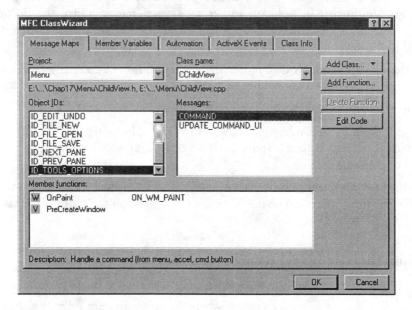

Figure 17-3: ClassWizard makes it easy to add a menu item handler.

Adding the function generates the following handler (the comment is from ClassWizard). Note that command handlers don't receive any parameter, nor do they return any value.

```
void CChildView::OnToolsOptions()
{
    // TODO: Add your command handler code here

}
```

Since command handlers are delivered in a completely random order, some processing cannot be designed to start in one command handler and terminate in another. As a result, an important rule to observe is to make each command handler *complete*: Whatever is started in the handler should be completed in that same handler. For instance, if a handler opens a file, and another one closes it, there is no guarantee that the second handler will ever be called. In fact, the second handler may be called before the first one! Hence, when coding a handler, always make sure that opened files are closed, allocated resources are freed, and so on.

Command handlers are arguably the *motion* of the application. A main window displays some data, which can usually be updated by the user (*e.g.*, the text of a word processor), but command handlers add all sort of processing on that data. As a result, command handlers are very diverse from each other. Here are some examples of typical command handlers:

- Some display a dialog box. For instance, the example above ("Tools/Options") would exactly do that in order to gather user's preferences. Once the dialog box is closed, the options are retrieved and applied on the application's data. Dialog boxes are detailed in the next chapter.

- Some alter the application's data representation (but not the data itself). In PocketWord, "View/Zoom" presents a zoomed-in or zoomed-out view of the document's data.

- Some interact with the clipboard (cut, copy, paste, etc.)

- Some display/hide secondary windows, such as split windows. For instance, in PocketExcel, "View/Split" splits the view into four smaller views, to see various regions of the same file.

- Some directly activate options. In PocketExcel, The option "View/Status Bar" shows/hides the status bar. The menu item is checked when the status bar is visible.

- And so forth.

17.1.3 Updating Menus At Run Time

An excellent method to let the user know that some menu items are non-operational is to disable them. Consider a report generator, where some reports are only available to some users, but not to others. Depending on the user id, some menu items might be enabled and others disabled (see Figure 17-4).

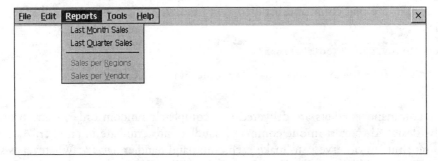

Figure 17-4: In this application, a few menu items are disabled because the user doesn't have the privilege to see the information.

By default, `CFrameWnd` disables all menu items that don't have any associated command handler in the application (or in MFC). Hence, if you add a custom menu item but no handler for it, the item will be disabled. You can override this behavior by setting `CFrameWnd::m_bEnableMenuItem` to `FALSE`, making all menu items enabled at any time, but this is rarely required. Selecting an enabled menu item that doesn't have a handler does nothing (which is confusing for the user).

Update Command Handlers

In addition to command handlers, you can add handlers to control the *appearance* of each menu item. In Figure 17-3, ClassWizard offers to add either a `COMMAND` or an `UPATE_COMMAND_UI` handler. Whereas the first one is used to add a command handler to process the command, the second adds an *update command handler* to alter the appearance of that same menu item. You know by now that command handlers are invoked when the user selects a menu item; update command handlers are invoked whenever the menu they belong to is shown[54].

An update command handler added by ClassWizard resembles the following (the comment is also from ClassWizard):

```
void CChildView::OnUpdateReportsSalesPerRegions(CCmdUI* pCmdUI)
{
    // TODO: Add your command update UI handler code here

}
```

There is always one parameter: a pointer to a `CCmdUI` object. This object represents the related menu item ("`Reports/Sales per Regions`" in this case). A few `CCmdUI` methods are available (listed in Figure 17-5), which directly modify the appearance of the menu item.

Menu Function	Description
`Enable()`	Enables, or disables, the menu item.
`SetCheck()`	Checks, or unchecks, the menu item.
`SetText()`	Changes the menu item caption (permanently).

Figure 17-5: Some `CCmdUI` methods to alter the appearance of menu items.

For instance, the last two menu items of the menu Reports (shown in Figure 17-4) need an `UPDATE_COMMAND_UI` to disable them if the user doesn't have the proper permission. Here is a possible implementation, which uses an hypothetical method called `UserHas`

---

[54] This is another MFC feature, handled by the main frame.

Permission(), which returns TRUE if the user has the specified permission, FALSE otherwise. As a result, each time the Reports dropdown menu is shown, those two menu items are updated according to the current user's permissions.

```
void CChildView::OnUpdateReportsSalesPerRegions(CCmdUI* pCmdUI)
{
    // TODO: Add your command update UI handler code here
    BOOL    bEnable = UserHasPermission(PERMISSION_SALES_PER_REGION);
    pCmdUI->Enable(bEnable);
}

void CChildView::OnUpdateReportsSalesPerVendor(CCmdUI* pCmdUI)
{
    BOOL    bEnable = UserHasPermission(PERMISSION_SALES_PER_VENDOR);
    pCmdUI->Enable(bEnable);
}
```

Menu items are very often dynamically updated at run-time using update command handlers. Usually, command and update command handlers provide enough functionality within an application. In other situations, menus need to be manipulated further, something that can be done using a CMenu object.

CMenu

MFC represents a menu via CMenu. Like most other MFC objects, it's a class that encapsulates a handle (in this case, an HMENU that refers to the resource within Windows), and that exposes some methods that essentially send messages to that handle. The main application menu can be obtained by calling GetMenu() on the main window:

```
CMenu * pMenu = AfxGetMainWnd()->GetMenu();
```

or, within the main frame:

```
CMenu * pMenu = GetMenu();
```

Given a pointer to the menu bar, you can obtain a temporary pointer to a dropdown menu by calling CMenu::GetSubMenu() and specifying a zero-based index. For instance, the following example returns a pointer to the third dropdown menu of Figure 17-2, the "View" dropdown menu:

```
CMenu * pMenu     = AfxGetMainWnd()->GetMenu();
CMenu * pViewMenu = pMenu->GetSubMenu(2);      // 3rd dropdown menu
```

If a dropdown menu contains a pop-up menu (i.e., a cascading menu), you can still invoke GetSubMenu() to access it. Given the pointer to the View menu of Figure 17-2, the next example obtains a pointer to the "Zoom" cascading menu. Note that separators count as one item:

```
CMenu * pZoomMenu = pMenu->GetSubMenu(8);     // 9th menu item
```

Unfortunately, `CMenu::GetSubMenu()` only works by position, not by item name. As a result, if you ever modify the menu structure (by adding or removing items), actual calls to `GetSubMenu()` will no longer work.

The pointer returned by `CWnd::GetMenu()` or `CMenu::GetSubMenu()` is temporary and is only valid within the current handler[55]. But it allows manipulating the underlying menu by calling some `CMenu` methods (listed in Figure 17-6) to add, remove or modify menu items.

Menu Function	Description
`AppendMenu()`	Adds a new menu item or a pop-pup menu at the end of a menu.
`InsertMenu()`	Inserts a new menu item or a pop-up menu at a specific position.
`ModifyMenu()`	Modifies the properties of a specific menu item.
`RemoveMenu()`	Removes a menu item at a specific position. If the item is a pop-up menu, that menu is not deleted (although it should previously be retrieved through `GetSubMenu()` to keep a reference to it).
`EnableMenuItem()`	Enables or disables a menu item. A disabled menu item is grayed and does not send a `WM_COMMAND` when selected.
`CheckMenuItem()`	Checks or unchecks a menu item.

Figure 17-6: A few `CMenu` methods to create, modify or delete menus at run-time.

The last two methods, which update menu items, are rarely needed if the menu items of your applications are updated through update command handlers (the common scenario).

Adding Menu Items

In Visual C++, starting a debugging session adds the `Debug` menu in the application, which is removed once the debugging session is completed. You can do the same on CE: modify a menu at run-time by adding (or removing) complete drop-down menus.

The next example adds a "`View`" dropdown menu, with two menu items: "`Graph`" and "`Numbers`". It starts by creating an empty popup menu, and appends two items. Each item is a string (instead of a separator, for instance), as indicated by `MF_STRING`. The item command identifiers have already been declared within Visual C++ (using the Resource Symbols dialog box, accessible from the `View` menu). Then the pop-up menu is added into the application menu, as the second dropdown menu (as indicated by the position, 2, and the `MF_BYPOSITION` flag). The `MF_POPUP` flags indicates that a pop-up menu is added (as

---

[55] Temporary pointers that are returned by MFC are deleted whenever the application becomes idle, even for a very brief period.

opposed to a string item), and requires the third parameter to be the menu handle (instead of the menu item command id). The last argument is the pop-up menu name, shown in the menu bar.

Note that the menu handle is obtained by calling CMenu::Detach(). This method returns the pop-up menu handle but also ensures that the pop-up menu is not destroyed when ViewMenu goes out of scope (as it would, otherwise):

```cpp
void CMainFrame::AddViewMenu()
{
    CMenu   ViewMenu;

    // Create a standalone pop-up menu
    ViewMenu.CreatePopupMenu();

    // Add the two items.
    ViewMenu.AppendMenu(
        MF_STRING,                // This item is a string
        ID_VIEW_GRAPH,            // Command id
        _T("&Graph"));            // Caption

    ViewMenu.AppendMenu(
        MF_STRING,
        ID_VIEW_NUMBERS,
        _T("&Numbers"));

    // Insert the pop-up menu into the application menu
    // on the third position
    GetMenu()->InsertMenu(
        2,
        MF_BYPOSITION | MF_POPUP,
        reinterpret_cast<UINT>(ViewMenu.Detach()),
        _T("&View"));
}

void CMainFrame::RemoveViewMenu()
{
    GetMenu()->DeleteMenu(2, MF_BYPOSITION);
}
```

Most CMenu methods accept either a menu item position within the menu (0 being the first), or a menu item identifier. For instance, CMenu::InsertMenu() requires the menu item before which the new menu is to be added. Since menu bar items do not have command identifiers, they can only be identified through their respective position. On the other hand, adding a menu item in a dropdown menu could be done by specifying a command identifier instead of a position. Usually, it is better to use command identifiers with dropdown menus with CMenu methods whenever this is possible, because those methods still work even if items are shuffled around later on.

You may have observed that the previous example was implemented in the main frame. You may choose otherwise, for instance by updating the menu from the view. In this case, you only have to call AfxGetMainWnd->GetMenu() to have a hold on the application menu bar. It's really a matter of personal preferences whether you handle the menu in the view or the frame (or somewhere else!)

Radio Menu Items

You can use menu items like radio buttons where selecting one item disables the others. On Figure 17-2, the Zoom menu items form a mutually exclusive group, where choosing one item automatically disables the others in the group. Also note that a dot, instead of a checkmark, is displayed on the left of the selected item.

Although CCmdUI provides a SetRadio() method, it simply calls SetCheck()[56]. But there's a workaround: whenever a menu item of the group is selected (*i.e.*, whenever the related command handler is invoked), obtain a pointer to the parent menu and invoke CMenu::CheckRadioMenuItem().

For instance, the code to handle the "50%" menu item of Figure 17-2 may resemble the following:

```
void CChildView::OnViewZoom50()
{
    .
    .
    .
    CheckZoomMenuItem(ID_VIEW_ZOOM_50);
}

// A private method that enables the specified menu item within the
// Zoom pop-up menu.

void CChildView::CheckZoomMenuItem(UINT uItemID)
{
    CMenu * pMenu = AfxGetMainWnd()->GetMenu();
    CMenu * pViewMenu = pMenu->GetSubMenu(2);
    CMenu * pZoomMenu = pViewMenu->GetSubMenu(8);

    pZoomMenu->CheckMenuRadioItem(
            ID_VIEW_ZOOM_50,        // First menu radio item of the group
            ID_VIEW_ZOOM_CUSTOM,    // Last menu radio item of the group
            uItemID,                // Radio menu item to check
            MF_BYCOMMAND);          // Previous args are command ids
}
```

---

[2] This is on CE only; it displays a dot on other Windows platforms.

17.1.4 Ownerdraw Menu Items

Windows CE supports ownerdraw menu items, *i.e.*, menu items that are not being drawn by the system but by a window (in your application), typically the main frame, the owner of the menu. This is the method to use in order to draw small icons next to some menu items.

Menu items cannot be set as ownerdraw using the resource editor; they must be set programmatically, by calling CMenu->ModifyMenu(), and specifying MF_OWNERDRAW as the second parameter. Alternatively, the style can be specified when calling CMenu::AppendMenu(), in which case the third parameter is not the caption but a user-defined 32-bit value (typically a pointer to some information describing the menu item).

Whenever an ownerdraw menu is to be shown, Windows CE sends two messages to the owner window: WM_MEASUREITEM, to identify the height and width of the item, and WM_DRAWITEM, to draw the item. They are handled, respectively, in CWnd::OnMeasureItem() and CWnd::OnDrawItem(), using the ON_WM_MEASUREITEM and ON_WM_DRAWITEM message map entries.

OnMeasureItem() receives a MEASUREITEMSTRUCT structure, which contains data to identify the menu item being drawn. The handler must store the item's width and height in the itemWidth and itemHeight members. The standard height of a menu item can be obtained by calling GetSystemMetrics(SM_CYMENU). The width of the item directly depends on the caption's length (in pixels). We'll see how to calculate that value in the forthcoming example.

OnDrawItem() receives a DRAWITEMSTRUCT structure, which also describes the menu item to draw. That structure contains a device context ready to be used and the rectangular coordinates of the item, in addition to the item identifier. The handler must draw the described item in all of the possible states: normal, selected, grayed, and checked.

The **Menu** sample (on the CD-ROM) implements an ownerdraw menu (the View menu introduced earlier), very similar to those found on desktops. Figure 17-7 illustrates the output.

Figure 17-7: An ownerdraw menu.

The key methods, OnDrawItem() and OnMeasureItem() are illustrated below. The two menu items are added by specifying a pointer to a structure (of type MENUITEMDATA) containing the menu item's caption (pszCaption) and an image index (nImageIndex) to be used with an image list (image lists are described in detail in Chapter 20).

```
// MainFrm.h

#pragma once

typedef struct
{
    LPCTSTR        pszCaption;              // Menu item caption
    int            nImageIndex;             // Menu item image index
} MENUITEMDATA, * LPMENUITEMDATA;

class CMainFrame : public CFrameWnd
{
    CImageList     m_MenuImageList;          // Image list
    MENUITEMDATA   m_MenuItemData[2];        // Two ownerdraw menu items

        .
        .
        .

};
```

```
// MainFrm.cpp

CMainFrame::CMainFrame()
{
    // Create the image list based on IBM_MENU_BITMAP,
    // which contains the two menu item bitmaps.
    m_MenuImageList.Create(IDB_MENU_BITMAP, 12, 1, RGB(0, 128, 128));

    // m_MenuItemData[0] is the "Graph" menu item
    m_MenuItemData[0].pszCaption  = _T("&Graph");
    m_MenuItemData[0].nImageIndex = 0;

    // m_MenuItemData[1] is the "Numbers" menu item
    m_MenuItemData[1].pszCaption  = _T("&Numbers");
    m_MenuItemData[1].nImageIndex = 1;
}

        .
        .
        .

void CMainFrame::AddViewMenu()
{
    CMenu   ViewMenu;

    ViewMenu.CreatePopupMenu();

    // Add two owner-draw menu items (ID_VIEW_GRAPH and ID_VIEW_NUMBERS),
    // passing as an 32-bit item data the address in m_MenuItemData.
```

```
    ViewMenu.AppendMenu(
            MF_OWNERDRAW,
            ID_VIEW_GRAPH,
            reinterpret_cast<LPCTSTR>(&m_MenuItemData[0]));

    ViewMenu.AppendMenu(
            MF_OWNERDRAW,
            ID_VIEW_NUMBERS,
            reinterpret_cast<LPCTSTR>(&m_MenuItemData[1]));

    GetMenu()->InsertMenu(2, MF_BYPOSITION | MF_POPUP,
            reinterpret_cast<UINT>(ViewMenu.Detach()), _T("&View"));
}

void CMainFrame::OnDrawItem(int nIDCtl, LPDRAWITEMSTRUCT lpdis)
{
    // Pass to parent when drawing anything else than the two menu items
    if (lpdis->CtlType != ODT_MENU || (lpdis->itemID != ID_VIEW_GRAPH &&
            lpdis->itemID != ID_VIEW_NUMBERS))
    {
            CFrameWnd::OnDrawItem(nIDCtl, lpdis);
            return;
    }

    // Get the item data, a ptr to MENUITEMDATA (see AppendMenu() earlier).
    LPMENUITEMDATA pItemData =
            reinterpret_cast<LPMENUITEMDATA>(lpdis->itemData);

    // Get the prepared device context and the rectangle to draw into.
    CDC *   pDC = CDC::FromHandle(lpdis->hDC);
    CRect   rcItem = lpdis->rcItem;

    // Fill the image area with the default menu background color.
    CRect   rect(rcItem);
    rect.right = rect.left + 15;
    pDC->FillSolidRect(rect, ::GetSysColor(COLOR_MENU));

    // Output the associated image.
    m_MenuImageList.Draw(pDC, pItemData->nImageIndex,
            rcItem.TopLeft() + CPoint(1, 1), ILD_NORMAL);

    COLORREF        nBkColor;

    if (lpdis->itemState & ODS_SELECTED)
    {
            // If the item is selected, draw a 3D border
            // around the image area.
            pDC->Draw3dRect(rect, RGB(255, 255, 255), RGB(128, 128, 128));

            // The background color is highlighted (usually dark blue)
            nBkColor = ::GetSysColor(COLOR_HIGHLIGHT);
    }
    else
            // The background color will be normal menu (usually gray).
            nBkColor = ::GetSysColor(COLOR_MENU);

    // Set rect to cover the text area (next to the image area).
```

```
        rect.right = rcItem.right;
        rect.left = rcItem.left + 15;

        // Fill the text area.
        pDC->FillSolidRect(rect, nBkColor);

        // Draw the text. The '&' is *magically* taken care of bu Windows.
        pDC->DrawText(pItemData->pszCaption, -1, rect + CPoint(1, 1), DT_LEFT);
}

void CMainFrame::OnMeasureItem(int nIDCtl, LPMEASUREITEMSTRUCT lpmis)
{
        // Get the item data, a ptr to MENUITEMDATA (see AppendMenu() earlier).
        LPMENUITEMDATA pItemData =
                reinterpret_cast<LPMENUITEMDATA>(lpmis->itemData);

        // Calculate the width of the text.
        CClientDC      dc(this);
        CSize          sz = dc.GetOutputTextExtent(pItemData->pszCaption,
                                _tcslen(pItemData->pszCaption)));

        // Set the width (plus some extra to leave a right margin) and
        // height (using default menu item height).
        lpmis->itemWidth  = sz.cx + 20;
        lpmis->itemHeight = ::GetSystemMetrics(SM_CYMENU);
}
```

17.2 ACCELERATORS

An accelerator is a shortcut to execute a command menu. For instance, many applications support Ctrl-O as an equivalent to the File/Open menu item. Accelerators are built with a resource editor (see Figure 17-8), which produces an accelerator table in the resource file (.rc), such as that one show below:

```
ID_APPACCEL ACCELERATORS PRELOAD MOVEABLE PURE
BEGIN
    "N",            ID_FILE_NEW,            VIRTKEY,CONTROL
    "O",            ID_FILE_OPEN,           VIRTKEY,CONTROL
    "S",            ID_FILE_SAVE,           VIRTKEY,CONTROL
    "P",            ID_FILE_PRINT,          VIRTKEY,CONTROL
    "Z",            ID_EDIT_UNDO,           VIRTKEY,CONTROL
    "X",            ID_EDIT_CUT,            VIRTKEY,CONTROL
    "C",            ID_EDIT_COPY,           VIRTKEY,CONTROL
    "V",            ID_EDIT_PASTE,          VIRTKEY,CONTROL
END
```

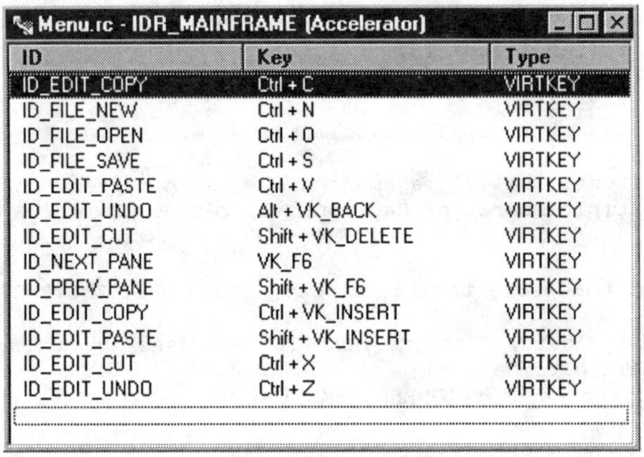

Figure 17-8: Visual C++'s resource editor allows adding accelerator tables.

AppWizard automatically generates a default accelerator table called `IDR_MAINFRAME` (the one shown above), automatically loaded by the main frame (via `CFrameWnd::LoadAccelTable()`). Then, each message being pumped by the application's main thread is passed to `CFrameWnd::PreTranslateMessage()`[57], where the translation accelerator-to-command takes place. The other classes (frame, view and document) only see of an accelerator the related command, not the accelerator itself.

From a development standpoint, it is not important whether a command comes from a menu item, a toolbar button, or an accelerator. All that's left for you to do is to customize that table by adding, updating and removing entries.

17.3 KEYBOARD

Windows sends multiple messages to a window when the keyboard is hit. Since there is one keyboard but many applications, there is an issue as to which window should receive keyboard messages. One solution is to simply notify all windows of keyboard events, but that is unpractical to say the least, as users are using one application at a time. The application being used is called the *active* application. It is easy to identify it, because its title bar is highlighted while the other applications' title bars are grayed. If the active application doesn't contain any control (only a graph, for instance), all keyboard messages are sent to the application window. On the other hand, if the application contains a few controls, one of them is designated as the *current*, and this control has the focus: all keyboard messages will go to that control. Controls usually represent the focus by displaying a thin dotted line, although edit controls show a caret (see Figure 17-9).

---

[57] That method internally calls `::TranslateAccelerator()`.

Windows makes sure that at least one window (or control) has the focus. If the user closes an application that had the focus, the focus is redirected to another window (otherwise keyboard messages would have nowhere to land).

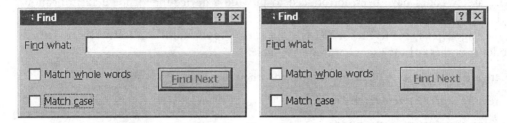

Figure 17-9: Focus usually represented by a thin dotted line around the control (left), but edit controls show instead a caret (right).

17.3.1 Special Keys

The TAB key moves the focus to the next control within a dialog box. That makes it easy to navigate from one control to another by simply using the keyboard. Another method is to position the mouse pointer on a control and click on it, or tap on a control. This also transfers the focus to the control clicked/tapped upon.

Another special key in a dialog box is the Enter key; when pressed, it invokes the *default push button*. A default push button is represented with a thicker border. By default, the OK button is the default push button, but you can choose any other button when designing the dialog box (this is just another button style attribute). However, the default push button moves with the focus. If the focus is on a push button, this button is also the default push button. This makes sense, since pressing the Enter key will go to it, like any other key. If the focus is on another type of control (say a list box), the original default push button, as designed in the dialog box, becomes the default one again. It remains default until the focus is moved onto another push button.

17.3.2 Scan Codes and Virtual Key Codes

At the hardware level, pressing and releasing a key generates a scan code that uniquely identifies the key. When the user presses a key, Windows sends the WM_KEYDOWN message to the active window (or control). If the key is held down long enough, a succession of WM_KEYDOWN messages will follow as well. When the key is released, Windows sends WM_KEYUP. Those messages are *keystroke messages*.

Internally, the application class translates keyboard messages as they are pumped (via `::TranslateMessage()`). Combinations of `WM_KEYDOWN` and `WM_KEYUP` produce `WM_CHAR` messages, which contain a *virtual key code*. `WM_CHAR` is a *character message*.

Virtual key codes have been introduced to provide a device-independent identification to keyboard keys. For instance, the Delete key code is `VK_DELETE` (VK stands for Virtual Key); the Page Up key is `VK_PRIOR`; F1 is `VK_F1`, etc. Applications can safely rely on virtual key codes regardless of the exact hardware available.

Here are two examples of the messages sent when the user presses some keys:

1. Pressing Shift+F1 generates:

    - `WM_KEYDOWN` for `VK_SHIFT`

    - `WM_KEYDOWN` for `VK_F1`

    - `WM_KEYUP` for `VK_F1`

    - `WM_KEYUP` for `VK_SHIFT`

2. Pressing `Shift+G` generates:

    - `WM_KEYDOWN` for `VK_SHIFT`

    - `WM_KEYDOWN` for `VK_G`

    - `WM_CHAR`: code 71 ('G')

    - `VM_KEYUP` for `VK_G`

    - `VM_KEYUP` for `VK_SHIFT`

Other keystroke and character messages are generated as well, such as `WM_SYSKEYDOWN`, `WM_SYSCHAR`, and `WM_SYSKEYUP`, which are generated when the `VK_MENU` key (typically `ALT`) is used along other keys.

17.3.3 Processing Keyboard Messages

All of these messages can be handled by any window, by adding the appropriate entries in the message map (using ClassWizard for instance). Applications that directly read keyboard input are mostly interested in character messages (`WM_CHAR`), whereas keystroke messages (`WM_KEYDOWN` , etc.) are usually passed to default processing.

However, remember that those messages are delivered to the window with the input focus. Most applications use controls (buttons, list boxes, etc.) and one of them usually has the focus, in which case the parent window never receives keyboard messages. A window is always free to ignore those messages; they will be passed to the ancestor class, which will redirect them to Windows itself for default processing. If your application doesn't have any specific keyboard processing requirements, all those messages can be simply ignored.

17.4 STYLUS

A stylus is an alternative to a mouse for small scale devices. For instance, when using a Palm-size PC while standing in line, using a mouse would not be quite practical. The stylus is then a better input device. However, some Windows CE devices also support mice.

The stylus generates mouse messages (see Figure 17-10) as the stylus tip is touching the screen.

Stylus Message	Description
WM_LBUTTONDBLCLK	The stylus has been double-tapped on the screen
WM_LBUTTONDOWN	The stylus has been applied to the screen.
WM_LBUTTONUP	The stylus has been released from the screen.
WM_MOUSEMOVE	The stylus is being dragged on the screen.

Figure 17-10: Stylus messages

Each message is relayed to the top-most window underneath the stylus tip. Hence tapping a push button sends the WM_LBUTTONDOWN message to the push button, not to its parent (which is under the push button).

Note that the WM_LBUTTONDBLCLK message is only sent for windows that have the CS_BLDCLKS class style (windows created with CFrameWnd, CWnd, and CView usually have it). For instance, in a view-only application generated by AppWizard, the child view contains the following code, which registers a window class with CS_DBLCLKS:

```
BOOL CChildView::PreCreateWindow(CREATESTRUCT& cs)
{
    if (!CWnd::PreCreateWindow(cs))
          return FALSE;

    cs.style &= ~WS_BORDER;
    cs.lpszClass = AfxRegisterWndClass(CS_HREDRAW|CS_VREDRAW|CS_DBLCLKS,
          NULL, HBRUSH(COLOR_WINDOW+1), NULL);

    return TRUE;
}
```

Handlers to those messages can be added with ClassWizard. Each handler receives two parameters: flags and the stylus position. Here is the default handler for WM_LBUTTONDOWN, as generated by ClassWizard:

```
void CChildView::OnLButtonDown(UINT nFlags, CPoint point)
{
    // TODO: Add your message handler code here and/or call default

    CWnd ::OnLButtonDown(nFlags, point);
}
```

The flags indicate whether the CTRL and SHIFT keys were pressed at the same time, by respectively setting the MK_CONTROL and MK_SHIFT bits. Consider a drawing application; it is often difficult to a draw a square that is truly square. That application may assist the user if the SHIFT key is pressed as the square is drawn, by making sure all edges are of equal length. The doordinates are relative to the upper-left corner of the window.

17.4.1 Dragging the Stylus

Stylus messages are not too often handled individually, but rather to provide the user with the ability to drag objects (or draw by dragging). Dragging is not too difficult. The idea is to maintain a Boolean that is set between a WM_LBUTTONDOWN and WM_LBUTTONUP. In the meantime, whenever a WM_MOUSEMOVE message is received, the Boolean indicates whether the user is dragging or not.

The following example illustrates how to draw a line from an initial position to the current stylus position. This is achieved by tapping on the window, establishing the initial position. As the stylus is dragged, the line is erased and redrawn from the initial point to the current position. This is repeated until the drag is completed, where a final line is drawn from the initial position to the final position.

```
class CChildView: public CWnd
{
    BOOL    m_bDragging;
    CPoint m_ptInit;
    CPoint m_ptPrev;
    .

    .
};

CChildView::CChildView()
{
    m_bDragging = FALSE;
}

void CChildView::OnLButtonDown(UINT nFlags, CPoint point)
{
    m_bDragging = TRUE;
    m_ptInit    = point;
    m_ptPrev    = point;
```

```
}

void CChildView::OnMouseMove(UINT nFlags, CPoint point)
{
    if (!m_bDragging)
    {
        CWnd ::OnMouseMove(nFlags, point);
        return;
    }

    if (point == m_ptPrev)
        return;

    EraseLine(m_ptInit, m_ptPrev);
    DrawLine(m_ptInit, point);

    m_ptPrev = point;
}

void CChildView::OnLButtonUp(UINT nFlags, CPoint point)
{
    if (!m_bDragging)
    {
        CWnd ::OnLButtonUp(nFlags, point);
        return;
    }

    EraseLine(m_ptInit, m_ptPrev);
    DrawLine(m_ptInit, point);

    m_bDragging = FALSE;
}
```

Here are the details. When the mouse is clicked, WM_LBUTTONDOWN is received. The m_bDragging indicator is automatically set to TRUE. The current mouse coordinates are stored in m_ptInit (the initial point position) and m_ptPrev (the previous mouse position).

As the mouse is moved (with the button down), WM_MOUSEMOVE messages are received. If m_bDragging it TRUE, then the left button is down; hence, the user is dragging. If the button is up (m_Dragging is FALSE), then this is a normal move, which is passed to the parent (CWnd) for default processing. If the new coordinates are different than the previous, then the previous line is erased, and a new line is drawn. Note than when the first WM_MOUSEMOVE message is received, m_ptPrev and m_ptOrig are the same, so nothing is in fact erased. But a line is drawn from m_ptOrig to point, the current mouse coordinates.

When the user releases the button, WM_LBUTTONUP is received. If the user is not dragging, the message is ignored. Otherwise, the previous line is erased and the final line is drawn. Also, m_bDragging is set to FALSE, to indicate that the user is not dragging any more. Accordingly, subsequent mouse messages will not produce any line drawing.

As you can see, it is up to the application to follow the mouse. Note that you are free to implement an alternative to dragging, since dragging is not always a good method. Touch pads are not always adequate, and some people may have problems doing such operations. An alternative to drawing in this application could be to require the user to tap twice: to indicate the start position and to mark the end position. As a result, the code would have to be slightly different than above.

Whichever approach you decide to use (you may also have a program option to let the user choose), you have to code it yourself. Windows will send you raw stylus messages, and it is up to you to implement the desired behavior.

17.4.2 Capturing the Stylus

Let's recall that stylus messages are received by the topmost window immediately underneath the stylus. When the stylus is moved outside a window, that window no longer receives stylus messages. That's a problem with the previous example. If the user drags the stylus outside the window, the window won't receive the WM_MOUSEMOVE message any more. Worse, WM_LBUTTONUP also won't be received if the user releases the stylus outside the window. Consequently, the flag m_bDragging would remain TRUE. The next time the stylus comes over the window and WM_MOUSEMOVE messages start pouring in again, the window will believe that the user is still dragging, because the flag m_bDragging is TRUE. In both cases, that will lead to some usability confusion for the user.

To prevent this situation, the window must keep receiving messages from the stylus even if it is outside the window. The application only needs these messages from the time the user started dragging until the drag is completed. Hence, once the user starts dragging, the application must tell Windows that it needs all messages until the stylus is released. Receiving all stylus messages regardless of its position (over the window or not) is called *capturing the mouse*, and is done by using CWnd::SetCapture() and CWnd::Release Capture().

SetCapture() indicates to Windows that stylus messages must be redirected to the calling window, wherever the stylus is. Later on, the window must call Release Capture() to restore the stylus its normal behavior. Care must be taken when using these functions. In particular, one has to make sure to call ReleaseCapture(), otherwise the stylus will be dedicated to one window only.

In the next example, the stylus is captured as soon as the WM_LBUTTONDOWN is received, *i.e.*, as soon as the user starts to drag. From that point and on, all stylus messages will be received, even if the stylus is moved outside the window. Whenever WM_LBUTTONUP is received, the capture is released, and the stylus regains its normal behavior. The modification simply consists of adding the capture call in two handlers of the previous example. The **LineDraw** sample, on the CD-ROM, implements this example.

```
void CChildView::OnLButtonDown(UINT nFlags, CPoint point)
{
    m_bDragging = TRUE;
    m_ptInit = point;
    m_ptPrev = point;

    SetCapture();
}

void CChildView::OnLButtonUp(UINT nFlags, CPoint point)
{
    if (!m_bDragging)
    {
            CWnd ::OnLButtonUp(nFlags, point);
            return;
    }

    EraseLine(m_ptInit, m_ptPrev);
    DrawLine(m_ptInit, point);

    m_bDragging = FALSE;

    ReleaseCapture();
}
```

Note that OnMouseMove() remains intact. As the stylus is dragged outside the window, the mouse coordinates will reflect the out-of-window position. Drawing lines can still be conducted as usual, since Windows ensures that the line is drawn within the window only.

In this example, it makes sense to capture the stylus from a usability standpoint: this is what most users would expect from such an application. On the other hand, there is no need to capture the stylus all the time. Take a word processor for instance: it really does not make sense to capture the stylus, since the user may use the stylus to activate other applications at any time. The rule of thumb is to capture the stylus mouse when the user is dragging (moving an object on the screen or drawing something), and release the capture when the drag is done.

17.4.3 Cursors

A cursor is a small image that reflects the current stylus or mouse position, if such devices are supported. But unlike desktops, most CE devices don't have a mouse, and don't have to show a cursor at all times.

Wait Cursor

The only occasion where a cursor might be shown on those devices is when some processing takes a few seconds to complete (such as connecting to a remote site). In this case, showing a wait cursor provides some reassuring feedback to the user that the device is not dead, but just working. The most famous wait cursor is, of course, the hourglass.

The simplest method to use a wait cursor is to use the CWaitCursor class. Just declaring an object of that type is all it takes to display the cursor, until that object goes out of scope (*i.e.*, the end of the function or block). For instance:

```
void CChildView::OnConnect()
{
    // Show a wait cursor
    CWaitCursor    wc;

    // Connect to the remote site (may take a few seconds)
    .
    .
    .

    // Upon leaving, the cursor is erased/restored.
}
```

An alternative is to use BeginWaitCursor() and EndWaitCursor(), which respectively show and hide the cursor. Both are CCmdTarget methods (CCmdTarget is the parent class of CWnd).

Custom Cursors

Applications that run on devices configured to support cursors may display various cursors at run-time.

CWinApp provides a few methods to load cursors. CWinApp::LoadCursor() loads a cursor designed in a resource editor (each custom cursor has an unique identifier). CWinApp::LoadStandardCursor() loads a predefined cursor, the most common being IDC_ARROW and IDC_WAIT.

17.5 OTHER INPUT DEVICES

A mouse is basically handled like a stylus, as they generate the same messages. Right-button events are treated like left-button ones.

Some CE devices are also equipped with a microphone to record voice and sound. Applications can use the voice Recorder Control, described in Section 19.4.3 to record and playback sound.

Chapter 18

Dialog Boxes, Property Sheets, and Message Boxes

Dialog boxes are a special type of window that typically contains a series of controls (combo boxes, edit boxes, buttons, etc.), and that are designed using a graphical dialog box editor, making the design process very easy. They are alternatives to regular windows, whose controls must be created and positioned programmatically, which is a tedious process. Their ease of use, combined with MFC support, make dialog boxes a very nice feature to use.

This chapter presents dialog boxes, but also property sheets, which elegantly combine multiple dialog boxes together. They are fully supported in MFC, easy to use, and are very useful when screen real estate is at a premium (and it is, under Windows CE!)

Finally, message boxes are described toward the end of this chapter. Message boxes are simplistic dialog boxes that display informational, warning or error messages, even questions. Their ease of use make them very convenient.

18.1 DIALOG BOXES

A dialog box is a non-resizable window that is used for gathering some information. A good example is the Open dialog box used by many applications, but also a custom one to collect customer information (see Figure 18-1). A new feature on CE allows you to add the "?" and "OK" buttons to the title bar to save space.

18.1.1 Overview

Dialog boxes are easy to use, easier in fact than using a regular window. A dialog box's appearance is based on a dialog template. Suffice it to say at this point that developers use a resource editor to graphically design the dialog box by filling it with any supported and user-defined controls. The result is encoded as a named dialog template in the resource file (.RES) and the executable image (.EXE).

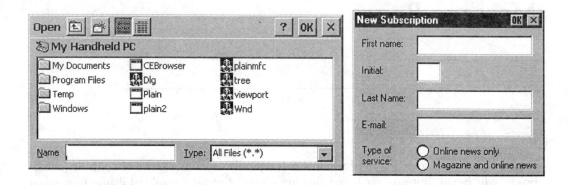

Figure 18-1: The Open dialog box. Such a dialog box is predefined within Windows, and is available to all applications. You can also develop your own dialog boxes, such as the one on the right.

Using dialog boxes gives two real advantages over regular windows. First, you do not need to worry about the actual screen resolution, since the dialog box is drawn by Windows (so Windows worries about that internally). Secondly, you do not need to hard code and guess the positions of the controls. You can imagine the pain of "manually" creating a window with 20 controls, while ensuring that all controls are fully aligned with respect to each other, both horizontally and vertically. In contrast, today's tools allow you to complete most dialog box layouts in minutes. Should the layout be later changed (say to enlarge a few edit boxes), only the resources need to be recompiled and bound to the application; no source code has to be altered and rebuilt.

Modal and Modeless Dialog Boxes

There are two types of dialog boxes: modal and modeless. Modal dialog boxes are by far more popular that modeless ones.

A modal dialog box retains the focus until it is closed, and the user can't access any other window within the same application while the dialog is active. This is ideal to gather some information and "suspend" the application until that information has been provided.

Consider opening a file, where the application must first obtain a file name to continue. It does so by presenting a dialog box where the user is invited to type in a file name. It makes sense to use a modal dialog box, since otherwise, the user could return to the application and continue working. Since the user started an operation (opening a file), using a modal dialog box forces the user to provide the necessary data to complete that operation. Hence, use a modal dialog box to gather data in order to complete some work. As mentioned earlier, this is the form of dialog box most applications are largely built with.

A modeless dialog box runs in parallel with the application. In PocketWord, the Find dialog box is modeless: while visible, the user can return to the text and make changes (see Figure 18-2). This requires more work from the application. For instance, Word must make sure that only one Find dialog box is shown at all times (otherwise the resulting pile of Find dialog boxes would quickly confuse the user). There are various methods an application can use to prevent this situation, but the application (not MFC) must implement them. We'll see one approach later on.

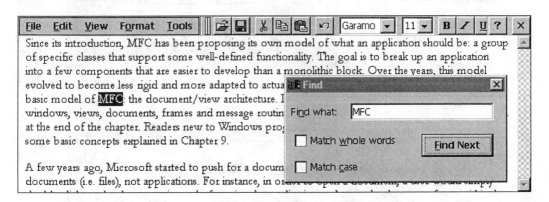

Figure 18-2: Using a modeless dialog box. In this case, the Find dialog box is modeless within PocketWord: the user can continue editing the text while the dialog box remains available.

Application developers (you and I) must decide ahead whether a dialog box is modal or modeless. This is purely a graphical user interface design consideration, but modal dialog boxes tend to make applications easier to use (since multiple visible windows – the application and one or more modeless dialog boxes – add a certain degree of confusion).

From a programming standpoint, modal and modeless dialog boxes have a lot in common, but they are managed differently from the application that is using them. Before explaining that kind of detail, let's first review how to design dialog boxes.

Designing Dialog Boxes

Dialog boxes are designed using the graphical editor embedded within Visual C++ (see Figure 18-3), or any other dialog box editor. This dialog box editor provides a control palette that allows selecting, positioning, and sizing controls onto the dialog box. In addition, users can specify the title, style and the dialog's main font. Each control can be individually customized using a Properties dialog box. The result is stored in the application resource file (`.rc`).

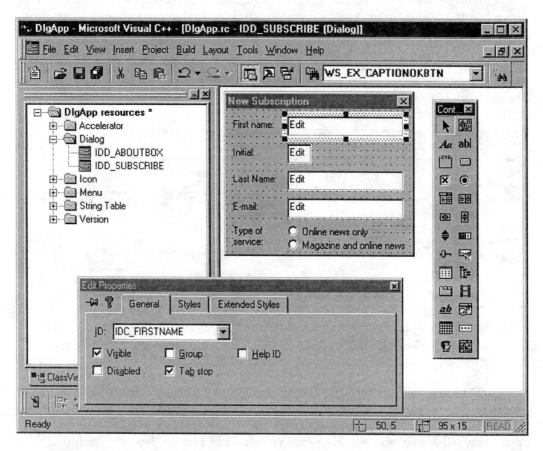

Figure 18-3: The dialog box editor within Visual C++ makes dialog box design too easy.

Dialog box coordinates are expressed as *dialog logical units* or DLUs. A DLU is based on the dialog box's main font, not pixels. What's really helpful is that changing the size of that font results in the entire dialog box and its content being automatically resized, preserving the same aspect ratio (see Figure 18-4). This can only be done at design time (not run time[58]), but this is still a time-saving feature. Each dialog box can have its own font, but it is better to use the same font for all dialog boxes within an application. A common font is MS Sans Serif 8-point.

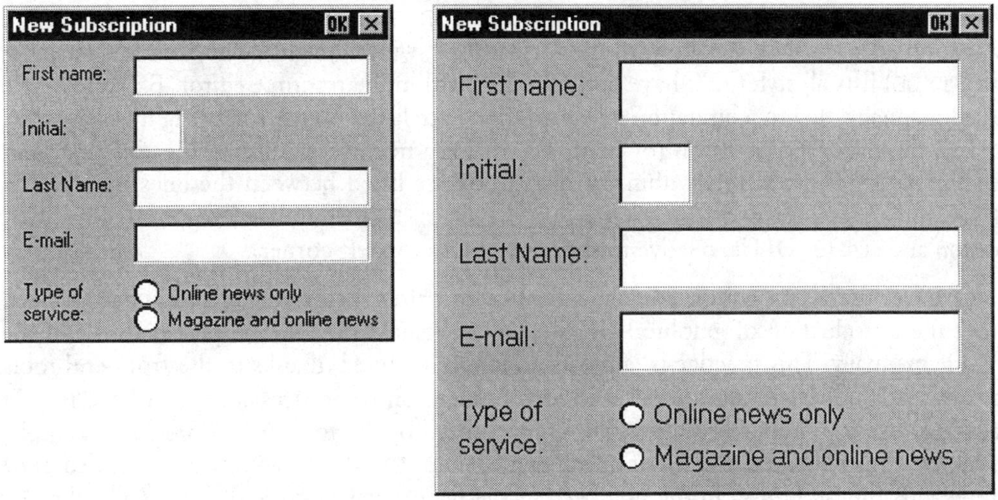

Figure 18-4: Two examples of the same dialog box, shown with different dialog font sizes. Changing the font resizes each control (buttons and static text) accordingly, but the size of the tile bar remains unchanged.

All the dialog editor does is to generate a script in the resource file (.rc) that describes the dialog box content. Below is the resource script of the dialog boxes shown in Figure 18-4.

```
IDD_SUBSCRIBE DIALOGEX 0, 0, 152, 108
STYLE DS_MODALFRAME | DS_CONTEXTHELP | WS_POPUP | WS_CAPTION | WS_SYSMENU
EXSTYLE WS_EX_CAPTIONOKBTN
CAPTION "New Subscription"
FONT 8, "MS Sans Serif"
BEGIN
        LTEXT           "First name:",IDC_STATIC,5,7,40,10
        EDITTEXT        IDC_FIRSTNAME,50,5,95,15,ES_AUTOHSCROLL
        LTEXT           "Initial:",IDC_STATIC,5,27,40,10
        EDITTEXT        IDC_EDIT2,50,25,20,15,ES_AUTOHSCROLL
        LTEXT           "Last Name:",IDC_STATIC,5,47,40,10
        EDITTEXT        IDC_EDIT3,50,45,95,15,ES_AUTOHSCROLL
        LTEXT           "E-mail:",IDC_STATIC,5,67,40,10
        EDITTEXT        IDC_EDIT4,50,65,95,15,ES_AUTOHSCROLL
        LTEXT           "Type of service:",IDC_STATIC,5,85,40,20,NOT WS_GROUP
        CONTROL         "Online news only",IDC_RADIO1,"Button",
```

---

[58] It is in fact possible to alter the font at run-time through a few tricks.

```
                    BS AUTORADIOBUTTON | WS GROUP | WS TABSTOP,50,85,69,10
        CONTROL     "Magazine and online news",IDC_RADIO2,"Button",
                    BS_AUTORADIOBUTTON,50,95,100,10
  END
```

In this example, the dialog box is identified by `IDD_SUBSCRIBE` (a plain identifier). The size coordinates (in DLUs) follow, in the format (0, 0, width, height). The next line (starting with `STYLE`) lists all styles that have been checked within the resource editor. Extended style (added manually, due to a limitation of Visual C++) are listed on the following line. The next line lists the dialog box caption (or title). The dialog's main font follows, the size first, and then the name. The controls within the dialog box are listed between the lines `BEGIN` and `END`. Controls are listed by their type (*e.g.*, `LTEXT`, `EDITTEXT`, etc.), caption, identifier, position and size (in DLUs, relative to the dialog box's top left corner).

One can use a text editor, edit the `.rc` file, and alter such a dialog box script. In fact, before the introduction of graphical IDEs (such as Visual C++), developers had to edit the `.rc` file manually. This practice is (almost) no longer required, thanks to the front-end tools that are available. There are a few exceptions though: on some occasions, you have to edit that file to use a an available feature, but unrecognized by the tool. In the previous example, Visual C++ provides no means of specifying the `WS_EX_CAPTIONOKBTN` extended style (which adds the `OK` button in the title bar), so the feature has to be added manually, directly in to the `.rc` file. If you intend to edit that file from Visual C++: from File/Open, select the `.rc` file, but make sure the option "Open as" is set to "Text", not "Auto". Using the former option opens a text file (which you can edit and close once done), whereas "Auto" results in the `.rc` being scanned again and made accessible via the resource editor.

CDialog

Dialog boxes are supported in MFC via the `CDialog` class. Once a dialog box is designed in Visual C++, invoking ClassWizard allows creating a new class, derived from `CDialog`, representing that dialog box. It is a good convention to use the dialog box's title as the dialog class name and terminate that name with `Dlg` (*e.g.*, the "Subscribe" dialog class is named `CSubscribeDlg`). The related header and source files are generated in files whose names are the dialog box class, minus the prefix "C". For instance, the `CSubscribeDlg` class resides in `SubscribeDlg.h` and `SubscribeDlg.cpp`. The default implementation provides basic functionality.

Using a modal dialog box is extremely simple: it only requires including the dialog box header file, creating an instance, and calling `CDialog::DoModal()`, as shown in the following example.

```
#include "SubscribeDlg.h"

void CChildView::OnSubscribe()
{
    // Instantiate a dialog box class. This doesn't show the dialog box.
    CSubscribeDlg  dlg;

    // Show the dialog box and "wait" until it is closed.
    dlg.DoModal();

    // When this point is reached the dialog box has been closed.
}
```

CDialog::DoModal() triggers some complex processing (all internal). First, it does not require any parameters, such as where to show the dialog box on the screen (the dialog box is responsible for its positioning; more on this later). Second, it loads the related resource template, creates the dialog box on the screen, creates the controls within the dialog, and lets the user navigate within the dialog box, either by clicking on the controls or using the TAB key to move from one control to the following. The call returns only when the user closes the dialog box. How the user closes the dialog box depends on the dialog box itself, although this is typically done by clicking title bar buttons such as "OK" or "X" (which is the equivalent of "Cancel"). The function returns the control identifier that forced the dialog box to be terminated (*e.g.*, IDOK, IDCANCEL, etc.)

During the execution of CDialog::DoModal(), the application continues to receive messages. The only difference is that the user input is limited to the dialog box. If the dialog box sends a message to the application window, the message will be processed normally while the dialog box is shown. The following dialog box example sends a message to its parent when processing OnOK():

```
void CPaymentDlg::OnOK()
{
    if (m_pParentWnd->SendMessage(WM_CHECKPAYMENT) == FALSE)
    {
        AfxMessageBox(_T("Payment cannot be checked."), MB_ICONSTOP);
        return;
    }

    .
    .
    .
}
```

The return value of DoModal() is important, since it identifies whether the user wants to continue or cancel the operation. For instance, if an user sets some options through a dialog box but clicks Cancel, the application must ensure that no change takes place. This is done by checking the value returned by CDialog::DoModal(), as shown below:

```
#include "SubscribeDlg.h"

void CChildView::OnSubscribe()
{
    CSubscribeDlg  dlg;

    // Display the modal dialog box. If the user closes it by clicking
    // the X in the title bar, DoModal() will return IDCANCEL. If this
    // is the case, simply return. If, on the other hand, the user clicks
    // 'OK' to close it, the returned value will be IDOK. In that case
    // continue with the subscription.
    if (dlg.DoModal() != IDOK)
        return;

    // Continue with subscription
    .
    .
    .
}
```

18.1.2 Enhancing Modal Dialog Boxes

Unless you use a dialog box to display information only, with a single "OK" button to close it (kind of a fancy message box), you are likely to implement some functionality within the dialog box itself. Also, it is common to add member variables to represent the controls within the dialog box. The next sections will explore those topics.

Processing Messages

Upon creation, but before being visible, a dialog box receives two messages: WM_CREATE and WM_INITDIALOG. WM_CREATE is not very useful, since the controls are not created yet, making them inaccessible. However, shortly after, the controls are internally created and WM_INITDIALOG is sent, which is handled in CDialog::OnInitDialog(). This handler is the ideal place to initialize the controls, such as adding strings in an otherwise empty combo box. The following example initializes the dialog box shown in Figure 18-5:

```
BOOL CPaymentDlg::OnInitDialog()
{
    // Call parent first
    CDialog::OnInitDialog();

    // Make that dialog the active window.
    SetForegroundWindow();

    // Get a pointer to the ccredit card type combo box. The cast
    // is needed since CWnd::GetDlgItem() returns (CWnd *).
    CComboBox *     pComboBox =
            reinterpret_cast<CComboBox *>(GetDlgItem(IDC_CCARDTYPE));
```

```
    // Add some strings into the combo box.
    pComboBox->AddString(_T("Amex"));
    pComboBox->AddString(_T("Mastercard"));
    pComboBox->AddString(_T("Visa"));

    // Make sure the focus is on the 'Bill me' button
    CButton *      pButton =
         reinterpret_cast<CButton *>(GetDlgItem(IDC_BILLME));

    pButton->SetFocus();

    // Return FALSE, since we have set the focus.
    return FALSE;
}
```

Figure 18-5: An initialized dialog box. In this case, a few strings have been added to a combo box.

The implementation of OnInitDialog() should always call the parent first, followed by a call to CWnd::SetForegroundWindow() (which makes the dialog box the active window). The focus is automatically set on the first control if the function returns TRUE; if the focus is set to a specific control (as it is above by calling CWnd::SetFocus() on the desired control), the method must return FALSE.

Once the dialog box is initialized and visible, CDialog::DoModal() takes over and internally manages the dialog box. What happens then depends on what the user does. Typically, the user interacts with the controls: selecting a list box item, clicking a button, entering text in an edit control, etc. Controls themselves react by sending notifications to the dialog box for each significant event such as those just mentioned. Chapters 19 and 20 describe those notifications in detail. What's important to know at this point is that the dialog box has to handle notifications of interest.

The CDialog class already implements handlers for the notification sent by the push buttons identified IDOK and IDCANCEL. The handlers are respectively CDialog::OnOK()

509

and `CDialog::OnCancel()` and both internally call `CDialog::EndDialog()`, which closes the dialog box (but they do <u>not</u> destroy the `CDialog`-based object itself). `CDialog::EndDialog()` requires one argument: the identifier of the control that has sent the notification forcing the dialog box termination (*e.g.*, `IDOK`, `IDCANCEL`). This is also the value returned by `CDialog::DoModal()`.

Applications can directly call `CDialog::EndDialog()`, but this is rarely needed. On the other hand, it is very common to override `CDialog::OnOK()`. The most common scenario is to validate the content of the controls within the dialog box before returning. For instance, in a data-entry dialog box which requires all fields to be specified, all fields can be checked one by one to ensure that they contain valid data. If some errors are found, error messages can be displayed (using message boxes) and the dialog box is left active instead of being closed. The next example makes sure that if user chose a credit card payment, all credit card information is provided. Otherwise, the focus is moved onto the control to enter information into, and the dialog box is set to remain visible and active.

```
void CPaymentDlg::OnOK()
{
    // If the 'Credit Card' radio button isn't checked,
    // call the parent and return
    CButton *      pButton =
            reinterpret_cast<CButton *>(GetDlgItem(IDC_CREDITCARD));

    if (pButton->GetCheck() == 0)
    {
            CDialog::OnOK();
            return;
    }

    // Make sure the credit card combo box contains a valid selection.
    // If not, display an error message box, move the focus on it,
    // and return without calling parent to leave the dialog box on.
    CComboBox *    pComboBox =
            reinterpret_cast<CComboBox *>(GetDlgItem(IDC_CCARDTYPE));

    if (pComboBox->GetCurSel() == CB_ERR)
    {
            AfxMessageBox(
                    _T("Please specify the credit card type."), MB_OK);

            pComboBox->SetFocus();
            return;
    }

    CEdit * pEdit;

    // Make sure the credit card number has been specified.
    pEdit = reinterpret_cast<CEdit *>(GetDlgItem(IDC_CCARDNO));

    if (pEdit->GetWindowTextLength() == 0)
    {
```

```
        AfxMessageBox(
                _T("Please enter the credit card number."), MB_OK);

        pEdit->SetFocus();
        return;
    }

    // Make sure the credit card expiration date has been specified.
    pEdit = reinterpret_cast<CEdit *>(GetDlgItem(IDC_CCARDEXPDATE));

    if (pEdit->GetWindowTextLength() == 0)
    {
        AfxMessageBox(
                _T("Please enter the credit card expiration date."),
                MB_OK);

        pEdit->SetFocus();
        return;
    }

    // Call parent to close this dialog box.
    CDialog::OnOK();
}
```

This approach is also very object-oriented. Take it from the application's standpoint: it invokes a dialog box to gather some information. If that dialog box returns IDOK (for success), then the application can assume that it obtained all the desired data. Hence, the dialog box is perceived as a black box that gathers *and* validates data, making it easier to use and especially re-use in other applications.

On the other hand, it is less common to override CDialog::OnCancel(). After all, if the user wants to cancel (*i.e.*, abort processing), let it be. One exception, though, is to confirm the cancellation in the case of a complex data-entry dialog box that may have taken some time to fill up, in case the user inadvertently clicked Cancel. The next example handles IDCANCEL by prompting the user if the dialog box should really gets closed. This shows the message box on Figure 18-6.

```
void CPaymentDlg::OnCancel()
{
    // Get a confirmation from the user.
    if (AfxMessageBox(
            _T("This offer won't last forever!\n")
            _T("Are you sure you want to miss such a good deal?"),
            MB_YESNO | MB_ICONQUESTION) == IDYES)

        // The user really wants to close it, so call parent to do so.
        CDialog::OnCancel();
}
```

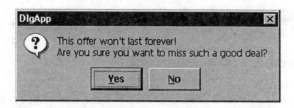

Figure 18-6: Showing a message box upon canceling a dialog box[59].

Adding Member Variables

The previous example illustrated how a dialog box works with its controls and how it handles some of their notifications. The dialog box is self-contained, and the application invoking the dialog box does not have to know anything about the dialog box implementation. In that regard, the dialog box can be used in another application by pasting the dialog box template and adding the related `.h` and `.cpp` files to the project.

The only thing left is to store the dialog box information into some variables that the calling application can retrieve and process. For instance, consider the File Open dialog box. Upon closing the dialog box the filename must be somehow returned to the calling function. After all, this is why the dialog box has been called in the first place ...

MFC has been designed to handle this situation very elegantly. To stay in line with an object-oriented approach, one can define member variables in the `CDialog`-derived class, and MFC generates enough code to associate these member variables to the actual controls. What's more, at specific points during the execution of a dialog box, MFC will keep the variables and the related controls synchronized.

Adding variables is simple. Consider the Payment dialog box (Figure 18-5) that contains a check box, two radio buttons, a combo box, and two edit controls, respectively identified `IDC_BILLME`, `IDC_PAYMENTMETHOD`, `IDC_CREDITCARD`, `IDC_CCARDTYPE`, `IDC_CCARDNO` and `IDC_CCARDEXPDATE`. By invoking ClassWizard over the dialog box, you can select the Member Variables panel and add variables for each listed control (see Figure 18-7). Note that since the radio buttons form a group (a feature described in Chapter 19), only the first button's identifier shows up (so `IDC_CREDITCARD` is not shown).

---

[59] Of course, marketing- and sales-oriented folks will want to change the exact message content, but coming up with something like "Hmm, this change will take a few days ... " may cool them off.

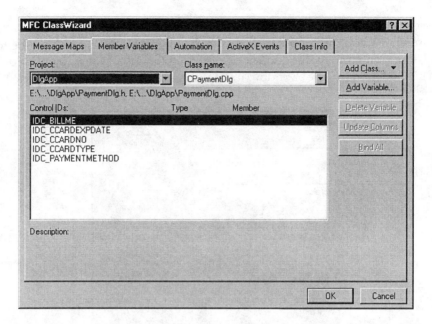

Figure 18-7: Visual C++'s ClassWizard can be invoked on a dialog class (here, CMyDlg) in order to add member variables for each of its controls.

A variable is added by first selecting a control (such as IDC_BILLME) and clicking the "Add Variable..." button, which displays the "Add Member Variable" dialog box (see Figure 18-8). A member variable requires three attributes to be specified:

- The member variable name. The name will be written as is into the dialog box class definition (in the .h file).

- The category, either Value or Control (more on this in a second).

- The variable type, which depends on the category (for a check box, ClassWizard proposes BOOL). The chosen type become the variable's type in the dialog box class definition.

A *value* variable represents the current value of the control. For instance, for an edit control, a value variable can be either a CString (the string contained in the edit control), an int (the string converted into an integer), a DWORD, etc. For a list box or a combo box, a value variable can only be a CString, being the current selected string. For a check box, the value is a BOOL (checked or uncheckled). For a group of radio buttons, only one variable is required, and it contains 0 if the first button is checked, 1 if the second button is checked, etc. A value variable is ideal when only the value of the control is of interest to the application, not the control itself. Value variables are used within most dialog boxes.

A *control* variable is an MFC object representing the control: CEdit, CListBox, etc. This is useful to access the control itself (*e.g.*, to disable/enable the control, set the focus on it, etc.) Using a control variable also allows retrieving the value within, by using a control-specific method (CEdit::GetWindowText(), CListBox::GetCurSel(), etc.)

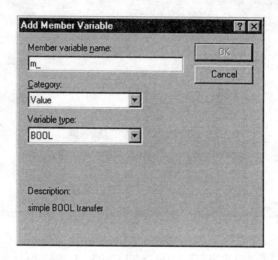

Figure 18-8: Given a control, an associated member variable is created by specifying a name, a category (value or control), and a variable type (which depends on the category).

It is possible to have both a value variable and a control variable referring to the same control, which provides full access to the value and the control itself. Because one acts on a value and the other on the control, there is no interference between the two. However, adding two or more variables of the <u>same</u> category (value or control) on the <u>same</u> control is not recommended.

Using Value Member Variables in the Application

Once member variables are created, the next issue is to use them. Figure 18-9 shows the variables added for the Payment dialog box. Notice how the variable names closely match the related control's identifier (a good convention to adopt). The variables are automatically added into the dialog's header file, so there's nothing to edit at this point.

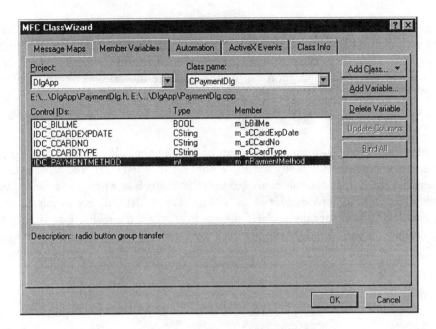

Figure 18-9: The variables for the Payment dialog box.

At run-time, invoking the dialog box for the first time will show it with empty edit controls, which is fine at this point, since the user is expected to fill in all fields. Upon closing the dialog box, MFC ensures that the member variables are updated to reflect the content of the edit controls. Hence, once `CDialog::DoModal()` returns, the application can use the member variables and process them, as shown in the following example:

```
void CChildView::OnSubscribe()
{
    CSubscribeDlg  SubscriptionDlg;

    if (SubscriptionDlg.DoModal() != IDOK)
        return;

    CPaymentDlg              PaymentDlg;

    if (PaymentDlg.DoModal() != IDOK)
        return;

    // If provided, validate the credit card information
    if (PaymentDlg.m_nPaymentMethod == 1)
        ValidateCreditCardInfo(
                PaymentDld.m_sCardType,
                PaymentDlg.m_sCardNo,
                PaymentDlg.m_sCardExpDate);
}
```

In the case where a customer invokes the same information later, it would be preferable to display an initialized dialog box, showing the values previously entered for that customer. By default, the dialog box class constructor resets all member variables added through ClassWizard. However, an application can optionally store the dialog box values after each call to `CDialog::DoModal()`, and subsequently use those values prior to call `CDialog::DoModal()`, in order to initialize the related controls when the dialog box is shown.

The next example is an improved version of the previous. It initializes the dialog box before displaying it (the fields being initially empty on the first call), and stores the dialog box values after the call. Those values are fed into the dialog box when it is called again. The values are stored in member variables of the calling class, `CChildView` in this example. In this situation, MFC automatically updates the controls when the dialog box is shown. The **DlgApp** sample, on the CD-ROM, implements that very same example, with other material as well.

```
struct SPAYMENT
{
    BOOL            m_bBillMe;
    CString         m_sCCardExpDate;
    CString         m_sCCardNo;
    CString         m_sCCardType;
    int             m_nPaymentMethod;
};

class CChildView : public CWnd
{
    SPAYMENT        m_Payment;                  // To store dialog box variables
    .
    .
    .
};

void CChildView::OnSubscribe()
{
    CSubscribeDlg   SubscriptionDlg;

    if (SubscriptionDlg.DoModal() != IDOK)
            return;

    CPaymentDlg             PaymentDlg;

    // Initialize the dialog box' value variables
    PaymentDlg.m_bBillMe            = m_Payment.m_bBillMe;
    PaymentDlg.m_sCCardExpDate      = m_Payment.m_sCCardExpDate;
    PaymentDlg.m_sCCardNo           = m_Payment.m_sCCardNo;
    PaymentDlg.m_sCCardType         = m_Payment.m_sCCardType;
    PaymentDlg.m_nPaymentMethod     = m_Payment.m_nPaymentMethod;

    if (PaymentDlg.DoModal() != IDOK)
            return;
```

```
    // Store the dialog box' value variables into member variables
    m_Payment.m_bBillMe          = PaymentDlg.m_bBillMe;
    m_Payment.m_sCCardExpDate    = PaymentDlg.m_sCCardExpDate;
    m_Payment.m_sCCardNo         = PaymentDlg.m_sCCardNo;
    m_Payment.m_sCCardType       = PaymentDlg.m_sCCardType;
    m_Payment.m_nPaymentMethod   = PaymentDlg.m_nPaymentMethod;

    // If provided, validate the credit card information
    if (PaymentDlg.m_nPaymentMethod == 2)
         ValidateCreditCardInfo(
              PaymentDlg.m_sCCardType,
              PaymentDlg.m_sCCardNo,
              PaymentDlg.m_sCCardExpDate);
}
```

Hence, to summarize, MFC transfers data back and forth between value variables and the controls, upon creating and closing a dialog box. Indeed, there is some magic that relates a C++ data variable and a control within MFC. That magic is called DDX/DDV (data transfer/data validation), and it is triggered by CDialog::UpdateData() (see Figure 18-10) If you closely examine the code generated by ClassWizard, you will notice a function called CYourDialog::DoDataExchange(). This is the magic function that glues controls and value variables together. That function is called by Updatedata(), and in other occasions, directly by MFC.

When CDialog::UpdateData() is called with FALSE, as it is in CDialog::OnInitDialog(), the value member variables are transferred into their corresponding controls (ClassWizard generates code to associate controls with value variables and vice-versa). Hence, if a value variable is set to _T("Visa"), the associated control (say an edit control) will be initialized to _T("Visa") when CDialog::UpdateData() is called with FALSE.

Calling the method with TRUE does the opposite: it extracts the content from the controls, converts them if it has to, and copies it into the member variables. A conversion example is the conversion of a string into an integer. Should the validation fail, a dialog box is automatically displayed. What's more, CDialog::OnOK() internally calls CDialog::UpdateData(TRUE), forcing all member variables to be updated upon exiting the dialog box.

In the previous scenario (a simple data entry dialog box), this implementation works very well: the application optionally initializes a few value member variables, invokes CDialog::DoModal(), and retrieves the new values out of the same member variables. From a programming standpoint, all the data transfer within the dialog box is done within MFC, requiring zero extra lines of code in your application.

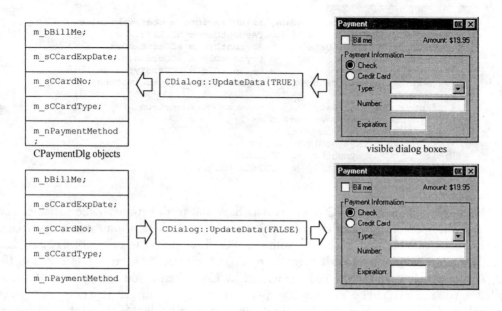

Figure 18-10: `CDialog::UpdateData()` transfers data from value member variables to controls in either way.

Using Value Member Variables in the Dialog Box

Value variables can also be used directly within the dialog box, in a notification handler, for instance. If you remember the `CPayment::OnOK` handler example, controls are directly accessed (via `CWnd::GetDlgItem()`) in order to retrieve their value. Since the dialog box now contains member variables associated with those controls, those variables can instead be used.

But there's a catch. A member variable and its associated control are only synchronized (either way) after a call to `CDialog::UpdateData()`, which is called by default when the dialog box is shown and closed, but not in between. That means that a method referring to a value variable only sees the content of the last update, not the actual associated control's value.

Fortunately, all it takes is to call `CDialog::UpdateData()` with `TRUE` to update the value variables based on the associated controls, or `FALSE` to update the controls based on the associated value variables. Here is the `CPayment::OnOK()` method, this time using member variables. Note that the **DlgApp** sample demonstrates both approaches.

```
void CPaymentDlg::OnOK()
{
    // Update the member variables based n the actual controls' content.
    UpdateData(TRUE);

    // If the 'Credit Card' radio button isn't checked,
    // call the parent and return
    if (m_nPaymentMethod != 1)
    {
        CDialog::OnOK();
        return;
    }

    // Make sure the credit card combo box contains a valid selection.
    if (m_sCCardType.IsEmpty())
    {
        AfxMessageBox(
            _T("Please specify the credit card type."), MB_OK);

        GetDlgItem(IDC_CCARDTYPE)->SetFocus();
        return;
    }

    // Make sure the credit card number has been specified.
    if (m_sCCardNo.IsEmpty())
    {
        AfxMessageBox(
            _T("Please enter the credit card number."), MB_OK);

        GetDlgItem(IDC_CCARDNO)->SetFocus();
        return;
    }

    // Make sure the credit card expiration date has been specified.
    if (m_sCCardExpDate.IsEmpty())
    {
        AfxMessageBox(
            _T("Please enter the credit card expiration date."),
            MB_OK);

        GetDlgItem(IDC_CCARDEXPDATE)->SetFocus();
        return;
    }

    // Call parent to close this dialog box.
    CDialog::OnOK();
}
```

The result is that using member variables usually simplifies coding. But also note that on the minus side, using a value member variable does not allow accessing the control, to set the focus for instance. As a result, that example ends up still calling `GetDlgItem()`. Control variables can solve that, as we are about to see.

Here are a few tips to remember when using value variables:

- `CDialog::OnInitDialog()` always calls `UpdateData(FALSE)` in order to update the controls based on the value member variables. Hence, even if you don't provide your own `OnInitDialog()`, the default implementation initializes the controls to the values specified before the call to `CDialog::DoModal()`.

- If you do provide `CYourDlg::OnInitDialog()`, always call the parent's implementation first to update the controls as described.

- `CDialog::OnOK()` always calls `CDialog::UpdateData(TRUE)` to update the value member variables based on the controls' current value. Hence, even if you don't provide your own `IDOK` handler, the value member variables are all synchronized upon terminating the dialog box, and are available when `CDialog::DoModal()` returns.

- If you implement `CYourDlg::OnOK()` to validate member value variables (like the previous example), make sure to call `UpdateData(TRUE)` first.

- In any dialog's handler, if you need to access a value variable, always call `CDialog::UpdateData(TRUE)` first, to synchronize all the value variables with their corresponding controls. Equally, if you update a value variable, always call `CDialog::UpdateData(FALSE)` to update the related controls.

- Each call to `CDialog::UpdateData()` updates all variables, which is sometimes an overhead when only one variable is needed. In that case, it might be better off using a control variable, and accessing the variable directly, without calling `CDialog::UpdateData()`. This is explained in the next section.

Using Control Member Variables

Control member variables provide a direct access to controls, and are handled differently. For one, they can only be used within the dialog box, where controls do exist. That means that you cannot use them in your application before or after the call to `CDialog::DoModal()`, since these controls do not exist (nor does the dialog box itself).

Here is an example. Say we add a control variable for the payment type combo box (we'll see how soon) called m_cCardType, of type `CComboBox`. Consider the following:

```
class CPaymentDlg : public CDialog
{
    CString  m_sCCardType;              // Value variable
    ComboBox m_cCCardType;              // Control variable
    .
    .
    .
};

void CChildView::OnSubscribe()
{
    CPaymentDlg              PaymentDlg;
```

```
    PaymentDlg.m_sCCardType =  _T("Visa");                        // OK

    PaymentDlg.m_cCCardType.AddString(_T("Visa"));               // ERROR

    if (PaymentDlg.DoModal() != IDOK)
        return;

    m_Payment.m_sCCardType = PaymentDlg.m_sCCardType;            // OK

    int CardTypeSelection = PaymentDlg.m_cCardType.GetCurSel(); // ERROR
}
```

Because `PaymentDlg.m_sCCardType` is a value variable (a `CString`), the application can access it outside `CDialog::DoModal()` as explained in the previous section. So far so good. But since `PaymentDlg.m_cCCardType` is a `CComboBox` member variable, it cannot be accessed outside `CDialog::DoModal()`, because the related combo box just doesn't exist; it only exists within the duration of `CDialog::DoModal()`. Worse, those are run-time errors (they crash the application), not compiler errors.

In fact, control variables can be accessed within the dialog box implementation of `OnInitDialog()`, `OnOK()`, `OnCancel()` and any other handler that is invoked when the dialog box is active. The next example initializes the combo box control in `OnInitDialog()`:

```
BOOL CPaymentDlg::OnInitDialog()
{
    CDialog::OnInitDialog();

    // Directly use a control variable to access a control.
    m_cCCardType.AddString(_T("Amex"));
    m_cCCardType.AddString(_T("Mastercard"));
    m_cCCardType.AddString(_T("Visa"));

    .
    .
    .
}
```

Given the availability of control member variables, there are few reasons to rely on `CWnd::GetDlgItem()`, although the function could be called if needed (but this is unlikely when a control variable is available). In fact, a control variable is a substitute to calling `CWnd::GetDlgItem()` each time the variable must be accessed

If you opt to use for `CWnd::GetDlgItem()` (instead of control variables), be aware that that method creates and returns a *temporary* instance. The pointer is only valid within the current function, and cannot be stored (say, in a member variable) and used later on. Also, it's *always* a good practice to test that the returned value is not `NULL` (during development, through an ASSERT), in order to detect any inconsistency between the identifier used in the application and the exact control identifier. For example:

```
CButton *  pButton = reinterpret_cast<CButton *>(GetDlgItem(IDC_BILLME));
ASSERT(pButton != NULL);

pButton->SetFocus();
```

The pointer can be used for accessing the control, but also to get or set the value, by calling the appropriate method, such as CListBox::GetCurSel(), or CWnd::Get WindowText() for an edit control. But again, the same can be achieved with a control variable. The only potential advantage is improved performance. Calling CDialog:: UpdateData() updates *all* value variables, even if only one or two are truly needed at the moment of the call. Hence calling CDialog::UpdateData() adds some overhead. Accessing one or two variables through CWnd::GetDlgItem() is sometimes faster. The rule of thumb is to consider using this method only when there are a lot of member variables (20+) and only a few need to be accessed.

18.1.3 Working with Modeless Dialog Boxes

Modeless dialog boxes are also implemented with the CDialog class, but they are not driven by CDialog::DoModal(), nor are they closed by CDialog::EndDialog().

A modeless dialog box becomes alive by calling CDialog::Create(), passing the dialog box identifier and a pointer to the parent. This method can be invoked from the parent or within the dialog box's constructor, whichever is most convenient (the first approach is more common). Unlike CDialog::DoModal(), CDialog::Create() returns immediately, making both the dialog box and the application accessible to the user.

Because the dialog box may exist at any point in time, it is important to ensure that the variable representing the dialog box has a broader application scope. Typically, this excludes making it a local variable (because of the limited scope). A common approach is to use dynamic memory, and store the pointer within a member variable of the application class, view or frame. Using a pointer makes it easy to determine if an instance has already been created or not, by simply comparing the pointer against NULL.

A modeless dialog box is destroyed by calling CWnd::DestroyWindow(), at any point in time. This method can be called in the dialog box's destructor or directly by the parent, whichever is more appropriate. A popular scenario is to have the dialog box sending an user-defined message to its parent upon being closed by the user, and let the parent deletes the dialog box and the class instance, and reset its internal pointer to NULL. That approach is illustrated in an example below.

The dialog box implementation itself is almost identical. You can use member variables (both value and control variables), invoke CDialog::UpdateData() as required, implement any handler (such as OnInitDialog()), and so forth. One important difference, though: always override OnOK and OnCancel. The default implementation calls EndDialog() in both cases, which must not be called for modeless dialog boxes. Instead of calling the parent implementation, send a message to the parent window to signal the dialog box termination. This technique is illustrated below.

A Modeless Dialog Box Example

The next example implements the modeless CNewsOptionsDlg dialog box. It can be invoked and created from a menu item. When dismissed, it sends a message to its parent, which must delete it. The **DlgApp** introduced earlier also implements a modeless dialog box.

```
// NewsOptionsDlg.h

// User-defined message sent to parent upon termination
const WM_CLOSING_OPTIONS_DLG = WM_USER + 100;

class CNewsOptionsDlg : public CDialog
{
    CWnd * m_pParent;
public:
    CNewsOptionsDlg(CWnd* pParent);        // Constructor *needs* parent
    BOOL    Create();                      // Simpler Create() method

    enum { IDD = IDD_NEWSOPTIONS };        // From ClassWizard

    virtual void OnOK();
    virtual void OnCancel();

            .                              // More ClassWizard stuff
            .
            .
};

inline CNewsOptionsDlg::Create()
{
    return CDialog::Create(IDD, m_pParent);
}
```

```
// NewsOptionsDlg.cpp

CNewsOptionsDlg::CNewsOptionsDlg(CWnd* pParent):
    CDialog(CNewsOptionsDlg::IDD, pParent)
{
    ASSERT(pParent != NULL);
    m_pParent = pParent;
}
```

```
     .
     .
     .

BOOL CNewsOptionsDlg::OnInitDialog()
{
    CDialog::OnInitDialog();
    CenterWindow();
    return TRUE;
}

void CNewsOptionsDlg::OnOK()
{
    m_pParent->PostMessage(WM_CLOSING_OPTIONS_DLG);
}

void CNewsOptionsDlg::OnCancel()
{
    m_pParent->PostMessage(WM_CLOSING_OPTIONS_DLG);
}
```

```
// ChildView.h

#include "NewsOptionsDlg.h"

class CChildView : public CWnd
{
    // Pointer to dialog box
    CNewsOptionsDlg *       m_pNewsOptionsDlg;
     .
     .
     .
    // Handler for custom dialog box message
    void OnClosingOptionsDlg(WPARAM, LPARAM);
};
```

```
// ChildView.cpp

CChildView::CChildView()
{
    // No dialog box yet
    m_pNewsOptionsDlg = NULL;
}

CChildView::~CChildView()
{
    // If the dialog box is active, delete it.
    if (m_pNewsOptionsDlg)
    {
            // Modeless dialog boxes are automatically destroyed upon
            // termination, but the class itself must be deleted.
            ASSERT(m_pNewsOptionsDlg->m_hWnd == NULL);
            delete m_pNewsOptionsDlg;
    }
}
```

```
// The message map must contain an entry to handle the notification
// sent by the dialog box upon its termination.
BEGIN_MESSAGE_MAP(CChildView,CWnd )
      .
      .
      .

    ON_MESSAGE(WM_CLOSING_OPTIONS_DLG, OnClosingOptionsDlg)
END_MESSAGE_MAP()

// A method called to create the modeless dialog box.
// If the dialog box doesn't already exist, it is created and made
// visible. If it already exists, it is brought on top of the app.
void CChildView::OnOptions()
{
    if (m_pNewsOptionsDlg == NULL)
    {
        m_pNewsOptionsDlg = new CNewsOptionsDlg(this);
        m_pNewsOptionsDlg->Create();
        m_pNewsOptionsDlg->ShowWindow(SW_SHOW);
    }
    else
        m_pNewsOptionsDlg->SetForegroundWindow();
}

// Dialog box termination notification, which destroys the dialog box.
// It is very important (due to some MFC logic) to specify the two
// parameters WPARAM and LPARAM with handlers called via ON_MESSAGE();
// otherwise, the application might crash.
void CChildView::OnClosingOptionsDlg(WPARAM, LPARAM)
{
    ASSERT(m_pNewsOptionsDlg != NULL);     // The dialog must exist by now

    m_pNewsOptionsDlg->DestroyWindow();    // Delete the dialog box
    delete m_pNewsOptionsDlg;              // Delete the C++ object
    m_pNewsOptionsDlg = NULL;              // Reset pointer
}
```

18.2 COMMON DIALOG BOXES

Windows CE directly implements some predefined dialog boxes that are used by many applications. Using these predefined dialog boxes provides many advantages: no need to re-invent them, ease of use, and consistent look and feel.

Four common dialog boxes are supported on Windows CE (see Figure 18-11):

- **Open,** to select a filename to open and **Save As,** to assign a file name to a document to save.

- **Print,** to print a document.

- **Color,** to pick a standard or custom color.

- **Find and Replace,** to locate some text and, optionally, replace it.

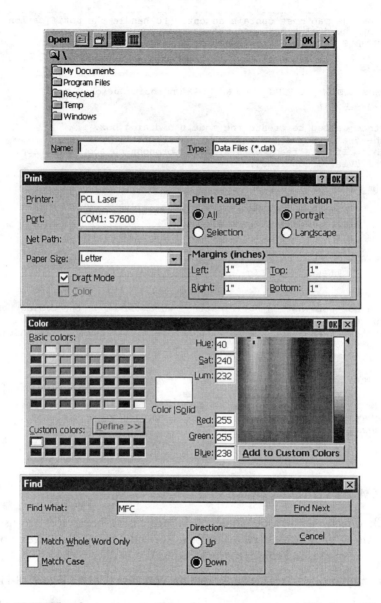

Figure 18-11: The four common dialog boxes supported on Windows CE. In a bottom down order: Open (also Save As), Color, Print, and Find.

These dialog boxes are also directly supported by MFC, which essentially provides wrapper classes that ease their use. These classes are CFileDialog, CColorDialog, and

`CFindReplaceDialog`, `CPrintDialog`, and their use is demonstrated in the **CommDlg** sample, on the CD-ROM.

18.2.1 CFileDialog

The `CFileDialog` class implements both the File Open and File Save common dialog boxes. The typical usage is to pass the proper parameters to the constructor and invoke `DoModal()`, as shown below.

```
// This handler is called when the user wants to import data into the
// application. To do so, a file name is first obtained.,

void OpenFile()
{
    // Construct an Open file dialog box.
    CFileDialog    dlg(TRUE,                  // Open
                    _T(".dat"),            // Default extension
                    _T("Default"),         // Default file name
                    OFN_FILEMUSTEXIST      // Flags
                                          // Filter
                    _T( "Data Files (*.dat)|*.dat|")
                    _T("All Files (*.*)|*.*||"),
                    this);                 // Parent

    // Invoke the dialog box, return if user cancels.
    if (dlg.DoModal() != IDOK)
            return;

    // Obtain the full path
    CString        m_sFilName = dlg.GetPathName();
}
```

The first parameter to `CFileDialog::CFileDialog()` is a Boolean that selects between the Open (`TRUE`) or Save As (`FALSE`) dialog box. The second parameter is the default extension to be added to the name, if none is entered by the user. The third parameter is the name to be shown by default. The next parameter is a combination of flags that dictate some of the behavior of the dialog box. In the example above, the flag specifies that the file must exist (`OFN_FILEMUSTEXIST`). The following parameter is a filter specification, which controls what files are shown in the dialog box. A filter specification consists of a description, followed by a vertical bar and a corresponding file extension. Extra specifications can be added by separating them with vertical bars. The filter must end with two vertical bars. In the example above, there are two filter specifications: "`Data Files (*.dat)`", associated with .dat files, and "`All Files (*.*)`", associated with `*.*`. Finally, the last argument is the parent window, usually `this`.

Like any other dialog box, it becomes visible by invoking `DoModal()`. The method returns `IDOK` or `IDCANCEL`; in the latter case, the operation must be considered aborted.

On success (IDOK), CFileDialog offers a few methods to extract the file name entered/selected by the user (see Figure 18-12).

CFileDialog Method	Description	Example (\TEMP\MYFILE.DAT)
GetPathName()	Returns the full path name	\TEMP\MYFILE.DAT
GetFileName()	Returns the file name	MYFILE.DAT
GetFileExt()	Returns the file extension	DAT
GetFileTitle()	Returns the file title	MYFILE

Figure 18-12: The file name entered in a CFileDialog can be retrieved through a few methods:

The class also implements a few predefined handlers to control the user interaction with the list control embedded in the dialog.

18.2.2 CColorDialog

The CColorDialog box implements the standard color dialog box. It is very easy to use, as shown in the following example:

```
COLORREF ChooseColor(COLORRED InitialColor)
{
    // Construct the dialog, passing the color to be initially selected.
    CColorDialog   dlg(InitialColor);

    // Invoke the dialog box, returning on Cancel.
    if (dlg.DoModal() != IDOK)
            return;

    // The new color is available via CColorDialog::GetColor()
    return dlg.GetColor();
}
```

The constructor accepts an initial color, which will be selected when the dialog box is shown. It accepts optional arguments, such as flags to control the appearance, and the parent window (NULL works fine).

The dialog box is shown by invoking CDialog::DoModal(), which returns either IDOK or IDCANCEL. In the former case, the color chosen by the user can be retrieved by calling CColorDialog::GetColor(). The returned color is of type COLORREF.

CPrintDialog

The CPrintDialog can be used in two modes that I call "visible" and "quiet".

In the visible mode, the Print dialog box (as shown in Figure 18-11) is displayed. The member variable m_pd (of type PRINTDLG) can be configured to customize the appearance of the dialog box. The following example illustrates this approach:

```
void OnPrint()
{
    CPrintDialog    dlg(FALSE);

    if (dlg.DoModal() != IDOK)
            return;

    // Prepare printing
    .
    .
    .
}
```

The second approach consists of retrieving, from the registry, the default printer settings, without displaying the dialog box. The next example shows this technique:

```
void OnPrintUsingDefault()
{
    CPrintDialog    dlg(FALSE);
    dlg.GetDefaults();

    // Prepare printing
    .
    .
    .
}
```

In both cases, a device context can be retrieved from the CPrintDialog dialog by calling GetPrinterDC(). This method returns a device context handle based on the selected printer. To follow MFC's mood, it is best to attach this device context handle to a CDC object, and use this CDC object to print. As a bonus, the CDC object delete the handle when deleted. Here's a CDC-based print implementation:

```
class CCommonView: public CView
{
    CDC     m_PrinterDC;
    .
    .
    .
};

void CCommonView::OnStartPrinting()
{
    // Let the user set the printing parameters
    CPrintDialog    dlg(FALSE);
```

```
    if (dlg.DoModal() != IDOK)
            return;

    // Obtain a printer device context
    HDC      hPrinterDC = dlg.GetPrinterDC();
    ASSERT(hPrinterDC != NULL);

    // Attach it to a CDC object
    m_PrinterDC.Attach(hPrinterDC);
}

void CCommonView::OnEndPrinting()
{
    // When printing's over, release the printer device context.
    m_PrinterDC.DeleteDC();
}
```

18.2.3 CFindReplaceDialog

Unlike the other common dialog boxes seen so far, the CFindReplaceDialog dialog box is modeless. The application must invoke Create() (instead of DoModal()), and process a specific message whenever the user interacts with the dialog. This message is not a constant, and requires an extra step to be handled via message maps.

The exact message id is obtained by calling ::RegisterWindowMessage() with the FINDMSGSTRING constant. This constant is unfortunately undefined in CE, but it can be found on other platforms; it is shown in the following example:

```
#define FINDMSGSTRING _T("commdlg_FindReplace")

class CCommonView : public CView
{
    static UINT          WM_FINDREPLACE;// Message id
    CFindReplaceDialog * m_pFindDlg;    // Dialog box pointer (modeless)
    CString              m_sPrevString; // Previous searched string

public:



    // Find/Replace dialog box registered message handler.
    LRESULT OnFindReplace(WPARAM wParam, LPARAM lParam);
};

UINT CCommonView::WM_FINDREPLACE;

CCommonView::CCommonView()
{
    // Get the registered FINDMSGSTRING window message in WM_FINDREPLACE
```

```
    WM FINDREPLACE = ReqisterWindowMessaqe(FINDMSGSTRING);

    // No modeless dialog box yet.
    m_pFindDlg = NULL;
}
```

Note in this example that the dialog box is also declared as a member variable. Indeed, since it is going to be modeless, it cannot be used as a local variable, as we did for the other common dialog boxes. The dialog box is shown (in modeless mode) by calling `Create()`, as shown below, typically in response to the Edit/Find menu item:

```
void CCommonView::OnEditFind()
{
    if (m_pFindDlg == NULL)
    {
        m_pFindDlg = new CFindReplaceDialog;
        m_pFindDlg->Create(TRUE, m_sPrevString, NULL, FR_DOWN, this);
    }

    m_pFindDlg->SetForegroundWindow();
}
```

The dialog box sends the message id obtained in the constructor (`m_FindMessage` in the example) to its parent whenever the user interacts with the dialog box (clicking Find Next, OK or Cancel). Use the `ON_REGISTERED_MESSAGE` macro in the message map to handle the message:

```
BEGIN_MESSAGE_MAP(CCommonView, CView)
    //{{AFX_MSG_MAP(CCommonView)
    ON_COMMAND(ID_EDIT_FIND, OnEditFind)
    //}}AFX_MSG_MAP
    // Standard printing commands
    ON_COMMAND(ID_FILE_PRINT, CView::OnFilePrint)
    ON_REGISTERED_MESSAGE(WM_FINDREPLACE, OnFindReplace)
END_MESSAGE_MAP()
```

The handler for the dialog box message is responsible for finding (or replacing) the text. Also, since the handler is called upon the dialog box termination, it can also perform some cleanup. The next example demonstrates a simplistic implementation:

```
LRESULT CCommonView::OnFindReplace(WPARAM wParam, LPARAM lParam)
{
    LPFINDREPLACE pFindReplace = reinterpret_cast<LPFINDREPLACE>(lParam);

    if (pFindReplace->Flags & FR_DIALOGTERM)
    {
        m_pFindDlg->DestroyWindow();
        delete m_pFindDlg;
```

```
            m_pFindDlg = NULL;

        return 0;
    }

    m_sPrevString = pFindReplace->lpstrFindWhat;
    AfxMessageBox(pFindReplace->lpstrFindWhat);

    return 0;
}
```

It is important to note that the function must receive the WPARAM and LPARAM parameters, and return an LRESULT value, because that's the way MFC executes the call. Not doing so can very likely crash the application, especially in Release mode.

Finally, as usual with a modeless dialog box, the parent's destructor must clean up when closed, as shown below:

```
CCommonView::~CCommonView()
{
    // The dialog box has been deleted by MFC, but not the C++ object.
    if (m_pFindDlg != NULL)
        delete m_pFindDlg;
}
```

18.3 PROPERTY SHEETS

A property sheet appears as a dialog box containing a few tabs, each tab showing some controls (Figure 18-12). Property sheets are also called tabbed dialog boxes. Property sheets are ideal to group together related application features or attributes, such as options, profiles, settings, etc.

Property sheets have OK and Close buttons on the top right corner, but unlike other Windows platforms, there is no Apply button.

Internally, a property sheet is a collection of property pages, each based on a dialog template (like a dialog box), within a Tab control. Clicking OK means that all selections on all pages (not only the current one) are applied at once. Similarly, clicking Close discards all changes done within the property sheet.

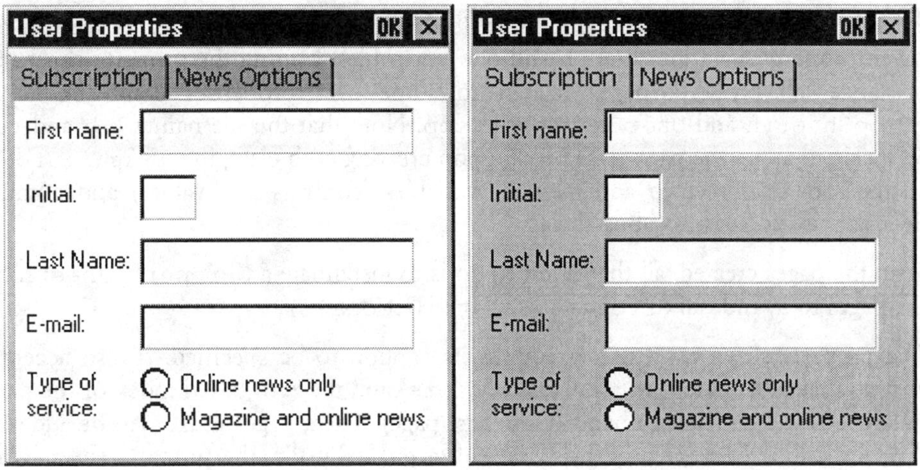

Figure 18-12: The same property sheet shown on a P/PC (left) and an H/PC (right). They are obviously very similar. Property sheets includes a caption (title), an OK and Close buttons, and one tab per property page.

18.3.1 Creating Property Sheets and Pages

MFC provides some very good support for property sheets and pages. CPropertySheet implements the property sheet functionality. Although it is used pretty much like a dialog box (its methods resemble those of CDialog), CPropertySheet is in fact derived from CWnd. On the other hand, each page is based on a dialog box template and is implemented using CPropertyPage, which is derived from CDialog.

Using a property sheet starts by creating each page within Visual C++, using the dialog box editor. Pages can vary is size (*i.e.*, height and width), but the property sheet will be displayed large enough to accommodate the largest page(s). However, it is a good idea to adjust all pages to the same size, because it makes it easier to align and center the controls, and to obtain a consistent look across the pages. It also recommended not to use OK and Cancel buttons on individual pages, since the user may get confused with those displayed by the property sheet. Finally, test the sheets on the target device (if possible), since property sheets larger than the screen are hard to deal with from a user's standpoint.

Then, using ClassWizard, a new class must be created for each dialog template. It is important to specify CPropertyPage as the parent class instead of CDialog in order to obtain the proper behavior. Also, it is a good convention to terminate the name with "Page" (*e.g.,* CSubscribePage), to distinguish them from dialog box classes. Each property page class can be generated in its own .h and .cpp files by default, although this is inconvenient if an application uses many property sheets and/or many pages per sheet, as it simply makes too many files to deal with. Instead, some developers prefer to keep all pages of a given property sheet into one `.h` and one `.cpp` files, bearing the property sheet name. For instance, all property pages related to some user properties could be kept in `UserPropSheet.h` and `UserPropSheet.cpp`. Note that the file names (`.h` and `.cpp`) can be specified along the page class name, upon creating each class, in `ClassWizard`. This is also the tool of choice to add member variables (controls and values) and command handlers, as it is for `CDialog`-based class.

With the pages created, all that is left to do is to instantiate a `CPropertySheet` object, add the pages to it, and call `CPropertySheet::DoModal()`.

The property sheet constructor requires its caption to be specified. It also accepts an optional pointer to its parent window (usually `this`) and the zero-based index of the page to be initially selected (the default being 0, the first page). Then, pages must then be added into the sheet by calling `CPropertySheet::AddPage()`. Finally, the property sheet is made visible by calling `CPropertySheet::DoModal()`. Only the selected page is in fact internally created; the other pages are not created yet (and do not receive `WM_INITDIALOG`). In fact, a property page is only internally created when the user selects it for the first time. `CPropertySheet::DoModal()` returns `IDOK` or `IDCANCEL`, like a dialog box, when the user closes the property sheet.

The next example illustrates the use of a property sheet. It assumes that two pages have already been created with ClassWizard, and that they lie in their respective `.h` and `.cpp` files.

```
#include "SubscriptionPage.h"     // Page definition
#include "NewsOptionsPage.h"      // Page definition

void CChildView::OnShowProperties()
{
    CPropertySheet          PropSheet(_T("User Properties"), this);
    CSubscriptionPage       Page1;
    CNewsOptionsPage        Page2;

    // Value member variables can be initialized for each page here.

    PropSheet.AddPage(&Page1);
    PropSheet.AddPage(&Page2);

    if (PropSheet.DoModal() == IDCANCEL)
            return;

    // Value member variables can be retrieved and processed
    // for each page here.
}
```

You can derive a new property sheet class if you wish to encapsulate the creation parameter(s), and let the application use the new, simplified class. You can go one step further and make the pages member variables as well. These member variables cannot be encapsulated (*i.e.*, kept private) because the application needs to have access to each page's member variable (unless you provide *enough* methods in your sheets to access them). The next example illustrates this approach. In this implementation, the page classes are generated by ClassWizard in the same `.h` and `.cpp` files that hold the property sheet code, namely `UserPropSheet.h` and `UserPropSheet.cpp`.

```cpp
// UserPropSheet.h

#pragma once

// CSubscriptionPage, generated by AppWizard.
class CSubscriptionPage : public CPropertyPage
{
    .
    .
    .
};

// CNewsOptionsPage, generated by AppWizard.
class CNewsOptionsPage : public CPropertyPage
{
    .
    .
    .
};

// CUserPropSheet, added by developer
class CUserPropSheet : public CPropertySheet
{
    DECLARE_DYNAMIC(CUserPropSheet)

public:

    CSubscriptionPage       m_Page1;
    CNewsOptionsPage        m_Page2;

    CUserPropSheet(CWnd * pParentWnd);
    virtual ~CUserPropSheet();

protected:

    DECLARE_MESSAGE_MAP()
};
```

```cpp
// UserPropSheet.cpp

#include "stdafx.h"
#include "psheet.h"
#include "UserPropSheet.h"

///////////////////////////////////////////////////////////////////////
// Code for CSubscriptionPage goes here
```

```
.
.
.
////////////////////////////////////////////////////////////////////////
// Code for CNewsOptionsPage goes here
.
.
.


////////////////////////////////////////////////////////////////////////
// CUserPropSheet

IMPLEMENT_DYNAMIC(CUserPropSheet, CPropertySheet)

CUserPropSheet::CUserPropSheet(CWnd * pParentWnd) :
    CPropertySheet(_T("User Properties"), pParentWnd, 0)
{
    AddPage(&m_Page1);
    AddPage(&m_Page2);
}

CUserPropSheet::~CUserPropSheet()
{
}

BEGIN_MESSAGE_MAP(CUserPropSheet, CPropertySheet)
END_MESSAGE_MAP()

// CUserPropSheet handlers go here
```

Hence, an application can use such a property sheet as follows:

```
#include "UserPropSheet.h"        // Property sheets (and included pages)

void CChildView::OnShowProperties(WPARAM, LPARAM)
{
    CUserPropSheet          PropSheet(this);

    // Value member variables can be initialized for each page here.

    if (PropSheet.DoModal() == IDCANCEL)
        return;

    // Value member variables can be retrieved and processed
    // for each page here.

}
```

Whether you choose the first approach (without encapsulation) or the second (with encapsulation) is up to you. I personally prefer the latter, because it makes the property sheet just a little bit easier to re-use (*i.e.*, fewer details to remember). The **PSheet** sample, on the

536

CD-ROM, combines both approaches: each page is implemented in its own source file, but a derived property sheet encapsulates their use.

18.3.2 Using Property Sheets

Most messages are sent to the active page as the user interacts with the property sheet. For instance, if the user clicks on a push button on the active page, the BN_CLICKED notification is sent to that page (see Chapter 19 for control notifications). You can use ClassWizard to install handlers within each page, as you would do for a dialog box. Don't forget to call UpdateData() to update the member variables and/or controls in your handlers. Note that DoDataExchange() (introduced in Section 18.1.2) is automatically invoked when switching from one page to another, keeping controls and value variables in synch.

Most of the interaction with the property sheet itself is handled by Windows, although MFC calls a few virtual property page methods as events unfold:

- Upon showing the property sheet, CPropertyPage::OnSetActive() is called for the page initially selected. That method must return TRUE to let the page be active. If, for some reason, the page cannot be displayed, FALSE can be returned. The property sheet will automatically select another page, and invoke OnSetActive() for that page and so on. If all OnSetActive() methods for all pages return FALSE, the property sheet is not shown.

- When switching to another page, CPropertyPage::OnKillActive() if first called for the page that was selected, and CPropertyPage::OnSetActive() is called for the newly selected page. These two methods typically return TRUE, indicating that the switch can be done. However, OnKillActive() can conduct some validation in order to make sure that the page is correct; on error, FALSE must be returned in order to maintain the active page selected (and cancel the switch).

- When clicking OK, CPropertyPage::OnKillActive() is first called for the selected page. Then, CPropertyPage::OnOK() is called for all pages that have been made active. This method doesn't return a value; to prevent the property sheet from being closed, OnKillActive() must return FALSE.

- When clicking Cancel, CPropertyPage::OnQueryCancel() is invoked on behalf of the active page. This method must return TRUE to allow the cancellation, or FALSE to maintain the property sheet alive. If it returns TRUE, CPropertyPage::OnReset() is called for all pages that have been made active.

Within a property page message handler (or virtual methods such as those we just discussed), calling CWnd::GetParent() returns a pointer to the property sheet itself.

Given that pointer, a few methods are available to programmatically alter the behavior of a property sheet (see Figure 18-13).

CPropertySheet Method	Description
GetActiveIndex()	Returns the zero-based index of the active page
GetPage()	Returns a pointer to the specified page (CPropertyPage)
GetActivePage()	Returns a pointer to the current page (CPropertyPage)
SetActivePage()	Sets the specified page as active.
RemovePage()	Removes a page from the property sheet.
GetPageCount()	Returns the page count.

Figure 18-13: The most commonly used CPropertySheet methods.

18.3.3 Modeless Property Sheets

Property sheets can be modeless, pretty much the same way as dialog boxes. As usual, create the pages and add them to the property sheet by calling CPropertySheet::AddPage(). Then invoke CPropertySheet::Create() instead of CPropertySheet:: DoModal(). The function immediately returns, making the application and the sheet running concurrently.

When the modeless sheet is closed (upon the user clicking OK or Cancel), it can notify the application by sending an user-defined message. The handler to this message, in the application, would simply invoke CWnd::DestroyWindow() to terminate the property sheet, exactly as it is with a modeless dialog box, as seen earlier.

18.4 MESSAGE BOXES

A message box is a small modal dialog box, with an icon, a text message, and a combination of push buttons (see Figure 18-14).

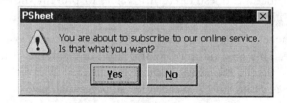

538

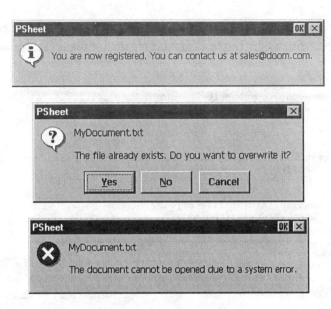

Figure 18-14: A few message boxes.

Message boxes can be slightly customized, as shown on the figure above: four different icons can be used, as well as a different combination of buttons. The text is a plain text string that automatically wraps within the message box. You can use '\n' to break the string, as shown above after "MyDocument.txt".

Their limited functionality makes messages boxes extremely easy to use. Simply call AfxMessageBox(), passing the text to be displayed within the message box, and a combination of styles. Figure 18-15 list a few common styles, whereas Appendix C (Section C.1.3.) contains the complete list.

Style Category	Style Value	Description
Types		
	MB_OK	Displays one button: OK
	MB_YESNOCANCEL	Displays three buttons: Yes, No and Cancel
Icons		
	MB_ICONEXCLAMATION	Displays the exclamation mark icon
	MB_ICONINFORMATION	Displays the information icon
	MB_ICONWARNING	Displays the warning icon
	MB_ICONSTOP	Displays the stop icon

Figure 18-15: A few message box styles, which can be combined together.

The following example shows the four message boxs shown in Figure 18-14. Note that sometimes a string is written over two lines, but both parts form a single, continuous string.

```
AfxMessageBox(
    _T("You are about to subscribe to our online service.\n")
    _T("Is that what you want?"),
    MB_YESNO | MB_ICONEXCLAMATION);

AfxMessageBox(
    _T("You are now registered. You can contact us at sales@doom.com."),
    MB_ICONINFORMATION);

AfxMessageBox(
    _T("MyDocument.txt\n\nThe file already exists. ")
    _T("Do you want to overwrite it?"),
    MB_YESNOCANCEL | MB_ICONQUESTION);

AfxMessageBox(
    _T("MyDocument.txt\n\n")
    _T("The document cannot be opened due to a system error."),
    MB_ICONHAND);
```

If you want a fancier message box (with a bold font, images, other icons, etc.), you have to implement either a dialog box or a window meeting your requirements.

SUGGESTED READINGS

Fowler, GUI Design Handbook

> This book is essentially a reference guide that reviews all existing GUI items that are available in today's operating systems: check boxes, combo boxes, entry fields, menus, etc. What's interesting is that each item is described in terms of what it is good for, how to test the usability, and further references.

Galitz, The Essential Guide to User Interface Design

> The book proposes design guidelines to build clear and easy to understand user interface applications, such as selecting the proper type of windows, menus, controls, colors, icons, etc.

Microsoft, The Windows Interface Guidelines for Software Design

> This is one of the best books to design user interfaces *à la* Microsoft. For instance, Chapter 8 explains some rules to respect when designing secondary windows, such as dialog boxes and property sheets. The text is easy to read, and contains numerous figures to illustrate the topics. A must for enthusiastic graphical user interface developers.

Chapter 19

Windows Controls

This chapter explains the Windows controls, the specialized windows that are reused throughout most applications to provide a consistent look and feel. Figure 19-1 shows several in a dialog box. They are implemented within Windows CE and are available to all applications. MFC also supports those controls, making them very easy to use.

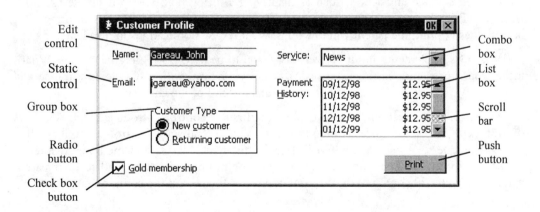

Figure 19-1: The original Windows controls, described in this chapter.

This chapter explains how to use the original Windows controls (buttons, edit controls, combo boxes, list boxes, scroll bars, and static controls), as well as a few other controls unique to CE. The next chapter focuses on the common controls, also called advanced controls.

19.1 CONTROL OVERVIEW

Controls are called *child windows*, child in the sense that they are attached to a parent window (more on that in a second) and *window* because they *are* windows. Everything that has been said so far about a window can also be said about a control.

Controls are attached to a parent because their purpose is to perform one or a few specific actions. They usually don't have a title bar, or a menu, and they don't provide enough functionality to act as applications themselves. Hence they need a parent to implement the core application functionality. Take scroll bars for instance: the purpose is limited to gathering some input to provide a relative position given an arbitrary range; they cannot be applications by themselves. Controls do need a parent window to "host" them, such as a dialog box, which implements some core functionality.

Controls are autonomous regarding their own functionality. When a push button is tapped, the push button repaints itself with a pushed down look to provide some feedback to the user, and returns to its normal appearance when the stylus is released. In fact, a parent window doesn't have to do anything at all once a control has been created.

Controls maintain a special dialogue with their parent, making them interactive. When tapped upon, besides repainting itself, a button does something else: it *notifies* its parent window that it has been tapped upon. Upon receiving the notification (which is a message), the parent may take any action, such as displaying a dialog box. Here's a simple example: when the Print button is tapped, it notifies its parent window, which starts printing. The button doesn't print; the parent window does. We'll review notifications in detail later.

Windows implements about 30 controls, ready to be used "as is" in applications. What's more, you can extend existing controls or create your own, with a unique appearance and behavior. We'll discuss extending controls toward the end of the chapter.

In the following sections, we will explore the first six controls introduced with Windows (buttons, edit boxes, list boxes, combo boxes, scroll bars, and static controls) as well as some controls unique to Windows CE. We'll describe the MFC classes and methods to interact with them from a programming standpoint, and the notifications they send to their parent window. Chapter 20 continues on the same topic, but focuses on the common controls.

19.2 WORKING WITH WINDOWS CONTROLS

Before diving into the details of some controls, let's present some attributes common to all of them.

19.2.1 Managing Controls in Dialog Boxes

Controls are very easy to use with dialog boxes. To start with, the dialog box layout (with all its controls) is constructed using a dialog box editor, such as the one bundled in Visual C++, or Visual Basic. At run-time, the dialog box automatically creates the controls, and upon termination, automatically destroys them. Furthermore, since MFC adds the concepts of value and control variables, accessing controls is as simple as using member variables (Chapter 18 presents the complete picture regarding dialog boxes.) Those are the reasons why the vast majority of controls are used within dialog boxes.

19.2.2 Managing Controls in Plain Windows

In some rare circumstances, controls must be created in a plain window. Consider an existing application whose main window displays a graph. As part of some enhancement, a Print button must be added on the lower right corner. We may argue whether a button should be placed there, but let's assume it has to be done that way. Since the window already exists, redesigning the window to make it dialog-based is not really an option.

Creating Controls – The Old Way

If controls are to be used in non-dialog-based windows, they must be created program-matically. As mentioned before, controls are windows. Hence, in C/Win32, all controls can be created using ::CreateWindow() or ::CreateWindowEx(), like any other window. One of the parameters to these two functions is the Window class name (not to be confused with a C++ class name). Calling ::CreateWindow(_T("LISTBOX"), ...) creates a list box; calling ::CreateWindow(_T("BUTTON"), ...) creates a button, etc.. Class names such as "LISTBOX", "BUTTON", etc. are pre-registered class names, recognized by Windows CE. The class name is used to identify the window procedure that will manage the control, and each window procedure is implemented differently, all within Windows.

Creating Controls – The MFC Way

In MFC, calling CWnd::Create(_T("LISTBOX"), ...) also creates a list box, because this method is essentially a wrapper to ::CreateWindowEx(). But MFC designers, in their quest of hiding as many details as possible, derived new classes that make control creation and manipulation easier. All these control classes are derived from CWnd. As a result, all CWnd methods that are explained in Chapter 15 directly apply to *all* controls. Each control class implements a Create() method that is as simple as it can get. Although the parameters vary from one control to another, all Create() methods require at least four arguments:

1. The style, which defines the appearance and behavior. This includes predefined windows styles (*e.g.*, WS_VISIBLE), as well as the control-specific style attributes (*e.g.*, LBS_STANDARD, valid with a list box control). Window and control styles are listed in Appendix C.

   We'll see control-specific styles as we explore each control, but make sure you specify WS_VISIBLE (it is off by default); otherwise, the control won't show up. It is a good practice to specify WS_CHILD, although most controls' Create() methods do so automatically (using WS_CHILD is required with control windows).

   Extended styles (WS_EX_xxx) cannot be specified with the control"s Create() methods, but you can call CWnd::ModifyStyleEx() immediately after creating the control to turn some of them on. Note that you can also call CWnd::ModifyStyle() later on to enable or disable regular style attributes. This method is especially useful with some recent controls, since the resource compiler doesn't recognize all styles, and they must be programmatically turned on to be used (more in Chapter 20).

2. The control's coordinates, expressed as a CRect, which determines the position and size of the control within the parent window. The coordinates must be relative to the parent's client area. For instance, specifying CRect(10, 10, 110, 40) positions the control's top left corner at (10,10), in pixels, in the parent's client area.

   One issue that quickly comes up is the difficulty of establishing the control coordinates, since it is difficult to align controls without a graphical tool. Your life can really become miserable if you have to create a bunch of controls and guess their positions. Be prepared to go through the edit-compile-run-whine cycle more than once.

3. The parent window (as a CWnd *). This is the window that will receive the notifications when sent. This parameter must be the control's parent window, usually this.

4. The control identifier, which must be unique in respect with the other controls of the same parent. You must "manually" create identifiers when creating controls programmatically. In an AppWizard-generated application, you can easily create unique ids from by choosing *Resource Symbols* from the *View* menu. The dialog box that is shown allows you to add new identifiers in a snap. If this option is disabled (such as when you work on an application written from scratch), remember that you can use any positive value, as long as there isn't any other control with the same identifier within the same window.

The following example creates two identical list boxes, the first one using CWnd, the second using CListBox. The purpose is to demonstrate that they are equivalent, since CWnd::Create() is never used with controls in practice.

```
class CMyWnd: public CWnd
{
    CWnd          m_cListBox1;              // First listbox
    CListbox      m_cListBox2;              // Second listbox
    .
    .
    .
};

int CMyWnd::OnCreate(LPCREATESTRUCT lpcs)
{
    if (CWnd::OnCreate(lpcs) == -1)        // Call parent
            return -1;

    CRect  rect(10, 10, 60, 50);           // Hypothetical position

    cListBox1.Create(
            _T("LISTBOX"),                 // Predefined class name
            _T(""),                        // Title (none is required)
            WS_VISIBLE | LBS_STANDARD,     // Style
            rect,                          // Position and size
            this,                          // Parent window
            IDC_LISTBOX1);                 // Application-defined identifier

    cListBox2.Create(
            WS_VISIBLE | LBS_STANDARD,     // Style
            rect,                          // Position and size
            this,                          // Parent window
            IDC_LISTBOX2);                 // Application-defined identifier
}
```

Note that the second call, CListBox::Create(), takes fewer parameters than the first call, CWnd::Create(), a more generic call. Internally, CListBox::Create() invokes CWnd::Create() but it provides the first two parameters (class name and caption), which are always the same for list boxes: _T("LISTBOX") and _T(""). The advantage of using CListBox::Create() is that developers don't need to know the predefined class name of the controls they want to use. That's one detail less to remember.

Using Member Variables for Controls

In this example, the parent window creates its two controls in OnCreate() (the handler from WM_CREATE). This is the ideal spot to create controls in plain windows, since the parent window exists, but is not visible yet.

The parent window is using two member variables to represent the controls. Very importantly, those variables are member variables, not local to `OnCreate()` (we'll see why in just a minute). Always use member variables when creating controls.

It is very, very important to understand that declaring a control variable does not create the control. In the example above, declaring `m_cListBox1` and `m_cListBox2` only declares C++ variables. There are no Win32 system calls executed by doing so, unless a window (or a list box) is being created. Hence, until the call `CWnd::Create()` or `CListBox::Create()` are executed, no window-related operations can be executed using those variables. For instance, calling `CListBox::GetCurSel()` before calling `Create()` fails on both variables[60].

Destroying Controls

The parent window doesn't have to explicitly delete its controls, as this happens automatically. Hence, when the parent window is deleted, so are the controls.

If you need to delete the controls before the parent window is closed (a very rare scenario), know that controls can be destroyed by calling `CWnd::DestroyWindow()`. This is a method inherited from `CWnd`, and it works with all controls.

`CWnd`'s destructor deletes the attached window if it hasn't been deleted yet. This destructor (and behavior) is inherited by all controls as well. Hence, in the example above, if `m_cListBox1` and `m_cListBox2` were local variables, they would automatically destroy the related list boxes when going out of scope, when `OnCreate()` terminates.

19.2.3 Interacting with Controls

Because they are windows, controls react to messages, whether their parent window is a dialog box or not. When the user taps on a push button, what the button really sees is a `WM_LBUTTONDOWN` (left mouse button down) message; the button reacts by repainting itself with a pushed down look. All of this happens without the parent window being aware of anything.

But controls do not *only* react to mouse events. Their parent can send them messages too. For instance, to change the text of a push button, the parent window must send the message `WM_SETTEXT` along the text string address in `lParam`. When that message is received, the control repaints itself with the new text.

Sending that kind of message in MFC is the same as in the SDK, although the syntax is slightly different. Instead of sending a message to the control such as:

---

[60] Doing so in debug mode generates an assertion failure message box, because the variables are not associated with controls yet.

```
HWND          hButtonWnd;
    .
    .
    .
::SendMessage(hButtonWnd, 0, (LPARAM) _T("&Print"));
```

the parent window can invoke `SetWindowText()` over a `CButton` object:

```
CButton      cButton;
cButton.SetWindowText(_T("&Print"));
```

The first method (`::SendMessage()`) requires the programmer to know what the `wParam` and `lParam` arguments are, which are message-dependent (in this case, respectively zero and the string pointer). Given that there are hundreds of messages, it is easy to specify wrong parameters, and the compiler can't help. A few macros have been introduced in the SDK to make these calls safer to use and improve readability, but the door is still open for problems. For instance, consider wrongfully sending the message `LB_INSERTSTRING` (which is normally sent to a list box to add a string) instead of `WM_SETTEXT` to a push button: the compiler will not complain, but the text in the button won't get updated any time soon!

MFC solves all these problems by providing methods for each control class. For instance, a `CButton` has about ten methods to interact with them (*e.g.*, `CButton::SetState()`, `CButton::SetCheck()`, `CButton::SetButtonStyle()`, etc.) – but it doesn't have an `AddString()`. As a result, by using a `CButton`, developers are restricted to valid operations only. Typically, MFC provides as many C++ wrapper methods than there are supported messages.

In addition, remember that because controls are derived from `CWnd`, all `CWnd`'s methods are inherited as well. For instance, calling `CWnd::SetWindowText()` or `CWnd::EnableWindow()` on a `CButton` works perfectly well. That's because a button works with the messages sent by those `CWnd` wrapper methods.

19.2.4 Control Notifications

Controls are used for specific reasons: to gather input, to display information in a certain format, or both. What makes them useful is their eagerness to communicate essential information.

Sending and Handling Notifications

When some significant event takes place on a control, that control sends a notification message to its parent (see Figure 19-2). Each type of control has a predefined set of notification messages. For instance, tapping on a button results in the button sending the BN_CLICKED notification to its parent window. Notifications for all controls are listed in Appendix D.

The parent responds to these notifications by taking any relevant action. For instance, when the parent receives the BN_CLIKED notification from the *Print* button, the parent may start the print process.

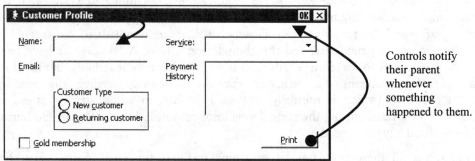

Figure 19-2: Controls send notifications to their parent, which in turn may send them messages to update their appearance or change their behavior.

Notifications are automatically sent by controls. There is usually nothing to do, from a programming standpoint, for controls to send notifications[61]. They always do. That's their nature. This behavior is rooted deep in Windows.

Notifications, like other messages, are received and handled via message maps. For instance, the parent window of a button labeled *Print* can have the following entry to handle the button notification BN_CLICKED:

```
// In MyWnd.h

class CMyWnd: public CWnd
{
```

---

[61] Some controls requires the style xxx_NOTIFY to be set in order to send extra notifications, as we will see later.

```
public:
    . . .
    afx_msg void OnPrint();              // Handler
declaration
};
```

```
// In MyWnd.cpp

BEGIN_MESSAGE_MAP(CMyWnd, CWnd)
    . . .
    ON_BN_CLICKED(IDC_PRINT, OnPrint)      // Message map entry
    . . .
END_MESSAGE_MAP()

void CMyWnd::OnPrint()                      // Handler
implementation
{
    // Handle BN_CLICKED from the IDC_PRINT push button by
printing
}
```

First, the handler must be declared in the class definition. The handler prototype depends on the notification (more on that later). `afx_msg` defines nothing, it's purely informational. The message entry also depends on the notification. In this case, the `ON_BN_CLICKED` entry associates the `BN_CLICKED` notification from the `IDC_PRINT` control to the handler `CMyWnd::OnPrint`. If another button is clicked, that entry will not be used, because the control id (`IDC_PRINT` in this case) won't match. Hence, message map notification entries take into account the notification *and* the control identifiers.

Visual C++'s ClassWizard has been designed to manage parent windows' message maps. For instance, invoking ClassWizard on a dialog box allows adding handlers for all notifications from all its controls. Unfortunately, in some rare occasions, ClassWizard doesn't support specific notifications, and you must add message map entries and handler definitions manually.

Notification Details

The `BN_CLICKED` notification is perhaps one of the simplest. The notification model evolved with Windows, particularly with the introduction of Windows 95 and the common controls, detailed in the next chapter.

The original Windows controls send notifications through a `WM_COMMAND` message. The accompanying parameters are detailed in Figure 19-3. During the pre-MFC era, applications had to decipher those parameters themselves.

WM_COMMAND Parameter	Description	Example
HIWORD(wParam)	Notification code	BN_CLICKED
LOWORD(wParam)	Control identifier	IDC_PRINT
lParam	Control handle	Internal control handle

Figure 19-3: When sending WM_COMMAND to send a notification, each control prepares wParam and lParam as shown above. This presents a consistent notification mechanism, which many message map entries (such as ON_BN_CLICKED) are based upon.

Using WM_COMMAND was enough with these controls, because no further information had to be passed along the notification. One exception was the scroll bar, which needs to pass the position of the thumb button when it gets moved. Since wParam and lParam were already used to hold notification data, new messages were introduced: WM_VSCROLL and WM_HSCROLL. With those messages, wParam contains a 16-bit scroll code and a 16-bit position, and lParam is the control handle (for identification). We'll see scroll bars in Section 19.3.5.

Common controls uses another message (WM_NOTIFY), described in the next chapter.

19.3 WINDOWS CONTROLS

Now that we understand what controls are, how to interact with them, how and why they send notifications, let's review each control from an MFC standpoint, one by one. The following figure summarizes the controls described in this chapter.

Category	Name	MFC Class
Window Controls		
	Push Button	CButton
	Check Box	CButton
	Radio Button	CButton
	Group Box	CButton
	Edit Control	CEdit
	List box	CListBox
	Combo Box	CComboBox
	Scroll Bar	CScrollBar
	Static Control	CStatic
Miscellaneous		
	HTML Viewer Control	*Not implemented in MFC*
	Rich Ink Control	*Not implemented in MFC*
	Voice Recorder Control	*Not implemented in MFC*

Figure 19-4: The original Windows controls and some other controls, described in this chapter.

The remaining of this section and Section 19.4 explains these controls by describing the following:

- **Specific creation parameters, including the most popular style attributes.** The complete list of style attributes can be found, for each control, in Appendix C.

- **The operations they support.** Only the most common operations are detailed by explaining some class methods. Explaining all methods would just provide too much material.

- **The notifications worth handing.** Again, only the most important notifications are described in this chapter. Appendix D contains the complete list of notifications for all controls.

Examples are presented all along.

19.3.1 CButton

There are four types of buttons, all implemented using the CButton class (see Figure 19-5):

- **Check box**, which is represented by a small square followed by some text (Items 1, 2 and 3 on Figure 19-5). The text can be on the left of the square as well. Check boxes are used by the user to indicate some preferences (such as to use or not use a spell checker in a word processor).

- **Group box** (yes, this is implemented as a button!), which doesn't provide any functionality other than displaying a grayed frame with an optional caption (Item 4 on Figure 19-5). They add clarity by regrouping controls together.

- **Radio buttons**, usually laid out in groups, in which only one is selected at any time (Items 5 and 6 on Figure 19-5). These buttons are used for the user to make a single selection within a group.

- **Push buttons**, which can display a text caption or an image (Item 7 on Figure 19-5). When clicked upon, push buttons trigger an action (via a notification handled by the parent). The parent usually gathers the status of all check boxes, radio buttons and other controls, and performs the selected action.

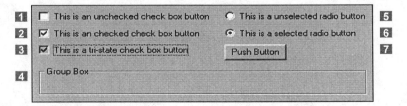

Figure 19-5: The types of buttons that are available via CButton.

Creating Buttons

If you choose to create a button programmatically, call `CButton::Create()` and specify the button caption in addition to the four arguments presented in Section 19.2.2 (style, rectangle, parent, and id). The caption is the text associated with the button. For instance, for a check box, this is the text displayed next to it; for a group box, this is the text listed in the top line, etc.

Use the styles `BS_PUSHBUTTON`, `BS_CHECKBOX`, `BS_RADIOBUTTON` and `BS_GROUPBOX` to create a push button, check box, radio button, and group box, respectively. The `BS_3STATE` style creates a three-state check box (checked, unchecked, and indeterminate).

The styles `BS_3STATE`, `BS_CHECKBOX` and `BS_RADIOBUTTON` create buttons whose appearances do not change automatically when the user clicks on them. For instance, clicking on an unchecked `BS_CHECKBOX` button results in a notification sent to the parent (`BN_CLICKED`), but the button remains unchecked. To become checked, the parent must call `CButton::SetCheck(1)`, as we'll see shortly. This contrasts with `BS_AUTO3STATE`, `BS_AUTOCHECKBOX` and `BS_AUTORADIOBUTTON` buttons, which send notifications when clicked upon, but also automatically change their state (the parent doesn't have to do anything). It is common to use auto-changing buttons in applications.

Here is an example of the creation of a button in a plain window:

```
// Assume CMyWnd declares: CButton m_cButton;

void CMyWnd::OnCreate(LPCREATESTRUCT lpcs)
{
    CRect   rect(10, 10, 40, 20);           // (Guessed) position

    m_cButton.Create(
            _T("&Print"),                   // Caption
            WS_VISIBLE | WS_TABSTOP |       // Visible and tab stop
            BS_PUSHBUTTON,                  // Button style: push button
            rect,                           // Position and size
            this,                           // Button's parent window
            IDC_PRINT);                     // Button identifier
    .
    .
    .
}
```

Button States

Buttons have three distinct states:

- The *focus* state indicates whether the button is receiving the keyboard input. This applies to check boxes, radio buttons, and push buttons. This state is represented with a thin dotted line around the text in the button (the *focus rectangle*). The user moves the focus between controls by clicking on them or by using the TAB key while in a dialog box. The focus can be explicitly set to a window by calling CWnd::SetFocus().

- The *push* state indicates whether the button is pushed or not. This state applies to push button, check box (including three-state), and radio button. This state is represented differently depending on the control. A pushed push button will appear with sunken edges (instead of raised), whereas the background of a check box or radio button is dimmed when pushed.

- The *check* state determines if the item is checked or not. A normal check box and radio buttons can be checked or unchecked, but a three-state check box can also be indeterminate. The square box of an indeterminate three-state check box appears as dimmed, with or without a check mark. The check state of automatic buttons (those created with the BS_AUTOxxx style) automatically changes when the user clicks of them, whereas the parent window must make the change itself for non-automatic button.

The current state can be obtained programmatically by calling CButton::GetState(), and changed by calling CButton::SetState(). The check state can also be obtained by calling CButton::GetCheck(), and changed through CButton::SetCheck(). One reason to programmatically alter the state (even with automatic buttons) is, for example, when the user selects an option that checks a series of check boxes. For instance, some windows present a "Check All" button to check a series of check boxes; upon receiving the BN_CLICKED notification from the "Check All" button, the parent window may check all check boxes programmatically.

Grouping Radio Buttons

Radio buttons are usually grouped together, and the selection is normally mutually exclusive within the group (selecting one deselects any other selected in the group). Note that the grouping does not happen graphically (putting a frame around some buttons does not make them radio buttons), it's a style attribute: WS_GROUP. The first radio button of a group must have the style WS_GROUP, as well as the control that follows the last button, based on the order of creation. Also, to be able to move onto a radio button group using the TAB key, make sure the first button of the group also has the WS_TABSTOP style.

Figure 19-6 demonstrates the use of WS_GROUP. That window contains two groups of radio buttons (red – green – blue) and (Windows CE 1.0 – Windows CE 2.0 – Windows CE 2.1). The first button of each group (Controls 2 and 6), as well as the control that follows each group (Controls 5 and 9) must have the WS_GROUP attribute set.

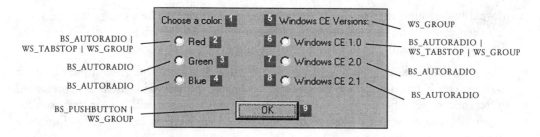

Figure 19-6: Radio buttons are grouped via the `WS_GROUP` style. It must be set for the first radio button of the group and the very next control following that last radio button of the same group. The order in which controls have been created is shown in numbered, grayed boxes.

Button Notifications

The most important notification is `BN_CLICKED`, sent when a button is tapped. As a matter of fact, most user commands are passed via menu, toolbar, and... push buttons. For instance, suppose the user is presented with a form to buy some products. The parent window doesn't have to be involved as the user enters information (in edit control, detailed below) and makes his/her choice (by checking a few check boxes, radio buttons, etc.). However, when the button "Buy" is clicked, the parent queries all controls, and processes the purchase.

Other notifications (listed in Appendix D) exist for backward compatibility only and can be ignored.

19.3.2 CEdit

An edit control is a rectangular window in which the user can enter input from the keyboard. A parent window uses an edit control to gather keyboard input, instead of processing keyboard messages, or calling C functions like `getch()`. On Figure 19-1, edit controls are displayed next to "Name:" and "Email:".

An edit control receives input only when it has the focus, that is, when the user taps on it or by using the TAB key. When an edit control has the focus, it displays a small caret to indicate the insertion point.

Creating Edit Controls

You create an edit control by calling `CEdit::Create()` and specifying the four arguments listed in section 19.2.2. A few interesting styles are listed in Figure 19-7.

Edit Styles	Description
ES_AUTOHSCROLL	Scroll the edit content if the user reaches the end of line.
ES_MULTILINE	Supports multiple lines of text.
ES_PASSWORD	Displays '*' (by default) for each character entered. This is useful to read passwords.
ES_UPPERCASE	Converts typed characters to uppercase.
ES_READONLY	Makes the edit control read-only. Contrarily to static controls, user can still select the text within the control.

Figure 19-7: Popular edit control styles.

Here's an example of an edit control creation:

```
CEdit   cEdit;
CRect   rect(10, 10, 40, 20);

cEdit.Create(
        WS_VISIBLE | WS_TABSTOP |      // Visible and tab stop
        ES_UPPERCASE,                  // Edit style: make it uppercase
        rect,                          // Position and size
        this,                          // Edit's parent window
        IDC_NAME);                     // Edit identifier
```

Text Buffer

An edit control automatically manages an internal buffer on the local heap (that the application doesn't have to allocate or free). That buffer may hold up to 30,000 characters. A parent window can set the text of an edit control by calling `CWnd::SetWindowText()`. Conversely, it can obtained the already-entered text by calling `CWnd::GetWindowText()`.

The number of entered characters in the control is obtained by calling `CWnd::GetWindowTextLength()`. The maximum number of characters that can be entered can be limited by calling `CEdit::SetLimitText()`, and obtained through `CEdit::GetLimitText()`. These calls do not affect the characters that have already been entered. When the user types more than what is allowed, the control sends the EN_MAXTEXT notification to its parent. There is usually no need to handle this notification, as the control will not accept the extra input by itself anyway.

Text Selection

Text selection and clipboard operations (clear, cut, copy, and paste) are the control's responsibility. These operations can be programmatically invoked by the parent window as well, by respectively using CEdit::Clear(), CEdit::Copy(), CEdit::Cut(), and CEdit::Paste(), but this is very rare.

The user may select a few contiguous characters within a control. The parent window can call CEdit::GetSel() to retrieve the index of the first and last characters selected. Also, range of characters can be selected programmatically by calling CEdit::SetSel(). The selected portion can be replaced by other text by calling CEdit::ReplaceSel().

Since edit controls are very good at managing text selection themselves, applications are usually not involved in that activity.

Modifiable and Read-only Text

An edit control sets an internal flag whenever it is modified. A parent window can call CEdit::GetModify() to determine if the user made any change to the control. This is convenient, when reading back a form, to identify the fields that the user updated. The parent may reset the flag by calling CEdit::SetModify().

The text is by default writable, but it might be set as read-only. For instance, when displaying a form about a record, the record identifier field might remain read-only to prevent the user from changing it. An edit control can be created as read-only (by using the ES_READONLY style attribute), or can be set as read-only after creation by calling CEdit::SetReadOnly(). To know if the control is already read-only, the parent calls CWnd::GetStyle() and checks if the ES_READONLY flag is set.

Password Text

Passwords and other sensitive information can be entered by setting the ES_PASSWORD style. When doing so, any input is displayed as an asterisk. The asterisk can be replaced by any other character specified in CEdit::SetPasswordChar(). The character being used is returned by GetPasswordChar().

Margins and Tab Stops

The left and right margins can be set. Each margin is expressed as a width (in pixels) that is left blank. Margins can be set by calling CEdit::SetMargins() and specifying the two margins (left and right), in pixel units. CEdit::GetMargins() returns a DWORD, whose LOWORD() is the left margin and HIWORD(), the right one.

Tab stops can be in multiline edit control by calling CEdit::SetTabStops(), specifying either an fixed interval or an array of intervals. The call must be followed by a call to CWnd::Invalidate(), since setting tab stops does not redraw the window.

The default settings are usually acceptable, resulting in these methods being rarely used.

Undoing Operations

Edit controls support an undo feature. Calling `CEdit::Undo()` reverses the last operation done by the user. Calling `CEdit::EmptyUndoBuffer()` resets the undo flag, preventing the last operation from being undone. A parent window can call `CEdit::CanUndo()` to determine whether the last operation can be undone.

Multiline Edit Controls

Edit controls support only one line of text by default. But they can support multiple lines when the style `ES_MULTILINE` is set. And in this case, you can control whether the Return key is interpreted by the control itself or by the dialog box (the default). In the first case (by setting the `ES_WANTRETURN` style), pressing Return inserts a new line in the edit control; in the second case, pressing Return triggers the default push button.

The Notepad application is essentially composed of a window whose client area is a multiline edit control that accepts return key as a new line character.

Edit Control Notifications

A notification commonly handled in interactive applications is `EN_KILLFOCUS`, sent when the user moves the focus out of the control.

Whenever the notification is received, the parent may validate the data entered in the edit control on-the-fly. If something is wrong, the parent may display an error message box, and move the focus back to the control by calling `CWnd::SetFocus()`. If this approach is retained, remember that there must be one message map entry (`ON_EN_KILLFOCUS`) per edit control to validate as such.

Another scenario is to gather information, again on-the-fly. Consider a data entry window, which requires a customer id. As soon as the user has entered the id, the parent fetches the information and displays it the customer profile on the screen. This makes the application slightly easier to use: there is no need to add a button called "Load" for instance; tabbing out automatically loads.

19.3.3 CListBox

A list box is a control that displays a series of strings. In Figure 19-1, a list box is shown above the Print button. An optional scroll bar is displayed if the number of strings exceeds the size of the list box (as shown). A string can be selected by tapping on it.

Creating List Boxes

You create a list box by calling CListBox::Create() and specifying the four arguments specified in Section 19.2.2. Figure 19-8 shows some popular styles.

List Box Styles	Description
LBS_MULTICOLUMN	A horizontal scroll bar is used instead of a vertical one.
LBS_MULTIPLESEL	More than one string can be selected.
LBS_STANDARD	The most popular style. The list box is sorted and sends notifications whenever strings are clicked or double-clicked.
LBS_USETABSTOPS	Expands tab stops when drawing strings.

Figure 19-8: Popular list box control styles. Windows CE does not support owner-drawn list boxes.

Here is an example creating a list box:

```
CListBox        cListBox;
CRect           rect(10, 10, 40, 20);

cListBox.Create(
        WS_VISIBLE | WS_TABSTOP |     // Visible and tab stop
        LBS_STANDARD,                 // Listbox style: std listbox
        rect,                         // Position and size
        this,                         // Listbox's parent window
        IDC_HISTORY);                 // Listbox identifier
```

String Operations

A string is added to the end of the list box by calling CListBox::AddString(). For instance, a database application can retrieve the content of a table line by line, and insert them, one by one, in a the list box. Note that if the list box has the LBS_SORT style set, the string is inserted based on the alphabetical order. The method returns the zero-based index in the list of the newly-inserted string. Only one string can be inserted per line. The list box displays the string by itself and doesn't require the parent window to do so. Strings are also called items, especially in the documentation.

A string can be inserted at a specific, zero-based position, by calling CListBox::InsertString(). Doing so pushes the other strings downward. Conversely, calling CListBox::DeleteString() removes a string from the list box based on its zero-based position, pulling the following strings up.

`CListBox::GetCount()` returns the number of items in the list box, whereas `CListBox::ResetContent()` empties the list box at once. It is faster to call `Reset Content()` once than to repeatedly call `DeleteString()` for each string to remove.

The list box repaints itself after each modification, a convenient feature that leaves the list box constantly up to date. But that can cause a problem if there are hundreds of strings to insert or delete, because (re)painting will occur hundreds of times, slowing down the application. Perhaps you've faced the situation yourself on other Windows platforms, where it takes a few seconds (even minutes) for the list box to get filled. If you expect to insert many strings at once (more than ten), painting can be turned off by calling `CWnd::SetRedraw(FALSE)`. Painting is turned on again once the insertion is completed, by calling `CWnd::SetRedraw(TRUE)`, which also refreshes the list box. Hence, drawing occurs only once. Since insertion operations are much faster than painting, the user will not notice any delay. This tip also applies when deleting many items.

Searching Strings

If the user presses a key while a list box has the input focus (*i.e.*, when an item is shown/selected with a focus rectangle), the list box selects the next item that starts with that key. For instance, if the user taps on a list box and presses 'B', the first entry starting with 'B' will be selected. Pressing 'B' again selects the next entry that starts with 'B', and so on. Selection restarts at the top once it reaches the bottom. This behavior is integrated right into the list box, and doesn't require any support from your application.

Your application can also search strings itself. `CListBox::FindString()` searches for a string starting with the specified prefix, from a specified position (-1 for the entire list), and returns the index of the first matching entry (or `LB_ERR` if not found). For instance, if the list contains "Audi", "Bentley", "BMW" and "Mercedes" in that order, finding "B" returns 1, the zero-based index of "Bentley". The current selection is not altered by the search.

If an exact string is searched (instead of any string matching a prefix), use `CListbox::FindStringExact()`. In the example above, search for "B" would return `LB_ERR` (no match), whereas "Bentley" would return 1. This call doesn't affect the selection either.

Finally, to search for an exact string and select it if found, use `CListBox::SelectString()`. It too returned a zero-based index if a match is found; otherwise, it returns `LB_ERR` and the selection is left unmodified.

Single Selection

A list box usually has a single item being selected (displayed as white letters on a dark blue background by default).

The user changes the selection by clicking on an item, which results in the LBN_SELCHANGE (selection changed) notification being sent to the parent window. Upon receiving that notification (if handled), the newly-selected item is returned by calling CListBox::GetCurSel(), which returns the zero-based index of the currently selected item. If there isn't any item selected, it returns LB_ERR.

Setting the selection is done by calling CListBox::SetCurSel(). Note that doing so does not trigger the LBN_SELCHANGE notification to be sent to the parent.

An application can also make use of CListBox::GetSel(), passing an item index, to determine if that item is selected or not. It returns non-zero if selected, 0 if not.

Multiple Selection

List boxes support multiple selections if the style LBS_MULTIPLESEL is set (it isn't by default, leading to single selection). An example of a multiple-selection list box is one displaying many files, which can be selected in order to open all of them at once.

CListBox::GetCurSel() and CListBox::SetCurSel() do not apply to multiple-selection list boxes. Instead, CListBox::GetSelItems() and CListBox::SetSel() must be used.

CListBox::GetSelItems() returns the selected state of all items at once. It requires an array of integers, whose content will hold the indices of the selected items. For instance, if the items 1, 3, 4, and 6 are selected in a multiple-selection list box, CListBox::GetSelItems() fills a 4-integer array with 1, 3, 4, and 6. The number of selected items is returned by calling CListBox::GetSelCount(). This method can be used for allocating an array prior to call GetSelItems(), as shown in the following example:

```
void CMyDlg::CalculatePayments()
{
    // Construct and initialize an array that contains the listbox'
    // selected item indices.
    int    nCount = m_cHistory.GetSelCount();
    int *  aItems = new int[nCount];

    m_cHistory.GetSelItems(nCount, aItems);

    // Process the selected items in aItem
    .
    .
    .
```

```
    delete [] aItems;
}
```

`CListBox::SetSel()` sets the selection state of an item. It requires an item index and a Boolean, which must be TRUE to select the item, or FALSE to deselect it. This method only affects the specified item, leaving all other items intact. If a range of items are to be selected or deselected at once, one can call `CListBox::SetItemRange()`, which accept a selection Boolean, and the indices of the first and last items. The following example deselects all items at once:

```
    m_cListBox.SetItemRange(FALSE, 0, m_cListBox.GetCount()-1);
```

Item Operations

An application can retrieve the string content of an item by calling `CListBox::GetText()`, specifying a zero-based index and either a pointer to a buffer or a reference to a CString object. This method is very useful for the parent to know which string has been selected. For instance, upon receiving the LBN_SELCHANGE notification, the parent can call that method to identify the string, and display extra information about it. GetText() also accepts a string pointer (instead of a CString). That buffer must be long enough to accommodate the string about to be read. Call `CListBox::GetTextLen()` to obtain the length if any given string.

Applications may associate a 32-bit value (such as an index or a pointer) to each item in a list box. For instance, each item of a list box containing a list of names may refer to a structure (or object) describing each person. `CListBox::SetItemData()` associates a 32-bit DWORD value to the specified index, whereas `CListBox::GetItemData()` retrieves that same value. The next example is a parent window handler for LBN_SELCHANGED. It identifies the newly selected item and gets the associated 32-bit value, which is in this case an index into an array of information data:

```
void CMyWnd::OnSelChange()
{
    // Get the current selection, return on error.
    int nSel = m_cListbox.GetCurSel();

    if (nSel == LB_ERR)
            return;

    // Get the associated DWORD
    DWORD   dwData = m_cListbox.GetItemData(nSel);

    // Use it as an index into an internal array to access and display
    // more information about the selected item
```

```
      SMOREDATA *      pMoreData = m SomeDataArray[dwData];

      . . .
}
```

For this example to work, the application must have associated a 32-bit value for each string initially inserted.

In other cases, it might be preferable to store a pointer instead of a 32-bit DWORD value. For instance, a pointer to some extra data might be associated with each item and retrieved later on. Use CListBox::SetItemDataPtr() and CListBox::GetItemDataPtr() to associate and retrieve respectively a pointer value with/from an item. Note that the associated pointer is in fact a cast 32-bit DWORD value; these functions internally are not different than SetItemData() and GetItemData(). The following example is a variation of the previous example.

```
void CMyWnd::OnSelChange()
{
    // Get the current selection, return on error.
    int nSel = m_cListbox.GetCurSel();

    if (nSel == LB_ERR)
          return;

    // Get the related information (assuming it has been
    // associated before)
    SMOREDATA *     pMoreData =
          static_cast<SMOREDATA *>(m_cListbox.GetItemDataPtr(nSel));

    . . .
}
```

List Box and Item Appearance

You can control the interpretation of the tab character when a list box has the LBS_USETABSTOPS style (see Figure 19-9). By default, tab stops are set to two dialog units. These units are based on the default font size; call ::GetDialogBaseUnits() to obtain the number of pixels per unit.

Figure 19-9: One list box without LBS_USETABSTOPS and another one with it.

To set each tab stop on a specific unit, call `CListBox::SetTabStops()`, specifying the new unit. For instance, specifying 12 means to align each character following a tab on the next dialog unit a multiple of 12. To set each tab stop on various units, call the same method, but passing an array of integers, each representing a dialog unit alignment measure. Finally, calling that method with no arguments resets each tab stop at every two dialog units.

When a list box contains more items than it can display, a vertical scroll bar is displayed for the user to navigate throughout the list. You can ensure that a specific item is visible by calling `CListBox::SetTopIndex()` with the index of the item that should be the first displayed in the list box. For instance, if a list box is designed to hold about 10 items, an item can be displayed in the middle of the list box by displaying the 4th item before it at the top (making the target item the 5th in the list). Conversely, `CListBox::GetTopIndex()` returns the index of the first visible item

The height of each item can be set by calling `CListBox::SetItemHeight()`, which accepts an item index and a height in pixels. Windows CE does not support variable-size items (the index must be zero), so the method is applied on all items at once. Conversely, the height is returned by calling `CListBox::GetItemHeight()`, again passing an index of 0.

MultiColumn List Boxes

When a list box has the `LBS_MULTICOLUMN` and `WS_HSCROLL` set, the list expands horizontally, and it displays a horizontal scroll bar instead of a vertical one (see Figure 19-10). All the other methods seen earlier still apply identically.

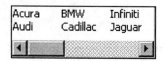 

Figure 19-10: The same list box, with and without the `LBS_MULTICOLUMN` style. Default is without.

The width of each column is set to some default, but it can be altered by calling `CListBox::SetColumnWidth()` and specifying a width in pixel units.

When the list box has more items than it can display and the horizontal scroll bar is shown, `CListBox::GetHorizontalExtent()` returns the width (in pixels) by which the list bar can be scrolled horizontally. Conversely, `CListBox::SetHorizontal Extent()` sets that width. These two functions are rarely used.

List Box Notifications

Two notifications are interesting, but they are only sent if the style LBS_NOTIFY is set; otherwise, the list box remains mute.

The first notification is LBN_SELCHANGE, sent whenever the user changes the selection. Application may then query the selected item and display supplemental information about it in other controls next to the list box.

The other notification, sometimes handled, is LBN_DBLCLK, which is sent when an item is double-tapped. The parent can handle this notification by opening a dialog box that shows more information about the tapped item.

19.3.4 CComboBox

A combo box combines two controls into one: an edit control, always shown, and a list box, which may be dropped (shown) or retracted (not shown). Figure 19-1 shows a retracted combo box next to "Service:". There are three styles of combo boxes, which determine how they can be used (see Figure 19-11).

Combo Box Type	Writable Edit control?	Retractable list box?
Simple	Yes	No
Dropdown	Yes	Yes
Droplist	No	Yes

Figure 19-11: The three combo box types.

Combo boxes are used when space is tight, a frequent situation with Windows CE. Consequently, simple combo boxes, which always display their list box and occupy more room, are not as popular as the others. A dropdown combo box is chosen over a droplist when the user can enter a non-listed choice (the droplist limits the user to choose an existing string in the list box).

Creating Combo Boxes

You create a list box by calling CListBox::Create() and specifying the four arguments specified in Section 19.2.2. Figure 19-12 shows some popular styles.

Combo Box Styles	Description
CBS_DROPDOWN	A dropdown combo box.
CBS_DROPDOWNLIST	A droplist combo box
CBS_SIMPLE	A simple combo box
CBS_SORT	Sorts the strings in the list box

Figure 19-12: Popular list box control styles. Windows CE does not support owner-drawn combo boxes.

The next example creates a combo box:

```
CComboBox       cComboBox;
CRect           rect(10, 10, 40, 20);

cComboBox.Create(
        WS_VISIBLE | WS_TABSTOP |   // Visible and tab stop
        CBS_DROPDOWN,               // Combobox style: drop down
        rect,                       // Position and size
        this,                       // Combobox's parent window
        IDC_SERVICE);               // Combobox identifier
```

List Box-Like Operations

Combo boxes implement the same list box string methods seen earlier, namely `AddString()`, `DeleteString()`, `InsertString()`, `ResetContent()`, `FindString()`, `FindStringExact()`, and `Select String()`.

Combo boxes only support single-selection. Hence `GetCurSel()` and `SetCurSel()` are supported.

Each item can be associated with a 32-bit data, making the following methods fully supported: `SetItemData()`, `SetItemDataPtr()`, `GetItemData()` and `GetItemDataPtr()`.

Other methods are implemented they same way they are with list boxes: `GetCount()`, `GetTopIndex()`, `SetTopIndex()`, `GetHorizontalExtent()`, and `SetHorizontalExtent()`.

Text operations have been brought in too: `LimitText()`, `GetItemHeight()`, and `SetItemHeight()`.

The text of a specific item in the combo box can be retrieved by calling `CComboBox::GetLBText()`, whereas the length of an item is returned via `CComboBox::GetLBTextLen()`.

Edit Control-Like Operations

`CWnd::GetWindowText()` retrieves the text selected in the edit control part of the combo box. The maximum length of the text that can be entered can be limited by calling `CComboBox::LimitText()`.

Unique Combo Box Operations

A few operations are truly unique to combo boxes. `CComboBox::ShowDropDown()` accepts a Boolean that determines if the list box is shown (TRUE) or not (FALSE). Conversely, `CComboBox::GetDroppedState()` returns TRUE if it is visible, FALSE otherwise.

Combo boxes may use an extended user interface that makes them easier to use by the user. When that extended interface is active, tapping on the edit control of a dropped-down combo box shows the list box; pressing the down arrow also shows the list box. This behavior is activated by calling `CComboBox::SetExtendedUI(TRUE)`.

Section 20.2.1 describes how to add a combo box within a command bar.

ComboBox Notifications

Figure 19-13 lists some notifications sent by combo box controls. Those notifications are rarely handled.

Notification Message	Description
`CBN_DROPDOWN`	The list box is about to be made visible
`CBN_EDITCHANGE`	The edit control has been changed and updated
`CBN_SELCHANGE`	The selection is about to be changed in the list box.

Figure 19-13: The most common combo box notifications.

19.3.5 CScrollBar

Scroll bars are narrow controls that consist of a scroll area, a scroll box (also called the thumb), and arrows on both ends. They represent the relative position of the information being displayed against the whole document. Scroll bars can be either horizontal or vertical. Scroll bars shouldn't be confused with sliders (described in the next chapter). There are two styles of scroll bars on Windows CE:

- The *old-style* scroll bars were those used in pre-Windows 95 systems. The thumb is fixed in size (kind of square), and the scroll bar range, which must be specified programmatically, is limited to 16-bit values. This limitation causes problems if the scroll bar represents a wide range, as we will see. Although this is a problem more likely to be found on larger Windows platforms, it may also surface on some Windows CE applications, especially since CE is now running on larger screens. `CScrollBar` implements that type of scroll bar, which is no longer popular today.

- The *new-style* scroll bars (such as the one shown in Figure 19-1) provide a thumb whose size against the scroll bar itself indicates how much of the whole document/image is being viewed. Also, these scroll bars remove the range limitation. MFC doesn't provide a class for those scroll bars, but the example presented in this section introduces a reusable class, `CScrollBar32`, that implements them.

Both styles are described in this section.

Using Scroll Bars

Scroll bars are never used alone. In some cases, they are integrated in other controls (edit controls, list boxes, combo boxes, etc.), which manage them automatically. For instance, if ten items are added in a list box that has room for five, the list box automatically displays and manages the scroll bar. From a programming standpoint, this functionality comes free. In some other cases, scroll bars can be added in a parent window to provide scrolling capabilities.

There are three methods of using scroll bars, depending on the scrolling requirements and the application's structure:

- If you use a document/view application, and you wish to make the view scrollable (horizontally, vertically, or both), use a `CScrollView` instead of a `CView`. This method is the easiest to use, once you know a few essential tricks (presented below) to make it work right.

- If you want to add scrolling capabilities to a plain window other than a view, add the style `WS_HSCROLL` and/or `WS_VSCROLL` when creating the window. This will add scroll bars within the window, which will send `WM_HSCROLL` and/or `WM_VSCROLL` when used by the user. The window is responsible for painting according to the scroll bar position though.

- If you want to scroll only a part of a window (not the entire window), you can create a scroll bar control, which will also send `WM_HSCROLL` and/or `WM_VSCROLL` when used. Your application is responsible for scrolling whatever must be scrolled.

These methods are described in detail in the following paragraphs.

Method 1: Using CScrollView

If you use a document/view application, specify that the view must be derived from CScrollView, instead of a plain CView, on Step 4 in ClassWizard. This will generate an OnInitialUpdate() method that invokes CScrollView::SetScrollSizes(), the key method that lets the view know when and how to display scroll bars:

```
// Default OnInitialUpdate(), from AppWizard

void CSbViewView::OnInitialUpdate()
{
    CScrollView::OnInitialUpdate();
    CSize sizeTotal;
    // TODO: calculate the total size of this view
    sizeTotal.cx = sizeTotal.cy = 100;
    SetScrollSizes(MM_TEXT, sizeTotal);
}
```

You must calculate, within that function, the total width and height of the view. For instance, if you are reading a bunch of numbers in order to produce a graph, you may arbitrarily determine that the highest bar would be 300 pixels high, and that each bar width is ten pixels. You could access the document to find out how much data there is to display, how many bars that will produce, and hence, the total width of the graph. For instance, assuming that 40 bars are to be displayed, the total width is 400 (pixels). Therefore, you would set sizeTotal.cx to 400 and sizeTotal.cy to 300. Then, depending on the actual size of the view, CScrollView may or may not display scroll bars: if the visible view is greater than 400x300, no scroll bars are shown; if the size is smaller (either vertically, horizontally, or both), the scroll view automatically displays scroll bars. However, although you can forget about scroll bars, there are two other issues to address: redrawing properly, and mouse coordinates.

Although CScrollView can scroll the view, the image will not redraw properly. For instance, Figure 19-14 illustrates a view that simply calls CDC::Ellipse(0, 0, 1000, 1000) and that has slightly been scrolled in both directions. The drawing code is shown below:

```
void CSbViewView::OnInitialUpdate()
{
    CScrollView::OnInitialUpdate();
    CSize sizeTotal;

    // Use 1000x1000, to draw an ellipse of that size.
    sizeTotal.cx = sizeTotal.cy = 1000;

    SetScrollSizes(MM_TEXT, sizeTotal);
}
```

```
void CSbViewView::OnDraw(CDC* pDC)
{
    pDC->Ellipse(100, 100, 900, 900);
}
```

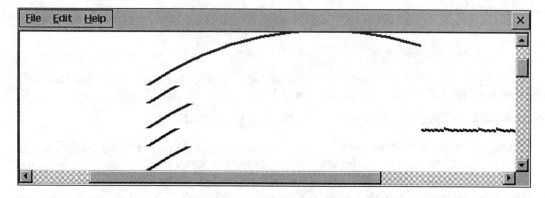

Figure 19-14: A CScrollView scrolls, but drawing requires some attention.

The source of the problem is that OnDraw() is unaware that the view has been scrolled, a problem that can be fixed in OnPrepareDC(). This function is automatically called just before OnDraw() in order to adjust the device context if needed. Implement OnPrepareDC() as follows:

```
void CSbViewView::OnPrepareDC(CDC* pDC, CPrintInfo * pInfo)
{
    // Although the scroll view scrolls, the viewport origins are not
    // set properly. Make the adjustment here.
    CPoint pt = GetScrollPosition();
    CPoint ptPrev;

    ::SetViewportOrgEx(pDC->m_hDC, -pt.x, -pt.y, &ptPrev);
}
```

Note that if you add the function with ClassWizard, make sure that the function declaration exactly matches the one shown above. It didn't in my case (the CPrintInfo * argument was missing), resulting in the function not being called until fixed.

The other problem is to interpret mouse/stylus coordinates when the view is scrolled: the coordinate passed to OnLButtonDown() is *always* relative to the window's top left corner, whether the view is scrolled or not. But if the view is fully scrolled in both directions, clicking in the lower right corner should return the total image size, not the window bottom right corner as it does now.

This problem can easily be fixed by adding the returned value of GetScroll Position() to the mouse coordinate, as shown in this handler:

```
void CSbViewView::OnLButtonDown(UINT nFlags, CPoint point)
{
    // Adjust the point by taking into account the scroll position(s).
    point += GetScrollPosition();

    .
    .
    .
}
```

With these two fixes, using a scrollable view actually becomes fun! The **EasyScrl** sample, on the CD-ROM, implements this technique.

Method 2: Adding WS_HSCROLL and/or WS_VSCROLL

If you use a plain window (not a view) that needs to be scrolled horizontally and/or vertically, add the window styles WS_HSCROLL and/or WS_VSCROLL upon creating the window (*i.e.*, when calling Create() or in PreCreateWindow()). The window will automatically have a horizontal and/or vertical scroll bar(s). But they do nothing by themselves: the window must manage the range of each scroll bar and the scroll bar notifications.

The range of a scroll bar specifies by how much it can scroll. This measurement is completely application-dependent. The total size of the image must be established for the range to be calculated, as shown in the first method. For instance, if a 40-bar chart is to be drawn, and each bar's width is ten pixels, the total width is 400 pixels. You must also know the size of the window itself (what is later referred to as the *page*). This is the window's client area, which can be obtained by calling CWnd::GetClientRect(). Although CE doesn't support resizable Windows, WM_SIZE is still sent after creation, along the window's size. This is a good place to set the scroll bar range. Besides, this makes the code more portable on other Windows platforms, where windows are indeed resizable. In order to set the range, call CWnd::SetScrollInfo(), passing the scroll bar type (SB_VERT or SB_HORZ), and a SCROLLINFO structure (see Figure 19-15), which sets the scroll range attributes.

Type	Member	Description
UINT	cbSize	Always set to sizeof(SCROLLINFO).
UINT	fMask	Scroll bar parameters to set or retrieve.
int	nMin	Minimum scrolling position.
int	nMax	Maximum scrolling position.
UINT	nPage	Page size, *i.e.*, the visible area.
int	nPos	Scroll bar thumb position. This is updated only when the user strops dragging the thumb. Use nTrackPos to determine the position during a drag.
int	nTrackPos	Immediate tracking position when dragging the thumb.

Figure 19-15: The SCROLLINFO structure.

The most important fields are nMin, nMax, nPage, and nPos, which respectively control the minimum range, maximum range, page size, and position. Here's how to set those values for an horizontal scroll bar, assuming that the window's client area width is W_w and the total image's width is W_i, where the image is larger than the client area (*i.e.*, $W_i > W_w$):

- Set nMin to 0

- Set nMax to W_i

- Set nPage to W_w

- Limit the scroll position to [0, W_i - W_w + 1] (inclusive) when processing scroll bar messages, described hereafter.

The next example sets the range in OnSize():

```
void CMainWindow::OnSize(UINT nType, int cx, int cy)
{
    CFrameWnd::OnSize(nType, cx, cy);

    SCROLLINFO    si;
    si.cbSize = sizeof(si);
    si.fMask  = SIF_PAGE | SIF_RANGE;
    si.nMin   = 0;

    if (cx < m_szTotal.cx)
    {
        // The window's width is smaller than image's width.
        // Set the scroll bar range range.
        si.nPage     = cx;
        si.nMax      = m_szTotal.cx;
        m_nMaxScroll = m_szTotal.cx - cx + 1;

        // Set the line as the tenth of the width, and
        // set the page as the actual width.
        m_nLineSize  = cx / 10;
        m_nPageSize  = cx;
    }
    else
        // The image entirely fits: no scroll bar.
        si.nMax = 0;

    // Set the scroll range of the HORIZONTAL scroll bar.
    SetScrollInfo(SB_HORZ, &si);
}
```

Finally, your window must respond to the notifications sent by the scroll bar and move the image. Actually, scroll bars don't send notifications; they instead send two specific messages: WM_HSCROLL (from horizontal scroll bars), and WM_VSCROLL (from vertical scroll bars). They are respectively handled by CWnd::OnHScroll() and CWnd:: OnVScroll(), and require entries in the message map (ON_WM_HSCROLL and ON_WM_ VSCROLL). Their default implementation (in CWnd) does nothing useful.

Each message handler receives three parameters: a scroll bar code (shown in Figure 19-16), a position (valid when the user is moving the thumb), and a pointer to a CScrollBar (which can be ignored).

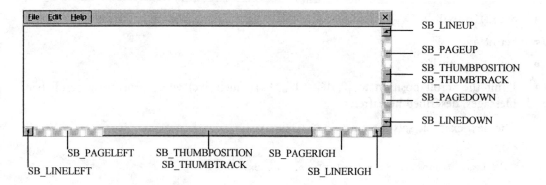

Figure 19-16: Scroll codes indicates how the user interacts with scroll bars. SB_THUMBTRACK is sent as the user drags, whereas SM_THUMBPOSITION is sent when the drag is over.

Upon receiving these messages, the window responds by shifting the image and, very importantly, positioning the thumb to the new position (otherwise it will return to its original position). The main problem is not moving or scrolling the image, it's flickering. A simple implementation may simply invalidate the client area, and repaint everything, taking into account the new scroll position (by calling ::SetwindowOrgEx(), as seen earlier). However, if the user drags the scroll bar button, the window may not repaint fast enough (especially for complex images), in addition to the annoying flickering that will harass the user!

The best way to scroll an image is to call CWnd::ScrollWindow(), which requires the amount to scroll by (in pixels), vertically and horizontally. These values directly depend on the new scroll position, and by how much the image is already scrolled. The call moves the image as required, and WM_PAINT is placed in the queue to repaint only the small portion that became invalid (see Figure 19-17). A well-designed OnPaint() can take advantage of such a small invalid area by only redrawing that small portion. The result will be a responsive, flicker-free, scrolling window.

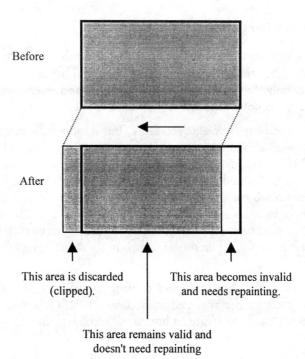

This area is discarded (clipped).

This area becomes invalid and needs repainting.

This area remains valid and doesn't need repainting

Figure 19-17: Scrolling a window via `CWnd::ScrollWindow()` is an efficient technique, since it moves the image without flickering, and invalidates only a small portion.

This technique is demonstrated in the **ScrlGrph** sample (see Figure 19-18), which implements a scrolling graph in a plain, non document/view application.

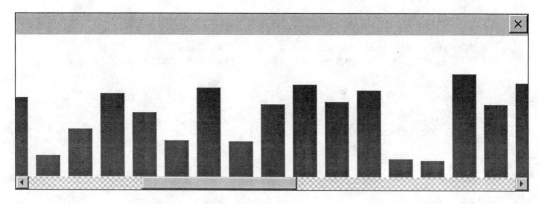

Figure 19-18: A scrolling graph in a non document/view application.

Method 3: Using Scroll Bar Controls

Both methods seen so far scroll an entire window. If what you want is to scroll a part of it, neither approach will satisfy you. Instead, you can add a scroll bar control, and respond to its messages by scrolling only the portion of interest. This method resembles the previous one, except that the scroll bar is not embedded in the window, but is a control by itself.

MFC provides a scroll bar class, CScrollBar, but it unfortunately implements the *old-style* scroll bars, those with a fixed-size thumb, limited to a 16-bit range. Those scroll bars are really obsolete. One alternative is to use a CScrollBar object, but rely on CWnd::SetScrollInfo() and CWnd::GetScrollInfo() to access it. These two methods will give your scroll bar the contemporary look everybody expects. To make things easier, the **Sb32** sample includes a wrapper class called CScrollBar32, which can be used pretty much like a CScrollBar (except one detail we are about to see). Unless mentioned otherwise, the methods explained hereafter apply to both CScrollBar and CScroll Bar32.

You can create a scrollbar like any other control: by calling Create(). This method only requires the four arguments specified in Section 19.2.2. Only two scroll bar-specific styles are available: SBS_HORZ, to create an horizontal scroll bar, and SBS_VERT, to create a vertical one.

You can position the scroll bar anywhere on the window. However, you must query the system to obtain their standard size. The standard width of a vertical bar and the standard height of an horizontal bar can be obtained by calling ::GetSystemMetrics() with SM_CXVSCROLL and SM_CYHSCROLL respectively. The next example creates an horizontal scroll bar.

```
int CChildView::OnCreate(LPCREATESTRUCT lpcs)
{
    if (CWnd::OnCreate(lpcs))
          return -1;

    // Create a vertical scroll bar.
    CRect   rect(100, 10, 100 + ::GetSystemMetrics(SM_CXVSCROLL), 90)

    m_cScrollBar.Create(
          WS_VISIBLE | SBS_VERT,          // Visible and vertical
          rect,                           // Position
          this,                           // Parent window
          IDC_SCROLLBAR);                 // Control id

    .
    .
    .


    return 0;
}
```

You can use the same approach in a dialog box, by placing a scroll bar at the desired position. Either way, you must calculate and set the scroll bar range. How this is done depends on the type of scroll bar your application is based on (*i.e.*, CScrollBar or CScrollBar32).

Using Old-Style Scroll Bars

The common scenario is to set a range equal to the width of the graphic minus the width of the visible portion. For instance, in Figure 19-19, the graphic is 600 pixels wide (a value the application can calculate), but the client area's width is 480. The range can be set to 120 (600 – 480). As the user interacts with the scroll bar, the position will range from 0 to 120, regardless of the actual size of the scroll bar[62]. This exact amount indicates by how many pixels the original image must be scrolled. If the scroll bar thumb is on the left (at position 0), the left portion of the image must be shown (a); if the thumb is in the middle (at position 60), the center of the image must be shown (b); if the thumb is on the right (at position 120), the right portion must be shown (c).

CScrollBar implements a few methods to work with the range, but bear in mind that these methods limit the range to a 16-bit value (although this is usually enough on CE devices – at least *today*). If you are interested in a larger range, jump to the next section *Using New-Style Scroll Bars*.

The first method is CScrollBar::SetScrollRange(), which establishes the minimum and maximum values of the scroll bar button. The range can be retrieved by calling CScrollBar::GetScrollRange(). SetScrollRange() is specific to CScrollBar.

The current scroll bar button position can be obtained at any moment by calling CScrollBar::GetScrollPos(). The position can be either set by the user (by dragging it) or programmatically, by calling CScrollBar::SetScrollPos().

Using New-Style Scroll Bars

In order to use the modern scroll bar, one can rely on CScrollBar32::SetScrollRange(), which requires the page size and the minimum and maximum range values, as explained earlier. CScrollBar32::GetScrollRange() retrieves those values.

---

[62] The scroll bar internally performs calculations to return the specified range based on it's actual width.

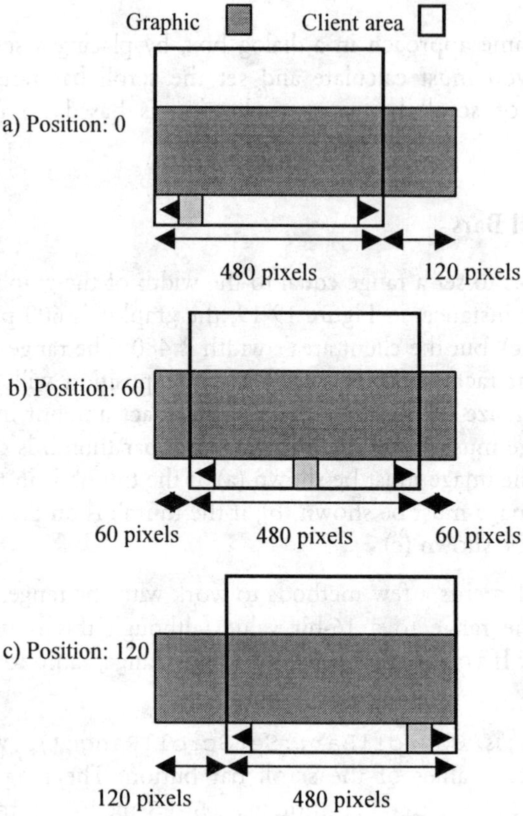
Graphic
Client area
a) Position: 0
480 pixels
120 pixels
b) Position: 60
60 pixels
480 pixels
60 pixels
c) Position: 120
120 pixels
480 pixels

Figure 19-19: The range is usually the width of an image minus the visible width. The scroll position then indicates by how much the original image must be scrolled.

Disabling Scroll Bars

In some applications, the image's width can vary because of various factors, such as a zoom capability. At some point, the image within those application may suddenly fit the visible area, rendering the scroll bar(s) useless. The issue then becomes whether the scroll bar(s) should simply be disabled (*i.e.*, grayed) or simply hidden.

A scroll bar can be hidden by calling `SetScrollRange(0, 0)`, or even `CWnd::ShowWindow(SW_HIDE)`. Hiding scroll bars is acceptable, but some users do not like controls that appear/disappear - it gives an impression of inconsistency. The alternative is to disable the scroll bar: leaving it there, but grayed and non-operational.

A scroll bar can be entirely disabled by calling `CWnd::EnableWindow(FALSE)`. As an alternative, the arrows on each extremity can individually be disabled, while maintaining the scroll bar enabled, by calling `CScrollBar::EnableScrollBar()`. Disabling arrows that way is unusual, though.

19.3.6 CStatic

Static controls display static information, *i.e.*, data that essentially does not change nor react to user input. Under Windows CE, static controls are used in dialog box to display text or bitmaps, as an alternative to drawing them programmatically (by processing `WM_PAINT` for instance). Once a static control is created, it repaints itself whenever it has to, like any other control, making their use simple.

Creating Static Controls

You create a button by calling `CButton::Create()` and specifying the text to display in addition to the standard four arguments (listed in Section 19.2.2). The text can be `NULL` to display a bitmap.

You can set and retrieve the text of a static control by calling `CWnd::SetWindowText()` and `CWnd::GetWindowText()` respectively. Similarly, you can set and retrieve the bitmap handle of a static control by calling `CStatic::SetBitmap()` and `CStatic::GetBitmap()`. The next example demonstrated a call to `CStatic::SetBitmap()`:

```
CStatic     Static;
CRect       rect(. . .);

Static.Create(
    NULL,                           // No text
    SS_BITMAP | WS_VISIBLE,         // The static shows a bitmap
    rect,                           // Coordinates
    this,                           // Parent window
    IDC_STATIC);                    // -1

CBitmap     Bitmap;

Bitmap.Loadbitmap(IDB_MYBITMAP);    // From the resource file.
Static.SetBitmap(Bitmap);           // Displays the bitmap
```

Static controls do not send notifications unless the `SS_NOTIFY` style is on, but in most cases, they are just ignored.

19.4 OTHER CONTROLS

There are three controls that are available on Windows CE, which aren't considered common controls, and that aren't supported by MFC, either (it is very likely that they will in the next release, though). These controls, HTML Viewer, Ink, and Voice Recorder, are briefly reviewed in this section, along some examples.

19.4.1 HTML Viewer Control

Windows CE provides a control to display HTML data, which can be obtained either from a web page or a file. Windows CE's own Internet Explorer is in fact based on it. This is not an ActiveX control, nor does it expose any COM interface. The control is implemented in `HtmlView.dll`; related messages, notifications, and structures are defined in `HtmlView.h`, and a library is provided in `HtmlView.lib`.

Sample **HtmlApp** (see Figure 19-20) uses this control, and provides a wrapper class called `CHtmlCtrl`. This class only provides the functionality required for that example: creating the control and displaying some HTML data. It could easily be extended to handle the other messages that the control natively supports (refer to your platform's `HtmlView.h` for the list of messages).

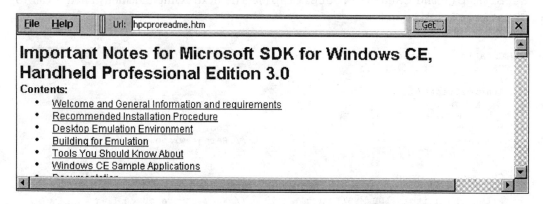

Figure 19-20: An application using the HTML Viewer control.

It is up to the application to load an HTML page from the web or a file. The text can then be passed to the control by sending the `DTM_ADDTEXT` message (or calling `CHtmlCtrl::AddText()`). This can be repeated more than once for a single page (a very useful feature when loading data by chunks). Once the page has fully been inserted, send the `DTM_ENDOFSOURCE` (or call `CHtmlCtrl::EndOfSource()`) to signal the its completion.

The control sends various notifications (also listed in `HtmlView.h`) to its parent window (in this example, the frame): when the user taps a link, when a image is required, or when a sound must be played. But notifications are not sent properly (the window handle isn't the HTML Viewer control - as it should be - but a child's control). As a result, notifications can't be handled by MFC's logic, nor can they be reflected to the control itself (in this case, the `CHtmlCtrl` class). Fortunately, this problem can be resolved simply by applying the following fix in the parent window's `OnNotify()` handler:

```
BOOL CParentWnd::OnNotify(WPARAM wParam, LPARAM lParam, LRESULT* pResult)
{
    if (wParam == HTML Control Id)
    {
            NMHDR * pNMHDR = reinterpret_cast<NMHDR *>(lParam);
            pNMHDR->hwndFrom = Handle of the HTML Control;
    }

    return CFrameWnd::OnNotify(wParam, lParam, pResult);
}
```

This fix is applied in the **HtmlApp** sample, which is based on a `CHtmlCtrl`.

19.4.2 Ink Control

Virtually all PC companion devices provide a touch screen and a stylus. In order to read stylus input, Windows CE provides the Ink Control, shown in Figure 19-21. This control is very complete: it has its own menu (which can be turned off) and users can directly type *and* draw. It's almost a complete application in itself!

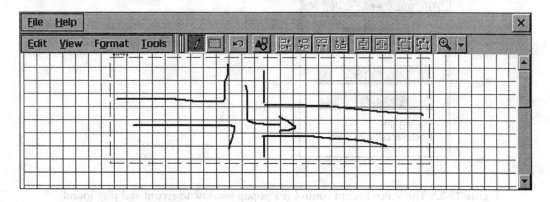

Figure 19-21: User can write and draw using the Ink control.

The control maintains the data in its own buffer, which the application can read and store in a file. Later, that data can be passed back to the control to be displayed again. An application could potentially interpret that data if required.

The **Rich Ink** sample is a simple application that displays an Ink control, whose content can be saved in a file, and eventually re-opened. Since MFC doesn't support a class for that control, a wrapper class, called `CInkCtrl`, is provided for convenience.

Starting with Windows CE 2.1x, the control's header and library files are in `Inkx.h` and `Inkx.lib`, respectively. On the previous CE versions, those files are `RichInk.h` and `RichInk.lib`.

But pay attention here: an enhanced ink control, called the Rich Ink control, has been introduced with CE 2.1x, which now uses `RichInk.h` and `RichInk.lib`. This enhanced control is not available on previous versions.

19.4.3 Voice Recorder Control

The Voice Recorder control is a small window that allows the user to record and play sound files (typically `WAV` files), on devices equipped with a sound card and a microphone (see Figure 19-22). Palm-size PCs are the prime candidates for that control, which is in fact a pop-up window that directly interacts with the user. Once visible, the user can click a button to start recording and another to stop. The control may have an OK and Cancel buttons as well.

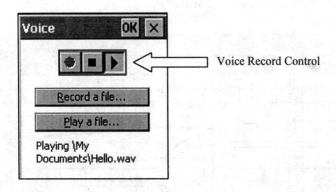

Figure 19-22: The Voice Record control is a popup window to record and play sound files.

The control requires a file name, where the sound is recorded and played from. The same file can be used for both operations. As the user interacts with the control, notifications are sent to the parent window to indicate what actions are taking place (*e.g.*, start playing, stop playing, etc.) The parent window can also send messages to start recording and playing programmatically.

Since MFC doesn't provide any class, the **Voice** sample uses a wrapper class called `CVoiceCtrl`. Unlike other controls, this one doesn't have an id (although it does have a window handle). This prevents the parent's ability from processing notifications through its message map. The solution simply consists of calling a specific handler whenever a notification is received from the control (in the parent's `OnNotify()`), using the control's handle to identify it:

```
BOOL CVoiceDlg::OnNotify(WPARAM wParam, LPARAM lParam, LRESULT* pResult)
{
    NMHDR * pNMHDR = reinterpret_cast<NMHDR *>(lParam);

    // If the notification comes from the Voice control, simply
    // call OnNotifyVoice().
    if (pNMHDR->hwndFrom == m_pVoiceCtrl->GetSafeHwnd())
    {
            OnNotifyVoice(reinterpret_cast<NMHDR *>(lParam), pResult);
            return TRUE;
    }

    return CDialog::OnNotify(wParam, lParam, pResult);
}

void CVoiceDlg::OnNotifyVoice(NMHDR *pNMHDR, LRESULT* pResult)
{
    switch (pNMHDR->code)
    {
    case VRN_RECORD_START:
        .
        .
        .
    }
}
```

Given the nature of the control, it is perhaps best to use that control like a modeless dialog box, *i.e.*, to create it when needed, and delete it when either a close notification is received or when it is no longer required. You can create the control by calling `CVoiceCtrl::Create()`, which requires some style attributes (as usual), a `CPoint` (the top left corner of the window), a file name, and the parent window. The control can later be closed by calling `CWnd::DestroyWindow()`.

19.5 CUSTOMIZING CONTROLS

Using controls offers the advantage of presenting a consistent user interface. However, some developers find them too consistent, and prefer to add extra features to enhance them. Well, it turns out that MFC and Windows have enough room to allow just that. The next paragraphs explain various techniques to enrich existing controls.

19.5.1 Changing Control Colors

One of the most common changes is to alter the color of some controls. The easiest method to alter the text and background color of the controls seen in this chapter is to implement CWnd::OnCtlColor() in the parent window. When painting themselves, just after allocating a device context, controls send a WM_CTLCOLOR message to their parent for it to customize the device context about to be used. For instance, every edit control sends WM_CTLCOLOREDIT to its parent just before being drawn. The first parameter is a pointer to the device context that the control will use to paint itself; by altering that device context, the parent window alters the appearance of the control.

The next example is a dialog box-based application that displays two edit controls. Both have green text, but only the first one has a yellow background. Refer to the **CtlColor** sample for an example of such an implementation.

```
BEGIN_MESSAGE_MAP(CCtlColorDlg, CDialog)
    .
    .
    .
    ON_WM_CTLCOLOR()
END_MESSAGE_MAP()

HBRUSH CCtrlsDlg::OnCtlColor(CDC* pDC, CWnd* pWnd, UINT nCtlColor)
{
    if (nCtlColor == CTLCOLOR_EDIT)
    {
        // First call default
        HBRUSH hBrush = CDialog::OnCtlColor(pDC, pWnd, nCtlColor);

        // Override the text color to green
        pDC->SetTextColor(RGB(0, 128, 0));

        // The Name edit control must have a yellow background.
        // All other edit controls use the default color background.
        if (pWnd->GetSafeHwnd() == m_cName.m_hWnd)
        {
            pDC->SetBkColor(RGB(255, 255, 196));
            return (HBRUSH) m_Brush;
        }
        else
            return hBrush;
```

```
    }

    // For controls other than edit, use default colors.
    return CDialog::OnCtlColor(pDC, pWnd, nCtlColor);
}
```

Controls can also process that message themselves through reflection, as explained in Section 19.5.4.

19.5.2 Owner-Drawn Buttons

Buttons provide more flexibility by supporting an owner-drawn style attribute (BS_OWNERDRAWN). Normally, buttons paint themselves. But setting this style indicates that the parent window – not the button itself – will display the button in the window. Thus, instead of sending WM_PAINT to the button, Windows sends WM_DRAWITEM to the parent window. The message is sent along a structure DRAWITEMSTRUCT that provides enough information (control id, a device context set up for the control, a rectangle of the client area, etc.) for the parent window to paint the control.

There are two methods to handle that message. The first approach is to implement a handler, namely OnDrawItem(), in the parent window. Upon being called, the parent retrieves the information it needs from the structure and draws the control as needed. But there are two disadvantages to that method. First, this handler is called for all buttons that have the BS_OWNERDRAW attribute set. Hence, this handler must first identify which button in being painted, potentially resulting in a big switch(). Secondly, this is not quite object-oriented. If the same button's look is to be used in a few other windows, the handler must be copied into each of those windows. And if there is already such a handler in place (to handle the representation of other buttons), handlers must be merged together. This is of course not insurmountable, but it just adds some development overhead.

The second approach solves both problems, though. The default implementation of OnDrawItem (in CWnd) sends the message to the control specified in the DRAWITEM STRUCT structure, resulting in CButton::DrawItem() being called by the application framework. This method by default simply asserts (i.e., ASSERT(FALSE);), because a basic CButton doesn't know how the associated owner-drawn button must be painted. Instead, you must create a new class, derived from CButton, that implements DrawItem() and use that class with each owner-drawn button.

For example, here is the implementation of CODButton, an owner-drawn button that is red instead of gray (see Figure 19-23). This button class is implemented in the **CtlColor** sample.

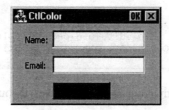

Figure 19-23: An owner-drawn button.

```
// ODButton.h

#pragma once

class CODButton: public CButton
{
public:
    //{{AFX_VIRTUAL(CODButton)
    public:
    virtual void DrawItem(LPDRAWITEMSTRUCT lpDrawItemStruct);
    protected:
    virtual void PreSubclassWindow();
    //}}AFX_VIRTUAL

protected:
    //{{AFX_MSG(CODButton)
    //}}AFX_MSG

    DECLARE_MESSAGE_MAP()
};
```

```
// ODButton.cpp

#include "stdafx.h"
#include "CtlColor.h"
#include "ODButton.h"

#ifdef _DEBUG
#define new DEBUG_NEW
#undef THIS_FILE
static char THIS_FILE[] = __FILE__;
#endif

BEGIN_MESSAGE_MAP(CODButton, CButton)
    //{{AFX_MSG_MAP(CODButton)
    //}}AFX_MSG_MAP
END_MESSAGE_MAP()

// This virtual function is called when this object is attached
// to the control, upon the parent dialog box's initialization.

void CODButton::PreSubclassWindow()
{
```

```
        // Make sure the button has the BS OWNERDRAW style.
        ModifyStyle(0, BS_OWNERDRAW);

        // Call default.
        CButton::PreSubclassWindow();
}

// Called to drawe the button. Draw the button in red!

const COLORREF      BTN_COLOR  = RGB(192, 0, 0);
const COLORREF      BTN_HILITE = RGB(255, 160, 160);
const COLORREF      BTN_SHADOW = RGB(64, 0, 0);

void CODButton::DrawItem(LPDRAWITEMSTRUCT lpdis)
{
    CString s;
    GetWindowText(s);

    CRect   rcFocus;
    CRect   rcItem(lpdis->rcItem);
    CDC         dc;

    dc.Attach(lpdis->hDC);

    if (lpdis->itemState & ODS_FOCUS)
    {
            rcFocus = rcItem;
            rcFocus.DeflateRect(3, 3);

            CPen *       pPrevPen =
                    (CPen *) dc.SelectStockObject(BLACK_PEN);

            CBrush *       pPrevBrush =
                    (CBrush *) dc.SelectStockObject(NULL_BRUSH);

            dc.Rectangle(rcItem);

            dc.SelectObject(pPrevBrush);
            dc.SelectObject(pPrevPen);

            rcItem.DeflateRect(1, 1);
    }

    if (lpdis->itemState & ODS_SELECTED)
    {
            dc.FillSolidRect(rcItem, BTN_COLOR);
            dc.Draw3dRect(rcItem, BTN_SHADOW, BTN_HILITE);

            rcItem.OffsetRect(1, 1);
    }
    else
    {
            dc.FillSolidRect(rcItem, BTN_COLOR);
            dc.Draw3dRect(rcItem, BTN_HILITE, BTN_SHADOW);
    }

    dc.SetBkMode(TRANSPARENT);
```

```
    dc.DrawText(s, rcItem, DT_LEFT | DT_CENTER | DT_VCENTER);

    if (lpdis->itemState & ODS_FOCUS)
            dc.DrawFocusRect(rcFocus);

    dc.Detach();
}
```

Back to the parent (say a dialog box), use ClassWizard to generate a CButton member variable. Open the dialog box's header file, include "ODButton.h" and replace "CButton" by "CODButton". That's it! Here is such a parent's class definition:

```
// CCtlColorDlg.h

#include "ODButton.h"                  // CODButton class definition

class CCtlColorDlg : public CDialog
{
    CBrush  m_Brush;

public:
    CCtlColorDlg(CWnd* pParent = NULL);

    //{{AFX_DATA(CCtlColorDlg)
    enum { IDD = IDD_CTLCOLOR_DIALOG };
    CODButton       m_cSendEmail;       // ClassWizard initially put CButton
    CEdit           m_cName;
    //}}AFX_DATA

    .
    .
    .

};
```

19.5.3 Extending Controls

Beyond changing the appearance of a control, you might want to enhance the behavior of a control. For instance, consider a data entry dialog box, where a bunch of numbers must be entered. It could be useful to have an edit control that only accepts digits '-', '(', and ')' (to read telephone numbers) and beeps when trying to enter something else. Granted, there is an edit control in Windows, but it is friendlier than that: it reads just about everything.

A solution is to write a new edit control from scratch, by creating a class derived from CWnd, with OnPaint() to draw the control in response to WM_PAINT, OnChar() to process keys in response to WM_CHAR, and so on. To make that control well adapted, it should also send WM_CTLCOLOREDIT to its parent, in case the text and/or background color should be altered (as seen earlier). That approach can sure work, but that's a lot of work given the fairly simple objective.

What we really want is to build on top of an edit control, *i.e.*, simply process WM_CHAR differently (to filter out undesirable characters). Well, thanks to MFC, all we have to do is to implement an approach similar to the owner-drawn button: create a new class (say CTelEdit), derived from CEdit, that processes WM_CHAR the way we need (by discarding non-digit characters).

Here is such an implementation of CTelEdit:

```
#pragma once

class CTelEdit : public CEdit
{
public:

    //{{AFX_VIRTUAL(CTelEdit)
    //}}AFX_VIRTUAL

protected:
    //{{AFX_MSG(CTelEdit)
    afx_msg void OnChar(UINT nChar, UINT nRepCnt, UINT nFlags);
    //}}AFX_MSG

    DECLARE_MESSAGE_MAP()
};
```

```
// TelEdit.cpp

#include "stdafx.h"
#include "CtlColor.h"
#include "TelEdit.h"
#include <ctype.h>

#ifdef _DEBUG
#define new DEBUG_NEW
#undef THIS_FILE
static char THIS_FILE[] = __FILE__;
#endif

BEGIN_MESSAGE_MAP(CTelEdit, CEdit)
    //{{AFX_MSG_MAP(CTelEdit)
    ON_WM_CHAR()
    //}}AFX_MSG_MAP
END_MESSAGE_MAP()

void CTelEdit::OnChar(UINT nChar, UINT nRepCnt, UINT nFlags)
{
    // Call parent (to accept the key) only if it is a digit.
    if (_istdigit(nChar))
        CEdit::OnChar(nChar, nRepCnt, nFlags);
}
```

Then, in a dialog box, use ClassWizard to generate CEdit control variables, and replace them with CTelEdit, making them edit controls that only accept digits. You can also create controls programmatically (by using Create()), as long as you are using your own classes (*e.g.*, CODButton, CTelEdit)[63].

If what you have in mind is a control that is even more different than the existing controls, you can create your control from scratch, by deriving it from CWnd. This is more complicated, since you must handle everything: painting, focus, selection, cut and paste, etc., in addition to the primary functionality you want to implement. But this is still an option to consider if your control needs to be completely different than what's available. There are also numerous third-party controls (called *custom controls*), and one of them may fit your needs.

19.5.4 Message Reflection

MFC's message routing redirects notifications emitted from a control to the control itself, or rather, to the associated C++ class. We saw earlier than WM_CTL_COLOREDIT is sent from an edit control to its parent. We also saw that we can extend an edit control by using a class derived from CEdit. But we can also combine both, thanks to *message reflection.*

Generally speaking, whenever a control sends a message to its parent and the parent doesn't handle the message, the control will have a chance to handle it itself. For instance, if the parent of CTelEdit doesn't process WM_CTL_COLOREDIT, the message will be reflected to CTelEdit. The rule to remember is that a message is not reflected if the parent handles it. But this is acceptable: a control may exhibit a default behavior, which the parent can override.

Let's see an example of processing WM_CTL_COLOREDIT right into CTelEdit. Assume for the sake of simplicity that the class has a CBrush member variable called m_Brush, initialized in the constructor.

```
BEGIN_MESSAGE_MAP(CTelEdit, CEdit)
    .
    .
    .
    ON_WM_CTLCOLOR_REFLECT()
END_MESSAGE_MAP()

HBRUSH CTelEdit::CtlColor(CDC* pDC, UINT nCtlColor)
{
    // Set text to red
    pDC->SetTextColor(RGB(255, 0, 0));
```

---

[63] Either approach consists in *subclassing* the Windows control, *i.e.*, reroute messages internally sent to your C++ object's message map in your application.

```
    pDC->SetBkMode(TRANSPARENT);

    // Return the background brush
    return &m_Brush;
}
```

Other messages can be reflected as well (*e.g.*, `WM_DRAWITEM`, `WM_HSCROLL`, `WM_VSCROLL`, etc.), including `WM_COMMAND` (commands) and `WM_NOTIFY` (notifications). Those two are of special interest.

When extending control classes, it is not uncommon to handle some reflected commands and notifications, to keep the processing within the derived class rather than in the parent. For instance, consider the case where a dialog box displays a button labeled *Start* Whenever that button is clicked, some processing is triggered, and the button's label becomes *Stop*. When clicked again, the processing stops, and the button reverts to *Start* and so on. Simply put, the button toggles its label when clicked upon, in addition to notifying its parent as usual. Without reflection, the parent must toggle the button upon receiving the notification. But with reflection, that's something the button can take care of.

The reflection of `WM_COMMAND` and `WM_NOTIFY` can be processed in two different ways, both different than what we've seen so far (with `WM_CTLCOLOR`):

- By using `ON_COMMAND_REFLECT` and `ON_NOTIFY_REFLECT`, the control processes the reflected notification and prevents the parent from receiving it. Hence, the parent only receives a notification only if it isn't processed by the control itself.

- By using `ON_COMMAND_REFLECT_EX` and `ON_NOTIFY_REFLECT_EX`, the control first processes the reflected notification, and the return value (a Boolean) determines whether the also parent receives the notification (`FALSE`) or not (`TRUE`).

In both scenarios, the control has the final word regarding who processes the command or notification.

The next example illustrates the toggling button described earlier. It uses `ON_COMMAND_REFLECT_EX` to first process the notification (toggle its own caption), but it lets the parent receive the notification as well, to do whatever processing is required. From the parent standpoint, plain `BN_CLICKED` notifications are received as usual. This example is implemented in the **CtlColor** sample.

```
// ToggleButton.h

#pragma once

class CToggleButton : public CButton
{
    CString         m_sAltCaption;

public:
```

```
    void           SetAltCaption(LPCTSTR pszAltCaption);

protected:
    afx_msg BOOL OnClicked();

    DECLARE_MESSAGE_MAP()
};

inline void CToggleButton::SetAltCaption(LPCTSTR pszAltCaption)
{
    m_sAltCaption = pszAltCaption;
}
```

```
// ToggleButton.cpp

#include "stdafx.h"
#include "ToggleButton.h"

BEGIN_MESSAGE_MAP(CToggleButton, CButton)
    ON_CONTROL_REFLECT_EX(BN_CLICKED, OnClicked)
END_MESSAGE_MAP()

BOOL CToggleButton::OnClicked()
{
    // Switch the caption
    CString sNewCaption = m_sAltCaption;
    GetWindowText(m_sAltCaption);
    SetWindowText(sNewCaption);

    // Also let the parent process it by returning FALSE.
    // Otherwise (returning TRUE), the parent would not receive it.
    return FALSE;
}
```

Professing reflected commands and notifications right in the controls is truly object-oriented. The same control can be reused in other applications without any change.

SUGGESTED READINGS

Fowler, *GUI Design Handbook*

> This book is essentially a reference guide that reviews all existing GUI items that are available in today's operating systems: check boxes, combo boxes, entry fields, menus, etc. What's interesting is that each item is described in terms of what it is good for, how to test the usability, and further references.

Galitz, *The Essential Guide to User Interface Design*

The book proposes design guidelines to build clear and easy to understand user interface applications, such as selecting the proper type of windows, menu, controls, colors, icons, etc.

Microsoft, *Windows CE Programmer's Guide*

All common controls are described, although not in full detail, and strictly in Win32 terms (not MFC). However, some details are occasionally revealed, which might help getting the most out of those controls.

Chapter 20

Advanced Controls

This chapter focuses on advanced controls, also known as the common controls (see Figure 20-1). Some of these controls have been introduced with Windows 95, others with recent releases of the Microsoft Internet Explorer. They are different than the original Windows controls in many regards. First, they implement a lot more functionality and versatility, to a point where applications can be built just by using some of them. Second, they usually pass information when sending notifications to the parent window, and the parent window, which can respond to them. Third, their improved capabilities require more programming, although the controls have been well designed to prevent any overhead.

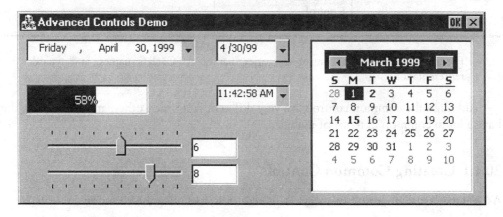

Figure 20-1: Some popular common controls.

20.1 WORKING WITH THE COMMON CONTROLS

MFC supplies a class for each common control, which are grouped in four categories (see Figure 20-2). MFC's implementation doesn't only consist of wrapper classes; some classes contains a lot of code, which you get free by deriving classes from them.

Category	Name	MFC Class
Foundation Controls		
	Command Bar	CCeCommandBar
	Toolbar	CToolBarCtrl, CToolBar
	Property Sheet	CPropertyPage, CPropertySheet
	Tab Control	CTablControl
	Rebar	CReBar
File Controls		
	Header Control	CHeaderCtrl
	Image List	CImageList
	Tree View	CTreeCtrl
	List View	CListCtrl
Scale Controls		
	Spin Box	CSpinButtonCtrl
	Trackbar (Slider)	CSliderCtrl
Information Controls		
	Progress Bar	CProgressCtrl
	Data and time Picker	CDateTimeCtrl
	Status Bar	CStatusBarCtrl, CStatusBar
	Month Calendar Control	CMonthCalCtrl
	Tooltip	CToolTipCtrl

Figure 20-2: Windows control categories, names, MFC class names, and typical representation.

Although the common controls are very different from each other, at least visually, they have a lot in common in terms of usability.

20.1.1 Creating Common Controls

As you may recall, there are two ways to use controls, including the common controls:

• Insert them into a dialog box (using a dialog box editor), and optionally use control member variables to manipulate either their content or the controls themselves. This approach is very popular.

- Create them programmatically. This approach requires invoking their respective `Create()` method, which typically takes four parameters: style attributes, a position rectangle (in parent's client coordinates), the control id, and the parent window, usually `this`.

This is not different that what we've seen in the previous chapter, since the common controls are ... controls.

20.1.2 Notifications

We saw in the previous chapter that the original controls send their notifications via a `WM_COMMAND` message. The only exception is the scroll bar control, which uses `WS_HSCROLL` and `WS_VSCROLL` instead to pass additional information.

The common controls also need to pass all sorts of information to their parent, but adding new messages was rejected because there would be too many of them. Furthermore, as we will see shortly, some parents may respond to notifications the common controls send. As a result, an extensible standard solution was desired. That led to the introduction of `WM_NOTIFY`.

`WM_NOTIFY` is the notification message sent by the common controls, instead of `WM_COMMAND` or other messages. Future controls will certainly use it as well. `wParam` is the control identifier, whereas `lParam` is a pointer to a `NMHDR` structure, listed in Figure 20-3.

Type	Member	Description
HWND	hwndFrom	Handle of the control that sent the notification.
UINT	idFrom	Identifier of the control that sent the notification.
UINT	nCode	Notification code, which is control-dependent.

Figure 20-3: The `NMHDR` structure, sent along `WM_NOTIFY`.

Each control must initialize that structure in order to send a notification. Since all controls that send `WM_NOTIFY` respect that rule[64], all notifications can be properly interpreted.

But that's only half of the story. A common control needs to send more information along with its notification. For instance, if the user clicks on [+] in a tree view in order to expand a branch, the tree view notifies the parent *before* expanding by sending the `TVN_ITEMEXPANDING` notification (via `WM_NOTIFY`), and specifying an `NM_TREEVIEW` structure, shown in Figure 20-4:

---

[64] Actually, not all of them do. Some of the controls listed in Section 19.4 are non-conforming.

Type	Member	Description
NMHDR	hdr	NMHDR structure. The nCode field contains the unique notification identifier.
UINT	action	Action flag.
TV_ITEM	itemOld	Item's previous state or zero if unused.
TV_ITEM	itemNew	Item's new state or zero if unused.
POINT	ptDrag	Mouse position, in client coordinates, when the event took place.

Figure 20-4: The NM_TREEVIEW structure, sent along with WM_NOTIFY by a tree view control when the user tries to expand a branch.

The parent's handler (that you implement), like any other WM_NOTIFY handler, expects a pointer to an NMHDR structure (we'll see the details in a minute). In this case, pointing to an NM_TREVIEW structure is acceptable since its very first field *is* an NMHDR structure. By looking at the nCode field (in NMHDR), it can be determined that the notification type is TVN_ITEMEXPANDING, in which case it can safely be assumed that the pointer is not only pointing to an NMHDR structure, but to an NM_TREEVIEW one.

The notifications based on WM_NOTIFY are also handled in the message map. Unlike the original control notification entries, only one type of message map entry is required: ON_NOTIFY(). The following example handles TVN_ITEMEXPANDING:

```
// In MyWnd.h

class CMyWnd: public CWnd
{
public:
    . . .
    // Handler declaration
    afx_msg void OnItemExpandingMyTree(NMHDR* pNMHDR, LRESULT*
pResult);
};
```

```
// In MyWnd.cpp

BEGIN_MESSAGE_MAP(CMyWnd, CWnd)
.
.
.
    ON_NOTIFY(TVN_ITEMEXPANDING, IDC_TREE, OnItemExpandingMyTree)
END_MESSAGE_MAP()
```

```
void CAboutDlg::OnItemExpandingMyTree(NMHDR* pNMHDR, LRESULT* pResult)
{
    NM_TREEVIEW* pNMTreeView = (NM_TREEVIEW*) pNMHDR;

    // Process the item expansion.
    .
    .
    .

    // Set *pResult to FALSE to allow the expansion or collapse,
    // or TRUE to prevent it.
    *pResult = FALSE;                     // Allow the expansion/collapse
}
```

Note the prototype in the class definition: it receives a pointer to an NMHDR structure and a pointer to an LRESULT (a long value). The message map entry is ON_NOTIFY and requires the notification code, the control id, and the handler. Hence, the handler is only called for *that* notification from *that* control. In this handler, the pointer can safely be cast to an NM_TREEVIEW pointer, because that is what the tree view control sends. ClassWizard can add handlers for you, and it will even cast the pointer.

If you write the handler by yourself, make sure that you are casting to the proper data structure, as listed in the help for the notification. Each control usually sends their own structure for all of their notifications. For instance, tree view notifications are delivered with an NM_TREEVIEW structure.

The parent may also respond to the control by returning a value through *pResult. This value will be interpreted by the control in order to take the proper action. In this example, setting *pResult to TRUE would direct the control not to expand/collapse the tree branch clicked by the user. The value to return in *pResult depends on the notification itself, and some controls simply ignore the content of *pResult.

Under the hood, the control sends a WM_NOTIFY message using SendMessage(), passing its own control identifier in wParam and the notification-dependent structure in lParam. The message map interprets the message and calls the parent handler, passing lParam (cast as an NMHDR *) and a pointer to an LRESULT. As the parent handler executes, the control is blocked on SendMessage(), which completes when the parent's handler terminates. The value set in *pResult becomes the returned value of SendMessage(). The control regains control, and proceeds according to the returned value. This behavior is buried in the common controls, but MFC smoothes the edges.

The remaining of this chapter describes the common controls listed in Figure 20-2.

20.2 FOUNDATION CONTROLS

The foundation controls contain or manage other controls. For instance, a tab control can contain buttons, edit controls, list boxes, etc. The foundation controls are described in the following sections, except the property sheet, which is described in Chapter 18.

20.2.1 Command Bar

The command bar is a control exclusive to Windows CE that combines the application menu, a toolbar, and optional adornments (the Help (?) and Close (X) buttons, on the right side of the command bar). Figure 20-5 shows a typical command bar.

Figure 20-5: A typical command bar, with a menu and toolbar buttons.

Creating a Command Bar

When creating an application in Visual C++, AppWizard lets you decide what type of command bar your application can have among the following four types (see Figure 20-6):

1. **Basic CommandBar.** This command bar only contains a menu with File, Edit, and Help. There isn't any toolbar button, but there is a Close (**X**) button.

2. **CommandBar with toolbar buttons**. This command bar carries the same menu, but adds four toolbar buttons: Cut, Copy, Paste, and About.

3. **Internet Explorer ReBars**. Very popular, this style allows moving the previous four-button toolbar. It also generates an empty, but moveable, dialog bar which can be used to provide additional buttons, combo boxes, etc.

4. **MFC 2.0-compatible CommandBar.** This option is only enabled with document-based applications, and it generates a toolbar similar to #2. Visually, the toolbar has a few more toolbar buttons, and internally, the command bar uses backward-compatible calls.

A command bar relies on a toolbar resource, which can be edited within Visual C++ in order to customize them. Each button is assigned a command id, which results in a WM_COMMAND message sent to the application when tapped (like menu items). Whichever command bar style you choose, the code that creates it always resides in the application's main frame, typically MainFrm.cpp.

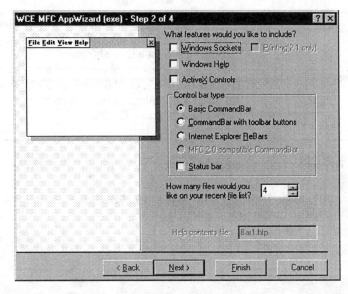

Figure 20-6: Step 2 of AppWizard can generate four types of tool bars (from top to bottom): basic command bar; command bar with toolbar buttons; Internet Explorer rebar, and MFC2.0-compatible CommandBar.

The command bar is a `CCeCommandBar` object, whose `Create()` method only requires the application window (`this`). Then a few methods are available to customize the toolbar, listed in Figure 20-7.

CCeCommandBar Method	Description
InsertMenuBar()	Inserts a menu bar in the command bar. The method requires a menu identifier.
LoadToolBar()	Inserts a toolbar in the command bar. The method requires a toolbar identifier.
AddAdornments()	Adds the rightmost buttons in the command bar. It can be invoked without parameter (to add a Close button), with

	CMDBAR_HELP (to add Help and Close buttons) and/or CMDBAR_OK (to add OK and Close buttons). Every bar must have at least a Close button.
InsertComboBox()	Adds a combo box in the command bar. The method requires the width, combo box identifier, a button position (to insert the combo box before), combo box style (see Appendix C, Section C.2.7).
InsertSeparator()	Adds a separator button.

Figure 20-7: Some CCeCommandBar methods.

For instance, the next example (not generated by AppWizard) creates an empty command bar with a Close button (see Figure 20-8):

```
class CMainWindow: public CFrameWnd
{
    CCeCommandBar    m_CommandBar;
    .
    .
    .
    afx_msg int     OnCreate(LPCREATESTRUCT lpCreateStruct);
    afx_msg void    OnPaint();
};

int CMainWindow::OnCreate(LPCREATESTRUCT lpCreateStruct)
{
    // Call parent first, return on error
    if (CFrameWnd::OnCreate(lpCreateStruct) == -1)
            return -1;

    // Then create an empty command bar, return on error
    if (!m_CommandBar.Create(this))
            return -1;

    // Add a Close button.
    m_CommandBar.AddAdornments();
}

void CMainWindow::OnPaint()
{
    CPaintDC        dc(this);

    dc.SelectStockObject(BLACK_BRUSH);
    dc.Ellipse(0, 0, 100, 100);
}
```

It is important to note that the command bar overlaps the client area. For instance, the previous code, which outputs a circle from (0, 0) to (100, 100), produces the output shown in Figure 20-8.

Figure 20-8: The command bar overlaps the client area. This circle is drawn from (0,0) to (100, 100).

There are two methods to deal with this situation:

(a) Right after creating the command bar in OnCreate(), the frame window can obtain is window position by calling GetWindowRect(). The top of the visible client area is then the bottom value of that rectangle. The rest of the application (specifically OnPaint()) can then be designed to work within the visible portion only. This method is demonstrated in the next example:

```
int CMainWindow::OnCreate(LPCREATESTRUCT lpCreateStruct)
{
    if (CFrameWnd::OnCreate(lpCreateStruct) == -1)
            return -1;

    if (!m_CommandBar.Create(this))
            return -1;

    m_CommandBar.AddAdornments();

    // Position the command bar.
    RecalcLayout();

    // Get the position of the command bar in the client area.
    CRect    rectCommandBar;

    m_CommandBar.GetWindowRect(rectCommandBar);
    ScreenToClient(rectCommandBar);

    // Assume m_rectVisible is a member variable of type CRect

    GetClientRect(m_rectVisible);
    m_rectVisible.top = rectCommandBar.bottom;

    // The rest of the application must draw within m_rectVisible.
```

```
      return 0;
}
```

(b) The frame window can create another window that covers the visible client area (as calculated in the previous step). That child window then implements the core functionality (not the frame). Because the command bar doesn't overlap, the child window is easier to implement, since the coordinate (0,0) is the window's top left corner, not the command bar's (when using a device context within that window). This method is actually retained in view-based applications (the view is a separate window below the command bar).

Accessing the Command Bar from CFrameWnd

Previous MFC implementations manipulated the command bar through a few `CFrameWnd` methods, such as `AddComboBoxString()`, `InsertComboBox()`, etc. These methods still exist, but for backward-compatibility only. For instance, these methods are used when generating an MFC 2.0-compatible command bar using AppWizard. Invoking any of those methods internally forces the frame to instantiate a `CCeCommandBar` object and invoke methods upon it.

It is preferable not to use these methods in new applications any more, and directly work on a `CCeCommandBar` object, as shown above.

Interacting with the Command Bar

The command bar sends messages to its parent window. Hence, menu and toolbar commands go to the frame window, which reroutes them to the view, document, frame, etc. (as explained in Chapter 15, Section 15.6). ClassWizard is the tool of choice to add handlers to any of those classes.

20.2.2 CToolBarCtrl and CToolBar

A tool bar is a series of controls, usually push buttons, but also combo boxes for instance, that sits next to the menu, in the application's command bar. They are good for accessing often-used or repeatedly-used functions using the stylus. Refer to Figure 20-6 for examples. Two MFC classes deal with tool bars:

- `CToolBarCtrl` is a class that strictly wraps the Win32 toolbar control. Most methods are inlined and simply send a message to the underlying toolbar control. For instance:

```
_AFXCMN_INLINE BOOL CToolBarCtrl::EnableButton(int nID, BOOL bEnable)
{
```

```
    ASSERT(::IsWindow(m_hWnd));
    return (BOOL) ::SendMessage(m_hWnd, TB_ENABLEBUTTON, nID,
        MAKELPARAM(bEnable, 0));
}
```

- CToolBar is class that relies on the same underlying toolbar control, but that provides a high-level API, in addition to extra functionality that provides a better integration within the MFC architecture (such as initializing a toolbar using a toolbar resource id). Because internally both classes use the same toolbar control, CToolBar provides a method that returns a CToolBarCtrl& for low-level toolbar functions, if required.

Nonetheless, most CE applications use neither, since a toolbar is typically inserted into the command bar by calling CCeCommandBar::LoadToolbar(). However, in some cases, an application can use a CToolBar in order to add a toolbar into a rebar control, described in the following section.

Both classes provides methods to get or set some of the properties of the controls they contain, but most applications use plain toolbars.

20.2.3 CReBarCtrl and CReBar

A rebar, also called Internet Explorer rebar, is a container to other controls, but also toolbars, dialog bars, and command bars. It contains multiple bands, each of which has a gripper and its controls (see Figure 20-6 for an example). A rebar is ideal to provide various bars that the user can position at will.

Like toolbars, rebars come in two flavors: CeRebarCtrl is a wrapper class whose methods send rebar messages to the underlying rebar control, whereas CReBar provides a higher-level API, better integrated within the MFC architecture. CReBar only contains three methods, shown in Figure 20-9.

CReBar Methods	Description
Create()	Creates a rebar control.
AddAdornments()	Adds a Close button, and optionally a Help and OK button.
GetReBarCtrl()	Returns a reference to CeRebarCtrl in order to provide low-level access to the rebar, if needed.
AddBar()	Adds a band to the rebar.

Figure 20-9: CReBar methods.

AppWizard uses a CReBar control when generating an application with Internet Explorer ReBars (see Figure 20-5). It also generates a default command bar to hold the menu, a default tool bar (with a grip), and a default dialog bar, also with a grip, as shown on Figure 20-6. The code is as follows:

```
class CMainFrame : public CFrameWnd
{
    CCeCommandBar   m_wndMenuBar;          // Command bar
    CToolBar        m_wndToolBar;          // Toolbar (+ grip)
    ialogBar        m_wndDlgBar;           // Dialog bar (+ grip)
    CReBar          m_wndReBar;            // ReBar to hold the three bars
    .
    .
    .
}

int CMainFrame::OnCreate(LPCREATESTRUCT lpCreateStruct)
{
    // Call parent first.
    if (CFrameWnd::OnCreate(lpCreateStruct) == -1)
         return -1;

    // Create a command bar and insert the IDR_MAINFRAME menu into it.
    if (!m_wndMenuBar.CreateEx(this) ||
       !m_wndMenuBar.InsertMenuBar(IDR_MAINFRAME))
          return -1;

    // Create a tool bar and load the IDR_MAINFRAME tool bar resource.
    if (!m_wndToolBar.CreateEx(this) ||
       !m_wndToolBar.LoadToolBar(IDR_MAINFRAME))
          return -1;

    // Create the dialog bar. This is based on a dialog box template
    // labeled IDR_MAINFRAME.
    if (!m_wndDlgBar.Create(this, IDR_MAINFRAME,
         CBRS_ALIGN_TOP, AFX_IDW_DIALOGBAR))
          return -1;               // fail to create

    // Create the rebar and add the command bar, the tool bar and the
    // dialog bar. Also add a Close button.
    if (!m_wndReBar.Create(this) ||
       !m_wndReBar.AddBar(&m_wndMenuBar, NULL, NULL, RBBS_NOGRIPPER) ||
       !m_wndReBar.AddBar(&m_wndToolBar) ||
       !m_wndReBar.AddAdornments())
          return -1;

    return 0;
}
```

As mentioned earlier, given a CRebar, an application can retrieve a CReBarCtrl& to perform low-level operation on a band. For instance, the following example adds some text to the dialog bar (see Figure 20-10):

```
    // In CMainFrame::OnCreate(), before the final 'return 0;'

    // Get access to the rebar control.
CReBarCtrl& cReBar = m_wndReBar.GetReBarCtrl();

    // Initialize a REBARBANDINFO to set the text of band #2, which is
    // the dialog bar.
    REBARBANDINFO  BandInfo;
    BandInfo.cbSize = sizeof(BandInfo);
    BandInfo.fMask = RBBIM_TEXT;
    BandInfo.lpText = _T("Connection Speed:");
    cReBar.SetBandInfo(2, &BandInfo);
```

Figure 20-10: Adding the text "Connection Speed:" to a dialog bar in a rebar control.

`CReBarCtrl()` provides numerous methods to query or alter the apperance of the control and its bands in addition to `SetBandInfo()` shown in the previous example.

There's one issue when using a dialog bar within a command bar: the dialog bar's controls will send their notifications to the dialog bar itself, not the main frame, which is where they should go. The solution is to reroute `WM_COMMAND` messages to the parent frame (not necessarily the immediate parent, which can be a `CRebar`). For instance, if the command bar has a button, the `BN_CLICKED` notification will go the main frame first (which will reroute it to the view, the document and the application window as well).

The following illustrates a class called `CCeDialogBar` than implements this feature. The **Bar3** sample, on the CD-ROM, implements this class to handle dialog bar messages throughout the application (frame, view, and application class).

```
// CeDialogBar

#pragma once

class CCeDialogBar : public CDialogBar
{
public:
    BOOL OnCmdMsg(UINT nID, int nCode, void* pExtra, AFX_CMDHANDLERINFO*
pHandlerInfo);
};
```

```
// CeDialogBar.cpp

#include "stdafx.h"
#include "CeDialogBar.h"
```

```
BOOL CCeDialogBar::OnCmdMsg(UINT nID, int nCode, void* pExtra,
AFX_CMDHANDLERINFO* pHandlerInfo)
{
    // Pass to parent first
    CWnd * pParent = GetParentFrame();
    ASSERT(pParent != NULL);

    if (pParent->OnCmdMsg(nID, nCode, pExtra, pHandlerInfo))
            return TRUE;

    return CDialogBar::OnCmdMsg(nID, nCode, pExtra, pHandlerInfo);
}
```

Then simply replace all instances of `CDialogBar` by `CCeDialogBar` in the main frame class definition, such as the one shown below:

```
// MainFrm.h

#pragma once

#include "ChildView.h"
#include "CeDialogBar.h"

class CMainFrame : public CFrameWnd
{
    .
    .
    .

    CCeCommandBar           m_wndMenuBar;
    CToolBar                m_wndToolBar;
    CCeDialogBar            m_wndDlgBar;     ; To reroute commands to frame
    CReBar                  m_wndReBar;
    CChildView              m_wndView;
    .
    .
    .
};
```

20.2.4 CTabCtrl

A tab control presents a set of dividers with one of them being active, or on top of the others (see Figure 20-11). As the user selects tab, the control sends notifications to its parent to inform that the user is switching tab. However, the control doesn't switch the *content* of the tabs: the application must process the tab switch notifications and display whatever is suitable for the newly-selected tab (typically a bunch of controls).

A single tab usually contains some text, but it can also contain an image or both. A 32-bit user-defined value can also be associated (and later retrieved) with a tab. Such a value might be a pointer to some other application's data to perform some validation, for instance.

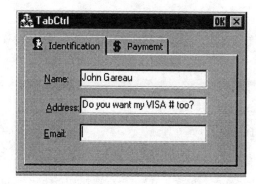

Figure 20-11: A typical tab control with two tabs; each tab contains an image and some text. Images are optional.

Adding a Tab

CTabCtrl provides an overloaded CTabCtrl::InsertItem() to insert tabs. All require a zero-based tab insertion position (tabs can be inserted in any order). Some require the tab text, others the text and the image, etc. Internally, all these methods fill up a TCITEM structure (listed in Figure 20-12) and send a message to the underlying control.

Type	Member	Description
UINT	mask	Specifies what following members are valid.
DWORD	dwState	Current state.
DWORD	dwStateMask	Which bits in dwState are valid.
LPTSTR	pszText	Tab text.
int	cchTextMax	Size of buffer pointed to by pszText.
LPARAM	lParam	User-defined 32-bit value associated with the tab.

Figure 20-12: The TCITEM structure.

Consider, for instance, the following version of InsertItem() (in afxcmn.inl), which requires a tab position, the tab text, and an image:

```
BOOL CTabCtrl::InsertItem(int nItem, LPCTSTR lpszItem, int nImage)
{
    ASSERT(::IsWindow(m_hWnd));
    return CTabCtrl::InsertItem(TCIF_TEXT|TCIF_IMAGE, nItem, lpszItem,
        mage, 0);
}
```

This function is simply a front-end to another version that fills up a TCITEM structure and sends a message to the underlying control:

```
BOOL CTabCtrl::InsertItem(UINT nMask, int nItem, LPCTSTR lpszItem,
    int nImage, LPARAM lParam)
{
    ASSERT(::IsWindow(m_hWnd));

    TCITEM item;
    item.mask = nMask;
    item.iImage = nImage;
    item.lParam = lParam;
    item.pszText = (LPTSTR) lpszItem;

    return (BOOL)
        ::SendMessage(m_hWnd, TCM_INSERTITEM, nItem, (LPARAM) &item);
}
```

Controlling the Tab Appearance

Ideally, each tab should be displayed with an image and a text. This is not always possible on small scale devices, although `CTabCtrl::SetPadding()` may help reducing the amount of wasted space between images and texts. The default padding is otherwise adequate.

A tab control uses a `CImageList` (described in Section 20.2.5) to locate its images when some are specified. Note that some tabs may have an image and others not, but it is better to provide some consistency and either use images with all tabs or not at all.

One aspect that is entirely left to the application is what to show when a tab is selected. The tab control will limit itself in raising the chosen tab, period. There are many approaches to update the tab content. An application may show a series of controls for a given tab, and when switching to another tab, hide them and show the series of controls associated with the other tab. This approach works fine when each tab contains very few controls (one or two for instance). However, in real-world applications, each tab typically contains five, if not ten controls on average. In that situation, it is best to use a dialog box template for each tab, and show the dialog box associated with the selected tab. Such an implementation will be demonstrated in just a minute.

Removing a Tab

Two methods are available to remove tabs. The first one, `CTabCtrl::DeleteItem()`, requires a position and deletes the corresponding tab. The second, `CTabCtrl::Delete AllItems()`, deletes all items at once. Whatever is associated with a tab (controls, dialog box templates, etc.) must be freed by the application.

Notifications

Tab controls send two important notifications:

- TCN_SELCHANGING is sent by the tab control whenever the user tapped on another tab but before that tab becomes selected. The parent window can call CTabCtrl::GetCurSel() to identify the tab that is still selected, and perhaps perform some validation. For instance, consider a tab that displays a customer entry form: the parent may ensure that a valid customer number has been entered before allowing the user to go to another tab. The handler can return FALSE (via *pResult) to let the tab control know that the tab can be switched, or TRUE to prevent the switch.

- TCN_SELCHANGE is sent when the switch has been done. GetCurSel() can be called to identify the new tab now shown. The application must handle this notification by hiding the content of the previous tab and showing the content of the new tab. Keep reading to see how.

A Dialog-Based Tab Control

The main issue when using a tab control is to manage the content of each tab, as the user switches from one to another. One solution - easy to use - is to associate a dialog box template (designed in Visual C++ for instance) to each tab. Whenever a tab is shown, the template is turned into a modeless dialog box (with no border), properly positioned within the tab control. When switching to another tab, the dialog box is hidden, and another dialog box, based on the next tab's template is shown. To make this approach really easy to use, the **TabCtrl** sample (on the CD-ROM) uses CDlgTabCtrl, a reusable class that supports dialog-based tabs, and that can be used instead of CTabCtrl. It provides additional methods to add one "page" at a time, each page being based on a dialog template identifier, and optionally, a CDialog-derived box object (to hold the dialog's member variables).

The following example is the implementation of the TabCtrl sample, shown in Figure 20-11. This is a dialog box that uses CDlgTabCtrl. It inserts two pages in the tab control, respectively based on the IDD_IDENTIFCATION and IDD_PAYMENT dialog box templates (both designed in Visual C++). A dialog box variable, m_IdentDlg, generated with ClassWizard, is associated with the first page to access member variable. This is not a requirement though, as no dialog box variable is associated with the second page. In real-world application, it is very likely that each page would have a dialog box variable associated with it.

```
#include "DlgTabCtrl.h"
#include "IdentificationDlg.h"

class CTabCtrlDlg : public CDialog          // Parent dialog box
{
    CDlgTabCtrl              m_CustomerTab;  // Tab control
    CImageList               m_ImageList;    // Tab control's image list
    CIdentificationDlg       m_IdentDlg;     // Associated with 1ˢᵗ page
    .
    .
    .
```

```
};
BOOL CTabCtrlDlg::OnInitDialog()
{
    CDialog::OnInitDialog();


    .
    .          // Other MFC initialization stuff
    .

    // Create an image list (which hold the tab images), and
    // associate it with the tab control
    m_ImageList.Create(IDB_TABIMAGES, 16, 0, RGB(0, 128, 128));
    m_CustomerTab.SetImageList(&m_ImageList);

    TCITEM tcItem;

    // Add the first page, with an image and some text.
    // Also associate m_IdentDlg with that page to access
    // the member variables if required.
    tcItem.mask = TCIF_TEXT | TCIF_IMAGE;
    tcItem.iImage = 0;
    tcItem.pszText = _T("Identification");
    m_CustomerTab.AddPage(&tcItem, IDD_IDENTIFICATION, &m_IdentDlg);

    // Add a second page, with an image and some text, but
    // without a dialog box object.
    tcItem.mask = TCIF_TEXT | TCIF_IMAGE;
    tcItem.iImage = 1;
    tcItem.pszText = _T("Paymemt");
    m_CustomerTab.AddPage(&tcItem, IDD_PAYMENT);

    // Other methods are available. For instance, to add a tab
    // with just some text, you can do this:
    //      m_CustomerTab.AddPage(_T("Payment"), IDD_PAYMENT);


    .
    .
    .


    return TRUE;
}
```

The parent window (your application) still receives the TCN_SELCHANGING notifications to perform some validation and prevent the switch if necessary. For instance, the example below prevents the user from switching from the Identification tab unless a name is entered. Note the call to UpdateData(), which is essential to update the member variables.

```
void CTabCtrlDlg::OnSelchangingCustomerTab(NMHDR* pNMHDR,
    LRESULT* pResult)
{
    // When switching off from the first tab, make sure a name is provided.
    // Use m_IdentDlg to accept the first tab's member variables.
```

```
*pResult = FALSE;                        // Allow the switch by default.

// Call GetCurSel() to identify which tab we are switching from.
if (m_CustomerTab.GetCurSel() == 0)
{
        // Update the dialog box (VERY IMPORTANT, see Chapter 18)
        m_IdentDlg.UpdateData(TRUE);

        if (m_IdentDlg.m_sName.IsEmpty())
        {
                AfxMessageBox(
                        _T("Please provide the name of the customer."));
                *pResult = TRUE;        // Prevent the switch.
        }
}
}
```

Internally, CDlgTabCtrl maintains an array of modeless dialog boxes, one per tab, all positioned within the tab control. It also handles TCN_SELCHANGED in order to detect when the user switched tabs. When that happens, the dialog box associated with the tab being switched off is hidden, whereas the dialog box associated with the tab being selected is made visible. All dialog boxes are deleted when the tab control is destroyed.

20.2.5 CImageList

An image list control is a collection of images. It is not visible by itself; it is instead used with other controls, such as the tab control we just described, the tree view (Section 20.3.1), the list view (Section 20.3.2) and header (Section 20.3.3). You can also use an image list to draw images programmatically, a better alternative to loading multiple bitmaps or icons for drawing.

The purpose of an image list is to ease the manipulation of a large set of images (as opposed to a large amount of individual images). An image list can be initialized from a bitmap (designed in a resource editor) and it provide methods to add/remove images, display images with some special effects, etc. Since each image within the image list is referenced via a zero-based index, an image list is basically an array of images.

There are five overloaded CImageList::Create() methods, but the most common accepts the following five parameters:

1.   A bitmap identifier or name. Such a bitmap usually contains as many images as required by the application.

2.   The width of a single image (in pixels) within that bitmap. The width is used internally to identify each individual image (where they start, where they end). Common values are 16 or 18 (see Figure 20-13), but they can be of any size

3. The growth factor, if images are to be added in the image list at run-time. This is uncommon, as image lists are typically created with a bitmap containing all the images the application needs.

4. The color mask, a COLORREF value. Images can later be drawn by applying some special effects to all pixels of that color. Consider Figure 20-13: the background color (green) is the color (0, 128, 128). By specifying that value as the mask, it is later possible to draw individual icons while specifying that the background (*i.e.*, all pixels of color (0, 128, 128)) be not rendered, resulting in a transparent background.

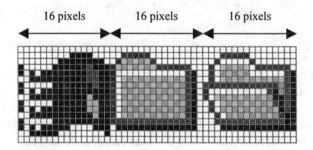

Figure 20-13: A 48x16 bitmap used with an image list. In this case, there are three images, each with a width of 16 pixels.

The following example creates an image list for the bitmap depicted above:

```
// Somewhere in the header file:
// CImageList     m_ImageList;

m_ImageList.Create(IDB_DIRECTORIES, 16, 1, RGB(0, 128, 128));
```

One created, you can call CImageList::GetImageCount() to obtain the number of individual images that are available, if required. The count is based on the bitmap's width and the width specified as the second argument.

Using Image Lists

When using image lists with other controls (the common case), there is no need to worry about drawing images, since these controls take care of using and drawing images internally. All that is left for you to do is to create the image list and associate it with the controls. Hence, if you only intend to use an image list with a control, there is nothing else to do beyond creating the list!

```
// Somewhere in the header file:
// CTreeCtrl        m_TreeCtrl;

m_TreeCtrl.SetImageList(&m_ImageList, TVSIL_NORMAL);
```

Drawing Images

On rare occasions, though, you might want to use an image list as a convenient image placeholder, and draw by yourself. For instance, if you are programming an application that needs to displays a lots of icons, you may instead use one single image list, instead of loading tens – if not hundreds – of individual icons.

Drawing a specific image is easily achieved by calling `CImageList::Draw()`. That method requires a pointer to a device context (`CDC *`), an image index within the image list (0 being the first image, 1 the second, etc.), a point representing the top-left position of the image within the specified device context, and a drawing style (see Figure 20-14). Make sure that you create the image list with a mask (as seen earlier), in order to use interesting drawing effects.

Drawing Style	Description
`ILD_BLEND25, ILD_FOCUS`	Blends the image with 25% of the system highlight color. The image list must contain a mask for this style to be effective.
`ILD_BLEND50, ILD_SELECTED, ILD_BLEND`	Blends the image with 50% of the system highlight color. The image list must contain a mask for this style to be effective.
`ILD_MASK`	Draws the mask.
`ILD_NORMAL`	Draws the image, applying the default background color to the mask. If the background color is `CLR_NONE`, the background is transparent.
`ILD_TRANSPARENT`	Draws the image, using the mask to draw a transparent background.

Figure 20-14: Image list drawing styles.

The most common style is `ILD_NORMAL`, which draws the image, replacing the mask with the default background color. That color can be set and retrieved by calling `CImageList::SetBkColor()` and `CImageList::GetBkColor()`.

For an icon-like effect, the background color can be set to `CLR_NORE`, in which case the background is transparent. Alternatively, using the flag `ILD_TRANSPARENT` with `CImageList::Draw()` provides the same result.

20.3 FILE CONTROLS

The file controls are often used for displaying file-related information, such as the file browser shown on Figure 20-15, described later on and implemented in the **FBrowser** sample. The left pane is a tree control (CTreeCtrl) displaying a file hierarchy, whereas the right pane consists of a list control (CListCtrl) displaying the content of the selected directory in the tree control. The list control includes a header control (CHeaderCtrl), which sits at the top of the list control. The tree and list controls both internally use an image list control (CImageList) in order to display the small bitmaps associated with each entry.

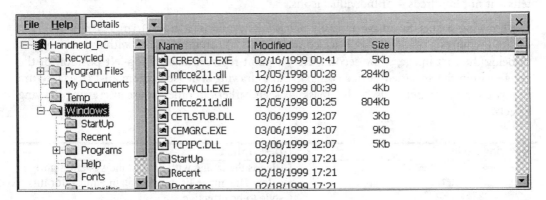

Figure 20-15: A file browser that uses a tree view, list view, and header controls.

These controls are so complete that the application actually contains very little code, as we'll see later.

20.3.1 CTreeCtrl

The tree control is a very popular control, whose purpose is to display information using an hierarchy. Some examples are the directories and files of a device, a C++ class hierarchy, an employee chart, an inventory, office locations, etc.

The tree control internally implements a lot of functionality while being surprisingly easy to use. Here's how it works: your application inserts one item at a time in the control, specifying the name of the item and its parent item, along other optional parameters. The parent item is used by the control to establish the hierarchy. Once items are inserted, the user can select items, expand or collapse them, and so on, without requiring any involvement from your application (*i.e.*, the control fully manages itself).

614

The tree control sends many notifications to its parent (your application) upon the operations conducted by the user (such as selecting an item, expanding a branch, etc.) The parent may react by displaying new information, adding more items in a branch about to be expanded, etc., pretty much the same a tab control interact with its parent. We'll see some examples of handlers later.

Creating a tree control is not even challenging. `CTreeCtrl::Create()` takes the usual parameters: style, position and size (a `CRect`), the parent window (usually `this`), and a control identifier. Some popular styles are listed in Figure 20-16.

Tree Styles	Description
TVS_HASLINES	Lines connecting items are shown.
TVS_LINESATROOT	Lines connecting item to the tree's root are shown.
TVS_HASBUTTONS	Items with sub-items are shown with a [+]/[-] sign.
TVS_SHOWSELALWAYS	The selected item is always made visible (the tree automatically scrolls if it has to).

Figure 20-16: Some very popular tree view control style attributes.

Inserting and Deleting Items

Call `CTreeCtrl::InsertItem()` to insert an item in a tree. This method is overloaded (it has different set of parameters), but the easiest is the following:

```
HTREEITEM InsertItem(
    LPCTSTR        lpszItem,
    int            nImage,
    int            nSelectedImage,
    HTREEITEM      hParent = TVI_ROOT,
    HTREEITEM      hInsertAfter = TVI_LAST);
```

The first parameter is the item text. The second parameter, an index into an image list, identifies the image for that item. The third parameter, also an index into an image list, is the image to display when the object is selected. For instance, selecting a directory in the File Browser displayed earlier shows an opened folder, as opposed to a closed folder by default. The next to last parameter is the parent item, the default being the tree root. Finally, the last parameter is the item after which the new item is added, the default being the last.

This calls requires an image list to be associated with the tree control. Each call to `CTreeCtrl::InsertItem()` as described above will implicitly rely on that image list. If you don't want to use images with an item, then you don't have to associate an image list to the control, and you can use another `Create()` method that doesn't require an image index.

Each insertion returns an item handle, whose type is HTREEITEM. There is no need to store those returned handles. One exception is during initialization: a item handle can be stored into a local variable in order to be specified as the parent of other items being inserted. For instance:

```
HTREEITEM  hRootHandle;

// Insert a root item (the parent is implicitly TVI_ROOT)
hRootHandle = m_TreeCtrl.InsertItem(_T("CObject"), . . .);

// Insert a child item (use hRootHandle as the parent)
m_TreeCtrl.InsertItem(. . , hRootHandle, . . .);
```

As mentioned earlier, once the items are inserted, the control itself handles the user interaction. From an application standpoint, all there is to do is to handle the control notifications.

You can remove an item by calling CTreeCtrl::DeleteItem(), and passing the item handle. The entire tree can be emptied at once by calling CTreeCtrl::DeleteAll Items().

Tree Control Notifications

Whenever some user interaction happens (*e.g.*, the user clicked on [+] to expand an item), the control first notifies the parent window. Four potentially interesting notifications are TVN_SELCHANGING (the selection is about to be changed), TVN_SELCHANGED (the selection has changed), TVN_ITEMEXPANDING (an item is about to expand or collapse) and TVN_ITEMEXPANDED (an item has expanded or collapsed). Each notification is sent along a NM_TREEVIEW structure (see Figure 20-17).

Type	Member	Description
NMHDR	hdr	Common notification information.
UINT	action	Notification-specific action flag.
TVITEM	itemOld	Information about the old item state. If unused, the structure's members are all set to zero.
TVITEM	itemNew	Information about the new item state. If unused, the structure's members are all set to zero.
POINT	ptDrag	Mouse coordinates at the time the notification was sent.

Figure 20-17: The NM_TREEVIEW structure.

Let's look at an example to understand how that works. Say the user clicks on the [+] of an item, in order to expand it. Before the expansion takes place, the tree control sends the

TVN_ITEMEXPANDING notification. In order to receive the notification, the parent must have the following entry in its message map:

```
ON_NOTIFY(TVN_ITEMEXPANDING, IDC_TREE, OnItemExpandingTree)
```

The handle is defined as follows:

```
void CMyWnd::OnItemExpandingCarTree(NMHDR * pNMHDR, LONG * pResult)
{
    NM_TREEVIEW *  pTreeView = (NM_TREEVIEW *) pNMHDR;

    // Handle the notification here
    . . .

    *pResult = 0;                           // Allow the expansion
}
```

The first parameter to this notification handler is actually a pointer to an NM_TREEVIEW (as described by the online documentation about the TVN_ITEMEXPANDING notification). The member itemNew of the structure is the item handle (of type HTREEITEM) of the item *about* to be expanded. I mentioned earlier that there is no need to store the item handles, and that was because notifications pass enough information to identify the items of interest.

The handler may perform some processing such as adding the child items into the item about to be expanded. For instance, when an item representing a directory is about to be expanded, the parent window may access that directory, read its content, and populate the tree accordingly. It is better to read directories when they are about to be expanded, instead of reading the entire disk (or network) when initializing the control.

This handler may also affect the outcome of the underlying operation (here, an expansion). For this notification, passing zero in *pResult means that the expansion can take place. On the other hand, passing a non-zero value prevents the expansion from taking place. For instance, if the directory cannot be read (not enough permission), the handle may first display a message box indicating the permission problem, and then return a non-zero value for the control not to expand the item (should it already contain any child items).

Refer to the online documentation (with Visual C++) in order to correctly interpret the content of the NM_TREEVIEW structure. For instance, when handling TVN_SELCHANGING, the itemOld member designates the currently selected item, whereas itemNew is the item about to receive the selection. On the other hand, when processing TVN_ITEMEXPANDING, itemOld is not used, and itemNew described the item being expanded (or collapsed).

The TVITEM Structure

Tree notifications pass information about items by using a `TVITEM` structure (see Figure 20-18). In fact, most `CTreeCtrl::InsertItem()` overloaded methods are internally implemented by initializing an `TVITEM` structure and sending a message, along the structure's address, to the underlying tree control. That structure was formerly called `TV_ITEM`. Most of these members are self-explanatory and we'll see how to use them later. But before doing so, let's review two members: `state` and `stateMask`.

Type	Member	Description
UINT	mask	Defines what fields within the structure are valid.
HTREEITEM	hItem	The item handle referred to by this structure.
UINT	state	Item state.
UINT	stateMask	State mask.
LPTSTR	pszText	Item text.
int	cchTextMax	The number of characters in pszText.
int	iImage	Index in an image list to display the image of the item in a non-selected state.
int	iSelectedImage	Index in an image list to display the image of the item in a selected state.
int	cChildren	Indicates whether a button [+] or [-] is displayed, even if the item does not have child items.
LPARAM	lParam	An application-defined 32-bit value.

Figure 20-18: The `TVITEM` structure.

Each tree control item has an internal state:

- Bits 0-7 contain the state flags, among them: `TVIS_BOLD`, `TVIS_EXPANDED`, `TVIS_FOCUSED`, `TVIS_SELECTED`, etc.

- Bits 8-11 specify an image overlay, to be superimposed on the item's default image. Keep these bits to 0 if no overlay is to be used.

- Bits 12-15 defines the image index, in the control's image list.

If you want to change the state flags, say to set `TVIS_BOLD` on an item, you need to update the `state` member. But if you simply set `state` to `TVIS_BOLD`, all the other bits will be set to zero. The `stateMask` is used to specify what bits you are about to set, without affecting the other bits. The alternative would to first query the actual state and then change the specific bits. By using the state mask, there is no need to get the actual state initially.

The last member, `lParam`, allows the application to associate an arbitrary 32-bit value to each item. This can be a pointer to a structure holding more information for each item.

An application can retrieve a TVITEM structure by calling CTreeCtrl::GetItem(), and passing a HTREITEM (obtained in a notification for instance). Conversely, an application can modify an existing tree item by calling CTreeCtrl::SetItem() and specifying a TVITEM structure. There are also numerous CTreeCtrl methods that retrieve or set specific information about an item, but they internally rely on GetItem() or SetItem() to accomplish their duty. Some of these methods are GetItemState(), GetItemText(), GetItemData(), etc., as well as the SetXXX counterpart.

Other Tree Control Methods

The user normally selects an item by clicking on it, but the same result can be achieved programmatically by calling CTreeCtrl::SelectItem() and specifying an item handle. CTreeCtrl::GetSelectedItem() returns the item currently selected.

Other CTreeCtrl methods are available to alter the appearance of the control. For instance, the graphical indentation can be changed (although this is not often required) by calling CTreeCtrl::SetIndent().

The control background color can be set by calling CTreeCtrl::SetBkColor(), and retrieved through CTreeCtrl::GetBkColor(). Similarly, the text color can be set and retrieved by calling CTreeCtrl::SetTextColor() and CTreeCtrl::GetText Color() respectively.

Saving Memory with Text Callback

By default, a tree control internally allocates memory (from the local heap) to store the item strings as they are inserted. This is very useful because the application doesn't have to store the strings itself. For instance, when populating a directory tree, the application can read and insert filenames one by one, without storing them in some data structures.

On the other hand, if the application internally maintains the set of strings, inserting them in the tree control results in wasted space because the control allocates memory to hold these strings as well. To prevent this duplication, an application can pass LPSTR_TEXTCALLBACK instead of a string when inserting an item. This directs the tree control not to allocate any memory. In return, the tree control will request the string in order to draw it. This request is sent using the TVN_GETDISPINFO notification.

The following example illustrates such an insertion and a TVN_GETDISPINFO handler. The functions call in italics are hypothetical functions that do what their name suggests:

```
void CMyWnd::OnCreate()
{
    ReadData();
```

```
      for (int i = 0; i < GetDataCount(); i++)
            m_TreeCtrl.InsertItem(i, LPSTR_TEXTCALLBACK, 0);
}

void CMyWnd::OnGetDispInfo(NMHDR * pNMHDR, LRESULT * pResult)
{
    NMTVDISPINFO * pNMTVDISPINFO = (NMTVDISPINFO *) pNMHDR;

    // Fill in the text, if that is what is required.
    if (pNMHDR->item.mask & TVIF_TEXT)
    {
            // Retrieve the text based on the specified HTREEITEM
            LPCTSTR pszText = GetDataString(pNMHDR->item.hItem);

            // Set the text directly into the structure.
            pNMHDR->item.pszText = pszText;
    }

    // *pResult is ignored by the control.
}
```

CTreeCtrl and CTreeView

In addition to CTreeCtrl, applications can use CTreeView to represent hierarchical data. The purpose of CTreeView is to simplify the implementation of a document/view application whose main view is a tree control.

A CTreeView is first and foremost a view, making it usable in an document/view architecture. But it also manages an internal CTreeCtrl, whose size always fully covers the view. Calling CTreeView::GetTreeCtrl() returns a reference to that internal view, allowing the application to add items in the control, which are then shown in the view.

The FBrowser sample, shown in Figure 20-12, uses such a view.

20.3.2 CListCtrl

A list control is a graphically- and functionally-enhanced list box. It can display its content using four different layouts (see Figure 20-19):

1. As small icons with text, with multiple items per line

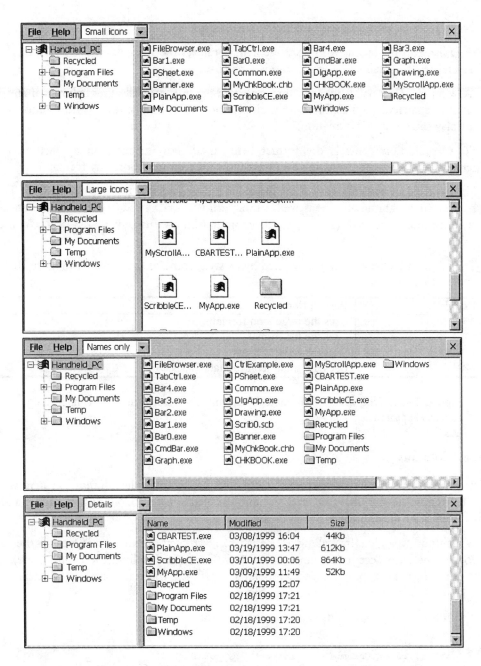

Figure 20-19: A list control can be displayed in different formats (from top to bottom): small icons, large icons, list, and report.

2. As large icons with text, with multiple items per line

3. As a list, *i.e.*, small icons with text, one item per line, no other columns. On CE, this resembles the small icon format, and is rarely used.

4. As a report, *i.e.*, small icons with text, one item per line, with all other columns if any. This format actually is a table, with multiple lines and columns. It is very useful to display categorized information.

Your application controls the format being used. For instance, an application may restrict a list as a report (*i.e.*, a table), or it may allow the user to choose any format.

List controls are typically added in a dialog box, using a dialog box resource editor. They can be created programmatically as well: simply call `CListCtrl::Create()` and specify the style, position and size (a `CRect`), the parent window (usually `this`) and a control identifier.

The format of a list control is governed by its style, some of them listed in Figure 20-20.

List Styles	Description
LVS_ICON	Uses the large icon format.
LVS_LIST	Uses the list format.
LVS_REPORT	Uses the report format.
LVS_SMALLICON	Uses the small icon format.

Figure 20-20: One of the four mutually exclusive attributes that determines a list controls appearance.

Adding Columns

A list control displays one *item* per line. It can also display multiple columns per item when using the report view; in this case, each column is called a *subitem*. Columns should be added immediately after the control has been created.

A column is added by calling `CListCtrl::InsertColumn()`. One of the two overloaded methods accepts a column index (zero-based), a heading (the column title), the alignment (left, right or centered), which default to left, the width (in pixels), and finally, the index of the sub-item associated with the column.

The following example adds two columns to a list:

```
m_ListCtrl.InsertColumn(0, "Name", LVCFMT_LEFT, 120);
m_ListCtrl.InsertColumn(1, "Attribute", LVCFMT_LEFT, 60);
```

The other `CListCtrl::InsertColumn()` method requires a filled `LVCOLUMN` structure. This structure contains essentially the same parameters (alignment, width, etc.).

A column's width can later be obtained by calling `CListCtrl::GetColumnWidth()`, and set by calling `CListCtrl::SetColumnWidth()`.

A column can be deleted by calling `CListCtrl::DeleteColumn()`.

Inserting and Deleting Items

Each line is an item, and is zero-based. If the list contains columns, the corresponding data for a given item is called a subitem, and they are one-based.

`CListCtrl` implements a few `InsertItem()` methods depending on the data to be inserted. The most common `CListCtrl::InsertItem()` method accepts three parameters:

- The zero-based item index (0, 1, 2, ...)
- The item text. You can use `LPSTR_TEXTCALLBACK` to prevent the control from allocating memory to store the string internally, if the application maintains all the strings itself. In that case, the control sends the `LVN_GETDISPINFO` to query the string prior to display it.
- An index into the associated image list.

None of the provided `InsertItem()` methods can be used to insert sub-items. Setting sub-items can be done by calling `CListCtrl::SetItemText()`, passing the index of an existing item, the sub-item position, and the text.

The following example inserts one item and fills one sub-item (*i.e.*, the second column for that item).

```
m_ListCtrl.InsertItem(0, TEXT("\Windows"), 0);
m_ListCtrl.SetItemText(0, 1, TEXT("Read-write"));
```

An application can call `CListCtrl::GetItemCount()` to determine the item count in the list. This doesn't take into account sub-items.

Items can be deleted individually by calling `CListCtrl::DeleteItem()`, or all at once by calling `CListCtrl::DeleteAllItems()`.

Using Image List Controls

Each item can be associated with an image. Since two sizes are possible (small or large), two image lists (each using its respective bitmap) must be associated with the list, using a flag indicating which one is small and which one is large, as follows:

```
// Assume that m_ImageListSmall and m_ImageListLarge are both
// CImageList objects, a m_ListCtrl is of type CListCtrl.

// Create an image list for small and large images.
m_ImageListSmall.Create(IDB_FILES_SMALL, 16, 1, RGB(0, 128, 128));
m_ImageListLarge.Create(IDB_FILES_LARGE, 32, 1, RGB(0, 128, 128));

// Associate the image lists to the list ctrl.
m_ListCtrl.SetImageList(&m_ImageListSmall, LVSIL_SMALL);
m_ListCtrl.SetImageList(&m_ImageListLarge, LVSIL_NORMAL);
```

When displaying large icons, the LVSIL_NORMAL image list is accessed to obtain the images for each item; in all other modes, the LVSIL_SMALL image list is used instead. Naturally, both image lists must contains the same number of images, and the images in one list must match the other's. For instance, Figure 20-21 shows the two bitmaps used with the previous example:

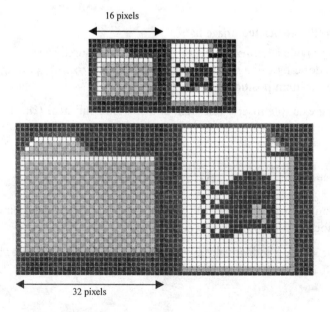

Figure 20-21: Two image lists are required with a list control to display small and large icons.

The LVITEM Structure

Notifications pass information about items by using a LVITEM structure (see Figure 20-22). Many other CListCtrl methods internally use that structure as well: InsertItem(), GetItemText(), SetItemText(), etc.

Type	Member	Description
UINT	mask	Indicates which of the following members are valid.
int	iItem	Zero-based item index.
int	iSubItem	One-based sub-item index (see below).
UINT	state	Item state (focused, selected, etc.).
UINT	stateMask	Mask when setting or retrieving state.
LPSTR	pszText	Item text.
int	cchTextMax	Item text size.
int	iImage	Image list index.
LPARAM	lParam	32-bit user-defined data for that item.

Figure 20-22: The LVITEM structure.

The members are used in a way similar to the tree control. An application can retrieve information about an item by calling CListCtrl::GetItem(), and set an item by calling CListCtrl::SetItem().

Sorting Items

CListCtrl::SortItems() can be called in response to LVN_COLUMNCLICK, a notification sent when a column header is clicked in the report mode. It requires two parameters, a comparison function, which must be either global or static, and a 32-bit user-defined value. Internally, SortItems() sorts the list by calling the comparison function, passing three arguments: two item values to compare and the 32-bit user-defined value.

The two item values are in fact the 32-bit user-defined data that can be associated with each item. This is typically a pointer to a structure describing the item in details. The third parameter is typically set to contain the column number to determine what to sort upon. This method is used with the **FBrowser** sample.

Other List Control Attributes

The width of a column, in a list or report view, can be changed by calling CListCtrl::SetColumnWidth(), and can be retrieved through CListCtrl::GetColumnWidth().

The space between icon, in an icon view, can be set to prevent overlapping by calling CListCtrl::SetIconSpacing().

The control's background color can be set by calling CListCtrl::SetBkColor(), and retrieved through CListCtrl::GetBkColor(). Similarly, the text color can be set and retrieved by calling CListCtrl::SetTextColor() and CListCtrl::GetText Color() respectively. Also, the text background color can be set and retrieved by calling CListCtrl::SetTextBkColor() and CListCtrl::GetTextBkColor().

List Control Notifications

We just saw that LVN_COLUMNCLICK is a notification sent when the user clicks on a column. And that's about the only one of interest. If sorting is not a desired feature, notifications can be ignored.

CListCtrl and CListView

MFC provides a view called CListView, that internally manages a CListCtrl. This is the same concept as described earlier regarding CTreeCtrl and CTreeView. A CListView is used in the example presented in Section 20.3.4.

20.3.3 CHeaderCtrl

A header control is usually positioned above columns of texts and provides a title. They can be enlarged by the user to customize their appearance. Header controls are usually embedded into a list control or a list view, in which case the parent control/view fully manages the header control. As a result, applications rarely manipulate header controls themselves.

Nonetheless, it is sometimes useful to access this embedded header control, in order to change its appearance, for instance (by calling CWnd::ModifyStyle()). You can create a header control yourself by calling CHeaderCtrl::Create(), or use one in a dialog box. You can even call CListCtrl::GetHeaderCtrl() to obtain a pointer to the embedded header control within a list control. From that point, you can call any CWnd method as well as the methods described in Figure 20-23:

CHeaderCtrl Method	Description
GetItemCount()	Retrieves the number of items (column header).
GetItem()	Retrieves item information.
SetImageList()	Associates an image list.
SetItem()	Sets item information.

Figure 20-23: A few CHeaderCtrl methods.

Header controls send notifications, but they are usually handled by the parent list control. Again, header controls are almost never directly or indirectly used by applications.

20.3.4 The FBrowser Sample

The **FBrowser** sample is a simple file browser, shown on Figure 20-15. Its purpose is not to implement a full browser, but rather how to use the tree, list, and image controls. The main frame consists of a splitter window whose left pane is a tree view and the right pane a list view. The application has been generated from AppWizard using a single-document architecture, without document support. Two classes have been added using ClassWizard: CDirectoryView, derived from CTreeView, and CFileView, derived from CListView. The frame has been cleaned up to throw away the default view (called CChildView).

20.4 SCALE CONTROLS

Two controls are available to help the user choose a value within a range or scale: the spin button control (CSpinButtonControl) and the slider control (CSliderCtrl).

20.4.1 CSpinButtonCtrl

A spin button is a control with a pair of up and down arrows (see Figure 20-24). It can be combined with an edit control, in order to allow the user to increase or decrease the value displayed in the edit control by tapping on the arrows, in addition to typing into the edit control. They are called spin button because keeping the stylus on either arrow spins the value very quickly. They are also called up-down controls.

Figure 20-24: A spin button, merged within an edit control.

They are ideal when used with consecutive, predictable numbers. If more than ten increments are possible, consider using slider controls, as some users do not find it convenient to wait until the desired number is reached.

CSpinButtonCtrl are created either in dialog boxes, or by calling Create() and specifying the usual four arguments. Popular styles are listed in Figure 20-25.

CSpinButtonCtrl Style	Description
UDS_ALIGNLEFT	Fits the spin button within the buddy control, along the left edge.
UDS_ARROWKEYS	Increment/decrement the value when the arrow keys are tapped.
UDS_AUTOBUDDY	Selects the previous window (in the Z order) as the buddy. When designing a dialog box, make sure the spin control follows the chosen buddy (such as an edit control).
UDS_SETBUDDYINT	Updates the buddy window (using WM_SETTEXT message) when the position changes.

Figure 20-25: Some of the most common CSpinButtonCtrl styles.

The Buddy Control

Spin controls are usually associated with a buddy edit control that displays an actual value. This edit control can automatically be updated whenever the user taps on the spin button's arrows, without custom code to back this feature up. Call CSpinButtonCtrl::Set Buddy() to specify the buddy window (as a CWnd *). Even better, you can specify the style UDS_AUTOBUDDY, in which case the spin control attaches itself to the previous control (which must be the targeted edit control). The buddy control can be retrieved by calling CSpinButtonCtrl::GetBuddy().

By default, the buddy window displays decimal numbers (using base 10). You can call CSpinButtonCtrl::SetBase() to set the base to 16 in order to display hexadecimal numbers.

Setting the Range

Oddly, the default range is 0 for the maximum and 100 for the minimum. Since the maximum value is inferior than the minimum value, tapping the up arrow decreases the values whereas tapping the down arrow increases it.

There are two methods to modify the minimum and maximum values. CSpinButtonCtrl::SetRange() accepts a 16-bit minimum and maximum values, whereas CSpinButtonCtrl::SetRange32() accepts 32-bit values.

Note that it is common to specify a maximum value superior to the minimum value, in order for the up arrow to increase the value and the down arrow, to decrease it.

You can control the acceleration (if the range covers large numbers) by calling CSpinButtonCtrl::SetAccel(), passing an array of UDACCEL structures. This structure contains an amount of time (in seconds) before the increment is set to the specified value. Here is an example that increases the increment every other second by 10 (*i.e.*, 10, 100, 1000, up to 10000):

```
UDACCEL     Accel[] =
{
    {2,     10},                         // After 2sec, increase by 10
    {2,     100},                        // After 4sec, increase by 100
    {2,     1000},                       // After 6sec, increase by 1000
    {2,     10000}                       // After 8sec, increase by 10000
};

const int ACCEL_COUNT = sizeof(Accel) / sizeof(UDACCEL);

m_SpinButton.SetAccel(ACCEL_COUNT, Accel);
```

The control then manages the acceleration all by itself.

Spin Button Notifications

Spin button controls send WM_HSCROLL or WM_VSCROLL (depending on the control's orientation) when the position is being changed.

Additionally, spin buttons send the UDN_DELTAPOS notification when the position (and the buddy's value) is about to change. It sends an NMUPDOWN structure which contains the actual position and the proposed change. The parent may accept the change by setting *pResult to 0, or prevent it by using a non-zero value.

Spin buttons are almost always associated with an edit control, both managing the notifications in a satisfactory way. As a result, parent windows are rarely concerned with spin control notifications.

20.4.2 CSliderCtrl

A slider control displays a scale and an indicator, and lets the user choose a precise value from a continuous range of values (see Figure 20-25). It is better to use a spin control if there are fewer than ten choices, or is the range is not continuous. Slider controls are also called track bars.

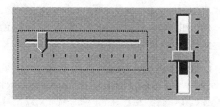

Figure 20-25: Slider controls. The right one also displays a range to provide some information to the user as to what range of values is the best.

CSliderCtrl can be used in dialog boxes or created by calling Create() (with the usual four arguments). Figure 20-26 lists some styles commonly used:

CSliderCtrl Style	Description
TBS_AUTOTICKS	Displays tick marks based on the slider range.
TBS_BOTH	Displays tick marks on either side of the slider. This can be used with either TBS_HORZ or TBS_VERT.
TBS_HORZ	Horizontal slider.
TBS_VERT	Vertical slider.

Figure 20-26: Some common CSliderCtrl styles.

Slider Positions

Whether the slider is shown with tick marks or not, a slider maintains an internal minimum-maximum range which is set to 0 and 100 by default. Call CSliderCtrl::SetRange() to specify custom minimum and maximum range values.

The thumb motion is discrete, not continuous: it moves from one position to another, called thumb positions. Given the range, the slider will automatically establish the thumb stop positions at each interval of one. For instance, if the slider control occupies 200 pixels, there will be a stop position every other pixel for a 100-unit range. The smaller the distance is between two stops, the more fluid the thumb motion is.

The thumb position is always on a thumb stop, never in between. The current position can be retrieved by calling CSliderCtrl::GetPos(), and programmatically set by calling CSliderCtrl::SetPos(). The position is always within the specified range.

Displaying Tick Marks

By default, independent of the range, two tick marks are shown: on the left and right edges of the slider control (for a horizontal slider, top and bottom for a vertical one).

If the style TBS_AUTOTICKS is set, you can call SetTicFreq() to display a tick at every specified unit of thumb stops. For instance, assuming a range (0, 100), SetTicFreq(10) displays a tick at position 0 (the left most), 10, 20, etc, up to 100.

Alternatively, you can keep that style off, and display tick marks at some specified positions. For instance, if you want to have the default two ticks plus one in the middle (using a range 0-100), you can call CSliderCtrl::SetTic(50).

Increasing the Thumb's Motion Fluidity

Tick marks do not affect the motion of the slider thumb; the range does. When using a small range on a larger slider, the thumb moves in large steps, instead of moving smoothly. You can increase the fluidity of the thumb by increasing the range and adjusting the position when reading it.

For instance, consider a large slider control that has a range of 1 to 4, with a tick displayed every unit (see Figure 20-27-a). Given the range, there are only four thumb stops (on each tick mark), breaking the motion in large steps. The motion can be rendered much more fluid by using instead a range from 10 to 40, with a tick interval of 10 (see Figure 20-27-b). The value returned by GetPos(), once divided by 10, returns a value in the range 1 to 4.

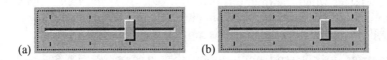

(a)   (b)

Figure 20-27: Thumb fluidity can be smoothed by increasing the range. In (a), the range is 1 to 4, with a tick interval of 1, and the thumb can only be positioned on a tick. In (b), the range is 10 to 40, but with a tick interval of 10, providing a better thumb motion.

The example shows up how to set up each slider:

```
// The left slider is set up using a range from 1 to 4.
// GetPos would then return a value in that range.
m_cRoughSlider.SetRange(1, 4);
m_cRoughSlider.SetTicFreq(1);

// To make the slider more fluid, the range is set to 10 to 40,
// with ticks every 10 units. The value returned by GetPos()
// will be between 10 and 40, so it must be divided by 10
// to obtain a range 1 to 4.
m_cSmoothSlider.SetRange(10, 40);
m_cSmoothSlider.SetTicFreq(10);
```

Buddy Controls

When the range is considerable, the user may not know the exact value at the current indicator position. It is then useful (for the user) to display the actual value (obtained by calling CSliderCtrl::GetPos()) in an adjacent control, such as a read-only edit control or a static control.

Sliders support the notion of buddy controls, *i.e.*, a control that always reflects the actual indicator position. Up to two buddies can be specified for each slider (on each side). A single control is set as a slider's buddy by calling `CSliderCtrl::SetBuddy()`, passing a pointer to the control (`CWnd *`), and a position indicator (`TRUE` for left/top, `FALSE` for right/bottom). This call positions the specified control next to the slider. However, the buddy is not updated automatically as the thumb is moved. The parent window (or dialog box) must handle the slider notifications and update the buddy.

`CSliderCtrl::GetBuddy()` returns the buddy based on the requested position (`TRUE` for left/top and `FALSE` for right/bottom).

Slider Messages

Sliders send messages when the thumb is being moved. However, most applications are not concerned with those notifications: they only need the actual position. One exception is to update the buddy control(s), as the thumb is moved, since this is not achieved automatically.

Slider controls do not send notifications; they rely on `WM_HSCROLL` (for horizontal sliders) and `WM_VSCROLL` (for vertical sliders).

Here is an example of a handler used to update a right buddy control with the actual value of the slider. This example assumes that there is only one slider control, represented by a control variable named `m_cSlider`:

```
void CCtrlDlg::OnHScroll(UINT nSBCode, UINT nPos, CScrollBar* pScrollBar)
{
    // Ignore scroll messages from anybody but the slider.
    if (pScrollBar->GetSafeHwnb() != m_cSlider.m_hWnd)
          return;

    // Get the position as a string.
    CString sText;
    sText.Format(_T("%d"), m_cSlider.GetPos());

    // Get the right buddy and sets its text.
    CWnd * pWnd = m_cSlider.GetBuddy(FALSE);
    ASSERT(pWnd != NULL);

    pWnd->SetWindowText(sText);
}
```

20.5 INFORMATION CONTROLS

A few controls are available to provide information and feedback to the user:

- The progress bar (`CProgresCtrl`)

- The date and time picker (CDateTimeCtrl)
- The month calendar control (CMonthCalCtrl)
- The status bar control (CStatusBarCtrl)

20.5.1 CProgressCtrl

A progress bar informs the user about an ongoing operations (see Figure 20-28). They should be used whenever an operation lasts for more than five seconds. Shorter operations may simply use an hourglass cursor. Some progress bars are displayed in a small popup window, along a *Cancel* button to interrupt the operation. The progress control is one of the few that doesn't send notifications to its parent.

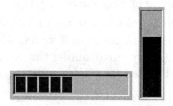

Figure 20-28: Horizontal and vertical progress controls.

Progress bars are usually displayed horizontally, but you can specify the style PBS_VERTICAL to make them vertical.

Many applications use a progress control that shows a percentage as it advances as shown in Figure 20-1. This is not a standard feature available through Windows or MFC, but it can easily be implemented by creating a new control that extends the progress control. Section 20.6.4 provides all the details.

Setting the Range

Like slider controls, progress bars are based on a range. Call CProgressCtrl::SetRange() to specify the minimum and maximum range values, which respectively default to 0 and 100.

Changing the Position

There are three methods to move the position of a progress bar, depending on how progression is measured:

- **Incremental**: call CProgresCtrl::SetStep() to establish an increment amount, which is applied whenever CProgressCtrl::StepIt() is called.

This last call causes the control to repaint itself to reflect the change. There is one caveat, though: stepping beyond the maximum limit wraps back to the minimum limit, which defeats the purpose of a progress bar. Use this approach when you can establish ahead the exact number of calls to `StepIt()`.

For instance, if 10 operations must be conducted, the range can be set from 0 to 10, the step is set to 1, and `StepIt()` is called once each operation is completed.

In this case, the progression is represented in terms of completed operations.

- **By an offset**: call `CProgressCtrl::OffsetPos()` to pass a positive of negative offset, which is applied on the current position. The new position always remains within the range bounds. This method is ideal when variable-length operations are to be run, and the total can be known ahead.

  For instance, when downloading a file of 100Kb via a serial connection, the progress bar's range can be set from 0 to 100. The file may actually be read by chunks, as time-outs may occur during the download. Every time a chunk is read, the total count is used to update the progress control.

  In this scenario, the progression is represented in terms of data having been processed.

- **By a specific value**: call `CProgressCtrl::SetPos()` to set the position to a specific value. This is appropriate when used with a timer when the total duration can be estimated.

  For instance, if a second thread is started to monitor some conditions for 15 seconds, the progress bar's range can be set from 0 to 15 and a 1-second timer can be installed. Every time the timer sends a message, an internal counter is incremented by one and its value is used to advance the progress bar. Since timers are not so reliable, the application may actually calculate the exact time and update the progress bar accordingly.

  Under this approach, the progression is represented in terms of elapsed time.

The current position can be obtained by calling `CProgressCtrl::GetPos()`.

20.5.2 CMonthCalCtrl

The month calendar control displays a monthly calendar, allows the user to navigate through months (by tapping on the visible month) and years (by tapping on the visible year), and supports the notion of "current date" (see Figure 20-29).

Figure 20-29: The month calendar control is very complete, yet easy to use.

The control doesn't require any special attributes to be displayed as shown. Interestingly enough, the control may show more than one month of the current year if its size so allows (up to twelve months). Today's date is always selected (and shown) when the control is initially displayed, but you can select another date by calling CMonthCal::SetCurSel() (more on this in a minute).

Using CMonthCalCtrl

Although you can add a month calendar control is a dialog box using Visual C++, ClassWizard will not let you add a control variable for it (ClassWizard doesn't recognize that control). Here's what to do to add a control variable in a dialog box:

(a) In the dialog header file, include Afxdtctl.h and declare a month calendar control variable:

```
#include "Afxdtctl.h"

class CCtrlDlg : public CDialog
{
    CMonthCalCtrl  m_cMonthCal;
    .
    .
    .
};
```

(b) Add a DDX_Control statement in DoDataExchange(), under the comments for ClassWizard:

```
void CCtrlDlg::DoDataExchange(CDataExchange* pDX)
{
    CDialog::DoDataExchange(pDX);
    //{{AFX_DATA_MAP(CCtrlDlg)
```

```
        .
        .
        .
    //}}AFX_DATA_MAP
    DDX_Control(pDX, IDC_MONTHCALENDAR1, m_cMonthCal);
}
```

(c) That's it! You can then access the control variable as usual.

Setting a Date Range

The date range determines what months the user can navigate through. For instance, a range can be set to cover all months of a given year, restricting the user in selecting dates within that year.

You can set a date range limit by calling `CMonthCalCtrl::SetRange()`, and specifying two `CTime` objects, or two `SYSTEMTIME` structures, representing the minimum and maximum dates. Pass `NULL` pointers to remove the range.

The next example sets a 6-month range, from January 1999 to June 1999, using `CTime` objects. The year and month fields are naturally very important. Day fields are less important, since months are always displayed in full. Nevertheless, days limit the selection by preventing the days before the start dates and after the ending dates from being selected. For instance, if the ending time is June 15, days beyond the 15 (*e.g.*, June 20) can't be selected.

```
// m_cMonthCal is a CMonthCalCtrl object.

CTime       StartTime(1999, 01, 01, 00, 00, 00);
CTime       EndTime(1999, 06, 30, 00, 00, 00);

m_cMonthCal.SetRange(&StartTime, &EndTime);
```

Even if today's date is out of the range, today's date will automatically be shown when displaying the control for the first time by default. You can display another month (within the range) by selecting an appropriate date. The next example makes sure that January 1999 is shown by selecting 01/15/99:

```
CTime       InitTime(1999, 01, 15, 00, 00, 00);

m_cMonthCal.SetCurSel(InitTime);
```

Call `CMonthCalCtrl::GetRange()` to obtain the actual range (the minimum and maximum) or `CMonthCalCtrl::GetMonthRange()` to get the number of months between two dates.

Today

A month calendar control displays by default today's date at the bottom. The feature can be disabled be setting the attribute MCS_NOTODAY. Also, today's date on the calendar is displayed with a red border, unless the MCS_NOTODAYCIRCLE style is on. The two styles are independent of each other.

The date shown as today's date can be set by calling CMonthCalCtrl::SetToday() and passing a pointer to either a CTime object or a SYSTEMTIME structure. To make sure that the new date is also visible, call CMonthCal::SetCurSel() with the same value.

CMonthCalCtrl::GetToday() retrieves that date.

Appearance

You can change the first day of the week (that is, the day represented on the leftmost column) by calling CMonthCalCtrl::SetFirstDayOfWeek(). Use 0 for Monday, 1 for Tuesday and so on, up to 6 for Sunday. The default is as defined by LOCALE_IFIRSTDAYOFWEEK.

You can also display the week number on the left by setting the MCS_WEEKNUMBERS. Unfortunately, this can't be done in a dialog box editor, since the style is not recognized by the resource compiler. You can, however, add a control variable (as explained before) and set the style by calling CWnd::ModifyStyle() in CYourDlg::OnInitDialog(), as follows:

```
BOOL CCtrlDlg::OnInitDialog()
{
    CDialog::OnInitDialog();
    .
    .
    .
    // Display week numbers
    m_cMonthCal.ModifyStyle(0, MCS_WEEKNUMBERS);
    .
    .
    .
}
```

The month color can be set by calling CMonthCalCtrl::SetColor(). The first parameter is an area code (e.g., MCSC_MONTHBK for the month background, MCSC_TEXT for the text, etc.) and the second is the color as an RGB value (e.g., COLORREF(255, 0, 0) for red).

Selection

For single-selection calendar month control (which is the default), call `CMonthCalCtrl::GetCurSel()` to obtain the currently-selected date, returned in either a `CTime` object or a `SYSTEMTIME` structure. As mentioned earlier, call `SetCurSel()` to select and display a given day.

For multiple-selection calendar month control (*i.e.*, with the `MCS_MULTISELECT` style), call `CMonthCalCtrl::GetSelRange()` to obtain the minimum and maximum range values, specified as a pair of either `CTime` objects or `SYSTEMTIME` structures.

Displaying Days in Bold

Special days can be displayed in bold (an operation called setting the day state) if the `MCS_DAYSTATE` style is set. For instance, holidays, pay days, anniversaries, etc. can all be highlighted by your application. This is done in two steps.

The first step consists of indicating the day states for the month(s) currently shown in the control, including the months partially displayed (if any). Call `CMonthCalCtrl::GetMonthRange()`, with two time buffers (`CTime` or `SYSTEMTIME`) and the `GMR_DAYSTATE` flag to know how many months are being shown and the exact first and last date. For instance, that call for Figure 20-29 would return a value of 3 (months), the start date being 02/28/99 and the end date, 04/10/99. Note that the returned value is not always 3; it can be 2 (if the first of the current month starts on a Sunday for instance), or more, since the control can be sized to display up to 12 visible months.

Then fill an array of `MONTHDAYSTATE` structures, one for each visible month. A `MONTHDAYSTATE` structure is a 32-bit value, where each bit (0 to 30) corresponds to one day (1 to 31). If a bit is set, the corresponding day is displayed in bold. The first `MONTHDAYSTATE` will be applied to the first visible month (even if shown partially), the second, to the second month, etc.

Finally, call `CMonthCalCtrl::SetDayState()`, passing the number of structures and the array. You must pass as many structures as there are visible months (*i.e.*, the same value returned by `GetMonthRange(..., GMR_DAYSTATE)`), otherwise the call fails. The next example highlights March 2 and 15 on Figure 20-29:

```
CTime            StartTime;
CTime            EndTime;

int nVisibleMonth = m_cMonthCal.GetMonthRange(
                    StartTime,        // First visible date
                    EndTime,          // Last visible date
                    GMR_DAYSTATE);    // Based on all visible months

ASSERT(nVisibleMonth == 3);
```

```
MONTHDAYSTATE          mdStates[3];

mdStates[0] = 0;                        // End of February
mdStates[1] = (1 << 14) | (1 << 1);    // March 15th and 2nd
mdStates[2] = 0;                        // Beginning of April

m_cMonthCal.SetDayState(3, mdStates);
```

But as soon as the user taps on the left or right arrow to display other month(s), that day state setting completely vanishes, even if the user comes back to the initial months. This brings us to step 2.

As the user navigates from month to month, the control sends the MCN_GETDAYSTATE notification, passing an NMDAYSTATE structure (shown in Figure 20-30). The handler must essentially repeat the process described above: fill an array of MONTHDAYSTATE structures and store the address of that array in the prgDayState member of the NMDAYSTATE structure. The cDayState member indicates how many months are visible (including partial months) and hence, the size of the requested array.

Type	Member	Description
NMHDR	nmhdr	Information about the notification message.
SYSTEMTIME	stStart	Starting date.
int	cDayState	Total number of months to provide.
LPMONTHDAYSTATE	prgDayState	Array of MONTHDAYSTATE values, one per month.

Figure 20-30: The NMDAYSTATE structure.

The following example makes sure that March 2nd and 15th, as well as April 30th are always highlighted. Note that the MONTHDATSTATE array is a member variable, to ensure that it persists once the handler returns. Also note the SETDAYSTATE helper inline, which improves code readability.

```
class CCtrlDlg : public CDialog
{
    CMonthCalCtrl  m_cMonthCal;
    MONTHDAYSTATE  m_mdState[3];  // To handle MCN_GETDAYSTATE
    .
    .
    .
};

// An helper function to set/reset a day in a MONTHDAYSTATE value.

inline void SETDAYSTATE(MONTHDAYSTATE& mds, int nDay, BOOL bSet = TRUE)
{
    ASSERT(nDay >= 0 && nDay <= 31);
```

```
      nDay--;

      if (bSet)
            mds |= (1 << nDay);
      else
            mds &= ~(1 << nDay);
}

void CCtrlDlg::OnMonthCalGetDayState(NMHDR * pNMHDR, LRESULT * result)
{
      NMDAYSTATE* pDayState= (NMDAYSTATE *)pNMHDR;

      // Three months are shown at most (given the control's size).
      // If the control is enlarged, more months will be visible, and
      // this code will have to be adjusted to process those months.
      ASSERT(pDayState->cDayState <= 3);

      // Initialize the array.
      for (int i = 0; i < 3; i++)
            m_mdState[i] = 0;

      // Set the bits depending on the first month being shown:
      switch (pDayState->stStart.wMonth)
      {
      case 2:                              // mdState[0] must be February
            SETDAYSTATE(m_mdState[1], 2);  // March 2
            SETDAYSTATE(m_mdState[1], 15); // March 15
            SETDAYSTATE(m_mdState[2], 30); // April 30
            break;

      case 3:                              // mdState[0] must be March
            SETDAYSTATE(m_mdState[0], 2);  // March 2
            SETDAYSTATE(m_mdState[0], 15); // March 15
            SETDAYSTATE(m_mdState[1], 30); // April 30
            break;

      case 4:                              // mdState[0] must be April
            SETDAYSTATE(m_mdState[0], 30); // April 30
            break;
      }

      // Store the address in the structure. It is better to use
      // a member array, which persists when the handler returns.
      pDayState->prgDayState = m_mdState;
}
```

20.5.3 CDateTimeCtrl

The date and time picker control displays a combo box showing a date or time. Clicking the arrow shows a month calendar control to select a new date (see Figure 20-31).

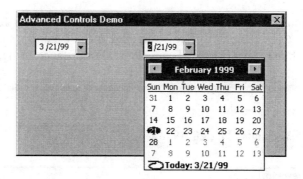

Figure 20-31: Date-time picker controls.

A few interesting attributes are `DTS_LONGDATEFORMAT`, to display the date using a long format (*e.g.*, "Sunday, December 20, 1998") instead of using a short format (the default), and `DTS_TIMEFORMAT`, which shows a time instead of a date.

Like the month calendar control, the date time picker control is not well recognized by ClassWizard nor the resource compiler. As a result, you must insert by yourself the control variable you wish to use with that control, as explained with the month calendar control. You also have to include `Afxdtctl.h` when doing so. Some style attributes must be set by calling `CWnd::ModifyStyle()`, again because of some limitations of the resource compiler.

Setting and Getting the Date and Time

Call `CDateTimeCtrl::SetTime()`, passing either a `CTime` object or a `SYSTEMTIME` structure, to set the time within the control. The control automatically repaints itself with the specified time.

On the other hand, you can retrieve the time within the control by simply calling the `CDateTimeCtrl::GetTime()` method, which requires the same parameters.

You can also set a time range limit by calling `CDateTimeCtrl::SetRange()`, and specifying two `CTime` objects: the minimum and maximum. Pass `NULL` pointers to remove the range. Call `CDateTimeCtrl::GetRange()` to obtain the actual range.

Formatting the Date and Time

Three predefined styles are available to display the date and time using different formats: `DTS_LONGDATEFORMAT`, `DTS_SHORTDATEFORMAT`, and `DTS_TIMEFORMAT`.

Nonetheless, you can use a custom representation, by passing a formatting string to `CDateTimeCtrl::SetFormat()`. The string can include quote-delimited user-defined text and some predefined codes listed in Figure 20-32. For instance, using:

```
"'Today is: 'HH':'m':'s ddddMMMdd', 'yyy"
```

causes the following to be shown:

"Today is: 20:29:31 Sunday Dec 20, 1998"

Code	Description
d	The one- or two-digit day.
dd	The two-digit day. Single-digit day values are preceded by a zero.
ddd	The three-character weekday abbreviation.
dddd	The full weekday name.
h	The one- or two-digit hour in 12-hour format.
hh	The two-digit hour in 12-hour format. Single-digit values are preceded by a zero.
H	The one- or two-digit hour in 24-hour format.
HH	The two-digit hour in 24-hour format. Single-digit values are preceded by a zero.
m	The one- or two-digit minute.
mm	The two-digit minute. Single-digit values are preceded by a zero.
M	The one- or two-digit month number.
MM	The two-digit month number. Single-digit values are preceded by a zero.
MMM	The three-character month abbreviation.
MMMM	The full month name.
t	The one-letter AM/PM abbreviation (that is, AM is displayed as "A").
tt	The two-letter AM/PM abbreviation (that is, AM is displayed as "AM").
y	The one-digit year (that is, 1998 would be displayed as "8").
yy	The last two digits of the year (that is, 1998 would be displayed as "98").
yyy	The full year (that is, 1998 would be displayed as "1998").

Figure 20-32: The predefined formatting codes. Additionally, 'X' can be used for callback formatting, but that is unusual.

Accessing the Drop-Down Month-Calendar Control

A month calendar control is created whenever the user clicks the drop-down button. At that moment, the control sends the `DTN_DROPDOWN` notification, which can be handled by the parent window (or dialog box). The handler can access the month calendar control by calling `CDateTimeCtrl::GetMonthCalCtrl()`. The returned value is a temporary pointer (which is meaningful within the handler only), and can be used to access the related control.

Note that the font of the month calendar control can be directly set and obtained via the date-time control, by respectively calling `CDateTimeCtrl::SetMonthCalFont()` and

CDateTimeCtrl::GetMonthCalFont(). Similarly, the color of the month calendar control can be set and retrieved by calling CDateTimeCtrl::SetMonthCalColor() and CDateTimeCtrl::GetMonthCalColor().

Data Time Control Notifications

Besides DTN_DROPDOWN, a date time picker control sends DTN_DATETIMECHANGE, when a change is detected in the control.

20.5.4 CStatusBarCtrl and CStatusBar

A status bar is a horizontal window, displayed at the bottom of an application window, that displays status information, such as help menu commands, the current operation taking place, the cursor position, etc. Figure 20-33 shows a typical status bar.

Figure 20-33: A typical status bar displays an informational message on the left, and the Caps Lock key status on the right.

AppWizard has an option to generate a default status bar, such as the one shown before. The main frame (or the application window) creates it by using a CStatusBar member variable and calling Create(this).

CStatusBar and CStatusBarCtrl

Like the rebar and toolbar controls, MFC provides two classes for the status bar control. CStatusBarCtrl is essentially a C++ class wrapper around the underlying status bar, whose methods send messages; CStatusBar, commonly used in applications, provides enhanced methods and a better integration with the document/view architecture. Most applications use CStatusBar.

Panes and Indicators

A status bar is composed of panes. Default status bars contain two: an informational message on the left, a CAPS LOCK indicator on the right. Panes can easily be customized.

Immediately after creating the toolbar, the main frame invokes `CToolBar::Set Indicators()`, passing an array whose elements describe the panes that compose the toolbar. The following code is generated from AppWizard:

```
class CMainFrame : public CFrameWnd
{
    CStatusBar              m_wndStatusBar;
    .
    .
    .
};

static UINT indicators[] =
{
    ID_SEPARATOR,           // status line indicator
    ID_INDICATOR_CAPS
};

int CMainFrame::OnCreate(LPCREATESTRUCT lpCreateStruct)
{
    .
    .
    .
    if (!m_wndStatusBar.Create(this) ||
            !m_wndStatusBar.SetIndicators(indicators,
            sizeof(indicators)/sizeof(UINT)))
    {
            TRACE0("Failed to create status bar\n");
            return -1;      // fail to create
    }

    return 0;
}
```

In this example, the array (called `indicators[]`) contains `ID_SEPARATOR` and `ID_INDICATOR_CAPS`. `ID_SEPARATOR` has a special meaning when used as the first element in the array (as it is in this example): it means that the first pane will be used to display status messages (such as "`Ready`"), but also menu item prompts when the user navigates through the menu. When used in another position in the array, it inserts some space between two panes. `ID_INDICATOR_CAPS` is the "CAPS" string resource id; by passing a string resource id, a pane large enough to accommodate the string is created. And it turns out that the main frame monitor the keyboard and updates the pane according to the status of the CAPS LOCK key[65].

You can add your own panes by adding your own string ids. Note that it is very, very common to leave `ID_SEPARATOR` as the first pane, but don't hesitate to remove the CAPS pane if it is not required.

---

[65] `CFrameWnd` actually contains such code for `ID_INDICATOR_CAPS`.

The next example uses a 4-pane status bar. The second and third pane are updated with the stylus coordinates when the user taps in the client's area, whereas the last one shows "ALT" if the menu (or ALT) key is pressed. This example is implemented in the **Cstmsbar** sample.

```
// In MainFrm.cpp . . .

BEGIN_MESSAGE_MAP(CMainFrame, CFrameWnd)
    .
    .
    .
    ON_UPDATE_COMMAND_UI(ID_ALT_INDICATOR, OnUpdateAltIndicator)
END_MESSAGE_MAP()

static UINT indicators[] =
{
    ID_SEPARATOR,
    ID_XPOS_INDICATOR,              // "x = ???" string id
    ID_YPOS_INDICATOR,              // "y = ???" string id
    ID_ALT_INDICATOR                // "ALT" string id
};

int CMainFrame::OnCreate(LPCREATESTRUCT lpCreateStruct)
{
    .
    .
    .
    if (!m_wndStatusBar.Create(this) ||
            !m_wndStatusBar.SetIndicators(indicators,
            sizeof(indicators)/sizeof(UINT)))
    {
            TRACE0("Failed to create status bar\n");
            return -1;      // fail to create
    }

    // Enlarge the second and third panes and make them pop-up.
    m_wndStatusBar.SetPaneInfo(1, ID_XPOS_INDICATOR, SBPS_POPOUT, 60);
    m_wndStatusBar.SetPaneInfo(2, ID_YPOS_INDICATOR, SBPS_POPOUT, 60);

    return 0;
}

// This handler is called whenever the application becomes idle.
// It shows "ALT" in the status bar whenever the menu key is pressed.
// pCmdUI in this case represents the last status bar pane, whose
// id is specified in the message map along this handler.

void CMainFrame::OnUpdateAltIndicator(CCmdUI * pCmdUI)
{
    pCmdUI->Enable(::GetKeyState(VK_MENU) < 0);
}

// A public function called by the view when the stylus is tapped.

void CMainFrame::UpdateStatusBarPanes(CPoint pt)
```

```
{
    CString s;

    s.Format(_T("x = %d\n"), pt.x);
    m_wndStatusBar.SetPaneText(1, s);

    s.Format(_T("y = %d\n"), pt.y);
    m_wndStatusBar.SetPaneText(2, s);
}
```

```
// In ChildView.cpp . . .

void CChildView::OnLButtonDown(UINT uFlags, CPoint pt)
{
    // Get a pointer to the parent frame
    CMainFrame *   pFrame = static_cast<CMainFrame *>(GetParentFrame());
    ASSERT(pFrame != NULL);

    // Call a frame's public method to update the status bar.
    pFrame->UpdateStatusBarPanes(pt);
}
```

The output of this example is shown below:

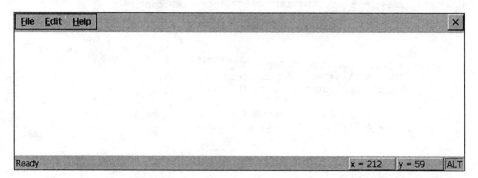

Figure 20-34: A customized status bar.

20.6 CUSTOMIZING COMMON CONTROLS

Some of the common controls detailed in this chapter can have their appearance and behavior customized to meet specific requirements.

20.6.1 Using Existing Control Features

Some controls already provide specific methods to customize their appearance. For instance, CListCtrl, CReBarCtrl and CMonthCalCtrl support methods to alter the color of their text and background color. Once the color is set, there is nothing else to do for the control to use that color. The only drawback is that the new color is applied systematically to all items, and cannot instead be applied selectively.

20.6.2 Owner-Drawn Controls

Some controls support an owner-drawn style attribute. These controls are the header, list, tree, tab, status bar, and command bar's menu items. When that attribute is set, they send WM_DRAWITEM to their parent. Because the default's parent implementation is to call the control's DrawItem(), you can also derive some classes to create objects in MFC that draw themselves, without relying on their parent. The procedure as identical to the one described in Section 19.4.2. It is a little bit demanding though, since all items must be painted, even those that are shown using their default appearance.

It's always fun to change the appearance of existing controls, but it's important to limit the number of fonts and colors. Using 18 colors and 14 fonts within the same list control will certainly confuse more than one user.

20.6.3 Custom Draw Services

A new method is available for command bands, header, list, tool bars, track bars, and tree: custom draw services. This approach is more flexible than those seen so far: it gives the parent (or the related MFC object itself via message reflection) the choice from among the following:

- Painting items entirely;
- Specify some of the drawing resources, but let the underlying control actually paint;
- Let the control paint as usual;

    for one, a few, or all items within the control.

Each of those controls sends the NM_CUSTOMDRAW notification to the application during the *paint drawing stage*. There are multiple drawing stages, each identified by a unique value, as shown in Figure 20-35.

Drawing Stage	Identifier	Sent
Control pre-painting	CDDS_PREPAINT	Before the control is drawn.
Control post-painting	CDDS_POSTPAINT	After the control is drawn.
Control pre-erasing	CDDS_PREERASE	Before the control is erased.
Control post-erasing	CDDS_POSTERASE	After the control is erased.
Item pre-painting	CDDS_ITEMPREPAINT	Before an item is drawn.
Item post-painting	CDDS_ITEMPOSTPAINT	After an item is drawn.
Item pre-erasing	CDDS_ITEMPREERASE	Before an item is erased.
Item post-erasing	CDDS_ITEMPOSTERASE	After an item is erased.

Figure 20-35: Drawing stages.

On receiving the CDSS_PREPAINT stage, the application must return a value of CDRF_NOTIFYITEMDRAW in order to receive item notifications. Then, the control sends notifications with the a stage of CDDS_ITEMPREPAINT for each item to paint. The handler can do the following:

- Entirely paint the item by using the specified device context. It must then return CDRF_SKIPDEFAULT to let the control know that the item has been painted.

- Alter drawing parameters, but let the control draw. The application must then return CDRF_NEWFONT (if the font and, optionally, the text colors, have been changed) or CDRF_DODEFAULT (if nothing or only the colors have been changed).

- Let the control draw the item using current default item settings. The handler simply has to return CDRF_DODEFAULT.

The following example customizes the appearance of a tree view (see Figure 20-36). Items that have child items are drawn using a special font, and the selected item's text is displayed in yellow (on blue). The other items are left intact. This example is implemented in the **CstmDraw** sample.

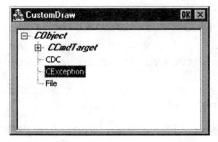

Figure 20-36: A custom draw tree control.

```
// CustomDrawDlg.h

class CCustomDrawDlg : public CDialog
{
    CFont   m_Font;                    // Special font

public:
    .
    .
    .

protected:
    // Message map declaration goes here
    .
    .
    .
    afx_msg void OnMfcTreeCustomDraw(NMHDR * pNMHDR, LRESULT * pResult);
```

```
    DECLARE_MESSAGE_MAP()

private:
    LRESULT CustomDraw(LPNMTVCUSTOMDRAW lcd);
};
```

```cpp
// CustomDrawDlg.cpp

 .
 .
 .

BEGIN_MESSAGE_MAP(CCustomDrawDlg, CDialog)
    //{{AFX_MSG_MAP(CCustomDrawDlg)
    //}}AFX_MSG_MAP
    ON_NOTIFY(NM_CUSTOMDRAW, IDC_MFCTREE, OnMfcTreeCustomDraw)
END_MESSAGE_MAP()

BOOL CCustomDrawDlg::OnInitDialog()
{
    .
    .
    .

    // Create the font for parent items
    LOGFONT lf;
    memset(&lf, '\0', sizeof(LOGFONT));
    lf.lfHeight = -10;
    lf.lfWeight = FW_BOLD;
    lf.lfItalic = TRUE;
    _tcscpy(lf.lfFaceName, _T("MS Sans Serif"));

    m_Font.CreateFontIndirect(&lf);

    // Add some entries in the tree control
    HTREEITEM hObject =
            m_cTreeCtrl.InsertItem(_T("CObject"));

    HTREEITEM hCmdTarget =
            m_cTreeCtrl.InsertItem(_T("CCmdTarget"), hObject);

    m_cTreeCtrl.InsertItem(_T("CWnd"), hCmdTarget);

    m_cTreeCtrl.InsertItem(_T("CDC"), hObject);
    m_cTreeCtrl.InsertItem(_T("CException"), hObject);
    m_cTreeCtrl.InsertItem(_T("File"), hObject);

    return TRUE;
}

// Handler invoked when the tree control sends NM_CUSTOMDRAW.
// pNMHDR points in fact to an NMTREEVIEW (because this is a
// tree view notification).

void CCustomDrawDlg::OnMfcTreeCustomDraw(NMHDR * pNMHDR,
    LRESULT * pResult)
{
```

```
    LPNMTREEVIEW   pnmtv = reinterpret_cast<LPNMTREEVIEW>(pNMHDR);

    switch (pnmtv->hdr.code)
    {
    case NM_CUSTOMDRAW:
            // When custom drawing, pNMHDR points on a NMTVCUSTOMDRAW
            // structure, which is a custom draw structure for
            // tree views.
            *pResult =
                    CustomDraw(reinterpret_cast<LPNMTVCUSTOMDRAW>(pNMHDR));

            break;

    // Process other notifications here
    }
}

// Custom tree control drawing.

LRESULT CCustomDrawDlg::CustomDraw(LPNMTVCUSTOMDRAW lcd)
{
    // On control prepainting, notify the control that item
    // notifications are requested.
    if (lcd->nmcd.dwDrawStage == CDDS_PREPAINT)
            return CDRF_NOTIFYITEMDRAW;

    // Process item prepainting notifications
    if (lcd->nmcd.dwDrawStage == CDDS_ITEMPREPAINT)
    {
            // The item can safely be cast into an HTREEITEM in this case.
            HTREEITEM       hItem =
                    reinterpret_cast<HTREEITEM>(lcd->nmcd.dwItemSpec);

            // Set the color to yellow if the item is selected
            if (lcd->nmcd.uItemState & CDIS_SELECTED)
                    lcd->clrText = RGB(255, 255, 128);

            // If the item has some children, select our font.
            // Otherwise use default font.
            if (m_cTreeCtrl.ItemHasChildren(hItem))
            {
                    CDC     dc;
                    dc.Attach(lcd->nmcd.hdc);
                    dc.SelectObject(&m_Font);
                    dc.Detach();

                    // Let the control know that the font has been changed.
                    return CDRF_NEWFONT;
            }
    }

    // Let the control do its default processing. Note that the default
    // processing relies on the text color, which might have been modified.
    return CDRF_DODEFAULT;
}
```

650

Since notifications can be reflected, the code can actually be implemented right in a derived class, making it self-contained. This class can then be re-used as is in any other application.

20.6.4 Extending Existing Classes

Speaking of notification reflection, a few controls are prime candidates for that. Consider the tree control. We saw in Section 20.3.1 that it sends a notification when an item is about to be expanded. Assuming the tree displays a file hierarchy, it could handle that notification itself, and go ahead and read the directory about to be shown. The files obtained by reading that directory are then added as child items of the item about to be expanded. Once completed, the handler returns "Go for it", and the control shows the newly inserted items.

Another case where extending an existing control is desirable is to change the appearance of a control that doesn't provide any facility to do so natively. A good example is the progress bar control: it doesn't provide any method to customize its look. Nonetheless, many applications use a nice-looking progress bar that indicates the percentage as it advances (see Figure 20-37). Such a custom control can easily be implemented by deriving a new class from `CProgressCtrl`, and re-implementing `OnPaint()`. This will produce a progress bar control that you can use exactly like any other progress bar, except that it will look different. The progress bar shown below is implemented in `CPctProgressCtrl`, a "percentage" progress control. This progress bar is implemented in the **Ctrl** sample.

Figure 20-37: A custom progress control.

SUGGESTED READINGS

See section "Suggested Readings" in Chapter 19

Part V

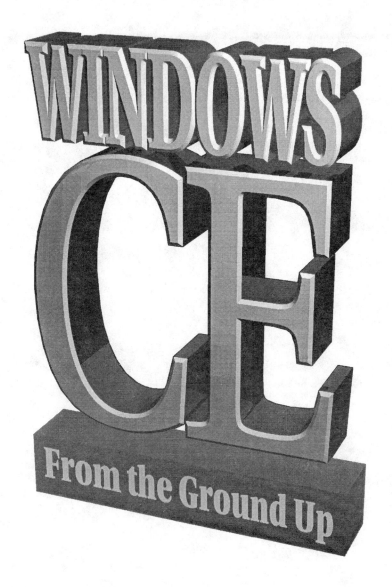

More Application Development

Chapter 21

The Shell

The shell is the system component that manages the user interface, and allows the user to run applications and switch among them. There is no standard shell across all Windows CE devices: each type of platform must have its own.

H/PCs and Palm-size PCs are delivered with shells that resemble those found on Windows 9x/NT. Those "standard" shells and the related API are described in this chapter.

Also, some Windows CE features formerly implemented in the shell are detailed in this chapter: user notifications, low-memory condition management, and clipboard operations. These features have now been moved into other modules in order to be available on shell-less systems. Nevertheless, they are described in this chapter because they *appear* as an integral part of the shell.

21.1 WINDOWS CE SHELLS

H/PCs and Palm-size PCs have each their own distinct shell, but they have closely been designed upon the ones found on Windows 9x and NT (see Figure 21-1).

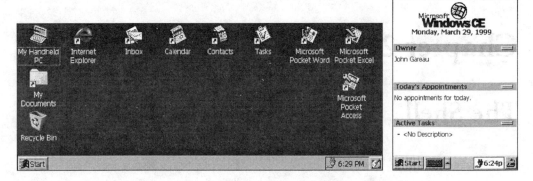

Figure 21-1: The H/PC and Palm-size PC shells.

Although a few differences set them apart, these two shells share a lot of attributes, discussed in the following sections.

21.1.1 Shell Namespace

The H/PC shell has been designed to present multiple types of objects to the user: files and directories, but also folders, shortcuts (links), printers, etc. Those shell objects are called *shell items*. Each item is programmatically represented by an id, called an item identifier, whose type is ITEMIDLIST.

An application can retrieve information about any shell object by calling ::SHGetFileInfo(). Despite the name, this function works on folders and directories as well. It requires a file name, some file attributes (usually 0), a pointer to an SHFILEINFO structure (listed in Figure 21-2), the size of that structure, and a series of flags that identify what information to retrieve (see Figure 21-3).

Type	Member	Description
HICON	hIcon	File icon.
int	iIcon	Index of the icon image in the system image list.
DWORD	dwAttributes	Object attributes.
char	szDisplayName[]	Object name, as shown in the shell.
char	szTypeName[]	Object description.

Figure 21-2: The SHFILEINFO structure.

Flag	Description
SHGFI_ATTR_SPECIFIED	Indicates that the dwAttributes member of the SHFILEINFO structure at psfi contains the specific attributes that are desired.
SHGFI_ATTRIBUTES	Retrieves the attributes of the file.
SHGFI_DISPLAYNAME	Retrieves the file's display name.
SHGFI_EXETYPE	Retrieves the executable type of the file.
SHGFI_ICON	Retrieves the icon associated with the file.
SHGFI_ICONLOCATION	Retrieves the icon location.
SHGFI_LARGEICON	Retrieves the large icon.
SHGFI_LINKOVERLAY	Places a link overlay on the icon.
SHGFI_OPENICON	Retrieves the open icon.
SHGFI_PIDL	The path specified in the pszPath parameter is a pointer to an ITEMID list.
SHGFI_SELECTED	Displays the icon in selected state.
SHGFI_SHELLICONSIZE	Retrieves the icon size used by the shell.
SHGFI_SMALLICON	Retrieves the small icon.
SHGFI_SYSICONINDEX	Retrieves the system icon index.
SHGFI_TYPENAME	Retrieves the file's type name.
SHGFI_USEFILEATTRIBUTES	The file attributes passed in the dwFileAttributes parameter should be used.

Figure 21-3: The flags that can be passed to ::ShGetFileInfo().

Here are two functions that retrieve file information (file type and small icon). The first function (GetFileIconType()) requires an existing file name, and the second (GetExtIconType()), a file extension. In both cases, the returned icon must be deleted by calling DestroyIcon().

```
BOOL GetFileIconType(LPCTSTR pszName, HICON * pIcon, CString& sType)
{
    SHFILEINFO  shfi;

    // Get information about the specified file. The file must
    // exist for the call to succeed.
    if (!SHGetFileInfo(
            pszName,
            0,
            &shfi,
            sizeof(SHFILEINFO),
            SHGFI_ICON | SHGFI_SMALLICON | SHGFI_TYPENAME))
            return FALSE;

    // Extract icon and type name.
    *pIcon = shfi.hIcon;
    sType  = shfi.szTypeName;
```

```
    return TRUE;
}

BOOL GetExtIconType(LPCTSTR pszExt, HICON * pIcon, CString& sType)
{
    SHFILEINFO  shfi;

    // Get information about the specified extension.
    // Use the SHGFI_USEFILEATTRIBUTES flags to force the assumption
    // that the file exists and doesn't need to be accessed as such.
    if (!SHGetFileInfo(
            pszExt,
            FILE_ATTRIBUTE_NORMAL,
            &shfi,
            sizeof(SHFILEINFO),
            SHGFI_USEFILEATTRIBUTES |
            SHGFI_ICON | SHGFI_SMALLICON | SHGFI_TYPENAME))
            return FALSE;

    // Extract icon and type name.
    *pIcon = shfi.hIcon;
    sType  = shfi.szTypeName;

    return TRUE;
}
```

These two functions could be used to gather information about an existing file, or about a specific file extension. These functions can be found in the **Shell** sample.

```
HICON   hIcon1, hIcon2;
CString s1, s2;

// Get information about "\FileBrowser.exe"
GetFileIconType(_T("\\FileBrowser.exe"), &hIcon1, s1);

// Get information about the ".doc" files.
GetExtIconType(_T(".doc"), &hIcon2, s2);

.
.
.

// Destroy the icons.
DestroyIcon(hIcon1);
DestroyIcon(hIcon2);
```

21.1.2 Folders

A folder is a collection of shell items. It can contain directories, files, shortcuts, applets, printers, and even other folders. Folders are internally maintained on the file system, as we'll see before long.

Each Windows platform has its own set of system folders, each with a specific role. For instance, the Control Panel folder is collection of system applets. Other examples of folders are the "Recycle Bin" (deleted files), "My Handheld PC" (folder hierarchy), "My Documents" (user documents' default directory), etc.

An application might be interested in obtaining the locations of those folders (*i.e.*, where they reside on the file system), in order to add, update, or remove items from them. For instance, when saving a file, the default directory could be the one corresponding to "My Documents".

An application can determine the location of any of these system folders by calling ::SHGetSpecialFolderLocation(). That function takes three arguments: a window handle (NULL is fine), a constant identifying what folder's location is to be retrieved, and an ITEMIDLIST pointer.

On an H/PC, the returned item identifier is allocated by the shell using a COM interface called IMalloc. This interface must be used by the application to delete the item identifier when no longer required (not doing so would result in memory leaks). Hence, an application must first obtain a pointer to that IMalloc interface, as we'll see shortly.

On a P/PC, the returned identifier is simply a constant, since the IMalloc interface is not implemented on that shell.

Given the item identifier, the related path name can be obtained by calling ::SHGetPath FromIDList(). Once the path is obtained, an application can use normal file system calls (described in Chapter 11) to update items.

::SHGetPathFromIDList() requires three arguments: a window handle (NULL), an item identifier, and a buffer of at least MAX_PATH characters to store the path name.

The next example demonstrates the use of those shell functions by returning the path of a system folder. Two functions are listed: one for an H/PC, and the other, for a P/PC. These functions can be found in the **Shell** sample.

```
// Lookup a shell folder on an H/PC.

LPCTSTR HPCShellFolderLookup(int nFolder, LPTSTR pszPath)
{
    LPMALLOC        pMalloc;

    if (!SUCCEEDED(SHGetMalloc(&pMalloc)))
            return NULL;

    LPITEMIDLIST    pidlFolder;
    LPCTSTR         p;

    if (SUCCEEDED(SHGetSpecialFolderLocation(
            NULL,
            nFolder,
```

```
                    &pidlFolder)))
      {
            SHGetPathFromIDList(pidlFolder, pszPath);
            pMalloc->Free(pidlFolder);

            p = pszPath;
      }
      else
            p = NULL;

      pMalloc->Release();

      return p;
}

// Lookup a shell folder on an P/PC.

LPCTSTR PPCShellFolderLookup(int nFolder, LPTSTR pszPath)
{
      LPITEMIDLIST    pidlFolder;
      LPCTSTR         p;

      if (SUCCEEDED(SHGetSpecialFolderLocation(
            NULL,
            nFolder,
            &pidlFolder)))
      {
            SHGetPathFromIDList(pidlFolder, pszPath);
            p = pszPath;
      }
      else
            p = NULL;

      return p;
}
```

Figure 21-4 lists some valid constants and their values on an H/PC and a P/PC:

IDL Constant	H/PC (Example)	Palm PC (Example)
CSIDL_BITBUCKET	\Recycled	N/A
CSIDL_CONTROLS	\Recycled	N/A
CSIDL_DESKTOPDIRECTORY	N/A	N/A
CSIDL_DESKTOP	\Windows\Desktop	N/A
CSIDL_DRIVES	\	\
CSIDL_FAVORITES	\Windows\Favorites	\Windows\Start Menu
CSIDL_FONTS	\Windows\Fonts	\Windows\Fonts
CSIDL_NETHOOD	N/A	N/A
CSIDL_NETWORK	N/A	N/A
CSIDL_PERSONAL	\My Documents	\My Documents
CSIDL_PROGRAMS	\Windows\Programs	\Windows\Start Menu\Programs
CSIDL_PRINTERS	N/A	N/A
CSIDL_RECENT	\Windows\Recent	N/A
CSIDL_SENDTO	N/A	N/A

CSIDL_STARTUP	\Windows\StartUp	\Windows\StartUp
CSIDL_STARTMENU	N/A	\Windows\Start Menu
CSIDL_TEMPLATES	N/A	N/A

Figure 21-4: Constants used with ::SHGetSpecialFolderLocation() on an H/PC and a P/PC.

There is a quicker way though to add items in the recently-used documents folder, which is accessible from the Start menu: ::SHAddToRecentDocs(). This function adds the document specified by either its path name or an ITEMIDLIST pointer. The first argument, SHARD_PATH or SHARD_PIDL, determines the type of the second, a path name or an ITEMIDLIST.

21.1.3 Shortcuts

Shortcuts give direct access (or link) to a file that physically resides in another directory. It is common to use shortcuts on the desktop itself to run frequently-used applications. For instance, on Figure 21-1, shortcuts on the H/PC appears as large icons with a small upright arrow in the bottom left corner.

A shortcut is created by calling ::SHCreateShortcut(). The first parameter is the shortcut name (which must end with the ".LNK" extension). The second parameter is the file name the shortcut is referring to. Any file can be referred to.

Given a shortcut name, you can retrieve the associated file name by calling ::SHGetShortcutTarget(). Three parameters are required: the shortcut name, a buffer to store the referred file name and the buffer length. A minimum length of MAX_PATH should be used.

The next example implements AddShortcutToDesktop(), a function that adds a shortcut to an application on the desktop of an H/PC. That function can be found in the **Shell** sample.

```
BOOL AddShortcutToDesktop(LPCTSTR pszFilePath, LPCTSTR pszLinkName)
{
    TCHAR   szShortcutLnk[MAX_PATH];

    if (ShellFolderLookup(CSIDL_DESKTOP, szShortcutLnk) == NULL)
        return FALSE;

    _tcscat(szShortcutLnk, pszLinkName);

    return SHCreateShortcut(
        const_cast<LPTSTR>(szShortcutLnk),
        const_cast<LPTSTR>(pszFilePath));
}
```

For instance, invoking the function as follows

```
AddShortcutToDesktop(_T("\\FileBrowser.exe"), _T("\\FileBrowser.lnk"));
```

creates a shortcut named "`FileBrowser`" on the desktop, using the application icon found in `FileBrowser.exe`. Tapping twice on the shortcut starts the application. This example assumes that the application ("`FileBroser.exe`") is on the root directory ("`\`").

Note that the shortcut name can be any string, as long as it ends with "`.lnk`". For instance, specifying "`My Browser.lnk`" as the second parameter would created a shortcut named "`My Browser`", with the same application icon.

21.2 TASKBAR

Both H/PC and P/PC shells have a taskbar (see Figure 21-1), similar to the one found on desktops.

In fact, the H/PC taskbar is just about identical to a desktop taskbar: it has a Start button, window buttons (each of which representing an application), a date and time panel, and a Desktop button. The date and time panel, in addition to providing immediate access to data and time information, can display icons, called annunciators, which indicate that a user notification is active and must be acknowledged. Annunciators are described in the following pages.

On the other hand, a Palm-size PC has a Start button, an Input Panel button, a date and time panel (with annunciators) and a Desktop button. Running applications are not shown in the task bar, but are instead accessible from the Start menu. As a matter of fact, the shell brings a running application up front if the user attempts to run a second instance via the Start menu, limiting applications to one instance only. The shell also handles the Palm PC hardware navigation control buttons: Action, Exit, Rocker, and Apps.

21.2.1 Adding and Deleting Taskbar Icons

Applications can also add icons – called status indicators – in the date and time panel, and receive messages when the user taps on them (see Figure 21-5):

- A single tap should display a pop-up window that controls the related object. For instance, clicking on a speaker icon displays a volume meter.

- A double-tap should automatically trigger the default command.

Application

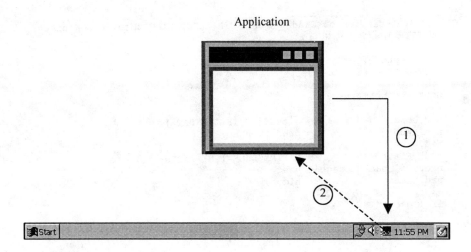

Figure 21-5: When an application adds a status indicator (1), the taskbar sends a message back to the application when the user taps on the icon (2). The application processes the notification as desired.

An application can add a status indicator (an icon) by calling `::Shell_Notify Icon()`, which sends a notification to the shell. Two parameters are required: the message to send (`NM_ADD`, `NM_MODIFY` or `NM_DELETE`) and a pointer to a `NOTIFYICONDATA` structure (listed in Figure 21-6). We'll see how to initialize that structure in a second.

Type	Member	Description
DWORD	cbSize	Always `sizeof(NOTIFYICONDATA)`.
HWND	hWnd	Window to be notified when the user taps on the icon.
UINT	uID	Application-defined value to uniquely identify an icon when a notification is received from the shell. Useful for applications that display multiple icons.
UINT	uFlags	Describes which of the following fields are valid.
UINT	uCallbackMessage	Notification sent back to the application by the shell.
HICON	hIcon	Icon to add, modify or delete.
WCHAR	szTip[64]	Tip to display on the icon.

Figure 21-6: The `NOTIFYICONDATA` structure.

When adding an icon, the structure must specify the handle to the window that is adding the icon, an arbitrary 32-bit, user-defined icon identifier, and an 16x16 icon handle. The next example adds an icon:

```
BOOL AddStatusIndicator(CWnd * pWnd, UINT uID, UINT uMsg, HICON hicon,
    LPCTSTR lpszTip = NULL)
{
    ASSERT(pWnd->GetSafeHwnd() != NULL);
    ASSERT(hIcon != NULL);

    NOTIFYICONDATA nid;

    nid.cbSize           = sizeof(NOTIFYICONDATA);
    nid.hWnd             = pWnd->m_hWnd;
    nid.uID              = uID;
    nid.uFlags           = NIF_MESSAGE | NIF_ICON;
    nid.uCallbackMessage = uMsg;
    nid.hIcon            = hicon;

    if (lpszTip)
    {
        nid.uFlags |= NIF_TIP;
        _tcscpy(nid.szTip, lpszTip);
    }

    return Shell_NotifyIcon(NIM_ADD, &nid);
}
```

A window could invoke that function by first loading an icon (in OnCreate() for instance):

```
const UINT WM_TBNOTIFICATION = WM_USER + 100;

int CMyWnd::OnCreate(LPCREATESTRUCT lpcs)
{
    if (CWnd::OnCreate(lpcs) == -1)
        return -1;

    .
    .
    .

    // Load the application's 16x16 icon in m_hImage (a HANDLE).
    m_hImage = LoadImage(
        AfxGetInstanceHandle(),            // App's instance
        MAKEINTRESOURCE(IDR_MAINFRAME),    // Icon id
        IMAGE_ICON,                        // Type of image
        16,                                // Desired width
        16,                                // Desired height
        0);                                // Unused

    // Add the icon in the date and time panel.
    AddStatusIndicator(
        this,                              // Window to notify
        0,                                 // Icon id (app-defined)
        WM_TBNOTIFICATION,                 // Notification msg
        static_cast<HICON>(hImage));       // Icon

    return 0;
}
```

Removing the icon from the data and time panel is done as follows:

```
BOOL RemoveStatusIndicator(CWnd * pWnd, UINT uID)
{
    ASSERT(pWnd->GetSafeHwnd() != NULL);

    NOTIFYICONDATA nid;

    nid.cbSize = sizeof(NOTIFYICONDATA);
    nid.hWnd   = pWnd->m_hWnd;
    nid.uID    = uID;

    return Shell_NotifyIcon(NIM_DELETE, &nid);
}
```

Upon exiting, the application should remove the icon from the task bar. The next function does exactly that:

```
void CMyWnd::OnDestroy()
{
    RemoveStatusIndicator(this, 0);              // Remove the icon

    DestroyIcon(static_cast<HICON>(hImage));     // Destroy the image.
    CWnd::OnDestroy();                           // Call parent
}
```

All those functions are implemented in the **Shell** sample.

21.2.2 Processing Taskbar Notifications

Taskbar notifications are only sent for icons that have been added with a callback message (*i.e.*, with the NIF_MESSAGE flags). If an icon has been added without such a message, no notification is sent.

Whenever the user moves the stylus (or the mouse) over a tray icon, the system sends the associated callback message to the window that inserted that icon. The wParam parameter specifies the application-defined icon identifier, and the lParam parameter specifies the related mouse message (WM_LBUTTONDOWN, WM_LBUTTONUP or WM_MOUSEMOVE). As specified earlier, handlers for those messages should implement a standard behavior, as shown in the following example:

```
BEGIN_MESSAGE_MAP(CMainFrame, CFrameWnd)
    .
    .
    .
    ON_MESSAGE(WM_TBNOTIFICATION, OnTbNotification)
END_MESSAGE_MAP()
```

```
LRESULT CMainFrame::OnTbNotification(WPARAM wParam, LPARAM lParam)
{
    // wParam is the annunciator id, lParam is stylus/mouse message

    switch (lParam)
    {
    case WM_LBUTTONDOWN:
            DisplayTrayMenu();
            break;

    case WM_LBUTTONDBLCLK:
            CarryDefaultAction();
            break;

    default:
            // Ignore
            ;
    }

    return 0;
}
```

21.2.3 Executing Applications

The shell also provides a function, ShellExecuteEx(), to open a file, whether it is an executable or a data file. This function in fact applies a "verb" to the specified file name; the default verb is "Open", but other application-dependent verbs are supported.

The next example implements a function that opens the specified file, passing optional parameters:

```
BOOL ShellOpenFile(LPCTSTR pFile, LPCTSTR pParams = NULL)
{
    SHELLEXECUTEINFO        sei;

    memset(&sei, '\0', sizeof(sei));
    sei.cbSize = sizeof(sei);
    sei.lpFile = pFile;
    sei.lpParameters = pParams;
    sei.nShow = SW_SHOW;
    sei.hInstApp = AfxGetInstanceHandle();

    return ShellExecuteEx(&sei);
}
```

For instance, this function could be used to load an application or open a document, as follows:

```
    // Execute FileBrowser.exe
```

```
ShellOpenFile( T("\\FileBrowser.exe"));

// Locate the application that works with .doc files (i.e. Word),
// start it, and load MyFile.doc.
ShellOpenFile(_T("\\MyFile.doc"));
```

21.3 USER AND APPLICATION NOTIFICATIONS

Windows CE devices are designed to notify (or alert) the user of some scheduled events. For instance, an Appointment application can start flashing an LED to remind the user of an imminent meeting. Another example is to run an application at 5:00 PM every day to automatically download quotes in a spreadsheet from a remote site.

Windows CE incorporates six new functions to implement user and application notifications.

21.3.1 User Notifications

Applications that need to get the user's attention at a specific moment can do so by using user notifications. Those notification are triggered upon a timer event, and are ideal for reminders or to-do lists, for example. When that time is reached, the operating system places the application's icon in the annunciators panel and notifies the user (we'll see how in a second). The user may then acknowledge the notification and start the application. An important point to remember is that the application is only started when the notification is acknowledged by the user.

`::CeSetUserNotification()` creates and registers a notification to be activated at a specific time. The function takes a notification handle (0 for a new notification), the path name of the related application, the time the notification is to be triggered (a SYSTEMTIME pointer) and a pointer to CE_USER_NOTIFICATION structure that describes how the notification should take place.

This CE_USER_NOTIFICATION structure is typically initialized by calling `::CeGetUserNotificationPreferences()`, which shows a dialog box that presents the valid options given the hardware (see Figure 21-7). The user can select his/her preferences among the following options:

- Play a wave file (.wav)

- Flashing a light-emitting diode (LED)

- Displaying a dialog box. That dialog box contains an **OK** button to acknowledge the notification or a **Snooze** button to be notified again in five minutes.

- Vibrate the device.

667

CeSetUserNotification() returns a notification handle, which can by used again to modify the notification parameters. The notification can be deleted at any moment by calling CeClearUSerNotification() and passing the notification handle.

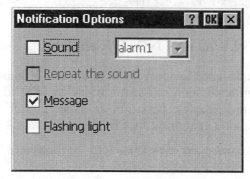

Figure 21-7: The dialog box shown by ::CeGetUserNotificationPreferences().

If the use chose to display a dialog box, clicking **OK** acknowledges the notification to Windows CE, which starts the application. On the other hand, if the user acknowledges the notification by taping the annunciator icon, the started application must call ::CeHandleAppNotifications() to acknowledge the notification. This function only requires the application's name.

The **Notif** sample implements an example of these features.

21.3.2 Application Notifications

An application can be scheduled to run upon a specific event or at a specified time. This type of notification automatically starts the application, and doesn't have to be acknowledged by the user. There are two calls to trigger an application, one being event-based, the other being timer-based.

The first call is CeRunAppAtEvent(), which runs an application when a specific event is detected. The call takes two parameters: the application full path name and the event (see Figure 21-8).

Event	Description
NOTIFICATION_EVENT_NONE	No events – remove all event registrations for this application
NOTIFICATION_EVENT_SYNC_END	When data synchronization finishes
NOTIFICATION_EVENT_DEVICE_CHANGE	When a PC Card device is changed
NOTIFICATION_EVENT_RS232_DETECTED	When an RS232 connection is made
NOTIFICATION_EVENT_TIME_CHANGE	When the system time is changed
NOTIFICATION_EVENT_RESTORE_END	When a full device data restore completes

Figure 21-8: Events that can trigger the execution of an application.

The second call is CeRunAppAtTime(), which runs an application at a specific time. It also takes two parameters: the application name and a SYSTEMTIME time.

The **Notif** sample implements an example of these features.

21.4 Managing Low-Memory Conditions

Under low-memory conditions, Windows CE sends WM_HIBERNATE or WM_CLOSE to the applications, as explained in Section 8.3.1. Actually, these messages are sent by the shell, which periodically monitors memory usage. When the remaining memory falls under a certain threshold, the H/PC shell sends WM_HIBERNATE whereas the P/PC shell directly sends WM_CLOSE. Those messages are sent at any moment.

Upon receiving WM_HIBERNATE, an H/PC application should release as much memory as it can. For instance, icons and bitmaps can be released, as well as some application data (in a temporary file). WM_HIBERNATE is eventually followed by WM_ACTIVATE, in which case the discarded or saved data should be loaded again.

On a Palm-size PC, upon receiving WM_CLOSE, an application should save all the data in a temporary file, and pass the message back to CE, which will then terminate the application. Consequently, whenever such an application is restarted, it should always check if data has been saved and restore it if so, bringing the user to where he/she was when the application was closed.

An application can also inform the user of low-memory conditions by invoking an OEM-defined low-memory dialog box through ::SHShowOutOfMemory(). An example of this dialog box is shown in Figure 21-9. This could be done when one of the memory-allocation functions (detailed in Chapter 8) fails. The function requires the dialog box owner's handle (NULL is fine) and 0 (the second parameter is a reserved value). The next example invokes the out-of-memory dialog box:

```
void DoSomething()
{
    SMYSTRUCT *     p = new SMYSTRUCT[1024];

    if (p == NULL)
    {
            SHShowOutOfMemory(NULL, 0);
            return;
    }

    .
    .
    .

    delete [] p;
}
```

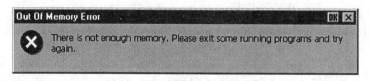

Figure 21-9: An out-of-memory dialog box.

21.5 CLIPBOARD

The clipboard is a memory area, maintained by Windows CE, that applications use to exchange data among themselves. For instance, most applications provide an Edit menu with the Cut, Copy, and Paste menu items. Cut and Copy transfer data into the clipboard, whereas Paste brings the clipboard's data into the application. The clipboard is shared among all processes in the system.

The clipboard serves as a temporary repository for formatted data. Applications are responsible for representing and maintaining the application data. For instance, most applications typically support some selection, which is the data that can be cut or copied into the clipboard. When data is cut, it is up to the application to delete the data from its own memory; when pasting, the application must add the data into its memory and display it on the screen.

Applications can store/retrieve data to/from the clipboard using some predefined Windows formats, listed in Figure 21-10. Additionally, applications can define their own custom format. It is common for an application to store a single piece of data using multiple formats. When the data is pasted, an application can try to find one format that is understood. For instance, a bitmap image can be saved as a bitmap handle or binary text; an application may paste the data using either format, whichever the application has been designed to handle.

Value	Description
CF_BITMAP	A HBITMAP handle.
CF_DIB	A BITMAPINFO structure, follows by the bitmap bits.
CF_ENHMETAFILE	A HENHMETAFILE handle.
CF_METAFILEPICT	A METAFILEPICT structure.
CF_OEMTEXT	A null-terminated string, using the OEM character set.
CF_PALETTE	An HPALETTE handle. When some data requiring a palette are placed in the clipboard, the palette would also be specified.
CF_PENDATA	Pen extension data (Microsoft Windows for Pen Computing.)
CF_RIFF	Audio data.
CF_SYLK	Microsoft Symbolic Link (SYLK) data.
CF_TEXT	A null-terminated ASCII string.
CF_WAVE	Audio data (standard wave formats).
CF_UNICODETEXT	A null-terminated UNICODE string.

Figure 21-10: Supported clipboard data formats.

21.5.1 Copying Data to the Clipboard

Assuming that the user selected some data and invoked a Copy operation (from the Edit menu for instance), an application has to follow a few simple steps to store the data in the clipboard.

First, the application must call OpenClipboard(), passing the current window's handle (AfxGetMainWnd()->m_hWnd), and then, EmptyClipboard(), to remove any data left if any.

The application then stores the data in the clipboard by calling SetClipboard Data(), which requires a data format (see Figure 21-10) and a data handle. If a data structure is to be passed, make sure it is allocated via LocalAlloc(). Once that call returns, the system owns the data; the application can still read it, but it cannot and must not free it. An application can call SetClipboardData() for each format being stored in the Clipboard.

Finally, the application closes the Clipboard by calling CloseClipboard().

The next example places a Unicode string in the clipboard:

```
BOOL CopyTextToClipboard(LPCTSTR pszText)
{
    // Allocate a buffer throuhg LocalAlloc() and copy the string in it.
    LPTSTR pClipboardText = (LPTSTR)
        LocalAlloc(LMEM_FIXED, (_tcslen(pszText) + 1) * sizeof(TCHAR));
```

```
        tcscpy(pClipboardText, pszText);

    // Store the data in the clipboard.
    OpenClipboard(AfxGetMainWnd()->m_hWnd);
    EmptyClipboard();

    HANDLE hData = SetClipboardData(CF_UNICODETEXT, pClipboardText);

    CloseClipboard();

    return (hData != NULL);

    // No need to free pClipboardText
}
```

21.5.2 Pasting Data from the Clipboard

Pasting data starts by opening the clipboard, by calling OpenClipboard(), as described above.

Then, the application can query the clipboard to determine whether is specific format is there, by invoking IsClipboardFormatAvailable(), passing as the unique parameter the desired format (see Figure 21-10). The function returns TRUE if the data has been stored using that format.

If a suitable format is supported, the application calls GetClipboardData(), passing the desired format. This function returns a system-allocated handle that the application can use to copy data into a local buffer. The returned handle should not and must not be freed. If the data is to be copied in some buffers, the application must either allocate those buffers (using LocalAlloc() for instance), or call GetClipboardDataAlloc(), which internally calls LocalAlloc() and stores the clipboard data in it. In both cases, the allocated data is then owned by the application and must eventually be freed.

Once done with the clipboard, the application must call CloseClipboard().

The next example pastes a Unicode string from the clipboard:

```
BOOL PasteTextFromClipboard(CString& s)
{
    // See if the clipboard contains an UNICODE string first.
    if (!IsClipboardFormatAvailable(CF_UNICODETEXT))
        return FALSE;

    OpenClipboard(AfxGetMainWnd()->m_hWnd);

    HANDLE hClipboardText = GetClipboardDataAlloc(CF_UNICODETEXT);

    CloseClipboard();

    // On error, return FALSE.
    if (hClipboardText == NULL)
```

```
        return FALSE;

    s = reinterpret_cast<LPCTSTR>( hClipboardText);
    LocalFree(hClipboardText);

    return TRUE;
}
```

21.5.3 Registering a Custom Clipboard Format

Besides the format listed in Figure 21-10, applications can use their own data representation with the Clipboard. This is required when a custom data structure is being manipulated via the Clipboard.

In order to do so, applications must first obtain a clipboard format (an UINT value), which will be specified when storing and retrieving data from and to the Clipboard. This is done by calling `RegisterClipboardFormat()` and specifying a descriptive string. Naturally, if the format has already been registered, the same clipboard format is returned. The name is <u>not</u> case-sensitive.

The next example copies and pastes an application-defined structure. The functions to access the clipboard follow.

```
// An application-defined structure.
struct SMYSTRUCT
{
    .
    .
    .
};

// Copies an SMYSTRUCT to the clipboard.

void foo()
{
    // Declare an SMYSTRUCT structure and initialize it.
    SMYSTRUCT      ms;
    .
    .
    .

    // Register a new custom format.
    UINT           uLabelFormat = RegisterClipboardFormat(_T("SMYSTRUCT"));

    // Copy ms into the clipboard.
    CopyDataToClipboard(&ms, sizeof(ms), uLabelFormat);
}

// Paste an SMYSTRUCT from the clipboard.

void bar()
{
```

```
    SMYSTRUCT *     pms, ms;

    // Obtain the custom format.
    UINT            uLabelFormat = RegisterClipboardFormat(_T("SMYSTRUCT"));

    // Get the data from the clipboard.
    // The buffer must be freed by calling LocalFree().
    PasteDataFromClipboard(reinterpret_cast<LPVOID *>(&pms), uLabelFormat);

    // Copy the buffer into a local buffer.
    memcpy(&ms, pms, sizeof(ms));

    // Release the buffer allocated by
    LocalFree(pms);

    // Work on ms
    .
    .
    .
}
```

The two functions to access the clipboards are listed below. They resemble those seen earlier (for Unicode strings):

```
BOOL CopyDataToClipboard(LPVOID pData, BYTE cbSize, UINT uLabel)
{
    LPVOID pClipboardData = (LPTSTR) LocalAlloc(LMEM_FIXED, cbSize);
    memcpy(pClipboardData, pData, cbSize);

    OpenClipboard(AfxGetMainWnd()->m_hWnd);
    EmptyClipboard();

    HANDLE hData = SetClipboardData(uLabel, pClipboardData);

    CloseClipboard();

    return (hData != NULL);
}

BOOL PasteDataFromClipboard(LPVOID * pData, UINT uLabel)
{
    if (!IsClipboardFormatAvailable(uLabel))
        return FALSE;

    OpenClipboard(AfxGetMainWnd()->m_hWnd);

    HANDLE hClipboardData = GetClipboardDataAlloc(uLabel);

    CloseClipboard();

    if (hClipboardData == NULL)
        return FALSE;

    // Pass the allocated buffer to the caller, which must
    // call LocalFree() on it.
```

```
    *pData = reinterpret cast<LPVOID>(hClipboardData);

    return TRUE;
}
```

21.5.4 Other Clipboard Functions

The Clipboard API supports other functions, listed in Figure 21-10, although they are used infrequently.

Clipboard Function	Description
GetClipboardFormatName()	Returns the name of the specified format.
GetOpenClipboardWindow()	Returns the handle of the window that currently has the clipboard opened.
CountClipboardFormats()	Returns the number of formats currently available in the clipboard.
EnumClipboardFormats()	Returns the number of available formats in the clipboard.
GetClipboardOwner()	Returns the current owner of the clipboard, typically the last window to have stored data in it.
GetPriorityClipboardFormat()	Given an array of formats, returns the first format found in the clipboard.

Figure 21-11: Other clipboard functions.

SUGGESTED READINGS

Microsoft, *Windows CE Programmer's Guide*

> Chapter 27 describes some details of the H/PC shell, whereas Chapter 32 describes the Palm-size PC's. Among the details are the exact task bar specifications (*e.g.*, size in pixels), type of input, etc.

675

Chapter 22

Porting Desktop Applications to Windows CE

A key Windows CE design feature is the use of the same API found on other Windows platforms: Win32. However, because this API is only partially supported on CE, porting applications from Windows 9x or NT is rarely a straight-forward process. Even MFC-based applications cannot be ported too easily, because MFC has also been put on a low-calorie diet.

This chapter reviews the most important hardware and software differences between the desktop implementation of Windows and Windows CE, providing hints as to where to look for potential problem areas. It also explains the typical problems encountered when porting applications and how to work around those difficulties.

22.1 HARDWARE CONSIDERATIONS

When looking at an embedded system connected to a few sensors (such as a PC/104 or a Motorola MBX board), it is pretty clear that Windows CE lives in an environment quite different that its cousins 9x and NT. Even Palm-size PCs and Handheld PCs, which look pretty much like small-scale desktops – after all, some of them have a colored screen, a keyboard, and a few MB of memory – actually have their own traits and impose some constraints when developing and porting applications.

The areas that require the most attention are memory, power, input devices, and screens, all explored below.

22.1.1 Memory

You will be pleased (or not, depending on where you stand) by the vast amount of memory Windows CE provides. After all, most deeply embedded systems run in kilobytes of ROM and RAM, if not less. On the other hand, desktop developers may feel pinched when realizing that their target device *only* has 4MB of RAM; indeed, that's a sharp drop from the typical 64MB-to-256MB desktop. Furthermore, the lack of hard disk (specifically, of a paging file) truly limits the virtual memory to what physical memory has to offer, not a byte more. As a result, you must do your best to limit the use of physical memory.

Here are a few tips that can help reducing your application's appetite for memory:

- Limit RAM requirements. This is achieved by various means: re-using variables instead of declaring multiple variables and using them once, analyzing the memory allocated for variables and optimizing it (see Chapter 8 for details), trying to free temporary data as soon as it is no longer used, and so forth.

- Use simplified graphics over complex ones, which produces leaner code. Since the screen is typically very small, it is acceptable to produce graphics that are "good enough" rather than top-notch graphics that do not provide more information, but that require much more code to implement.

- Use a C++ class library (such as MFC) and re-use your own objects as much as possible in order to eliminate code duplication.

- Along the same line, code that you re-use from one application to another should reside in dynamic-link libraries (DLLs). Visual C++, for instance, provides a Wizard to help you write DLLs very quickly. Using DLLs makes the application size smaller overall The only drawback is to make sure that DLLs are present along with the applications, since otherwise the applications cannot run.

- If you are implementing some sort of complex algorithms to solve a specific problem, it may not hurt to browse a few books, which often propose ready-to-use functions that have been designed to be as tight and efficient as possible.

- Process WM_HIBERNATE. Non-CE applications do not implement this message, so it has to be added whenever an application is ported. Use the macros UNDER_CE or _WIN32.WCE to compile conditional code under CE only.

22.1.2 Power

Most Windows CE devices are powered by batteries, so energy resources are limited. For instance, a Palm-size PC can run about 10 to 15 hours (spread over many days) on two AAA batteries. There are three factors that substantially determine the longevity of the batteries:

- Whether the screen is lit (which quickly drains the batteries). This is more of a user issue, and applications can't do anything about it.

- The use of various devices, such as modems. Again, the user usually controls their use, but applications may also minimize their use on some occasions. For instance, when performing an on-line registration, it is better to gather the user information and then use the modem to transmit that information, rather than first start the modem, read user input (which may take a while), and then transmit the data.

- Using excessive CPU cycles, typically by looping until some conditions are detected (a situation also called *busy-waiting*). For instance, when waiting for an event to occur, always make sure a thread is blocked, instead of spinning in a loop. A typical scenario is a thread that needs to introduce some delay before completing some work. It is far better for that thread to sleep for a little while (by calling `Sleep()`), or to wait on some synchronization objects (mutexes, event flags or critical sections), which are cost-free operations, rather than looping with frenzy. See Chapter 7 for more details.

An application can also query the energy available by invoking `GetSystem PowerStatusEx()`. This function returns information about the battery condition (whether they are charging or not, the percentage of charge remaining, the time remaining, etc.)

22.1.3 Input Devices

Because Windows CE can come in practically any form and shape, an application cannot simply assume that there is always a keyboard and a mouse. These two input devices might not be present; instead a touch screen and a microphone might be the means of input (consider a Palm-size PC for example). Under these conditions, it is quite hard to write a generic application that can run on *any* Windows CE platforms.

If a given software is to be targeted to various CE devices, it might be a good idea to provide multiple versions of that software, each version being adapted to some input devices. Specialized applications such as those will contain less code than a generic application that is ready to use a multitude of input devices, only to find out that one or two are indeed available.

It is practically impossible to port an application to Windows CE without making changes here and there. On the same ground, using diverse Windows CE configurations makes it almost impossible to use the exact same application without making the necessary changes.

22.1.4 Screens

Screens on Windows CE devices are quite different than what is commonly found on desktops today (video adapters with a resolution as high as 1600x1200 on 21-inch monitors ...). In fact, CE devices might have been designed to work without any screen.

For those devices that come with a screen, it is very likely that the resolution will not only be smaller than those found on desktops, it may also be odd-shaped, such as higher than wider (an unusual ratio on desktops). Moreover, fewer colors are available, not to mention that some devices only provide grayscales. All these factors largely impact the user interface. Whereas desktops invite you to add as much as you can think of by being resourceful (in screen size, RAM, etc.), CE resources are scarce and applications must follow the trend.

Less screen real estate means less information presented. Typical CE applications windows do not carry a title bar, nor a status bar, and merge their menu and toolbars by using the new command bar. But equally important, you should resist the urge to add any information that is not essential. If you carefully observe the applications shipped with Handheld PCs and Palm-size PCs, you can see how plain those applications are: no bells and whistles; they just do what they were meant to do, no more, no less. That's really the philosophy to adopt. Too many programs today are hard to use because of the extra functions in menus, buttons, and the like. For users new to an application, a rich variety of functions may be overwhelming. Furthermore, because CE devices may run short of resources, there are really no reasons not to keep an application as vanilla as possible.

Here are a few tips that may help keeping your applications slim:

- Clearly limit the functionality of an application. For instance, a Note Taker takes notes, nothing else. And once the application is coded, it is better to move on to another application instead of trying to enhance the old one. Users will eventually dictate what to add.

- Do not use a title bar or status bar, unless your application cannot live without it.

- Submenus (such as a File submenu) should have between two and seven items, optimally three or four. A one-item submenu should be combined with another submenu, whereas a long submenu should be broken up into two or more submenus.

- Use toolbar buttons for the very most important functions, not just for the sake of having buttons. Three or four buttons may be all it takes.

- The client area should remain relatively empty: limited use of icons and bitmaps, and one or two fonts, no more. When looking at an application, it should be clear what information is being conveyed.

- Do not use bitmapped or colored background, as that can make foreground information harder to discern.

- Consider using property sheets as opposed to overpopulated dialog boxes.

Perhaps the simplest rule, but the toughest for you to learn, is to see and use an application from a user's perspective. It is often frustrating to have to simplify an application that we thought was perfect, but doing so can make the application better and easier to use.

22.2 SOFTWARE

Although there is no official number, it is estimated that Windows CE supports more than 1000 functions of the original Win32 API, as defined on Windows NT[66]. Some people have suggested 1500. The simplified API is the result of an effort to minimize the memory requirements on CE.

But regardless of the exact number, what really matters is that functions used in some desktop applications are not available on CE. That will translate into compiler and linker errors. And because Win32 is the lowest API available to applications, any change to it produces a ripple effect to any C/C++ run-time libraries, including MFC. As a result, you face a reduced-API constraint in every direction you look, requiring more changes to your desktop applications being ported onto CE.

Additionally, because of some specific features of Windows CE, a small set of new functions has been added; applications that take advantage of these functions become CE-dependent.

This section will review the most important changes in the Win32 API, the C/C++ run-time libraries and MFC. It also exposes the new functionality that is available to CE applications. It starts by reviewing the most important change: the mandatory use of Unicode.

22.2.1 Unicode

Windows CE needs to support multiple alphabets, since it is being sold in international markets. Using ASCII as the default character set (as it is on Windows 9x) was immediately out of the question. Instead, Windows CE has been built with Unicode, which is a much more extended character set than ASCII.

---

[66] According to "Windows CE Programmer's Guide" (see Suggested Readings, at the end of this chapter).

ASCII characters are represented by 8-bit values (*i.e.*, char, in C/C++), for a total of 256 possible permutations (*i.e.*, distinct characters). Unicode uses 16-bit values (*i.e.*, unsigned short, in C/C++), for a total of 65536 different possible characters. The first 256 match those of ASCII, making Unicode compatible with it. But the larger range of Unicode gives enough room to incorporate a variety of extra glyphs and symbols.

Unicode-Based Applications

Unicode-based applications interact with Windows by using Unicode strings instead of ASCII strings, independently of the programming language they have been built with (see Figure 22-1). Specifically:

- All Win32 system calls that have one or more string parameters require Unicode strings, not ASCII strings. For instance, SetWindowText() requires the text to be a Unicode string, not an ASCII string.

- Window messages that contain string(s) contain Unicode strings, not ASCII strings. For instance, WM_CREATE passes a CREATESTRUCT structure, which contains two Unicode string pointers. On Windows 9*x*, these pointers are ASCII pointers.

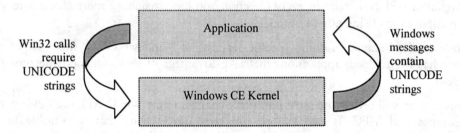

Figure 22-1: Windows CE and applications exchange strings in Unicode, not ASCII.

Windows NT, which supports both ASCII and Unicode applications, identifies at load time which character set the application is expected to use, and internally uses that character set when exchanging messages at run time. Windows CE only supports Unicode-based applications, whereas Windows 9*x* is the opposite: only ASCII-based applications are supported[67].

That doesn't mean that Unicode-based applications (on NT and CE) cannot use ASCII strings; it only means that ASCII strings cannot be used with the Win32 API nor received from Windows messages. We'll see in a short while why ASCII remains useful in some cases.

---

[67] Actually, there is some Unicode support within Windows 98, but not enough to run Unicode-based applications.

Making an Application Unicode-Based

From a C/C++ programming standpoint, Unicode is enabled by defining the Unicode symbol (which is defined by default with all Windows CE tools). Defining this symbol eventually leads the compiler to use Unicode strings in all the relevant data structures and the linker, to use Unicode-based libraries.

Unfortunately, the use of Unicode is not that easy and transparent. You must be aware of the difference between the character sets when coding your applications. There are two main issues: using the proper Unicode string representation (instead of the ASCII representation), and using the proper Unicode string functions. That last issue you will notice the most.

Unicode C/C++ Representation

Let's address the first issue: Unicode character representation. Every C/C++ programmer knows that a string such as "ABC" generates a four-byte string in memory, as shown in Figure 22-2-a. The equivalent in Unicode is shown in Figure 22-2-b, where each character truly is a 16-bit value, spanning two bytes, resulting in an 8-byte string. Note that such a string ends with a 16-bit null character, not an 8-bit one.

(a)

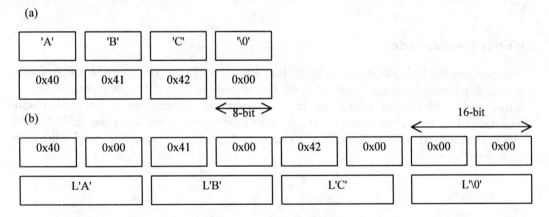

(b)

Figure 22-2: ASCII strings are represented with 8-bit characters vs. Unicode strings, which use 16-bit characters (represented here in little-endian).

So, how is such a string represented in a program? Microsoft's compiler supports the L prefix, which stands for *long* character. Consider the following:

```
'a'        // The letter 'a' in Ascii (one byte)
"abc"      // The string "abc" in Ascii (four bytes, including null)
L'a'       // The letter 'a' in Unicode (two bytes)
```

```
L"abc"      // The string "abc" in Unicode (eight bytes, including null)
```

Adding the L prefix to a character or a string tells the compiler to produce a Unicode string in memory.

Using Unicode Functions

Using Unicode strings is one thing; invoking functions working with Unicode strings is another. Consider strlen(), the function that returns the character count of an ASCII string. This function scans and counts 8-byte values until it hits an 8-bit NULL; it then returns the character count. The exact same logic, applied to a Unicode string, will not work. Referring back to Figure 22-2-b, strlen() will stop on the second byte, which is, in fact, the first half (in little-endian) of the first character. Moreover, invoking strlen() with a Unicode string will result in a compiler error, as the function expects an ASCII pointer (char *), not a Unicode pointer (unsigned short *).

To remedy to that problem, Microsoft provides *wide string* functions, a set of C functions that operates on Unicode strings only. For instance, wcslen() accepts a pointer to a Unicode string (*i.e.*, unsigned short *) and returns the character count. There is in fact a Unicode version of every ASCII function found in the C library: wcslen(), wcscpy(), etc.

Writing Portable Code

This support for Unicode is fine in itself, but is not enough to write portable applications across Windows platforms, because string representations and function names differ, as shown earlier. Instead of asking you to use conditional compilation all over, Microsoft introduced two equivalent macros that take care of the conversion when required: _T and TEXT. In ASCII, they do nothing, but in Unicode, they add the L prefix. Consider the next example:

```
_T("abc")
```

On Windows 9x, the previous string is an ASCII string (*i.e.*, "abc"), but on CE, it is an Unicode string (L "abc"). But more important, the *same code* can be used as is on both platforms, while using the proper character set.

This approach has been pushed further. A new character type has been introduced, called TCHAR. This type, along other useful types and macros, is defined in Tchar.h, which is made available for all Windows platforms. In ASCII (when UNICODE is not defined), TCHAR is simply char; otherwise (when UNICODE is defined), TCHAR is WCHAR, which is ultimately unsigned short. Hence, the following code works on all Windows platforms:

```
TCHAR        szMyString[32];        // A 32-TCHAR string
```

On Windows 9*x*, this is a 32-byte string, but on CE, it is a 32-short string (or a 64-byte string). But on any system, it holds 32 *characters* (ASCII or Unicode).Other new types are also implemented (in winnt.h) to make portability a non-issue (see Figure 22-3).

Type	Description
LPTSTR	Pointer to a TCHAR string
LPCTSTR	Pointer to a constant TCHAR string

Figure 22-3: Other generic TCHAR-related types.

By using TCHAR and the related types, developers can produce applications that are portable across all Windows platforms, without changing a single line of code regarding string conversions.

And there's more. Remember strlen() and wcslen()? To make code portable, Tchar.h defines a bunch a macros that wrap either type of functions. For instance, _tcslen() is a macro that is wcslen() if UNICODE is defined (as it is on CE), and strlen() otherwise. Hence, the following code becomes portable:

```
#include "tchar.h"

int nCount = tcslen(_T("MyString"));        // Get character count

// nCount is 8 in both ASCII andr UNICODE.
```

Figure 22-4 lists some popular macros and their corresponding implementations on Unicode and ASCII.

Portable Function Name	Unicode Equivalent	ASCII Equivalent
_tcscat()	wcscat()	strcat()
_tcschr()	wcschr()	strchr()
_tcscmp()	wcscmp()	strcmp()
_tcscpy()	wcscpy()	strcpy()
_tcslen()	wcslen()	strlen()
_istdigit	iswdigit()	isdigit()
_istspace()	iswspace()	isspace()
_totupper()	towupper()	toupper()
_totlower()	towlower()	tolower()

Figure 22-4: A few popular macros to handle strings in both ASCII and Unicode.

Tips and Traps

There are still a few traps you must be aware of, even if all the macros mentioned above are used consistently:

- Applications can no longer assume that the size of a character is one byte in Unicode. For instance, when allocating a 256-character buffer, the following declaration

```
LPTSTR      p = malloc(256);
```

  only allocates room for 128 Unicode characters. A better implementation is to rely on sizeof(TCHAR), which produces the adequate result whichever character set is selected:

```
LPTSTR      p = malloc(256 * sizeof(TCHAR));
```

- Another potential problem is alignment. Since some CPUs slow down when accessing a short or an odd address, Unicode strings must be aligned accordingly on even addresses. This is normally not a problem, as compilers will do that automatically. However, packed structures, which do not contain padding bytes, may cause a problem. Consider the following structure declaration:

```
#pragma pack(push, 1)                       // No byte padding

struct MyStruct
{
    UINT8           uCode;                  // An 8-bit code
    TCHAR           szName[8];              // An 8-character string
};

#pragma pack(pop)                           // Restore padding
```

Figure 22-5 (a) shows how this structure gets represented in memory. Figure 22-5 (b) shows the same structure, as if the pragma directives were not there. In (a), szName turns out to start on an odd address, a situation to avoid for performance considerations.

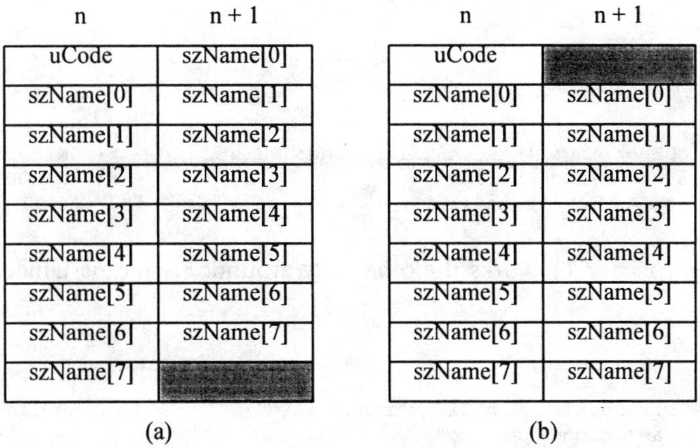

n	n + 1
uCode	szName[0]
szName[0]	szName[1]
szName[1]	szName[2]
szName[2]	szName[3]
szName[3]	szName[4]
szName[4]	szName[5]
szName[5]	szName[6]
szName[6]	szName[7]
szName[7]	███████

(a)

n	n + 1
uCode	███████
szName[0]	szName[0]
szName[1]	szName[1]
szName[2]	szName[2]
szName[3]	szName[3]
szName[4]	szName[4]
szName[5]	szName[5]
szName[6]	szName[6]
szName[7]	szName[7]

(b)

Figure 22-5: Unpadded structures may result with unaligned Unicode strings.

- Finally, it might not be possible to systematically convert all data structures to Unicode. For instance, if a structure represents the format of some data exchanged with a remote computer on the network, the structure must remain intact if the remote program cannot be updated as well. The local application would then have to convert the data structures to/from ASCII as required.

How About Using ASCII?

One type of Windows CE application can still largely work in ASCII: console applications. The stdio C library (*e.g.*, printf(), gets(), etc.) is available to console applications and it works in ASCII only. Hence, ASCII strings must be used with these functions, as it always has. Nonetheless, Win32 calls made from a console application still and always will require Unicode strings. Here is an example of mixing ASCII and Unicode strings within a console application:

```
char        szName[32];                              // ASCII
TCHAR       szBuffer[128];                           // UNICODE

printf("Enter your name: ");                         // ASCII
gets(szName);                                        // ASCII

wsprintf(szBuffer, _T("The name is %S"), szName);    // MIX (see below)

MessageBox(NULL, szBuffer, . . .);                   // UNICODE
```

The Win32 wsprintf() function has been updated to support a new format specification, %S, in addition to %s. Whereas %s formats an Unicode string, %S formats an ASCII string. Here's an example:

```
TCHAR       szBuffer[128];

wsprintf(
    szBuffer,                                           // UNICODE
    _T("UNICODE string: %s\n, ASCII string: %S\n",      // UNICODE
    L"This is an Unicode string",                       // UNICODE
    "This is an ASCII string");                         // ASCII
```

Paradoxically, `printf()` works the other way around: `%S` means Unicode whereas `%s` means ASCII:

```
printf(
    "Unicode string: %S\n, ASCII string: %s\n",         // ASCII
    L"This is an Unicode string",                       // UNICODE
    "This is an ASCII string");                         // ASCII
```

It sounds more complicated than it really is. With just a little bit of practice, especially with console applications, you will become comfortable in either mode. The basic rule is to remember that Win32 functions require Unicode strings whereas C (`stdio`) functions require ASCII strings.

22.2.2 The Win32 API

There are a lot fewer Win32 functions supported on CE than on other Windows platforms. This book has so far exposed the API that is supported. What's *not* supported has deliberately been left aside to prevent any confusion. It turns out that the core functionality has been left pretty much intact, allowing developers to write fine Windows applications. What's gone are the extra, the redundant, or fancy calls that wouldn't really fit in a tighter environment such as Windows CE. Listing all the functions that are gone isn't practical nor interesting; what is more useful perhaps is to list the categories of functions that did not make it. Section 22.2.4 also lists some of those categories (from an MFC standpoint).

Windows CE does <u>not</u> support the Win32 functions related to the following:

- ASCII versions of the Win32 system calls

- Many GDI advanced graphical functions (bezier curves, etc.)

- Some common dialogs (font and page setup)

- Some common controls (*e.g.*, animated controls, check and drag list boxes, hot keys, tool tips, and mini frames)

- Direct Access Objects (DAO)

- Multiple-Document Interface (MDI)

- Open Database Connectivity (ODBC)
- Some of Object Linking and Embedding (OLE)
- Metafiles
- Semaphores
- Event logging
- Named pipes
- Security
- Message API
- Structure Exception Handling (SEH) (*i.e.*, Microsoft's extensions to C++: __try, __except and __finally)
- And others.

Moreover, the API not mentioned in this list is not necessarily available as is. For instance, numerous Registry API functions are not present in CE (although the most important ones are). What that means is that your applications may not recompile very well the first time; expect a battery of minor changes here and there to fix those errors.

22.2.3 C/C++ Run-Time Libraries

It would be equally futile to list an exhaustive list of the unavailable C/C++ library functions, since new functions are supported with every release of the operating system binaries and libraries. Instead, all functions (supported or not) have been grouped into categories, and each category is reviewed below. This may help you identifying early in the porting process what aspects of the applications to port may require your attention. But ultimately, your tools (compiler and linker) will tell you what's permitted and what's not.

The following list contains the categories of functions that <u>are</u> generally available:

✓ **Argument access** (*e.g.*, va_arg, va_start, va_end).

✓ **Character classification** (*e.g.*, isalnum(), iswalnum(), isalpha(), iswalpha(), etc.)

✓ **Data conversions** (*e.g.*, abs(), _itoa(), mbstowcs(), _wtoi(), etc.), but a few are absent, especially those dealing with floats and doubles (*e.g.*, atof(), strtod(), etc.). Consider using sprintf() or _gcvt() as a substitute.

✓ **Floating-point** (*e.g.*, abs(), acos(), asin(), etc.).

✓ On a few **memory allocation** functions made it (*e.g.*, _alloca(), malloc(), realloc(), free() and _msize()). All others are gone (calloc(), _heapchk(), etc.)

✓ **Memory-buffer manipulation** (*e.g.*, memcmp(), memcpy(), memmove(), memset(), etc.).

✓ Most **stream file I/O** functions made it (*e.g.*, fopen(), fclose(), printf(), scanf(), putc(), gets(), etc.). Those that were removed are less popular (*e.g.*, rewind(), setvbuf(), tmpfile(), etc.).

✓ **String manipulation**, for both ASCII and Unicode (*e.g.*, strcat(), wcscat(), strcmp(), wcscmp(), etc.). Multibyte functions are omitted, however (*e.g.*, mbscat(), mbscmp(), etc.).

Conversely, the following categories of functions are <u>not</u> provided with Windows CE. You may use instead some Win32 functions (when available) or some third-party libraries:

✗ **Byte classification** (*e.g.*, _ismbbalnum(), _ismbbalpha(), etc.)

✗ **Debug** (*e.g.*, _CrtCheckMemory(), _CrtDumpMemoryLeaks(), etc.)

✗ **Directory control** (*e.g.*, _chdir(), _chdrive(), _getcwd(), _mkdir(), _rmdir(), etc). Use instead the Win32 directory functions CreateDirectory() and RemoveDirectory() (described in Section 11.4). Remember that since there is no concept of current directory, there are no Win32 calls to set or get it.

✗ **Error and exception handling** (*e.g.*, _set_unexpected(), terminate()).

✗ **File handling**, both handle-based (*e.g.*, _chsize(), _filelength(), _isatty(), _locking() and _fstat()) and path-based (_access(), _waccess(), _chmod(), _wchmod(), _stat(), _umask(), etc.). Most of the functionality just isn't there (for instance, there is no protection on CE to set with _chmod() or _umask()).

✗ **Low-level file I/O** (*e.g.*, _open(), _read(), _write(), _close(), etc.). Use the Win32 equivalent instead (CreateFile(), ReadFile(), WriteFile(), CloseHandle(), etc.).

✗ **Process and environment control** (*e.g.*, abort(), atexit(), _execl(), _execv(), _getpid(), _pipe(), raise(), signal(), _spawnl(), _spawnv(), system()). However, these are available: setjmp(), longjmp(), exit(), atexit().

✗ **Searching and sorting** (*e.g.*, bsearch(), _lfind(), _lsearch()). One exception: qsort() is available.

✗ **Time** (*e.g.*, clock(), ctime(), _wctime(), gmtime(), localtime(), mktime(), strftime(), time(), etc.). The type time_t is defined and only difftime() is available. Use Win32 time functions instead.

Most of the available functions are listed in `stdlib.h`. However, some header files are gone; for instance, since there are no C time functions, `time.h` is not part of the distribution. This will very likely impact some files being ported.

22.2.4 MFC

MFC for CE has not been saved from the purge, since it is largely built on top of the Win32 API. Compared to MFC 6.0 (for *9x*/NT):

- 88 classes are fully supported (that's the good news!)

- 53 classes have been modified, by dropping some methods to reflect some of the functionality that is now gone or that can be duplicated via other calls.

- 86 classes have been eradicated, either because they are irrelevant on CE or because there is an alternate way to produce the same result (more on this later).

- Six (6) classes have been added, which add command bar, object store database and socket functionality.

These modifications are such that the vast majority of MFC applications will not recompile under CE without being modified. The next sections detail some of the most common problems. The poster included with this book shows the MFC hierarchy for Windows CE, including the classes that are supported, modified, removed, and added.

Unsupported Classes

Since quite a lot of MFC classes are just unsupported, applications that rely on them will have to be modified. The classes conspicuous by their absence are those related to MDI applications, some common control classes (*e.g.*, CRichEditCtrl, CCheckListBox), traditional database support (via ODBC or DAO), some Internet classes (*e.g.*, CHttpServer, CGopherLocator), various OLE classes (*e.g.*, COleDataSource, COleServerItem), etc. The good news is that more MFC classes are supported compared to the previous version (provided with VCCE 5.0).

Limited Graphical Operations

The original device context class (CDC) content is rich: it contains about 180 member variables and functions. For CE, it's been significantly reduced in functionality, largely because CE supports less sophisticated graphics than *9x*/NT. All CDC classes but CMetaFileDC are supported, minus the functionality dropped from CDC:

- A dozen or so methods have been modified to support simpler graphic operations. For instance, BitBlt() only supports 4 of the 15 raster operations; ExtTextOut() supports fewer options; and so forth.

- Nonessential functions (a total of 86) have simply been eradicated from CDC. Among the casualties are Bezier drawings, color floodings, mapping mode settings, redundant text methods (TextOut() has been removed since ExtTextOut() and DrawText() are available), extended operations

691

(`TabbedTextout()`, `GetOutputTabbedTextExtent()`, etc.), and helper methods (*e.g.*, `PtInRect()` can be obtained by checking whether a point is within a rectangle). Some graphical functions such as `Arc()`, are gone, again because they can be emulated otherwise. All this imposes more work on developers.

- Curiously, some CDC methods are not implemented whereas their Win32 counterparts are. For instance, methods to set window and viewport origins aren't implemented, but Win32 functions to do so are available. If some functionality is not found in MFC, it would be a good idea to double-check what's available using Win32.

- Windows origins cannot be modified, although viewport origins now can. This impacts applications that support scrolling. For instance, applications relying on window origins for scrolling now have the use of the viewport origins, but that overall causes little impact. Older versions of CE did not even support viewport origins, making scrolling a real issue.

- The only mapping mode still supported is `MM_TEXT`, where logical coordinates correspond to physical coordinates (pixels). Many applications use that mode, so they remain unaffected. Those that use other mapping modes will require some rework (and recalculation).

Overall, most applications should be relatively immune to these changes. It is only those applications with fancy graphics that will have to be simplified and/or re-coded.

Limited GDI Resources

The GDI classes (`CPen`, `CBrush`, `CBitmap`, `CFont`, `CRgn` and `CPalette`) have been downsized to reflect the changes done to the underlying Win32 API.

- `CPen` only supports cosmetic pens (of a width of 1 and a single color); geometric pens (with brush patterns and fancy styles) have been zapped.

- `CBrush` no longer supports hatched, hollow and pattern brushes.

- `CBitmap` impose a few restrictions: OEM bitmaps are not supported; resource bitmaps are read-only; and so on.

- `CFont` is largely unaffected, other than TrueType and Raster font cannot co-exist on the same system.

- `CRgn` are only useful to manipulate square rectangles (elliptical regions are not supported)

All these changes are easy to fix in most programs, because they usually require simplifying the code when porting it over CE.

More Annoyances

Other changes throughout the MFC hierarchy are listed below. These changes are minor, but they still prevent applications from being ported "as is":

- CWinApp, the application class, has been slightly modified. A few member variables are either absent or uninitialized. The methods to load cursors are gone. Regarding help, only OnHelp() made it; the other methods, such as OnHelpIndex(), have been dropped.

- Menus are supported with fewer options: bitmap and disabled menu items are not supported (although grayed menu items are). Context help for menus are not supported either. Once created, menus are shown in the command bar by using CFrameWnd::InsertMenu(), which is a new CE-exclusive method.

- Group boxes (which are in fact static controls), used for surrounding a group of related controls (push buttons, radio buttons, text, lists, etc.) must be created after the controls they surround; otherwise those controls will be hidden underneath. This happened in many applications.

- Asynchronous sockets (CAsyncSocket) do not fully support asynchronous event notifications in CE (in particular, the CAsyncSelect() method has been dropped). Microsoft recommends using the newcomer class CCeSocket instead of the classes CAsyncSocket and CSocket. This new class, in addition of being derived from CSocket, supports the following asynchronous events: socket ready for reading, incoming connections, and connection completed.

- Since Windows CE does not support wizards, property sheets do not have any wizard functionality.

- A few common dialog boxes (CFontDialog, CPageSetupDialog, and the OLE dialog boxes) are not supported.

- Twelve (12) control classes have been modified: CButton, CComboBox, CEdit, CListBox, CListCtrl, COleControl, CReBarCtrl, CSpinButtonCtrl, CStatic, CStatusBarCtrl, CTabCtrl and CToolBarCtrl. The changes largely have to do with features that have been dropped, such as style options that are no longer available. For instance, owner-drawn list boxes and combo boxes are not supported. Other changes have to do with eliminating redundancy. For instance, CButton controls cannot display bitmaps or cursors, but CBitmapButton, which is fully supported, can display bitmaps.

22.2.5 New Functionality

The few features unique to CE naturally come with a few new functions added to the supported Win32 API. These functions are unique to CE, and are not to be found on any other Windows platform. As a result, using them makes an application fully CE-dependent and not portable.

The API has been extended to include the following features:

- Command bars, a new screen space saver functionality that merges menus and toolbars together.

- Object Store database management API (see Chapter 10 for details). These functions allows accessing databases, as well as inserting, modifying and deleting records.

- ICMP API (detailed in Chapter 12). These few high-level functions implement a "ping" functionality, which allows a computer to query another one on the network.

- And assorted others.

MFC encapsulates some of this new functionality into new or existing classes.

SUGGESTED READINGS

Microsoft, Windows CE Programmer's Guide

> The book reviews most of the Win32 API available on CE. That same information is available with most online help, shipped with Platform Builder and MSDN.

Chapter 23

Using Visual Basic

There is an alternative to application development using C with the SDK, or C++ with MFC: Visual Basic 6.0[68]. Visual Basic is what Microsoft wants just about every developer to use, because this is the ideal language to host various COM-compliant objects and plug them together. Indeed, the strength of Visual Basic is its simplicity and ease of use ... when put in the context it's been designed for. But that advantage becomes a disadvantage when trying to develop powerful applications that require more than working with object's attributes and methods.

This chapter presents an overview of Visual Basic (not specific to any platform), highlights its pros and cons, and reviews the version available for CE development. It also explains an adaptation of Scribble (introduced in Chapter 15) to Visual Basic.

23.1 OVERVIEW OF VISUAL BASIC

For those of you whose most recent memory about Basic is when you were booting a 64KB IBM PC (the model that came before the PC XT, a little less than 20 years ago, whose ROM contained a Basic interpreter), you'll be quite surprised to see that the language has kept up with the software technologies of the '90s: procedures, user-defined types, local variables, object-oriented programming, access to the Win32 API, COM support, etc. Visual Basic is alive and kicking, largely because Microsoft wanted a language any folk with an interest in computers would understand and use. Today, there are indeed hordes of programmers well versed in that language. This section presents the most important concepts of Visual Basic

---

[68] There used to be a second alternative to MFC/C++: Visual J++ 1.1. However, for some obscure reasons, the material about it was pulled off of Windows CE's site in early 1999.

(which you can skip if you are an experienced Visual Basic programmer), and concludes by examining some limitations of the Windows CE version.

23.1.1 Forms

Visual Basic is based on *forms* (windows). A new project starts with an empty form (*i.e.*, a plain window), upon which you drag controls, pretty much the same way a dialog box is built using Visual C++. But the comparison stops here.

Figure 23-1 is the Visual Basic IDE, which is differtent than Visual C++'s. Besides the menu and tool bar, there are four panels shown here. The Toolbox is on the left side, the middle window contains the project's initial form, the top right window is the Project window (the Workspace in Visual C++), and the Properties window, below the Project window, shows the properties of the object being selected (here, the Form1 form). Visual C++ also has a property window, but Visual Basic objects have considerably more properties to deal with.

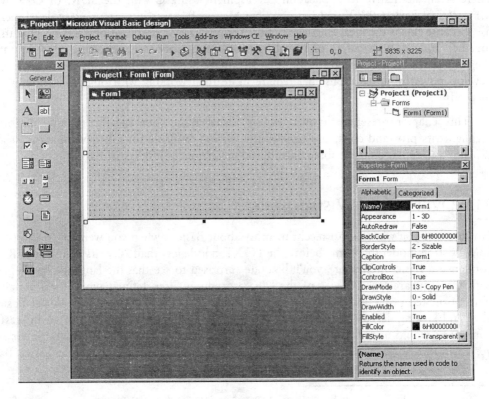

Figure 23-1: A Visual Basic project starts by designing a form.

Visual Basic has "Visual" in its name because you start working with visual items (forms, controls, etc.) and end up adding some code to "activate" them, whereas with Visual C++, you start coding before adding resources[69] (see Figure 23-2). For instance, double-clicking on a form opens a code window for that form, which is to be stored in a .frm file named after the form (see Figure 23-3). As the project progresses, developers spend more and more time writing code than designing forms.

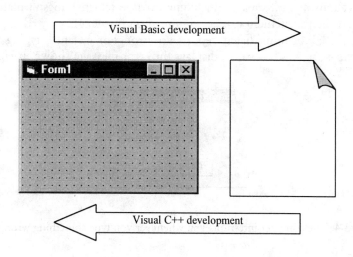

Figure 23-2: Visual Basic developers start with visual items, whereas Visual C++ developers start with the code.

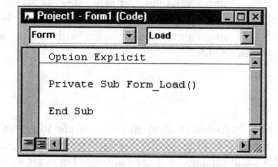

Figure 23-3: The initial code associated with a form. The top right combo box lists all available methods that can be inserted (a simplified equivalent of Visual C++'s ClassWizard).

---

[69] Visual C++ probably got its name to build on the success of Visual Basic, because there's not much "visual" about it.

A code window is not just a plain text file, as a `.h` and `.cpp` file is. The top part is the declaration part, where global variables are declared. This is followed by procedures and functions. The thin horizontal line between the declaration part and the procedure (and between subsequent procedures) in Figure 23-3 is automatically added by the code window. In fact, the editor is carefully analyzing everything you type.

Another departure from C++ is that this code window is not format-free. For instance, in C++, the locations of white spaces (including carriage returns) doesn't matter, but it does in Visual Basic. A single statement can be continued on the next line by adding an "_". If the "_" is omitted, the editor immediately reports an error. For instance, typing an incomplete assignment (such as "a = <Enter>") displays the error message shown in Figure 21-4.

Figure 23-4: The compiler interrupts you whenever you type something wrong.

23.1.2 Modules

Source code is normally implemented in forms, but it can also be implemented in a separate *module* (a separate `.bas` file). Global variables and procedures within a module can be made public (widely accessible within the project) or private (only accessible from the procedure within the module only). C programmers are familiar with the concept, by using static variable and functions within a C file.

23.1.3 Controls

A form in itself is inert; it becomes alive when controls are added to it. And that's where Visual Basic scores: there is a wide availability of controls designed for Visual Basic. Microsoft even provides small catalogs of those controls. There are three types of controls:

- The intrinsic controls, provided with Visual Basic, are the initial Windows controls (static, edit, list box, etc.), plus a few others (Timer, Data, etc.) These controls are shown in the default control toolbox (see Figure 23-5).

- The ActiveX controls, provided as separate `.ocx` files, are integrated within the tool box as needed. Visual Basic provides some of those controls (such as the list view control), and there are many, many third-party controls commercially available.

- "Insertable" objects, such as an Excel spreadsheet or a Word document.

All those controls give Visual Basic developers a vast choice when developing applications. Because those objects expose numerous properties, many Visual Basic applications just provide a form to put those controls on and provides the glue between them, passing information from one control to another.

Figure 23-5: Visual Basic's original toolbox.

23.1.4 Objects

In addition to controls, Visual Basic supports *objects*. Like objects in C++, they are a combination of code and data, treated as a single unit. In the Visual Basic terminology, an object is anything that fits that definition (a control, a form, even an entire application), whereas a control is an object that must be contained within a form object.

Objects have many properties (*i.e.*, attributes), which can be set at design and run time. For instance, on Figure 23-1, the form's properties are shown in the Properties window. The third property is `BackColor`, which can be changed, at design time, to any other color. The form will use that color when shown.

The ability to initialize the appearance and behavior of all the controls and forms at design time helps reducing the amount of code significantly. This is a strong contrast with Visual C++, where only a few attributes can be set a design time, requiring more coding to set the other attributes at run-time.

This is not to say that properties cannot be read and modified at run-time in Visual Basic. On the contrary: all properties can be accessed at run-time (we'll see more about properties before long).

23.1.5 Classes

The concept of objects naturally evokes the notion of classes for C++ programmers. Well, it does too for Visual Basic programmers!

Class Modules

Visual Basic supports a special type of module called a *class module*. Like a C++ class, a class module defines a pattern to create objects, which are instances of that class. This is different than the modules described earlier, which implement one instance of the global variables declared within. Within a class module, variables and procedures can be public and private, providing class encapsulation.

Each class module resides in its own source file (like a module, but using the .cls extension), and the file name names the class. Objects are instantiated by using the new statement (which is not an operator as in C++) and specifying the class module name (or file name).

Here is a simple class file (Class1.cls) that has one private string variable, a class initializer (same as a constructor in C++) and one function returning the left part of the string variable. Note that comments start with a single apostrophe ('This is a comment).

```
' Class1.cls

Private strName As String

Private Sub Class_Initialize()
    strName = "Class1"
End Sub

Public Function LeftName(Length As Long) As String
    LeftName = Left(strName, Length)
End Function
```

A form could use that class by creating an instance of it, by using the New statement. Internal reference counts are maintained and objects are automatically deleted when no longer referenced.

700

```
Private Sub Form_Load()
    Dim MyClass As New Class1          ' Allocate a class1 object
    MsgBox MyClass.LeftName(3)         ' Invoke Class1.LeftName

    ' The Class1 object is deleted when returning from this proc.
End Sub
```

Encapsulation and Properties

Like modules, class modules can have private variables, the equivalent of class attributes in C++. A class module can hence encapsulate its internal data. In C++, member variables are usually always kept private, providing get/set functions if required. Visual Basic goes one step further and implements properties to access them. Consider the following class (Class1) and form (Form1):

```
' Class1.cls

Private strName As String              ' Private class variable

Property Get Name() As String          ' "Get Name" property
    Name = strName
End Property

Property Let Name(NewName As String)   ' "Let Name" property
    If NewName = "" Then
        strName = strName
    Else
        strName = NewName
    End If
End Property
```

```
' Form1.frm
Dim MyClass As New Class1

Private Sub Form_Load()
    MyClass.Name = "MSDN"              ' Invokes "Let Name" property
    MsgBox MyClass.Name               ' Invokes "Get Name" property
End Sub
```

In Form_Load(), assigning a value to MyClass.Name invokes the Let Name property, which can perform some validation, provide default values, etc. Obtaining the value from MyClass.Name (by calling MsgBox in this example) invokes the Get Name property, which can process the data if needed before returning it. This is a powerful and elegant alternative to providing methods such as GetName or SetName in order to support encapsulation, although some developers prefer to use the latter approach.

Objects can also have one default property (or method) to simplify coding. For instance, a text control (*i.e.*, an edit control) can be set simply by assigning a string to it, instead of using a property or invoking a method.

```
Text1 = "John Doe"
```

Interfaces and Polymorphism

Visual Basic supports the notion of interfaces (*à la* COM), where a class module contains abstract methods (*i.e.*, public procedure without code). This class module can be used as an interface in other class modules. The result is an object with one or multiple interfaces, exactly the way COM likes it.

Furthermore, Visual Basic supports the concept of references to generic objects. Interfaces are implemented in that case using late binding at run-time, providing some polymorphism.

23.1.6 Handling Window and Control Messages

Events are the equivalents of Windows messages in MFC/C++, and they are handled within a form in Visual Basic when they are *raised*. For instance, a form can have objects (an instance of a certain class module); events raised by that object can be handled right in the form. Parameters can be passed as well, without any reference whatsoever to wParam and lParam (the technical jargon is left for C/C++ programmers only!)

Events are also used for control commands and notifications. For instance, consider a form that has a command button (*e.g.*, a push button), labeled Command1; while editing the form, double-clicking on the button adds the following handler in the form's code window:

```
Private Sub Command1_Click()

End Sub
```

Window messages are considered events too, and can be handled through predefined procedures. For instance, one can add the Form_Paint() predefined procedure to handle WM_PAINT (although Visual Basic refers to it as the "paint event").

```
Private Sub Form_Paint()
    Circle (230, 90), 40
End Sub
```

As a radical departure from MFC/C++, objects can be used instead of handling Windows messages. For instance, in order to use a timer, an MFC/C++ application sets a timer and handles WM_TIMER. In Visual Basic, a Timer control is instead added to the form; at run-time, this timer is not visible, but it fires events at a specific interval (which is a property), which are handled in a specific event handler.

Overall, events bring the event-driven nature of Windows within Basic programs.

23.1.7 Win32 Interface

Visual Basic provides a direct access to the Win32 API defined in "Coredll.dll". This dynamic-link system library contains the interface to all system calls available to the application. For example, a Basic application can call CreateFile(), like in C/C++.

23.2 VISUAL BASIC FOR WINDOWS CE

So far, Visual Basic has properties that make it not so basic after all. Its numerous features narrow the gap with other "advanced" languages such as C++. Unfortunately, that's only true on desktops.

Visual Basic designers had to take into account the small amount of memory (compared to desktops) that is typically found on Windows CE devices. As a result, it was impossible to support the entire set of Visual Basic features, and a lot had to go. The bad news is that casualties are everywhere: fewer objects, fewer controls, fewer properties, fewer methods, fewer events, fewer general functions, fewer predefined constants, and even fewer statements (about 2/3 are gone). One of the most significant casualties is the (lack of) support for class modules, with all the goodies related to them. Encapsulation also takes a hit since the Private keyword means nothing on Windows CE (everything is public).

There is no doubt that porting existing applications from NT (or 9x) to CE will be quite challenging for anything but trivial applications. This could even be worse than porting MFC applications to CE (the subject of Chapter 22), since MFC provides a good abstraction, and MFC's diet has been less severe than Visual Basic's.

Overall, Visual Basic for CE is still very capable at exploiting third-party components and integrating them in on single application. This, combined with its ease of use, are the real strengths of Visual Basic.

On the other side, it is arguably inadequate for large or complex projects, because the IDE itself and the language are just not powerful enough to meet the challenges associated with those projects[70]. Also, the simplicity mentioned earlier comes at a price of performance degradation and memory consumption.

23.3 AN EXAMPLE

One piece of code is better than one thousand explanations, so here is the implementation of Scribble (see Figure 23-6), whose MFC/C++ implementation is described in Chapter 15. The application has three forms: the main window (`frmScribble.frm`), the `PenWidths` dialog box (`frmPenWidths.frm`) and the About dialog box (`frmAbout.frm`). It uses two modules (not class modules through): `Constants.bas` (to hold a few constants, a kind of `Resource.h`), and `Lines.bas`, which stores lines in memory and interacts with data files.

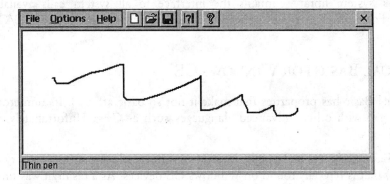

Figure 23-6: Scribble for Visual Basic.

The **Scribble** sample (in the Chap23 directory o the CD-ROM) contains the project for the HPC and HPC Pro.

SUGGESTED READINGS

Holzner, Visual Basic 6 Black Book

> One of the best book on the subject for experienced programmers (most other books on Visual Basic start very slooooooowly). The book also has a problem solving approach, which helps applying concepts quickly. Beware that there is no mention of the limitations found on CE, so many topics and examples do not apply.

---

[70] The built-in compiler only performs a limited checking, resulting a numerous run-time errors during development. Also, there are no elaborate architectures, like the document/view architecture found in VC++.

Chapter 24

Windows CE Profiling

Windows CE includes a version of the kernel – `Nkprof.exe` – that supports profiling, a diagnostic facility that provides information about application and kernel execution times. This article presents what types of profiling Windows CE supports and how to use it to obtain some useful information about the workings of your CE system.

24.1 PROFILING SUPPORT IN WINDOWS CE

Windows CE directly supports three profiling methods:

- The *Monte Carlo* profiler interrupts the system on a regular basis and determines what kernel routines execute. It is useful to see where the kernel spends its time, but it is not very useful for application development because it does not interpret application addresses. Nonetheless, it is possible to develop a tool that would report that information, as we will see shortly.

- The *Instrumented Kernel* profiler analyzes kernel calls – KCALLs for short – when preemption is turned off, a condition where threads are prevented from running. This impacts the execution of Interrupt Service Threads (ISTs), since a ready-to-run IST would be blocked until preemption is turned on again. The profiling returns the minimum, maximum, and average times where preemption is off. These values establish the IST latency time, *i.e.*, the longest period a ready-to-run IST is blocked by the kernel. This information is very useful for real-time system designers, as it indicates the longest time (the worst case) an IST – any IST – may be held before having a chance to process some events.

- The *Hardware-Assisted* profiler tracks process and thread creation and termination, as well as thread switches, which is useful to identify which threads run, and when, within a given application.

The first two methods require two easy steps: building the profile-enabled version of the kernel and using a terminal emulator to get the output from the debug port. The last approach is more complex, as it requires writing an application to obtain the results. Luckily, a sample application is readily available with Platform Builder 2.11.

24.2 INSTRUMENTED KERNEL AND MONTE CARLO PROFILING

The profile-enabled version of the kernel (`Nkprof.exe`) directly supports Instrumented Kernel and Monte Carlo profiling, which can be activated thanks to some enhancement in the keyboard driver. Hence, the first step is to build that profile-enabled version of the kernel. This can be done by setting a few environment variables and building a new kernel:

```
SET WINCEPROFILE=1
SET WINCEMAP=1
SET IMGNODEBUGGER=1

CD %_TARGETPLATROOT%\Kernel
Build -cfs
Makeimg
```

`WINCEPROFILE` indicates to `Makeimg.exe` to use `Nkprof.exe` as the kernel instead of `Nk.exe` when producing `Nk.bin`. As a matter of fact, `Romimage.exe` (invoked via `Makeimg.exe`) outputs the following during the build:

Windows CE ROM Image Builder v1.0 Copyright Microsoft 1995.

WINCEPROFILE=1 Using nkprof.exe for kernel.

The sample keyboard device drivers of the ODO and PC-Based platforms directly support commands to activate and deactivate profiling, as shown in Figure 24-1.

Key	Description
F8	Starts Monte Carlo profiling, in RAM buffers.
F9	Starts Instrumented-Kernel profiling.
F11	Starts Monte Carlo profiling with symbol lookups in the profiler ISR.
F12	Stops profiling.

Figure 24-1: Keys to activate/deactivate the profiler. This feature is directly available in the sample keyboard drivers provided with Platform Builder 2.11

The drivers rely on two documented system calls. ProfileStart() takes two arguments (a sample interval, in microseconds, and a profiling mode), and starts Instrumented Kernel and Monte Carlo profiling. ProfileStop() stops the Windows CE profiling and outputs a profile report through the debug serial port, which can be seen by connecting a terminal emulator. The report generator is built in within Windows CE and cannot be customized.

Any application or driver (such as the provided keyboard drivers) may invoke these functions, as long as the underlying kernel is Nkprof.exe. Figure 24-2 shows the output produced by pressing F11 (to start the profiling), waiting a few seconds, and then pressing F12 (to stop profiling)

```
Total samples=547
Module          Hits            Percent
------------    ----------      -------
nk.exe               12           2.1
ddi.dll               2           0.3
coredll.dll           1           0.1
UNKNOWN             532          97.0
Hits        Percent Address  Module      Routine
----------  ------- -------- ----------  ------------------------
       9          1 802057ad nk.exe      : OEMWriteDebugString
       2          0 8020da64 nk.exe      : KCall
       2          0 016b3fb3 ddi.dll     :?EmulatedBlt
       1          0 80204c68 nk.exe      : WaitForStatus
       1          0 01aebf09 coredll.dll : SplitFreeBlock
```

Figure 24-2: The report being output on the debug serial port after starting and stopping the profiler, by respectively pressing F11 and F12. The module labeled UNKNOWN is in fact an application eating CPU cycles.

There are a few drawbacks, through. First, the report includes information about the kernel only, not the applications (collectively shown as UNKNOWN). Hence, you cannot directly measure how applications perform. The alternative is to invoke ProfileStart() with PROFILE_BUFFER (or pressing F8), which stores the samples in memory. These samples correspond to program counters, obtained on a periodic basis, which can later be retrieved and interpreted by an application. Unfortunately, the PC-based platform uses a conflicting memory location that sometimes hangs the system. You will have to update the PC-based profiling support (in the OAL) and the memory configuration if you eventually opt to use for that method. Furthermore, the actual PC-based implementation only supports fixed sampling period, despite ProfileStart() that accepts any value. Again, you can change the OAL to implement that functionality. Finally, the KCALL profiling (activated via F9) did not produce any output most of the time for reasons that are not clear. Let's hope that the next releases of CE will fix those issues.

24.3 HARDWARE-ASSISTED PROFILING

Hardware-Assisted profiling monitors a different series of events, and requires a different approach. Here's how it works: an application provides the kernel with five functions, that are called back by the kernel when the following events take place (one function per event):

- A thread is created
- A thread is terminated
- A process is created
- A process is terminated
- A thread-switch occurred

Each of these functions is invoked with some parameters to help identify the thread or process the event is related to. For instance, when a thread is created, the thread creation callback is called with the handle of that thread. That information can be registered by the callback in some application-defined structure, to be later displayed.

The implementation is non-trivial, though. Because the functions are called back by the kernel, they indeed run in kernel mode, not in user mode. That imposes a few limitations on the implementation of these functions:

- Exceptions cannot occur, including page fault. Hence, the functions must reside in a dynamic-link library (DLL) which is to be loaded by an application via `LoadDriver()`, a method that prevent page faults.
- The functions run in kernel mode. Consequently, all pointers must be mapped via `MapPtrToProcess()`, because the functions are not invoked from slot 0.
- System calls are not allowed when executing the functions. This is not a problem though, as callback functions simply record events in memory buffers and terminate.

24.3.1 Building A Hardware-Assisted Version of the Kernel

This profiling method works with ordinary kernels. And to make it easier to use, Microsoft provides a library, called `Schedlog.lib`, which can be linked with the kernel. This library is not essential, but using it provides more information to each function when called back. Building a kernel with that library is easy:

```
SET SCHEDLOG=1
SET WINCEREL=1

CD %_TARGETPLATROOT%\Kernel
```

```
Build -cfs
Makeimg
```

24.3.2 Implementation Details

As mentioned earlier, the callback functions must reside in a DLL (which is to be run in kernel mode), whereas the application's core resides in a normal program (which runs in user mode). An example of such an application and DLL is provided with Platform Builder 2.11, in %_WINCEROOT%\Public\Common\Oak\Utils\Schedlog: Sclogldr (the application that loads the DLL) and Sclogdl (the DLL that sets up the profiling session).

Upon initialization, the application loads the DLL by calling LoadDriver(). The DLL in turn initializes a SCHEDLOG_ENABLE structure, defined in %_WINCEROOT%\Public\ Common\Oak\Inc\Schedlog.h, by assigning the address of the functions to be called back. These functions are all in the DLL as well. The structure also holds a 32-bit, application-defined value, passed as a parameter to each function when called back. This 32-bit value typically points to a user-application structure that holds counters, for instance.

The profiling session starts within the DLL by calling KernelIOControl(). The OAL provided on PC-based platforms and ODO respond by enabling the profiling. If you use a custom port of Windows CE, you will have to add this functionality into your implementation of OEMIoControl(). The DLL then sleeps for a predetermined period of time, during which the functions are called back as events take place. These functions can record anything useful. Once the sleep is over, another call to KernelIOControl() terminates the profiling session. This method is illustrated in Figure 24-3.

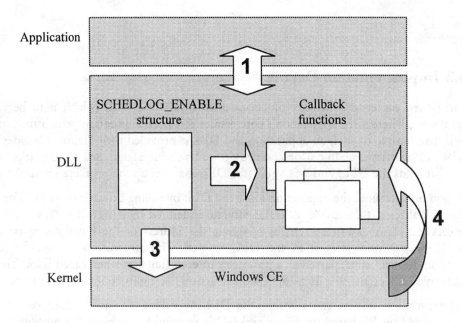

Figure 24-3: Hardware-assisted profiling. The application loads the DLL (1). A `SCHEDLOG_ENABLE` structure is then initialized to contain the address of some callback functions (2). The profiling session is started (3), during which the kernel calls the functions back (4), which register the profiling events.

This method is very flexible and powerful, because you may collect whatever data you want, whenever the functions are called back. The application may then interpret that data once the profiling session is over and display a report or some graphs.

To summarize, Monte Carlo profiling can reveal some useful information about applications, but it requires reworking some of the OAL. The Instrumented Kernel is extremely useful as it provides interrupt latency times, crucial for time-sensitive applications, when it works... The Hardware-Assisted profiling requires developing a simple application to collect information, but it gives precise insights regarding who is running when. These tools are all valuable to monitor application and system execution times, especially when considering that the next major version of Windows CE will be enhanced to meet real time requirements.

References

CAMPBELL, J.: *C Programmer's Guide to Serial Communications*, Second Edition, Sams Publishing, 1993

FOWLER, S.: *GUI Design Handbook*, McGraw-Hill, New York, NY, 1998

GALITZ, W.: *The Essential Guide To User Interface Design*, Wiley Computer Publishing, New York, NY, 1996

GAREAU, J.: "Advanced Embedded x86 Programming: Paging", *Embedded Systems Programming*, pp. 62-83, Vol. 11, No. 6, June 1998

GAREAU, J. and LABROSSE, J.: "Developing Applications with Windows CE 2.10", *Embedded Systems Programming*, pp. 46-59, Vol. 11, No. 11, October 1998

GAREAU, J.: "Porting MFC Applications to Windows CE", *Windows CE Tech Journal*, pp. 30-37, Vol. 1, No. 3, September 1998

HOLZNER, S.: *Visual Basic 6 Black Book*, The Coriolis Group, Scottsdale, AR, 1998

INTEL CORP. : *Pentium® Processor Family Developer's Manual, Volume 3: Architecture and Programming Manual*, Order Number 241430, 19957

KOON, J.: *USB Peripheral Design*, Annabooks, San Diego, CA, 1998

LABROSSE, J.J.: *iC/OS The Real-Time Kernel*, R&D Publications, Lawrence, KS, 1992

LABROSSE, J.J.: *Embedded Systems Building Blocks*, R&D Publications, Lawrence, KS, 1995

McKUSICK, M.K., LEFFLER, S.J., KARELS, M.J. and QUATERMANN, J.S.: *The Design and Implementation of the 4.4BSD UNIX operating System*, Addison-Wesley, 1996

MICROSOFT CORP.: *Microsoft Windows CE Programmer's Guide*, Microsoft Press, Redmond, WA, 1996

MEYER, S.: *Effective C++ Second Edition*, Addison Wesley Longman Inc., Reading, MA, 1998

MURRAY, J.: *Inside Windows CE*, Microsoft Press, Redmond, WA, 1998

PETZOLD, C.: *Programming Windows Fifth Edition*, Microsoft Press, Redmond, WA, 1999

PIETREK M., "Peering Insert the PE: A Tout of the Win32 Portable Executable File Format", *Microsoft Systems Journal*, March 1994, Miller-Freeman

PIETREK M., "Remove Fatty Deposit from your Applications Using Our 32-bit Liposuction Tools", *Microsoft Systems Journal*, October 1996, Miller-Freeman

PROSISE, J.: *Programming Windows 95 With MFC*, Microsoft Press, Redmond, WA, 1996

ROGERSON, D.: *Inside COM*, Microsoft Press, Redmond, WA, 1997

RIPPS, D.: *An Implementation Guide to Real-Time Programming*, Yourdon Press Computing Series, Englewood Cliffs, NJ, 1989

RICHTER, J.: *Advanced Windows*, Third Edition, Microsoft Press, Redmond, WA, 1997

SELLS, C.: *Windows Telephony Programming*, Addison Wesley Longman Inc., Reading, MA, 1998

SOLOMON, D.: *Inside Windows NT*, Second Edition, Microsoft Press, Redmond, WA, 1998

STEVENS, R.: *UNIX Network Programming: Volume 1*, Second Edition, Prentice-Hall, Englewood Cliffs, NJ, 1997

STEVENS, R.: *UNIX Network Programming: Volume 2*, Second Edition, Prentice-Hall, Englewood Cliffs, NJ, 1998

STROUSTRUP, B.: *The C++ Programming Language*, Third Edition, Addition Wesley, Reading, MA, 1997

TANENBAUM, A.: *Computer Networks*, Third Edition, Prentice-Hall, Englewood Cliffs, NJ, 1996

TANENBAUM, A.: *Modern Operating System*, Prentice-Hall, Englewood Cliffs, NJ, 1992

TURLEY, J.: *Advanced 80386 Programming Techniques*, McGraw-Hill, Berkeley, CA, 1988

PRATA, S.: *The Waite Group's C Primer Plus*, Third Edition, Macmillan computer Publishing, 1998

Appendix A

An Overview of C++ for C Programmers

C++ is often referred to as a "better C". Perhaps the most important difference between C++ and C is the object-oriented nature of C++, which is known to improve application design and implementation when applied properly. It also incorporates many other features that help simplify system and application development. This appendix reviews the most important characteristics of C++, for those of you already familiar with C programming. You will certainly enjoy the fact that C++ is 100% backward-compatible to C, allowing you to master C++ step by step.

A.1 OBJECT-ORIENTED CONCEPTS

Object-Oriented Programming (OOP, not oops!) is about breaking the functionality of an application into objects, each of which implements a specific functionality. The interaction of the objects with each other produces a complete application.

A good example is a Microsoft Foundation Class (MFC) application. It is essentially composed of four objects, each of which plays its very own role (see Figure A-1):

- The *application object* implements the application initialization, the message loop, and termination. There's no window associated with it, but it works hand in hand with the other objects described below. This class really drives the application.

- The *main frame* object implements the main window, also called the application window. This is the window that features the title bar, the command bar, a client area, and a status bar, if any. However, the user interaction with the command bar is also redirected to the other classes by this main frame object.

- The *view* object implements a window that entirely covers the main frame's client area. The sole purpose is to implement the application's user interface by displaying the application's data (text, graph, etc.)

- The *document* object implements all the data structures required to hold the application data. It is not concerned with the representation of that data because that's the purpose of the view only. The document may internally access various data repositories (files, databases, the network, etc.) to load and store the application's data, and the exact implementation does not need to be known by the other classes.

Taken individually, each class is not enough to implement a complete application. But joined together, they constitute a normal application. You can focus on one object at a time, which is simpler than it is to work on the entire application as a whole, as was required with traditional C and SDK Windows programming.

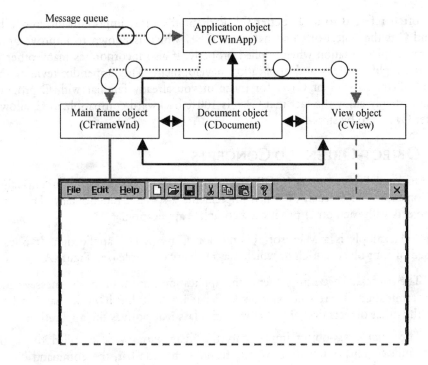

Figure A-1: The main four classes of an MFC application (the names in parentheses are the MFC base class names). There are other architectures available, which use other classes. A solid line indicates a direct access between two classes. Windows messages (WM_xxx) are represented by small circles, and the dotted lines indicate the basic message flow (which is enhanced within MFC).

Furthermore, each of these objects implement some mechanic that needs to be implemented in every Windows application. By reusing these objects, you can directly benefit from this functionality, giving you more time to focus on the unique functionality of your own applications. Reusability is a key concept of object oriented programming.

OOP starts with an object-oriented design (OOD), whose goal is to produce a model of the solution to implement. This is typically done by breaking a complex problem into smaller ones that can be addressed individually. Whereas C++ provides the tools for OOP, fewer tools are available for OOD. Should an OOD be inconsistent, incomplete, or incorrect, OOP will simply materialize these shortcomings. Hence C++ (and OOP in general) should not be seen as a programming paradigm that guarantees an adequate implementation, but rather as a means to implement OOD efficiently. The Suggested Readings section identifies some valuable references about OOD and OOP.

A.2 CLASSES

All C developers are familiar with structures (struct), which group together a series of variables that have a common purpose. C++ extends the concept by introducing *classes*. A C++ class is a data structure with special properties, all described in just a moment. But to start with, consider that a class is a structure, only with the word class instead of struct, and the addition of the word public. Consider the next example, which implements a printer front-end, used throughout this appendix (see Figure A-2), using both a structure and a class.

```
// A C/C++ structure that describes a printer front-end.
struct SPrinter
{
    char    szFullName[128];
    int     nPortNo;
};

// A C++ class that is the exact equivalent.
class CPrinter
{
public:                                    // Explained later
    char    szFullName[128];
    int     nPortNo;
};
```

We'll review the differences between structures and classes in detail toward the end of this appendix.

Once defined, classes are used exactly like structures, *i.e.*, by declaring variables of a class type, and accessing the member variables using the "." operator, such as:

```
CPrinter    MyPrinter;
```

```
MyPrinter.szFullName[0] = '\0';
```

Declaring such a variable is said *to create an instance of a CPrinter class*, or to *instantiate a CPrinter object*. Hence, `MyPrinter` is an *object* of type `CPrinter`. That's what an object is: a class instance, no more, no less[71].

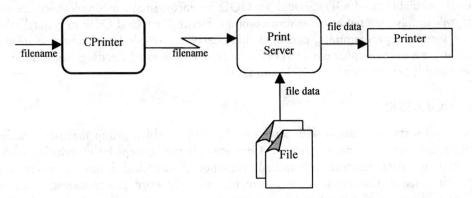

Figure A-2: The examples in this appendix implement some printer front-ends by using a class called `CPrinter`. This object receives file names to print and sends them to a remote print server, using some communication means (WinSock, etc.) That print server eventually accesses the files and prints them one by one.

A.2.1 Member Variables and Member Functions

Classes, like structures, hold variables. But they can also hold functions. Consider this implementation of `CPrinter`:

```
// A printer class, which acts as a front-end to a print server.
class CPrinter
{
public:
    char    szFullName[128];            // e.g. \\PrintServer\laser1
    int     nPortNo;                    // To communicate with print srvr
};

// Based on a printer name, obtain a communication port no (nPortNo)
// in order to communicate with the corresponding print server.
```

---

[71] Some people tend to "humanize" objects by saying that they are entities that "live" by themselves. Those are just abstractions that have confused more than one developer as far as I am concerned. I prefer to express an object as what it really is from a programming and pragmatic standpoint.

```
void InitializePrinter(CPrinter * pPrinter, char * pszName)
{
        .
        .
        .
}

// Print a test page. A special command is sent to the print server.
void PrintTestPage(CPrinter * pPrinter)
{
        .
        .
        .
}

// Print a file. The file name is sent to the print server.
void PrintFile(CPrinter * pPrinter, char * pszFileName)
{
        .
        .
        .
}

// Release the connection to the print server
void UninitializePrinter(CPrinter * pPrinter)
{
        .
        .
        .
}

// Let's print something.
void PrintSomething()
{
    CPrinter        MyPrinter;

    InitializePrinter(&MyPrinter, "\\\\PrintServer\\laser1");

    PrintTestPage(&MyPrinter);
    PrintFile(&MyPrinter, "MyFile.txt");

    UninitializePrinter(&MyPrinter);
}
```

Note that all functions naturally require a pointer to a CPrinter class in order to work on a given printer (such as MyPrinter). Since these functions are so dependent on that class, they can be incorporated right into it. Consider this next implementation:

```
class CPrinter
{
public:
    // Same member variables
    char    szFullName[128];
    int     nPortNo;
```

```
    // Member functions, working on this class' member variables only.
    void    InitializePrinter(char * pszName);
    void    PrintTestPage();
    void    PrintFile(char * pszFileName);
    void    UninitializePrinter();
};

// Based on a printer name, obtain a communication port no (nPortNo)
// in order to communicate with the corresponding print server.
void CPrinter::InitializePrinter(char * pszName)
{
    .
    .
    .
}

// Print a test page. A special command is sent to the print server.
void CPrinter::PrintTestPage()
{
    .
    .
    .
}

// Print a file. The file is sent to the print server.
void CPrinter::PrintFile(char * pszFileName)
{
    .
    .
    .
}

// Release the connection to the print server
void CPrinter::UninitializePrinter()
{
    .
    .
    .
}

// Let's print something.
void PrintSomething()
{
    CPrinter        MyPrinter;

    MyPrinter.InitializePrinter("\\\\PrintServer\\laser1");

    MyPrinter.PrintTestPage();
    MyPrinter.PrintFile("MyFile.txt");

    MyPrinter.UninitializePrinter();
}
```

The class itself now directly contains functions. The functions are such that they implicitly work on a CPrinter. Functions defined within a class are called member functions, whereas the variables are called member variables. In OOP terminology, they are respectively called *methods* and *attributes*. Those member functions are then implemented by prefixing each of them with CPrinter::, as shown above.

In PrintSomething(), note how the member functions are invoked *on behalf of* MyPrinter. For instance, MyPrinter.InitializePrinter() invokes the member function CPrinter::InitializePrinter(). &MyPointer does not have to be specified any more, because the compiler passes it implicitly (more on this later). Consequently, CPrinter::InitializePrinter() can directly use szFullName and nPortNo, on behalf of MyPrinter. Here's a hypothetical implementation of that function:

```
void CPrinter::InitializePrinter(char * pszName)
{
    strcpy(szFullName, pszName);
    nPortNo = GetPortNo(pszName);          // Returns a port no.
    OpenPortNo(nPortNo);                   // Opens a communication channel
}
```

If another CPrinter object is instantiated, say Printer2, invoking Printer2.InitializePrinter() calls the same exact member function, but it implicitly works this time on Printer2's member variables. This is illustrated in this example:

```
void PrintSomethingElse()
{
    CPrinter        Printer1;
    CPrinter        Printer2;

    // Invoke InitializePrinter(), which will work on Printer1.
    Printer1.InitializePrinter("\\\\PrintServer\\laser1");

    // Invoke InitializePrinter(), which will work on Printer2.
    Printer2.InitializePrinter("\\\\PrintServer\\laser2");
}
```

The real advantage of using member functions is simplicity: their limited scope (the class' member variables) clearly delimits their implementation, giving them a very precise and unambiguous role. Furthermore, using member functions eliminates namespace contention. In C, from a practical standpoint, a function can't be called Initialize(), because it will likely clash with another function of the same name in some libraries. But by using member functions, CPrinter::InitializePrinter() can be replaced with CPrinter::Initialize(), since there is no other function called Initialize() *within* the class, and it is pretty clear, in that context, that Initialize() initializes ... a printer.

A.2.2 Hidden Pointer

Behind the scenes, each member function receives a hidden parameter, which is a pointer to the instance they have been invoked upon. Within a member function, member variables are directly accessed using that pointer, but this is hidden from you by the compiler. You can reference this hidden pointer, however, and its name is always this (*i.e.*, the "current object").

For instance, the following statements (which are what you could write):

```
void CPrinter::Initialize(char * pszName)
{
    strcpy(szFullName, pszName);
    nPortNo = GetPortNo(pszName);           // Returns a port no.
    OpenPortNo(nPortNo);                    // Opens a communication channel
}

void PrintSomething()
{
    CPrinter        MyPrinter;
    MyPrinter.Initialize("\\\\PrintServer\\laser1");
    .
    .
    .
}
```

are hypothetically generated by the compiler as follows (the compiler automatically adds the code written in bold, not you):

```
void CPrinter::Initialize(CPrinter * this, char * pszName)
{
    strcpy(this->szFullName, pszName);
    this->nPortNo = GetPortNo(pszName);
    OpenPortNo(nPortNo);
}

void PrintSomething()
{
    CPrinter        MyPrinter;
    CPrinter::Initialize(&MyPrinter, "\\\\PrintServer\\laser1");
    .
    .
    .
}
```

You can see that invoking a member function really consists of calling a function and passing the address of a variable as the first parameter. Again, this parameter is hidden to you, but it can be referred to using this, as shown above. Note that the actual implementation by the compiler may vary. For instance, instead of using a parameter, the object can be specified by using a dedicated register.

A.2.3 Constructors and Destructors

The `CPrinter` class contains one initialization function and one uninitialization (or termination) function, `CPrinter::Initialize()` and `CPrinter::Uninitialize()`. In this particular implementation, they must be called to respectively establish a link with a remote print server and close that link. However, you are required to invoke them explicitly (as shown in `PrintSomething()`). Not invoking `CPrinter::Initialize()` would prevent printing, so you are likely to identify the problem and add the call. But forgetting to call `CPrinter::Uninitilize()` would prevent some resource from being released, but you may never realize the mistake.

C++ extends classes furthermore by introducing constructors and destructors. A constructor, if present[72], is automatically invoked upon instantiating the class. Conversely, a destructor, if present, is automatically invoked when the class instance(*i.e.*, the object) goes out of scope. The idea is to give any object a chance to initialize/uninitialize itself no matter what, without requiring you to do it explicitly.

In this new `CPrinter` class definition, the initialization and uninitialization functions give way to a constructor (whose name is always the same as the class) and a destructor (whose name is always "~" followed by the class name):

```
class CPrinter
{
public:
    char    szFullName[128];            // e.g. \\PrintServer\laser1
    int     nPortNo;                    // e.g. 1 for port #1

    CPrinter(char * pszName);           // Constructor
    ~CPrinter();                        // Destructor

    void PrintTestPage();
    void PrintFile(char * pszFileName);
};

// (Constructor)
// Based on a printer name, obtain a communication port no (nPortNo)
// in order to communicate with the corresponding print server.
CPrinter::CPrinter(char * pszName)
{
    strcpy(szFullName, pszName);
    nPortNo = GetPortNo(pszName);       // Returns a port no.
    OpenPortNo(nPortNo);                // Opens a communication channel
}
```

---

[72] Even if you don't provide any constructor or destructor, the compiler generates default ones.

```
// (Destructor)
// Release the connection with the remote server.
CPrinter::~CPrinter()
{
    ClosePortNo(nPortNo);                    // Close the comm. channel
}

// Print a test page. A special command is sent to the print server.
void CPrinter::PrintTestPage()
{
    .
    .
    .
}

// Print a file. The file is sent to the print server.
void CPrinter::PrintFile(char * pszFileName)
{
    .
    .
    .
}

// Let's print something.
void PrintSomething()
{
    // Be declaring an CPrinter variable, the constructor is
    // automatically called with the specified argument.
    CPrinter        MyPrinter("\\\\PrintServer\\laser1");

    // At this point, MyPrinter() is already initialized.

    MyPrinter.PrintTestPage();
    MyPrinter.PrintFile("MyFile.txt");

    // Just before returning, MyPrinter's destructor is invoked,
    // as MyPrinter goes out of scope. The communication is terminated.
}
```

Constructors and destructors allow the class designer to ensure that regardless how their object is used, it is properly initialized and uninitialized. This gives objects some sort of self-containment.

A.2.4. Encapsulation

The CPrinter class definition contains some member attributes (szFullName and nPortNo) that can be manipulated by some other code. For instance, you could execute the following:

```
// Let's print something.
void PrintSomething()
```

```
{
    CPrinter        MyPrinter("\\\\PrintServer\\laser1");

    // Directly access nPortNo. This alters the state of the object,
    // and prevents it from working properly.
    MyPrinter.nPortNo = -1;

    MyPrinter.PrintTestPage();            // Won't print
    MyPrinter.PrintFile("MyFile.txt");    // Wont' print

    // Destructor may fail, since it will attempt to close an
    // invalid port no.
}
```

Now why would someone do that? Communications are too often the weak link in a team of developers, and one might have misinterpreted the role of nPortNo. In reality, this is quite unlikely in such a straightforward example, but it may happen in a class that contains tens of member attributes.

The CPrinter class designer may help prevent this situation, by *encapsulating* the member variables. Consider this new CPrinter class definition:

```
class CPrinter
{
private:                                  // What follows is private
    char    szFullName[128];
    int     nPortNo;

public:                                   // What follows is public
    CPrinter(char * pszName);
    ~CPrinter();

    void    PrintTestPage();
    void    PrintFile(char * pszFileName);
};
```

By adding the private *access control*, the two member variables that follow are only accessible from the member functions declared within that class. In particular, any other function cannot access those member variables. On the other hand, making all member functions public (as in this example) means that those functions can be called from any other function. Consider the following:

```
CPrinter::CPrinter(char * pszName)
{
    strcpy(szFullName, pszName);        // OK (within a member function)
    nPortNo = GetPortNo(pszName);       // OK (within a member function)
    OpenPortNo(nPortNo);                // OK (within a member function)
}

void PrintSomething()
```

```
{
    CPrinter        MyPrinter("\\\\PrintServer\\laser1");

    MyPrinter.nPortNo = -1;              // ERROR (not a member function)
    MyPrinter.PrintTestPage();           // OK, PrintTestPage() is public
}
```

It is common to declare `private` member variables that shouldn't be modified by code other than member functions. This is so common, in fact, that private is *on* by default in class definitions (until now, we had to add `public` to make them public). Also, member functions that are used internally and that should not be called by other code are also declared `private`. Here is an example of a typical class definition that uses private member variables and functions:

```
class CPrinter
{
    // The following is automatically private by default,
    // and can only be used by any member functions.

    char      szFullName[128];
    int       nPortNo;

public:
    // The following is public i.e. callable from non-member functions.

    CPrinter(char * pszName);
    ~CPrinter();

    void      PrintTestPage();
    void      PrintFile(char * pszFileName);

private:
    // The following is private i.e. callable by member functions only

    int       ConnectToServer(char * pszName);
};
```

This approach is called *encapsulation*, where private member variables and functions are made inaccessible from non-member functions (see Figure A-3). The objective is to expose variables and functions that can be called, but to hide variables and functions that are implementation-related. Should that implementation change (while retaining the same public variables and functions), no code outside the class is impacted. It is very common in OOD/OOP to encapsulate *all* variables (*i.e.*, make all variables private) and only expose a specific set of functions (which may internally use private functions).

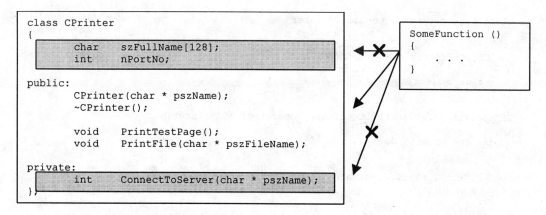

Figure A-3: Encapsulation prevents non-member functions from accessing private member variables and functions (which are shown grayed).

Consider CPrinter; the public member functions are independent of the implementation. Should that implementation change (let's say by writing file names to print in a database and using a database handle instead of a communication port), applications can still use CPrinter as before. On the other hand, making nPortNo public automatically reveals some implementation details; if some applications directly access the variable (and they will, since they can[73]), the implementation cannot be changed without breaking those applications.

Note that encapsulation is an OOD issue; C++ indifferently allows you to make member variables private or public. Again, C++ is a tool that reflects some OOD design.

A.2.5 Inheritance

C++ classes are a significant enhancement over plain old structures. But what if we want to extend an existing class? For instance, CPrinter implements two functions; what if we want to add a new member function, called EjectPage()?

Well, if we own the source code of CPrinter, we can directly make the modification there. But this assumes access to the source code (not always possible if the code resides in a library), and it opens the door to the introduction of bugs (inadvertently). Inheritance is a solution that eliminates both that risk and the need to access the source code.

Consider the CEjectPrinter class, which is *derived* from CPrinter, and can eject a page:

---

[73] That's a supposition, but one that tends to be true in real life.

```
class CEjectPrinter: public CPrinter
{
public:
    CEjectPrinter(char * pszName);

    void    EjectPage();
};

CEjectPrinter::CEjectPrinter(char * pszName) : CPrinter(pszName)
{
    // Not much to do
}

void CEjectPrinter::EjectPage()
{
    .
    .
    .
}
```

This definition means that CEjectPrinter *is a* CPrinter. Everything found in a CPrinter will be found in a CEjectPrinter (see Figure A-4). CEjectPrinter is said to be a *derived class*, whereas CPrinter, in this case, is called a *base class* or a *parent class*.

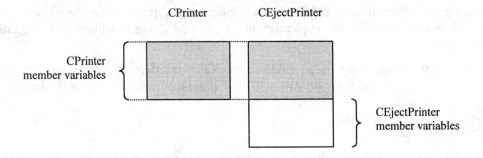

Figure A-4: Inheritance allows a new class (CEjectPrinter) to fully inherit from a base class (CPrinter), while adding its own distinctiveness[74].

Note that CEjectPrinter's constructor accepts a file name, which is simply passed to the parent class' constructor, which will perform as usual.

Deriving a class from an existing class implies that the new class inherits both the member and function variables of the class it is derived from. Consider the following example, a slightly modified version of PrintSomething():

---

[74] Sounds like "We will add your biological and technological distinctiveness to our own. You will be assimilated. Resistance is futile." – The Borg Collective (Star Trek: First Contact).

```
// Let's print something.
void PrintSomething()
{
    CEjectPrinter  MyPrinter("\\\\PrintServer\\laser1");

    MyPrinter.PrintTestPage();          // CPrinter::PrintTestPage()

    // Eject an extra page
    MyPrinter.EjectPage();              // CEjectPrinter::EjectPage()

    MyPrinter.PrintFile("MyFile.txt");  // CPrinter::PrintFile()

    // Eject an extra page
    MyPrinter.EjectPage();              // CEjectPrinter::EjectPage()
}
```

Since `CEjectPrinter` is a `CPrinter`, `CPrinter`'s public member functions can be invoked (`PrintTestPage()` and `PrintFile()`). `CPrinter`'s public member variables could be accessed if there were any. But additionally, `CEjectPrinter`'s public member functions (and variables, if any) can be accessed as well (*i.e.*, `EjectPage()`)

The biggest advantage of this derivation is that `CEjectPage` automatically receives the functionality of a `CPrinter`, without having to duplicate it, and without having to have to access `CPrinter`'s source code (to cut and paste). Furthermore, the code added in the `CEjectPage()` member function is isolated from `CPrinter`'s member functions, reducing the risk of altering `CPrinter`'s implementation[75]. `CPrinter`'s member variables and functions that are private remain private to `CPrinter`, and cannot even be accessed from `CEjectPrinter`. In fact, `CEjectPrinter` can only use public members of `CPrinter`. All in all, `CEjectPrinter` gains the full functionality of `CPrinter` but also extends it by adding an extra function to eject a page. `CPrinter` has been easily and safely reused, even if its source code is not available.

If `CPrinter`'s designers would have liked to make a member function private to non-member functions but public to derived classes, they could have made that function *protected*. Consider the following:

```
class CPrinter
{
    char    szFullName[128];
    int     nPortNo;

public:

    CPrinter(char * pszName);
    ~CPrinter();
```

---

[75] In fact, `CEjectPrinter` would not even be able to alter a fully encapsulated `CPrinter`.

```
        void PrintTestPage();
        void PrintFile(char * pszFileName);

protected:
    // The following is only available to member functions of
    // CPrinter and derived classes.

    int     SendCommand(char * pszCmd);
};

class CEjectPrinter: public CPrinter
{
public:
    CEjectPrinter(char * pszName);
    void EjectPage();
};

void CEjectPrinter::EjectPage()
{
    SendCommand("EJECT");                    // OK (parent's protected)
}

// Let's print something.
void PrintSomething()
{
    CEjectPrinter  MyPrinter("\\\\PrintServer\\laser1");

    MyPrinter.PrintTestPage();
    MyPrinter.PrintFile("MyFile.txt");
    MyPrinter.EjectPage();

    MyPrinter.SendCommand("RESET");          // ERROR (object's protected)
}
```

In this example, CEjectPrinter, being derived from CPrinter(), can use protected functions, as is they were public. On the other hand, PrintSomething() cannot invoke protected functions, as if they were private. Protected methods are useful to implement some functionality that must be made available to derived classes, but not to other functions.

A.2.6. Polymorphism

After reviewing CEjectPrinter, its designer concluded that having to ask developers to invoke EjectPage() all the time was not ideal. After all, developers used to CPrinter simply call PrintTestPage() and PrintFile(), and nothing else. So, that designer decides to make EjectPage() private, and re-implements PrintTestPage() and PrintFile() as follows:

```
class CEjectPrinter: public CPrinter
{
```

```
public:
    CEjectPrinter(char * pszName);

    void    PrintTestPage();
    void    PrintFile(char * pszFileName);

private:
    void    EjectPage();
};

void CEjectPrinter::PrintTestPage()
{
    CPrinter::PrintTestPage();          // Call parent's implementation
    EjectPage();                        // Call private EjectPage()
}

void CEjectPrinter::PrintFile(LPCTSTR pszFileName)
{
    CPrinter::PrintFile(pszFileName);   // Call parent's implementation
    EjectPage();                        // Call private EjectPage()
}

void CEjectPrinter::EjectPage()
{
    SendCommand("EJECT");               // Unchanged
}

void PrintSomething()
{
    CEjectPrinter  MyPrinter("\\\\PrintServer\\laser1");

    MyPrinter.PrintTestPage();          // Will print and eject.
    MyPrinter.PrintFile("MyFile.txt");  // Will print and eject.
}
```

Before going any further, note the syntax to invoke the parent's implementation, in `PrintTestPage()` and `PrintFile()`. Not prefixing the parent's methods by the parent class name would result in a recursive invocation (*i.e.*, a function calling itself), eventually leading to a crash.

With this modification, the class is easier to use, since developers familiar with `CPrinter` can now use `CEjectPrinter` the exact same way. This is certainly an improved design over the previous implementation.

However, there is that function out there, called `TestPrinter()`. This function has been written a long time ago as follows, and can be called to test a `CPrinter` object:

```
void TestPrinter(CPrinter * pPrinter)
{
    pPrinter->PrintTestPage();
    pPrinter->PrintFile("TestFile.txt");
}
```

729

If a `CPrinter` object is passed to `TestPrinter()`, `CPrinter::PrintTest Page()` and `CPrinter::PrintFile()` are invoked on behalf of that object. Fine so far. But because `CEjectPrinter` *is a* `CPrinter`, it is perfectly legitimate to invoke `TestPrinter()` with a `CEjectPrinter` object, as follows:

```
void TestAllPrinters()
{
    CPrinter        Printer1("\\\\PrintServer\\laser1");
    CEjectPrinter   Printer2("\\\\PrintServer\\laser2");

    TestPrinter(&Printer1);              // OK
    TestPrinter(&Printer2);              // OK
}
```

From within `TestPrinter()`, `pPrinter` is indeed a pointer to a `CPrinter` (see Figure A-5), whether it has been called with a `CPrinter` or a `CEjectPrinter` object.

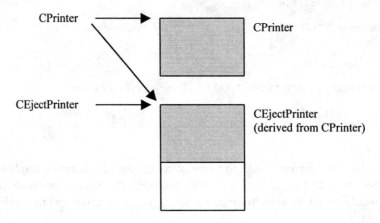

Figure A-5: A `CEjectPrinter` being a `CPrinter`, it can be referenced by either a (`CPrinter *`) pointer, or a (`CEjectPrinter *`) pointer. On the other hand, a `CPrinter` object can only be referenced by a (`CPrinter *`) pointer.

But invoking `TestPrinter()` with a `CEjectPrinter` object will invoke the same methods: `CPrinter::PrintTestPage()` and `CPrinter::PrintFile()`, because all `TestPrinter()` knows about the object is that it is a `CPrinter` (no other assumption is made). But ideally, `TestPrinter()` should invoke `CEjectPrinter::PrintTest Page()` and `CEjectPrinter::PrintFile()` when a `CEjectPrinter` object pointer is passed. Polymorphism and virtual methods solve that problem. Consider this new implementation of `CPrinter`:

```
class CPrinter
{
    char    szFullName[128];
    int     nPortNo;

public:

    CPrinter(char * pszName);
    ~CPrinter();

    virtual void PrintTestPage();
    virtual void PrintFile(char * pszFileName);

protected:

    int     SendCommand(char * pszCmd);
};
```

By adding the keyword `virtual` to a member function, any reference to that function later on is done by looking up in a table in order to identify the exact function to call.

First it is important to know that once a function is declared virtual, the same function in all derived classes is automatically virtual as well. For instance, the same functions in `CEjectPrinter` are virtual, even if the keyword virtual is not shown as such in the `CEjectPrinter`'s class definition:

```
class CEjectPrinter: public CPrinter
{
public:
    CEjectPrinter(char * pszName);

    void    PrintTestPage();              // virtual, even if not specified
    void    PrintFile(char * pszFileName);// virtual, even if not specified

private:
    void    EjectPage();
};
```

Back to `TestPrinter()`. Because `PrintTestPage()` and `PrintFile()` in `CPrinter` are known to be virtual, the compiler will generate enough code to determine the exact type of the object and invoke the proper functions.

Hence, invoking `TestPrinter()` with a `CPrinter` object results in the invocation of `CPrinter::PrintTestPage()` and `CPrinter::PrintFile()`; however, passing a `CEjectPrinter` object instead results in calling `CEjectPrinter::PrintTestPage()` and `CEjectPrinter::PrintFile()` (see Figure A-6). Using a pointer to an object and calling different methods depending on the real object pointed to is called *polymorphism*. `TestPrinter()` will work with any `CPrinter`-derived class, and will always invoke the proper functions, even for classes created way after `TestPrinter()` has been compiled[76]! That is an extremely powerful feature that allows legacy code (*e.g.*, `TestPrinter()`) to work with newer code (a new `CPrinter`-derived class).

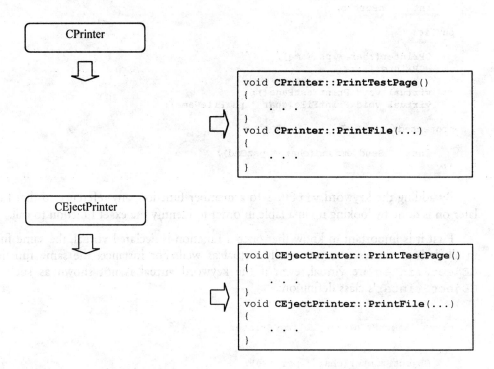

Figure A-6: Polymorphic methods (virtual member functions) can be invoked upon different classes derived from a base class. In this example, passing a `CPrinter` or a `CEjectPrinter` object to `TestPrinter()` results in different functions being invoked.

A.2.7 Polymorphism and Function Tables

It seems almost magical that methods are called based on the exact nature of an object. The implementation is quite simple though, and relies on function tables.

In a class definition, whenever one or more functions are declared virtual, the compiler generates a function table (sometimes called *vtbl*, for virtual function table) for that class. That table contains the address of the class' virtual functions, and maintains one hidden

---

[76] As long as `TestPrinter()` has been compiled using a `CPrinter` class definition containing virtual functions.

pointer in the class to that table (see Figure A-7). This pointer is usually the very first member variable of the class (although it is hidden to programmers), but compiler designers may make it the last if they want (or any position for that matter). At any point in time, there is one and only one function table for a given class, but there might be zero, one or many instances of that class, all referring to the same table.

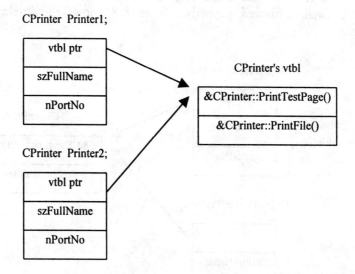

Figure A-7: Each instance of a CPrinter class contains a member that points to an unique *vtbl*, which contains the address of CPrinter's virtual functions.

Whenever a virtual function is invoked from an object, the compiler generates an indirect call to the function table. The following call:

```
pPrinter->PrintTestPage();
```

becomes on an x86 (using Visual C++ 6.0, non-optimized code):

```
mov    eax, DWORD PTR _pPrinter$[ebp]    ; eax <- pPrinter
mov    edx, DWORD PTR [eax]              ; edx <- pPrinter's &vtbl[0]
mov    ecx, DWORD PTR _pPrinter$[ebp]    ; ecx <- pPrinter (i.e. this)
call   DWORD PTR [edx]                   ; vtbl[0] function call
```

This implementation makes the *vtbl* pointer the very first member of the class (second line), and passes the object via a register (third line). If CPrinter::PrintTestPage() was not virtual, the code would be as follows:

```
mov    ecx, DWORD PTR _pPrinter$[ebp]      ; ecx <- pPrinter (i.e. this)
call   CPrinter::PrintTestPage             ; direct invocation
```

One can see that using a virtual function adds an indirection, which results in a few extra assembly language instructions[77].

A class derived from a class containing virtual methods will automatically have a function table as well, initialized properly. Figure A-8 shows the implementation of CEjectPrinter.

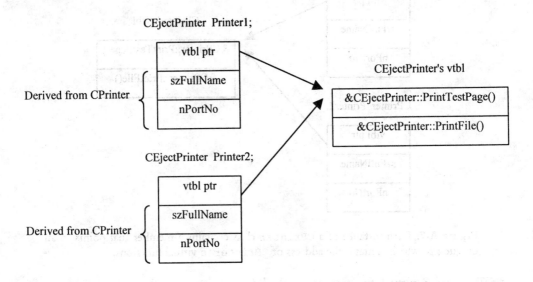

Figure A-8: CEjectPrinter objects also have a pointer to a unique CEjectPrinter function table, in addition to the member variables inherited from CPrinter.

Note that the *vtbl* pointer is at the same location (*i.e.*, first member variable) than in CPrinter. Hence, the same indirect call, when pPrinter refers to a CEjectPrinter object, results in the CEjectPrinter's *vtbl* being referred to, resulting in a call to CEjectPrinter::PrintTestPage(), not CPrinter::PrintTestPage().

Polymorphism is a very powerful feature, but it leads to the following question: what member functions should be made virtual when designing a particular class? Again, this is a design issue: the designer must imagine how developers will use the class, and what methods

---

[77] Some people have rejected C++ (and remained faithful to C) because of that overhead. I personally believe that if performance is such an issue, those people should directly code in assembly language. I consider this overhead completely negligible, given the immense benefit of virtual functions.

might have to be re-implemented in derived classes. OOD and OOP being iterative activities, it is common for non-virtual methods to eventually become virtual. In the meantime, a rule of thumb is to make methods virtual when in doubt.

A.2.8 Multiple Inheritance

A class may be derived not only from one class as we've seen so far, but from multiple classes. Consider the following class, CDonePrinter, which is a printer that notifies the user when the printing is done:

```
class CWindow
{
    .
    .
    .
    void    DisplayMessage(char * pszFormat, ...);
};

class CDonePrinter: public CPrinter, public CWindow
{
public:
    void    PrintTestPage();
    void    PrintFile(char * pszFileName);
};

void CDonePrinter::PrintTestPage()
{
    CPrinter::PrintTestPage();
    DisplayMessage("The test page has been printed");
}

void CDonePrinter::PrintFile(char * pszFileName)
{
    CPrinter::PrintFile(pszFileName);
    DisplayMessage("The file '%s' has been printed", pszFileName);
}
```

In this example, CWindow is a class that implements DisplayMessage(), a method that displays a window containing a string. CDonePrinter is derived from both CPrinter and CWindow (see Figure A-9) and uses methods from both classes.

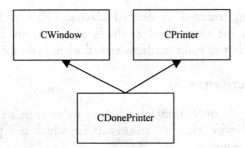

Figure A-9: CDonePrinter is a class that inherits from CWindow and CPrinter. This is a case of multiple inheritance, where CDonePrinter is *both* a CWindow *and* a CPrinter.

A.2.9 Other Important Class Features

There are other important concepts related to classes, reviewed here briefly:

- An *abstract class* provides an interface without exposing any implementation details. A class is abstract when it contains one or more *pure* virtual functions (using the initializer "= 0"). The following example shows CBasePrinter as an abstract class, and CPrinter, derived from it.

```
class CBasePrinter
{
public:
    virtual void PrintTestPage() = 0;                    // Pure virtual
    virtual void PrintFile(char * pszFileName) = 0;      // Pure virtual
};

class CPrinter: public CBasePrinter
{
    .
    .
    .

public:

    CPrinter();
    ~CPrinter();

    void PrintTestPage();                                // Implemented
    void PrintFile(char * pszFileName);                  // Implemented
};

void main()
{
    CBasePrinter    MyPrinter1;                           // Error
    CPrinter        MyPrinter2;                           // OK
}
```

Being abstract, CBasePrinter can never be instantiated. A class derived from it can be instantiated only if it implements *all* CBasePrinter's pure methods. Because CPrinter define those methods as non-pure, CPrinter can be instantiated.

- In a case of multiple inheritance, where multiple base classes are derived from another base class, this base class is replicated (see Figure A-10-a). This base class can be set as a *virtual base class* (by deriving classes from it using public virtual BaseClass), in which case it is not replicated (see Figure A-10-b).

A.3   OTHER C++ FEATURES

C++ includes numerous features that makes it a preferred language over C.

A.3.1   Variable Declarations

Local variables can be declared anywhere, not only at the beginning of a block of code (after the open curly brace). Consider the following:

```
void TestAllPrinters()
{
    CPrinter              Printer1("\\\\PrintServer\\laser1");
    TestPrinter(&Printer1);

    CEjectPrinter  Printer2("\\\\PrintServer\\laser2");
    TestPrinter(&Printer2);
}
```

In this case, Printer2 is declared in the middle of the function, closer to where it is being used. This often eases the reading of complex functions, by declaring variables when they are truly needed.

Variables can also be declared in statements, and used afterward:

```
void PrintArrayOfFiles(char ** ppFiles, int nCount)
{
    printf("Printing %d files\n", nCount);

    CEjectPrinter  Printer("\\\\PrintServer\\laser1");

    for (int i = 0; i < nCount; i++)
            Printer.PrintFile(ppFiles[i]);

    // i can be used from now on like any other local variable.

    if ((CPrinter * pDefaultPrinter = GetDefaultPrinter()) == NULL)
            pDefaultPrinter = &Printer;

    // pDefaultPrinter can also be used here.
    .
    .
    .
}
```

(a)

```
class CBaseObject
{
    ...
};

class CWindow: public CBaseObject
{
    ...
};

class CPrinter: public CBaseObject
{
    ...
};

class CDonePrinter: public CWindow,
                    public CPrinter
{
    ...
};
```

(b)

```
class CBaseObject
{
    ...
};

class CWindow: public virtual CBaseObject
{
    ...
};

class CPrinter: public virtual CBaseObject
{
    ...
};

class CDonePrinter: public CWindow,
                    public CPrinter
{
    ...
};
```

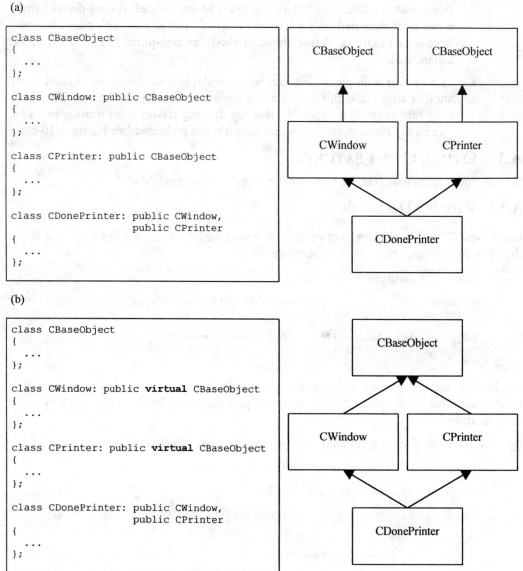

Figure A-10: Both CWindow and CPrinter are derived from some base class called CBaseObject. In (a), CBaseObject is replicated twice in CDonePrinter. In (b), when using CBaseObject as a virtual base class, CBaseObject exists once in CDonePrinter.

A.3.2 References

Every C programmer at some point has wished to get rid of the pointers, this infamous source of countless bugs. Newcomers to C find greater satisfaction in understanding pointers than finding answers to the meaning of life ...

C++ answered the call and introduces references, which are synonymous for variables. Consider the following:

```
CEjectPrinter  MyPrinter("\\\\PrintServer\\laser1");
CEjectPrinter& ThePrinter = MyPrinter;          // Reference to MyPrinter
```

From a compiler standpoint, `ThePrinter` is a synonym for `MyPrinter`. There is only one variable (`MyPrinter`), and using `ThePrinter` is just like using `MyPrinter`. References are mostly used when passing arguments to functions. Consider this new implementation of `TestPrinter()` and `TestAllPrinters()`:

```
void TestPrinter(CPrinter& Printer)
{
    Printer.PrintTestPage();
    Printer.PrintFile("TestFile.txt");
}

void TestAllPrinters()
{
    CPrinter        Printer1("\\\\PrintServer\\laser1");
    TestPrinter(Printer1);

    CEjectPrinter  Printer2("\\\\PrintServer\\laser2");
    TestPrinter(Printer2);
}
```

This apparently passes `CPrinter` objects by value (instead of by address). At least, that's what the syntax suggests (albeit the "`!&`"). Internally, one can think of references as being pointers[78], making this implementation the equivalent of the previous pointer-based version. Parameters passed via references are often passed by address (not by value) internally, but they are coded using a value-like syntax, instead of pointers. Whichever the implementation, a reference is not a variable in itself, but a reference to another existing variable. Code is easier to write and performance is maintained.

References can also be returned by functions, such as shown below:

```
// Global variables
CPrinter    Printer1("\\\\PrintServer\\laser1");
```

---

[78] Although remember that references cannot be manipulated as pointers.

```
CPrinter      Printer2("\\\\PrintServer\\laser2");
CPrinter      Printer3("\\\\PrintServer\\laser3");

/// Return a reference to a printer (a global variable in fact),
//  based on the desired location.
CPrinter& ChoosePrinter(int nLocation)
{
    switch (nLocation)
    {
    case BUILDING_A:
            return Printer1;

    case BUILDING_B:
            return Printer2;

    default:
            return Printer3;
    }
}

void DoSomething()
{
    // Obtain a reference to a printer, based on BUILDING_A location.
    // Printer is not a new object, but solely a reference to either
    // Printer1, Printer2 or Printer3, declared globally.
    CPrinter&     Printer = ChoosePrinter(BUILDING_A);
    Printer.PrintTestPage();
}
```

There are a few traps, though:

- Do not forget the "&" in the parameter list, otherwise, you end up creating a local new object. In the following example, the "&" has been omitted; as a result, `Printer` is a new object, a copy of what has been passed as an argument:

```
void TestPrinter(CPrinter Printer)          // This creates a new object
{
    Printer.PrintTestPage();
    Printer.PrintFile("TestFile.txt");
}
```

- Do not return a reference to a local variable. The following code returns a reference to an object that no longer exists when the call terminates. This is a sure bug and most compilers will emit a warning.

```
CPrinter& ChoosePrinter(int nLocation)
{
    CPrinter      Printer1("\\\\PrintServer\\laser1");
    CPrinter      Printer2("\\\\PrintServer\\laser2");
    CPrinter      Printer3("\\\\PrintServer\\laser3");
```

```
    switch (nLocation)
    {
    case BUILDING_A:
            return Printer1;                    // That's a no-no.

    case BUILDING_B:
            return Printer2;                    // No-no-no

    default:
            return Printer3;                    // No-no-no-no
    }
}
```

A.3.3 Function and Operator Overloading

Most developers have run into the situation where a function is invoked with a different set of parameters. In the next example, three functions perform the same operations, but on different types:

```
void Print_Number(int nNumber);              // Print a number
void Print_Real(float fReal);                // Print a real
void Print_String(LPCTSTR pszString);        // Print a string
```

C++ allows reusing the same function name, as long as the parameter list differs. This is call *function overloading*. Hence, the following example is valid:

```
void Print(int nNumber);
void Print(float fReal);                      // Fine in C++
void Print(LPCTSTR pszString);               // Fine in C++
viod Print(intnNumber, float fReal);         // Fine in C++
```

When invoking Print(), the compiler will choose the appropriate function, promoting (*i.e.*, casting) types as necessary, if possible. If no function can be matched, the compiler rejects the call as ambiguous.

Note that functions cannot only differ by their return type; they must differ by their parameter list. Hence, the following is incorrect:

```
void Print(int nNumber);
int Print(int nNumber);                       // Error: already defined
```

Operators can also be overloaded. Consider the "<<" operator (bitwise logical left shift). It can elegantly be used as an "I/O" operator with the CPrinter class to send a file to a CPrinter, instead of calling PrintFile():

```
class CPrinter
{
    .
    .

    .
    void    PrintFile(char * pszFileName);
    void    operator<<(char * pszFileName);        // Overloading <<
    .

    .
    .
};

// Define the << operator as a call to PrintFile().
void CPrinter::operator<<(char * pszFileName)
{
    PrintFile(pszFileName);
}

void PrintSomething()
{
    CPrinter        MyPrinter("\\\\PrintServer\\laser1");

    MyPrinter.PrintFile("MyFile1.txt");    // Print a file

    MyPrinter << "MyFile2.txt";            // Print another file
}
```

A.3.4 New Cast Operators

Casting is a simple fact of life for C programmers, to explicitly convert one type to another. However, casting is often overused and a common source of errors. C++ introduces new casting operators that are easier to spot in source code, and that are more specialized (they don't radically substitute one type for another one, even completely unrelated, as it is in C). Although C-style casting still works, it is recommended to use the following C++ cast operators:

- The `static_cast` operator casts related types, such as a void pointer to a non-void one, or from an `int` to `float`. For instance:

```
int     i = 5;

float   f1 = i;                            // warning
float   f2 = static_cast<float>(i);        // ok

char * p1 = malloc(10);                    // error
char * p2 = static_cast<char *>(malloc(10));   // ok
```

- The `reinterpret_cast` operator performs a bit-copy and does not check for type compatibility. This is the most risky C++ cast operator. For instance:

```
unsigned        uAddr = 0xffff0000;
void *          p1 = uAddr;                      // error
void *          p2 = reinterpret_cast<void *>(uAddr); // ok
```

- The `dynamic_cast` operator allows navigating within a hierarchy by accessing a parent class, a derived class, or sibling class in a case of multiple inheritance. This operator is based on some compiler-generated run-time type information (RTTI) and may require special compiler options and libraries [79]. Here's an example, to be used with the example shown in Section A.2.8.

```
void TestIfPrinter(CWindow * pWindow)
{
    if (CPrinter * p = dynamic_cast<CPrinter *>(pWindow))
        p->PrintTestPage();
}
```

- The `const_cast` operator throws away the `const` qualifier. This is required when a constant variable is passed as an argument to a function that requires a non-constant value (assuming that the function is not going to alter the variable). For instance:

```
void ResetPrinter(const CPrinter * pPrinter)
{
    CPrinter * p = const_cast<CPrinter *>(pPrinter);

    p->ResetPrinter();              // ok, even if it is a non-const function
}
```

A.3.5 And There's Much More

The ultimate reference is the book from the C++ author, listed in the Suggested Reading section. The book contains more than 900 pages, so there is obviously a lot of material to cover. Here are a few other features that may require your attention:

- Namespaces
- Exceptions
- Templates
- Streams
- And more

---

[79] That's the case with Visual C++ 5.0. However, VCCE 5.0 does not provide libraries to support RTTI for Windows CE applications.

A.3.6 And What About Structures?

Early in this appendix, I quickly dismissed structures and plunged right into classes. But it turns out that structures have been significantly enhanced in C++. In fact, a structure is exactly the same as a class, except that by default, a structure makes its members public, whereas a class makes them private. Hence, structures can have member functions, can be derived from other structures (even from classes and vice-versa!), virtual functions can be used, and so on.

There are two schools of thoughts regarding structures. Some simply suggest never to use them anymore, since using classes *is* the way to go. Others suggest to use structures as they are in C: plain data structures that contain a set of public member variables (but no member functions or private members). The latter approach has been retained on Windows (for backward compatibility with C applications).

But it's really your own call whether you fully exploit structures or not when designing applications. My recommendation? Use them in a way you feel comfortable. Personally, on Windows, I use structures as they are implemented in C.

SUGGESTED READINGS

Stroustrup, The C++ Programming Language

> This is the ultimate source regarding C++, written by its very own creator. Complete and accurate, you'll find answers to all your questions, but it requires all your attention when reading it. It contains the exact syntax of the language, for those interested (compiler designers, etc.). It stays away from the implementation of commercial compilers, forcing the reader to stick with the standard.

Appendix B

An Overview of COM for C++ Programmers

Most Windows CE developers can write awesome applications without worrying about COM, Microsoft's Common Object Model. However, it is increasingly becoming difficult to avoid it. For instance, Windows CE Services notifications are COM-based. COM is in fact the result of some intensive design work at Microsoft, and is clearly the development path ahead. This appendix demystifies COM by describing what it is and what it looks like from a programming standpoint.

The description that follows assumes some familiarity with C++ classes and multiple inheritance. Not that COM strictly requires it (COM can be used in many programming languages), but COM is clearly a natural extension to C++, retrofit to work with other programming languages. For that reason, I chose to explain COM using a pragmatic C++ approach, instead of using some abstract (*i.e.,* vague and mysterious) concepts.

B.1. THE COMMON OBJECT MODEL (COM)

Let's say that a co-worker of yours implements a C++ class and that he/she gives you the corresponding header (.h) and library (.lib) files. That's all you need to use it: you simply have to look the class definition to identify what methods are available, their parameters, and the value they return. From a syntax standpoint, you simply rely on what C++ has to offer (*i.e.,* some C++ function calls) to invoke those methods. Because your co-worker did not provide an HTML help file, you might have to ask him/her one or two questions, but that's about it. You link the library to your application and *voilà*! Well, that is true if you are programming in C++ too...

But let's say you are using Visual J++ to write your application. The library that implements the class might still be useful, but the header file is not at all, because it is not written in Java. Furthermore, sharing objects between the two languages is not natively supported on either side[80]. Bottom line: your coworker's C++ object is useless in that case.

The problem is neither the Visual Basic application or the C++ class; it's the interface between both. In that case, the major issue is that the programming languages don't match.

Even if you were to use C++, you could run into another important issue: name mangling incompatibility. Say your coworker is using Visual C++, but you are using Borland C++. Each compiler decorates function calls (a method such `CPicture::DrawCircle` becomes `?DrawCircle@CPicture@@UAGJXZ` in Visual C++), but they do it in their own way, *i.e.*, in a way that is incompatible with other compilers[81]. Given a function call, your compiler will generate some decorated name, whereas your coworker's library contains the same functions, but decorated differently. The result? Link errors. The only solution is to share the source code, but this is not possible when the code is written by a software vendor that wants to make a buck.

And that's not all. Say your coworker and you decide to work in C (say *adiós* to the name decoration problem). Then you really have to study the header file carefully, to determine how the object is implemented. Some objects could be implemented as structures whereas others as function tables. The point is that there is no uniform object representation in C (nor in many other languages). Hence, there can still be some incompatibility between your code and your coworker's library.

To make things worse, imagine that you don't know *who* wrote the header file and library. Hence, you're on your own if you don't understand the implementation...

To summarize, without some specifications regarding how to write and implement objects, it is impossible to develop components that can be used in various programming languages or compilers.

The Common Object model (or COM) is a specification to write reusable components in various programming languages. By following that specification, a Visual C++ programmer can write a component (an object) that can be used in another C++ application, but also in a C or Visual Basic application as well[82].

The key to this interoperability is based on *interfaces* and *components*. Interfaces define formal sets of functions, whereas components implement one or many of those interfaces in some programming language. Applications, written in any language that supports COM, then simply access components via the interfaces they implement.

---

[80] Although Java directly supports calls to C functions, which could provide indirect access to C++ objects.

[81] Method decoration is not part of the C++ standard, so compiler vendors can do what they want.

[82] Maniacs can even use COM objects in assembly language!

A word of caution, though. COM solves all the problems mentioned above and is a powerful technology; however, many developers feel overwhelmed by it. But like anything else, taking one chunk at a time is usually the best way to get to the end.

B.1.1   Interfaces

An interface is the specification (or the definition) of a set of related functions, where each function is described by its returned value, function name, and parameters. For instance, the Shape interface may define a set of functions to draw shapes (circles, squares, etc.) Quite importantly, an interface doesn't dictate anything regarding the implementation; it just describes some functionality.

Interestingly enough, interfaces do not have version numbers, therefore eliminating any problem related to version incompatibility. Extending an interface (by adding new functions for instance) results in a totally new, unrelated interface with its own name and IID (more on this later).

Interface Definition

Since interfaces are to be used in any language, Microsoft provides a new language to define interfaces. This language is called the Interface Description Language (IDL), and is based on the Open Software Foundation (OSF) Distributed Computing Environment (DCE) specification that defines remote procedure calls. This language contains extensions that are COM-specific (to support distributed objects).

The next example (IShape.idl) illustrates the IShape interface, which is derived from IUnknown (more on this interface soon) and two methods: DrawCircle() and DrawSquare().

```
// IShape.idl

[
    object,
    uuid(5ee7dcb0-c6bd-11d2-a7ad-00104b22d0c6),
    helpstring("IShape Interface"),
    pointer_default(unique)
]

interface IShape: IUnknown
{
    import "unknwn.idl" ;

    HRESULT DrawCircle([in] int l, [in] int t, [in] int r, [in] int b);
    HRESULT DrawSquare([in] int l, [in] int t, [in] int r, [in] int b);
};
```

This file can be fed to an IDL compiler, which outputs source files in the proper language. For instance, Visual C++ contains `Midl.exe`, which produces some header and implementation files, which can be used in C/C++ applications.

Note that you may directly write your interface in your favorite programming language, bypassing the IDL process. This is fine as long as the object is used with that language only. Should the object be used in another language, then an IDL definition is likely to be required to generate the proper definitions for that other language.

Interface Binary Standard

Regardless of the programming language, an interface must be implemented according to some very specific rules, called the interface binary standard. Those implementation rules are really what makes COM a usable technology.

Here are some of those rules, depicted in Figure B-1.

- Interfaces are accessed via pointer (they are not instantiated, whereas components can).

- Functions within an interface must be implemented using a function table, *i.e.*, an array of function pointers. This table is usually called *vtbl* (for virtual function table).

- Each function has an associated calling convention. On a given platform, it is usually the same for all functions, but it can vary if required.

- Each function of the interface must be called by passing, as the last parameter, a pointer to this object instance itself (the equivalent of `this` in C++). This pointer points to the object itself, which is composed of a *vtbl* pointer, followed by the object variables.

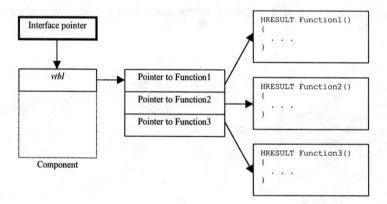

Figure B-1: The COM interface binary standard specifies that an interface is referred to via a pointer, which points to another pointer (within a component, in fact) that references a function table. Each entry in that table references the actual function implementation.

Experienced C++ programmers are probably very familiar with this model. Compiler vendors for other languages are required to adopt the same rules in order to support COM, making it possible to share objects independently of the underlying programming language.

Interface Identifiers

Interfaces are identified by a name in applications. By convention, interface names start with an "I", *e.g.*, IShape (in contrast, component definitions start with "C", *e.g.*, CPicture). Since the name is meaningful with the current compiler (not across compilers or languages), a 128-bit Globally Unique IDentifier (GUID) is also associated with each interface. When used with an interface, this identifier is called an IID (interface identifier). The IID is listed in the IDL file (see7dcb0-c6bd-11d2-a7ad-00104b22d0c6 in the above example).

There is one important constraint about GUIDs: they must be unique in the universe! To obtain such a unique GUIDs, developers typically rely on some development tools. For instance, Visual C++ provides Uuidgen.exe, which generates such a unique number. The next example demonstrates the use of Uuidgen.exe to generate a 128-bit unique GUIDs.

```
E:\>uuidgen
5ee7dcb0-c6bd-11d2-a7ad-00104b22d0c6

E:\>uuidgen
161576b0-c6be-11d2-a7ad-00104b22d0c6
```

C++ Representation

In C++, an interface is represented by an abstract base class, where each function part of the interface is declared as pure virtual (*i.e.*, = 0). However, in C, an interface is a structure containing a pointer to a table containing function pointers. The common denominator is that a function table is present (it is automatically generated in C++ when a class implements virtual functions), as required by COM.

B.1.2 Components

A component is an instantiation of a data structure that implements one or more interfaces. Unlike interfaces, it can (and usually does) contain member variables.

Interface and Component Representation

An interface is represented as a "plug-in jack" on either the left or right side of a component, itself represented by a square. The name of the interface is often written next to the jack.

The `IUnknown` interface, when implemented in itself, is represented on top of the object (see Figure B-2).

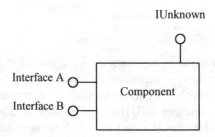

Figure B-2: COM representation of a component and the supported interfaces.

Using Interfaces

Given a component, an application must query a pointer to a supported interface. COM specifies that each component must implement `QueryInterface()`, which returns a valid pointer if the interface is supported or `NULL` otherwise. Applications typically know ahead what interface they intend to use, and hence query specific ones. An interface is queried using its 128-bit GUID.

Components that implement multiple interfaces return a distinct pointer per interface. That pointer is then referenced to invoke functions, defined by the interface, but implemented by the component.

Component Implementation

All COM objects must implement the `IUnknown` interface, which provides two types of services:

- Querying interfaces within the object, using `QueryInterface()`.
- Maintaining a reference counter, using `AddRef()` and `Release()`. Since a single object can be referenced by multiple clients, a reference count must be maintained to support a dynamic de-allocation. Whenever a client gets access to an object, the reference count is incremented; whenever the clients no longer needs to access the object, the reference count is decrements. When the count reaches zero, the object can be deleted since no one is referencing it.

B.1.3 An Implementation Example

To conclude this COM overview, here is the implementation of two interfaces and one component. IShape is an interface to draw shapes (circle, squares, etc.). ICanvas is also an interface, to create a visible area, paint it, and eventually destroy it. These two interfaces are implemented in one object called CPicture.

The example is kept as simple as possible; non-essential details (such as drawing shapes) have been deliberately omitted for brevity.

COM Component Representation

From a COM standpoint, all these definitions yield to one component, CPicture, which implements two interfaces, IShape and ICanvas. The representation of that component is shown on Figure B-3.

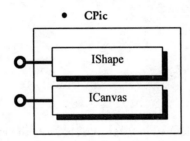

Figure B-3: The CPicture COM component.

Source Code

The IShape interface is defined using the IDL language, in IShape.idl. The MIDL compiler generates IShape.h (the class definition) and IShape_i.c (the IID declaration), which are not shown.

```
// IShape.idl - Definition of the IShape interface.
// This file must be compiled using MIDL.EXE.

[
    object,
    uuid(5ee7dcb0-c6bd-11d2-a7ad-00104b22d0c6),
    helpstring("IShape Interface"),
    pointer_default(unique)
]
```

```
interface IShape: IUnknown
{
    import "unknwn.idl" ;

    HRESULT DrawCircle([in] int l, [in] int t, [in] int r, [in] int b);
    HRESULT DrawSquare([in] int l, [in] int t, [in] int r, [in] int b);
};
```

Similarly, the `IShape` interface is defined using IDL, in `IShape.idl`:

```
// ICanvas.idl - Definition of the ICanvas interface.
// This file must be compiled using MIDL.EXE.

[
    object,
    uuid(161576b0-c6be-11d2-a7ad-00104b22d0c6),
    helpstring("ICanvas Interface"),
    pointer_default(unique)
]

interface ICanvas: IUnknown
{
    import "unknwn.idl" ;

    HRESULT CreateCanvas();
    HRESULT PaintCanvas();
    HRESULT DestroyCanvas();
};
```

The `CPicture` component is defined in `Picture.h`. Note the inclusion of `IShape.h` and `ICanvas.h`, both generated by the MIDL compiler:

```
// Picture.h - Definition of the CPicture component.

#include <objbase.h>

#include "IShape.h"                    // Generated from IShape.idl
#include "ICanvas.h"                   // Generated from ICanvas.idl

class CPicture: public IShape, public ICanvas
{
    HANDLE          m_hCancas;         // Some attributes
    int             m_cx,m_cy;
    LONG            m_nRef;            // Reference count

public:

    CPicture();
    ~CPicture();

    // IUnknown interface implementation
    virtual HRESULT __stdcall QueryInterface(const IID &,void **);
```

```
    virtual ULONG      stdcall AddRef();
    virtual ULONG    __stdcall Release();

    // IShape interface implementation
    virtual HRESULT __stdcall DrawCircle(int l, int t, int r, int b);
    virtual HRESULT __stdcall DrawSquare(int l, int t, int r, int b);

    // ICanvas interface implementation
    virtual HRESULT __stdcall CreateCanvas();
    virtual HRESULT __stdcall PaintCanvas();
    virtual HRESULT __stdcall DestroyCanvas();
};
```

Finally, the component itself is implemented in Picture.cpp. That's where the interfaces are implemented, too:

- The three IUnknown methods: QueryInterface(), AddRef(), and Release();

- The IShape methods: DrawCircle() and DrawSquare();

- The ICanvas methods: CreateCanvas(), PaintCanvas(), and Destroy Canvas().

```
// Picture.cpp - Implementation of the CPicture component

#include "Picture.h"

CPicture::CPicture()
{
    m_hCancas = NULL;
    m_cx = m_cy = 0;
    m_nRef = 0;
}

CPicture::~CPicture()
{
}

HRESULT __stdcall CPicture::QueryInterface(const IID& iid,void ** ppv)
{
    if (iid == IID_IUnknown)
    {
        *ppv = static_cast<IShape *>(this);
    }
    else if (iid == IID_IShape)
    {
        *ppv = static_cast<IShape *>(this);
    }
    else if (iid == IID_ICanvas)
    {
        *ppv = static_cast<ICanvas *>(this);
    }
    else
    {
        *ppv = NULL;
```

```
               return E NOINTERFACE;
    }

    static_cast<IUnknown *>(*ppv)->AddRef();
    return S_OK;
}

ULONG __stdcall CPicture::AddRef()
{
    return InterlockedIncrement(&m_nRef);
}

ULONG __stdcall CPicture::Release()
{
    if (InterlockedDecrement(&m_nRef) == 0)
    {
            delete this;
            return 0;
    }

    return m_nRef;
}

HRESULT __stdcall CPicture::DrawCircle(int l, int t, int r, int b)
{
    .
    .

    .
    return S_OK;
}

// Other CPicture methods follow
.
.
.
```

C++ Class Representation

From a C++ standpoint (that is, when putting COM aside), these classes form the hierarchy shown in Figure B-4.

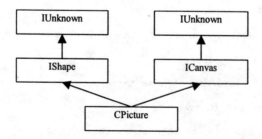

Figure B-4: The C++ class hierarchy. Note that in this case of multiple inheritance, IUnknown, found in each interface, is not a virtual base class.

C++ Memory Representation

The hierarchy shown above relies on two function tables, one for `IShape` within `CPicture`, and one for `ICanvas` within `CPicture`. Any instance of `CPicture` contains two pointers (one for each table), and the attributes (member variables). Figure B-6 shows two instances of `CPicture` (Picture1 and Picture2), both referring to the function tables generated by the compiler.

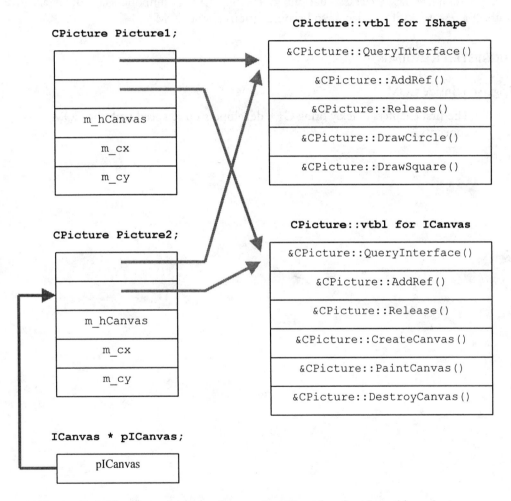

Figure B-6: The C++ classes implementation. Note that function tables exist once, and they are referred to by each instance of `CPicture` (`Picture1` and `Picture2`) An interface pointer (`pIShape`) points to an entry within a component, which would be referring the related *vtbl*.

B.1.4 Other Features

The COM specification goes much further than components interfaces, although those are the key concepts. There are other topics, such as object factories, component containment and aggregation, servers, Automation, and more. DCOM (Distributed COM) allows accessing remote objects (*i.e.*, objects on remote computers) transparently (through some Remote Procedure Calls). Finally, Microsoft provides ATL (Active Template Library), a set of C++ template-based classes that allows creating COM components. All in all, give yourself a few weeks if you decide to become serious about COM.

SUGGESTED READINGS

Rogerson, Inside COM

> The first chapters quickly bring C++ developers up to speed with the COM concepts.

Appendix C

Window and Control Styles

The following sections describe the window and control styles supported by Windows CE. These styles can be specified upon creating a window by calling `CWnd::Create()` or they can be enabled/disabled by calling `CWnd::ModifyStyle()`.

Extended styles are also shown (*e.g.*, `WS_EX_xxx`). Those styles can be specified by calling `CWnd::CreateEx()` or `CWnd::ModifyStyleEx()`.

C.1   WINDOW STYLES

The following sections describe the styles of basic windows, non-client areas, and message boxes.

C.1.1 Basic Window Styles

Basic Window Style	Description
WS_CHILD	Specifies a child window (such as a control). `CWnd::Create()` always adds that style.
WS_POPUP	Specifies a pop-up window.
WS_VISIBLE	Specifies a window that is initially visible. If this style is not specified, the window is not visible.
WS_DISABLED	Specifies a window that is initially disabled. A disabled window doesn't receive input from the user.
WS_CLIPCHILDREN	Excludes the area occupied by child windows when drawing in a parent window. Windows CE windows always have the `WS_CLIPCHILDREN` style.
WS_CLIPSIBLINGS	Excludes the area occupied by sibling windows above a window.
WS_GROUP	Specifies the first control of a group of controls. This style is primarily used with radio buttons.
WS_TABSTOP	Specifies a control that can receive the keyboard focus when the user presses the TAB key. All controls in a dialog box should have this style.
WS_EX_NOACTIVATE	Specifies that a window cannot be activated. If a child window has this style, tapping it does not cause its top-level parent to activate. Although a window that has this style will still receive stylus events, neither it nor its child windows can get the focus.
WS_EX_NODRAG	Specifies a stationary window that cannot be dragged by its title bar.
WS_EX_NOANIMATION	Prevents a window from showing animated exploding and imploding rectangles and from having a button on the taskbar.
WS_EX_TOPMOST	Creates a window that will be placed and remain above all non-topmost windows.

C.1.2 Non-Client Area Styles

Non-Client Area Style	Description
WS_BORDER	Specifies a window with a thin-line border.
WS_CAPTION	Specifies a window with a title bar and border.
WS_DLGFRAME	Specifies a window with a dialog box border style. A window with this style cannot have a title bar.
WS_HSCROLL	Specifies a window with a horizontal scroll bar.
WS_VSCROLL	Specifies a window with a vertical scroll bar.
WS_OVERLAPPED	Specifies a window with the WS_BORDER and WS_CAPTION styles.
WS_SYSMENU	Uses in conjunction with the WS_CAPTION style, adds the standard Close (X) button to a window title bar..
WS_EX_CAPTIONOKBTN	Includes an OK button in the title bar.
WS_EX_CLIENTEDGE	Specifies a window with a border with a sunken edge.
WS_EX_CONTEXTHELP	Includes a Help button (?) in the title bar of the window.
WS_EX_DLGMODALFRAME	Specifies a window with a thick border.
WS_EX_OVERLAPPEDWINDOW	WS_EX_CLIENTEDGE | WS_EX_WINDOWEDGE Specifies a window with a three-dimensional border style.
WS_EX_STATICEDGE	This style should be used for items that do not accept user input.
WS_EX_WINDOWEDGE	Specifies a window border with a raised edge.

C.1.3 Message Box Styles

The following styles can all be combined.

Button Style	Description
MB_ABORTRETRYIGNORE	The message box contains three buttons: Abort, Retry, and Ignore.
MB_OK	The message box contains one button: OK.
MB_OKCANCEL	The message box contains two buttons: OK and Cancel.
MB_RETRYCANCEL	The message box contains two buttons: Retry and Cancel.
MB_YESNO	The message box contains two buttons: Yes and No.
MB_YESNOCANCEL	The message box contains three buttons: Yes, No, and Cancel.
MB_DEFBUTTON1	The first button is the default button (default).
MB_DEFBUTTON2	The second button is the default button.
MB_DEFBUTTON3	The third button is the default button.

Icon Style	Description
MB_ICONASTERISK, MB_ICONINFORMATION	The icons is lowercase letter 'i' in a circle.
MB_ICONEXCLAMATION, MB_ICONWARNING	The icon is an exclamation point.
MB_ICONERROR, MB_ICONHAND, MB_ICONSTOP	The icon is a stop sign.
MB_ICONQUESTION	The icon is a question mark.

Window Style	Description
MB_APPLMODAL	The user must respond to the message box before continuing working with the window.
MB_SETFOREGROUND	The message box becomes the foreground window.
MB_TOPMOST	The message box is created with the WS_EX_TOPMOST window style.

C.2.   ORIGINAL CONTROL STYLES

The following table shows the styles supported by Windows CE for the original controls.

C.2.1   Push Button Styles

Push Button Style	Description
BS_BOTTOM	Places the text at the bottom of the button rectangle .
BS_CENTER	Centers the text horizontally in the button rectangle.
BS_DEFPUSHBUTTON	Makes the button the default push button.
BS_LEFT	Left-aligns the text in the button rectangle.
BS_NOTIFY	Enables a button to send BN_DBLCLK, BN_KILLFOCUS, and BN_SETFOCUS notification messages to its parent window.
BS_OWNERDRAW	Makes the button an owner-drawn button.
BS_PUSHBUTTON	Makes the button a push button.
BS_RIGHT	Right-aligns text in the button rectangle.
BS_TOP	Places text at the top of the button rectangle.
BS_VCENTER	Vertically centers text in the button rectangle.
WS_TABSTOP	The user can tab into the control.

C.2.2 Radio Button Styles

Radio Button Style	Description
BS_AUTORADIOBUTTON	Creates a radio button that, when selected by a user, clears all other buttons in the same group (see WS_GROUP below).
BS_RADIOBUTTON	The button is a radio button.
BS_LEFT	Left-aligns the text in the button rectangle on the right side of the check box.
BS_RIGHT	Right-aligns the text in the button rectangle on the right side of the check box.
BS_RIGHTBUTTON	Positions a check box square on the right side of the button rectangle.
WS_GROUP	Indicates the start/end of a radio button group. The first radio button of a group must have that style, as well as the control following the last radio button of the same group.
WS_TABSTOP	The user can tab into the control. Only the first radio button of a group needs that style.

C.2.3 Check Box Styles

Check Box Style	Description
BS_3STATE	The button is a check box button with three state: checked, unchecked, and indeterminate.
BS_AUTO3STATE	Same as BS_3STATE, except that clicking on the button automatically changes the state.
BS_AUTOCHECKBOX	The button is a check box button with two states: checked and unchecked. Clicking on the button automatically toggles the state.
BS_CHECKBOX	The button is a check box button with two states: checked and unchecked.
BS_LEFT	Left-aligns the text in the button rectangle on the right side of the check box.
BS_RIGHT	Right-aligns text in the button rectangle on the right side of the check box.
BS_RIGHTBUTTON	Positions a check box square on the right side of the button rectangle.
WS_TABSTOP	The user can tab into the control.

C.2.4 Group Box Styles

Group Box Style	Description
BS_GROUPBOX	The button is a group box.

C.2.5 Edit Control Styles

Edit Control Style	Description
ES_AUTOHSCROLL	Allows more text to be entered by displaying a scroll bar.
ES_AUTOVSCROLL	Scrolls text up one page when the user presses the ENTER key on the last line.
ES_CENTER	Centers text in a multiline edit control.
ES_COMBOBOX	Indicates that the edit control is part of a combo box
ES_LEFT	Left-aligns text.
ES_LOWERCASE	Converts all characters to lowercase as they are typed into the edit control.
ES_MULTILINE	The control is a multiline edit control.
ES_NOHIDESEL	Shows the selection (if any), even if the control does not have the focus.
ES_NUMBER	Accepts only digits to be typed into the edit control.
ES_OEMCONVERT	Converts text typed in the edit control from the Windows CE character set to the OEM character set, and then converts it back to the Windows CE set.
ES_PASSWORD	Displays an asterisk (*) for each character typed into the edit control.
ES_READONLY	Makes the control read only.
ES_RIGHT	Right-aligns text in a multiline edit control.
ES_UPPERCASE	Converts all characters to uppercase as they are typed into the edit control.
ES_WANTRETURN	Specifies that a carriage return be inserted when the user presses the ENTER key while typing text into a multiline edit control in a dialog box (by default, the Enter key triggers the dialog box's default push button).
WS_TABSTOP	The user can tab into the control.

C.2.6 List Box Styles

List Box Style	Description
LBS_DISABLENOSCROLL	When a list box doesn't contain enough items to use a scroll bar, the scroll bar is hidden. This style makes the scroll bar disabled instead.
LBS_EXTENDEDSEL	Enables the user to select multiple items by using the SHIFT key and the mouse.
LBS_MULTICOLUMN	Specifies a multicolumn list box.
LBS_MULTIPLESEL	Allows multiple items to be selected.
LBS_NOINTEGRALHEIGHT	By default, a list box is slightly resized by CE to display an exact number of items. Setting this style indicates to CE not to resize the list box, *i.e.*, use the coordinates exactly as specified.
LBS_NOREDRAW	Disables the redrawing mode of the listbox.
LBS_NOSEL	No selection can take place.
LBS_NOTIFY	Allows sending the LBN_SELCHANGE and LBN_DBLCK notifications.
LBS_SORT	Items are sorted alphabetically.
LBS_STANDARD	LBS_NOTIFY	LBS_SORT	WS_VSCROLL	WS_BORDER
LBS_USETABSTOPS	Converts tab characters ('\t') into tab stops.
LBS_WANTKEYBOARDINPUT	Specifies that the owner of the list box receives WM_VKEYTOITEM messages when the user presses a key and the list box has the input focus. This enables an application to perform special processing on the keyboard input.
WS_TABSTOP	The user can tab into the control.

C.2.7 Combo Box Styles

Combo Box Style	Description
CBS_AUTOHSCROLL	Allows more text to be entered by displaying a scroll bar.
CBS_DISABLENOSCROLL	When the combo box doesn't contain enough items to use a scroll bar, the scroll bar is hidden. This style makes the scroll bar disabled instead.
CBS_DROPDOWN	The combo box is a dropdown combo box.
CBS_DROPDOWNLIST	The combo box is a droplist combo box.
CBS_LOWERCASE	Converts any uppercase characters typed into the edit control of a combo box to lowercase.
CBS_NOINTEGRALHEIGHT	By default, a combo box is slightly resized by CE to display an exact number of items. Setting this style indicates to CE not to resize the combo box, *i.e.*, use the coordinates exactly as specified.
CBS_OEMCONVERT	Converts text typed in the combo box edit control from the Windows CE character set to the OEM character set and then back to the Windows CE set. This style is most useful for combo boxes that contain file names. It applies only to combo boxes created with the CBS_DROPDOWN style.
CBS_SORT	Items are sorted alphabetically.
CBS_UPPERCASE	Converts any lowercase characters typed into the edit control of a combo box to uppercase
WS_TABSTOP	The user can tab into the control.

C.2.8 Scroll Bar Styles

Scroll Bar Styles	Description
SBS_HORZ	Designates a horizontal scroll bar.
SBS_VERT	Designates a vertical scroll bar.

C.2.9 Static Control Styles

Static Control Styles	Description
SS_BITMAP	A bitmap is displayed instead of text.
SS_CENTER	Centers the text within the control.
SS_CENTERIMAGE	The four sides are adjusted to accommodate the bitmap.
SS_ICON	An icon is displayed instead of some text.
SS_LEFT	Left-aligns text within the control.
SS_LEFTNOWORDWRAP	Same as SS_LEFT, except that text is not wrapped after the first line (it is clipped).
SS_NOPREFIX	Prevents the interpretation of the ampersand (&) characters as shortcut prefix character.
SS_NOTIFY	Sends the STN_CLICKED notification when clicked/tapped upon.
SS_RIGHT	Right-aligns text within the control.

C.3   COMMON CONTROL STYLES

The following tables list the styles for the following common controls: up down control, date and time picker, month calendar, tab control, header, tree view, list view, progress bar, toolbar, and rebar. The next table shows some styles sharing the common controls.

C.3.1   Basic Common Control Styles

Basic Common Control Styles	Description
CCS_ADJUSTABLE	Enables a toolbar's built-in customization features, which enable the user to drag a button to a new position or to remove a button by dragging it off the toolbar. In addition, the user can double-click the toolbar to display the Customize Toolbar dialog box, which enables the user to add, delete, and rearrange toolbar buttons.
CCS_BOTTOM	Positions the control at the bottom of the parent window, and sets the widths as the parent's width.
CCS_NODIVIDER	Prevents a 2-pixel highlight from being drawn at the top of the control
CCS_NOMOVEY	The control can move and resize horizontally only. This is useful for header control, for instance.
CCS_NOPARENTALIGN	Prevents the control from automatically moving to the top or bottom of the parent window. Instead, the control keeps its position within the parent window despite changes to the size of the parent. If the application also uses the ccs_top or ccs_bottom styles, it adjusts the height to the default, but does not change the position and width of the control.
CCS_NORESIZE	Prevents the control from using the default width and height when setting its initial size or a new size. Instead, the control uses the width and height specified in the request for creation or sizing.
CCS_TOP	Positions the control at the top of the parent window.
CCS_LEFT	Positions the control at the left of the parent window.
CCS_RIGHT	Positions the control at the right of the parent window.
CCS_NOMOVEX	The control can move and resize vertically only.
CCS_VERT	The control is vertical.

C.3.2 Toolbar Styles

Toolbar Style	Description
TBSTYLE_CUSTOMERASE	Creates a toolbar that generates NM_CUSTOMDRAW notification messages when it processes WM_ERASEBKGND messages.
TBSTYLE_FLAT	Creates a flat toolbar, in which both the toolbar and the buttons are transparent. Button text appears under button bitmaps.
TBSTYLE_LIST	Places button text to the right of button bitmaps. This style can only be used with the TBSTYLE_FLAT style. In Windows CE, the TBSTYLE_LIST style creates a toolbar with variable width buttons. If you want to use the TBSTYLE_LIST style with fixed width buttons, you can override the default behavior by sending a TB_SETBUTTONSIZE or TB_SETBUTTONWIDTH message.
TBSTYLE_TRANSPARENT	Creates a transparent toolbar, in which the toolbar is transparent, but the buttons are not. Button text appears under button bitmaps.
TBSTYLE_WRAPABLE	Creates a toolbar that can have multiple rows of buttons. Toolbar buttons can wrap to the next line when the toolbar becomes too narrow to include all buttons on the same line. Wrapping occurs on separation and non-group boundaries.
TBSTYLE_BUTTON	Creates a toolbar button that looks like a standard Windows CE push button.
TBSTYLE_CHECK	Creates a button that toggles between the pressed and not pressed states each time the user clicks it. The button has a different background color when it is in the pressed state.
TBSTYLE_CHECKGROUP	Creates a check button that stays pressed until another button in the group is pressed.
TBSTYLE_GROUP	Creates a button that stays pressed until another button in the group is pressed.
TBSTYLE_AUTOSIZE	Calculates a button width based on the text of the button, not on the size of the image.
TBSTYLE_DROPDOWN	Creates a drop-down list button.
TBSTYLE_SEP	Creates a separator, which provides a small gap between button groups. A button that has this style does not receive user input.

C.3.3 Rebar Styles

Rebar Style	Description
CCS_VERT	Causes the control to appear vertically at the left side of the parent window.
RBS_AUTOSIZE	Specifies that the layout of a band will automatically change when the size or position of its control changes. When the layout changes, the control sends an RBN_AUTOSIZE notification.
RBS_BANDBORDERS	Displays narrow lines to separate adjacent bands
RBS_FIXEDORDER	Displays multiple bands in the same order at all times. A user can move bands to different rows, but the band order is static.
RBS_SMARTLABELS	Displays the icon for a band that has one only when the band is minimized. If a band has a text label, the label is displayed only when the band is in its restored state or in its maximized state. Windows CE is the only Windows-based OS that supports the RBS_SMARTLABELS style for rebar controls.
RBS_VARHEIGHT	Displays a band at the minimum required height, when possible. Without this style, the command bands control displays all bands at the same height, using the height of the tallest visible band to determine the height of other bands.
RBS_VERTICALGRIPPER	Displays the size grip vertically, instead of horizontally, in a vertical command bands control. This style is ignored for command bands controls that do not have the CCS_VERT style.

C.3.4 Tab Control Styles

Tab Control Style	Description
TCS_BOTTOM	Displays the tabs at the bottom of the control. If the TCS_VERTICAL style is also specified, this style is interpreted as TCS_RIGHT.
TCS_BUTTONS	Displays all tabs as buttons with no border drawn around the display area.
TCS_FIXEDWIDTH	Specifies that all tabs are the same width. You cannot combine this style with the TCS_RIGHTJUSTIFY style.
TCS_FLATBUTTONS	Changes the appearance of a selected tab to indented while other tabs appear to be on the same plane as the background. This style only applies to tab controls that have the TCS_BUTTONS style.
TCS_FLIP	Flips all tabs from top to bottom or left to right.
TCS_FOCUSNEVER	Creates a tab control that never receives the input focus.
TCS_FOCUSONBUTTONDOWN	Specifies that a tab which, when selected, receives the input focus.
TCS_FORCEICONLEFT	Aligns an icon with the left edge of a fixed-width tab. This style can only be used with the TCS_FIXEDWIDTH style.
TCS_FORCELABELLEFT	Aligns a label with the left edge of a fixed-width tab; that is, it displays the label immediately to the right of the icon instead of centering it. This style can only be used with the TCS_FIXEDWIDTH style, and it implies the TCS_FORCEICONLEFT style.
TCS_MULTILINE	Displays multiple rows of tabs, if necessary, so that all tabs are visible at once.
TCS_MULTISELECT	Specifies that multiple tabs can be selected by holding down CTRL when selecting a tab. This style only applies to tabs that have the TCS_BUTTONS style.
TCS_OWNERDRAWFIXED	Specifies that the parent window is responsible for drawing tabs
TCS_RAGGEDRIGHT	Leaves a ragged right edge by not stretching a row of tabs to fill the entire width of the control. This style is the default.
TCS_RIGHT	Displays multiple tabs vertically on the right side of controls that use the TCS_VERTICAL style. If the TCS_VERTICAL style is not specified, this style is interpreted as TCS_BOTTOM.
TCS_RIGHTJUSTIFY	Increases the width of each tab, if necessary, so that each row of tabs fills the entire width of the tab control. This style is valid only when used with the TCS_MULTILINE style.
TCS_SCROLLOPPOSITE	Specifies that unused tabs move to the opposite side of the control when a new tab is selected.
TCS_SINGLELINE	Displays only one row of tabs. The user can scroll to see more tabs, if necessary. This style is the default.
TCS_VERTICAL	Displays multiple tabs vertically on the left side of the control. This style is valid only when used with the TCS_MULTILINE style. To make tabs appear on the right side of the control, combine this style with the TCS_RIGHT style.

C.3.5 Tree View Styles

Tree View Style	Description
TVS_CHECKBOXES	Enables items in a tree view control to be displayed as check boxes. This style uses item state images to produce the check box effect.
TVS_DISABLEDRAGDROP	Prevents the tree view control from sending TVN_BEGINDRAG notification messages.
TVS_EDITLABELS	Enables the user to edit the labels of tree view items.
TVS_HASBUTTONS	Displays plus (+) and minus (-) buttons next to parent items. The user taps the buttons to expand or collapse a parent item's list of child items. To include buttons with items at the root of the tree view, you must also specify the TVS_LINESATROOT style.
TVS_HASLINES	Uses lines to show the hierarchy of items.
TVS_LINESATROOT	Uses lines to link items at the root of the tree view control. This value is ignored if TVS_HASLINES is not also specified.
TVS_SHOWSELALWAYS	Uses the system highlight colors to draw the selected item.
TVS_SINGLESEL	Specifies that when a new tree view item is selected, the selected item will automatically expand and the previously selected item will collapse.

C.3.6 List View Styles

List View Style	Description
LVS_ALIGNLEFT	Specifies that items are left-aligned in icon view and small icon view.
LVS_ALIGNTOP	Specifies that items are aligned with the top of the list view control in icon view and small icon view.
LVS_AUTOARRANGE	Specifies that icons automatically remain arranged in icon view and small icon view.
LVS_BUTTON	Specifies that item icons look like buttons in icon view.
LVS_EDITLABELS	Enables item text to be edited in place. The parent window must process the LVN_ENDLABELEDIT notification message.
LVS_ICON	Specifies icon view.
LVS_LIST	Specifies list view.
LVS_NOCOLUMNHEADER	Specifies that no column header is displayed in report view, which is the default view.
LVS_NOLABELWRAP	Displays item text on a single line in icon view. By default, item text may wrap in icon view.
LVS_NOSCROLL	Disables scrolling, so all items must be displayed within the client area.
LVS_NOSORTHEADER	Specifies that column headers do not work like buttons. This style is useful if clicking a column header in report view does not carry out any action, such as sorting.
LVS_OWNERDATA	Creates a virtual list view control.
LVS_OWNERDRAWFIXED	Enables the owner window to paint items in report view. The list view control sends a WM_DRAWITEM message to paint each item; it does not send separate messages for each subitem. The itemData member of the DRAWITEMSTRUCT structure contains the item data for the specified list view item.
LVS_REPORT	Specifies report view.
LVS_SHAREIMAGELISTS	Specifies that the control does not destroy the image lists assigned to it when it is destroyed. This style enables the same image lists to be used with multiple list view controls.
LVS_SHOWSELALWAYS	Always shows the selection highlighted, even if the control is not activated.
LVS_SINGLESEL	Enables only one item to be selected at a time. By default, multiple items can be selected.
LVS_SMALLICON	Specifies small icon view.
LVS_SORTASCENDING	Sorts items based on item text in ascending order.
LVS_SORTDESCENDING	Sorts items based on item text in descending order.
LVS_EX_CHECKBOXES	Enables items in a list view control to be displayed as check boxes. This style uses item state images to produce the check box effect.
LVS_EX_FULLROWSELECT	Specifies that when an item is selected, the item and all its subitems are highlighted. This style is available only in conjunction with the LVS_REPORT style.
LVS_EX_GRIDLINES	Displays gridlines around items and subitems. This style is available only in conjunction with the LVS_REPORT style.

`LVS_EX_HEADERDRAGDROP`	Enables drag-and-drop reordering of columns in a list view control. This style is only available to list view controls that use the `LVS_REPORT` style.
`LVS_EX_SUBITEMIMAGES`	Enables images to be displayed for subitems. This style is available only in conjunction with the `LVS_REPORT` style.

C.3.7 Header Control Styles

Header Control Style	Description
`HDS_BUTTONS`	Causes each header item to look and behave like a button. This style is useful if an application carries out a task when the user clicks an item in the header control.
`HDS_DRAGDROP`	Enables drag-and-drop reordering of header items.
`HDS_FULLDRAG`	Causes the header control to display column contents even while a user resizes a column.
`HDS_HIDDEN`	Creates a header control that you can hide by setting its height to zero. This style is useful when you use the control as an information container instead of a visual control.
`HDS_HORZ`	Creates a horizontal header control.

C.3.8 Up-Down (Spin) Control Styles

Up-Down Control Style	Description
UDS_ALIGNLEFT	Positions the up-down control next to the left edge of the buddy window. The buddy window is moved to the right and its width is decreased to accommodate the width of the up-down control.
UDS_ALIGNRIGHT	Positions the up-down control next to the right edge of the buddy window. The width of the buddy window is decreased to accommodate the width of the up-down control.
UDS_ARROWKEYS	Causes the up-down control to process the UP ARROW and DOWN ARROW keys on the keyboard.
UDS_AUTOBUDDY	Automatically elects the previous window in the z-order as the up-down control's buddy window. In Windows CE, the window must be an edit control.
UDS_HORZ	Causes the up-down control's arrows to point left and right instead of up and down.
UDS_NOTHOUSANDS	Refrains from inserting a thousands separator between every three decimal positions.
UDS_SETBUDDYINT	Causes the up-down control to set the text of the buddy window, using the WM_SETTEXT message, when the position changes. The text consists of the position formatted as a decimal or hexadecimal string.
UDS_WRAP	Causes the position to wrap if it is incremented or decremented beyond the end or beginning of the range.

C.3.9 Slider (Trackbar) Control Styles

Slider Control Style	Description
TBS_HORZ	Creates an horizontal slider (default).
TBS_VERT	Creates a vertical slider.
TBS_AUTOTICKS	Displays a tick mark for each increment.
TBS_NOTICKS	No tick marks are shown.
TBS_BOTTOM	Displays the tick marks below an horizontal slider.
TBS_TOP	Displays the tick marks above an horizontal slider.
TBS_RIGHT	Displays the tick marks on the right of a vertical slider.
TBS_LEFT	Displays the tick marks on the left of a vertical slider.
TBS_BOTH	Displays the tick marks on either side on the slider.
TBS_ENABLESELRANGE	Displays a selection range within the slider.

C.3.10 Progress Bar Styles

Progress Bar Style	Description
PBS_SMOOTH	Displays progress status in a smooth scrolling bar instead of the default segmented bar.
PBS_VERTICAL	Displays progress status vertically, from bottom to top.

C.3.11 Month Calendar Control Styles

Month Calendar Control Style	Description
MCS_DAYSTATE	Specifies that the month calendar will send MCN_GETDAYSTATE notifications to request information about which days should be displayed in bold.
MCS_MULTISELECT	Enables the user to select a range of dates. By default, the maximum range is one week. You can change the maximum selectable range using the MCM_SETMAXSELCOUNT message.
MCS_NOTODAY	Creates a month calendar that does not display a Today selection.
MCS_NOTODAYCIRCLE	Creates a month calendar that does not circle the current date
MCS_WEEKNUMBERS	Displays the week number, from 1 through 52, to the left of each week in the calendar.

C.3.12 Date and Time Picker Styles

Date and Time Picker Style	Description
DTS_APPCANPARSE	Enables the owner to parse user input. When a Date Time Picker control has this style, a user can make changes within the client area of the control by pressing the F2 key. The control sends a DTN_USERSTRING notification message when the user is finished editing.
DTS_LONGDATEFORMAT	Displays the date in long format. The default format string for this style is defined by LOCALE_SLONGDATEFORMAT, which produces output like "Friday, April 19, 1999."
DTS_SHOWNONE	Enables the control to accept "no date" as a valid selection state. This state can be set with the DTM_SETSYSTEMTIME message or verified with the DTM_GETSYSTEMTIME message.
DTS_SHORTDATEFORMAT	Displays the date in short format. The default format string for this style is defined by LOCALE_SSHORTDATE, which produces output like "4/19/99."
DTS_TIMEFORMAT	Displays the time. The default format string for this style is defined by LOCALE_STIMEFORMAT, which produces output like "5:31:42 PM." An up-down control is placed to the right of the DTP control to modify time values.
DTS_UPDOWN	Places an up-down control to the right of a DTP control to modify time values. This style can be used instead of the drop-down month calendar, which is the default style.

C.3.13 Status Bar Styles

Status Bar Style	Description
CBRS_TOP	The status bar is located at the top of the frame window.
CBRS_BOTTOM	The status bar is displayed at the bottom of the frame window.
CBRS_NOALIGN	The status bar is not resized when the parent is.

Appendix D

Control Notifications

The following sections describe the control notifications supported on Windows CE.

D.1 WINDOWS CONTROLS

This section lists the notifications for the Windows original controls.

D.1.1 Button Notification

Notification message	Message-map Entry	Description
BN_CLICKED	ON_BN_CLICKED	The button has been clicked.

D.1.2 Edit Notifications

Notification message	Message-map Entry	Description
EN_CHANGE	ON_EN_CHANGED	The user has taken an action that may have altered the text in the control. The notification is sent after that action has been done and the control, updated.
EN_ERRSPACE	ON_EN_ERRSPACE	Not enough internal memory could be allocated.
EN_HSCROLL	ON_EN_HSCROLL	Sent after the user clicked the horizontal scroll bar (if any) but before the control is updated.
EN_KILLFOCUS	ON_EN_KILLFOCUS	The user moved the focus to another control. The parent window may perform an immediate validation if required.
EN_MAXTEXT	ON_EN_MAXTEXT	Sent when no character can be inserted anymore, either because the maximum count has been reached, or because the edit control is not large enough and is not scrollable.
EN_SETFOCUS	ON_EN_SETFOCUS	The user moved the focus on the control.
EN_UPDATE	ON_EN_UPDATE	The text has been altered and is about to be redisplayed. The parent window may resize the control if required.
EN_VSCROLL	ON_EN_VSCROLL	Sent after the user clicked the horizontal scroll bar (if any) but before the control is updated.

D.1.3 List Box Notifications

Notification message	Message-map Entry	Description
LBN_DBLCLK	ON_LBN_DBLCLK	The user double-clicked on a string. Sent if the LBS_NOTIFY style is set only.
LBN_ERRSPACE	ON_LBN_ERRSPACE	The list box does not have enough memory to execute the request.
LBN_KILLFOCUS	ON_LBN_KILLFOCUS	The list box lost the input focus.
LBN_SELCANCEL	ON_LBN_SELCANCEL	The selection is canceled. Sent if the LBS_NOTIFY style is set only.
LBN_SELCHANGE	ON_LBN_SELCHANGE	The selection is about to change. Sent if the LBS_NOTIFY style is set only.
LBN_SETFOCUS	ON_LBN_SETFOCUS	The list box gained the input focus.
WM_VKEYTOITEM	ON_WM_VKEYTOITEM	The list box receives a WM_KEYDOWN message. Sent if the LBS_WANTKEYBOARDINPUT style is set only.

D.1.4 Combo Box Notifications

Notification Message	Message-map Entry	Description
CBN_CLOSEUP	ON_CBN_CLOSEUP	The list box has been closed
CBN_DBLCLK	ON_CBN_DBLCLK	The user double clicked an item in the list box
CBN_DROPDOWN	ON_CBN_DROPDOWN	The list box is about to be made visible
CBN_EDITCHANGE	ON_CBN_EDITCHANGE	The edit control has been changed and updated
CBN_EDITUPDATE	ON_CBN_EDITUPDATE	The edit control has been changed and is about to be updated
CBN_SELCHANGE	ON_CBN_SELCHANGE	The selection is about to be changed in the list box.

D.1.5 Scroll Bar Messages

Message	Message-map Entry	Description
WM_HSCROLL	ON_WM_HSCROLL	A horizontal scroll bar has been used.
WM_VSCROLL	ON_WM_VSCROLL	A vertical scroll bar has been used.

D.1.6 Static Control Notifications

The following notifications are only sent when a static control has the SS_NOTIFY attribute set.

Notification message	Message-map Entry	Description
STN_CLICKED	ON_STN_CLICKED	The static has been tapped
STN_DBLCLK	ON_STN_DBLCLK	The static has been double-tapped

D.2   Common Controls

This section lists the notifications for the common controls. All of them share the notifications listed in the following table, in addition to their specific notifications.

Notification message	Message-map Entry	Description
NM_CLICKED	ON_NOTIFY	The control has been clicked.
NM_CUSTOMDRAW	ON_NOTIFY	The control needs to be drawn.
NM_KEYDOWN	ON_NOTIFY	A key has been pressed.

D.2.1 Tool Bar Notifications

Notification message	Message-map Entry	Description
TBN_BEGINDRAG	ON_NOTIFY	A button started to get dragged.
TBN_DROPDOWN	ON_NOTIFY	A TBSTYLE_DROPDOWN button has been clicked.
TBN_ENDDRAG	ON_NOTIFY	A button is no longer dragged.
TBN_GETBUTTONINFO	ON_NOTIFY	Requests information about a button.

D.2.2 ReBar Notifications

Notification message	Message-map Entry	Description
RBN_AUTOSIZE	ON_NOTIFY	The rebar resized itself.
RBN_BEGINDRAG	ON_NOTIFY	A band started to get dragged.
RBN_ENDDRAG	ON_NOTIFY	A band is no longer dragged.
RBN_HEIGHTCHANGED	ON_NOTIFY	The height changed.
RBN_LAYOURCHANGED	ON_NOTIFY	The layout changed.

D.2.3 Tab Control Notifications

Notification message	Message-map Entry	Description
TCN_KEYDOWN	ON_NOTIFY	A key has been pressed.
TCN_SELCHANGE	ON_NOTIFY	The selection has changed.
TCN_SELCHANGING	ON_NOTIFY	The selection is about to change.

D.2.4 Tree View Notifications

Notification message	Message-map Entry	Description
TVN_BEGINDRAG	ON_NOTIFY	A drag operation just started.
TVN_BEGINLABELEDIT	ON_NOTIFY	A label is about to be edited.
TVN_DELETEITEM	ON_NOTIFY	An item has been deleted.
TVN_ENDLABELEDIT	ON_NOTIFY	A label has been edited.
TVN_GETDISPINFO	ON_NOTIFY	Some item information is requested.
TVN_ITEMEXPANDED	ON_NOTIFY	An item has expanded.
TVN_ITEMEXPANDING	ON_NOTIFY	An item is about to be expanded.
TVN_KEYDOWN	ON_NOTIFY	A key has been pressed.
TVN_SELCHANGED	ON_NOTIFY	The selection has changed.
TVN_SELCHANGING	ON_NOTIFY	The selection is about to change.
TVN_SETDISPINFO	ON_NOTIFY	An item has been updated.

D.2.5 List View Notifications

Notification message	Message-map Entry	Description
LVN_BEGINDRAG	ON_NOTIFY	A drag operation just started.
LVN_BEGINLABELEDIT	ON_NOTIFY	A label is about to be edited.
LVN_COLUMNCLICK	ON_NOTIFY	A column has been clicked.
LVN_DELETEALLITEMS	ON_NOTIFY	All items were deleted.
LVN_DELETEITEM	ON_NOTIFY	One item was deleted.
LVN_ENDDRAG	ON_NOTIFY	The drag operation has ended
LVN_ENDLABELEDIT	ON_NOTIFY	A label has been edited.
LVN_GETDISPINFO	ON_NOTIFY	Some item information is requested.
LVN_INSERTITEM	ON_NOTIFY	An item has been inserted.
LVN_ITEMACTIVATE	ON_NOTIFY	An item has been activated.
LVN_ITEMCHANGED	ON_NOTIFY	An item has changed.
LVN_ITEMCHANGING	ON_NOTIFY	An item is about to be changed.
LVN_KEYDOWN	ON_NOTIFY	A key has been pressed.
LVN_MARQUEEBEGIN	ON_NOTIFY	A selection using a bounding box (marquee) just began.
LVN_ODCACHEHINT	ON_NOTIFY	The content of a virtual list view has changed.
LVN_ODFINDITEM	ON_NOTIFY	A particular callback item must be found.
LVN_ODSTATECHANGED	ON_NOTIFY	An item or a range of items have changed.
LVN_SETDISPINFO	ON_NOTIFY	An item has been updated.

D.2.6 Header Notifications

Notification message	Message-map Entry	Description
HDN_BEGINDRAG	ON_NOTIFY	A drag operation just started.
HDN_BEGINTRACK	ON_NOTIFY	A divider drag operation just started.
HDN_DIVIDERDBLCLK	ON_NOTIFY	A divider has been double-clicked.
HDN_ENDDRAG	ON_NOTIFY	The drag operation has ended
HDN_ENDTRACK	ON_NOTIFY	The divider drag operation has ended
HDN_GETDISPINFO	ON_NOTIFY	Some item information is requested.
HDN_ITEMCHANGED	ON_NOTIFY	An item has changed.
HDN_ITEMCHANGING	ON_NOTIFY	An item is about to be changed.
HDN_ITEMCLICK	ON_NOTIFY	An item has been clicked.
HDN_ITEMDBLCLICK	ON_NOTIFY	An item has been double-clicked.
HDN_TRACK	ON_NOTIFY	A divider is being dragged.

D.2.7 Up-Down Control Notifications

Notification message	Message-map Entry	Description
UDN_DELTAPOS	ON_NOTIFY	The position is about to change.

D.2.8 Slider Control Notifications

Message	Message-map Entry	Description
WM_HSCROLL	ON_WM_HSCROLL	A horizontal scroll bar has been used.
WM_VSCROLL	ON_WM_VSCROLL	A vertical scroll bar has been used.

D.2.9 Progress Bar Notifications

Progress bars do not send notifications.

D.2.10 Month Calendar Notifications

Notification message	Message-map Entry	Description
MCN_GETDAYSTATE	ON_NOTIFY	Requests information about days to be displayed in bold.
MCN_SELCHANGE	ON_NOTIFY	The selection has changed.
MCN_SELECT	ON_NOTIFY	An explicit data selection has just been made.

D.2.11 Date Time Notifications

Notification message	Message-map Entry	Description
DTN_DROPDOWN	ON_NOTIFY	The embedded month calendar is about to be displayed.
DTN_CLOSEUP	ON_NOTIFY	The embedded month calendar is about to be closed.
DTN_DATETIMECHANGE	ON_NOTIFY	The date changed.
DTN_FORMAT	ON_NOTIFY	Requests text to display.
DTN_FORMATQUERY	ON_NOTIFY	Requests the maximum text length to display.
DTN_USERSTRING	ON_NOTIFY	The control has been edited.
DTN_WMKEYDOWN	ON_NOTIFY	The user types in a callback field.

D.2.12 Status Bar Notifications

Notification message	Message-map Entry	Description
SBN_SIMPLEMODECHANGE	ON_NOTIFY	The simple mode changed.

Appendix E

Microsoft Coding Conventions

There are two important coding conventions commonly found in the vast majority of C/C++ Windows applications:

- Hungarian Notation
- Windows data types

These important conventions are described in the following pages.

E.1 HUNGARIAN NOTATION

Microsoft has been using what is called today the *Hungarian Notation*, where a variable is prefixed by one or two lowercase letters that describe the type. The following table lists the most common notations.

Prefix	Associated Data Type
b	BOOL
br	BRUSH or CBrush
by	BYTE
C	class
c	char (or TCHAR)
cb	byte count
dw	DWORD
f	BOOL (flag)
fn	function address
g_	global variable
h	HANDLE, HWND, etc.
i	INT (usually an index)
l	LONG
lp	long pointer. This is obsolete, but still in use. Use p instead.
m_	member variable
n	short, INT
p	pointer (usually combined with another prefix e.g. pszName)
pt	POINT or CPoint.
rc	RECT or CRect
S	struct
s	string
sz	null-terminated string
sz	SIZE or CSize
u	UINT
w	WORD
wnd	CWnd
x	x-axis position
y	y-axis position

E.2. WINDOWS DATA TYPES

Windows defines a data type for just about every data representation (except user-defined ones). This has proven to make code quite portable across Windows platforms, especially during the transition from 16-bit Windows 3.x to 32-bit Windows 95/NT.

New data types are constantly added as the API grows; the following table lists some of the most popular types. I recommend that you use them to minimize portability issues across Windows platforms.

Windows Data Types	Description (`typedef`, `#define`, etc.)
`__TEXT(quote)`	`L##quote`
`__T(quote)`, `_T(quote)`	`__TEXT(quote)`
`BOOL`	`int`
`BYTE`	`unsigned char`
`CALLBACK,` `WINAPI,` `APIENTRY,` `PASCAL`	`__stdcall`
`CHAR`	`char`
`COLORREF`	`DWORD`
`CONST`	`const`
`DWORD`	`unsigned long`
`FALSE`	`0`
`FLOAT`	`float`
`HANDLE`	`void *`
`HGLOBAL, GLOBALHANDLE`	`HANDLE`
`HLOCAL, LOCALHANDLE`	`HANDLE`
`HRESULT`	`LONG`
`INT`	`int`
`LONG`	`long`
`LPARAM`	`LONG`
`LPCRECT`	`const RECT *`
`LPCTSTR`	`LPCWSTR (in UNICODE)`
`LPCVOID`	`CONST void *`
`LPLONG`	`long *`
`LPSHORT`	`short *`
`LPTSTR`	`LPWSTR (in UNICODE)`
`LPVOID`	`void *`
`LRESULT`	`LONG`
`PBOOL, LPBOOL`	`BOOL *`
`PBYTE, LPBYTE`	`BYTE *`
`PCWSTR, LPCWSTR`	`CONST CHAR *`
`PDWORD, LPDWORD`	`DWORD *`

PFLOAT	FLOAT *
PINT, LPINT	int *
PLONG	LONG *
POINT	struct tagPOINT
	{
	LONG x;
	LONG y;
	}
PPOINT, LPPOINT	POINT *
PRECT, LPRECT	RECT *
PSHORT	SHORT *
PSIZE, LPSIZE	SIZE *
PUCHAR	UCHAR *
PUINT	unsigned int *
PULONG	ULONG *
PUSHORT	USHORT *
PVOID	void *
PWCHAR, PWSTR, LPWSTR	WCHAR *
PWORD, LPWORD	WORD *
RECT	struct tagRECT
	{
	LONG left;
	LONG top;
	LONG right;
	LONG bottom;
	}
SHORT	short
SIZE	struct tagSIZE
	{
	LONG cx;
	LONG cy;
	}
TBYTE, TCHAR	WCHAR (in UNICODE)
TRUE	1
UCHAR	unsigned char
UINT	unsigned int
ULONG	unsigned long
USHORT	unsigned short
VOID	void
WCHAR	wchar_t
WORD	unsigned short
WPARAM	UINT

Appendix F

Modules and Components

The core functionality of Windows CE, including the API implementation, resides in distinct modules. Some of those modules can be even further broken down into components. You can reduce the size of a Windows CE image by picking only the modules and components that you need. This appendix lists all configurable modules (Section F.1) and components (Section F.2), in alphabetical order. Modules that are not configurable (kd, ebot, nkprof, etc.) are not shown. The exact list of modules and components is contained within `%_PUBLICROOT%\Common\Cesysgen\Makefile`.

F.1 MODULES

Module	Description	Components	Required	New in CE 2.10?
afd	Protocol manager			
arp	Address resolution protocol			
atadisk	ATA disk support			
cegsm				
ceramdrv	RAM disk driver module			✓
cmd	Command processor			✓
comm	Communication applet (in the control panel)			✓
commctrl	Common controls			
commdlg	Common dialogs			✓
commg	Communication control			✓

	panel applet (portrait)			
console	Consoles			✓
control	Control panel			✓
coredll	Operating core DLL	accel_c coreimm coreloc coremain coresioa coresiow coresip corestra corestrw cryptapi fileinfo fileopen fmtmsg fmtres lmem mgdi_c rectapi rsa32 serdev shcore shexec shmisc shortcut tapilib thunks wavelib wmgr_c	✓	
corelibc	Core C library	ccrtstrt		
ctlpnl	Control panel helper process			✓
cxport	common transport utilities			
device	Installable device manager			
dhcp	Dynamic Host Configuration Protocol			
dualio	PCMCIA client diver module for the Socket Communications Dual Serial I/O			
elnk3	Elink Ethernet driver			
fatfs	FAT file system	fatmain fatui		
filesys	File system	fsdbase fsheap fsmain fspass fsreg fsysram		
gwes	Graphics, Events and Windowing subsystem	accel audio btnctl calibrui caret cascade cdlctl clipbd cmbctl column cursor cursor8 defwndproc dlgmgr dlgmnem drawmbar edctl edimefe edimejpn foregnd gcache getpower gsetwinlong gwectrl eshare gwesmain hotkey icon iconcurs idle imgctl immthunk journal kbdui lbctl loadbmp loadimg loadstr mcursor mcursor8 menu menuscrl mgalias mgbase mgbitmap mgblt mgblt2 mgdc mgdibsec mgdraw mgdrwtxt mgfe		

		mgpal mgpalnat mgprint mgrast mgrast2 mgrgn mgtci mgtt mgwinmgr mnotapui moverlap msgbeep msgbox msgbox28 msgque nclient nled notify oom oomui sbcmn scbctl startui startup stcctl syscolor tchui timer uibase winmgr wmbase		
hwxjpn	Japanese handwriting			✓
hmxusa	English handwriting			
inetcore	Windows Internet DLL core			
inetftp	FTP protocol			
intl	Regional settings applet			✓
intlg	Regional settings applet (portrait)			✓
ircomm	IrDA communication			
irdastk	IrDA stack			
main	Keyboard control applet			✓
msfilter	Sample ACM filter			✓
ndis	NDIS network module			
ne2000	NE2000 network module			
netbios	Netbios over TCP/IP			
netdetect	Ping			
netui	Network user interface			
network	Network control applet			✓
networkg	P/PC network control applet			✓
nk	Windows CE kernel		✓	
ntlmssp	NT Lan Manager Security Service Provider			
ole32	OLE support	com docfile exp msf ole232 olemain stg		
oleaut32	OLE Automation			
parallel	Parallel port driver			✓
passwrd	Password control applet			✓
passwrdg	Password control applet (portrait)			✓
pcl	PCL printer driver			
power	Power control applet			✓
powerg	Power control applet (portrait)			✓
ppp	Point-to-point protocol			
prnerr	Printer port error			✓

	information and dialog			
prnport	Printer transport layer			
proxim	Proxim network card driver			
redir	Network redirector (WNet)			
remnet	Remote networking			
Rnaapp	Remote networking application support			
rsabase	RSA encryption			
schannel	SSL/PCT secure socket layer			
screen	Screen control applet			✓
screeng	Screen control applet (portrait)			✓
secur32	Security Support Provider Interface			
shell	Debugging shell			
sipcpl	SIP control applet			
softkb	SIP device driver			
sounds	Sound control applet			
soundsg	Sound control applet (portrait)			
splusa	USA speller			✓
sramdisk	SRAM (PCMCIA) card			
system	System control applet			✓
systemg	System control applet (portrait)			✓
tapi	Telephony API			
taskman	Task manager			✓
tcpstk	TCP/IP stack			
termctrl	Terminal			
toolhelp	Debugger support			
trueffs	TrueFFS block device driver			✓
unimodem	TAPI service provide for AT command modems			
usbd	USB module			✓
usbmouse	USB mouse driver			✓
uuid	UUID support			
waveapi	Multimedia sound			
wininet	Internet API support			
winsock	Winsock services	sslsock		
xircce2	Xircom Ethernet driver			

F.2   COMPONENTS

Component	Description	Module	Required	New in CE 2.10?
accel	Accelerator	gwes		
accel_c	Create accelerator table (new in 2.10)	coredll		✓
asyncio		coredll		
audio	Audio	gwes		
btnctl	Button control	gwes		
calibrui	Touch screen calibration U/I	gwes		
caret	Caret	gwes		
cascade	Cascading menu	gwes		
ccrtstrt		corelibc		
cdlctl	Candidate list control	gwes		
clipbd	Clipboard	gwes		
cmbctl	Combo box	gwes		
column	Column	gwes		
com	Component Object Model interface	ole32		
corecrt	Core C run-time	coredll		
corecrtw		coredll		
coreimm	Input method manager	coredll		
coreloc	National language support	coredll		
coremain	Base functionality	coredll	✓	
coresioa	Stdio functions (ASCII)	coredll		✓
coresiow	Stdio functions (UNICODE)	coredll		✓
coresip	Soft-input panel	coredll		✓
corestra	sprintf-like formatting (ASCII)	coredll		✓
corestrw	sprintf-like formatting (UNICODE)	coredll		✓
cryptapi	Crypt API	coredll		
cursor	Cursor API	gwes		
cursor2	Cursor support	gwes		
cursor8	Cursor support	gwes		✓
defwindowproc	Default window procedure	gwes		
dlgmgr	Dialog manager	gwes		
dlgmnem	Dialog mnemonics	gwes		
docfile	OLE docfile	ole32		
drawmbar	Menu	gwes		
edctl	Edit control	gwes		
edimefe	Far East edit control.	gwes		✓
edimejpn	Japanese edit control	gwes		✓
exp	OLE storage	ole32		
fatmain		fatfs		
fatui		fatfs		

fileinfo	ShGetFileInfo API	coredll		✓
fileopen	GetOPenFileName and GetSaveFileName API	coredll		✓
fmtmsg	Message format	coredll		
fmtres	Win32 error messages	coredll		✓
foregnd	Foreground window component	gwes		
fpemul	Floating-point emulation			✓
dsdbase	Database functionality	filesys		
fsheap	Heap file system	filesys		
fsmain	File system main	filesys		
fspass	Password API	filesys		
fsreg	Registry API	filesys		
fsrglite		filesys		
fsysram	RAM and ROM file systems	filesys		
fsysrom	ROM file system (MINKERN, MININPUT configurations)	filesys		
gcache	GWES initialization	gwes		
getpower	Battery power	gwes		
gsetwindowlong	GetWindowLong and SetWindowLong	gwes		
gwectrl	GWES base	gwes		
gweshare	GWES shared routines	gwes		
gwesmain	GWES main component	gwes		
hotkey	Hot Key component	gwes		✓
icon	Icons	gwes		
iconcurs	Mouse cursors	gwes		
idle	System idle	gwes		
imgctl	Image list control	gwes		
immthunk	Thunking	gwes		
journal	Simple journaling	gwes		✓
kbdui	Keyboard interface	gwes		
lbctl	List box control	gwes		
lmem	Local heap	coredll	✓	
loadbmp	Bitmap loading	gwes		
loadimg	Image loading	gwes		
loadstr	String loading	gwes		
locusa	USA-specific	coredll		
mcursor	Mouse cursor	gwes		
mcursor1	Standard window cursor movement	gwes		
mcursor8	Standard window cursor movement	gwes		
menu	Menu	gwes		
menuscrl	Scrolling menu	gwes		
mgalias	Font face name aliasing	gwes		✓
mgbase	Font face name aliasing	gwes		✓
mgbitmap	GDI bitmap	gwes		
mgblt	BitBlt	gwes		

mgblt2	Bitmap transfer API	gwes		
mgdc	Device context	gwes		
mgdi_c	GDI support	coredll		
mgdibsec	CreateDIBSection	gwes		
mgdraw	Drawing	gwes		
mgdrawtxt	Text drawing	gwes		
mgfe	Far East mgdi routines	gwes		
mgpal	Palette support	gwes		
mgpalnat	Natural palette	gwes		
mgprint	Printing support	gwes		
mgrast	Raster font	gwes		
mgrast2	Raster font support	gwes		
mgrgn	Drawing regions	gwes		
mgtci	Character translation	gwes		✓
mgtt	TrueType font	gwes		
mgwinmgr	Window management support	gwes		
mnoover	menu support	gwes		
mnotapui	User interface support	gwes		
moverlap	Overlapped menu	gwes		
msf	OLE storage	ole32		
msgbeep	Message beep	gwes		
msgbox	Message box	gwes		
msgbox2	2bpp message box			
msgbox28	2bpp and 8bpp message box	gwes		
msgque	Message queue	gwes		
mtapui	Tap menu user interface (not used in any configuration)			
nclient	Non-client window area	gwes		
nled	Notification led	gwes		
notify	User notification	gwes		
ole232	OLE services support	ole32		
olemain	OLE main			
oom	Out-of-memory	gwes		
oomui	Out-of-memory user interface	gwes		
rectapi	GDI rectangle support	coredll		
rsa32	RSA encryption	coredll		
sbcmn	Scroll bar support	gwes		✓
scbctl	Scroll bar control	gwes		
serdev	Serial device support	coredll		
shcore	Core shell	coredll		✓
shellapis	Shell API	coredll		
shexec	Shell API support	coredll		✓
shmisc	Shell API support	coredll		✓
shortcut	shell shortcut support	coredll		✓
sslsock	SSL Winsock	winsock		

startui	Startup dialog	gwes		
startup	Startup	gwes		
stcctl	Static control	gwes		
stg	OLE lightweight storage (not used in any configuration)	ole32		
syscolor	Color	gwes		
tapilib	TAPI support	coredll		
tchui	Touch screen user interface	gwes		
thunks	Kernel to Win32 thunks	coredll	✓	
timer	Base timer	gwes		
uibase	User interface base	gwes		
uuid		ole32		
wavelib	Multimedia support	coredll		
winmgr	Window manager	gwes		
wmbase	GWES base	gwes		
wmgr_c	Window manager	coredll		

Appendix G

Samples on the CD-ROM

The accompanying CD-ROM contains some samples referred to in various chapters, summarized in the following table.

Unless noted otherwise, all samples are targeted to Windows CE 2.11.

Chapter	Sample	Description	API	Tools
7				
	Slbridge	Demonstrates the use of event flags to control the traffic light of a single-line bridge	Win32	PB
8				
	VirtMem	Demonstrates virtual memory allocation, query and release.	Win32	PB
10				
	DB	Databases	Win32	PB
	Regdemo	This application demonstrates most registry calls applications can use.	Win32	PB
11				
	ListFile	Lists all files on the CE device.	Win32	PB
	MapFile	File system map I/O API	Win32	PB
12				
	WNet	Uses the WNet API to list desktop resources and connect a remote device locally.	Win32	PB
	Inet	Uses the WinInet API to send HTTP and FTP requests.	Win32	PB
	SockCli	A Winsock application that implements a client. This application runs on CE and works with SockSvr.	Win32	PB

	SockSvr	A Winsock application that implements a server. This application runs on NT and works with SockCli.	Win32	VC++
	Icmp	Implements a Ping application using CE's ICMP protocol.	Win32	PB
13				
	Ras	Establishes a RAS connection to a RAS server. This application is functionally equivalent to Remnet.	Win32	PB
	Rapidemo	A desktop (NT) application that makes some remote calls using RAPI.	Win32	VC++
	MyCeDll	A Windows CE dynamic-link library (DLL), used with Rapidemo	Win32	PB
	Dcc	Demonstrates the connection manager.		
14				
	Hellow32	Displays "Hello Win32"	Win32	VC++
	Hellomfc	Displays "Hello MFC". This is the MFC counterpart of "hellow32".	MFC[1]	VC++
15				
	Scribble	A document/view application to scribble. This is an adaptation of the Scribble tutorial provided with Visual C++, for Windows CE.	MFC[3]	VC++
16				
	Drawing	Demonstrates drawing primitives.	MFC[1]	VC++
	Rects	Draws random rectangle. It shows how drawing can be optimized by identifying visible areas to paint.	MFC[1]	VC++
17				
	Menu	Shows ownerdraw menu items, how to alter menus at run-time and how to use check radio buttons.	MFC[2]	VC++
	Linedraw	Shows how to capture the mouse/stylus.	MFC[2]	VC++
18				
	DlgApp	Demonstrates how to use modal and modeless dialog boxes.	MFC[2]	VC++
	PSheet	Uses a simple property sheet.	MFC[2]	VC++
	CommDlg	Uses four common dialog boxes: Open, Color, Find and Replace, and Print.	MFC[2]	VC++
19				
	Ctrls	Demonstrates how to use and interact with controls in a dialog-based application.	MFC[4]	VC++
	EasyScrl	Shows how to scroll graphs without flickering in a CScrollView.	MFC[3]	VC++
	ScrlGrph	Shows how to scroll graphs without flickering in a plain window, using scroll bar controls.	MFC[1]	VC++

	Sb32	Shows how to use a scroll bar control to scroll multiple windows at once.	MFC[1]	VC++
	HtmlApp	Implements an HTML control class to display web pages. This application's child view is in fact replaced by the HTML control. It also uses a custom dialog bar that passes notifications to the main frame.	MFC[2]	VC++
	RichInk	Implements an Ink control class to record hand-written strokes. This application's child view is replaced by the HTML control.	MFC[2]	VC++
	Voice	Implements a Voice control class to record and play sounds. This demo is targeted to Windows CE 2.01 for Palm-size PCs.	MFC[4]	VC++
20	CtlColor	Demonstrates how to change control colors, how to extend controls, how to use owner-draw buttons and how to add message reflection.	MFC[4]	VC++
	TabCtrl	Implements a dialog-based tab control.	MFC[4]	VC++
	FBrowser	An Explorer-like application for CE, that combines a tree view and a list view controls.	MFC[2]	VC++
	Cstmsbar	Implements a custom status bar.	MFC[2]	VC++
	Bar3	Demonstrates how to customize rebars and how to reroute dialog bar control commands.	MFC[2]	VC++
	Ctrl	Demonstrates the use of various common controls, as well as a custom progress bar.	MFC[4]	VC++
21	CstmDraw	Shows how to implement custom-drawn controls using custom draw services.	MFC[4]	VC++
	Shell	Adds a status indicator in the system tray.	MFC[2]	VC++
23	Notif	Demonstrates how to use notifications. This demo is targeted to Windows CE 2.01 for Palm-size PCs.	MFC[4]	VC++
	Scribble		N/A	VB

[1] Application written from scratch, without a view nor a document, which demonstrates a specific concept.

[2] Application generated by AppWizard, with a child view but without a document, with a few handlers added through ClassWizard.

[3] Like [2], but with a document (*i.e.*, based on the document./view architecture).

[4] Dialog-based application generated from AppWizard.

Index

Notes

Notes

Notes

Notes

Notes

Notes

Notes

Notes

The author and publisher appreciate your comments and suggestions.
You may contact us at info@annabooks.com

For information regarding books, classes, workshops, and conferences regarding
Windows CE engineering, please see http://www.annabooks.com.

For information regarding Windows CE system integration, drivers, operating system
adaptation, application porting, or Windows CE licensing, please see
http://www.annasoft.com.

Annabooks
11838 Bernardo Plaza Ct.
San Diego, California, USA 92128
619-673-0870